Russian Politics and Society

'Already a standard in the field, this third edition of Richard Sakwa's *Russian Politics and Society* represents a provocative yet balanced account of the country's political development and degeneration. The coverage is impressively comprehensive, rendering its subject both accessible to lay readers and engaging for the specialist. The book is superbly informed by one of Russia's most astute analysts.'

Professor Michael Urban, University of California, Santa Cruz

'Sakwa's *Russian Politics and Society* is *the* place to begin to understand how Russia found itself in its current perilous position.'

Professor Ronald Grigor Suny, Department of Political Science, University of Chicago

'A remarkable achievement – comprehensive in scope and judicious in its interpretation, this is a satisfying portrait of the world's largest state as it enters a new millennium.'

Stephen White, University of Glasgow

Since it was first published in 1993, Richard Sakwa's *Russian Politics and Society* has become the most comprehensive and indispensable guide to contemporary Russian politics.

It is a key introduction to the subject, providing a readable account of Russian politics from the fall of communism to Vladimir Putin's administration. Using clear examples, maps, election results and recommendations for further reading, this is an ideal textbook for students.

For this third edition the text has been thoroughly updated and expanded to include the end of Yeltsin's government and his replacement by the dynamic Putin. The current edition includes:

- material revised and updated factually and theoretically throughout the book
- a history of Yeltsin's second term in office, and the impact of his successor Vladimir Putin
- two additional chapters on 'Cultural transformation' and 'Pluralism, elites, regime and leadership'
- a revised structure to take into account recent developments in Russian politics such as regional and federal reform, the second Chechen war, the renewed struggle for economic and social reform and the new impetus to achieve international integration
- a new select bibliography
- a companion website (see www.routledge.com/politics/textbooks) with supplementary material including the Russian Constitution and an extended bibliography.

Richard Sakwa is Professor of Russian and European Politics at the University of Kent at Canterbury. He has published many books on contemporary Russian politics, including *Soviet Politics: An Introduction* and *Gorbachev and His Reforms, 1985–1990*. He has also edited Ruslan Khasbulatov's *The Struggle for Russia*.

Russian Politics and Society

Third edition

Richard Sakwa

1	2	3	4	6	6	7	8	9	10	11	12	15

18, 3, 5, 6, 7, 8, 12, 13, 14, 4, 9, 10, 11

London and New York

First published 1993
Second edition published 1996
Third edition published 2002
by Routledge
11 New Fetter Lane, London EC4P 4EE

Simultaneously published in the USA and Canada
by Routledge
29 West 35th Street, New York, NY 10001

Routledge is an imprint of the Taylor & Francis Group

Typeset in Times by Taylor & Francis Books Ltd
Printed and bound in Great Britain by TJ International Ltd, Padstow, Cornwall

British Library Cataloguing in Publication Data
A catalogue record for this book is available from the British Library

Library of Congress Cataloging in Publication Data
Sakwa, Richard.
Russian politics and society/Richard Sakwa.–3rd ed.
Simultaneously published in the USA and Canada.
Includes bibliographical references and index.
1. Russia (Federation)–Politics and government–1991– 2. Post-communism–
Russia (Federation). 3. Former Soviet republics–Politics and government.
4. Post-communism–Former Soviet republics. I. Title.
JN6695 .S28 2002
320.947'09'049–dc21   2001048670

ISBN 0–415–22752–6 (hbk)
ISBN 0–415–22753–4 (pbk)

Contents

Figures

Tables

Preface to the third edition

Over a decade has passed since the fall of the Soviet communist system in 1991. In that time, Russia has been balanced between consolidating the democratic aspirations that accompanied the fall of the old regime and reproducing in new forms the authoritarianism that was overthrown at that time. There are undoubtedly major achievements recorded in these years. The basic framework of a democratic law-governed state has been established, enshrined in the constitution adopted in December 1993. Some of the fundamental institutions of such a state have also been established, together with a market-oriented economy. Relations with the former members of the Soviet Union have been strained, but no Yugoslav-style inter-state wars involving Russia have broken out, while Russia's relations with the rest of the world are now probably more balanced and stable than at any time in the past. There are, however, many aspects of Russia's post-communist evolution that give cause for concern. Although the framework and institutions of a democratic society have been established, political practices of leaders at all levels often undermine the spirit of democracy. This is most in evidence during elections, where the weakness of an independent media and civil society allows executive authorities considerable leeway. Above all, the wars in Chechnya (1994–6, 1999–) entailed untold suffering and abuse of human rights.

This book will try to provide a balanced analysis of post-communist Russian institutional, political and social development. The structure of this edition has changed considerably from earlier editions. Chapter 1, for example, now contains a brief summary of Soviet politics, a change made in response to comments from lecturers and others requesting some more historical context as background to contemporary developments. This edition has cut some of the material presented in the first two editions. For example, much of the detailed analysis of the events leading up to the violent confrontation of October 1993, and details of the evolution of the current constitution, has been removed. In addition to restructuring, the material has been updated to reflect events up to the early mid-term of Vladimir Putin's first presidency. Plenty of echoes of the earlier versions remain, but this edition focuses on the challenges facing Russia in the twenty-first century.

The restructuring and updating have been the relatively easy part. Far harder has been the attempt to make sense of it all. Already in the Preface to the second edition in 1996, I noted that the glad days of the early post-communist years (reflected to a degree in the tone of the first edition of 1993) had given way to foreboding about the erosion of Russia's tenuous democratic gains. I argued in 1996 that between the people and the state a regime based on Yeltsin personally had emerged that undermined the consolidation of the state and the autonomy of social institutions in one direction, and stunted the growth of an active civil society and representative system on the other. In 1996, only the outlines of a type of oligarchical capitalism that funded the regime and blurred the distinction between particularistic economic and general state interests were visible. The heyday of oligarchical capitalism and regime elitism lasted a bare two years, between Yeltsin's re-election for a second term in 1996 and the financial crash of August 1998. The appointment of Yevgenii Primakov as prime minister in September 1998, and even more the emergence of Putin as Yeltsin's successor in 1999, signalled the reassertion of a 'statist' line that sought to regain a relative autonomy for the state, freed from the deathly embrace of the oligarchs and Yeltsin's personalised 'courtly' style of regime rule. The reassertion of the state in the early 2000s, however, threatened further to undermine the free development of autonomous political institutions in society. Putin's advocacy of a liberal economic model appeared balanced by a rather more traditional model of politics.

This is the stage in which we now find ourselves. The question 'Is Russia a democracy?' resounds ever more insistently as press freedom appears under attack, the second Chechen war drags on, and the party and representative system is reorganised and, apparently, bent to the needs of an emerging state corporatist system. This book promises no simple answer to questions about the nature of Russian democracy. It will, however, try to provide the historical and institutional framework, some of the economic and social context, and to present the key debates and issues within which the reader can make up his or her own mind. If the book allows the reader to take a balanced and informed view of contemporary Russian politics, then it will have succeeded in its purpose.

Richard Sakwa
Canterbury
July 2001

Acknowledgements

The debts incurred in preparing a work of this size are too numerous to list. In addition to thanking all those who helped in the preparation of the first two editions of this book, I would like in particular to mention Roy Allison, Vladimir Amelin, Jonathan Aves, Edwin Bacon, Pavel Baev, Nikolai Biryukov, Philip Boobbyer, Mike Bradshaw, Archie Brown, Yitzhak Brudny, Tim Colton, Lena Danilova, Howard Davies, Al Evans, Alexander Filippov, F. Steven Fish, Vladimir Gelman, Leonid Gordon, Gabriel Gorodetskii, Chris Hamn, Vicki Hesli, Elena Hore, Eugene Huskey, Yurii Igritskii, Misha Ilin, Igor Klyamkin, Arbakhan Magomedov, Andrei Medushevskii, Marie Mendras, Lena Omel'chenko, Oksana Oracheva, Robert Orttung, Vladimir Pastukhov, Nicolai Petro, Hilary Pilkington, Sergei Prozorov, William Reissinger, Tom Remington, Neil Robinson, Stefan Rossbach, Peter Rutland, Andrei Ryabov, Thomas Saalfeld, Aleksei Salmin, Robert Sharlet, Liliya Shevtsova, Svetlana Sidorenko, Louis Skyner, Steven Solnick, Valerii Solovei, Kathryn Stoner-Weiss, Joan Barth Urban, Marcia Weigle, Harald Wydra and Andrei Zagorskii. I am particularly grateful for the support and encouragement given by Bruno Coppieters, Peter Duncan, Cameron Ross, Olga Sidorovich, Sergei Yerofeev and Stephen White. The faults, of course, remain my own. Craig Fowlie and Mark Kavanagh at Routledge, like their predecessors who have tussled with the gigantism inherent in Russian studies, once again displayed great patience and understanding as I tried to cut a crystal goblet out of jelly. I am most grateful for the secretarial and other assistance of Alison Chapman, Nicola Cooper and Jean Hudson at the University of Kent. It is my pleasure to thank the British Academy for their assistance in the preparation of this edition.

Note on style, spelling and transliteration

Words like Party are capitalised to indicate that the proper noun referred to is a concrete entity that existed or exists in the Soviet Union or Russia. The word 'democrat' is usually used without inverted commas, although the attempt by a particular group to appropriate the term for themselves is clearly problematical; similarly, for stylistic reasons, the use of 'self-styled democrat' or 'so-called democrat' is kept to a minimum.

The spelling of geographical areas tries to follow the changes, but in most cases has resisted the conversion back to Sovietised forms. Moldavia has thus become Moldova, and its capital Kishinev has become Chisinau, and there they stay despite the reversion to the earlier usage in the Russian media. The same goes for Belorussia's conversion to Belarus; Kirghizia's to Kyrgyzstan; Tataria's to Tatarstan; and Alma Ata's change to Almaty. However, where there is a standard American/British rendition of a name, this is the one used here. For example, Kiev rather than the Ukrainised Kyiv.

The transliteration system is the standard British one (a modified version of the Library of Congress system), used in most cases except when convention has decreed otherwise. The 'iu' letter becomes 'yu', 'ia' becomes 'ya', and at the beginning of names 'e' become 'ye' (Yevgenii rather than Evgenii). Thus, El'tsin becomes Yeltsin, Ekaterinburg is Yekaterinburg, and Riiazan is Ryazan;. The diacritical (representing the soft sign) is also omitted from the end of frequently used words like *oblast'* (region) and Belarus', and from the end of place names and proper nouns, thus Lebed rather than the more strictly accurate Lebed', and Rossel rather than Rossel', although when the soft sign is in the middle of a name (e.g. Luk'yanov, Zor'kin) it is retained.

Glossary of acronyms, acrostics and terms

ABM	Anti-Ballistic Missile treaty (1972)
Afghantsy	Those who fought in the Afghan war, 1979–89
APEC	Asia–Pacific Economic Co-operation forum
Apparatchik	Worker in the Communist Party's Central Committee apparatus
ASEAN	Association of South-East Asian Nations
ASSR	Autonomous Soviet Socialist Republic
CC	Central Committee
CEC	Central Electoral Commission
CEE	Central and Eastern Europe
CFDP	Council for Foreign and Defence Policy
CFE	Conventional Forces in Europe treaty (1990)
CFSP	Common Foreign and Security Policy
Chinovnik	(Tsarist) civil servant
CIS	Commonwealth of Independent States
CMEA	Council for Mutual Economic Assistance, Comecon
CPD	Congress of People's Deputies
CPRF	Communist Party of the Russian Federation
CPSU	Communist Party of the Soviet Union
CSCE	Conference on Security and Co-operation in Europe (see also OSCE)
Dedovshchina	Bullying, hazing
EAPC	Euro-Atlantic Partnership Council
EBRD	European Bank for Reconstruction and Development
ECHR	European Convention on Human Rights and Fundamental Freedoms
ECJ	European Court of Justice
ESDI	European Security and Defence Identity
EU	European Union
FC	Federation Council
FD	Federal district
FDI	Foreign Direct Investment
FEC	Fuel and Energy Complex (in Russian: TEK)
FIS	Foreign Intelligence Service (see SVR)
FSB	*Federal'noi sluzhby bezopasnosti*, Federal Security Service
FSK	*Federal'noi sluzhby kontrrazvedki*, Federal Counter-intelligence Service

GDP	Gross Domestic Product
GKChP	*Gosudarstvennyi komitet cherezvychainoi polozhenie*, established during the attempted *coup* of August 1991 (see also SCSE)
GKU	Main Monitoring Department (of the presidential administration)
Glasnost	Openness
GNP	Gross National Product
Grazhdanin	Citizen
GRP	Gross Regional Product
Guberniya	Province, unit of Tsarist administration
GU(U)AM	Georgia, Ukraine, (Uzbekistan), Azerbaijan and Moldova grouping
IFIs	International Financial Institutions
IMF	International Monetary Fund
INF	Intermediate Nuclear Forces Treaty (1987)
Ispolkom	*Ispolnitel'nyi komitet*, Executive Committee (of the soviets)
KGB	*Komitet gosudarstvennogo bezopastnosti*, Committee of State Security
Kolkhoz	Collective farm
Komsomol	*Kommunisticheskii soyuz molodezhi*, Young Communist League
Korenizatsiya	Indigenisation, nativisation
Krai	Territory, province
LDPR	Liberal Democratic Party of Russia
MD	Military District
MFA	Ministry of Foreign Affairs
MID	*Ministerstvo inostrannykh del*, Ministry of Foreign Affairs
MVD	*Ministerstvo vnutrennykh del*, Ministry of Internal Affairs
NACC	North Atlantic Co-operation Council
Nato	North Atlantic Treaty Organisation
Neformaly	Informals
NMD	National Missile Defence
Nomenklatura	The Communist system of political appointments, came to designate the class of office-holders
NPT	Non-proliferation Treaty (1968)
Obkom	*Oblastnoi komitet*, *oblast* committee (of the CPSU)
Oblast	Region
OECD	Organisation for Economic Co-operation and Development
Okrug	District
OMON	Special-purpose riot police
OSCE	Organisation for Security and Co-operation in Europe (the name for the CSCE from December 1994)
OVR	Fatherland–All Russia electoral bloc
PCA	Partnership and Co-operation Agreement
Perestroika	Restructuring
PfP	Partnership for Peace
PL	Party-list electoral system
Postanovlenie	Directive
Raion	District, borough

Rasporyazhenie	Executive order
RF	Russian Federation
Rossiyanin	Russian (in the civic sense)
RSFSR	Russian Soviet Federated Socialist Republic
Russkii	Russian (in the ethnic sense)
SALT	Strategic Arms Limitation (Talks) Treaty
SCO	Shanghai Co-operation Organisation
SCSE	State Committee of the State of Emergency (see also GKChP)
SMD	Single-member districts in elections
Sootechestvenniki	Compatriots
SPS	Union of Right Forces party
SSR	Soviet Socialist Republic
START	Strategic Arms Reduction (Talks) Treaty
SVR	*Sluzhba vneshnoi rezvedky*, Foreign Intelligence Service
TLE	Treaty Limited Equipment
UES	United Energy Systems, the electricity monopoly
Ukaz	Decree
UN	United Nations
UNDP	United Nations Development Programme
USSR	Union of Soviet Socialist Republics
VTsIK	Central Executive Committee
VTsIOM	All-Russian Centre for the Study of Public Opinion
VV	Interior Troops
WEU	Western European Union
WGF	Western Group of Forces
WTO	Warsaw Treaty Organisation, Warsaw Pact
WTO	World Trade Organization
Zemlya (pl. *zemli*)	Territory, comparable to the German *Länder*
Zemstvo	Unit of Tsarist local administration

Part I

The fall of communism and the rebirth of Russia

In this part we will examine two associated but nevertheless distinct processes. The first is the *dissolution* of the system of Soviet communism. We will provide a brief overview of the trajectory of Soviet politics, both noting its achievements and identifying some of its main failings, before examining the rise of Russia and its role in the breakdown of Soviet communism. In the second chapter, the focus will be on the *disintegration* of the Union of Soviet Socialist Republics (USSR). The emphasis shifts from issues of political organisation to the very shape of the state itself. The USSR was established in 1922 as an equal union of allegedly sovereign republics to give political form to the diversity of the new republic's peoples and nations. The system worked as long as there was a force standing outside the ethno-federal framework; and this force was the All-Union Communist Party (Bolsheviks) (VKP(b)), renamed the Communist Party of the Soviet Union (CPSU) at the Nineteenth Party Congress in 1952. With the launching of *perestroika* (restructuring) by the new General Secretary of the CPSU, Mikhail Gorbachev, in 1985, the Party gradually lost its integrative capacity as its own internal coherence dissolved, precipitating the disintegration of the state that it had overseen by the end of 1991. The dynamics of the relationship between dissolution and disintegration and the role of Russia in both is our central concern in this part.

1   Soviet communism and its dissolution

> But what I believe to be certain is this: if you were to give all these grand, contemporary teachers full scope to destroy the old society and build it anew, the result would be such obscurity, such chaos, something so crude, blind, and inhuman that the whole structure would collapse to the sound of humanity's curses before it could ever be completed.
>
> (Fyodor Dostoyevsky)[1]

Soviet communism was one of the most ambitious attempts at social engineering known to history. Coming to power in October 1917, the Bolshevik party under the leadership of Vladimir Il'ich Lenin sought to change every aspect of Russian politics and society. Armed with the ideology of Marxism, they launched the great communist experiment to build a society on fundamentally different principles from those that human history had hitherto seen. The ideology proclaimed the abolition of the market, the introduction of social, national and political equality, the direct and unmediated power of the working masses, and the spread of the revolution to all corners of the earth. In practice, of course, these ideals were tempered by the harsh realities of trying to build socialism in a relatively backward and isolated society. Communism in Russia was an experiment in the most profound sense, in that untested principles of social organisation were applied by one group over the rest of the community. The attempt to abolish the private ownership of the means of production, to overcome Russia's imperial legacy by granting autonomy to many of the peoples making up the nation, and to repudiate the whole tradition of Western state and law to create a fundamentally new politics, all this was a measure of the grandeur of Bolshevik ambition. For seventy-four years, the Soviet Union sought to create an alternative social order, in effect an alternative modernity, to that predominant in the West. In the event, what was established was a *mismodernised* society, creating institutions that were modern in form but repudiating modernity's spirit, above all political liberty and free thought. The Soviet system endured far longer than most of its early critics thought possible, but ultimately in 1991 came crashing down. The legacy of the failed experiment lives on in Russia today. Although the major formal aspects of the old system collapsed in 1991, great wedges of the old institutional and informal structure survived intact into the post-communist era. The successor regime did not enjoy a *tabula rasa* on which to build a new system. What emerged out of the fall of communism is a unique and fascinating hybrid. The bulk of this book is devoted to analysing the nature of this hybrid new political order, but this chapter will focus on the nature and fall of the communist system itself.

The Soviet system

In this section we will do no more than provide a brief outline of the main phases of Soviet power. The periodisation is used only to highlight the key developments. The Provisional Government, led in its final period by Alexander Kerensky, had replaced the imperial rule of Nicholas II in February 1917, but itself lasted a mere eight months. The October revolution was effectively four revolutions rolled into one:

- The first was the mass revolution, in which peasants sought land, soldiers (peasants in another guise) struggled for peace and workers strove for greater recognition in the labour process.
- The second was the counter-elite revolution, in which the alienated Russian intelligentsia repudiated the absolutist claims of divine rule by the monarchy and fought to apply what they considered to be more enlightened forms of rule. The Bolsheviks from this perspective were only the most ruthless and effective part of this counter-elite, challenging the bases of the old order in the name of the radical emancipation of the people in the name of a new set of social ideals.
- The third revolution was the national one. Already Poland and Finland had broken away from the Russian empire, but the Provisional Government's failure to respond to the national aspirations of Ukraine, the South Caucasian and the Central Asian republics was one of the reasons for its downfall.
- The fourth revolution was what could be called the revolution of internationalism. The Russian revolution reflected a trend of thought, exemplified by Marx, which suggested that the old-style nation-state was redundant and that, as capitalism became a global system, so social orders would gradually lose their national characteristics. From this perspective the revolution could just as easily have taken place in Berlin or Paris; it just happened to start in what Lenin called 'the weakest link in the imperialist chain', in St Petersburg and Moscow, but would according to him inevitably spread.

The inter-relationship and tension between these four levels of revolution are what make the Russian revolution so perennially fascinating, and it is these contradictions that we shall explore below. The Bolshevik seizure of power was followed by seven recognisable phases before the final period of reform and collapse from 1985.

Consolidation and compromise, October 1917–June 1918

The weeks following the revolution were followed by decrees granting the peasants land and declaring Russia's withdrawal from the First World War. This was accompanied by an assault against big business ('the Red Guard attack on capital'), as well as against the free press. The secret police, the Cheka, was established in December 1917. In the Treaty of Brest-Litovsk of March 1918, the Germans imposed crushing terms on Russia as Lenin gave up territory to buy time. This was a period in which various oppositional groupings *within* the revolution, like the coalitionists (in favour of broadening the government to include all parties represented in the soviets) and the Left Communists (who urged Lenin to wage a revolutionary war against Germany in the name of the internationalist principles of October), were defeated. It was also the period when movements *against* the revolution began to mobilise, in effect precipitating the Civil War. Between March–June 1918, Lenin sought to find a compromise with big business through his programme of 'state capitalism', an attempt that revealed his ruthless pragmatism (as the peace of Brest-Litovsk had done earlier) as the emancipatory goals of the mass revolution came into contradiction with the developmental goals of sections of what had now become the representatives of a new elite. The independent workers' movement was ruthlessly crushed by Bolshevik power. Lenin's model of socialism appeared to be that of the German war economy, a type of state capitalism where the state fulfilled the role of capitalists.

Civil War and War Communism, June 1918–March 1921

The attempts at compromise (and there remain questions over the degree of Lenin's commitment to broadening the base of the new regime) came to an end as the incipient Civil War broadened into wide-scale armed confrontation. The system known as War Communism developed, partially in response to the exigencies of fighting the war and the concomitant need to centralise authority and resources, but also reflecting aspects of Bolshevik utopianism such as the attempt to abolish private property over the means of production in its entirety. Nationalisation of enterprises was accompanied by the establishment of a Supreme Council of the Economy (Vesenkha) that tried, in Lenin's words, to hold the entire economic life of the country in its fist. To feed the cities and the Red Army (established in February 1918), a harsh system of grain expropriation operated against the peasantry. The new political system also became increasingly centralised, provoking the emergence of the Democratic Centralist opposition that demanded the introduction of the separation of powers within the regime itself, with greater autonomy for local soviets and lower-level party committees. This was a period characterised by an unstable mix of ideological extremism and pragmatism, reflected by 1920, for example, by the attempt to abolish money, which had become largely worthless anyway. With the Civil War effectively over by mid-1920, the momentum of Bolshevik ideological extremism continued for another few months, showing itself, for example, in the war against Poland that sought to spread the revolution at the point of the Red Army's bayonets. The intensification of grain requisitioning, the militarisation of labour (a policy advocated by the commissar of war, Leon Trotsky) and the closure of urban markets provoked peasant uprisings (notably in Tambov region) and, most significantly, demands by workers at the Kronstadt naval base in the Gulf of Finland for 'soviets without Bolsheviks'.

The New Economic Policy (NEP), March 1921–9

In response to the threat to the regime, Lenin at the Tenth Party Congress in March 1921 convinced his party to reverse its policies and make concessions to the peasantry. Compulsory grain deliveries were now replaced by a tax in kind, allowing peasants to sell grain surpluses in a restored market. A limited degree of producer autonomy was introduced as part of the NEP. To secure the regime's flanks in this 'retreat', however, Lenin imposed draconian discipline within the party through a 'ban on factions', adopted at the same congress. Although the Workers' Opposition since 1920 had been complaining about the curbs on free speech within the party, and had tried to broaden the base of the regime by restoring elements of the mass revolution by granting broad economic rights to the trade unions, they were now not only defeated but the very idea of opposition was proscribed. The distinction between opposition *to* the revolution, by various forces outside the regime, and opposition *within* the system by those seeking to explore alternative policy options was extinguished, and the door opened to Stalin's monocratic rule.

The establishment of the USSR in December 1922 reflected a peculiar type of ethno-federalism, where 'union republics' like Ukraine, Belorussia (as it was known before changing its name to Belarus in 1991) and the Russian Soviet Federated Socialist Republic (RSFSR) came together to form a new state whose legacy of dual federalism (with representation based on both territorial and ethno-federal principles) lives on to this day in Russia. Lenin died in January 1924 and, in the jockeying for power that followed, Stalin proved the most adept at exploiting the political closure of the regime bequeathed by Lenin to secure his power against Trotsky, Bukharin and other Bolshevik leaders. At first, Stalin supported Bukharin's moderate policies within the framework of NEP, but by the late 1920s, despite the evident success of NEP in restoring industry and prosperity to the countryside, sought ways to go beyond its limitations. The regime was effectively hostage to the peasants' willingness to sell grain on the market. At the same time, already in 1924 Stalin had announced the idea of 'socialism in one country', effectively renouncing Lenin's internationalism and establishing the priority of Soviet state interests above those of the international revolution. Stalin insisted that Russia could not only *begin* the transition to socialism, but could go on to *complete* its construction by its own efforts. To do this required resources from the countryside to pay for the investment required.

Revolution from above and Stalin's rule, 1929–53

Stalin's 'third revolution' (following those of 1905 and 1917) was directed initially against the peasantry, forcing them into collective farms (*kolkhozy*), making it easier to extract grain from them in order to fund industrialisation. The five-year plans for crash industrialisation were launched within the framework of the state planning agency, Gosplan. The principles of command and administer were now universalised to every aspect of economic and social life, including the arts and personal life. The role of terror and the secret police climaxed in the great purges of 1937–8. Nevertheless, the rudiments of a modern industrial economy were built, although at great cost. The distortions of the Stalinist command economy, the destruction of the most active people in the countryside, the neglect of the service sector, the reduction of money to an internal accounting unit and the relative isolation of the Soviet economy from world development all left the post-communist Russian economy with severe structural problems. It was this economy, however, that provided the sinews of war to defeat the Nazi German invasion of June 1941, and the USSR emerged victorious in May 1945 as part of the winning alliance with the Western powers. This alliance soon crumbled into the Cold War as it became clear that Soviet power had come to stay in the Eastern European countries liberated from fascism by the Red Army, but now to be ensnared in the Soviet communist experiment.

Khrushchev and attempts at reform, 1953–64

Stalin's death in 1953 left his successors with several major dilemmas. The country had been governed by the personalised rule of a morbidly suspicious dictator for several decades, and the institutions of governance, including the CPSU, had been reduced to little more than shells. In the economy, Stalinist command methods were clearly stifling innovation and preventing the system from moving beyond the primary phase of industrialisation to become more complex, intensive and technologically sophisticated. At the same time, millions remained incarcerated in the *gulag*, the term used by Alexander Solzhenitsyn to describe the great archipelago of labour camps that stretched across the country like islands in the sea. In his 'Secret Speech' of 25 February 1956 at the Twentieth Party Congress, Nikita Khrushchev began to lift the lid on some of Stalin's crimes, including the deportation of whole peoples in 1944 (the Chechen, the Ingush, the Balkars and others). De-Stalinisation was a recognition of the need for change, but it was also an attempt to limit the change to a condemnation of the man, Joseph Vissarionovich Stalin, and not of the system that had allowed such a man to terrorise his own population for so long. In the event, Khrushchev's reforms, conducted under the slogan of returning to the alleged original purity of the revolution under Lenin, were deeply ambiguous and flawed, if for no other reason than (as we have seen) the October revolution consisted of at least four levels that were in tension with each other. There was no original grail to which Stalin's successors could return, as Gorbachev was to discover later. Khrushchev's erratic style of rule, moreover, had so thoroughly alarmed the defenders of the elite revolution that in October 1964 they ousted him.

Brezhnev and stagnation, 1964–82

Although in retrospect we view the long rule of Leonid Il'ich Brezhnev as General Secretary of the CPSU as a period of retrenchment and conservative reaction, some of the key features of the Khrushchev era were maintained, such as more attention to the needs of agriculture and the attempt to shift from producer to consumer goods. Nevertheless, most of the institutional innovations of the Khrushchev era, like the creation of some one hundred regional economic councils (*sovnarkhozy*) in an attempt to improve economic co-ordination, and initiatives to stimulate popular participation, were reversed: the Stalinist centralised ministries were restored and the stifling rule of local party committees, where jobs were effectively for life, was restored. The slogan of 'stability of cadres' encouraged complacency and corruption; extensive patronage networks ultimately even came to challenge the prerogatives of the party in making personal appointments (the *nomenklatura* system). The Brezhnev years can be seen as the Soviet system at its most 'normal', with no system-threatening external or internal threats. The challenge represented by the 'Prague Spring' of 1968 to democratise Soviet-style communism by introducing 'socialism with a human face', where the party's legitimacy to rule was to be achieved through effective policies and not to be derived in perpetuity from the very act of seizing power, was crushed by the Soviet-led Warsaw Pact invasion of August 1968. The stifling of sources of innovation and dynamism in Czechoslovakia was carried over into Soviet domestic policy, where 'dissent' was persecuted with single-minded ruthlessness by Yurii Andropov, at the head of the Committee for State Security (KGB) from 1967. Soviet-style communism was condemned now to an extended period of entropy, with no self-sustaining mechanism of growth or regeneration allowed to revitalise the system. A type of neo-Stalinism was restored, without mass terror but where the suffocating rule of the petty bureaucracy inhibited initiative and imbued the whole era with an aura of stagnation (*zastoi*).

The interregnum, 1982–5

Brezhnev's death in November 1982 provided his successor, Andropov, with the opportunity to experiment with ways of regenerating the system. His approach was that of 'authoritarian modernisation', employing the heavy-handed tactics of the secret policeman to defeat corruption and to kick-start the engine of economic growth. Fate, however, intervened to cut Andropov's innovations short, and his death in February 1983 allowed Konstantin Chernenko, one of the worst, oldest and most complacent of Brezhnev's acolytes, a brief period to restore the glories of the era of stagnation before his own death in March 1985 inaugurated an exhilarating period of change.

Perestroika

Gorbachev came to power committed to revitalising the Soviet Union. Within months, he launched the programme that he called *perestroika*, which in the space of six years moved from attempts to rationalise the system to a phase of liberalisation, and then on to a democratisation phase that began to transform the society and polity, but that culminated in a final stage of disintegration. Once changes began, they could not be constrained by regime-led reform, and by 1991 pressure for a radical change of system became overwhelming. The attempt in August 1991 by a group to hold back the tide of change precipitated the result that they had sought to avert: the dissolution of the communist system of government and, by the end of the year, the disintegration of the USSR.

   Perestroika was the last great attempt at communist reform. Even before coming to power, Gorbachev realised that the system was suffering from major problems, with declining economic growth, stultifying secrecy in scientific and political life, and with politics dominated by a corrupt elite. Visiting Canada in May 1983, Gorbachev shared his concerns with the Soviet ambassador there, Alexander Yakovlev, who would later become one of the architects of *perestroika*. Yakovlev reports that they spent hours discussing the disasters awaiting the Soviet Union if nothing was done: 'The most important common understanding…was the idea that we could not live this way anymore.'[2] By starting a 'revolution within the revolution' Gorbachev hoped to save the essentials of the system, above all the leading role of the Party and the planned economy. Greater responsiveness would be achieved by the use of *glasnost* (openness) and elements of competition through democratisation and limited marketisation.

Gorbachev believed that the old system remained viable; that it was a powerful motor that required only some fine tuning. *Perestroika*, he insisted, has 'been prompted by an awareness that the potential of socialism has been underutilized'.[3] The remoralising strain in *perestroika* was crucial. Gorbachev noted that the decision to launch *perestroika* was prompted in part by 'our troubled conscience'.[4] Despite the revolutionary language, his was essentially a reformist programme. His tragic fate was to act as the destroyer rather than the builder; the more he tinkered with the system, the deeper the crisis. His reform communism only exacerbated the problems of what was already a system in crisis, and worsened the legacy facing the post-communist governments. It fell to his successors in Russia and the other republics to rebuild economies and to nourish the fragile shoots of democracy that *perestroika* had encouraged. We shall examine below the three main phases of the old regime in its death agonies.

Rationalisation, 1985–6

In this phase some of the themes of Andropov's authoritarian reform programme were revived. As head of the KGB Andropov better than anyone knew the real state of affairs in the country. In the fifteen months of his leadership, he launched a campaign against corruption and attempted to tighten up on labour and and social discipline. To Andropov's programme Gorbachev added the notion of *uskorenie* (acceleration), seeking to rejuvenate the existing economic system by the vigorous application of old remedies. The government led by Nikolai Ryzhkov devoted yet more resources to investment and reinvestment (the improvement of old plant and facilities), imports were cut back and once again the needs of the long-suffering Soviet consumer were neglected. During this period, grand and ultimately meaningless programmes were announced, such as the promise that by the year 2000 every Soviet citizen would have an apartment of their own. The programme of acceleration sought both to reform the economy and increase output at the same time, contradictory demands that failed to achieve either.[5] The misconceived anti-alcohol campaign launched at this time, inspired by the 'conservative reformer' Yegor Ligachev, led to the increased production of bootleg liquor (*samogon*) and devastating losses to the budget revenues of central and regional authorities.

Rationalisation, according to László Póti, entails 'a series of superficial, partial and non-conceptual measures that, however, indicate a certain degree of unintentional discontent with the system'.[6] The period of rationalisation entailed a recognition of the problem accompanied by the belief that the solution lay within the framework of the existing system. Gorbachev, however, soon came to understand that more radical measures were required.

Reform, January 1987–March 1990

The second phase of *perestroika* can itself be divided into two sub-periods: a discussion phase from January 1987 to the Nineteenth Party Conference (28 June–1

July 1988) marked by debates over *demokratizatsiya* (democratisation) and the revelations of *glasnost*, a period that proved to be the high point of *perestroika*; and an implementation phase from summer 1988 to March 1990, which proved far more difficult than the reform communists anticipated. This reform phase corresponds to the stage of liberalisation discussed in the literature on transitions.[7]

In the discussion period, increasingly bold strategies for the political regeneration of the political system were debated in an attempt to tap the alleged hidden potential of the Soviet model of development. The January 1987 plenum of the Central Committee (CC) of the CPSU marked a watershed in the move away from authoritarian towards democratic reform. The plenum called for the extension of competitive elections in the workplace, the soviets and in the Party itself. In June 1987, a further plenum of the CC adopted a plan for the economic transformation of the country that focused on greater autonomy for enterprises and increased rights for workers to elect their own managers. Rather than strengthening the system, however, the revelations made possible by *glasnost* about the crimes of the past and the inadequacies of the present only undermined the legitimacy of the regime as a whole.

The Nineteenth Party Conference in June–July 1988 marked the transition to the implementation of programmes of reform. Attempts were made to formulate a grand strategy of political reform to modernise the entire system within the framework of one-party democracy and one-party parliamentarianism. Gorbachev's strategy was based on the CPSU retaining a predominant role;[8] but the Party was now to guide rather than to lead. The overall principal aim was to create a 'socialist legal state' with the separation of powers and a revived legislature. In December 1988, the USSR Supreme Soviet created a three-chamber Congress of People's Deputies (CPD), two chambers of which (the Soviet of the Union and the Soviet of Nationalities) were to be chosen in multi-candidate elections, while the third (what can be called the Soviet of Representatives) was to be made up of delegates from social organisations, including 100 guaranteed seats for the Communist Party. The full Congress was to meet twice a year while current parliamentary business was to be conducted by a smaller Supreme Soviet drawn from the CPD. This strange parliamentary model, devised by Gorbachev's old friend from his Moscow University days Anatolii Luk'yanov, represented a return to the dual system of a large and rather irrelevant Congress and smaller Central Executive Committee (VtsIK) that operated in the early Soviet years before being abolished by Stalin in 1936.

The semi-free elections of March 1989 for the new assembly saw the defeat of many communist officials and the return of some democrats, though they numbered no more than 400 out of a total of 2,250 CPD deputies (see the boxed text below). At the first convocation of the CPD in May 1989, Gorbachev was elected chairman of its new 542-member Supreme Soviet, a post he had achieved without facing the electorate at any stage. The Congress was the scene of vigorous debates, televised live to an enthralled nation, and appeared to mark the onset of effective parliamentary politics. The CPD and its Supreme Soviet passed a significant body of reformist legislation, with new laws on freedom of conscience and religious belief, and freedom of the press. The first steps were taken towards creating a law-governed state (*Rechtsstaat*), if not a democracy, something that distinguished *perestroika* from the rest of Soviet history. The structure of the new parliament, however, was deeply flawed – perhaps intentionally so. The Congress was unwieldy and, lacking the necessary committee structure, could not focus on key issues or set a coherent legislative agenda, while the Supreme Soviet became a permanent forum for wide-ranging debates but failed to establish the necessary routines for effective legislative activity (adoption *and* implementation) or for over-seeing the executive.

Election to the USSR Congress of People's Deputies, 26 March 1989

Background

- There were 2,250 seats, but only 1,500 were contested; the rest (750) were reserved for social organisations.
- The CPSU was allocated 100 seats, and the CPSU Central Committee drew up a list of exactly 100 (including Gorbachev).
- Eighty-five per cent of the candidates were communists, whereas in the previous election for the old Supreme Soviet they had comprised only 71.4 per cent. Thus 'democratisation' at this time had the paradoxical result of increasing the proportion of communists.

Electoral system

- Candidates had to obtain an absolute majority of the votes cast. If none achieved the threshold of 50 per cent, a run-off election was held between the two candidates with the most votes. The second vote usually took place a fortnight after the first ballot.

Result

- CPSU 1,931, non-CPSU 319.

Organisation

- In June 1989, the Congress elected a permanent Supreme Soviet of 542 members.
- The CPSU gained 475 seats, non-CPSU 67.

The Supreme Soviet was divided into two equal chambers with 271 seats apiece, the Council of the Union and the Council of the Nationalities.

The attempt to reconcile representative democracy with a leading role for the CPSU only rendered government incoherent. One-party democracy was a contradiction in terms, and the attempt to achieve the 'socialist pluralism of opinions' was challenged by the growth of genuine political pluralism in society. The very existence of the Soviet state in its old borders was challenged by the Baltic republics and others. Already in the final speech to the First Soviet Congress, Andrei Sakharov (an outstanding nuclear physicist who had worked to develop the Soviet atom bomb, but who had then become increasingly critical of the lack of political freedom in the system and consequently spent several years in internal exile in Gorkii) outlined a 'Decree on Power' that called for the repeal of the Party's constitutionally guaranteed right to a leading role, enshrined in Article 6 of the 1977 Soviet constitution, and sought to invert the relationship between the centre and the localities to guarantee that the laws of the former could only be implemented in the latter with their explicit authorisation.[9] The Decree on Power represented a revolutionary programme for the liquidation of the power of the *apparatchiki* (full-time Communist Party officials), insisting that:

> Any anti-legal interference by political parties, party-political organs and other social organisations in the work of state power and administration, the economic and socio-cultural activity of state enterprises, institutions and organisations must cease immediately and absolutely decisively.[10]

The Decree sought to separate the CPSU from state management, and in particular tried to end the practice whereby local Party leaders were simultaneously chairmen of local soviets (councils). Although challenged in the courts by Gorbachev, several local soviet chairmen resigned their Party posts.[11] In the great majority of cases, however, local soviet leaders right up to the *coup* of August 1991 were members of the local Party committee, and in numerous instances local Party leader as well.

The period was marked by accumulating failures, above all in the economic sphere. Reform plan followed reform plan, but none were consistently implemented. The country became increasingly ungovernable as Ryzhkov's relatively conservative government was unable to implement its own version of reform, in part because of Gorbachev's lack of support, while more radical alternatives were equally unacceptable. The emergence of an active workers' movement in the form of miners' strikes from June 1989 marked the point at which Gorbachev's strategy of reform from above was transformed into a revolution from below.

The reforms of this period can be defined as 'the substantial extension of the rationalisation measures in depth and rate with increased awareness of the tensions of the system, but still within that framework'.[12] Gorbachev's attempt to implement reforms within the framework of the one-party system proved unfeasible; the strategy of reform communism known as *perestroika* was not implemented because it was unimplementable. The period was characterised by a mass of contradictions, and it soon became obvious that one-party parliamentarianism was self-defeating. A 'socialist' legal state appeared to be an obstacle to the development of a genuine legal state in which the rights of citizens could be defended by law and in which powers were separated and defined. The reform consensus that existed in 1985 was undermined; by implementing self-defeating reforms, Gorbachev undermined the very concept of reform itself.

Transformation, March 1990–August 1991

The third phase was characterised by the dissolution of Gorbachev's definition of *perestroika* as a Party-led programme of reform and culminated in the *coup* of August 1991. From mid-1989, miners' strikes had demonstrated that new independent forces were entering the stage of Soviet politics. The 'vodka' riots of the New Year of 1990 were followed by a wave of demonstrations and the dismissal of unpopular regional Party leaders in Volgograd, Murmansk, Sverdlovsk, Tyumen and elsewhere under the pressure of mass protest. The politics of resentment against elite privileges were as strong as the hunger for democratic ideals.[13] This wave of protest culminated in a demonstration of perhaps half a million people in Moscow on 4 February 1990 calling for multi-party democracy.

The revolutions in Eastern Europe in the last months of 1989, following the inauguration of the first post-war non-communist government in Poland, led by Tadeusz Mazowiecki in August 1989, swept away the communist regimes in East Germany, Czechoslovakia, Bulgaria and Romania. Afraid that this might happen to them too, the Central Committee plenum of 5–7 February 1990 agreed to modify Article 6 to remove the constitutional monopoly of the CPSU on political power. This was confirmed by the third (emergency) meeting of the CPD on 14 March, which the next day strengthened Gorbachev's presidential powers. Thus the era of one-party rule, which had in effect lasted since October 1917, came to an end: free elections were introduced, the half-truths of *glasnost* gave way to genuine freedom of speech, and Party *perestroika* gave way to presidential *perestroika*. The transformation of the political system at last allowed liberalisation to give way to genuine democratisation.

This phase of *perestroika* could not be anything but a transitional period. It was characterised by intensified conflicts over economic policy, national issues and political strategies. Gorbachev had been able to consolidate his power faster than any previous Soviet leader, yet he still faced formidable opposition. Above all, the very forces he hoped to use to implement his reforms, the Party and the ministerial bureaucracy, resisted his policies, while he himself gave conflicting signals of what precisely these policies should be. In the early years of *perestroika*, Gorbachev had been able to mobilise a reform coalition of groups (including the military and the KGB) who, if not welcoming change, realised that some reform of the economy and the political system was essential if the Soviet Union was to meet the challenge of technological and social modernisation. However, by 1990 it was clear that the reform coalition was disintegrating and Gorbachev's own brand of communist reformism was losing support. Political life was becoming increasingly polarised, and Gorbachev's centrism was eroded from both sides.

A group of diehard reactionaries emerged, warning that Gorbachev's policies would lead to the betrayal of socialism and the destruction of the country. Already the letter in March 1988 by a Leningrad chemistry teacher, Nina Andreeva, had expressed the anger of the old generation. It urged a 'balanced' assessment of Stalinism and condemned the classless 'humanism' espoused by *perestroika*.[14] Conservatives like Ligachev were willing to accept some change but were intent on trying to salvage the Soviet past. The growing democratic movement also now diverged from *perestroika*'s reformism and was united if only on one thing, namely the need to transform the old structures of Soviet power and to introduce the basic features of a modern democratic system. Looming over all of these, however, was the growing unrest in the republics. The three Baltic republics (Estonia, Latvia and Lithuania) had never reconciled themselves to their incorporation into the Soviet Union in 1940 as part of the deal between Stalin and Hitler in August 1939 (the Nazi–Soviet Pact, and its various secret protocols), and now frustration with *perestroika* encouraged them to think of secession. Moldova had also been a victim of the Nazi–Soviet pact, while the Caucasian republics of Armenia and Georgia still hankered after the independence that they had lost as a result of Soviet invasions in 1921.

The democratic and national currents critical of Gorbachev's policies in 1988 found an individual around which opposition could focus. Already at the Twenty-seventh Party Congress in February–March 1986 Boris Yeltsin, at the time Party leader in Sverdlovsk *oblast* (region) and soon to be transferred to head the Moscow Party Organisation, had been the first top Party leader openly to condemn the privileges of the Party elite, and his stress on social justice earned him the soubriquet of a populist. Yeltsin's attack on the leading conservative, Ligachev, at the CC plenum on 21 October 1987 signalled the end of the monolithic rule of the CPSU and resulted in his dismissal as head of the Party in Moscow. His open confrontation with Ligachev, broadcast to millions on television, at the Nineteenth Party Conference on 1 July 1988 revealed the deep splits in the Party.[15] In the elections of March 1989, a tired and angry people gave him overwhelming support in Moscow (89 per cent of the vote) against the candidate of the old Party system, Yevgenii Brakov. In the Congress he was one of the leaders of the 400-strong Inter-regional Deputy's Group advocating the radicalisation of the reforms.

Perestroika-style institutions were duplicated in each of the USSR's fifteen republics. The elections to the Russian CPD of 4 March 1990 were relatively more democratic (although by no means free) than the Soviet elections of 1989, with nomination through social organisations dropped and the district registration meeting, used by officials in the 1989 Soviet elections to screen out undesirable candidates, abolished (see Chapter 5). Democratic groups achieved significant victories, assisted by the Democratic Russia electoral bloc established in January 1990 with branches in all major Russian towns. Some 20 per cent of the seats in the Russian Congress were won by democrats,[16] taking 63 out of 65 seats assigned to Moscow in the Russian parliament, and 25 out of 34 in Leningrad.[17] The economist Gavriil Popov came to head the Moscow soviet, in Leningrad the law professor Anatolii Sobchak came to power, and in Sverdlovsk (Yeltsin's home town) the democrats took control. There was a marked regional dynamic to the elections, with half of the establishment candidates north of Moscow's latitude suffering defeat, whereas south of that line hardly any did so. The pattern of the 1990s whereby voters above the 55th parallel tended to vote for reformists and those in the south for conservatives was already established.

As long as the struggle was between a decaying old regime and a rising new order, the democrats could muster a majority against the communist old guard. Even before August 1991, the second and third echelons of the ruling elite began to throw in their lot with the rising alternative as the rule of the *nomenklatura* (the class of people appointed by or deriving their status from the Communist Party) ebbed away: 'workers and intelligentsia, collective farmers and military officers, militiamen and former dissidents, Party secretaries in enterprises and non-party informals' were all moving over to the other side of the barricades against the higher officials of state and Party who, because of the distorted electoral process of 1990, were elected in almost equal numbers to the Congress.[18] The 'new class' of which Milovan Djilas had spoken was finally coming into its own;[19] born under Stalin, freed from the terror under Khrushchev, given job security under Brezhnev,

Figure 1.1 The USSR in 1991

harangued by Gorbachev in the cause of a restructured humane socialism, this class now cast aside the final shreds of communist ideology and claimed the role of the universal (middle) class of modernity.

The emergence of Russia

Russian predominance in the USSR did not necessarily mean that the Soviet state governed in the interests of Russia – a point made with great force by 'dissidents' like Solzhenitsyn and then taken up by the democratic insurgency in the late 1980s with Yeltsin at their head.[20] In institutional terms the RSFSR had been dissolved into the amorphous USSR. The other fourteen republics had been endowed with the attributes of statehood in the form of republican governments, parliaments and Communist Party organisations, and had developed distinct national identities even within the centralised framework. Russia, however, lacked its own Academy of Sciences, its KGB, its Ministry of Internal Affairs (MVD), its trade union or Komsomol organisations, its own national television and radio stations or even its own national capital. Its Council of Ministers was firmly subordinated to the Soviet government and lacked many of the ministries and departments present in other republics.

Above all, until 1990 the RSFSR had no Party organisation of its own, even though it made up 58 per cent (10.6 million) of the CPSU's membership of nineteen million members. A separate Russian Party organisation had been abolished with the adoption of the Union Treaty of December 1922 setting up the USSR, when Lenin had argued that the threat of 'great Russian chauvinism' would thus be diminished. The problem of the political representation of Russians themselves was ignored until Khrushchev in 1956 established a Russian Bureau, but this also was abolished in 1966. Russian communists lacked direct representation and were managed by All-Union Party bodies,[21] reinforcing the view in other republics that 'Soviet' meant 'Russian' while adding to the sense of grievance felt in Russia itself. As Ruslan Khasbulatov, the speaker of the Russian parliament between 1991–3, notes: 'The lack of rights and the grievous condition of Russia itself was a result of the deliberate policy of the central administration, which "dissolved" the republic in All-Union Party, economic and administrative structures.'[22] The history and traditions of Russia and its peoples were distorted and specifically Russian interests overlain by those of the Soviet system.

Already towards the end of *perestroika*, in response to stirrings of national consciousness, attempts were made to give shape to the aspirations for Russian statehood. On 27 July 1989, Russia's last communist prime minister, Alexander Vlasov, informed the Russian Supreme Soviet of plans to give greater economic autonomy to Russia, reminding deputies that Russia accounted for 60 per cent of Soviet GNP yet less than half of national income produced by Russia was left in the republic, whereas other union republics retained virtually all the national income they produced. He informed deputies of plans to increase Russia's sovereignty by the creation of new institutions that existed at the All-Union level but not yet at the republican level. These included a separate Russian Academy of Sciences, various social institutions, ministries, as well as a new television channel to cater to Russian needs.[23] The Leningrad Party organisation on 26 August called for the creation of a separate Russian Party organisation, but warned against any attempts to convert the CPSU into a confederation of republican parties.[24] In response to these demands, in December 1989 a 'Russian Bureau' of the CPSU was once again created, headed by Gorbachev himself. This half-measure satisfied few since the structural asymmetries between Russia and the other republics remained. It was this that provided the impetus for the establishment of Russian sovereignty.

At the first meeting of the Soviet Congress in May 1989, the idea that Russia itself could leave the Union was first mooted. In an impassioned speech the writer Valentin Rasputin spoke of environmental and moral issues, and warned of the growing anti-Russian sentiments in some of the other republics:

> Russophobia is spreading in the Baltic and Georgia, and it has penetrated other republics as well....Anti-Soviet slogans are combined with anti-Russian ones, and emissaries from Lithuania and Estonia travel about with such slogans, seeking to create a united front.

In such circumstances, he warned the non-Russian republics:

> Perhaps it is Russia which should leave the Union, since you hold her responsible for all your misfortunes....Without fear of being called nationalists, we [Russians] could then pronounce the word *Russian* and speak openly about our national self-awareness; we could end the mass corruption of the soul of our youth, and we could finally create our own Academy of Sciences.[25]

Such sentiments inspired deputies at the first convocation of the Russian Congress on 29 May to elect Yeltsin, after three ballots and by a margin of only four votes, chairman of the Russian parliament.[26] Gorbachev had bitterly opposed such an outcome, not trusting Yeltsin's political judgement and fearing that he would use Russian aspirations to further his own ambitions. To a degree his concern was justified, and henceforth the search for Union-wide solutions to the country's problems would give way to each republic trying to find its own way forward. It was clear that Gorbachev's attempts to revive the Soviet system through reform communism had failed; the Union republics of the USSR began to take responsibility for their own affairs. The blockage on democratic breakthrough at the all-Union centre encouraged the insurgency against the communist regime to take on national forms.

The most important manifestation of this was the adoption by the Russian legislature on 12 June 1990, by an overwhelming majority, of the Declaration of State Sovereignty of the RSFSR, whose principles were to lie at the basis of post-communist government in Russia. The Declaration stated that Russia was 'a sovereign state, created by historically united nations'; that 'RSFSR sovereignty is the unique and necessary condition for the existence of Russian statehood'; that 'the RSFSR retains for itself the right of free departure from the USSR'; and stressed the priority of the Russian constitution and laws over Soviet legislation.[27] The proclamation of state sovereignty, in Zverev's words, was 'psychologically rooted in the Russian people's unwillingness to carry the burden of empire'.[28] To paraphrase Stalin, Russia's insurgency was national in form but democratic in content. Gorbachev took a very different view, arguing later that 'Yeltsin's irresponsible actions' triggered the ensuing avalanche of sovereignty declarations – known as the 'parade of sovereignties' and the accompanying 'war of the laws' – that precipitated the disintegration of the Soviet Union.[29]

Gorbachev and others insist that the Declaration laid the foundations for the collapse of the USSR. This interpretation is categorically rejected by Khasbulatov (at the time Yeltsin's deputy chairman of the Russian Supreme Soviet), who insisted 'The Declaration [did] not, in essence, deal with sovereignty at all, but only with decentralisation of the excessively centralised Union state'. He noted how much remained under Soviet control: 'the combined armed forces, common rail network, airlines, defence' and much more, 'practically all the basic functions which make a state a state'.[30] This may well be true, but the Declaration acted as a spur to the other union republics (as well as to the autonomous republics within Russia) to adopt their own sovereignty declarations. By the autumn of 1990, the 'war of the laws' between the union authorities and components of the USSR was in full spate, ultimately undermining the integrity of the state. The assertion that in his struggle with Gorbachev Yeltsin destroyed the Soviet Union perhaps exaggerates the role of personalities in the titanic shift of geopolitical relations in Eurasia.

The centre of political life gradually shifted to Russia and the other republics as politics became 'renationalised'. The creation in June 1990 of the hard-line Communist Party of the RSFSR (CP RSFSR), headed by Ivan Polozkov, finally gave separate representation for the 58 per cent of CPSU membership who were in Russia; but it was also an attempt by the conservatives to build a separate power base to thwart Gorbachev's more radical reforms. In the event, they achieved little except to encourage Yeltsin and the Russian parliament to redouble their efforts to strengthen the Russian state as an instrument in the struggle against the Soviet Party regime. In 1990, Russia also gained its own Academy of Sciences, trade union and Komsomol organisations, and in May 1991 a Russian republic KGB was established. The struggle against the communist monopoly increasingly focused on 'democracy in one republic' rather than on Gorbachev's apparently futile attempts to democratise the Union and its institutions. The Declaration of State Sovereignty of 12 June 1990, as noted, marked the turning point in relations between the republics and the Union as Russian statehood was formally reborn and Russian laws were to take precedence over Union legislation. The Decree on Power that followed achieved what the democrats had earlier hoped that the Soviet Congress would do, namely assume the full powers of the state. The decree stipulated the separation of the Communist Party from the government in Russia and outlawed the 'party-political system of leadership' in the state, in enterprises, the KGB and the army. A resolution adopted at the same time forbade leading state officials to hold other posts, including those in political or social organisations.[31] Russia became a state-in-waiting.

Other republics followed Russia's lead, and on 16 July Ukraine adopted an extremely radical declaration of sovereignty, passed unanimously by its parliament, calling for multi-party democracy, a separate national army and respect for human rights. The precise meaning and juridical status of these declarations remained unclear, but they demonstrated that Gorbachev's attempts to negotiate a new

'Union Treaty' for the USSR would have to take into account the aspirations of the republics for autonomy. Declarations of sovereignty were not restricted to Union republics but began to be adopted by autonomous republics and even by regions and boroughs in Moscow and other cities. The 'war of the laws' focused above all on the contested jurisdictions of Union and republican power. As the Soviet administrative system came apart at the seams, both the republics and the centre claimed priority for their laws, leading in most cases to the implementation of neither.

The emergent Russian state became the main opposition to the decaying Soviet regime, and, as Khasbulatov noted, 'we find ourselves in an unprecedented situation in world history: a legitimate government in opposition'.[32] Gorbachev had planned a gradual deconcentration of power to society, yet his hesitancy in relinquishing the concept of Party rule – and indeed his failure to split the CPSU at the Twenty-eighth Party Congress in July 1990 and place an avowedly Social Democratic party at the head of the democratic transformation of the USSR – meant that as power leaked away from the old 'administrative-command' system (as the Soviet order was dubbed by democrats at this time) it was absorbed by the republics. As in 1917, the many layers of the revolution interacted in unpredictable ways. In the republics there was an upsurge of civic activity as a plethora of social organisations were established, known as *neformaly* (informals) in Russia. The rebirth of civil society was accompanied by the growth of pathological aspects of 'uncivil society' including virulently nationalist and racist movements. At the same time, the remnants of official structures used the new freedom to engage in the spontaneous privatisation of state property. Solnick likens the 'breakdown of hierarchy' at this time to a 'bank run' as Party officials began to prepare their 'golden parachutes' by 'stealing the state'.[33] In most republics, moreover, old communist elites managed to convert themselves into nationalists and continued to rule on the basis of the new ideology. The sovereignty of the republics indicated not the triumph of democracy and civil society but the establishment of the borders within which both might later develop.

Popular insurgency and regime decay

Despite a host of difficulties, such as complex registration laws and harassment, numerous parties were established in this period of insurgency. Gorbachev's 'socialist pluralism of opinions' was now superseded by structured political conflict and the veritable rebirth of politics.[34] The problem soon became one not of the lack of alternatives but the sheer abundance of new parties that failed to coalesce into a coherent force that could challenge the CPSU or provide the basis for viable government.[35] The decline of the Inter-regional Group of Deputies prefigured the decline of the USSR CPD itself. The democratic deputies, led by Yeltsin and Sakharov, were greatly outnumbered by the rest of the 2,250 deputies, whom the radical democrat Yurii Afanas'ev dubbed the 'aggressively obedient majority'.[36] The group was weakened by splits over national issues, with the Baltic delegation barely participating at all; and over tactics – the degree to which reform should remain within the one-party system. By late 1990, they had lost direction and coherence, especially with the death of Sakharov in December 1989.

Gorbachev's inability to convert the CPSU into a genuine instrument of reform was one of the main reasons for the failure of *perestroika*.[37] Although the Party had given up its monopoly on power in March 1990, this did not indicate a sudden conversion to democracy. As late as March 1991, the CPSU was still giving orders to government ministries, a year after having given up its constitutional 'leading role'. The old regime at this time tried to co-opt the resurgent Russian nationalism for its own purposes, but succeeded only in stimulating reactionary Russian nationalism and awakening the aspirations to statehood of some of the minorities within Russia. The CPSU sponsored various 'front' organisations, like the United Front of Workers (OFT), which tried to appeal to the loyalist instincts of blue-collar workers, and sought to influence the new parties established after March 1990. The USSR had moved from one-party rule to a limbo of non-party governance as the CPSU refused to move out of the way to allow new forces to take over. The Communist Party still claimed to be the only force that could fill the political vacuum, although itself now riven by the fragmentation that had gripped the rest of the country.

One of the cardinal principles that had kept the Party together was democratic centralism, an institutional theory that suggested participation of lower bodies in the decisions of higher ones but which in practice imposed a rigid hierarchical subordination.[38] Lenin's 1921 'ban on factions', as we have seen, prohibited horizontal contacts between Party cells. Gorbachev now weakened this element of democratic centralism, allowing an upsurge in factional activity. A Democratic Platform emerged calling for the radical democratisation of the CPSU, while the Marxist Platform demanded a return to a purer form of Marxian socialism.[39] The Party also began to split into its constituent national parts. In December 1989, the Lithuanian Communist Party under Algirdas Brazauskas broke away from the national CPSU in the belief that only by allying with domestic nationalists could it hope to retain a voice in Lithuanian politics. At the Twenty-eighth Party Congress in July 1990, Gorbachev had to fight hard to have his draft democratic programme of the Party adopted, with the CP RSFSR distinguishing itself by its dogged conservatism. The Party seemed constitutionally unable to reform itself, and, thus, far from being in the vanguard of reform, it lagged behind and indeed obstructed change.

The Central Committee of the CPSU, although much changed at the Congress, remained solidly conservative. At the same Congress the Politburo, a body that had in effect been the supreme government of the country, was radically transformed. Membership shifted from professional-territorial to largely territorial representation, composed now of the heads of the republican and some regional Party organisations, and certain key officials. At a stroke the Politburo was reduced in power, and the Party was crippled as a functioning political machine. As the linchpin of the Soviet political system, the CPSU had always been more than a political party. It was the Party's full-time apparatus, staffed by half a million *apparatchiki*, which was the effective core both of the Party and the state, while a million more were on the Party's teaching staff in the dense network of Party schools and departments of 'social science' in colleges. The ability of the rest of the membership to influence policy was severely limited by democratic centralism. During *pere-stroika* Gorbachev tried to broaden the influence of the rank-and-file by democratising the Party through the use of elections, and at the same time sought to weaken the grip of the Party bureaucracy by strengthening state bodies and the legislature.[40]

The CPSU's popularity fell sharply from its peak at the height of *perestroika*, and by May 1990 only 18.8 per cent of the electorate would have voted for it if there had been elections.[41] The Party began for the first time to suffer a financial crisis.[42] Party members themselves were disillusioned, and only 27 per cent stated that if given a choice they would join a second time.[43] Party membership peaked in October 1988 when it stood at 18.9 million members and 416,000 candidates, a total of 19.3 million.[44] In 1989, for the first time since the purges membership actually fell;[45] in the last quarter of 1989 alone 279,000 communists failed to renew their membership, and another 670,000 failed to do so by 1 April 1990.[46] Communists in Armenia and Azerbaijan left *en masse*, and few in the rest of the country felt moved to join what was increasingly perceived as a discredited organisation. This was a period marked therefore by mass defections, with membership falling to some 15 million by August 1991.

By the time of the August 1991 *coup*, the CPSU had lost its ideological and organisational integrity and had failed in its attempts to 'repartise' itself; that is, to convert itself from a state structure to a campaigning political organisation.[47] The CPSU was marginalised, its membership was falling, it was splitting into various factions, and communist dominance was challenged by numerous informal groups and movements, accompanied by the emergence of genuine pluralism in intellectual and political life. The Communist Party was by definition an expansive and monopolistic body that had left civil society, the proper sphere for political parties, after October 1917 and had occupied the state; it was now faced with the prospect of being ousted from its strongholds in the factories, the army and the KGB to become a normal parliamentary party subject to the vagaries of electoral politics. Gorbachev on this crucial issue could not follow his usual centrist position, because the centre had disappeared and he had to come off the fence: either Party rule or genuine multi-party politics. His failure to choose in time only protracted the crisis, preventing either side from taking the initiative and weakening his own position.

Gorbachev's economic policy was marked by similar equivocations. By 1990, he had broadly decided in favour of establishing a market economy, but like most of the population he was unwilling to face the hardships – or the political price – that would inevitably accompany the transition. Gorbachev's failure in September 1990 to support the plan proposed by the team led by Stanislav Shatalin and including Grigorii Yavlinskii and Yegor Gaidar, envisaging a rapid transition to the market in '500 days', was in retrospect probably the moment when the USSR passed the point of no return and could no longer be held together. The plan called for an end to price controls, fiscal and monetary discipline to contain inflation, and rapid privatisation. It envisaged the conversion of the USSR into an economic union with only loose political ties between the constituent republics. Under pressure from conservatives, the plan was rejected by Gorbachev in favour of a much-diluted programme proposed by a different team. Yeltsin had supported the Shatalin plan, and its failure led him to launch Russia's own economic reforms in November 1990. It appeared that no single economic programme could work for all of the USSR; but if every republic had to devise its own reform plan, then what was the point of Gorbachev's 'renewed union'?

Communist hard-liners now launched the so-called 'winter offensive' of 1990–1. Isolated from the radical democrats and fearing the hard-line reactionaries, Gorbachev became hostage to the conservatives. This was reflected in personnel policy. The liberal Vadim Bakatin was replaced as minister of the interior (MVD) with the pugnacious Boris Pugo, and on 27 December 1990 Gorbachev forced parliament to accept Gennadii Yanaev as his vice-president. Even the usually compliant Soviet legislature, now chaired by Luk'yanov, baulked at ratifying the appointment of an official who epitomised the stagnation of the Soviet bureaucratic system. On 20 December 1990, Eduard Shevardnadze, who had been foreign minister since July 1985, resigned, warning darkly of the threat of a *coup*.

The conservative offensive was not limited to displacing liberal officials in Moscow but attempted to crush the nationalists in the republics. The low point of this period came with the storming of the Lithuanian TV building on 13 January 1991, in which fifteen people were killed. Gorbachev's role in these events is still not clear, publicly defending the ministers responsible for the bloodshed but denying any responsibility. He might well have gone along with what turned out to be a dress rehearsal for the events of August, and then at the last minute repudiated the attempt by the conservatives to seize power in Lithuania. In economic policy this period was if anything more catastrophic than what had come before. In December 1990, Ryzhkov was replaced as prime minister by Valentin Pavlov, a man who had earlier been minister of finance and had almost single-handedly destroyed the rouble by printing money as fast as the budget deficit grew. He now set about destroying the whole economy by his refusal to countenance a rapid advance to the market and by his poorly planned currency reform and price rises.

At the time of the crisis of January 1991, Yeltsin had not hesitated to rush to the Baltic states to declare his support for their independence. While often seen as no more than a ploy in his struggle with Gorbachev, Yeltsin's action nevertheless represented a remarkable repudiation of Moscow's traditional empire-building role and created the conditions for the relatively peaceful dissolution of what now came to be known as the Soviet 'empire'. Gorbachev's attempt to re-legitimise the authority of the Soviet Union in the following months by renegotiating the federation was always a fragile affair, having been delayed too long while he had been distracted by the excitement of foreign affairs and the struggle with his Party opponents. The referendum on 17 March 1991 on a renewed Union gave a notably ambiguous response (see the boxed text below). While 71.3 per cent of the RSFSR's 79.4 million turnout (75.1 per cent of the total electorate) voted 'yes' to a renewed federation, almost exactly the same number (69.6 per cent) voted in favour of a second question added to the ballot in Russia, the creation of a Russian presidency, which implicitly challenged the postulates of the first.

Referendum on a 'renewed Union' and a presidency in Russia, 17 March 1991

The question

- Voters were asked: 'Do you consider necessary the preservation of the Union of Soviet Socialist Republics as a renewed federation of equal sovereign republics, in which the rights and freedom of the individual of any nationality will be fully guaranteed?'

Participation

- Six republics boycotted the referendum: Armenia, Georgia and Moldova, and the three Baltic republics of Estonia, Latvia and Lithuania.
- This signified the *de facto* division of the USSR into at least two parts.

Turnout and results (USSR)

- In the USSR 147 million voted, 75.4 per cent of the electorate.
- Of those who voted, 112 million supported the idea of a 'renewed Union'.
- Thus 76.2 per cent of turnout supported the Union.

Turnout and results (Russia)

- In Russia out of a total registered electorate of 105,643,364, 79,701,169 took part, 75.4 per cent
- Of those who voted, 56,860,783 voted 'yes' and 21,030,753 voted 'no'.
- Thus 71.3 per cent supported the Union and 26.4 per cent did not.
- 2.3 per cent of ballots were spoiled.

On whether to establish a presidency in Russia

- A supplementary question was added in Russia: 'Do you consider necessary the introduction of the post of president of the RSFSR, elected by universal suffrage?'
- 69.85 per cent of the ballot voted for Russia to have a president.
- Of those who took part, 28 per cent voted against a presidency for Russia and for a renewed Union.
- 23.4 per cent voted for a Russian president but against the Union.
- 45.6 per cent voted for a president and for the Union.
- 2.1 per cent of votes were spoiled.

Source: *Izvestiya*, 26 March 1991, p. 2; *Pravda*, 27 March 1991; M. Gorbachev, *Soyuz mozhno bylo sokhranit'* (Moscow, izd. 'Aprel'-85', 1995), pp. 148–9.

The counter-attack of the conservatives was halted by a renewed wave of labour unrest. On 1 March 1991, a national strike of miners began with economic and political demands, including calls for the resignation of Gorbachev and Pavlov, and the dissolution of the USSR Supreme Soviet. Many mines continued to strike until early May 1991, and they were joined by workers in other industries in Belarus in April. All of this warned Gorbachev that alliance with the conservatives eroded his position. At the opening of the Third Russian (Emergency) Congress of People's Deputies on 28 March, called by the conservatives in an attempt to oust Yeltsin, Gorbachev ordered 50,000 MVD troops into Moscow to prevent a demonstration in support of Yeltsin, yet perhaps a quarter of a million people defied his ban. Gorbachev at this point turned once again to the reformists, and in the 'nine-plus-one' agreement of 23 April at his *dacha* at Novo-Ogarevo conceded greater power to the leaders of the nine republics involved and an accelerated transition to the market economy. Yeltsin went on to pacify the miners, and announced that the mines were to be transferred to Russia. The new Union Treaty between the republics of what had been the Soviet Union would be one built from the bottom up, founded on the sovereignty of the republics and relegating Gorbachev and the central government to a secondary role. The treaty was formalised on 23 July 1991 and was to have been signed by some of the republics on 20 August.

Yeltsin's position was consolidated on 12 June 1991 when, for the first time in history, Russia chose its president in a popular vote (see Table 1.1, below), with Alexander Rutskoi (the leader of the Communists for Democracy faction that had emerged at the Third CPD) selected as his vice-president. On the same day, Popov was elected mayor of Moscow with 65 per cent of the vote; in Leningrad Sobchak was elected mayor with 69 per cent (soon recruiting Vladimir Putin as his adviser and later deputy), and at the same time 54 per cent voted to rename the city St Petersburg. At his inauguration on 10 July 1991, Yeltsin proclaimed his readiness to embark on a far-reaching democratic transformation and the fundamental renewal of the Russian Federation (RF). He supported the plan for a restructured Union and promised co-operation with the other republics, but at the same time he stressed the sovereignty of the RSFSR and its role in the world, not simply as part of the USSR but as a sovereign state in its own right. He painted a vision of a reju-venated Russia 'rising from her knees' and drawing on its cultural and spiritual heritage and its great past, re-entering the world community freed of imperialist ambitions and embracing the principles of freedom, property, the rule of law and openness to the world.[48] Yeltsin appealed to Russian patriotism against the commu-nist regime, but at the same time offered a new synthesis of national self-affirmation and democratic aspirations.

Conclusion

Communism in the Soviet Union fell in 1991 with minimal resistance. Gorbachev's reforms during *perestroika* had undermined the system from within, and by 1991 formerly mighty institutions were no more than hollow shells.[49] The CPSU was riddled with factions and had lost not only its much-prized ideological unity but also its ability to rule. While Gorbachev's achievements in ending the Cold War and returning consciousness to the people by lifting the burden of fear ensure him his place among the greats in the pantheon of history, his legacy was profoundly flawed. In contrast to his predecessors at the head of the Soviet state, his political flexibility allowed the decoupling of ideology and power while his responsiveness to popular aspirations allowed the Soviet system to be transformed in a relatively

Table 1.1 First Russian presidential election, 12 June 1991

Turnout and participation:

The total number of registered electors was 106,484,518 and turnout was 74.7 per cent. With the exception of Tatarstan, where a boycott of the elections was organised resulting in a 40 per cent turnout, participation ranged from 65 per cent in Moscow and St Petersburg to 85 per cent in Kursk and Belgorod *oblasts*.

Yeltsin won over 50 per cent of the vote in the first round, so no second round was required.

Result:

Candidate	Votes cast	Percentages
1 Yeltsin, Boris	45,552,041	57.30
2 Ryzhkov, Nikolai	14,395,335	16.85
3 Zhirinovskii, Vladimir	6,211,007	7.81
4 Tuleev, Aman	5,417,464	6.81
5 Makashov, Albert	2,969,511	3.74
6 Bakatin, Vadim	2,719,757	3.42
Invalid votes	3,242,167	4.10
Total votes cast	79,507,282	100.00

Sources: 'Soobshchenie tsentral'noi izbiratel'noi komissii po vyboram Prezidenta RSFSR', *Izvestiya*, 20 June 1991; *Pravda*, 20 June 1991.

peaceful manner. His earlier insistence that the Communist Party should remain at the head of the reform process gradually gave way to a more pluralistic understanding of the process of political change.

Gorbachev's style, however, tended to achieve the maximum confusion for the minimum advantage. His approach to policy-making perpetuated the arbitrariness that had always characterised the Soviet system. While he had a broad strategic vision of overcoming world divisions, he lacked the ability to formulate a convincing middle-level range of policy options that could command popular support or address the immediate needs of a society in turmoil. By 1991, he had even lost the support of the Party's liberal wing while not retaining the trust of the conservatives. Later he admitted that 'I should have taken advantage of the stability and popular consensus that existed in the first stage of *perestroika*, and moved more swiftly towards a market economy'.[50] As politics took on a public and parliamentary form Gorbachev's mastery of bureaucratic intrigue became irrelevant. Gorbachev's tragedy was that he was unable to make the transition from Party functionary to national leader, and the longer he delayed making the choice, the less he was able to fulfil either.[51]

Communist rule rested on a dynamic link between ideology and organisation: although the ideology was subject to permanent modification (from Lenin's internationalism to Stalin's Soviet nationalism through to Brezhnev's complacent 'developed socialism'), and organisational forms evolved (from Lenin's Party-centredness to Stalin's cult of personality through to Khrushchev's revival of the Party as a functioning institution), the important element was the link itself; power justified by the appeal to an over-riding ideological imperative. When that link was broken by Gorbachev, the whole edifice of communist rule collapsed. This in turn precipitated the disintegration of the national territory. Russia was the central actor in the destruction of the USSR, although the Declaration of State Sovereignty of 12 June 1990 was not intended to signal the end of the USSR. Underlying the Declaration and those that followed in other republics was a desire to see the federal union with a strong centre give way to a confederation of sovereign and equal states. The Declaration, however, unleashed a destructive dynamic that ended with the disintegration of the country. Lacking roots in any national community, the USSR proved susceptible to nationalist mobilisation once the political grip of the CPSU weakened.

2 The disintegration of the USSR

Nothing destroyeth authority so much as the unequal and untimely interchange of power pressed too far, and relaxed too much.

(Francis Bacon)[1]

At the beginning of the 1990s, Henry Kissinger observed that 'The borders between the "centre" and the republics do not necessarily coincide with the borders between totalitarianism and democracy.'[2] This view was certainly at the core of Gorbachev's attempts to save the Union. Yeltsin, meanwhile, continued the assault on the CPSU, and its demise in August 1991 left the USSR vulnerable to the increasingly sovereign republics. On 20 July 1991, Yeltsin issued a decree banning party structures in government offices and enterprises, and he also proposed legislation that would ban the Party from the armed forces.[3] The legal basis for the decree was dubious, since the USSR law on public associations stated that only the courts could outlaw a party (presumably including its branches). 'Departification' meant that communist officials would have to choose between their party and jobs. The depoliticisation decree came into effect on 4 August, and the CPSU was still considering its response when the *coup* intervened. Even Gorbachev appeared to lose patience with the dogged unreformability of the Party, vividly in evidence at the last plenum of the CPSU's Central Committee on 25–6 July, and announced that an emergency Party congress would be held in December 1991 to adopt a radical new programme that would return the Party to its social democratic roots.[4] Gorbachev at last appeared to accept the necessity of splitting the Party and placing himself at the head of the radical reforming faction. In the event, conservatives sought to halt the dissolution of communist power by forceful means, but succeeded only in precipitating the disintegration of the country that they had sought to save.

The August *coup*

Conservatives realised that the Union Treaty, due to be signed on 20 August, would make the old structures of power redundant. In July, twelve leading politicians, writers and generals signed a 'Word to the People', written among others by Gennadii Zyuganov who would go on to lead the revived Communist Party of the Russian Federation (CPRF), which served as the manifesto of the *coup*. In emotional language the address warned of the:

The subject components of the Russian Federation

1. Kaliningrad Oblast	31. Ivanovo Oblast	61. Khanty-Mansi Okrug
2. Pskov Oblast	32. Kostroma Oblast	62. Yamalo-Nenetsk Okrug
3. Smolensk Oblast	33. Kirov Oblast	63. Taimyr Okrug
4. Bryansk Oblast	34. Ulyanovsk Oblast	64. Evenk Okrug
5. Kursk Oblast	35. Samara Oblast	65. Ust-Orda Buryat Okrug
6. Belgorod Oblast	36. Orenburg Oblast	66. Aga-Buryat Okrug
7. Voronezh Oblast	37. Chelyabinsk Oblast	67. Chukotsk Okrug (Chukot Republic)
8. Rostov Oblast	38. Kurgan Oblast	68. Koryak Okrug (Koryak Republic)
9. Volgograd Oblast	39. Sverdlovsk Oblast	69. Republic of Adygeya
10. Astrakhan Oblast	40. Perm Oblast	70. Republic of Karachai-Cherkessia
11. Saratov Oblast	41. Tyumen Oblast	71. Republic of Kabardino-Balkaria
12. Penza Oblast	42. Omsk Oblast	72. North Ossetian Republic
13. Tambov Oblast	43. Novosibirsk Oblast	73. Republic of Ingushetia
14. Lipetsk Oblast	44. Tomsk Oblast	74. Republic of Chechnya
15. Orël Oblast	45. Kemerovo Oblast	75. Republic of Dagestan
16. Kaluga Oblast	46. Irkutsk Oblast	76. Republic of Kalmykia-Khalmg Tangch
17. Tula Oblast	47. Chita Oblast	77. Republic of Karelia
18. Moscow Oblast	48. Amur Oblast	78. Mordova Republic
19. Moscow City	49. Sakhalin Oblast	79. Chuvash Republic
20. Tver Oblast	50. Magadan Oblast	80. Republic of Marri-El
21. Novgorod Oblast	51. Kamchatka Oblast	81. Republic of Tatarstan
22. Leningrad Oblast	52. Jewish Autonomous Oblast	82. Republic of Bashkortostan
23. St Petersburg City	53. Krasnodar Krai	83. Udmurt Republic
24. Murmansk Oblast	54. Stavropol Krai	84. Komi Republic
25. Archangelsk Oblast	55. Altai Krai	85. Republic of Komi-Altai
26. Vologda Oblast	56. Krasnoyarsk Krai	86. Republic of Khakassia
27. Yaroslavl Oblast	57. Khabarovsk Krai	87. Republic of Tyva
28. Vladimir Oblast	58. Maritime (Primore) Krai	88. Buryat Republic
29. Ryazan Oblast	59. Nenetsk Okrug	89. Republic of Sakha (Yakutia)
30. Nizhnii-Novgorod Oblast	60. Komi-Permyak Okrug	

Figure 2.1 The Russian Federation

enormous, unprecedented misfortune that has befallen us....Why is it that sly and pompous rulers, intelligent and clever apostates and greedy and rich moneygrubbers, mocking us, scoffing at our beliefs and taking advantage of our naivete, have seized power and are pilfering our wealth, taking homes, factories and land away from the people, carving the country up into separate parts...excommunicating us from the past and debarring us from the future...our differences are nothing in the face of the general calamity and distress, in the face of the general love for the homeland, which we see as a single, indivisible entity that has united fraternal peoples in a mighty state, without which we would have no existence. [5]

The Address urged the creation of a nationwide movement of resistance to enemies like 'thoughtless and inept parliamentarians' but was vague on what form this should take.

The attempted *coup* of August 1991 sought to resolve by forceful means the crisis of power and end the struggle of conflicting ideologies. The leading conspirators were Pavlov (prime minister), Vladimir Kryuchkov (head of the KGB), Dmitrii Yazov (minister of defence) and Yanaev (vice-president). On Saturday 17 August, they met and discussed the implications of the new Union Treaty. They were joined by Luk'yanov, who realised that the devolution of power to the republics would in effect mean the end of the old centralised structures, including probably the national parliament and with it his own job. On learning that Gorbachev was unaware of their plans, he refused formally to join them but agreed to write against the treaty and at the same time assisted the putschists by delaying the convocation of the Soviet parliament for a week.[6]

On Sunday 18 August, the plotters sent a delegation to Gorbachev in his holiday home in Foros in the Crimea. The group included Valerii Boldin, on Gorbachev's personal staff since 1981 and accepted almost as one of the family, Oleg Shenin, a member of the CC Secretariat, Oleg Baklanov, first vice-chairman of the Defence Council, and General Valentin Varennikov, commander-in-chief of ground forces. They sought a presidential decree establishing a state of emergency or agreement to hand over power to the vice-president. Gorbachev condemned their actions and refused to have anything to do with the plot, warning that 'You and the people who sent you are irresponsible. You will destroy yourselves, but that's your business and to hell with you. But you will also destroy the country and everything we have already done.'[7] Gorbachev's communications with the outside world were cut off, but there remains a suggestion that Gorbachev might have done more to try to prevent the *coup*; indeed, Amy Knight asserts that 'Gorbachev's claims that he was an innocent victim of the coup ha[ve] lost all credibility'.[8] Others argue that in the circumstances he could have done little more.[9]

On Monday 19 August, the country woke up to endlessly repeated announcements by the mass media about the imposition of a state of emergency. A declaration by the State Committee for the State of Emergency (SCSE) was read out, signed by the original four plotters now joined by another four: Pugo, the hard-line minister of the interior; Baklanov; Alexander Tizyakov, president of the Association of State Enterprises; and Vasilii Starodubtsev, chair of the government-sponsored Peasant's Union. Yanaev announced that Gorbachev was ill and unable to fulfil his duties, and thus he was taking over in the interim. Troops entered Moscow, and for three days the Russian White House, the seat of parliament and the presidency, was defended by citizens. The plotters had stumbled into launching the *coup* with very little real preparation, and they had sent the troops into Moscow with no detailed instructions about what they were supposed to do once they got there. As Yazov admitted during later interrogations, 'We had no real plan.'[10] Russians remarked at the time that the *coup* had been organised with the level of competence with which the country had been run for the last few years.

The Russian leadership acted far more resolutely. On 19 August, Yeltsin, Khasbulatov and Ivan Silaev (the Russian prime minister) drafted an 'Appeal to the Citizens of Russia', condemning the *coup* in no uncertain terms as 'a right-wing, reactionary, unconstitutional coup' and branding the SCSE an illegal body.[11] Within three days it was all over, defeated by the opposition of the Russian leadership, the heroism of the people who took to the streets unarmed against tanks, the resistance in the army, the media and the factories, and by the lack of resolution of the plotters themselves. For the first time since Stalin a major initiative had been launched by-passing the Party leadership, and thus the *coup* revealed the degree to which the Party had been marginalised. At the same time, neither the Politburo nor the Central Committee and its Secretariat defended their own General Secretary imprisoned in the Crimea. However paradoxical it might appear, this was in a sense a 'constitutional *coup*'. The plotters tried to present their actions as being in conformity with the constitution and thus sought to draw legitimacy from their formal legality. The 'manifesto' of the putschists played down the ideological appeal to communist values. Instead, they sought to ground their venture on Soviet nationalism, the attempt to maintain the Soviet Union as a centralised state, and hoped to gain popular support by playing on populist emotions, above all by denouncing the unpopular co-operatives and other new forms of business activity, which the Address quoted above had termed 'bloodsuckers'. The plotters were not reactionaries, realising that the clock could not be turned back to before 1985. They were willing to accept some of Gorbachev's reforms but insisted that the time had come to stop the retreat. They represented a return to Andropov's authoritarian reform and a rejection of Gorbachev's democratising reforms. The attempted *coup* was therefore a conservative one, trying to preserve the USSR and its political system but ready to accept some necessary changes. The plotters sought to find a path midway between the out-and-out reactionaries, who would not have objected to Stalin's return, and the reform communists of Gorbachev's ilk, who were allegedly betraying the achievements of Soviet socialism.

They hoped that Luk'yanov's delay in convening the USSR Supreme Soviet would allow the country to settle down and accept the *coup* as a *fait accompli*. There was only one problem for the plotters, and that was that Gorbachev refused to step down, even temporarily. In any event, Yeltsin and his colleagues in the Russian government insisted that the *coup* subverted the constitution, and on that basis launched a counter-*coup* that destroyed not only the putschists but also the whole system of Soviet power. On 22 August, anti-communist demonstrations took place around the country, and the headquarters of the CPSU in Old Square in Moscow was in danger of being stormed. The statue of Felix Dzerzhinskii, the founder of the KGB's forerunner, the Cheka, in front of the Lubyanka (the secret police headquarters) was removed with the assistance of the Moscow city authorities. The demonstrations on that day looked as if they might turn into a popular revolution against Party officials and institutions. In Moldova and the Baltic republics statues of Lenin were dismantled, and one after another the republics announced their independence.

Yeltsin transformed the *coup* into a revolution. At a session of the Russian parliament the next day, the CPSU was suspended in Russia by a stroke of Yeltsin's pen. The CC and Moscow City Communist Party offices in Old Square were sealed to stop documents being destroyed, and Yeltsin ordered a number of communist newspapers to stop publication, including *Pravda* and *Sovetskaya Rossiya*. The retreat of the Party turned into a rout. On 24 August, Gorbachev resigned as General Secretary of the CPSU and called for the dissolution of the Central Commitee. On 29 August, the USSR Supreme Soviet suspended the CPSU, and, on 6 November 1991, Yeltsin banned the Party in Russia.[12] Party organisations were forbidden in military units and state institutions, and the property and bank accounts of the CPSU were placed under the control of the Russian authorities. Amid revelations of the abuse of state and Party funds, on 26 August N. Kruchina, a key worker in the CC's International Department that had been illicitly funding foreign communist parties, committed suicide. Details emerged of a Party-funded shadow economy, a secret financial empire organised by a Business Directorate in the Central Committee to maintain its financial position even if the Party lost political power.[13] Some Party administrators involved in this activity committed suicide, and other highly placed officials also did away with themselves. The Party's links with other communist parties and its subversive activities became known.[14] Some of the old guard in state posts also committed suicide, notably Marshal S.F. Akhromeev on 24 August, in despair at seeing the destruction of his life's work in building the USSR.[15]

The failure of the attempt by conservatives to halt the tide of disintegration by staging a *coup* in August 1991 only accelerated the demise of the old system and the state. While the nature of the August *coup* remains controversial, its effect is clear: the collapse of the once all-powerful Communist Party and the disintegration of the Soviet Union itself. The *coup* was the final act of 'one of the cruelest regimes in human history'.[16] The Soviet system had destroyed the old Russian middle class and the cultural intelligentsia; it had destroyed the self-sufficient peasantry and Russia's agriculture; the system had squandered the vast natural resources of the country and the wealth accumulated from the past; and in its final act the cannibalistic regime devoured itself.

The disintegration of the USSR

The defeat of the putschists in the August 1991 revolution reinvigorated democratic aspirations and instilled a new pride in Russian statehood, symbolised by the ubiquitous presence of the pre-revolutionary Russian tricolour (white, blue and red), which became the symbol of Russian democracy and was later adopted as the official Russian flag. At the funeral of the three young men who had died in the defence of the White House Yeltsin stressed that 'this conspiracy, this coup, was directed above all at Russia, the federation, the parliament, the president. But the whole of Russia stood up in its defence.'[17] The *coup* was followed by what can be considered the fourth and final phase of *perestroika*: disintegration.

The *coup* justified a series of formally anti-constitutional measures adopted by the Russian and other republican governments. All the major institutions of the Soviet state were discredited, with the partial exception of the military. The system was no longer in crisis but in a condition of catastrophic breakdown; few of its institutions were capable of reform or regeneration and after the *coup* were destroyed in their entirety. There was an immediate sense of popular relief that at last some of the problems facing the country could be resolved free from communist interference. A poll conducted by the All-Union (Russian) Centre for the Study of Public Opinion (VTsIOM) on 7 September 1991 found that 46 per cent of Muscovites were more optimistic than in early August, 32 per cent were as before, and only 15 per cent less optimistic.[18] However, for the new system to be considered secure it had to base itself not only on the negative legitimation of having withstood the *coup*, but also on a positive programme. With the destruction of the common enemy, the communist regime, the democratic and national coalition in Russia disintegrated. How was the country to be governed, and indeed what country, Russia or the Soviet Union?

On his return from the Crimea early on 22 August, Gorbachev remarked that he felt as if he was returning to 'a different country'.[19] In political terms, the world had indeed changed radically, and the next few months revealed that Gorbachev himself was increasingly marginalised by the decomposition of the USSR. The centre had in effect destroyed itself, and the *coup* transformed the declarations of sovereignty of the republics into declarations of independence. Lithuania had declared its independence on 11 March 1990 and Georgia on 9 April 1991, and even as the *coup* progressed other republics joined them: Estonia on 20 August; Latvia on the 21st; Ukraine on the 24th; Belarus on the 25th; Moldova on the 27th; Azerbaijan on the 30th; Kyrgyzstan and Uzbekistan on the 31st; Tajikistan on 9 September; Armenia on the 23rd; and Turkmenistan on 27 October. This formally left only Russia and Kazakhstan in the Soviet Union. Kazakhstan in particular favoured a Union because of its own delicate ethnic balance, split almost equally between Russians and Kazakhs, and because of its high degree of economic integration with the rest of the country.

Following the suspension of the CPSU its property was sequestered, and the democratic forces indulged in a rather undignified scramble for the pickings. The magnificent headquarters of the Central Committee on Old Square was taken over by the Russian government, and sessions of the Russian Council of Ministers would henceforth be held in the former offices of the Politburo. Up and down the country former Party headquarters were taken over by local administrations and organisations, and the Party's offices in factories and offices were turned over to new purposes. Very soon the ubiquitous presence of the Communist Party, once feared but more recently reviled, was but a fading memory.

The next casualty after the CPSU was the semi-democratic USSR Congress of People's Deputies. Inaugurated in a fanfare of enthusiasm, rather than dismantling the apparatus of communist power the Congress had provided a patina of democratic legitimacy for that authority.[20] An Emergency Congress from 2–5 September put an end to itself and thus also to one of the major elements of *perestroika*-style politics. Its last act was a Declaration of Human Rights and Freedoms that committed the country to international standards of legal, citizenship, property and social rights, including the right to work, and religious freedom and the right to use one's own language.[21] In the context, however, it was meaningless since there were no institutions that could guarantee these rights; and how could the rights of citizenship be defended in a country that increasingly existed only in name? Hopes for a democratic USSR were disappointed, and in the opinion of the self-styled democrats were probably unrealisable since empires and democracy are by definition incompatible. However, the question that was to haunt post-communist state-building immediately arose: what if the USSR was not an empire in anything like the traditional colonial sense but the core of a multinational community that could have survived as a democratic confederal state? The latter was Gorbachev's view, of a broad nationalist-leftist bloc, and increasingly of many ordinary citizens.

The bankruptcy of existing Union institutions had been vividly exposed by the *coup*. The logic of the struggle against the communist 'centre' had undermined all attempts to create alternative *national* democratic institutions and had focused attention on establishing the state organisations of individual republics. In these circumstances only a strong centre could have managed the transition from Soviet unitarism to a genuine confederation, but in this matter (as in so many others) Gorbachev had equivocated for too long and lost the opportunity that might have existed in 1988–9. The absence of a clear demarcation between Union and Russian institutions now gave rise to a dangerous vacuum of authority. Russia in effect suffered from a form of dual power, with two presidents and two parliaments, which gave rise to a type of 'dual powerlessness' and a paralysis of government.[22] This hesitancy was illustrated by Yeltsin's own behaviour. Instead of taking advantage of the enormous boost to his own popularity given by victory over the *coup* by launching decisive measures (including possibly pre-term elections to Russia's parliament and regional soviets), to consolidate the democratic revolution, he went on vacation to Sochi to ponder the future and thus missed the opportunity. Khasbulatov notes that 'The extraordinary passivity of the state during this period [from August to late October] remains a mystery to me.'[23]

It is precisely Yeltsin's failure to dissolve the Russian parliament, ironically, for which he is most condemned. In his second volume of memoirs, however, Yeltsin questions whether elections at that time would really have brought forward 'good' deputies, and notes that his resistance to the sort of acts suggested by the democrats, like the abolition of the state security system and vigorous 'decommunisation' measures, was based on the fear of provoking popular violence against the old regime, an approach that might have 'turned August into another October 1917', with all of the attendant violence and bloodshed.[24] The spectre of October and the fear of popular mobilisation inhibited the deepening of the democratic revolution. Instead of harnessing the enthusiasm of August to effect radical change, politics focused on intra-elite intrigues and institutional wrangling – soon provoking, not surprisingly, popular disillusionment.

The Russian authorities now stumbled into a war of manœuvre with Gorbachev and what remained of the USSR: slice by slice, in a form of 'salami tactics', Russia took over the powers of the union. Four main provisional structures operated to fill the vacuum resulting from the collapse of the old regime:

1 The Congress was replaced by a new USSR Supreme Soviet made up of representatives from the republics. If nothing else, the new parliament was intended to act as a counter-weight to the Russian parliament.[25] The modified Supreme Soviet had the right to call a full Congress but never did so. Several republics failed to send delegates to the new USSR legislature, and few regretted its abolition in December 1991.

2 The most important body was the twelve-member State Council made up of the leaders of eleven republics (the three Baltic republics and Georgia did not participate) with Gorbachev in the chair as president of what remained of the USSR. Gorbachev's acceptance of the new system ranks among his highest achievements, but his position would have been stronger if he had accepted more emphatically the confederalisation of the Union before the *coup* rather than after. During the *coup*, all the structures on which he had relied betrayed him (the CPSU, the army, the KGB and the MVD), but even earlier Gorbachev's instincts led him to try to find a new power base, the collective authority of the presidents of the republics in the Novo-Ogarevo process that had given rise to the Union Treaty, and this was now formalised by the creation of the State Council. Leaders of the democratic opposition had long called for a 'round table' conference of the Eastern Europe sort, but the *coup* made it clear that the only round table that would have any meaning in the USSR would be one involving not political movements but the leaders of the republics. The State Council took the key strategic decisions in the interim, recognising the independence of the three Baltic republics, but delayed the recognition of the independence of Armenia, Georgia and Moldova or that of Ukraine.

3 The third transitional body was the State Council's Inter-Republican Economic Committee, headed from 16 September by the former prime minister of Russia, Ivan Silaev. The committee acted as the government of the USSR to provide central direction in the transition to the market. Silaev's appointment reflected tensions within Yeltsin's camp, especially since he was, together with the reform economist Yavlinskii, convinced of the need to maintain a single economic space in the old Union. To this end an economic accord between ten of the former Soviet republics (excluding the three newly independent Baltic states, and Armenia and Georgia) was signed in the Kazakhstani capital, Almaty (formerly Alma Ata), in October 1991.

4 The USSR presidency itself was the fourth transitional structure. Gorbachev in the immediate post-*coup* period looked out of touch with current realities, reiterating his commitment to the renewal of the Communist Party and to notions of a renewed socialism. He had expected to carry on as before, but he was soon disabused of this illusion. He was harried and bullied by Yeltsin in the Russian parliament on 23 August, and popular opinion held him partly responsible for the *coup* because of his appointment of conservatives and his equivocation over economic reform. Gorbachev's mastery of compromise now worked to his advantage as he tried to achieve some sort of centrist democratic consensus in the post-communist era, as reflected in his appointments to the new Political Consultative Council under the presidency. Moreover, it now seemed to be in the interests of the non-Russian republics to keep an independent centre alive, if only to act as a counter-weight to the power of Russia.

By the end of 1991, it was clear that the old centre could play only a very limited role in post-communist politics. Gorbachev's power was increasingly over-shadowed by the Russian government and by Yeltsin personally. The republics were unwilling to delegate functions to the centre now that they themselves could decide the terms and intensity of the relationship with each other and the federal state. In the early post-*coup* days, the republics reached agreements on co-operation in economic, scientific, ecological and human rights matters, and, above all, the principles of collective security and defence. However, these commitments, like the economic accords, remained vague and gave way to the republicanisation of politics. The creeping Russification of All-Union institutions that had been evident even before the *coup* now accelerated as Russian normative acts increasingly replaced Union laws. Already in April 1991, the coal industry had been transferred to the control of the Russian government in exchange for ending the miners' strikes, and now the process of Russia 'gathering in' economic responsibilities speeded up. The federal budget was largely funded by transfers from the Russian treasury, and when in late October the Russian Congress decided to stop financing most Union bodies (with the exception of the foreign, defence, railways and atomic industries ministries), the Union effectively came to an end. In mid-November, Yeltsin took over Soviet oil exports and the gold and diamond industries, most of which are on Russian territory. The transitional institutions had little authority to take, let alone implement, decisions. The Union presidency headed by Gorbachev and the old institutions continued as if by sufferance from Yeltsin, and enjoyed only as much authority as he was willing to grant them. To the alarm of the other republics, Russia began to take on the mantle of the old Union centre.

Since Russia had led the democratic struggle against the *coup* and against the communist regime as a whole, it came as a surprise to the leadership to find that the hostility of the other republics was now directed against itself; instead of reaping gratitude for defeating the communist regime, Russia found itself isolated. What Russia had started was now completed by Ukraine in its refusal to be associated with the recreation of a new Union or any other centre in Moscow. As the Ukrainian leader, Leonid Kravchuk, put it on 8 November:

> We will oppose any attempt to create central government bodies. We will not ratify a treaty if central government bodies of any kind whatsoever are hidden behind it. Indeed no Center of any kind should exist other than coordinating bodies that would be established by the states participating in the treaty process.[26]

Russia's failure quickly enough to realise the depth of the distrust that existed towards any strong power in Moscow, be it in a Soviet authoritarian guise or a Russian democratic one, led to several ill-considered acts. Yeltsin's press secretary, Pavel Voshchanov, for example announced soon after the *coup* that the borders of republics which declared their independence would be questioned. Russia, more-over, was in the process of swallowing up the Soviet state apparatus, raising fears that it sought to absorb territory as well. This only seemed to confirm the suspicions of the republics that Russia was now the imperial hegemon replacing the Soviet regime, and put paid to Russia's hopes of establishing a genuine confederation to replace the USSR. Moreover, the republican leaderships that had wavered during the *coup* sought to protect themselves from Moscow's retribution by wrapping themselves in anti-Russian and nationalist flags, a ploy that was remarkably successful in allowing renamed neo-communist regimes to remain in power in many republics.

The West favoured the continuation of the USSR in order to maintain a single economic and political space, and to minimise the dangers of conflicts and the proliferation of nuclear weapons. Gorbachev's domestic position, however, became increasingly untenable and ultimately he failed to find a role either for himself or for the union bureaucracy. He tried to reconstitute the centre by offering the leaders of the republics seats on the State Council, but the leaders themselves were under pressure in their own republics. The increasingly bankrupt Union bureaucracy remained in business by printing money, stoking inflation and making a dire economic situation even worse, prompting the republics (above all Russia; see Chapter 12) to adopt their own economic reform plans. Silaev was given the impossible task of initiating reform from within the existing structures in a way that would suit both the republics and the centre.

These contradictions came to a head over attempts to negotiate a new Union Treaty of twelve sovereign states in a reconstituted entity that would be the subject of international law. Gorbachev insisted on the continuation of what he called 'the Novo-Ogarevo process', the search for a new Union of Sovereign States (USS), and this on 14 November 1991 resulted in the fifth draft of the Union Treaty, which conceded yet more powers to the Union republics while retaining some central institutions such as a directly elected president and a bicameral legislature.[27] Support for confederation came from the president of Kazakhstan, Nursultan Nazarbaev, and Yeltsin, who considered the maintenance of some sort of Union in Russia's interests. Only the Central Asian states, Belarus and Russia were willing to attend the initialling ceremony to be held on 25 November. The problem was noted by Yeltsin at this meeting, 'Signing the treaty without Ukraine is useless. There would be no Union. Let's wait for Ukraine.'[28] The other republics, above all Ukraine, in the event refused to have anything to do with a renewed centre and the ceremony never took place. Hopes for a new Union Treaty foundered on the rocks of Ukrainian aspirations, and ultimately the whole Union, already weakened by Baltic independence, was broken by the attempt to keep Ukraine part of it. While Gorbachev, and indeed Yeltsin, insisted that a Union without Ukraine was meaningless, Ukraine nevertheless abstained from all active participation in negotiations until the presidential elections and referendum of 1 December 1991. Policy within Ukraine was led by its Western regions, above all Lvov, taken from Poland in 1945. According to Szporluk, it was at that time that ethnicity took precedence over modernisation in Soviet development: 'The seeds of the Soviet Union's decline were thus planted at the moment of the Soviet Union's greatest triumph – 1945.'[29] As Napoleon put it, 'Empires die of indigestion.' Already by late 1991, there were plans to issue a separate Ukrainian currency. The overwhelming vote on 1 December 1991 to confirm the provisional declaration of independence of 24 August, and the election of Kravchuk as president, demonstrated that the initiative had irrevocably passed to the republics.

If Ukraine and other republics refused to have anything to do with a new Union Treaty, then what was Russia to do? If Ukraine became independent and began to issue its own currency, there was a danger that Russia would be flooded by the surplus roubles of 52 million Ukrainians. Yeltsin adopted the strategy long advocated by his close adviser, Gennadii Burbulis, namely the development of specifically Russian, as opposed to Soviet, policies.[30] A number of consequences followed from this, including the appointment of a new radical government headed by Yeltsin personally in early November 1991 with Yegor Gaidar responsible for economic reform and later acting prime minister. Another was the pronunciation of the death sentence on the Soviet Union. All this was tantamount to a Russian declaration of independence.

On 7–8 December 1991, the leaders of the three Slavic republics (Russia, Ukraine and Belarus) met in a hunting lodge in the Belovezh Pushcha nature reserve in Western Belarus to discuss the future of the Union. Since the three countries were the original signatories of the Union Treaty of December 1922 that had created the USSR, they claimed the right to dissolve what they had once formed, although according to the Soviet constitution the only way that a republic could secede was by referendum.[31] The Belovezh Accords declared that 'The USSR as a subject of international law and as a geopolitical entity has ceased to exist' and announced the formation of a Commonwealth of Independent States (CIS).[32] The Accords were ratified by the Russian Supreme Soviet on 12 December. While coming as a shock to the rest of the world, the Ukrainians had long been considering the option: their ideas for a confederation had been dismissed by Gorbachev, and they plainly considered that attempts now to renegotiate the Union Treaty were futile.[33] No records of the meeting survive, but two factors clearly precipitated the decision: the need to accommodate Ukraine's drive for independence; and the perception of Russia's 'government of reforms' that they stood a much better chance to transform the economy on their own. For Yeltsin, moreover, the act of dissolution had two advantages: it put a summary end to the Gorbachev era; and he apparently believed that the CIS would become a new Union with a new president, himself.[34]

The signatories reaffirmed their commitment to 'the goals and principles of the UN Charter, of the Helsinki Final Act and of other CSCE [Conference on Security and Co-operation in Europe] documents' (Preamble). Despite the commitment to 'universally recognised norms concerning human rights', no method of implementing these goals was indicated. Article 3 expressed the commitment to the 'preservation and progress of the ethnic, cultural, linguistic and religious identity of national minorities', but stopped short of recognising their right to political self-determination. The agreement attempted to maintain the territorial *status quo*, and Article 5 forcefully committed the member states to 'recognise and respect the territorial integrity of each other and the inviolability of the existing borders within the Commonwealth', although there was to be free movement of people and information within the Commonwealth. Above all, Article 6 committed the member states to 'maintain a common military-strategic space under joint command, including unified control over nuclear weapons'.[35]

The Central Asian leaders, and in particular Nazarbaev, were disturbed by the creation of what appeared to be an exclusively Slavic union. They met on 12 December in Ashgabat, the capital of Turkmenistan, and resolved to join the new body. On 21 December, all eleven republics that would make up the new

Commonwealth met in Almaty. The eight that had not met in Belarus (Armenia, Azerbaijan, Kazakhstan, Kyrgyzstan, Moldova, Tajikistan, Turkmenistan and Uzbekistan) signed a Protocol making them equal High Contracting Parties with the original signatories. The Protocol committed them to the Belovezh Accords and rendered them founder members of the Commonwealth. On that day, Nazarbaev announced that the USSR was no more, although formally it ended on 31 December 1991. The presidents signed six documents addressing some of the key problems facing the post-USSR world. They established a single economic space, unified control of nuclear arms and strategic forces, pledged that the international treaties of the USSR would be upheld and that the existing borders would be respected. The documents, however, were declarations of intent rather than binding treaties. Above all, the Almaty Accords declared that the new Commonwealth 'is neither a state nor a supra-state entity'.[36] It lacked serious central co-ordinating institutions and in effect abolished 'the centre' altogether, facilitating the ratification of the accords by the respective republican parliaments. It appeared that the CIS was to be a transitional phenomenon to manage the change and secure the orderly disaggregation of military and economic structures. This at least was the view of Ukraine and some other republics, but, as we shall see (Chapter 16), Russia, Kazakhstan and some others hoped for rather more.

The disappearance of the USSR meant the abolition of the post of president, and thus Gorbachev's rule was over. It would be an exaggeration to suggest that Yeltsin agreed to the abolition of the USSR in order to remove his rival Gorbachev, yet the personal factor is important.[37] As time passes, the depth of Gorbachev's domestic unpopularity at the time is easily forgotten. A poll in late November found that he was the seventeenth most popular politician, barely squeaking in above the populist Vladimir Zhirinovskiii, and far behind the most popular figure, Yeltsin.[38] Gorbachev resigned on 25 December 1991, maintaining a statesmanlike pose and declaring his critical support for the new regime:

> There can be no justification whatsoever for my going into opposition either from a political point of view or when it comes to the interests of the country....As long as Russia follows the path of democratic change, I will not only support her I will defend her, particularly at this difficult stage.[39]

Gorbachev and Yeltsin came to an agreement whereby the former president would enjoy certain privileges as long as he kept out of active politics. He established an International Foundation for Socio-Economic and Political Studies, known as the Gorbachev Foundation, and invited many of his former colleagues to work in it, including Yakovlev and others of the *perestroika* generation.

Problems of state-building

Russia was faced with both a systemic and a national crisis. Not only did its political and economic institutions need to be rebuilt, but also a new state had to be made. Basic ambiguities surround the emergence of the contemporary Russian state. We speak of an independent Russia, but at what point did it actually become independent? The other Soviet successor states in 1990–1 declared their independence, whereas Russia, while declaring its sovereignty on 12 June 1990 and effectively seceding from the USSR on 8 December 1991, was the only state simply to emerge as the residual legatee of the Soviet state following the latter's dissolution in December 1991. The reborn Russian state, moreover, had no precedents; its borders corresponded to no previous historical entity and the polity was based on entirely new principles.

The insurgency against the communist regime took the form of a struggle for the restoration of Russian statehood (*gosudarstvennost*). The Russian concept of 'statehood' is alien to the Anglo-Saxon mind, suggesting both a strong state in domestic politics and a vigorous presence in foreign policy. Statehood was being returned to Russia in two senses: as a political state at last freeing itself from the suffocating tutelage of the Communist Party; and as a republic with the attributes of statehood separate from the USSR. Russia's rebirth as a political state entailed the development of the institutions of political sovereignty, such as an independent parliament, government and presidency. Russia's rebirth as a republic, however, was to be a complex process, involving the development of a new national identity distinct from the Tsarist or Soviet imperial past. The very name of the state changed, with the Sixth Congress in April 1992 adopting a constitutional amendment that abolished the name 'RSFSR' and introduced 'Russia' and 'Russian Federation' as names with equal legal validity.

While 1991 represented a fundamental moment of rupture in both geopolitical and governmental terms, elements of continuity, of course, remained. The primordial drive for territorial consolidation was accompanied once again by attempts to strengthen the state at the centre. State-building takes four practical forms, leaving aside for the moment questions of national and cultural identity: the ability to defend the national territory; effective integration of the centre and periphery; ordered relations between the institutions of governance; and elements of reciprocity between the state and society. The Tsarist system was found wanting on all four counts, having suffered repeated defeats in the Great War; while the Soviet system was certainly able to defend itself, probably against the rest of the world combined, it was less successful in the other three aspects. The reborn Russian state now faced these challenges, once again in the context of balancing influence abroad and political reconstruction at home.

Russia inherited 76 per cent of the USSR's territory, 61 per cent of its GNP and 51 per cent of its population. Over 25 million Russians, however, found themselves outside the borders of the new state, representing a large proportion of the 43 million (15 per cent of the total USSR population) who found themselves outside their titular state (see Table 2.1). At 148 million, Russia had the world's fifth largest population (after China, India, the United States and Indonesia), with 128 recognised nations and ethnic groups. Stretching 9,000 km from east to west, Russia covers one-eighth of the earth's land surface (17.1 million sq km, of which 1.3 million sq km is arable). Its borders range a total of 58,562 km, with 14,253 km bordering sixteen foreign states and 44,309 km coasting two oceans and eleven seas. The country is richly endowed with natural resources and a skilled workforce. Russia had 90 per cent of the oil, 80 per cent of the natural gas, 70 per cent of the gold production and 62 per cent of the elec-

Table 2.1 Population of the USSR, 1989

Republic	Population of republic	% of USSR pop.	Living in USSR (1,000s)	% of USSR pop.	Living in their own titular republic (1,000s)	(%)	Living outside their own titular republic (1,000s)	(%)
Russia	147,386,000	51.4	145,155	50.6	119,866	82.6	25,289	17.4
Estonia	1,573,000	0.5	1,027	0.4	963	93.8	64	6.2
Latvia	2,681,000	0.9	1,459	0.5	1,388	95.1	71	4.9
Lithuania	3,690,000	1.3	3,067	1.1	2,924	95.3	143	4.7
Moldova	4,341,000	1.5	3,352	1.2	2,795	83.4	557	16.6
Belarus	10,200,000	3.6	10,036	3.5	7,905	78.8	2,131	21.2
Ukraine	51,704,000	18.0	44,186	15.4	37,417	82.6	6,767	15.4
Armenia	3,283,000	1.1	4,623	1.6	3,084	66.7	1,539	33.3
Azerbaijan	7,029,000	2.5	6,770	2.4	5,805	85.7	965	14.3
Georgia	5,449,000	1.9	3,981	1.4	3,787	95.1	194	4.9
Kazakhstan	16,538,000	5.8	8,136	2.8	6,535	80.3	1,601	19.7
Kyrgyzstan	4,291,000	1.5	2,529	0.9	2,230	88.2	299	11.8
Tajikistan	5,112,000	1.8	4,215	1.5	3,172	75.3	1,043	24.7
Turkmenistan	3,534,000	1.2	2,729	0.9	2,601	93.8	64	6.2
Uzbekistan	19,906,000	6.9	16,698	5.8	14,142	84.7	2,556	15.3
Total	286,717,000	100	257,965	–	214,550	74.8	43,283	15.1

Sources: *SSSR v tsifrakh v 1989 godu* (Moscow, Finansy i statistika, 1990), pp. 36, 38; *USSR: Facts and Figures Annual*, ed. Alan P. Pollard, Vol. 15, (Gulf Breeze, FL, Academic International Press, 1991), p. 504.

tricity output of the former Soviet Union. The great majority of the research institutes and educational establishments are also to be found here. It is this fundamental geographical and material disproportion between Russia and the other successor states that made it so difficult to establish comfortable relations between them.

Although Russia may have inherited the bulk of the territory and resources, the political institutions bequeathed by the old system were fragile and disordered. In his keynote speech of 28 October 1991, Yeltsin lamented the weakness of Russian statehood and stressed the need to establish the legal basis for the new Russia,[40] but the struggle to carve out a post-imperial state was to prove long and arduous. Russia had been far more subsumed into the Soviet identity than the other republics, leading them (and many outsiders) to confuse Russia with the Soviet Union. The Russian language was the official state language, and Russians predominated at all levels of government and administration: Russians traditionally were the second secretaries of the republican Party organisations and usually headed the local KGB. Native cultures were Sovietised and the use of their languages, especially in higher educational establishments and in political life, was stymied by the use of the imperial lingua franca. Russians represented Soviet power and thus Sovietisation was often perceived as synonymous with Russianisation (the cultural domination of Russia), and in places Russification (the conscious attempt to suppress other cultures in favour of Russia's) as well.

The new republic was a truncated form of the larger Russia for which the White armies had fought during the Civil War of 1918–20, and which ultimately the Bolsheviks rebuilt after their victory and which was formalised by the Union Treaty of December 1922. The rebirth of Russian statehood was accompanied by the tension between internal state-building and external withdrawal. However arbitrary the borders that Russia inherited, the attempt to recreate the 'greater Russia' that had died in 1991 would entail a level of violence comparable to that accompanying the 'greater Serbia' ambitions of the 1990s in the former Yugoslavia. Thus, a smaller Russian statehood emerged in which the national-patriots could argue that the problems associated with building the institutions of an independent Russia internally were provoked by Russia's separation from some of its historical territories and peoples externally. It was along the line of this argument that much of post-communist Russian politics flowed.

Conclusion

In 1991, the communist experiment in Russia, one of the most sustained attempts in social engineering ever undertaken by humanity, came to an end. The revelations of *glasnost* encouraged the view that the whole Bolshevik period had been one gigantic 'mistake', reflected in the popular slogan of the time 'seventy years on the road to nowhere'. The Soviet Union did not just fall, it collapsed. The failure of *perestroika* turned into a catastrophic breakdown of society and economy. All the institutions that maintained Soviet statehood were shattered simultaneously: the Communist Party, the secret police, the economic apparatus and the state mechanism. All of this was in terrible fulfilment of George Kennan's prediction soon after the Second World War that 'Soviet power, like the capitalist world of its conception, bears within it the seeds of its own decay.' He warned that if 'anything were ever to disrupt the unity and the efficacy of the party as a political instrument, Soviet Russia might be changed overnight from one of the strongest to one of the weakest and most pitiable of national societies'.[41] This indeed came to pass, and the fall of the communist system in August 1991 was soon followed by the disintegration of the Soviet state.

The political reforms from 1985 precipitated a crisis of authority and deprived the administrative system of its accustomed rules and leadership. It soon became clear that Soviet institutions could not be reformed but had to be thoroughly remade. Interwoven like a double helix, the dissolution of the Communist Party entailed the disintegration of the Soviet state. The foundation of the CIS and the overthrow of the Soviet president, bypassing the constitution and the law, was the last act of the counter-*coup* launched in August 1991 and marked Yeltsin's conclusive triumph over his rival. It was legitimated by the fact that the majority of the eleven presidents who disposed of the USSR had been directly elected in their republics, whereas Gorbachev owed his position to bureaucratic manœuvring. The USSR Supreme Soviet was not convened as requested by Gorbachev, to give at least some legal form to what was after all not only the dissolution of the USSR but of a geopolitical area that had taken some 500 years to be 'gathered together'. Political expediency and national self-assertion combined to put an end to the

USSR, but somewhere along the line democracy was the casualty. Subsumed in the USSR for decades, Russia in December 1991 returned to claim its place in the community of nations. The psychological and political consequences of such a dramatic emergence have yet to work themselves out.

Part II

Political institutions and processes

The August *coup* of 1991 in Russia might be taken as a symbolic moment of rupture between the old and the new, year zero of the new order; but at the same time, while history might have accelerated, it did not move in leaps. Enormous continuities remained across the symbolic divide: Russia was not a *tabula rasa* on which the new authorities could write at will. One of the main themes of post-communist politics must necessarily be the interaction between continuity and change, between the existing conditions in society, the economy and politics, and the process of change itself reacting with these historically determined conditions. Matters are complicated, moreover, by the fact that post-communist Russia had two 'old regimes' against which to measure itself and on which to draw, the Tsarist and the Soviet. While it was by no means certain that the factors that had given rise to Bolshevism in the first place had been overcome, it was clear that the seventy-four years of Soviet power would profoundly influence the post-communist period: there could be no direct return to pre-revolutionary Russia.

In 1991, the self-declared 'democrats' came to power, but this did not necessarily entail the triumph of democracy, and it soon became clear that post-communism was a distinctive syndrome of its own and far from synonymous with democracy. The fall of the communist regime was a necessary but not a sufficient condition for the triumph of democracy in Russia. Between the collapse of the old order and the birth of the new there lay a period of disorientation and disorder, a new Time of Troubles like that in the first decade of the seventeenth century. The dissolution of communist power was accompanied by a crisis of governance threatening chaos and social disorder. The optimal balance between stability and transformation proved elusive as the Soviet crisis of governance reappeared in an accentuated form. The weakness of post-communist state institutions was not compensated by the growth of other mechanisms to achieve the 'reign of peace' in civil society, giving rise to an almost primeval pre-liberal struggle of all against all, as Hobbes would have put it. The distinctive feature of post-communist Russia was the almost palpable retreat of government: the high tide of state power under the Soviet regime ebbed and society was left exposed and vulnerable to its own morbid elements: venality, criminality and corruption. Once again it appeared that decrees were issued and laws passed only to be ignored by a society apparently living according to a different set of rules. The economic collapse and the threat of social disorder accompanying the transition from communism raised fears that, once again, as in 1917, the democratic experiment would be still-born.

3 The new constitutional order

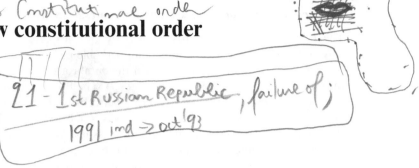

21 - 1st Russian Republic, failure of ;
1991 ind → oct '93

> Time has finally run out for communism. But its concrete edifice has not yet crumbled. May we not be crushed beneath its rubble instead of gaining liberty.
>
> (Alexander Solzhenitsyn)[1]

The re-emergence of a separate Russia out of the Soviet shell ranks as one of the great state-building endeavours of the twentieth century. Born out of the crisis attending the collapse of the USSR, the Russian state emerged with few immediate advantages. Its system of government had to be built from scratch, its constitution had to be rewritten, its legal system needed to move away from the punitive and vindictive ethos of the Soviet period, and its officialdom had to be retrained in the ways of a modern civil service. The priority for Russia was to establish the basic framework in which politics would be conducted, to establish the 'rules of the game', yet the struggle to adopt a new constitution would take until December 1993, and would include one of the most dramatic confrontations between branches of power seen in modern politics, the struggle between parliament and the presidency for supreme authority that culminated in the violent showdown of October 1993. It is with a brief analysis of this crisis that we begin and then examine the features of the new constitution and the associated development of constitutionalism and the rule of law.

Crisis and culminations: October 1993

With the demise of Soviet power in 1991, the one-dimensional conflict between the communist 'centre' and the insurgent 'democrats' ended, revealing structural weaknesses in the organisation of legislative power and exposing a crisis in relations between executive and legislative authority. This was a period that can be described as 'phoney democracy', with the people brought on as bit players in the drama of the struggle of president and parliament. The Russian legislature elected in March 1990 was designed neither to choose nor to control a government, let alone act as the supreme source of sovereignty. It did not have effective means to fulfil customary parliamentary functions like approving and overseeing budgets and legislation. The absence of the separation of powers worked both to the legislature's advantage, in that it had direct control over about half of state expenditure, and also to its disadvantage, as in its weak control over the executive.[2]

probs w/ legislature

Soviet parliamentarianism versus neo-Soviet presidentialism

The hesitant advance towards democracy of the *perestroika* years encumbered Russia with an unwieldy and largely unworkable parliamentary system. Russia was the only post-Soviet republic to retain the cumbrous two-tier legislative system for the elections of March 1990 (see Chapter 7). The Russian Congress was made up of 1,068 constituencies, of which 168 (15.7 per cent) were national-territorial and 900 (84.3 per cent) territorial. The Congress was to meet twice a year to legislate on the most important constitutional and other issues. With a two-thirds majority the Congress could alter the constitution, ratify changes in the name of the republic and cities, and change the powers of the presidency.[3] The Congress selected a smaller Supreme Soviet, the body properly known as the parliament, to examine current legislation and debate policies. By September 1993, the Supreme Soviet contained 248 voting members and 138 non-voting members working in committees and commissions, and thus a total of 386 officially worked in parliament on a permanent basis, although about a quarter of Supreme Soviet deputies were inactive. All Congress deputies over a five-year period were to have the opportunity of becoming members of the Supreme Soviet, but this did not work out in practice. In the three years of the Russian parliament it was renewed only twice, at the Sixth Congress in April 1992 and again at the Seventh in December 1992.[4]

The Supreme Soviet was headed by the chairman, a post that became vacant with Yeltsin's election as president in June 1991. Yeltsin's former ally Khasbulatov was the main candidate, but he encountered stiff opposition at the Fifth Congress in July 1991;[5] he was associated with the ethos of the old Party system and considered to have an abrasive personality. Having won his spurs during the *coup*, at the resumed Fifth Congress Khasbulatov was finally confirmed as 'speaker' (his favoured term for the post) on 28 October 1991 with 559 votes.[6] Khasbulatov's election did not put an end to Yeltsin's conflicts with the Russian parliament, and indeed intensified them as Khasbulatov, an economist by profession, sought to modify the government's economic reform programme and to defend the prerogatives of parliament – and his own.

Up to 1992, the Russian legislature was an accomplice to its own marginalisation: it voted to establish a presidential system at the Third Congress in April 1991, adopted the Law on the President at the Fourth on 24 May, and granted the presidency emergency powers to drive through reform by decree at the resumed Fifth Congress in November 1991. With the appointment in November 1991 of a non-party 'government of reforms', parliament was deprived of the right of detailed oversight over the work of the government. Although decrees and the appointment of key ministers required parliamentary approval, the legislature effectively lost control over policy and the government. Up to the Sixth Congress in April 1992, parliament largely acceded to the process of self-marginalisation. Parliament's 'marginalisation', however, was of a special type: the increased powers of the presidency were always clearly envisaged within the context of parliamentary supremacy. The Law on the President of May 1991 insisted that 'the president does not have the right to dissolve or suspend' the Congress or Supreme Soviet, he or she was to report at least once a year to the Congress, and their decrees were not to infringe existing legislation.[7] The extraordinary powers of the president were always regarded as temporary, so that when at the height of the struggle in 1993 parliament deprived the president of these powers, they were doing no more than what they were entitled to.

The struggle between parliament and the presidency in 1992–3, however, was always about more than legal issues. Sharpening differences over economic policy and state construction gave rise to the emergence of a 'red–brown' rejectionist front (leftists and nationalists), united in their opposition to the break-up of the USSR, radical economic reforms and Yeltsin's style of leadership and the team with which he worked. There was no clear rejectionist programme and instead the bloc reflected divergent interests; a common hostility to the new order represented by the August regime was enough to unite them in opposition to Yeltsin. At the same time, although independently, Khasbulatov and his colleagues sought to reverse the marginalisation of parliament as an institution, leading to profound political crisis at the Sixth (April 1992) and succeeding Congresses. At that Congress, for example, Khasbulatov condemned the cabinet's 'attack on democracy' and the dismissive attitude by ministers towards representative institutions.[8]

The crisis of governance did not derive from the personal qualities of the new leaders, the social context of the new politics or even long-term factors like the weakness of liberalism in Russia. More immediate political factors allowed the emergence of a type of dual power and ultimately provoked a constitutional crisis that led to bloodshed in the streets of Moscow in October 1993.[9] There remained a fundamental 'constitutional' crisis because the 1978 Russian constitution was heavily amended after 1990 and ended up granting both the executive and the legislative branches supreme state power.[10] Russia was *de jure* a parliamentary republic but *de facto* became a presidential republic. The balance between executive and legislative remained a matter of political struggle rather than constitutional law. The president's extraordinary powers were temporary and subject to the approval of parliament. Parliament itself enjoyed extensive powers under the existing constitution and, increasingly dominated by rejectionist groups, was able to block the executive's initiatives for constitutional change and economic reform.

Conflict between parliament and the presidency became endemic: personal factors played their part but structural factors were primarily responsible for the constitutional crisis that became a crisis of the state. Khasbulatov ruthlessly exploited his position as speaker to reward his supporters and make life uncomfortable for his critics. He enjoyed the power to manage the agenda, to manipulate the voting process on bills and amendments, to manage information flows, and controlled access to scarce resources and privileges such as foreign trips and offices. This did not render the Congress subservient to him, but it did mean that he exerted inordinate powers to shape its actions and agendas. Already in January 1992, Khasbulatov launched the first of his many broadsides against the 'shock therapy' approach to economic reform, condemning 'anarchical, uncontrolled price rises' and insisted that 'We are fed up with experiments.' He antagonised members of parliament as much as he did the president. The main charge against him was that instead of allowing parliament to act as an impartial forum for debate, he turned it into his own power base. Deputies claimed that Khasbulatov regularly exceeded his authority, others accused him of authoritarian methods of rule, and a growing number called for his replacement.[11]

The president himself failed to build consensus in parliament, not meeting with the leaders of the democratic movement for several months after the *coup*, and appeared to forget their earlier efforts on his behalf. Yeltsin's own rash and often ill-considered assaults on Congress narrowed the scope for compromise. The principles of parliamentary and presidential government are both equally valid, but the tragedy for Russia was that both were being pursued with equal vigour at the same time; like two trains approaching on the same track, the collision would be disastrous for both. While Khasbulatov certainly sought to turn the Russian parliament into his personal power base, the main reason for the crisis of legislative power in Russia was structural, primarily the legacy of the anti-parliamentarian essence of Soviet power and then, during *perestroika*, the incompetent approach to institutional reform. In establishing a powerful Congress Gorbachev hoped to balance the powers of the Communist Party; but the disappearance of the latter left the field clear for the former. The structure of parliament meant that it was an anti-parliamentary parliament, unable to work like a 'normal' representative and legislative body. The constitution, although heavily amended, still gave enormous powers to parliament, but the August 1991 settlement prescribed no institutional way to fulfil this role. The biannual Congress, as the 'highest state authority', enjoyed enormous powers and when in session could alter the constitution by a simple two-thirds majority, including depriving the president of his powers, or indeed, if they dared, abolishing the presidency entirely.[12] As long as the Congress wielded the enormous power to amend the constitution at will, and as long as the floor of the Supreme Soviet could be manipulated by the Presidium (which emerged as a type of parallel government) and by the speaker, no real parliamentary politics could emerge.

The distinctive feature of the crisis was that, while policy initiative lay with the presidential side, control over implementation and administration lay with parliament. This dualism was reflected in the very nature of the struggle, with parliament by necessity reduced to blocking measures: they had the power to impede presidential initiatives but lacked the power to develop policies – hence the growing irresponsibility of the Supreme Soviet's actions. The Congress and its Supreme Soviet were in the classical position of power without responsibility, but their power was essentially negative. Parliament failed to become an effective working body, with most of its legislation not direct-acting but requiring further regulations and decrees, offering enormous scope for the bureaucracy to hinder or to profit from them. The rejectionists, moreover, took full advantage of the moral and political collapse of the democratic challenge, intensifying the crisis of power at all levels.

Genesis of a tragedy

The conflict only gradually assumed the dimensions of a general crisis of power. At first Yeltsin grudgingly tolerated a degree of legislative oversight over his actions. He accepted the Supreme Soviet's repeal in November 1991 of the presidential decree imposing a state of emergency on Chechen-Ingushetia, but he over-ruled attempts by parliament to force the regional elections due on 8 December 1991. Parliament's reversal of Yeltsin's decree of 19 December 1991 merging the ministries of security and interior was allowed to stand. Parliament procrastinated over passing laws on such critical issues as privatisation, land reform and owner-ship, bankruptcy and the new constitution, and passed illiberal legislation on such issues as exchange controls. Rejectionist deputies opposed the reformers' reliance on economic aid from the West and sought more government intervention to preserve Russian industry, and in general were wary of the 'cosmopolitan' democracy that was allegedly being introduced into Russia. Khasbulatov became increasingly critical of the president's wide powers and sought parliamentary control over the government including the right to veto government appointments and policies.

Meetings of the Congress were times of high drama. The Sixth Congress in April 1992 failed to adopt a new constitution, placed even stricter controls over the progress of reform, and restricted the purchase and sale of land.[13] The Russian CPD appeared to be going the same way as the old Soviet Congress, acting as a brake rather than the motor of reform. Following the Sixth Congress Yeltsin threatened to hold a nationwide referendum on the new constitution and for the early dissolution of parliament (its term was due to end in March 1995) and new elections. A referendum was allowed if one-third of Congress deputies or one million members of the public asked for one. Even if Democratic Russia had collected the required signatures, the Supreme Soviet would still have had to agree to call a referendum. Thus there was stalemate and no legal way in which Yeltsin could dissolve Congress and call new elections.[14] In recognition of this Yeltsin rejoined the parliamentary process of drafting the new constitution, rather than holding a referendum and imposing his own.[15] Yeltsin, however, remained convinced that the Congress had outlived its purpose: 'In my opinion, it is an artificial, supra-parliamentary entity. Its very existence is a permanent basis for disrupting the balance between the legislative, executive and judicial branches.'[16]

Yeltsin's emergency powers had been granted for only one year and were due to expire on 1 December 1992, thus the Seventh Congress (1–14 December 1992) was if anything more tense than the Sixth. Divided into fourteen factions and with the balance of the 'marsh' (the centrist bloc composed largely of officialdom) having tilted even further towards the conservatives,[17] the reformers faced a formidable task. On 10 December, Yeltsin forced a showdown. In a short but threatening speech, he called for a referendum to decide who should have power, the president or parliament. He argued that the conservatives in the Congress had impeded the reforms, insisting that 'What they failed to achieve in August 1991, they decided to repeat now and carry out a creeping coup.'[18] On 11 December, Congress passed a resolution that emasculated Yeltsin's proposed referendum, passing a constitutional amendment that banned any plebiscite that could result in a vote of no confidence in any high-state body, or which could lead to its dissolution before its term of office had expired. Under the auspices of the chairman of the Constitutional Court, Valerii Zor'kin, a deal was brokered on 12 December in the form of a nine-point agreement that stood or fell together. A referendum was to be held in April 1993 on the adoption of the new constitution, with contentious points to be placed as options, and in the meantime the existing balance between executive and legislative was to be maintained. Nominations for the post of premier were to be put to the Congress for a non-binding popularity poll, and after some complex voting Victor Chernomyrdin replaced Gaidar as prime minister.

Russia appeared to have entered a vicious circle in which it could not have elections before the adoption of a constitution, but could not adopt a constitution before elections. The weakness of party politics meant that parliament itself as an institution took on a monolithic role as an actor in politics rather than as the vessel in which politics was conducted. In other words, politics was displaced into struggle *between* institutions rather than by consensual processes *within* them. Without changes to the structure of legislative power there could be no stable political development. The unstable compromise reached at the Seventh Congress was now comprehensively repudiated. Following desultory negotiations between Yeltsin and Khasbulatov, the Eighth Congress on 10–13 March 1993 failed to sanction the referendum or to establish the framework for the adoption of a new constitution. The Congress stripped Yeltsin of many of the powers granted to him earlier to implement economic reform. He was deprived of the right to issue decrees with the same force as parliamentary laws, to appoint presidential envoys or heads of administration, or to appoint government ministers without the approval of parliament. The government was granted the right to submit legislation directly to parliament (bypassing the presidency), a privilege that the Soviet government under Pavlov had sought not long before the *coup*. The presidency emerged limited and damaged by this bout with Congress.

In the last months of the old parliament Khasbulatov in effect organised an insurrection against Yeltsin and sought to use the combined forces of an eclectic rejectionist front to propel himself to power. He now proposed the establishment of a parliamentary republic at the centre and the restoration of the power of the soviets in the localities. Khasbulatov declared himself in favour of the restoration of a new form of Soviet power in which local executive authorities would be subordinated to local soviets, which would in turn be subordinated to the Presidium of the Supreme Soviet.[19] The president would be reduced to a figurehead, and the head of the legislature would in effect become chief executive.[20] Khasbulatov had long advocated the municipalisation of soviets to turn them into effective bodies of local self-government,[21] but this was taking his earlier ideas much further. Khasbulatov sought to establish a type of post-communist soviet power, echoing the slogan 'soviets without communists' of the Kronstadt insurgents of March 1921. On trips to the provinces he urged local soviets to resist the executive authorities, and by April 1993 he was boasting that he had restored Soviet power in the regions, and he soon tried to restore Soviet power in the centre as well.

Parliament's challenge left Yeltsin facing a conundrum, and as usual in a crisis he resolved on decisive action. In a broadcast on 20 March he announced a referendum for 25 April and the imposition of 'special rule' that would free him from legislative restraints, a declaration that was clearly unconstitutional. Despite the suggestion of a forceful resolution to the crisis, when the decree was published on 24 March it made no mention of the dissolution of Congress or the suspension of parliament. Zor'kin's attempts to mediate this time came to nothing, having discredited himself by rushing to condemn Yeltsin's 'special rule' even before seeing the decree. The Ninth Congress, called in response to Yeltsin's *démarche*, nevertheless met on 26 March in an atmosphere of extreme crisis. A meeting between Yeltsin and Khasbulatov on 27 March appeared to provide a solution by stipulating early presidential and parliamentary elections in autumn 1993. However, Congress on the next day angrily rejected the deal, and turned against Khasbulatov himself, with some 300 deputies voting for his resignation, and the vote to impeach Yeltsin fell only 72 short of the required two-thirds majority. Khasbulatov's own room for manœuvre had been drastically reduced, and the final day of the Ninth Congress on 29 March was marked by the passage of numerous acts stripping Yeltsin of his remaining powers.

The referendum of 25 April 1993 gave people four choices: support for president Yeltsin; support for his economic policies; and whether they favoured early presidential and parliamentary elections. The Ninth CPD stipulated that the vote required 50 per cent of the registered voters (not just a simple majority of those taking part) to be binding, but following an appeal the Constitutional Court ruled that only the last two questions required the higher threshold since they involved constitutional issues. In the event the turnout (64.5 per cent) and support for Yeltsin was higher than expected (see Table 3.1). Yeltsin received a ringing personal endorsement, with some 59 per cent of the turnout expressing confidence in him; even his policies, despite the hardship they had caused, were supported by 53 per cent of the vote. The 49 per cent vote for pre-term presidential elections and the thumping 67 per cent (43 per cent of the electorate) for early parliamentary elections, however, were not binding since they failed to reach the required 50 per cent of registered voters.

Table 3.1 Referendum, 25 April 1993

Turnout and participation:
Out of a total of 107,310,374 eligible voters, 69,222,858 actually voted, a turnout of 64.5 per cent.
Only Chechnya boycotted the referendum, while in Tatarstan nearly 80 per cent of the electorate ignored the vote, rendering the result there invalid.

Result (%):

	Yes		*No*	*Spoiled ballots*
% of vote	% of electorate	% of vote	% of electorate	%
1) Do you have confidence in the President of the Russian Federation, Boris Yeltsin?				
58.7	37.3	39.2	25.2	2.1
2) Do you approve of the socio-economic policies carried out by the President of the Russian Federation and the government of the Russian Federation since 1992?				
53.0	34.0	44.6	28.6	2.4
3) Do you consider it necessary to hold early elections to the Presidency of the Russian Federation?				
49.5	31.7	47.1	30.2	3.4
4) Do you consider it necessary to hold early elections of the people's deputies of the Russian Federation?				
67.2	43.1	30.1	19.3	2.7

Sources: *Rossiiskaya gazeta*, 6 May 1993; *RFE/RL Research Report*, Vol. 2, No. 21 (21 May 1993), p. 12.

Despite popular support for pre-term parliamentary elections revealed by the referendum, these were refused by the parliamentary leadership and the crisis deepened. While the result weakened Khasbulatov personally, the Supreme Soviet was increasingly radicalised by the conflict, and parliament as a whole over-estimated its strength, interpreting concessions as weakness. The politicisation of the struggle between parliament and presidency meant that the endemic constitutional crisis had been transformed into an overt political struggle for power. The extreme right, made up of nationalists and imperial restorationists, allied with the extreme left, neo-Bolshevik and Soviet rejectionists to defeat the centre. It appeared that the parliamentary leadership was engaged in a premeditated attempt to seize power, including the accumulation of weapons. Over the summer, Khasbulatov and Rutskoi toured the provinces, hoping to garner support. On a visit to the Far East Rutskoi declared that within two months he would be president. During a visit to Orël and Bryansk he insisted that an end to the confusion had to be made during the autumn, suggesting that the Congress would call for simultaneous pre-term parliamentary and presidential elections. He announced that an alternative policy programme was being developed that would allow the rebirth of Russia from the regions up.[22] More importantly, it is clear that parliament was planning to emasculate presidential power.

Interpreting the results of the April referendum as a renewed popular mandate, Yeltsin went on the offensive and sought to break the impasse by convening the Constitutional Assembly in June 1993, a tactic (as we shall see below) that was only partially successful. The draft of a new constitution was completed in July, but its adoption was blocked by some regional leaders. Yeltsin's failure on 18 September to convert the Federation Council into a fully fledged consultative-advisory body to replace parliament's existing Council of Nationalities triggered the final crisis.[23] On that very day, Khasbulatov escalated the personal vendetta by accusing Yeltsin of being a common drunkard. Since the referendum, Russian political life had descended to mutual mud-flinging amid accusations of corruption, a process encouraged by Rutskoi himself.[24] By a presidential decree of 1 September 1993, both Rutskoi and first deputy prime minister Vladimir Shumeiko, who had been trading insults, were suspended pending investigations into corruption.[25] The inner life of parliament itself had similarly degenerated, with a regime of fear against all of Khasbulatov's opponents. The more far-seeing deputies had already resigned their mandates. Parliament appeared unable to respond to the changes taking place in Russian life.

The new October

Finally, on 21 September 1993, Yeltsin took the dissolution option. Presidential decree No. 1400, 'On Gradual Constitutional Reform in the Russian Federation', dissolved the Supreme Soviet and the CPD, whose powers were to be transferred to a new Federal Assembly.[26] The existing Federation Council was to be vested with the functions of the upper chamber of the Assembly, while elections to the new lower chamber, the State Duma, were to take place on 12 December 1993. One of the reasons for Yeltsin's action was the failure of the Constitutional Assembly to adopt the new constitution, and it was now ordered to agree a final version with parliament's own Constitutional Commission (nominally headed by Yeltsin himself) by 12 December.[27]

The rejectionists greatly overplayed their hand, especially given the results of the April referendum. Khasbulatov and the deputies who supported him did not realise quite how detached they had become from popular opinion, and when they issued the call for the masses to come to defend the White House in September 1993, instead of the expected crowds a rather desultory few thousand assembled. Support for the parliamentary rejectionists was fragmented, and within parliament itself the picture is confused. Representatives of thirteen out of the fourteen factions remained in parliament, but it is clear that the number of deputies in the White House was falling sharply, some attracted by the promise of jobs in the presidential system and by generous retirement payments. The Tenth Congress was hastily convened, but while some deputies came the Congress lacked a quorum (the required number was swiftly decreased) since, among other reasons, Yeltsin had deprived them of free travel.

In the event it was the army that saved Yeltsin's fortunes. Violent demonstrations on Sunday 3 October soon gave way to insurrection, with armed marauders from the White House seizing the Mayor's office in the old Comecon building opposite. If at that point they had turned west and marched on the Kremlin they might well have been able to seize power. Instead the insurgents turned north into the suburbs to seize the Ostankino television centre. Here they encountered stiff resistance from the Interior Ministry forces defending the building, and became locked into a fire-fight lasting several hours. By the evening, Yeltsin had returned to the Kremlin from his dacha, and then spent a large part of the night urging the military commanders to crush the insurgency.[28] Having learnt the pitfalls of intervening in domestic political disputes, the military leadership was wary but finally agreed to take action, although a military force was only assembled with considerable difficulty and drew on numerous units and the Alpha security force. By dawn on 4 October, the White House was ringed by tanks and by the afternoon the rebel leaders headed by Rutskoi and Khasbulatov had surrendered and were incarcerated in the Lefortovo gaol. According to official statistics, 146 people died in the fighting.[29]

The results of the defeat of the Supreme Soviet were not long in coming. In the regions the traditional soviet-style legislatures were dissolved, allowing the regional executives to consolidate their powers as most created relatively subservient 'pocket' representative bodies to replace the old. Putin's subsequent attempt to rein in the regional bosses was in many ways a direct legacy of the events of October 1993. In the immediate term, Yeltsin placed temporary bans on some of the more extremist parties and newspapers, but his promise to hold parliamentary elections and a referendum on the constitution on 12 December 1993 was honoured (although the presidential elections promised for six months later were forgotten).

The Russian October of 1993 can be seen, for good or ill, as completing the revolution of August 1991. Neither the banning of the Communist Party nor the dissolution of parliament were strictly speaking constitutional acts, but while deficient in legality they clearly commanded a high degree of popular legitimacy. There are certain similarities between Yeltsin's act and that of president Fujimori in Peru in his *autogolpe* (self-*coup*) of April 1992, but perhaps a better analogy is with De

Gaulle's *démarches* from 1958 leading to the end of the parliamentary Fourth Republic and the establishment of the presidential Fifth Republic. Bitterly divisive though De Gaulle's acts may have been in the political community, the referendum of September 1958 showed overwhelming popular support (about 80 per cent of voters) for the new presidentialist constitution. In Russia, however, the violent denouement to the conflict irreparably damaged Yeltsin's reputation and undermined the legitimacy of the new constitutional order. Since the August 1991 *coup*, Yeltsin had appeared to many as too much of a destroyer, a *soi-disant* democrat employing Bolshevik methods to destroy Bolshevism.

The 1993 constitution

In countries like France the spirit of constitutionalism is enshrined not in any given constitution but in the constituent power (*pouvoir constituant*; and see Chapter 7) of the nation. The frequency with which France has changed its constitutions reflects the belief that no given constitution can constrain the constituent power of the French people: the French nation is considered to have existed long before any specific constitution.[30] In Russia the relationship between the constitution and the nation is far more ambiguous, reflecting the persistent syndrome of *displaced sovereignty*: instead of the basis of constitutional order being the sovereign people, it was arrogated by regimes of various type standing between the people and the state. This was evident in Russia's first experiment with constitutionalism between 1906 and the Revolution, and most forcefully in the Soviet period when popular sovereignty was proclaimed but then usurped by the Communist Party in the name of the higher goal of the pursuit of socialism, and then again, in a very different way, by Yeltsin's regime that pursued the cause of 'reform' as a meta-goal over and above any institutional expression of the popular will.

Soviet constitutionalism

Max Weber described the constitution (Basic Law) adopted for imperial Russia on 23 April 1906 as 'sham constitutionalism' because the Tsar's power allegedly was neither reduced nor effectively constrained.[31] In fact, a constitutional monarchy was introduced abolishing 'unlimited' (*neogranichennyi*) monarchical power, although the crown retained considerable powers.[32] The concept of sham constitutionalism is perhaps more appropriate to describe the Soviet era. The Soviet regime adopted constitutions in 1918 (for the RSFSR), 1924, 1936 and 1977, with the RSFSR adopting a slightly modified version on 12 April 1978. As the collective Tsar, the Communist Party placed itself above constitutional constraints, and its Statutes were in effect more important than the constitutions themselves. As Gorbachev put it:

> Of course the totalitarian regime disguised itself with democratic decorations: a constitution, laws of various kinds, and 'representative' bodies of government. In fact all the life activity of society was dictated and guided – from beginning to end – by the party structures, by the resolutions, decisions, and orders of the top echelons of the party.[33]

The Soviet system was sham constitutional because its constitutions did not do what constitutions are supposed to do, namely regulate the division of labour within the branches of the state, allocate functions between the centre and the localities, and provide a normative framework for the operation of the legal system.

The Soviet regime was pseudo-constitutional since it ignored the real balance of power in society, and in particular the leading role of the Communist Party. The 1918 constitution and its successors proclaimed 'all power to the soviets', but the actual mechanism whereby soviets were to exercise power and the role of the CPSU were left vague. Article 6 of the 1977 constitution defined the Communist Party as the 'leading and guiding force in Soviet society', but did not specify, and thereby limit, its functions. The Soviet polity actually operated according to the conventions of an 'unwritten constitution' of normative acts and administrative practices that left the formal constitution no more than declaratory window-dressing for the regime. The Soviet system had constitutions without the necessary framework of law that could achieve genuine constitutional government. Quite why the Soviet regime felt obliged to proclaim its adherence to constitutionalism remains a mystery, but part of the answer lies in the fact that the Soviet system, despite its repudiation of liberalism, felt constrained by its appeal to a democratic legitimation.[34]

In the last years of the Soviet regime Gorbachev sought through *perestroika* to achieve the renewal of the soviet representative system, the reorganisation of the higher bodies of state power, the reform of the electoral system, and to change the judicial-legal process in its entirety. In short, Gorbachev's programme represented a profound constitutional reform but one that was to be constrained by the concept of the 'socialist legal state'.[35] This programme was given legal form in the constitutional amendments of 1 December 1988, including the creation of the partially elected USSR Congress of People's Deputies, and on 9 June 1989 the CPD established a Constitutional Commission headed by Gorbachev.[36] In the event, the fall of the regime in late 1991 led to the abandonment of the Soviet constitution and the end of evolutionary reform. A precedent was set for constitutional transformation to take place in unconstitutional, indeed revolutionary, ways.

The genesis of the Russian constitution

The task now was to write Russia's first ever democratic constitution to consolidate the transformatory process. Russia drew on the experience of the West but ultimately the constitution and the legal system was tailored to Russian conditions. The drafting procedure was very different from that followed for the old Soviet consititutions in which a bureaucratic committee, with advice from experts and select groups, would propose a draft which was then publicised in a brief nationwide 'discussion' followed by a unanimous vote in the Supreme Soviet. The drafting of the new Russian constitution reflected the divisions of society and took a violent turn, as we saw above. Even in the best of times the designing of laws and institutions *ab initio* is an exhilarating but dangerous venture.[37] Numerous choices have to be made: between a unitary, federal or confederal system; a parliamentary or a presidential republic or something in between; the balance to be drawn between limited government and effective governance; the equation to be drawn between individual and group rights, between majorities and minorities. If rights are assigned to minority groups, then is there not a danger that members will identify with that community rather than as citizens of the larger state?

The birth of the new constitution was a long and painful process.[38] Four days after the revolutionary Declaration of Sovereignty of the RSFSR on 12 June 1990, the First Russian CPD on 16 June established a Constitutional Commission to prepare a document that would reflect Russia's new juridical and political status. The commission, made up of 102 MPs, was nominally chaired by Yeltsin with Khasbulatov its vice-chairman, but the main work was carried out by a smaller working group of some fifteen deputies chaired by the commission's secretary, Oleg Rumyantsev. The first version, rejecting the whole notion of socialism and communism, was ready by November 1990.[39] The draft declared that 'the Russian Federation is a sovereign, democratic, social and legal state of historically united peoples' (Art. 1.1) and broke decisively with Bolshevik traditions by defending the inviolable rights of the individual (Art. 1.3). Russia was defined as a 'social state' guaranteeing extensive collective and welfare rights based 'on the principles of social democracy and justice' (Art. 1.8). Not surprisingly, the draft was attacked as being 'anti-Soviet' and the Supreme Soviet refused to place it on the agenda for adoption by the Second CPD in December 1990.

Against the background of the 'winter offensive' by the so-called conservatives from late 1990, the Communists of Russia faction in the legislature prepared an alternative and more traditional draft constitution.[40] After much discussion the Constitutional Commission came out with a compromise draft in time for discussion by the Third Congress (28 March–4 April 1991), but by then the context had dramatically changed: the 17 March referendum established the post of a Russian president and the Communists of Russia split and a reformist faction (Communists for Democracy) emerged, led by Rutskoi. In June 1991, the Fifth Congress (first convocation) rejected the compromise draft, insisting that it failed to formulate Russia's rights against the centre and that it was full of contradictions, and instructed the commission to prepare another version.

The August 1991 *coup* and the subsequent dissolution of the Soviet system added a new urgency to the constitutional question, and the commission rapidly produced a second version,[41] which was presented by Rumyantsev to the Supreme Soviet on 10 October 1991.[42] With the fall of Soviet power, ideological issues, such as individual rights, civil society and judicial reform, were no longer so contentious, but new points of disagreement had emerged. These focused above all on the separation of powers on the horizontal level (between executive and legislative power), and on the vertical level (between the central authorities and components of the federation). The territorial organisation of the state proved particularly divisive since the draft sought to move away from Bolshevik ethno-federal principles towards a classic territorial federalism (see Chapter 9). As a result, the Supreme Soviet failed to muster the required 50 per cent of deputies to place the constitution on the reconvened Fifth CPD's agenda for approval.[43] In response, the Constitutional Commission met on 23 October and authorised Yeltsin to place a slightly revised draft before the CPD 'for discussion' (*k svedeniyu*), rather than adoption.[44] This he did on 2 November,[45] and Congress then instructed the commission to prepare yet another version in time for the Sixth Congress.

Work on the document was now torn between what appeared to be irreconcilable forces: on the one hand, most of the former autonomous republics rejected the Constitutional Commission's draft for failing to recognise their sovereign status; while, on the other, many of Russia's regions condemned it on the grounds that it gave excessive privileges to the republics. The working group sought to find a compromise, and on 2 March 1992 completed a third version that, after slight modifications, was published on 24 March.[46] This draft proposed a parliamentary republic but with broad powers for the president within the framework of parliamentary oversight and with the clear separation of powers between the executive, legislature and judiciary. As far as supporters of the legislature were concerned, 'In the absence of a civil society in our country, parliament and the Congress of People's Deputies are today virtually the only guarantors that can stop our country from plunging into a dictatorship of individuals.'[47] The signing of the three-tiered Federation Treaty on 31 March (see Chapter 9) appeared to resolve some of the sharpest conflicts over the federation.[48]

The Supreme Soviet this time placed the constitution on the agenda, recommending that it be adopted at its first reading to avoid exhaustive debate over individual clauses. However, the Sixth CPD, while rejecting alternative drafts, merely approved the general outline (*za osnovu*) of the commission's version, calling for yet more revisions.[49] Against the background of a sharp deterioration in relations between the president and parliament, including fears that Yeltsin might dissolve the legislature and put his draft to a national referendum, the Congress somewhat moderated its assault against the president's economic policies and political prerogatives, extending his right to rule by decree to the end of 1992 but forcing him to step down as prime minister. The Congress went on to make numerous amendments to the existing 'Brezhnev' constitution, including the bodily incorporation of the Federation Treaty.[50]

The constitutional process had now reached an impasse. Only the CPD had the right to amend or adopt the constitution, and Yeltsin's attempts to raise the million signatures necessary to hold a referendum did not offer a way out since adopting the constitution through a referendum was unconstitutional, and in any case required the approval of the Congress. The opposition in the Congress, on the other hand, used the right to make constitutional amendments with increasing boldness and for short-term political advantage. Of the 340 amendments made to the old constitution by early 1993, an astonishing 258 were adopted in 1992 alone.[51] The work of the commission continued, however, and it issued a fourth version on 11 November 1992.[52] Work on the new constitution continued in parallel with amendments to the old, allowing, according to Rumyantsev, a gradual convergence of the two. He claimed that this allowed a 'balanced and consistent modernisation of the legal space of the Federation' rather than a constitutional revolution,[53] an assessment that was too sanguine by far.

Fearing the loss of a powerful weapon in their struggle with the president, and hesitant to commit themselves to elections, the Seventh CPD in December 1992 once again failed to adopt the prepared draft constitution. According to Rumyantsev, this was a major mistake and allowed the president to seize the initiative and encourage other drafts that, according to Rumyantsev, were inferior to the parliamentary version in that they introduced numerous 'conjunctural' elements.

However long and convoluted the parliamentary version, Rumyantsev insisted, it was nevertheless permeated by a democratic spirit that was in sharp contrast to the Soviet-era constitutions.[54] Agreement had been reached at the Congress on putting the basic principles of the new constitution before the people in a referendum, but Khasbulatov's call in February 1993 for pre-term presidential and parliamentary elections ruptured the fragile compromise and once again opened up the question. The president now released details of his own, much more presidentialist, constitutional draft on the eve of the referendum of 25 April 1993.[55] This envisaged the abolition of the old Congress and Supreme Soviet, and their replacement by a bicameral legislature to be known as the Federal Assembly. The lower chamber (the State Duma) was to be elected on a proportional basis, while the upper (the Federation Council) was to be made up of the elected presidents of Russia's republics and the heads of regional administrations. Only the president's nomination for the post of prime minister was to be ratified by parliament, while all other ministerial appointments were to be approved 'in consultation' with the chamber. The president had the power to dissolve parliament and call new elections, while only the Federation Council had the right to impeach the president. The post of vice-president was to be abolished, and it was now made more difficult to amend the constitution. These ideas lay at the basis of the constitution adopted in December 1993.

An extended process of consultation followed in which the views of members of the federation were sought.[56] The results of the April 1993 referendum were interpreted as supporting the president's accelerated programme of constitutional change; and, indeed, following the referendum the struggle between the executive and the legislature now focused on the constitution.[57] By the same token, as both sides courted the regions and republics, the Russian constitutional process was ever more frequently likened to the Novo-Ogarevo process in which Gorbachev had tried to adopt a new Union Treaty but which precipitated the union's disintegration.[58] The presidential draft was presented to the Constitutional Commission on 6 May 1993, and on the next day rejected.[59] It remained unclear how his draft, or any other, could be adopted without the support of the existing Congress and Supreme Soviet.[60]

Work had continued on the Constitutional Commission's draft, and on 7 May 1993 the Commission approved the fifth 'Khasbulatovite' parliamentary version.[61] The equality of members of the federation was stressed 'apart from those allowed by the constitution'. Republics were recognised as states, enjoying the full panoply of state powers on their territory apart from those that remained the prerogative of the Russian Federation. Other federal units were labelled simply state-territorial formations. The upper house was to be called the Federation Council, while the lower house, the State Duma, was to be elected by a simple first-past-the-post system. The president was to become merely the ceremonial head of state and not head of the executive branch.[62] The draft was to be discussed by parliamentary committees and a final version was to be published by 15 October and discussed by a special convocation of the CPD to meet on 17 November.[63]

Yeltsin could not ignore this direct challenge to his constitutional status, and on 20 May he decided to finesse the constitutional question by taking up the option long advocated by the Russian Democratic Reform Movement led by Sobchak and Popov,[64] namely the convocation of a special Constitutional Assembly to accelerate the constitutional process.[65] However, whereas Popov had insisted that the Assembly should meet for only one purpose, the adoption of a new consitution, Yeltsin's Constitutional Assembly was intended to shape a draft that could then be sent round to members of the federation for their approval. The Constitutional Assembly opened on 5 June 1993 and was composed of some 750 representatives of the federation as well as from social organisations. In his opening speech Yeltsin likened the period to 1917 and insisted that the new Assembly was continuing the work of the Provisional Government in devising a democratic constitution for Russia, work brought to a violent end by the Bolshevik seizure of power and the dispersal of the Constituent Assembly in January 1918.[66] Yeltsin's attempt to base the rebirth of the Russian constitutional order on this tradition (the brief attempt to establish democracy in Russia in 1917), rather than the Tsarist, let alone the Soviet, was significant and symbolised the attempt to portray the Soviet period not just as an aberration but as fundamentally illegitimate; an interregnum in Russia's search for democracy. Indeed, his insistence that soviets and democracy were fundamentally incompatible was one of the factors that led to the final rift between himself and Khasbulatov.[67] Yeltsin branded the attempt by the Supreme Soviet to manage a smooth transition by maintaining continuity and observance of the existing constitution as being no more than 'a weapon in the hands of an illegitimate new ruling class, with whose assistance they try to retain their illegal power'.[68]

Despite the president's fighting talk, the work of the Assembly proceeded in a conciliatory atmosphere, and in its committees many of the ideas put forward by parliamentary representatives were adopted, giving rise to a 'mixed' form of government.[69] The Assembly came up with a new version on 12 July drawing on both the presidential draft of April 1993 and parliament's.[70] There was much on which they agreed, such as the rights and obligations of the citizen and the right to all forms of property, but they differed radically over the role of the president and parliament. The Assembly's version represented Yeltsin's last attempt to achieve some agreement with the old legislature over the constitution; the problem still remained of how to adopt it.[71] In an attempt to win over the regions, a Federation Council was established at a meeting in Petrozavodsk on 13 August of the Council of the Heads of the Republics, when Yeltsin called for the creation of a type of mini-parliament to resolve the constitutional crisis. The new Council was to consist of a representative apiece from the executive and legislative powers in each region and republic, making a total of 176 from the 88 subjects of the federation willing to participate (Chechnya refused).[72] At its first meeting on 18 September, however, Yeltsin failed to get them to sign a founding document.

The Supreme Soviet was still working to its own timetable of constitutional reform, ignoring the Constitutional Assembly. This attempt to give substance to a parallel constitutional process threatened to strip the president of his powers but proved a grave miscalculation. Yeltsin struck first, and as we have seen on 21 September 1993 dissolved the legislature and suspended the constitution. His action raised grave ethical issues: to what extent are unconstitutional acts valid in the attempt to establish the rule of law? The new constitutionalism was based on the view that the Soviet system was unreformable, and hence in a revolutionary process law is subordinate to political expediency. In other words, the constitution became a tool in the struggle for reform, an instrumental view that absolved the 'reformers' of the need to subordinate themselves to the rule of law. The tradition of 'displaced sovereignty' remained strong. From this perspective, current events were no more than the final triumph of the 'counter-revolution' against the Bolshevik usurpation of power in October 1917. This was in sharp contrast to the Gorbachevite view favouring continuity in the evolution from Soviet constitutional practices into the new democratic era. These two approaches reflected divergent views over the nature of the transition.

Following the dissolution of the Supreme Soviet, the Constitutional Assembly was reorganised to include a 'public chamber',[73] and shortly afterwards a 'state chamber' (the work of both was regularised on 11 October), to complete work on the constitution. The committee drew on the Constitutional Assembly's synthesis but also borrowed directly on earlier presidential and parliamentary drafts. The draft constitution was published on 10 November and, as expected, proposed a strongly presidential system and modified some of the privileges accorded the republics and regions when they had been able to take advantage of the struggle between the president and parliament.[74] A final section of the new version made a number of provisions for the transitional situation, stipulating that the president must serve his full term until June 1996 and thus ended speculation about pre-term presidential elections.

The constitutional referendum of 12 December 1993

It was this version that was placed before the people for approval on 12 December 1993 and became Russia's first democratic constitution. By a decree of 15 October, voters were asked to participate in a plebiscite on the constitution.[75] The support of the majority of the registered electorate, as stipulated by the 16 October 1990 referendum law, was no longer required for adoption but simply 50 per cent of those who voted,[76] although the minimum 50 per cent turnout was retained. The draft constitution was published on 10 November, and the question placed on the ballot paper on 12 December was a simple one: 'Do you support the adoption of the new Russian constitution?' This method of adopting the constitution is clearly open to criticism.[77] The use of the plebiscite is the favoured technique of dictators, and the judgement of a simple 'yes' or 'no' to a complex question is hardly the most democratic way of adopting such a crucial document. This was the method employed, however, by De Gaulle in 1958 to adopt the constitution establishing the Fifth Republic in France.

Official figures show that the constitution was supported by 58.43 per cent of the vote, thus exceeding the 50 per cent threshold required for adoption; while 41.6 per cent voted against (see Table 3.2).[78] The legitimacy of the constitution was weakened by the fact that only 30.7 per cent of the total electorate voted for the constitution, and in seventeen republics and regions the constitution was rejected.[79] There remain doubts over the accuracy of the official turnout figures, and the way that they were achieved, especially since the evidence (the ballot papers and area tallies) was swiftly destroyed. Nevertheless, Russia at last had a constitution. The constitution came into force on 12 December 1993, although it was only officially published in the Russian media on 25 December;[80] 12 December is now a national holiday, Constitution Day.

Table 3.2 Referendum on the constitution, 12 December 1993

Total electorate	106,170,835
Turnout	58,187,755 (54.8% of registered voters)
Valid votes	53,751,696 (50.6%)
Voting for the constitution	32,937,630 (58.43%)
Voting against	23,431,333 (41.6%)
Percentage of total electorate voting for the constitution	30.7%

Sources: *Rossiiskaya gazeta*, 21 December 1993, p. 1; *Byulleten Tsentral'noi izbiratel'noi kommissii Rossiiskoi Federatsii*, No. 1 (12) (1994), p. 38.

Basic principles of Russian constitutionalism

The Russian constitution of 1993 is liberal in its overall conception but some of its democratic procedures are flawed. The document reflected the tendency predominant under Yeltsin, namely the primacy of liberalism over democracy. Nevertheless, the constitution upholds basic principles of democratic state-building such as the separation of powers, defining the rights and duties of various levels of government. According to its critics, however, while the principle might have been upheld, the lack of balance in the separation of powers undermined the principles that it claimed to enshrine.

The new constitution is a liberal document, meeting world standards in its provisions for human and civic rights (outlined in its second chapter). It enshrines the civil rights of citizens, outlawing the incarceration of 'dissidents' and restricting the monitoring of correspondence and bugging of telephone calls. The constitution forbids censorship and guarantees freedom of the press. It allows Russians to travel abroad as a right, forbids the government from sending citizens into foreign exile or stripping Russians of their citizenship. It also promises freedom of movement within Russia, and enshrines 'the right to travel freely and choose one's place of stay and residence' (Art. 27), thus making the dreaded *propiska* residence permits unconstitutional (although Moscow city continued to apply the system). It also guarantees the right to private property, and thus seals this core aspect of the liberal revolution, including the right for citizens to buy and sell land (Articles 35, 36). Provision was made for an ombudsman for human rights, whose duties would be specified by a special law. The constitution is direct-acting, requiring no further legal enactments for its provisions to take effect, and thus the document remains the central reference point for legal and political processes in the country. Thus, the new document sought to overcome the legacy of legal arbitrariness of the Soviet years.

In addition, Russia was defined as a 'social state' (Art. 7) and numerous rights and entitlements were guaranteed to its citizens. The emphasis on social as well as political rights drew on the social-democratic element in Bolshevik thinking and on the 'social liberal' tendency in pre-revolutionary Russian thought, but fundamentalist liberals insist that 'social' is no more than a tame word for 'socialist'.[81] Whatever the inspiration, the degree to which these social rights can be fulfilled is disputed since entitlements to positive rights are even more difficult to enforce in a court of law than the negative rights concerning the inviolability of the individual. The listing of entitlements is alien to the Anglo-Saxon tradition but reflects the tendency in Continental social philosophy to assume that what is unregulated does not exist.

There is a more fundamental problem, however, than simply the abstract enumeration of political and social rights. Some of these rights are accompanied by qualifications that could be used to stifle political opposition. In particular, Art. 29.2 forbids the incitement of social, racial, national or religious hatred and has been cited as an unwarranted limitation on political and expressional rights. More seriously, the defence of state security or the legitimate rights of others (Art. 55.3) has been used for repressive purposes. Article 80 grants the president certain reserve powers as 'guarantor of the constitution', powers that could in certain circumstances be used to subvert the constitution (as has allegedly already been done in the two Chechen wars). The constitution failed to state that voting (except for the president, Art. 81.1) takes place on the basis of free and *equal* representation, thus making it impossible to appeal to the constitution to prevent, for example, constituencies varying greatly in the number of electors. Moreover, the proclamation of abstract promises of social justice, such as the right to free health care (Art. 41.1) and a 'decent environment' (Art. 42), might well be seen as undermining the very basis of trust on which a constitution rests. In this category come the guarantees for trial by jury (Art. 47.2) when this system came into general operation only much later, and the prohibition on 'the use of evidence obtained by violating federal law' (Art. 50.2). If these are not fulfilled, then what price all the other promises?

In a sharp break with the past the constitution makes no reference to any state ideology or religion and instead guarantees freedom of conscience, religion, thought and speech (Articles 28, 29) based on political pluralism and a multi-party system. However, this does not mean that the constitution is not an ideological document: it represents a clear commitment to certain values, including the notion of a 'social' and 'secular' state based on private property, the rule of law and popular sovereignty. However, the enunciation of the rationale behind these views is no longer as explicit as in earlier drafts. The section explicitly devoted to civil society was dropped, ostensibly for the sake of brevity. What was lost, however, was a clear repudiation of Russia's statist traditions and the commitment to the development of the sphere of freedom and autonomy associated with the notion of civil society.

The political system formalised by the 1993 constitution reflected numerous conjunctural factors. A constitution, ideally, reflects a popular consensus around certain principles and values, whereas this constitution contained elements that reflected only the concerns of a particular time and the interests of a particular group. Vitalii Tret'yakov, the trenchant editor of *Nezavisimaya gazeta*, argued that 'It is a constitution for presidents in general and for president Yeltsin in particular.'[82] Rumyantsev noted that 'When the president personally formulates foreign and domestic policy, one can say that the monarchical principle outweighs the democratic principle in the constitution.'[83] Konstantin Lubenchenko went even further in claiming that the constitution not only gave an overwhelming advantage to presidential power but actually 'codifies the existence of a totalitarian state that controls all spheres of the life of society'.[84] Thus, the main criticism of the 1993 constitution is its lack of balance in the separation of powers between branches of national government, above all granting the presidency excessive powers. In

Russia's early post-communist years, however, the question of 'balance' was not easily resolved, since 'balance' is something derived from the alignment of social and political forces. While the constitution embodies the principles of liberalism, it is predicated on the assumption that the strong president will also be a liberal. In the event of this not being the case the authoritarian elements embedded in the constitution will come into contradiction with its liberal provisions.

Criticism of the constitution focuses on the following issues: the inadequate legal defence of the civic and human rights of individuals; the lack of balance in the relationship between the executive and the legislative; the tension between federal and unitary principles in the relationship between the centre and localities and the large grey area of joint jurisdiction; the large area of rules and procedures (for example, governing elections) that are not written into the constitution but regulated by acts and decrees; and the lack of a realistic procedure for adopting constitutional amendments.[85] Other criticisms of the constitution include the charge that it is too long, infringing Talleyrand's dictum that 'A constitution should be short and unclear' [*sic*]. The authors of the United States constitution adhered to this principle, but the post-war framers of the West German constitution did not. The West German constitution (Basic Law, *Grundgesetz*) came into force on 23 May 1949 and in great detail established the country as a federal, social, legal state based on a parliamentary system of rule in which the president is the non-executive head of state. The constitution sought to avoid the mistakes of the Weimar republic and enshrined the principle that 'democracy must be able to defend itself', including a ban on parties that challenge the existing constitutional order. There was no place for referenda and other forms of plebiscitary democracy. In terms of length the new Russian constitution veers to the long side, but is much shorter than the unadopted Rumyantsev version.

These criticisms perhaps overstate the case. This constitution is very much a normative document, establishing the principles on which an ethically desirable state could be established rather than suggesting that it can be achieved immediately. If we accept Bogdan Kistiakovskii's argument that law and the state originally existed independently and that independent courts could be introduced under conditions of absolutism, so too today we can appreciate the new constitution in terms of asynchronicity in the introduction of the rudiments of liberalism, democracy and, indeed, social democracy. While Western democracies have spent the better part of the twentieth century introducing a social corrective to classical liberalism – until the rise of neo-liberalism in the 1980s – post-communist Russia faces the problem of enormously extended social, and indeed political, demands in conditions in which it lacks the ability to meet these demands, resulting in a gulf between aspiration and achievement. As in pre-revolutionary Russia, however, the tendency to subordinate law to the political struggle only creates more obstacles in the way of achieving the goal of a *pravovoe gosudarstvo* (a state ruled by law, *Rechtsstaat*), let alone a rule of law state (see below).

State, government and constitutional change

The adoption of the constitution was only the beginning of a constitutional process requiring the development of a whole system of laws and conventions. Legislative renewal was based on a division between federal constitutional laws (those defining constitutional principles and processes) and ordinary federal laws.[86] Constitutional laws are harder to adopt or amend than routine laws, requiring a two-thirds majority, whereas ordinary laws require a simple parliamentary majority. A vast programme of legislative activity awaited the new parliament, with the constitution itself alluding to ten constitutional laws, forty-four federal laws, five existing laws needing substantial changes to bring them into line with the new constitution, together with six acts governing the activity of the Federal Assembly itself and four dealing with the work of the president, a total of sixty-nine acts that would give legislative form to its general principles. Some of these acts were prepared by the presidential Commission for Legislative Suggestions, headed by Mikhail Mityukov, which had by 17 December 1993 drawn up a list of the required legislation.[87] The most urgent new laws were those governing states of emergency and martial law, on the prerogatives of the Constitutional and Supreme Courts, labour and tax laws, on social movements, on elections to the State Duma and on the composition of the Federation Council. Laws to be changed included those governing the status of the capital and the procuracy.

The presidential features of the constitution attracted much criticism. Zor'kin argued that the leading role of the Communist Party had been replaced by the one-man rule of the president, while Rumyantsev argued that the constitution gave legal form to the seizure of power.[88] For Victor Ilyukhin this was a 'constitution for the fascist future', while E. Volodin saw it as inaugurating 'the banana republic of Russia'.[89] A joint declaration of party leaders insisted that the constitution 'restores the authoritarian system in the Russian Federation'.[90] The actual operation of the new system of constitutional power, however, revealed that the constitution did not establish virtually unchecked executive power, as its critics had suggested would be the case. Both Yeltsin and Putin sought to rule with the consent of the Federal Assembly; the legislature itself for the first time in Russian history worked as a genuine parliament. With another president, however, the restraints on authoritarian rule might prove inadequate.

For the first time in Russian history a constitution made a serious attempt to define and limit state power. The final vestiges of the communist legacy were swept away as the new document promised economic liberalism and the democratic separation of powers. Yeltsin argued that the constitution was designed to lay down a 'firm, legal order' for a democratic state, marking an end to the 'dual power' between the presidency and the legislature.[91] The constitution sought to create a 'democratic, federal, rule-of-law state with a republican form of government' (Art. 1.1). The new version incorporated elements from the previous drafts, above all the section on human and civil rights, but significantly augmented presidential authority and limited the powers of parliament and the republics. The model of governance that emerges from the document is both pseudo-parliamentary and super-presidential, while the government itself has the potential to become a relatively autonomous third centre of power. (The constitution's provisions concerning the institutions of the state and federalism are discussed in the appropriate parts of this book.)

The debate over constitutional change is provoked by the perceived need to reduce the powers of the presidency. At present, Russia is considered to have a *change*

'super-presidential' system (see Chapter 5), although the degree to which there is a genuine separation of powers is sometimes forgotten. The problem is not so much that Russia lacks a separation of powers, but that they are unbalanced – and deliberately so, given the experience of conflict between 1991–3. Among the many plans for constitutional change is the idea that the president should be selected by the Federation Council; that the prime minister should be appointed by the Duma, which itself would enjoy enhanced powers; that the Duma should be granted the right to approve the prime minister's dismissal as well as nomination; removing the power ministries from direct subordination to the president and transferring oversight to the prime minister; and making attendance compulsory for the prime minister and ministers when requested by the Duma.

Some informal constitutional evolution has already taken place within the framework of the existing polity. While no formal change has taken place away from the presidentialist bias of the constitution, there has been a shift towards prime ministerial governance. It should be noted that some of what has now become convention can be formalised by the adoption of federal constitutional laws by the Federal Assembly without necessarily amending the constitution itself. In the last years of Yeltsin's rule, especially during Primakov's premiership, attempts were made to hammer out cross-party agreement on constitutional reform and the redistribution of power, but no consensus was achieved. According to Yegor Stroev, the speaker of the Federation Council, 'Today, no sensible person is in any doubt that our constitution needs correction.' He noted that while in theory the president had huge powers, in practice most of these powers ended at the walls of the Kremlin. Too many decrees, laws and ordinances were simply not implemented.

However, while constitutional changes may be desirable, the obstacles to their adoption are prohibitive. The constitution is much more difficult to change than Soviet-era constitutions, a feature that might well transform political conflict into a constitutional crisis. The constitution's ninth chapter discusses amendments and revisions, in effect making it easier to abolish the constitution than to amend it. Amendments to chapters 3–8 require a two-thirds majority of the State Duma, the support of three-quarters of the members of the Federation Council, and then ratification by the legislatures of no fewer than two-thirds of the subjects of the federation (Articles 108 and 136). Special rules apply to the 'fundamental' articles of the constitution, chapters 1 and 2, dealing with general rights, and chapter 9 itself, where changes require a three-fifths vote of both houses and a Constitutional Assembly, convened in accordance with federal constitutional law (Art. 135). This would, in principle, make it easier to change the 'inviolable' chapters than the others, not requiring the ratification of the subjects of the federation. According to some commentators, the difficulties attending constitutional revisions could lead to attempts to kill off the constitution as a whole and to start again.[92]

The deeper problem is that the Yeltsinite quasi-monarchical style of rule could be replaced by a form of populist parliamentarianism that would undermine even the existing meagre achievements in the shift towards a market economy and individual freedoms. On many occasions the Duma has passed resolutions that threatened the very basis of Yeltsin's foreign policy: denouncing the dissolution of the USSR at Minsk in December 1991; claiming the return of the Crimean peninsula from Ukraine; and supporting president Alexander Lukashenka of Belarus in even his most bizarre manœuvres. There appeared to be a consensus that the powers of the president should be limited and those of the government strengthened, but that the stick should not be bent too far towards irresponsible parliamentarianism. However, Putin at first set his face against any constitutional change, insisting that the present system should be allowed to bed down. In the event, he engaged in considerable quasi-constitutional institutional development, as in the establishment of seven federal districts and a State Council in 2000.

The Constitutional Court

Even the most splendid constitution on paper is valueless if there are no effective mechanisms to ensure compliance. The Law on the Constitutional Court of 12 July 1991 established a Court of fifteen independent judges, appointed for their personal qualities for a limited life term (up to the age of sixty-five), to deal with all the main questions of constitutionality but prohibited from examining political cases.[93] Drawing on the experience of the German Federal Constitutional Court, the Court's decisions are final and cannot be appealed.

Under its chairman, Zor'kin, the Court sought to mark out the centre ground that could establish civic peace and maintain the unity of the country. The court was thus accused of placing political considerations above the defence of the laws and constitution of Russia, though with such a malleable constitution the position of the Court was unenviable. The Court asserted its authority against the executive authorities when on 14 January 1992 it overturned a presidential decree establishing a joint ministry of security and internal affairs. The Court's attempt to modify the referendum held on 21 March 1992 in Tatarstan failed, although Zor'kin was vigorous in condemning the perceived threat to the unity of the country. Its ruling in November 1992 on the constitutionality of Yeltsin's ban on the Communist Party after the *coup* found a compromise solution that ruled that the ban on the Party apparatus had been constitutional, but not that on the rank-and-file organisations.

In December 1992, during Russia's first genuine *constitutional* crisis, when executive and legislative power were locked in conflict, the Court acted as a mediator and brokered a compromise, albeit not a durable one. The prestige of the Court was undermined when in January 1993 Zor'kin changed his mind and condemned the idea of a referendum as destabilising, and confidence in his judgement was further diminished when he rushed to condemn Yeltsin's announcement on 20 March 1993 of 'special rule' before seeing the document in question.[94] An even greater challenge to the Court's authority was posed by Yeltsin's decree of 21 September 1993 suspending the constitution. The decree urged the Court not to meet until the Federal Assembly began its work, but in the event ten out of the fourteen judges condemned the presidential decree,[95] and on 17 October Yeltsin decreed the suspension of the Court. The Court had tried to assert its authority to achieve the separation of powers, but the titanic struggle between executive and legislative authority marginalised the judiciary and trampled on the rule of law in its entirety. The Constitutional Court was placed in the invidious position of defending a discredited constitution. Its procedures, moreover, encouraged acts of political adventurism. The dissolution of the old legislature and the fate of the Court appeared to illustrate the old Russian principle that law is subordinate to politics.[96]

The 1993 constitution established a new Constitutional Court of nineteen judges (Art. 125), with the judges appointed by the Federation Council but nominated by the president. The Law on the Constitutional Court of 21 July 1994 provided the Court with a more restricted brief than its highly politicised predecessor, depriving it of the right to initiate cases itself. Designed to ensure that federal laws and decrees comply with the constitution, the Court lost some of its prerogatives concerning relations between the central authorities and components of the federation. Much-needed gate-keeping mechanisms were established to make appeals to the Court more difficult as part of the attempt to transform it into a more professional and less politicised body.[97] The Court now has a stable constitution to work with rather than the earlier constantly changing text.

The new law considerably reduced its scope for independent political activity. The judges were no longer allowed to accept matters for consideration on their own initiative, and the range of 'official entities' that could put matters to them was severely restricted. Whereas earlier any deputy (and there were over a thousand of them) could send questions, now this could only be done with the approval of one-fifth of the deputies of any one chamber or by a majority vote of the Federal Assembly as a whole. In certain respects, however, its authority was increased. A ruling by the Court, for example, on the constitutionality of a presidential decree, a government resolution or a parliamentary law, is final and cannot be appealed. Any legal act that is ruled as unconstitutional loses its force. The Court can deal with several cases simultaneously, usually considering similar cases together.

Some of the judges remained from the old Court, but the confirmation of the new took over a year to complete because the president's nominations were repeatedly rejected. Finally, on 7 February 1995 the Federation Council approved the nomination of the nineteenth judge and the court could commence its work.[98] Vladimir Tumanov was selected as chairman of the Constitutional Court, insisting that 'in the transitional period constitutional stability is the highest value', but he feared that lack of respect for the law was the gravest challenge facing the court.[99] On 25 January 2001, the law on the Constitutional Court was amended to extend the term of its judges from twelve to fifteen years and the age limit of seventy years was removed. The authority of the Constitutional Court remains high, although some of its rulings have been questioned (as over the legality of Yeltsin's first war in Chechnya). Yeltsin complied with every ruling of the Court, often instructing his representative there to withdraw proposals that were liable to be judged unconstitutional. This was not the case in general, though, and the new chairman of the Court, Marat Baglai in May 2001 called on the government to take additional measures to ensure that the decisions of the Court are implemented, something that was addressed in Putin's reform of the judicial system in 2001. Legislatures, which often ignore CC decisions, now have six months to respond; failure to do so after two warnings could lead to their dissolution. The new Court has focused overwhelmingly on individual rights (some three-quarters of its cases), and far less on issues dealing with the separation of powers and federalism, although under Putin the latter issue came to the fore. The Constitutional Court today is the cornerstone

cornerstone

of Russia's fragile democracy, regulating the federal, judicial and, effectively, political system as well.[100]

Constitutionalism, law and the state

Ralf Dahrendorf has distinguished between constitutional and normal politics; in the former, 'the hour of the lawyers' strikes as they attempt to root modern political society in a constitutional order, whereas, in the latter, legislative activity concentrates on managing the established system.[101] In Russia these two types of politics were superimposed on each other, provoking the October 1993 crisis. Questions of 'polity', the nature of the state, and 'policy', specific problems of public policy, became entwined.[102] The new constitution had to be prepared at a time of profound political and economic changes: the work of the lawyers was overseen by politicians. Zor'kin, chairman of the Constitutional Court, indeed argued that the crisis of power was 'a natural result of the policy of "shock therapy"'.[103] Constitution-making became part of the political struggle, and itself became the prize in the struggle between the executive and legislative authorities.[104]

The 1993 constitution established the foundations of the new polity, but the structure remained to be built. A constitutional system is a much broader concept than the constitution itself and reflects the ethical bases of society.[105] It is quite possible to have a constitution but no constitutional order (as under the Soviet regime), or to have a constitutional order but no constitution (as in Britain); the aim in Russia today is to combine the two. The legal functions of a constitution are only one among many, and this is particularly the case with this constitution that sought to repudiate the communist political and philosophical legacy and to establish the basis of a new constitutional order.

Rumyantsev frequently talked about the foundations of the constitutional order in Russia, the concept of *stroi* (system) in the broadest sense,[106] and he is right to do so. As V. Leontovich argued for pre-revolutionary Russia, it was the absence of a developed civil structure, 'something that is essential for any liberal constitution', that led to the disappearance of political freedom and the destruction of the constitutional system in Russia in 1917.[107] The constitutional process in Russia reflected contradictory processes of social development; a constitution can hardly be more effective than the society which it seeks to regulate. At the same time, this constitution is an act of deliberate political intervention in the evolution of the polity. The constitution was designed not to reflect an existing social order but to mould a new one, a task very different from that confronting the Founding Fathers in Philadelphia in 1787. The instrumental and normative elements in the document, the attempt to design a new social order, raised two fundamental questions: was the constitution drafted in terms of expediency rather than right?; and does the idea of order rather than freedom lie at its heart?

Constitutionalism and the law

The late Tsarist period was marked by an important debate by legal scholars and others over the concept of *pravovoe gosudarstvo* (a 'law-based state'). The Russian notion of *pravovoe gosudarstvo* is derived from the German concept of a

Rechtsstaat and thus differs from the Anglo-American concept of the 'rule of law'. As Donald D. Barry has noted, 'The concept of *Rechtsstaat* is based on the positivist assumption that the state itself is the highest source of law.'[108] Thus, a *pravovoe gosudarstvo*, as Harold J. Berman put it, 'is rule *by* law, but not rule *of* law'; the latter is sustained by the theory of natural law suggesting that there is a law higher than statutory law governing the normative acts of society.

Many of the more notable Russian moral philosophers and legal scholars condemned the positivist tradition, so strong in Germany. Solovyov, indeed, developed the notion of a type of social liberalism based on the idea of the 'right to a dignified existence' within the context of a society and state formally ordered by law, a view that sharply distinguished him from the revolutionary socialist challenge to Western liberalism but that brought him closer to Bismarck and Germany's *Rechtstaat* liberals.[109] Strong echoes of Solovyov's thinking can be found in Russia's new constitution. At the turn of the century, the name of Boris Chicherin is most strongly identified with the idea of a constitutional legal order and restraints on monarchical power, condemning the positivist tradition while calling for a type of defensive liberalism that he came to call 'liberal conservatism'. His views, also, are particularly resonant in the new constitution, as in his notion of 'liberal measures and strong government',[110] a formula adopted by Peter Stolypin when he was prime minister between 1906–11, by Yeltsin's first 'government of reforms' and then by Putin. Above all, his defence of the ethical attributes of the juridical sphere encompassed by civil society, and the notion of freedom that it represents, went far beyond Hegel's rather grudging acceptance of this sphere of conflicting private interests. It also firmly rejected Marx's critique, views that in effect make Chicherin the intellectual 'godfather', albeit unacknowledged, of Russia's new constitution.

The legal revolution has a dual character. The achievement of a *Rechtsstaat* in Russia today reflects the attempt in nineteenth-century Germany to limit the arbitrariness of the absolutist *Polizeistaat* (policy state). The term *Rechtsstaat* was used to describe Germany in the second part of the nineteenth century where a legalism devoid of democratic principle (positive law) predominated. If correct bureaucratic procedures were followed, then an act was legal, and thus in these terms Hitler's regime was legal since he used the provisions of the Weimar constitution to establish his rule. The Soviet police state in its way was governed by law but public power remained arbitrary.[111] Russia now sought to combine the principles of a *Rechtsstaat* with natural law, which suggests that there is a law higher than the state to which the state itself should be subordinate. This is the heart of the concept of constitutionalism; it is more than simply rule according to a constitution – as the 'sham constitutionalism' of the Soviet era amply demonstrated.

The establishment of a *Rechtsstaat* is *limiting*, but the establishment of the rule of law is *expansive*. The 'rule of law' is a concept associated with the Anglo-Saxon common-law tradition, whereas Russia is part of the Continental Roman law tradition: according to common law individual rights are defended by the courts; whereas in the Continental tradition they are enshrined in a constitution. Thus, to the Anglo-Saxon mind the registration of political parties and religious organisations might seem superfluous, since they are protected by common law and the courts on the principle that 'everything that is not forbidden is permitted'. The

→ Constitutionalism.

Continental system, however, relies on regulation to avoid conflict and to manage social affairs. The constitutional process in Russia today can therefore be seen as a dual revolution: both to achieve a *pravovoe gosudarstvo* (a state governing by law, based on the classical positivist conception of law) and to create a society governed by the rule of law to which the state itself is subordinated – in other words, genuine constitutionalism. It is this latter concept, based on the theory of natural law that has never taken root in Russia, that was acknowledged in the 1993 constitution.

For Russia the achievement of rule by law (if not yet the rule of law) would be no mean achievement. The gulf between aspiration and achievement remains large, but certain tangible advances towards the goal have been achieved, notably the adoption of the constitution itself. The system moved beyond the nebulous concept of 'socialist legality' towards a law-based state. The concept of law of the revived Russian constitutionalism is indebted to the debates of the late Soviet period. The aim here was above all to separate the Party from the state and to remake the state as an autonomous political and ordered entity. At the same time, the overweening powers of the state were to be limited by the establishment of legal safeguards for individual rights. Associated with the second project was the discourse of civil society, a concept that figured prominently in the draft version of the CPSU's final Programme and in early drafts of the new Russian constitution. There remains, however, a tension between attempts to reconstitute and at the same time to limit the state, a contradiction that emerged with full force under Putin.

Conclusion

The defeat of Khasbulatov's parliament in October 1993 put an end to a distinctive 'phoney democracy' phase, and opened the path to the establishment of a more stable political system. The adoption of a constitution is the core constitutive act of state-building and defines the ethical essence of a new state. The 1993 constitution provided Russian statehood with a coherent juridical form and stabilised the new political order. It proclaimed that 'The holder of sovereignty and the sole source of authority in the Russian Federation is its multinational people' (Art. 3.1). It provides the three key elements of a modern democratic state: popular sovereignty, including extensive civil rights for citizens; the separation of powers, although the accountability of the executive to the legislature is relatively weak and the division of powers between the federal authorities and the regions remains contested; and a set of norms that provides for the choice and accountability of executive authority to citizens. Russia has finally begun to overcome the long tradition of 'sham constitutionalism' to enjoy the genuine rule of law and the full exercise of constitutionalism. The Constitutional Court acts as the guarantor of the constitution, and its rulings have so far been authoritative if not always implemented in full.

The constitution represented the culmination of the democratic revolution against communism but at the same time became a casualty of this struggle as it became subsumed into self-sustaining (and self-serving) politics. The constitution, moreover, represented a conscious revolt against the alleged lack of a democratic political culture in Russia, but at the same time reflected the very cultural problematic that it sought to undermine. The constitution remained ideologised (in the

→) Chechnya .

traditional sense) in so far as it acted as an instrument of reform in the hands of 'the Bolsheviks of the marketplace'. There remains a long way to go before Russia's political life is fully constitutionalised. Sovereignty remains to a degree displaced, above all to executive authorities. The struggle for popular sovereignty and the full exercise of the powers of the instruments of that sovereignty (above all parliament and the courts) is at the same time a struggle for democracy, a struggle that continues to this day. As Viktor Sheinis noted, 'It is, of course, not enough to adopt a constitution in order to create a stable democratic society, but this is a necessary and, at present, urgent prerequisite.'[112] As long as the institutions of civil society and the associated 'habits of the heart', as Tocqueville put it, of a democratic and free people remain weak, the naturally predatory instincts of the state will find little resistance.

4 Law and society

Constitutional-pluralistic systems can be corrupted by too much oligarchy or too much democracy. In the first case, they become corrupt because a minority manipulates the institutions and prevents them from reaching their highest form, which is government by the people. The second type of corruption appears, on the other hand, when oligarchy is too eroded and the different groups push their claims too far and no authority able to safeguard the general interest remains.

(Raymond Aron)[1]

A legal (positivist) state is not necessarily a democratic one, but a democratic state is by definition governed by the rule of law. The task facing the Russian legal system was nothing short of revolutionary. The old Bolshevik system of jurisprudence, and the principles on which it was based, were clearly inadequate for a democratic market-based society, and thus a new system in its entirety had to be created. Even though the constitution-adopting process was marked by rupture, the reform of the legal system was far more evolutionary and in the event judicial reform moved slowly. Freed from communism, criminality rose to the surface, while the traditional metacorruption (of the system) took radically new forms during the grand privatisation of state assets in the 1990s. The security apparatus lost some of the prominence it had enjoyed in the communist years, but remained a significant presence. Progress towards the defence of human rights was patchy, with security agencies pursuing some high-profile persecutions of civic activists.

The legal system

Urban Russia since the judicial reform of 1864 had seen the development of a relatively free judiciary, Justices of the Peace (JPs) and the development of the jury system, but these achievements had been swept away by the Bolshevik regime. The Soviet regime restored the full powers of the procuracy and emphasised the primacy of social over civil rights. Only under Gorbachev did the judiciary begin to achieve a measure of political autonomy, but this had been precarious and it fell to the post-communist regime to consolidate judicial independence. Under the Soviet system each republic had its own legal code (as well as their own constitutions), but they varied little from all-Union standards. The struggle for statehood from 1990 had, naturally, been accompanied by legal conflicts between republican and Union legislation. During the 'war of the laws' of late 1990, the Russian Supreme Soviet insisted that Russian laws took precedence over all-Union laws.[2]

Only after the August *coup* did Russia seriously embark upon building a new legal system. The adoption of the constitution in 1993 provides the keystone for this endeavour.

The judicial system includes the procuracy, the *arbitrazh* courts (dealing with disputes between economic and other legally constituted organisations) and the normal criminal courts. There are two parallel systems: courts of general jurisdiction, dealing with cases of civil and criminal law; and arbitration (in effect, commercial) courts, regulating economic disputes. Both have their own system of trials, appellate and Supreme Court process. There are eighty-six regional courts of general jurisdiction and 2,000 district courts, soon to be joined by a revived system of JPs and a system of administrative courts. The *arbitrazh* system in the Soviet era had simply arbitrated between elements of a single vast bureaucracy, and questions were raised about its suitability for market conditions. At the end of the 1990s, a new system of administrative courts began to be introduced (twenty-one have been established so far) responsible for settling disputes over electoral law and between the federal and local authorities. The establishment of this separate system, with its own system of financing, was criticised by some civil rights activists as opening the door to kangaroo courts.

Legal institutions and their reform

Let us now examine the basic structure and institutions of the Russian legal system and the ways in which they are changing, and in the following sub-section evaluate the reforms.

The Civil (Criminal) Code

This is a federal law that prescribes, within the framework of the constitution, the detailed regulatory framework of a democratic market economy. The Duma adopted a new code, to replace the RSFSR one adopted in 1960, on 24 May 1996 and it came into force on 1 January 1997 with sections defending individual rights and freedoms, and regulating economic activity.[3] The Criminal Code adds up to a vast body of normative laws regulating everything from economic activity and the behaviour of public officials to civic behaviour. We quote the code below in the section on the struggle against corruption. There is also a Criminal (Civil) Procedural Code (UPK) that in 2001 underwent significant revision, above all to reduce the powers of prosecutors and to increase the power of lawyers and the rights of the accused. It sought to increase the independence of judges, although some feared that the price was greater dependence on the executive branch.

Supreme Court

The Supreme Court is the highest body in civil, criminal and administrative law. It oversees the work of all lower courts, and its judges (of whom there are twenty, assisted by forty-five lay assessors) are granted personal inviolability and can only be arrested with the permission of the Constitutional Court. The Supreme Court hears appeals against judgements of lower courts, and in exceptional cases may make judgements of its own. The Court is divided into three chambers to deal with civil, criminal and military cases, respectively.

Ministry of Justice

The judicial system is administered by the Ministry of Justice, drafting the laws and normative acts that regulate its work. The ministry is responsible for the training of judicial personnel, analysing statistics, and (under Putin) for ensuring the establishment of a 'single legal space' in Russia.

The Procuracy

Established in Tsarist times in 1702, the procuracy is at the heart of the Russian judicial system while at the same time one of its most contested instruments. Its powers were much reduced as part of Alexander II's legal reforms of 1864, but was reinstated to its former glory by Lenin in 1922. The 1995 Law on the Procuracy retained this body as 'the eye of the Tsar', although proclaiming the 'supremacy of law' (*verkhovenstvo zakona*).[4] The procuracy is responsible for the implementation of statutes by federal ministries, executive organs and officials, the observance of human rights by ministries and also commercial and non-commercial organisations. The Law on the Courts did not affect the procuracy, which still controls itself and its hierarchy of prosecutors. The body is considered a bastion of conservatism and most plans for legal reform (as with the changes to the UPK, noted above) include attempts to erode its powers. Its monopoly on managing a case at all stages will be broken and its supervisory functions will be restricted to cases where the state's interests are involved. It will lose the power to appeal against court decisions, or to restart investigations after sentencing, while the power to issue search and arrest warrants was to be transferred from prosecutors to the courts.

The Procurator-General is nominated by the president but formally his or her appointment and dismissal are the responsibility of the Federation Council. The fate of successive Procurators-General suggests that the independence of the judiciary remains tenuous. Valentin Stepankov resisted the dissolution of the legislature in September 1993, and was dismissed in the wake of the October events. Yeltsin bitterly opposed the Duma's 'amnesty' of 26 February 1994 for the instigators of the August 1991 *coup* and the October 1993 events, yet the new Procurator-General (Alexei Kazannik) felt it his duty to release the prisoners, but then resigned. The incident suggests scope for independence of the judiciary (and, incidentally, for parliament), but also illustrates the political pressures on the legal system. This was most apparent in Yeltsin's repeated attempts to dismiss Yurii Skuratov as Procurator-General from 1998, a move that was resisted by the Federation Council until finally they agreed to Dmitrii Ustinov as his replacement on 17 May 2000. Putin had hoped to appoint his ally Dmitrii Kozak to the post, but was forced to compromise. The procuracy was equally threated by regional leaders. The new constitution enshrined the rights of local elites over the judicial process (Art. 129.3). Local procurators are appointed by regional and republican authorities, facilitating corruption and undermining the independence of the judiciary. The separation of powers between the regions and the centre is flawed, and it was this that Putin sought to change.

Judges, the courts and impartiality

According to the constitution, judges of the Constitutional Court, the Supreme Court and the Supreme Arbitration Court (dealing with economic conflicts) are nominated by the president and endorsed by the Federation Council, and are meant to be irremovable during their tenure of office. The constitution sought to guarantee judicial independence (Articles 10, 120 and 124) but this might appear to lack substance in the absence of life tenure for judges or of provisions for financial autonomy. The Law on Judges regulates the activities of the 16,500 judges in courts of general jurisdiction and 2,500 arbitration judges. There remains a severe lack of judges, being at least 18 per cent under strength in 2000, and they are overburdened with cases (a five-fold increase since 1991). Court secretaries remain poorly trained and ill-equipped. The court system works extremely slowly, adding to the length of pre-trial detention. Sentences remain harsh with little concept of rehabilitation, while at the same time the number of complaints against judges witnessed a four-fold increase to 17,000 in the 1990s, above all for rude and abusive behaviour leading to the dismissal of ninety-five judges in 1999, twenty for falsifying records. A particular problem was the role played by the Chairs of Courts at the regional level, appointed for life and responsible for distributing cases. Although judges are appointed by the president, they can be dismissed by these Chairs. There are plans to limit their term of office to three to five years. A Judicial Academy is being established to remedy these problems, the salaries of judges are being raised to make the job more attractive and less susceptible to bribes, their immunity to prosecution will be restricted, selection and dismissal will be managed by a Qualification Collegium rather than the panel of judges, while the number of court personnel will be greatly increased.

The 1995 Federal Law on the Court System defended the independence of the judiciary and insisted that its rulings should conform to those legal provisions with the greatest juridical force (effectively, international law), and guaranteed judicial protection of rights and fair trial.[5] The decisions and actions (or inactions) of bodies of state power, local self-government, public associations and officials may be challenged in the courts. In practice, the lack of adequate funding of the judicial system threatens the independence of the judiciary as much as direct political interference. As for the latter, the 'telephone law' that was typical of the Soviet era, when the local Party boss would inform the presiding judge of the necessary outcome in sensitive cases, has far from disappeared in post-communist Russia, and indeed some have argued that it has increased between judges and appellate judges. Regional authorities have tended to make up the shortfall in finances of the court system, provoking a dangerous dependence of the courts on local authorities. The latter, particularly in Moscow and St Petersburg, rarely lose a case.

Trial by jury, acquittals and pardons

The first-ever congress of the Russian judiciary in October 1991 adopted a series of proposals for judicial reform, including the return to the jury system abolished by the Bolsheviks in October 1917.[6] A Law on Jury Trial allowed jury trials to take place in nine regions in which 4,000 cases have been heard, with one in five being acquitted (under standard procedures fewer than 1 per cent of cases end in acquittal, lower even than under Stalin when the acquittal rate ran at about 10 per cent). Some leading legal experts have turned against the jury system, arguing that popular involvement in the juridical process leads to perverse outcomes.[7] Revisions to the UPK are planned for the general introduction of jury trials by 1 January 2003.

Some of the harshness of sentencing policy had been tempered by the Presidential Pardons Commission. Its chair, Anatolii Pristavkin, noted that in pre-1917 Russia, with roughly the same population and the same crime rate, there were only 140,000 people in prison. He hoped that reform of the judicial system would overcome the 'gulag tradition' of incarcerating everyone found guilty of a crime.[8] However, under Putin almost no pardons were granted and on 27 December 2001 the Commission was abolished and its work transferred to 89 regional bodies.[9]

Pre-trial detention and the prison system

The civil courts are subordinate to the Ministry of Justice and have traditionally acted as branches of the state. There is now the right to appeal against arrest, but pre-trial detention centres remain over-crowded and only about a fifth of appeals lead to release. Some 2 million people are arrested each year, with some 270,000 going on to pre-trial detention in prisons (SIZOs) designed to hold 182,500, although 125,000 are released annually before going on to trial (nearly a quarter of those incarcerated).[10] A three-year wait (and longer) is not uncommon in a system where only about 75,000 cases are heard each year and where law courts do not have to meet any deadlines. It appears that torture is widespread in these detention centres, to elicit confessions, and only after this is the suspect arrested and able to enjoy the right to legal representation. Putin's reform of the judicial system sought to reduce the time that a suspect can be kept in gaol without trial to no more than twelve months.

Russia has a higher percentage of its population in gaol than any other country in the world. There are some 1,084,000 people in prison today, more than the total for the whole of the USSR in the late 1980s. Conditions in prisons remain appalling, with infectious diseases rampant including strains of TB resistant to antibiotics affecting some 10 per cent of the prison population. In fulfilment of commitments made on joining the Council of Europe, the prison system was transferred from the Ministry of the Interior (MVD) and placed under the jurisdiction of the Ministry of Justice. It appears that the incidence of torture has decreased.

The death penalty

Popular attitudes played their part in framing the new legal system, but law-making as such is not a democratic but an elitist pursuit; legal reform can be inhibited by vengeful popular prejudices. This applies particularly to the question of capital punishment, with public opinion surveys showing support for the death penalty running consistently between 65–80 per cent. The number of offences liable to capital punishment had traditionally been high, with some sixty capital offences in the 1960 RSFSR Criminal Code, and the USSR led the international league for the use of the death penalty. Between 1962 and 1989, 21,025 people (750 a year) were executed in the USSR, though during *perestroika* the number declined to 195 in 1990.[11] Some 95 per cent of those condemned were executed for first-degree murder, but doubts were cast on the competence of the courts to categorise the offence as such, and little account was taken of the mental state of the defendants. In addition, many wrongful verdicts were passed in the absence of juries and with no courts of appeal in the USSR. A temporary moratorium was placed on the death penalty in Russia on 2 February 1991, although since then some people were executed before the moratorium became permanent in 1996. Resistance in the Duma delayed passage of a law abolishing the death penalty for good, although Putin made clear his personal opposition to the death penalty.

Judicial independence and the rights of citizens

According to Tumanov, the first head of the new Constitutional Court, too much effort had been spent in the judicial reforms on establishing trial by jury, an aspect of criminal law covering only 1 per cent of the cases. The main emphasis, he argued, should have been placed on defending the rights of citizens, a much broader question. He insisted that judicial districts should not coincide with territorial areas (regions and republics), in order to preserve the independence of judicial authorities from local administrations. In pre-revolutionary Russia judicial districts encompassed several *gubernii*, and in the United States the fifty states are covered by only thirteen federal appellate court districts. This was impossible to do under Yeltsin since many of the legislators in the Federation Council, responsible for framing the judicial reforms, were at the same time regional bosses and were not in the least inclined to give up their powers.[12] The reforms of the federal system undertaken by Putin were directed precisely towards ensuring the uniformity of the exercise of law throughout the country, including plans to set up twenty-one federal judicial districts.

International context

International law has now been adopted as domestic law (see Art. 15.4 of the constitution). The international legal system is now fully part of Russian law, although there remains some discussion over what precisely is 'an international treaty of the Russian Federation' – Does it mean only treaties subject to ratification, intergovernmental treaties or interdepartmental minutes and protocols (if the latter, then any ministry can make and change law)? A further problem is the status of CIS agreements, particularly judgements issued by the Economic Court of the CIS. There is an emerging body of CIS law, something that is resisted by Ukraine. Russians now have the opportunity to take their case to the European Court of Human Rights, and several thousand cases have been lodged. No Russian has yet won a case there, but the threat has been sufficient in a number of cases to achieve a reversal of a judgement.

Legal reform and society

The Soviet system eliminated the independence of the judiciary; the legal system was subservient to the Party-state. Now the institutional context of the legal system has changed dramatically, and at the same time legal reform was accompanied by the internationalisation of Russia's political and economic systems. Russia became a full member of the Council of Europe in 1996, and its attempts to enter into contractual relations with international economic organisations such as the European Union (EU) and the International Monetary Fund (IMF) meant that Russian standards had to adapt to international ones. Communists had always understood that the law is a special kind of normative system, and the truth of this judgement was reflected in the comprehensive reorientation of the legal system based on a new set of values that has been attempted in post-communist Russia. Legal reform took place in the special conditions of the transition from a one-party system to a multi-party parliamentary democracy, accompanied by the transition from the command economy to the market. The social function of law played a prominent part in all the post-communist societies. Not only is law a method of exercising and controlling state power, establishing the rules for the conduct of competitive politics, but it bears a system of values enshrined in such principles as legal security, the freedom to own property, and the protection of rights.

The legislative activity of the Russian parliament operated within these constraints. There were seven key areas of legislation: the jurisdiction of state administrative bodies and the legal status of administrative bodies and political officials; constitutional reform and the establishment of a Constitutional Court; judicial reform, the rebuilding of the Russian legal system; laws regulating public life, the registration of political parties, laws on assembly and association, electoral regulations; laws on local government; laws concerned with the transformation of the economy, foreign trade and association laws, regulating the market economy, trading standards, accounting, tax, privatisation and land laws; and laws concerning the social sphere and welfare politics, social security, unemployment, benefits, labour laws. Despite the strained relations between the president and parliament throughout the 1990s, a large amount of legislation implemented this comprehensive programme for the radical transformation of the juridical basis for social activity.

Much of this legislative activity, however, was partial and distorted: social legislation lagged far behind economic laws, and acts were often drafted in an ambiguous manner leaving loopholes for the bureaucracy to exploit. The economic sphere was still over-bureaucratised, with a mass of regulations governing the operation of enterprises; instead of deregulation, too often there was yet more regulation. The principles of the new ownership structure were only haphazardly applied. There was as much an economic as a political need for a clear and consistent legal system, so that the economic community did not need to worry too much about political considerations and could instead concentrate on business. The defence of property rights remained weak, and the rights of minority shareholders were regularly flouted. Above all, there was still a very weak organised input of social influence on the drafting of laws. Social consultative mechanisms were embryonic, although compensated in part by the committees and commissions of the Federal Assembly that examined legislation and drew on expert opinion.

Putin's regional reforms sought to equalise citizenship throughout the federation by establishing a 'single legal space'. The reform of federal relations demonstrated that Putin's 'dictatorship of law' policy was a genuine attempt to ensure the rule of law. All courts – from the top down to the regional and lower courts – were now financed solely from the federal budget, thus eliminating the courts' financial dependence on regional governments, something that obviously compromised their independence. At the same time, the salaries of judges were raised to increase their level of 'professionalism' and 'honesty'. Yeltsin's misrule was nowhere more in evidence than in the judicial system. Despite endless plans, the Russian judiciary until well into the post-communist era remained stamped by its provenance in the Soviet era, something that was reflected in the low level of judicial defence of citizens' rights and freedoms. The judicial reforms being pushed through by the deputy head of the Kremlin administration, Dmitrii Kozak, sought to reduce the powers of the procuracy while increasing those of judges and widening the rights of lawyers and defendants.

Crime and the mafia

The Russian legal system was rebuilt against the background of a society edging towards ungovernability. The power vacuum left by the demise of the communist regime was exploited by criminal syndicates in which power, money and crime, according to Stephen Handelman, forged a 'seamless connection'. In his view, 'The Russian mafiya's (*sic*) connection with government, born of its symbiotic relationship with the former communist establishment, makes organised crime a dagger pointed at the heart of Russian democracy.'[13] The state had already been criminalised by the old elites, and now the arbitrariness of the Soviet system was converted into widespread societal lawlessness. The criminal gangs that had emerged under Stalin, the thieves' world (*vorovskoi mir*) with a code of honour enshrined in popular song, were ideally placed to exploit the disorder associated with the turn to capitalism. As one of them told Handelman:

> we outlasted Soviet power....The communists succeeded in grinding into powder the intelligentsia, the White Guards, the Baptists; they destroyed everything for the sake of their ideology, but they always failed to destroy us.[14]

The 'thieves in law' (*vory v zakone*, the fraternity of thieves whose strict code of criminal ethics forbade collaboration with the authorities – as opposed to the 'renegades', *suki*) were the basis for the explosion of organised crime. The authorities in many regions had effectively become mafia-like structures.[15] According to the MVD, in June 1997 there were some 9,000 organised criminal groups with some 100,000 members,[16] controlling banks, money exchanges and systematically subverting the state administration and new entrepreneurial activity. According to the Prosecutor General, Vladimir Ustinov, in early 2001 about 40,000 Russian enterprises, including a third of the country's banks, were controlled by criminal groups.[17] At least a quarter of Russia's business people were linked to the criminal world.[18] New and even more ruthless gangs drew freely on ex-servicemen, the KGB, the army and the militia to deal in pornography, narcotics, money laundering and protection rackets.[19] Already in the last years of *perestroika* senior officials of the old regime, most spectacularly in the Komsomol organisation, had begun the struggle for control of Russia's financial and industrial resources, and the anarchic post-communist economy provided rich pickings for them.

There had been a long-term rise in recorded crime since at least the mid-1970s, and this trend now accelerated. Under Gorbachev crime figures showed an alarming increase, and by 1991 this had reached awesome proportions accompanied by a sharp increase in motiveless crimes. A record 2.76 million crimes were recorded in 1992, a 27 per cent increase over the previous year, and the clear-up rate fell also.[20] The fear of crime etched itself deeply on the consciousness of the post-totalitarian society. In 1994, some 32,300 premeditated murders were recorded in Russia, double the 15,600 in 1990 and a rate considerably higher than that typical in Western Europe.[21] Contract killings in particular rose from 102 in 1992[22] to at least 2,500 in 1995, with some 6,500 others probably falling in this category.[23] These killings were marked by a chilling cold-bloodedness as former soldiers, accustomed to death in Russia's many 'little wars' (Afghanistan and Chechnya), profited from their 'professionalism'. Prominent victims included bankers and MPs, as well as the journalist Dmitrii Kholodov, blown up by an exploding briefcase in October 1994, the television star Vladislav List'ev, shot in the entrance hall to his apartment block in March 1995, and the democratic politician Galina Starovoitova, also shot in the entrance to her apartment block in St Petersburg in October 1998. The so-called mafia itself adapted to new circumstances, with criminal gangs gaining a legal foothold by registering as private detective agencies. Their international links also appear to have improved, helped by the enormous increase in the number of Russians travelling abroad, with Britain alone issuing 88,158 visas in 1994 compared to 11,500 in 1987. Fears of a 'tidal wave' of Russian organised crime engulfing Britain and the West, however, were exaggerated.[24]

Rising crime had prompted Yeltsin in 1992 to relax the controls on the bearing of arms, thus weakening the state's monopoly on firepower that had been imposed by the Bolsheviks soon after they came to power. Citizens now had the right to bear arms to protect themselves and their property. Businesses threatened by criminal gangs were forced to pay protection money to a 'roof' (*krysha*), but this in turn stimulated the proliferation of some 8,000 private security companies employing around 1.3 million people by 1995.[25] Official anti-crime organisations lost some of their best agents as an estimated one-third of the state's policemen, security officials and professional soldiers were attracted by better wages and prestige. The work of the courts was further impeded by the threats of criminals against witnesses and their families.

The development of the market and democracy in Russia had become fatefully entwined with organised crime. Criminal networks had entered the banking system, were in control of many companies, and distorted the evolution of market relations by extortion and protection rackets, thus forcing costly security operations.[26] Gangs were not only involved in typically gangsterish behaviour but also penetrated the 'legal' open economy; indeed, in post-communist Russian conditions it was very difficult to tell where the black economy (estimated to be roughly the same size as the official economy) ended and various shades of the grey economy began. In a report delivered to the Academy of Social Sciences in July 1997, Anatolii Kulikov, then Minister for Internal Affairs and also a Deputy Prime Minister, argued that 'Organised crime is dictating individual Russian industries how to behave on the market and controls whole areas of the country.' According to Kulikov, 'underworld godfathers are setting up closed syndicates and have them infiltrate the state's economic institutions'.[27]

While the old regime lacked freedom, it did at least ensure a degree of security. The new freedoms after the fall of communism were accompanied by such a degree of job and physical insecurity that many yearned for the order (*poryadok*) of Soviet times. The interpenetration of organised crime and politics led some to argue that Russia's second revolution had been 'stolen' by an unholy alliance of communists-turned-speculators and the criminal underworld. According to Handelman, whole regions and cities had fallen into the hands of criminal networks, senior officers happily traded weapons for cars, while the clandestine trade in nuclear materials threatened the rest of the world. He suggested that Russia had become a 'criminal state' run by and for criminals, while the honest lost out.[28] The Russian 'mafiya' was a distinctive product of the Soviet prison-camp system and the post-communist weakening of the state, whereas in Italy it was a well-organised product of long-term social development. The close connection between political and criminal elites originated in Soviet times but had grown in depth and scale after 1991. It would be an exaggeration, however, to argue that Russia had become a 'criminal state' since far too much remained beyond the control of criminal-political elites. It would be more accurate to say that Russia was a state marked by widespread criminality reaching into the upper echelons of central and local power; but this does not make Russia – any more than it makes Italy – a mafia state.

Corruption and metacorruption

According to Boris Fedorov, 'Corruption has permeated our entire society.... Corruption, that is a demand for remuneration, is encountered at every step.'[29] Corruption, however, is an ambiguous phenomenon. Georgy Satarov noted that it could be defined in the narrow sense as a transaction that involves a government official abusing a resource or property not in the interests of those who had placed responsibility in his hands but to the person who had bribed him (venal corruption); but it could also be defined more broadly as the degradation of power (metacorruption). He also stressed that there was a distinctively Russian phenomenon of 'corruption at the bottom', engaged in by the mass of the people to survive in a bureaucratised semi-market society, while 'corruption at the top' was the problem that usually most concerned Western writers. The two types of corruption in Russia linked up to create a type of 'social' corruption that was prevalent in Asian societies.[30] Yurii Levada noted that in popular perceptions corruption tended to become a catch-all bogeyman to describe various social ills such as the theft of state property, tax evasion, and links between oligarchs and politicians, in addition to the more narrowly defined bribery of government officials, cronyism and nepotism. Such a conceptual lack of precision, in his view, made it more difficult to fight corruption.[31] Russia's market-oriented corruption added a new layer to a deeply embedded 'culture of favours', to use Alena Ledeneva's term, based on *blat*, the system of informal contacts and personal networks that allowed people to obtain goods and services in the Soviet system.[32] Corruption and the shadow economy fed off each other, distorting classical market relations and poisoning basic transactions in daily life.[33]

Metacorruption and Yeltsin's regime

Russia is moving from metacorruption, that is a system which is corrupt in its very essence, to venal corruption; from a corrupt system to a system with corruption.[34] The communist system was metacorrupt in that it never subordinated itself to the rule of law (although after the initial revolutionary lawlessness it ruled by and through the law), characterised by its lack of accountability and the systematic enjoyment of privileges granted its leadership by the common ownership of the means of production.[35] Corruption was one of the reasons for the fall of communism.[36] A new form of metacorruption, however, has emerged rooted in the transition from a state-owned economy to a market-based system. The enormity of the attempt to disentangle the political process from its deep embedment in the economy, while at the same time structuring political life as an autonomous activity governed by the impartial rule of law and accountable to the electorate, can hardly be exaggerated. The extrication of the Russian state, on the one hand, from deep involvement in the economy and, on the other, from its dominance by a single party that governed for some seventy years in an arbitrary and voluntarist manner, represents an act of political reconstitution unprecedented in its scope and complexity. What has emerged, though, is a dual system where new forms of systemic metacorruption coexist with what we call venal corruption, the pursuit of individual gain out of the pursuit or attainment of public office. The World Bank calls the first sort 'state capture', and the second 'administrative corruption'.[37] Yeltsin's regime had the dual characteristics of both in good measure. Under Putin the metacorrupt features are being sharply curtailed as the policy process becomes less susceptible to social pressures and state capture is being reversed.

No clear line can be drawn between venality and metacorruption. The whole privatisation programme, for example, masterminded by Anatolii Chubais, was a huge exercise in transferring public goods into private assets. All sides of the Russian political spectrum, however, charge that privatisation favoured a small group of 'oligarchs', immiserated large sections of society and enriched Chubais's friends in the elite. From a structural perspective privatisation was considered a necessary component in establishing a market economy. Chubais insisted that the creation of a new middle class would create the social basis for democracy. Privatisation, however, hardly changed the behaviour of many of the new 'owners', and they continued to form alliances with state bureaucrats to gain resources and to shield them from hostile alliances of competing interests.

At the height of Yeltsin's rule the state itself engaged in corruption on a grand scale. In the 'loans-for-shares' scandal from November 1995 the state favoured certain 'insider' interests in the privatisation process in return for funds that would ensure that the machinery of government could continue to turn. Insider banks were granted shares in the country's top companies as collateral for loans to a desperate government, but it was understood by all that the government would default on the loans and the oligarchs would get the companies for a song. In this way Vladimir Potanin's Oneksimbank 'purchased' the giant Norilsk Nickel works (the world's largest), the Sidanko oil company, and the Northwest River Shipping Company, while the Menatep Bank got hold of Yukos, Russia's second largest oil company. The growing budget deficit was exacerbated by various tax exemptions granted to bodies like the Russian Orthodox Church for the import of alcohol and cigarettes, and above all to the National Sports Fund (NFS) established by presidential decree on 1 June 1992. Having been granted generous export quotas on a range of valuable raw materials, out of the billions of roubles that passed through its hands only a tiny proportion contributed to the development of sport, and not a single audit was conducted on the fund throughout its existence until its privileges were revoked in 1995.[38]

In the absence of a state able to enforce rules and to adjudicate between interests, organised crime stepped in to enforce contracts, regulate economic struggles and protect property rights. Corruption, in other words, worked from the top down and from the bottom up, squeezing honest business and endeavour almost entirely out of existence. The chaotic, arbitrary and punitive tax system, moreover, not only undermined the revenue-raising powers of the state but also drove small entrepreneurs as well as larger enterprises into the technically illegal activities of the black, grey and other-coloured sections of the economy. In the Central European countries the proportion of economic activity conducted outside the law tended to decrease after the early years of post-communism, but the mutually reinforcing development of organised crime and official corruption prevented this occurring in Russia (as well as Bulgaria and Ukraine).

The funding of political parties and electoral campaigns is at the sharp edge of political corruption. The best-known example of the latter is the 1996 presidential campaign in which the Yeltsin team (from March 1996 led by the ubiquitous Chubais) spent several dozen (if not thousands) times more money than the law allowed (each candidate could spend 14.5 billion old roubles, or $3.2 million). In February 1996, Russia's leading moguls, inspired by Boris Berezovskii, met at the Davos Forum in Switzerland and created a war chest to bankroll Yeltsin's re-election. The gulf between what the Yeltsin team actually spent on the campaign, whose upper estimates reach over $500 million,[39] and the modest sum that he declared is impressive.[40] There was no serious attempt to implement election and campaign laws – except against his opponents. The symbol of the campaign was not the ballot box but a cardboard box containing $538,000 in campaign cash that two of Chubais's aides were caught carrying out of the White House on 19 June, just three days after the first round of voting.[41] One of the two caught with the box was Sergei Lisovskii, one of the masterminds behind the campaign and head of the 'Premier SV' advertising agency, one of Russia's largest advertising companies. There have been allegations that he was somehow involved in the murder in 1995 of Vladislav List'ev, a television journalist and executive at ORT (Russia's main TV channel) who had temporarily frozen all advertising contracts, including that with Premier SV. Yeltsin's victory was due to more than electoral bribery and malpractice, above all arising out of fear of what a victory for the communists would entail, yet the shameless and extravagant promises and their equally brutal repudiation, and the illegal over-spending on the campaign indicated a profound corruption of the political process.

A year after the presidential elections, the charges of corruption focused on Chubais's own personal enrichment, with *Izvestiya* alleging that in February 1996, a month after he first left office, the Stolichnyi Savings Bank granted a five-year interest-free $2.9 million loan to his new Centre to Defend Private Property. The funds were allegedly used for his personal speculation in the treasury bills (GKO) market, allowing him to reap lucrative profits that he then pocketed.[42] In a letter to the paper Chubais did not dispute the facts but claimed (quite logically within the framework of what we call metacorruption) that what he had done was 'absolutely normal' in any democratic country.[43] His action was perhaps not strictly speaking illegal, but using funds donated for charitable purposes for personal speculation is irregular, to say the least. The whole story of Western 'aid' to Russia is similarly beset by a mixture of venality and systemic metacorruption.[44] There is a similar confusion over the legal status of the use of authors' 'advances' in the case of a number of officials in 1997. The story was linked to the intra-elite struggles over the Svyazinvest sale in July 1997, and led to the exposure of a $100,000 advance payment from Servina, a Swiss financial group with links to Potanin's Oneksimbank (the winner of the auction), to Alfred Kokh, head of the state property committee (GKI) responsible for the disbursement of state property, and led to his sacking in August 1997.[45] A similar case was exposed in November 1997 when five high officials, including Chubais, were together found to have received a $450,000 advance. Maksim Boiko, Kokh's successor at GKI, was forced to resign, but Chubais once again weathered the storm. Criminal charges were not filed against the officials on the grounds that there was no evidence that they had embezzled money from the state, although presumably Oneksimbank, in making the excessive payments, expected to receive something in return for its 'investment'.

At the heart of the metacorruption view of the Yeltsin regime is the notion of a 'party of power' closely entwined with financial-commercial interests. The concept of the 'party of power' is misleading in that it implies a coherence and unanimity among ruling groups that in actuality was never there, but the notion does at least indicate the prevalence of informal relations behind the allegedly democratic façade of elections and constitutional government. Although the 1996 presidential election encouraged a temporary coalescence in the face of the perceived communist threat, later events demonstrated just how fragmented it was. The 'Russia Our Home' (NDR) party, headed by Viktor Chernomyrdin, the former head of the huge utilities company Gazprom and Prime Minister from December 1992 until March 1998, suffered numerous splits, while economic elites engaged in bitter internecine warfare in which each side sought to mobilise the media and sections of the administration. The Svyazinvest auction revealed a complex pattern of alliances, with Potanin's Oneksimbank ranged alongside Chubais and First Deputy Prime Minister Boris Nemtsov (formerly governor of Nizhnii Novgorod *oblast*) against Boris Berezovsky of Logovaz and Vladimir Gusinsky of Mostbank. Gazprom is one of the most politically adroit companies in Russia, with its former head, Chernomyrdin, retaining close links with the company even as he served as Prime Minister. It is alleged that in the 1996 presidential elections Gazprom invested $450 million in Yeltsin's re-election campaign.[46] It was plans drawn up by Boris Nemtsov to challenge the privileges of the oligarchs, and in particular of natural monopolies like Gazprom, that by some accounts provoked the dismissal of Sergei Kirienko's government on 23 August 1998 and the attempt to restore Chernomyrdin as Prime Minister, thus gratuitously adding a political crisis to an already severe economic one (see Chapter 5).

Corruption in Russia is rooted in the political economy of the transition. Yves Mény has defined corruption 'as a clandestine exchange between two markets – the political and/or administrative market and the economic and social market'.[47] This definition, so pertinent to Russia, is at the core of John Girling's analysis of the issue:

> Corruption is the illegitimate reminder of the values of the market place (everything can be bought and sold) that in the age of capitalism increasingly, even legitimately, permeate formerly autonomous political and social spheres.[48]

For him corruption was more than a 'criminal' problem; it was a social one, derived in part from the incommensurability of the economic and political spheres that in practice eroded the distinction between public and private matters. Seen in this light, the spread of capitalism to Russia could not but subvert the realisation of the proclaimed democratic ideals together with good governance in its entirety. The close relationship between economic and political elites in a redistributionary system devoted to the privatisation of state assets with minimal legal controls and no public oversight could not but encourage not only venality but also metacorruption. What if Chubais was right, however, and that it did not matter how state property was disbursed as long as it was done quickly and created a substantial class (however narrow its composition) with a vital stake in the preservation of the post-communist order? In these circumstances corruption, ranging from the venal to the political, could be considered a progressive phenomenon. The common good could, it is argued, be achieved by metacorrupt means, something that is tautologically incoherent but is typical of the paradoxes of post-communism. Mayor Yurii Luzhkov's style of managing affairs in Moscow, where the city government took its cut of all deals and reinvested the proceeds in the city itself (like mayor Richard Daley in Chicago in an earlier epoch), suggested that metacorruption might be the price to pay to make the transition to capitalism irreversible.

Even more venal forms of corruption, moreover, can be considered functional. While the emergence of Yeltsinite metacorruption has been defended, by Chubais and his allies, as systemically progressive, allowing the rudiments of a capitalist system to be transferred to Russia and a middle class to emerge, a similar argument has been advanced by economists concerning venal corruption. Do its costs always out-weigh its benefits? Might it not encourage economic growth by subverting a stifling bureaucracy and allowing the accumulation of capital?[49] This may be the case in individual cases, but the evidence suggests that corruption deters foreign investment, and in Russia encouraged capital flight totalling at least $100 billion between 1991–8, dwarfing the $6 billion in foreign direct investment and the various painful International Monetary Fund (IMF) loans. If allowed to proliferate corruption ultimately undermines government itself as bureaucrats become more concerned with private profit than public duties. This has certainly been the case in Russia, where the very existence of the state was threatened by corruption, both meta and venal. For Leslie Holmes, indeed, corruption represented a distinctive type of crisis of the state.[50] The British consultancy Control Risks Group ranked Russia the most corrupt country in the world,[51] while Transparency International's Corruption Perception Index for 1997 placed Russia in 49th place,[52] not a healthy position for a country aspiring to great power status. By 2001, the Index saw Russia in 79th place out of ninety-one ranked countries, tying with Ecuador and Pakistan, although this was a slight improvement over the previous year when Russia was ranked 82nd.[53]

The 'political economy' approach to corruption is already well-established.[54] It stresses that political actors will act rationally to advance their (typically material) interests, usually at the expense of the public interest.[55] The approach focuses on the behaviour of agents, which in a situation where property rights were fluid and negative rights unenforced, allowed enormous scope for rent-seeking and corruption. Until 1998, the very management of state assets had been 'privatised', with some fifty authorised banks dealing with transfers from the state budget at the central and local levels, allowing unimaginable profits to be made at the state's expense – and above all at the expense of those whose wages were delayed as the banks speculated with funds designated for social purposes. Some ten so-called 'court' banks were at the heart of this system of financial manipulation. A system of tax benefits granted to so-called charitable foundations siphoned billions of roubles away from the state budget, as with NFS. In short, the Yeltsin regime allowed the state budget itself to become the object of private speculative manipulation, contributing to the bankruptcy of the state in mid-1998 and the effective default on foreign loans and the moratorium on servicing the domestic debt.

It is clear that the monopolies and financial groups exerted a disproportionate and direct influence on politics. Bureaucratic, political and economic corruption became entwined as the semi-feudal court politics around Yeltsin allowed a financial–industrial oligarchy to replace formal politics by a system of informal deals. The 'corridors of power' were no longer to be found in government ministries but in the softly carpeted executive suites of the new oligarchs. The very notion of 'lobbying' became pathetically inadequate to describe the way that whole areas of the state were colonised by external interests. Duma deputies allegedly were routinely bribed – in the words of one paper, 'everything can be bought and sold'.[56] The focus of political corruption, however, was the presidency – in a presidential system lobbying will inevitability focus more narrowly on the presidential apparatus than in the more complex multi-layered game typical of parliamentary systems. In Russia the relationship between special interest groups and the presidency was exceptionally close. The presidency was not only the source of 'reform' but was also at the apex of the meta-corruption with which it was accompanied.

The key issue increasingly became not the open contest between political parties but the struggles between the financial-industrial groups (FIGs). To succeed in the battle to gain the spoils of privatisation the FIGs and other conglomerates needed their own lobbyists within the political system and the ability to whip up media campaigns against their opponents. The major television stations and newspapers were owned in whole or in part by the economic moguls, like Vladimir Potanin, Boris Berezovsky and Vladimir Gusinsky, while the remaining electronic media is certainly dominated by the executive authorities, precluding investigative reporting on their activities. Classic cases of this were the struggles to control Svyazinvest in 1997 and NTV in 2000–1. The political process became less and less focused on the traditional instruments of politics like parliament, parties and the presidency, and was reduced to the law of the jungle of primitive economic empire-building. In an attempt to restore the presidency to its customary role under Yeltsin as balance-holder, in September 1997 he called in six of the top barons and ordered a ceasefire, but to little effect until Putin took up the struggle.

Anti-corruption measures

We argue that Yeltsin's regime had dual characteristics, both democratising and elite-dominated, venal and metacorrupt. It is these dual characteristics that made attempts at reform more than cosmetic, and ultimately allowed Putin to try to break with the previous system in its entirety. Under Yeltsin, however, anti-corruption campaigns often were little more than an instrument in intra-elite competition. A number of elements were involved in these anti-corruption campaigns.

The legal definition of corruption

In contrast to Russia's 1960 Criminal Code that made no mention of corruption, the new code at least recognises the problem. Article 291.1 criminalises the payment of bribes either directly or indirectly to an official whether in a state or private office, while 291.2 outlaws payments to an official to undertake wittingly illegal actions (or inaction). Article 292 defines 'administrative forgery' as an official inserting into official documents known falsehoods or distorting their contents out of mercenary or personal interest. Punishments ranged from a stiff fine to imprisonment. The very definition of the crime represented an important step in combating it, but few prosecutions have yet been brought against officials. In 1995, 3,504 charges were brought against corrupt civil servants, the great majority accused of bribery, while according to MVD statistics 700 cases had been found between 1995–8 linking bureaucrats to organised crime, although few prosecutions resulted.[57] A new law on government service came into effect on 1 January 1998 that defined the rights and obligations of civil servants and marked a small step towards overcoming the functional corruption that had defined the Russian state bureaucracy since at least the time of Peter the Great.[58] At the same time, although it is illegal for public servants to work in business, this is only irregularly policed. The enforcement of existing laws would be a significant contribution to fighting corruption.

Anti-corruption campaigns and income declarations

Budgetary constraints and problems of low morale inhibit the work of law enforcement agencies. The MVD, responsible for the militia, suffered a haemorrhage of experienced officers and was itself mired in criminality. The anti-corruption campaign waged by the minister of the interior, Kulikov, from mid-1995 revealed awesome depths of venality in the MVD. His high-profile campaign, including catching the traffic police red-handed in taking bribes, did little to change the structures that sustained the culture of bribe-taking.

The Yeltsin presidency launched a number of anti-corruption campaigns, but they tended to be a substitute for the kind of changes that would have genuinely tackled the problem.[59] Their primary purpose was symbolic and political. As Valerii Streletskii, the head of the anti-corruption section of the Presidential

Security Service in 1995–7, put it, 'We existed on two planes. On the one hand we carried out the war against corruption. On the other, we proceeded out of political interests.'[60] By 1998, Yeltsin had vetoed three Duma anti-corruption laws that might have threatened the interests of his newly enriched allies. A presidential decree of 4 April 1992 was the first official anti-corruption measure, focusing on petty crime in the civil service, and was followed by numerous equally ineffective campaigns. In his annual address to the Federal Assembly on 6 March 1997, Yeltsin acknowledged that corruption had undermined all levels of public service, noting that 'the criminal world has openly challenged the state and launched into open competition with it'.[61] The new anti-corruption campaign encompassed a number of measures, including a decree (drafted by Nemtsov) of 20 May 1997 that forced all government officials, members of parliament, public officials and political appointees to declare their incomes and assets (above all property holdings) in writing on special forms, and one of the sanctions for the first time against officials was the confiscation of personal property. From 1 January 1999, all government officials whose lifestyle exceeded their official incomes had to declare the source of their excess wealth. The actual declarations by leading officials at times verged on the farcical. Chernomyrdin, whose personal wealth in foreign bank accounts was reputed to be in the region of $5 billion, filed earnings of 1.4 million new roubles ($233,000) for 1997, a figure thirty-one times higher than that he had declared the previous year.[62] Yeltsin himself declared his 1997 income at 1.95 million new roubles ($320,000) derived mainly from his salary, royalties from his memoirs published in 1994 and interest on Russian bank accounts.[63]

As elsewhere, anti-corruption drives are used to punish opponents and to strengthen those politicians who can claim to have 'clean hands'. No campaign is complete without a few sacrificial lambs. The victims in this case were Sergei Stankevich, who had already been arrested in April 1997 in Warsaw on an international arrest warrant in connection with an ill-fated Red Square concert, and General Konstantin Kobets, the hero of August 1991 but who in May 1997 was charged with abuse of office, bribery and the illegal possession of firearms. Both had long ago left the top rank of government, and thus their prosecution did not taint the existing authorities. A notable element in any anti-corruption campaign was the use of *kompromat* (evidence of malfeasance) in power struggles among the elite to blacken (compromise) one's opponents. The battle of *kompromat* was waged from the highest to the lowest levels, and not only in Russia.[64]

Public supervision and transparency

From the above it is clear that effective anti-corruption campaigns have to be distanced from executive authorities. In keeping with the dual nature of Russian politics, there were moves in this direction. A General Control Inspectorate was established in 1992 to combat corruption, and its first head from March 1992, Yurii Boldyrev, proceeded to do so with gusto, exposing malfeasance in the Moscow mayor's office, GKI and, most notoriously, in the Western Army Group in the former East Germany. For his pains, Boldyrev was forced to resign as Comptroller General in March 1993.[65] Yeltsin had intended the anti-corruption campaign to be directed against his enemies, not his political allies.[66] And thus this case, as we suggested above with other anti-corruption campaigns, was politicised. In 1995, Boldyrev continued his lonely struggle against corruption as the deputy head of the Federal Audit Chamber. His exposure of the 'loans-for-shares' scam helped put an end to the practice, but the fact that the exposure of these cases hardly caused a ripple let alone a scandal indicates that we are dealing here with metacorruption, not 'simple' corruption. Under Putin the Audit Chamber was headed by Sergei Stepashin and now with presidential backing increased its oversight role over public expenditure, launching numerous investigations, including into the misappropriation of funds in Chechnya. There were plans to increase its powers (with the right to turn directly to the courts and to impose administrative penalties), but accompanied by a change in its status to bring it under presidential control. Instead of the Duma nominating its head, it would be the president (subject to Duma approval); and the president would enjoy the right to order the Audit Chamber to undertake investigations.[67]

In this context public oversight and media campaigns can have only a marginal role. It is not so much that the executive branch is too powerful, but that accountability for its actions is too weak. This is not a counsel for despair, and while what we described above is part of systemic metacorruption, we also argue that Russia is a dual system where venal forms of corruption can be challenged, and by doing so the legitimacy of metacorruption is also undermined. Already Yeltsin's March 1997 address to the Federal Assembly recognised the danger that metacorruption posed to his own power, and promised to abolish the system of authorised banks and replace them with a national treasury, and insisted that future privatisation auctions should be more transparent. Independent watchdog institutions play an important part in reversing the culture of corruption and ensuring that anti-corruption struggles are perceived as more than part of political gamesmanship. The struggle at least sustains an alternative normative system that refuses to accept corruption as 'normal' and upholds a concept of the public good. The abuse of the concept of civil society has led to it being abandoned by some analysts, yet Girling is absolutely right to argue that 'the emergence of "civil society" provides the potential for normative counter-claims'.[68] These claims, moreover, as Rutland and Kogan stress, must be rooted in the realities of the country itself. Only Russians, they insist, 'can come up with a formula for a "capitalism with a Russian face" that stands a chance of working in that country', and here legal abstractions should come to terms with the realities of political power: 'Unless one specifies the political conditions conducive to the emergence of a coalition in favor of battling corruption, reforms promoting the rule of law will remain mere castles in the air.'[69] The roots of political corruption lie not in the social psychology of Russians but in specific institutions, structures and practices, and well-formulated and implemented reforms can deal with it at that level.

Parliamentary and other forms of immunity

Many criminals had run for, and some were elected to, parliament to take advantage of the immunity from criminal prosecution that this conferred on them.[70] In many cases investigations have had to be dropped when the suspect successfully ran for office. Vitalii Savitskii, head of the Christian Democratic Union – Christians of

Russia (CDU/CR) bloc, had repeatedly advocated limiting parliamentary immunity for deputies from criminal prosecution.[71] His death just before the December 1995 elections in a car accident was considered suspicious by some. His cause continued to be fought, and by late 1998 there were concrete plans to lift the immunity from deputies indicted on criminal offences. Already the Constitutional Court ruled against attempts to grant deputies in regional legislatures immunity, ruling that only a federal law could decide the issue.[72] Managers of partially state-owned enterprises also enjoyed *de facto* immunity since their prosecution faced numerous legal obstacles, allowing the luxuriant growth of corruption. The business ethics of Russia's new semi-market economy in fact became part of the larger process of metacorruption.

Controlling campaign expenses

National elections to date have been accompanied by accusations that the CEC had failed to establish clear rules for the financing of electoral campaigns. In the December 1993 campaign, there had been confusion over how much a candidate could spend on themselves, allowing (it is claimed) corruption on a grand scale.[73] All candidates have to file financial declarations to the CEC or its equivalents at the local level stating the amount and source of campaign funds. Attempts to smear rivals with the charge that they received support from abroad (which is illegal) or foreign NGOs based in Russia have led to the publication of some of these.[74] Lobbying interests have 'invested' in candidates, hoping for a substantial return on their election. The failure of deputies to perform to expectations in this respect prompted business interests and other groups to participate directly in the December 1995 elections. The CEC has gradually refined the financial rules concerning elections, codified in the 2001 law on parties (see Chapter 8) but the problem, as before, remains consistent implementation.

More market or authoritarianism?

One of the leading analysts of the Russian 'transition', Anders Aslund, has argued that a rapid move to free markets would eliminate corruption.[75] The reduction of state intervention and bureaucratic interference would, in his view, remove some of the sources of distortion that allowed corruption to flourish. The analysis is undoubtedly correct in part, but needs to be balanced by an adequate understanding of the role that states play in regulating markets. A strong market required a strong state. It is at this point that more authoritarian solutions to the problem of corruption became increasingly popular. Already in 1998 Lebed, advancing a distinctive mix of authoritarian populism to resolve the economic crisis and the criminalisation of politics, won the governorship of Krasnoyarsk *krai*, while Luzhkov advanced a *dirigiste* model to tackle Russia's problems. Putin's response was a combination of market and discipline.

The historical and social roots of corruption go deep into Russian and Soviet history, and in the post-communist era threatened the whole democratisation process, undermining the rule of law, democracy, human rights and the very foundations of the emerging civil societies. Mény has argued that the prevalence of corruption undermines the democratic process itself, above all by encouraging a withdrawal from political participation and cynicism.[76] In Russia these features were apparent, with a widespread lack of trust in the new political elite and a grudging participation in the political process. A common attitude to the new leaders was that they were all thieves, but the very definition of what constituted theft was blurred in the context where the whole transitional regime was built on an *'enrichessez-vous'* programme. Despite the systemic corruption, at the individual level the communist system had been imbued by an ethos of public service, but this was now thrown out with the bath water of communism. The problem was exacerbated by the post-communist bias against idealism of whatever hue and by the dominance of a neo-liberal paradigm that elevated market forces into a new utopia.

Corruption extended not only into many areas of public administration but also into the law-enforcement and other security agencies, including in Russia the army. When combined with the increasingly transnational character of organised crime and the vast resources it was able to control, the very bases of state autonomy came under threat. With its roots in the communist period, contrary to expectations the fall of the regimes did not lead to the decline of corruption and organised crime but to their luxuriant growth in the new market conditions.[77] Criminal and bureaucratic forces in Russia have combined to form a new and ruthless power.

Corruption undermined the rudimentary systems of financial market regulation, discouraged foreign direct investment and contributed to the currency crises that unrolled out of East Asia from late 1997. Metacorruption distorted the whole economic system, and indeed a semi-reformed economy trapped between bureaucratic regulation and the market was clearly to the advantage of those who could take advantage of rent-seeking opportunities. While the struggle against corruption could to a degree become a public project, with the mobilisation of the media and social and international organisations (for example, Transparency International) to expose wrongdoing and to act as a watchdog to deter malfeasance by public officials, metacorruption could only be combated by systematic political action. Corrupt behaviour by public officials could be countered by judicial measures, whereas metacorruption required political reform. It is this Putin declared that he would do on coming to power.

The security apparatus and politics

From the very first days of Soviet power the security apparatus played a major role in the life of the state. As we saw in Chapter 1, barely a few weeks after coming to power Lenin on 20 December 1917 established the Cheka, the forerunner of the KGB. Despite some attempts to curb its powers, the security apparatus, through several changes of name, became the bedrock of Stalin's power and the guarantor of communist rule after his death. The KGB, reorganised in the early 1950s with more limited powers, penetrated society at all levels. In the final stages of *perestroika* the KGB under Kryuchkov worked with the Party elite to save the old system, trying to discredit the Russian leadership and isolating Gorbachev behind a wall of disinformation.[78]

The Russian authorities after the *coup* were faced with the challenge of how to put down this monster.[79] The republican branches of the KGB were transferred to the new states, and on 11 October 1991 the State Council abolished the central KGB (a decision formally ratified by the Supreme Soviet on 3 December) and its functions were divided between five agencies. About half of the KGB's 490,000 employees (some 240,000) were transferred to the Border Protection Committee, which after a number of reorganisations became the independent Federal Border Service in late 1993. Russia shares borders with eighteen states, five of which are in the CIS, and has over 60,000 km of border to defend. Some 11,000 km are new boundaries, emerging as a result of the dissolution of the USSR. Lacking resources to fortify the new frontiers, which stretch 7,559 km with Kazakhstan alone and another 2,245 with Ukraine (much of it not defined, let alone demarcated), Russia tried to make the outer borders of the CIS her own borders.

In October 1991, the Central Intelligence Service assumed the KGB's spying and counter-espionage functions, becoming after the fall of the USSR the Russian Foreign Intelligence Service (SVR). The SVR took over the KGB First Directorate's enormous network of foreign agents, electronic monitoring and communications networks, Space Intelligence Centre and much more. Academician Yevgenii Primakov, its first director, stressed that the SVR would not be under political, individual or corporate control, and its sole purpose would be to protect the state.[80] Its main functions were ensuring the non-proliferation of nuclear weapons, monitoring technology vital for the country, preventing regional conflicts, fighting international crime, and checking business partners of the Russian government. Following Primakov's elevation to the foreign ministry in January 1996, his replacement, Vyacheslav Trubnikov, was a career intelligence officer with a strong record of service to the Soviet regime. The other CIS states lacked sophisticated foreign-intelligence operations and were forced to rely on the Russians. The Law on Foreign Intelligence of 8 July 1992 subordinated the SVR to the president, with oversight by parliament and the Prosecutor's Office,[81] while the new law on foreign intelligence of December 1995 unequivocally subordinated the SVR to the president while stressing the importance of human rights.

The main successor organisation, at first headed by Vadim Bakatin, was the Inter-republican Security Service (ISS), which by a presidential decree of 19 December 1991 was swallowed up by the Russian Ministry of the Interior (MVD) to form a huge security apparatus called the Ministry of Security and Internal Affairs (MBVD – *Ministerstvo bezopastnosti i vnutrenykh del*), reminiscent of Stalin's monstrous People's Commissariat of Internal Affairs (NKVD). The merger was rejected by the Supreme Soviet and reversed by the Constitutional Court on 14 January 1992, and a separate MVD re-emerged, headed by Victor Yerin, and a new Ministry of Security (MB – *Ministerstvo bezopastnosti*) was created, headed by Yeltsin's ally, Victor Barannikov. The security agencies maintain huge parallel armies separate from the official military establishment. The MVD has some 70,000 Interior Troops (VV), with about half deployed in the defence of government establishments, while the other half, the OMON, was established during *perestroika* as a professional mobile strike force. The MB assumed the KGB's internal role and often appeared to be little different from its predecessor, taking over much of its structures and personnel. The ministry had 135,000 employees, 50,000 of them employed in counter-espionage; the rest, now that its services against dissidents and democrats were no longer required, turned their attention to crime.[82] The pervasive corruption within the MVD accentuated the role of the security apparatus.[83]

As the conflict between parliament and the president intensified, the MB's position became increasingly difficult, and while the MVD's Yerin pledged his loyalty to Yeltsin, Barannikov's attempts to maintain an independent role, together with corruption charges and the inadequacies of the Border Troops under his jurisdiction in fighting on the Tajik–Afghan border, led to his dismissal in July 1993. His replacement, Nikolai Golushko, was a career KGB officer, but his failure to warn the Kremlin of the gathering insurgency by parliamentary forces led to his own dismissal after the October 1993 events. He was replaced by Sergei Stepashin and, following the unexpected success of Zhirinovskii's nationalists in the 1993 elections, the MB on 21 December 1993 was reorganised to become the Federal Counter-Intelligence Service (FSK). The decree abolishing the MB argued that it had proved impossible to reform the agency, yet Yeltsin had done little to advance the cause of liberalisation, having used the agency to secure his own power base and foiling attempts by parliament to ensure oversight over state security and intelligence bodies.[84] The president, parliament and the Prosecutor General now share responsibility for oversight of security agencies.

The security agency soon recovered its confidence and often acted in a manner reminiscent of the KGB, in particular condemning foreign organisations in Russia as front organisations for the CIA. A leaked FSK document, for example, condemned the activities of foreign academic research centres in Russia as part of the United States' attempts to undermine Russia as a great power.[85] Yeltsin stressed the FSK's role in protecting Russia's economic interests to ensure that the country did not end up 'on the sidelines of the world economy'.[86] The FSK was responsible for the covert war against Djohar Dudaev in Chechnya from the summer of 1994, and it was Stepashin who on 7 December 1994 authorised aircraft to bomb Grozny in direct contravention of a ceasefire brokered by the defence minister, Andrei Grachev. The creation of the Federal Security Service (FSB) in the heat of the Chechen war,[87] and the appointment on 24 July 1995 of the former *Kommendant* of the Kremlin, Mikhail Barsukov, to replace Stepashin as its head, signalled a new prominence for the agency. The FSB absorbed several other security agencies, with a staff of some 77,640 (both officers and civilian personnel), and, although in principle subordinated to the government and president, the body remained dangerously independent and was authorised to conduct operations both at home and abroad (by which CIS states were meant). After several changes of leadership it was this body that propelled Putin to national prominence as its head between 1998–9, when he conducted a thorough reorganisation, including widespread dismissals, of its top staff.

The FSB appeared to recreate a monstrous multi-functional agency. Former KGB personnel permeated into many aspects of Russia's post-communist affairs and the new agencies inexorably extended their influence over Russian life. The Law on Security of March 1992, for example, endowed the MVD, the customs and revenue services, and even the transport sector among others, with security functions.[88] The July 1992 Law on the Federal Organs of State Security stated explicitly that the MB was 'a body of executive power', and endowed it with broad prerogatives to combat subversive activity against Russia by foreign agencies and domestic threats to constitutional order, territorial integrity and defence capability.[89] Former KGB censors and Party officials influenced the media, quite apart from using old contacts to line their pockets. In 2001, the FSB was once again given the power to investigate anonymous denunciations by citizens, an aspect of Soviet practices that was abolished with great fanfare in 1988 (and had in any case been limited in 1968), and ninety cities were closed to foreigners and other outsiders for 'security reasons'.[90]

Following the October 1993 events, a separate Presidential Security Service (PSB) was carved out of the Main Guard Directorate (GUO) to provide a military force loyal to the president; it was headed by Yeltsin's long-time personal security guard, Alexander Korzhakov. In December 1994, PSB troops marched across Moscow to raid the offices of Vladimir Gusinskii's MOST-bank, which among other things sponsored the independent television station NTV. Korzhakov at this time sought to intervene in crucial policy areas such as arms exports and high-technology transfers, and, stepping far beyond his official duties, wrote an intemperate letter to the prime minister warning against the removal of quotas on energy exports. Korzhakov apparently encouraged military intervention in Chechnya, no doubt hoping that a short victorious war would restore his master's fortunes in the presidential elections, while failure would only serve to confirm the need for the PSB and the security services to combat terrorism in Moscow. Korzhakov's role was likened to that of Rasputin in the dying days of the Tsarist regime, and his presence cruelly exposed the factional nature of Yeltsinite politics. Fearing defeat, Korzhakov in early 1996 advocated the cancellation of the forthcoming presidential elections but was over-ruled; he was fired following Yeltsin's success in the first round of the elections in June 1996.

The multiplicity of secret services suggested the emergence of a 'security state'. One commentator notes that Russia (and the CIS) is prey to a 'self-perpetuating Chekist culture'[91] that permeates the new social, political, economic and, indeed, criminal structures. Old habits die hard and, despite constitutional guarantees to the contrary, the last years of the Yeltsin presidency were marked by a revival of an autonomous role for the security services. The former head of the government apparatus, Vladimir Kvasov, argued that all telephones and offices in the White House (now the seat of the government) were bugged, and even Sergei Filatov, at the time head of the Presidential Administration, made the astonishing admission that he too might be under surveillance.[92]

The first Chechen war provided further evidence of the consolidation of a traditional security state and revealed the awesome implications of the reconstitution of a reborn security complex. The emergence of what came to be called 'the party of war' suggested that Russian politics was becoming increasingly militarised as the executive came under the influence of a security complex beyond parliamentary control. This militant group included the head of the PSB, Korzhakov, the head of the FSK, Stepashin, and the head of the MVD, Yerin. They were joined by the militant nationalities minister, Nikolai Yegorov, who had urged a forceful resolution of the Chechnya crisis but who became one of the first political casualties of the intervention, being sacked in late January 1995. The unity of the so-called 'power ministries', however, should not be exaggerated. Inter-service rivalries were pronounced and the inadequacies of the war effort brought home to Yeltsin the limits of the security apparatus and the awesome costs in domestic popularity and international isolation that their dominance would entail.

Primakov's appointment as prime minister in September 1998 was taken as a token of 'the resurgence of the KGB in the political life of the country' and a threat to Russian democracy.[93] Primakov's summary dismissal in May 1999, however, rather weakened the argument, although the important role played by people with a security background is significant, accompanied by the rise of the Security Council (see Chapter 5). Above all, Putin's natural political base lay in the security services, having served sixteen years in the KGB and then headed the FSB. There is no doubt that Putin drew on his former colleagues to provide muscle and personnel for his policies, although it would be an exaggeration to argue that politics under his leadership was 'securitised'.

Human and civil rights

The war in Chechnya and numerous cases where the civil rights of individuals have been abused has tarnished Russian democracy. Ever since the Helsinki Final Act of 1975 introduced a new order of legitimacy for the defence of civil rights, the issue has been at the centre of Soviet and Russian politics. The values enshrined by Helsinki, and developed by successive follow-up conferences until the one that began in Vienna in 1986, provided the normative and ethical basis for *perestroika* and for post-communist democratisation. The Organisation for Security and Co-operation in Europe (OSCE) and the Council of Europe remain the major international bodies ensuring and safeguarding the pan-European human rights regime (see also Chapter 15). There is a human rights element in many of Russia's international agreements: for example, there is a conditionality clause on human rights in the Partnership and Co-operation Agreement signed with the EU.

The European Convention on Human Rights and Fundamental Freedoms (ECHR), developed by the Council of Europe, became part of Russian law on its ratification on 5 May 1998. This was a revolutionary moment as West European norms were extended to the whole continent, and intensified as part of what is called the 'fourth generation' of rights (social, regional). This new stage in normative development was *conventional* (i.e. based on international conventions) rather than narrowly constitutional. Participation in these conventions is a powerful force, it has been argued, for the 'Europeanisation' of Russia; although others argue that Russia's membership of bodies such as the Council of Europe is premature. Surprisingly, Russia (unlike the UK) has not exercised its right of derogation in time of emergency (Art. 15) over Chechnya. Russia has, however, filed its first three 'observations' to the European Court of Human Rights over Chechnya, arguing that domestic remedies still remained to be explored and that criminal prosecutions would follow. The lack of energy in prosecuting abuses in Chechnya is in part a concession to the armed forces fighting against an enemy that itself is guilty of sustained human rights abuses; but this does not absolve Russia of its commitments in this area.

A number of cases have reflected the contradictions in Russia's human rights record. Alexander Nikitin for five years faced charges of divulging state secrets in contributing to a report by the Norwegian environmental group Bellona on the environmental dangers posed by rusting nuclear submarines in the Barents Sea. Acquitted by a St Petersburg court in December 1999, his case was only finally closed in September 2000 by the refusal of the Supreme Court to reverse the acquittal. The military journalist Grigorii Pasko was subjected to an equally long drawn-out series of trials and postponements over charges, first made in 1997, that he had committed state treason by disclosing information about the environmental dangers posed by the Pacific Fleet.

Putin's assertion about the 'dictatorship of law', although phrased in a neo-Soviet manner, in practice meant the universal application of law. In his comments to a conference of chairs of regional courts on 24 January 2000, Putin gave unqualified support for the principles enshrined in the radical 1992 proposals on judicial reform, and in introducing his reform of the federal system on 17 May he insisted that the 'dictatorship of law' meant the equally strict adherence to federal legislation and observance of the rights of citizens both in Moscow and the most remote region. His repeated avowals, however, did not allay concern and among other responses a conference of 350 human rights organisations in Moscow on 20–1 January 2001 warned, in the words of the veteran human rights activist Sergei Kovalev, of a drift to totalitarianism. A Democratic Conference in Moscow in June 2001 sought to unite 'democrats' in defence of human rights, although the meeting was divided over the degree to which it should move into opposition to the Kremlin.

The Duma has a Human Rights Ombudsman who issues annual reports on the state of human and civil rights in the country. The first appointment to this post was the well-known dissident Sergei Kovalev, but his experience in the post was an unhappy one: in March 1995, the Duma dismissed him, partly because of his trenchant criticism of the Chechen war. He was replaced by Oleg Mironov, a former communist who became a vigorous advocate of human rights, issuing hard-hitting reports condemning abuses. Over half of the 25,000 (up from 7,000 in 1998) cases received by his office in 2000 concerned the criminal justice system.[94] The presidential Human Rights Commission, headed under Putin by Vladimir Kartashkin, was sometimes accused of fostering a compliant civil society rather than encouraging autonomy for civic associations. From 2001, inter-regional human rights commissions were established in each of the seven federal districts to ensure that local laws corresponded to federal law in the sphere of human rights.

Conclusion

Russia's criminal justice system only fitfully protects the civil rights of the accused, the economic rights of corporate actors or the human rights of citizens.[95] It is for this reason that legal reform remains a cardinal aspect of the democratisation of Russia. The establishment of a *Rechtsstaat* (rule by law) in itself comprises a revolution. It means judicial review of legislation and executive acts, a system of citizen's rights, structures for the pluralistic interaction of groups, and, in the post-communist context of Russia, the development of a market economy; it does not necessarily mean democracy (the rule of law). Russia has made significant strides in becoming not only a state governed by law, but also a state of law. Many problems, however, remain, with the under-funding of the judicial system accentuating its lack of independence and inability to cope with the wave of crime that hit post-communist Russia accompanied by the rise of organised crime and the 'mafiya'. The security services remained overblown, and at times exerted untoward influence on the policy process. The contradiction between legal and political thinking remains acute, as does the tension between natural law and the writ of the constitution and normative acts.

5 The executive

A constitution is the property of a nation, and not of those who exercise the government.

(Thomas Paine)[1]

The dissolution of the Communist Party and the disintegration of the USSR created a power vacuum that was filled by a hegemonic presidency. The federal presidency in Russia sat at the head of a vast bureaucracy composed of dozens of agencies and thousands of administrators, although its reach in the regions (as we shall see in Part 3) was partial. A cabinet system coexists with a presidential one, with the constitution effectively making the president head of government. This is a bifurcated executive system: on the one hand, the president and his or her apparatus working from the Kremlin; and on the other, the prime minister and the government, based primarily in the White House (formerly the Supreme Soviet building) and Old Square (previously the headquarters of the Central Committee). The centre of political gravity returned to the Kremlin, which now adopted many of the institutions and functions of the Politburo of old. The presidency had its own security service, its own Security Council, administrative apparatus and much more. At the same time, out of the rubble of the Soviet regime many traditional features re-emerged, above all in the limited scope for the government itself. The Soviet administrative class only gradually took on the features of a modern civil service. The establishment of a powerful executive overshadowed not only the legislature but also the democratic gains that it claimed to advance.

The presidency

A presidential system emerged in the last Soviet years to compensate for the decline of the Communist Party, and later the presidential option looked increasingly attractive to overcome the crisis of reform in Russia. Under Yeltsin executive authority became relatively independent from the legislature, a trend given normative form by the 1993 constitution. Many functions of the old legislature, including some of its committees and commissions, were incorporated into the presidential system, providing yet another massive impetus to the inflation of the presidential apparatus. By the same token, some of the conflicts that had formerly taken place between the two institutions were now played out within the presidential system itself. No autonomy was granted to any particular leader or to the institution that they represented. The institutional aspects of this have been dubbed the politics of 'institutional redundancy' by Huskey.[2] The Russian presidency began to take on the features of the Tsarist or Soviet systems, with weak prime ministers responsible mainly for economic affairs, a minimal separation of powers and with politics concentrated on the leader. Under Yeltsin an unwieldy concentration of power was achieved, marked by corruption, clientilism and inefficiency. One of the challenges facing Putin was to improve the efficacy of the presidential administration itself.

Presidential versus parliamentary systems

The debate over the relative merits of parliamentary and presidential systems of government is far from academic in Russia. Advocates of parliamentary government, of the sort practised in Britain or Germany, stress that it encourages democratic forms of conflict resolution; the development of lively party systems; the clear formulation of alternative policy choices; the constant scrutiny of government and public administration; flexibility in the timing of elections if the government loses its majority or the confidence of parliament; and allows mistakes to be corrected and extremes to be tempered. They level three main arguments against presidential systems: over-dependence on the personality of the leader often giving rise to unpredictability; the way that they undermine the development of party systems; and the limits placed on the formulation of clear policy choices and alternative governments.[3] Arend Lijphart stresses the exclusive nature of presidential elections, based on the principle of the 'winner-takes-all'.[4] Juan Linz stresses the problem of 'dual democratic legitimacy', with independent electoral mandates for the executive and legislative branches, creating a situation in which 'a conflict is always latent and sometimes likely to erupt dramatically'.[5]

Presidentialists counter by insisting that parliamentary rule is a luxury afforded only to stable societies. In the immature post-communist democracies the attitudes and elites from the past were too strong, the tasks too urgent, the aggregation of interests too fluid, and the social bases for party systems too amorphous to allow parliamentary government. Partisans of presidential rule stress the need for a strong executive (the 'strong hand') to overcome overt and covert resistance in the transition to new forms of political and economic life. The sheer number of parties could not compensate for their organisational weakness and lack of influence in society, and the development of parliamentarianism was hesitant and contradictory. In these circumstances only a strong presidency could provide effective leadership to drive through the necessary reforms. In Russia, as Yeltsin noted in April 1992, the very unity of the country was at stake and could best be preserved by a strong executive.[6] In his defence of presidentialism in Russia Nichols argues that '*presidentialism is more likely than other arrangements to preserve processes of democratic consolidation in societies that are characterized by a lack of social trust*' [italics in original].[7] Presidential systems, moreover, were established in all twelve CIS states; Belarus in spring 1994 was the last of the post-Soviet states to establish an executive presidency. Rudimentary party systems, faction-ridden parliaments, and grave economic and social crises appeared to justify the strengthening of executive power, whereas in the Baltic republics and Central Europe parliamentary systems were established.

distrust of political parties =>
no hope for parliamentary sys.

Presidential and parliamentary forms of rule, however, do not necessarily have to be exclusive. Earlier drafts of the Russian constitution had favoured a mixed system along the lines of the semi-presidential system in France, where the president is directly elected by the people and the prime minister has to command a parliamentary majority. The president in France is elected by popular mandate for a five-year (formerly seven-year) term and conventionally enjoys the right to formulate foreign policy and aspects of domestic policy, but the government requires a majority in parliament and thus also enjoys a popular mandate. Such a division of powers within a dual executive is one that was much debated in the final Yelstin years; advocates of constitutional amendments fought to increase the autonomy of the prime minister and the government *vis-à-vis* the president.

The emergence of presidential rule

A presidential system emerged in the last Soviet years to compensate for the decline of the CPSU and the weakness of parliament.[8] Despite the resurrection of the revolutionary slogan 'all power to the soviets', the revived legislatures failed to live up to expectations. The constitutional amendments of 1 December 1988 made the USSR Congress the highest power in the land, and following the elections of March 1989 Gorbachev was elected chair of the new body; the basis of his rule began to shift from the Party to the new legislature. On the very day that the Communist Party officially lost its monopoly on power, 14 March 1990, the powers of the Soviet presidency were strengthened. An executive presidency independent of the legislature was established, and Gorbachev was elected to this post in an uncontested ballot by the CPD on 15 March 1990. His refusal to face national elections undermined the legitimacy not only of the post but marked the point where his credibility as a democratic reformer was fatally damaged. Presidential powers were increased during the course of the year, and at the Fourth USSR CPD in December 1990 the shift to presidential power was completed by the transformation of the old Council of Ministers into a more limited 'cabinet', with the prime minister and ministers nominated by the president and accountable to him.

The powers of the prime minister remained limited and the executive powers that were more properly the prerogative of the government were devolved to the Supreme Soviet's Presidium. While the powers of the presidency were greatly increased, the powers of the Soviet legislature were not correspondingly diminished. A new type of dual power emerged that was inherently unstable but manageable as long as the chairmanship of parliament was in safe hands. The chairman of the Soviet Congress, Luk'yanov, however, betrayed Gorbachev in August 1991, and later, after much the same system was reproduced in Russia, the struggle between the presidency and parliament dominated the first phase of Russia's independent statehood (see Chapter 3). When Yeltsin became chair of the Russian Supreme Soviet in May 1990, he gained executive authority but his powers were firmly subordinated to the legislature. The strengthening of parliament, designed initially to compensate for the declining power of the CPSU, was cut short by the emergence of presidential systems rooted in the newly 'empowered' legislatures but which gradually increased their own powers at the expense of the legislatures that had given them birth.

The presidential option looked increasingly attractive to overcome the crisis of reform in Russia. At the First CPD in May–June 1990, all factions united in favour of a strong leadership, and with Yeltsin's election to chair the Supreme Soviet a significant step was taken towards the development of the presidential system in Russia. In 1990, the Russian parliament passed some 150 acts affecting virtually every aspect of Russian life. Even so, Yeltsin insisted that the crisis of executive power remained acute.[9] Yeltsin's conservative opponents began to have second thoughts over the merits of a presidential system. They were outmanœuvred, however, by the opportunity offered by Gorbachev's referendum of 17 March 1991 on the 'renewed Union'. As noted (see Chapter 1), a second question was added to the ballot in Russia on a directly elected president. Russians voted by the same margin for the Union and a directly elected president of Russia.[10]

At the Third (Emergency) Congress Yeltsin, in one of those reversals of fortune that mark his career, turned the tables on those who had sought to curb his powers and emerged with a mandate for a strengthened presidency. On the opening day, 28 March 1991, Gorbachev tried to enforce his ban on marches by introducing troops into Moscow, but popular defiance showed him where power really lay, and soon afterwards he signed the Novo-Ogarevo 'nine-plus-one' agreement with Russia and the other republics. For the Congress and Yeltsin, too, the day proved decisive. The conservative bloc 'Communists of Russia', with their allies in the 'Rossiya' faction (together comprising about half the deputies), tried to keep the question of the presidency off the agenda. The unpopularity of the Soviet government (headed by Pavlov), and the increasingly stark conflict between allegiance to the unitary CPSU and aspirations for Russian sovereignty and statehood, led to a break in communist ranks. The Afghan war veteran and noted patriot, Alexander Rutskoi, defected and formed his own 'Communists for Democracy' faction. The balance now shifted in Yeltsin's favour, and not only were the proposed constitutional changes affecting the powers of the presidency accepted and arrangements made for elections on 12 June, but the Congress on its last day, 5 April, accepted Yeltsin's surprise demand for immediate powers to issue presidential decrees within the framework of existing legislation to hasten economic and political reform in Russia.

The necessary amendments were made to the constitution at the Fourth CPD on 22 May 1991. The principle of the division of powers was ratified and executive and judicial branches of the state were to be formed. The new president, elected for no more than two consecutive five-year terms, could not be a deputy or a member of a political party. He or she would head the executive branch and would be the highest official in the land, but was obliged to report to the Congress at least once a year. The president had the right to issue binding decrees and to suspend decisions of executive bodies if they contradicted the constitution or Russian laws. Both the Supreme Soviet and the Congress, however, could revoke presidential decrees, although the actual voting procedures to do this were not specified. The Congress could impeach the president by a two-thirds vote on a report by the Constitutional Court issued at the initiative of the Congress itself, the Supreme Soviet, or one of its chambers.[11] Thus, the extensive powers of an executive presidency were enshrined in law, but so too were a number of slow-acting time bombs.

The session adopted a law on the election of the president, and after an intense two-week campaign the first direct elections for Russia's presidency were held on 12

June 1991 (see Table 1.1). Yeltsin's decisive victory, polling 57 per cent of the vote and thus winning outright in the first round,[12] endowed his presidency with a popular legitimacy that Gorbachev's had lacked and helped him withstand the August *coup*. Instead of the largely ceremonial presidency, as in Czechoslovakia and Hungary, Russia found itself with an executive presidency on the American model. Victory gave Yeltsin freedom of manœuvre in relations with parliament and allowed him to confront the CPSU. However, as with the Soviet parliament earlier, while the authority of the presidency had increased, the powers of parliament had not correspondingly diminished.

Following his inauguration on 10 July, Yeltsin issued a flurry of presidential decrees, including the reappointment of Silaev as prime minister and the appointment of a number of ministers to the Russian government, the creation of a presidential administration, and a renewed onslaught against the CPSU by banning political parties from executive bodies. Yeltsin's heroic resistance to the *coup* seemed to justify the growth of presidential power, and the hastily reconvened Supreme Soviet in August granted him emergency powers to deal with the situation. He was granted yet more powers by the reconvened Fifth CPD (28 October–2 November 1991), including the right to reorganise the government, but now attempts were made to define the legal relationship between the president and the Supreme Soviet to avoid presidential power turning into dictatorship. On 2 November 1991, the Congress gave him the power for one year to appoint ministers and pass economic decrees without reference to parliament.[13] On 6 November, Yeltsin assumed the post of prime minister, in addition to his other responsibilities, and placed himself at the head of a 'cabinet of reforms' (see below), with the RSFSR Council of Ministers now officially called the Russian government.

While defending strong executive authority, Yeltsin's entourage recognised the need for some separation of powers to avoid a return to a new form of despotism that would once again exclude Russia, as they put it, from 'civilised society'.[14] The idea of 'delegated legislation', in which a government is allowed to rule for a time through decrees with the force of law, is used by democratic states in times of emergency (see also O'Donnell's notion of delegative democracy, Chapter 19). On these occasions, however, the legislature usually establishes limits to the emergency powers, overseen by a constitutional court, and a set period that can only be renewed with the assent of parliament. In Russia no such stable system emerged; the expanding powers of the presidency were at first delegated by parliament but thereafter were converted into a self-sustaining presidential system. The appeal to the logic of the struggle against communism, already seen during the insurgency phase in the form of 'wars of the laws' and declarations of sovereignty, perpetuated the legacy of administrative arbitrariness.

When in opposition Yeltsin had assaulted the old system with a hybrid programme encompassing a populist critique of the privileges of the power elite, an appeal to social justice, economic reform, the restoration of Russian statehood, and the radicalisation of democratic change. Once in power, however, he tempered these demands; no longer the challenger but the incumbent, Yeltsin soon came to rely on the instruments of the state rather than the mass politics of the street, though on occasion he was not averse to using the crowd. Yeltsin soon freed himself from the popular movement that had brought him to power. While this meant that he

Oct 1993

remained a free agent politically, it also suggested a failure to ensure an adequate institutional framework or political constituency to support the presidency. He failed to consult Democratic Russia over the choice of Rutskoi as his running mate for the presidential elections, nor did he consult with them over the formation of his government. Yeltsin went on to build the presidency on the basis of his personal authority, to the detriment of institutions and mass political structures. As Gorbachev had discovered earlier, strengthened presidential power is no guarantee of legitimacy or effective government.

Even before the *coup*, Yeltsin had prepared a series of decrees strengthening presidential power, and these were swiftly implemented in the following months. Executive authority became more independent of the legislature, though it remained constrained by law and regulated by parliament within the framework of 'delegated legislation'. Many questions remained, however, including the limits to presidential power. Would a strong executive encourage the development of democracy in society, or would it act as a substitute for popular democratic organisation? Would not the 'strong hand' inevitably take on aspects of the Bolshevism that it sought to extirpate, and perpetuate rather than overcome traditions of authoritarianism and arbitrariness? These fears appeared to be justified by the strengthening of presidential powers following October 1993. Many functions of the old legislature, including some of its committees and commissions, were incorporated into the presidential system; and some of the conflicts between the two institutions were now played out within the presidential system itself.

The Russian presidency began to take on the features of the Tsarist or Soviet systems, with weak prime ministers, a minimal separation of powers and with politics concentrated on the person of the leader, like a monarch in a court or the Politburo and its Central Committee apparatus. Once again an unwieldy concentration of power took place, marked by corruption and inefficiency. In addition, the Yeltsin presidency became enmeshed in a variety of informal power cliques, including the so-called 'oligarchs' who benefited from the disbursement of state property at knock-down prices, a group that in part overlapped with the 'family', which included Yeltsin's daughter Tatyana Dyachenko, Sibneft Oil Company executive Roman Abramovich, arch-oligarch Boris Berezovsky, presidential chief of staff Valentin Yumashev and his successor Alexander Voloshin. In ideological terms there was little to distinguish between the groups; their struggle was largely one for state resources.

The powers of the presidency

Russia's semi-presidential system was modelled on that of France, although with some important differences. The 1993 constitution grants the presidency extensive powers in naming governments, introducing legislation and making policy. The president is the head of state and the 'guarantor' of the constitution (Art. 80), elected for a four-year term with a maximum of two terms but without an age limit (Art. 81). The president nominates the prime minister and can chair cabinet meetings, proposes to the State Duma the director of the Central Bank, nominates to the Federation Council members of the Constitutional, Supreme and Supreme Arbitration Courts, and also nominates the Procurator-General. The president is also head of the Security Council, confirms Russia's military doctrine, appoints the commander-in-chief of the armed forces, and 'exercises leadership of the foreign policy of the Russian Federation' (Art. 86). The president is granted the right to introduce a state of emergency and suspend civil freedoms until new federal laws are adopted. The president reports annually to a joint meeting of the two houses of the Federal Assembly on the government's domestic and foreign policy. The president has the right to issue binding decrees (*ukazy*), which do not have to be approved by parliament, that have the power of law; they must not, however, contradict the constitution; and they are superseded by legislative acts. The powers of the presidency, therefore, are based on a combination of appointment powers and policy prerogatives.

Impeachment is extremely difficult, requiring a ruling on a demand by a Duma commission (set up with at least 150 votes) by both the Supreme and Constitutional Courts, to be confirmed by two-thirds of both the State Duma and the Federation Council, and can be initiated only in the event of 'treason or commission of some other grave crime' (Art. 93.1). The president has the right to veto legislation of the State Duma and in extreme circumstances to dissolve it (Art. 109, and see Chapter 6); if the Duma rejects the president's nomination for the post of prime minister three times, it is deemed to have dissolved itself. Given the sad history of the vice-presidency (Yanaev and Rutskoi), it is not surprising that the December 1993 constitution abolished the post. In the event of the president's incapacity or resignation, power is transferred 'temporarily' to the prime minister and new presidential elections must be scheduled within three months (Art. 92.2). The acting president is forbidden 'to dissolve the State Duma, to schedule referendums or to submit proposals on amendments to the Russian constitution or on revising its provisions' (Art. 92.3).

The government is subordinated to the president and, formally, does not have to represent the majority party or coalition in parliament (see below). The government is appointed by the president and responsible to him or her. Like the Tsar according to the 1906 constitution, who reserved to himself responsibility for foreign policy, control of the armed forces and the executive, the 1993 constitution (Art. 80) grants the president control over four key areas: security, defence, home and foreign affairs. Russia's presidency in effect acts as a duplicate government, with the functions of ministries often shadowed by agencies under the presidency. The prime minister therefore exerts only partial control over their own ministers, and is deprived of control over the so-called 'power ministries' responsible for domestic security. The president plays an active role in the policy process, initiating and vetoing legislation. Yeltsin used his decree powers with great gusto, issuing over 1,500 policy-relevant *ukazy* during his term in office.

The 1993 constitution sought to prevent a repetition of the conflict between executive and legislative authorities that had so nearly destroyed the Russian state. A strong and largely irremovable president was to act as the focus of stability, while the government was largely removed from the control of parliament. The problem of presidential systems, however, is their rigidity; it is almost impossible to change the president in mid-term without bringing down the regime itself. Parliamentary systems, on the other hand, allow more flexibility in forming governments and in responding to popular moods. This to a degree is precisely what the advocates of presidential government tried to avoid; only a strong executive, the reformers believed, could drive through the necessary transformation of the country. The politics of reform mimicked the future-oriented politics of the old regime, although with opposite effect.

The institutions of the presidency

Yeltsin's style in managing the political system was to ensure countervailing points of authority, and for much of his period in office this principle applied equally to his own administration. The number of units never remained stable for long, accompanied by the frequent turnover of presidential aides. It was only with the sacking of his long-time head of the Presidential Security Service and confidant, Alexander Korzhakov, in June 1996 that competing centres of power appear to have been removed, but new sources of competition soon emerged. Yeltsin's younger daughter, Tatyana Dyachenko, who during the 1996 presidential campaign emerged as a powerful politician in her own right, became one of the dominant figures of the second term. The presidential system since its inception has been in a process of constant modification. Below we shall look briefly at some of its main institutions and its associated bodies.

The Administration of Affairs

This is, as it were, the Kremlin's 'housekeeping' arm, allocating offices, goods and rewards, and responsible for payment of wages and the like. With its hands on the distribution of resources, this body exercises considerable influence over officials.

The Presidential Administration

This office is the core of the presidency, consisting of about forty specialised agencies through which the vast bulk of state management is achieved. One of the main agencies is the State-Legal Directorate (GPU), formed on 12 December 1991 to prepare the decrees and draft laws of the president.[15] The functions of the latter are now shared with the Ministry of Justice. The Main Monitoring Administration (GKU) was established on 5 August 1991 to oversee regional and republican administration, later becoming the Main Territorial Administration (GTU), responsible for overseeing regional affairs. Putin headed this department in 1997 before going on to lead the FSB. There were also foreign affairs and domestic policy departments. Many of these departments duplicated the work of the government, acting in effect as a shadow administration. A common theme among the many plans for reorganisation was the idea that the government should work exclusively on economic matters, while the presidential administration would focus on political matters, a division of labour that would, it was hoped, put an end to the competition between the two branches of the executive.[16]

The presidential administration was headed at first by Yurii Petrov, formerly Communist Party chief in Sverdlovsk and a typical representative of the so-called 'Sverdlovsk mafia', made up of Yeltsin's former associates from the Sverdlovsk Party organisation, on whom Yeltsin relied in his early years in power. Petrov was replaced by Sergei Filatov, formerly Khasbulatov's deputy in parliament, who in turn gave way on 15 January 1996 to the former nationalities minister, Nikolai Yegorov. Yegorov had been the president's representative in Chechnya from November 1994 to February 1995, during the most intense stage of the fighting. The appointment of the hard-line Yegorov indicated the strengthening of Korzhakov's position, long opposed by the liberal Filatov. The emergence of a shadowy half-world focused on the presidential chief of security, Korzhakov, did much to discredit Yeltsin's presidency. After a succession of changes in Yeltsin's final years, the appointment of Alexander Voloshin finally gave stability to the administration that continued into the Putin presidency.

The Kremlin property management department

This department, one of the more notorious agencies, was established in July 1991 to oversee the vast property empire that fell into the hands of the state with the demise of the Communist Party. In November 1993, it was separated from the presidential administration and on 2 August 1995 it took on the official status of a federal executive body.[17] The department manages the properties of all branches of federal authority, including payment of salaries to parliament members and court justices. It is responsible for the upkeep of 3 million square metres of floor space in office buildings in Moscow, including the Kremlin, the government's White House, the buildings of the State Duma and the Federation Council. It services the 12,000 top Russian officials. In addition, the department owns country houses, workshops, medical establishments, motor vehicle pools, hotels, the Rossiya Air Line that carries top officials of the Russian state, and properties belonging to the Russian state in seventy-eight countries. Its assets were estimated to be valued at some $500 billion, second only to those belonging to the Gazprom monopoly.

Pavel Borodin took over as acting head on 1 April 1993 with a staff of 350, and within five years he had increased the empire ten-fold. He supervised the reconstruction of the government's White House, damaged by the fighting of October 1993, as well as the Senate building in the Moscow Kremlin, where the president's apartments are located. Borodin wielded extraordinary influence as the keeper of presidential favours, and was at the heart of Yeltsin's court. Borodin personally supervised the restoration of the Grand Kremlin Palace, including the Catherine Hall, and it was this that was to provoke his downfall. The work cost perhaps up to $400 million, and was allegedly accompanied by the use of Swiss banks to launder kickbacks in return for Kremlin reconstruction contracts. It is alleged that Yeltsin's 'family', used in both the figurative and literal sense, received funded credit cards from the Swiss company Mabatex, involved in the refurbishment of the Kremlin. It was Borodin who had provided Putin with his entry into national politics by giving him a job in the presidential administration when he found himself jobless following Sobchak's electoral defeat in St Petersburg in 1996. One of Putin's first acts as president was to move him sideways to become State Secretary of the Union of Russia and Belarus, but in an act of hubris Borodin travelled to the United States for George W. Bush's inauguration in January 2001, and was promptly arrested in line with a long-standing Swiss arrest warrant in his name.

The Presidential Council

A State Council (Gossovet), named after the highest consultative body in the Russian Empire between 1810 and 1917, was established on 19 July 1991 as a consultative body responsible to the Soviet president to examine presidential decrees, to formulate priorities for government policy and to exercise a degree of control over presidential power.[18] A similar council was established under the Russian presidency and after a number of name changes following protests from parliament, ended up in February 1993 with a lower status and less autonomy as the Presidential Council. Yeltsin's main councillor, Burbulis, headed the State Council and in the space of eighteen months changed his job title five times.[19] Burbulis had taught 'scientific communism' in Sverdlovsk[20] when Yeltsin had been *obkom* first secretary there, and together both negotiated the rough passage through the democratic insurgency to the Kremlin. Having led Yeltsin's personal campaign staff in the presidential election of June 1991, Burbulis remained one of his closest advisers, taking on also the post of first deputy prime minister in late 1991, and was often represented, justifiably, as the *éminence grise* behind the new regime. He was one of the main architects of the first stage of the democratic transformation in Russia: the CIS as we saw in Chapter 2 had been Burbulis's idea, and he was also a strong advocate of Gaidar's shock economic policies. He became the target of bitter hostility, especially from parliament, and was gradually marginalised, until dismissed from all his substantive posts on 26 November 1992.

Chaired by the president, the Presidential Council's thirty-odd membership includes an eclectic list of the great and the good but even at its height played a marginal role in policy formation. The council as a whole, for example, opposed intervention in Chechnya but was over-ruled by the Security Council. In January 1996, a number of prominent members resigned, including Gaidar, academician Sergei Alekseev, the journalist Otto Latsis and Sergei Kovalev, who at the same time resigned from his post as head of the presidential Human Rights Commission in protest against Yeltsin's use of force, the secrecy surrounding state administration, ignoring of public opinion, and personnel changes. The same charges had been made against Gorbachev earlier, and indeed the shift of the intelligentsia from Gorbachev to Yeltsin in 1990–1 had played an important part in the dissolution of the old regime, and now Yeltsin found himself equally alienated from them. The Presidential Council was convened in February 1996 (effectively for the last time) to endorse Yeltsin's candidacy for a second presidential term. Although the council did so, the endorsement only came through gritted teeth, with some members subjecting Yeltsin to virulent criticism. Yurii Karyakin, for example, listed Yeltsin's shortcomings in considerable detail, and argued that he would only vote for Yeltsin because of the absence of a credible alternative. The council was not convened again under Yeltsin's leadership, and although it still exists, with the councillors enjoying the privileges that come from membership, its fate under Putin was unclear.

The Security Council (SC)

A Russian Security Council was established soon after Yeltsin's election as president in June 1991. It was then designed mainly as a consultative body as part of the presidential apparatus and operated in parallel with the government. When he took over direct control of the cabinet in November 1991, Yeltsin dissolved various structures that shadowed the government, including the SC. The Law on Security of 5 March 1992 reconstituted the SC as a body chaired by the president, while a law of 4 April 1992 endowed the Security Council with functions that included the drafting of basic policy guidelines and determining the key issues facing the president. The struggle with parliament prompted Yeltsin to strengthen presidential structures, especially in the field of security and foreign policy. By a decree of 3 June, the SC was re-formed to draft an annual report as the basic programmatic statement for executive bodies and to draft decisions.[21] The SC's jurisdiction was significantly broadened by a presidential decree of 7 July 1992, allowing it to issue orders to heads of ministries and local governing bodies, as well as controlling the activities of organisations involved in implementing the council's decisions.

Following the October 1993 events, the SC was brought under the exclusive control of the president and its membership regularised. According to the 1993 constitution, the president 'forms and heads the Security Council' with its status to be defined by federal law (Art. 83.g). Membership is drawn from the heads of the security, law enforcement and judicial agencies, and its staff is part of the Presidential Administration. The amended Law on Security stipulated that the SC was subordinate to the president and chaired by him, and its decisions were to be issued in the form of presidential decrees and instructions. The SC had no independent political standing other than as an instrument of presidential rule. Like the Politburo of old, the SC usually took decisions not by a majority vote but by consensus, thus avoiding individual responsibility by its members.[22] The SC appeared to be the core of that long-sought-for 'strong hand', the authoritarian political structure that could manage the system in the transition to a market economy. Opponents accused the SC of replicating Communist Party structures by fusing executive and legislative power, setting the agenda and controlling information to the president.

The SC's job is to prepare presidential decisions in the sphere of security, but security soon took on a rather broad definition. During the first Chechen war, the SC emerged as an important centre of power, by this time bringing together not only the president and its secretary (Oleg Lobov), but also the prime minister (Chernomyrdin), the foreign minister (Andrei Kozyrev) and the heads of the 'power ministries'. It was the SC that on 29 November 1994 (and confirmed on 7 December) resolved to use force against Chechnya (probably at defence minister Andrei Grachev's instigation), a decision taken by voting rather than by the usual consensual procedure.[23] The appointment of Alexander Lebed, the former head of the Fourteenth Army in Moldova, as secretary of the Security Council on 18 June 1996 was part of an electoral pact but was also a way of giving him an appropriate role in the new administration. In the event Lebed remained stubbornly independent, if not a maverick, and took a very broad view of his duties. Lebed combined the Security Council post with that of national security adviser. He was instrumental in the sacking of the widely despised Grachev, and replaced him with his ally Igor Rodionov. The scope of the Security Council's work was broadened by a presidential decree of 10 July, charging the council with defending Russia's vital interests in the social, economic, defence, environmental and informational spheres.[24] The Security Council's functions, however, were limited by the establishment on 25 July of a new body, the Defence Council, with a similar membership. The creation of the Defence Council was a classic piece of Yeltsin balancing, designed to counter the growth in the Security Council's status. Lebed sought to transform the Security Council from an advisory into a working body with real power. In his brief tenure Lebed was able to bring the first Chechen war to an end (the Khasavyurt agreement of 31 August 1996), but Lebed's confrontational style within two months led to his own dismissal on 17 October 1996, following which the Security Council went into decline. Putin briefly headed both the FSB and the SC, and on his elevation to the premiership he appointed his long-time associate Sergei Ivanov to take over. Under Putin the SC once again came into its own, becoming one of his main institutional supports and responsible for an ever wider range of tasks. The periodic rise and fall in the fortunes of the Security Council can be taken as indicative of the hesitant institutionalisation that has taken place in Russia. The council was intended as an instrument for implementing executive policy and to co-ordinate the work of other security agencies, but its political role reflected the character and status of its successive directors.

The government

Cabinet government is much more difficult to achieve in a presidential than in a parliamentary system. In the United States the post of prime minister is dispensed with altogether and the president chairs cabinet meetings. In France the president has the prerogative to appoint or dismiss the prime minister as long as the latter has the support of parliament, and it was a rudimentary version of this system that emerged in Russia. The prime minister is nominated by the president and then approved or rejected by the Duma, and is consulted in the appointment of ministers, who are responsible both to the president and parliament. Unlike in France, however, the Russian prime minister has no independent power base in parliament and thus 'cohabitation' (where the president and prime minister are of different political persuasions) cannot formally exist, although during Primakov's tenure (see below) a weak form of cohabitation did emerge.

Government, Duma and president

The Russian government is a direct descendent of the RSFSR Council of Ministers, but has greatly expanded in size and functions. The prime ministerial apparatus is another of those bureaucratic agencies that has swelled in the post-Soviet years, consisting now of some two dozen departments and over 1,000 full-time officials. The government is responsible both to parliament and to the president, but the precise balance of accountability remains unclear. Government in Russia consists of the chair of the government (the prime minister), a variable number of deputy prime ministers, usually responsible for a bloc of ministers, and federal ministries, generally with portfolios. Bodies like the presidential administration and the Security Council, as we suggested above, appear at times to usurp the role of the government. The government's lineage from the past is most visible in the institution of vice-premiers, who simulate the role of the old CPSU Central

Committee secretaries, although the presidential administration can also be seen to be the heir of the oversight functions once fulfilled by the Party apparatus.

Unlike conventional practice in the West, the ministries themselves are unable to make national decisions but have to prepare the appropriate documentation, which is then adopted as an act of the government as whole. In late 1992, two types of governmental bodies were established: ministries headed by members of the government who resign together with the prime minister; and departments headed by professional bureaucrats who are not members of the government and reporting directly to vice-premiers. A presidential decree of 14 August 1996 defined a ministry as a federal executive agency that enforces government policies and manages all activities in its defined sphere of influence, as well as co-ordinating the activities of other federal institutions in this sphere. At the sub-ministerial level there are a variety of special bodies, known as state committees, federal services or agencies, whose brief is usually technical and who lack direct access to the government but report through vice-premiers. These include professional bodies like the Patents Agency. Like most other post-Soviet institutions, the government has been subject to endless reorganisation.

Russia is not a parliamentary republic but neither is it fully a presidential one in the classical sense. The constitution states that the prime minister is appointed by the president with the consent of the State Duma. The premier forms his or her cabinet, which is then approved by the president, and the two share executive authority. In the United States the president is head of the executive, whereas according to Art. 110.1 executive power in Russia belongs to the government, but the head of the government works within the framework of presidential power. A hybrid 'tripartite' system emerged in which the government acts as a relatively autonomous centre of political authority in its own sphere, the president sets the overall direction of policy, while the Duma acts in a supervisory capacity and the ultimate source of public accountability by 'keeping the trust of the government', passing votes of no-confidence and confidence.

The office of prime minister, although overshadowed by the presidency in normal times, carries enormous advantages of incumbency, advantages that are greatly enhanced in the event of pre-term elections. According to the constitution, in the event of the demise or retirement of the incumbent president, the prime minister takes over and new elections are held within three months. Overshadowed by the succession, the campaign for the parliamentary elections of December 1999 began long in advance as potential presidential contenders sought to use them as primaries for the presidential elections that were initially due to have been held on 4 June 2000 but, following Yeltsin's resignation, were brought forward to 26 March 2000.

Executive power in Russia is thus exercised by the president and the government, a dual executive system with an unclear relationship between the two. The French constitutional axiom that 'The president presides and the government governs' does not translate easily into Russian practice, since the president does far more than 'preside'. Like its Soviet and Tsarist predecessors, the government is largely restricted to managing the economy and the social sphere, while the president is responsible for foreign, security and administrative issues. The constitution, as we have seen, endows the president with control over foreign and security policy as well as the main direction of domestic policy, and it is this article that provides the juridical basis for presidential rule. While Yeltsin's was an activist presidency, his poor health towards the end opened up the possibility of a new balance of power between the two wings of the executive, a development that Primakov tried to exploit. However, the young and vigorous Putin administration once again seized the initiative and reasserted the prerogatives of the presidency.

The prime minister is appointed by the president and endorsed by the State Duma and is in principle accountable to both – in principle because parliament's checking power is rather limited. If the president's nomination is three times refused by the Duma it is automatically dissolved and the president's choice is confirmed (Art. 111). The Duma's right to veto a nomination has been removed; but it can be assumed that in most circumstances a president would change the candidate after the previous candidate was rejected twice. A prime minister's resignation is tendered to the president rather than to the Duma. It is incumbent upon the prime minister to tender his or her resignation following presidential elections, but is not obliged to do so after parliamentary elections.

Soviet law since 1988 had stipulated that those who took up government posts were to resign their parliamentary seats, a principle reaffirmed by the 1993 constitution. Deputies cannot simultaneously be employed in the government or hold paid jobs in any field except teaching, scientific research and culture in general. Once the two-year transitional period ended, the principle was rigorously applied and nineteen deputies elected from the party-lists in 1995 resigned their seats. Kozyrev, elected to parliament from a single-member constituency in Murmansk, was forced to choose between resigning from the cabinet or giving up his legislative seat. The idea that ministers cannot simultaneously be MPs was designed to maintain the separation of powers, but this mechanical application of the rule (applied also in France) undermines the ability of parties to form a government, weakens the solidarity that binds together the governing party in countries like Britain and Germany, inhibits the Duma's ability to question ministers on a daily basis, and weakens the government's capacity to explain its policies in parliament.

A no-confidence vote in the government can be initiated by a Duma deputy at any time, but the signatures of one-fifth of all Duma members are required for a motion to be placed on the agenda. A no-confidence motion is adopted by a simple majority of total Duma membership (Art. 117.3), which then sets in train a complex process of confrontation. The president has two choices: either accept the motion, dismiss the government and nominate a new prime minister for the Duma's approval; or disagree with the Duma. If within three months the Duma once again expresses its lack of confidence in the government, then the head of state can either sack the government or dissolve the Duma by ordering new elections. The threat of dissolution is at the centre of presidential power, protecting the government and restraining the Duma out of fear of provoking pre-term elections. Article 109, however, modifies the dissolution option by stating that Article 117 cannot be activated to dissolve the Duma in the year following its election or in the six months before a presidential election. This would imply that in its first year or before a presidential election the Duma could dismiss one government after another with impunity, only having twice to vote a motion of no-confidence and not even having to wait three months between the two votes. The dissolution option can be activated in a second manner, this time on the initiative of the government itself. The prime minister can ask the Duma for a vote of confidence; if the Duma fails to vote in support of the government, the president must either dissolve the Duma or dismiss the government, a decision that must be taken within seven days of the vote.

Despite its reduced powers under the constitution, the Duma has proved able to define its own agenda. Governments in a rudimentary way have tended to reflect some of the main concerns of the Duma. In particular, strategic allies have been sought amongst the parties in the Duma that would make governance possible, especially by offering ministerial portfolios to parties that were apparently in opposition to the government itself (e.g. the CPRF). This did not prevent the Duma holding a vote of no-confidence in the government following 'black Tuesday' (a sudden fall in the value of the rouble on 11 October 1994), and again on 21 June 1995 in protest against the Budennovsk crisis (when hostages were seized by Chechen guerrillas). Chernomyrdin countered by tabling a confidence motion, which if not passed would have led to either the Duma or the government falling within a week. Threatened by imminent dissolution, a second vote of no-confidence on 1 July failed (just) to pass, and thereupon Chernomyrdin withdrew his confidence motion. Increasingly exasperated by Putin's neo-liberal economic policies, the communists tabled a no-confidence motion on 17 March 2001, provoking threats of an early dissolution and pre-term elections.

The unclear relationship between the political complexion of the Duma and the composition of the government is probably not sustainable in the long term, and the most logical resolution of the problem is for the government to be based on a parliamentary majority. Of course, given a fragmented and divided Duma with no stable majority, this would be problematical; the architects of the 1993 constitution took precisely this problem into account in drafting the articles on the relationship between government and parliament. If the government, moreover, became an independent political institution, relations with the president would become even more complicated. In the United States the problem is resolved by abolishing the institution of the prime minister entirely, and subordinating ministers directly to the president, who chairs cabinet meetings. The present Russian system is unsatisfactory from many perspectives, hence the plans for constitutional reform that focus precisely on this issue, but there remains the danger that some of the solutions may well exacerbate the problem of accountability and coherence.

Prime ministers and their policies

In the nine years of Yeltsin's presidency Russia had six prime ministers and eight governments, three of which were under Viktor Chernomyrdin (see Table 5.1). His predecessor, Yegor Gaidar, had never been confirmed by parliament and had thus remained an 'acting' PM. The rapid turnover of prime ministers in 1998–9 reflected the depth of the financial crisis that engulfed the country at this time and the search for a suitable successor. Yeltsin feared the emergence of a powerful and independent premier and ensured their subordination to his will. We will briefly characterise the personalities and policies of the prime ministers.

Table 5.1 Russia's prime ministers

Name	Period in office	Comments
Ivan Silaev	June 1990–26 September 1991	The office of premier remained largely 'Soviet' with few powers
Boris Yeltsin	November 1991–June 1992	Combined the premiership with the presidency
Yegor Gaidar	15 June–14 December 1992	'Acting' PM only since never confirmed by parliament
Victor Chernomyrdin	14 December 1992–23 March 1998	Russia's longest-serving PM, presided over two major changes of government (August 1996, March 1997)
Sergei Kirienko	24 April–23 August 1998	Only confirmed by the Duma in late April, and thereafter overwhelmed by the financial crisis
Yevgenii Primakov	9 September 1998–12 May 1999	Made an uncomfortable partner to Yeltsin, was dismissed at the first opportunity
Sergei Stepashin	19 May–9 August 1999	Very much an interim figure
Vladimir Putin	9 August–31 December 1999; acting president and PM January–May 2000	Exercised authority far beyond that typically allowed a PM by Yeltsin
Mikhail Kasyanov	May 2000–	Considered at first a holdover from the Yeltsin period but in the event survived far longer than anticipated

Russia's first 'prime ministers': Silaev and Yeltsin

Ivan Silaev had been appointed Russian prime minister in June 1990, but on 26 September 1991 resigned to head the new Inter-Republican Economic Commission, in effect becoming prime minister of the USSR. This was obviously an unsatisfactory situation, with unclear leadership in both the USSR and Russia. The Russian premiership was left vacant until on 6 November 1991 Yeltsin himself assumed the post, declaring that he would take responsibility for the implementation of reforms while allowing him full scope to use presidential decrees to drive forward the economic transformation. The constitutional status of the Russian government, however, remained ambivalent. As long as Yeltsin had been chairman of the Supreme Soviet there appeared to be no problem with the government's subordination to the Russian parliament. Once a strong presidency had emerged, however, and in the absence of a new constitution, conflict was bound to arise as Yeltsin sought to remove the government from legislative control.

In November 1991, the Fifth CPD allowed the president to form a government with only minimal legislative accountability. Yeltsin won the right to appoint his own cabinet, and ministers did not have to gain parliamentary approval.[25] Yeltsin appointed a team of radicals to create a 'government of reforms' whose core was drawn from a group of academics close to Burbulis. Chief among them was Gaidar, thirty-five, the minister for finance and economics who had worked with Yavlinskii and Shatalin, authors of doomed economic reform plans in the Gorbachev era, but who took a more marked neo-liberal free-market line. Gaidar had been a Senior Research Fellow at the Institute of Economics, from whence he brought several colleagues into the government, including Alexander Shokhin; a group accused by their opponents of being theoreticians who did not understand how society actually worked. Soon afterwards, Russia took over all the USSR ministries and enterprises on its territory, and the scene was set for a radical attempt at social transformation.

Gaidar now launched a radical economic reform programme, promulgated largely by presidential decrees rather than legislative acts. Yeltsin's strategy from late 1991 was directed towards 'a policy of breakthrough', shock therapy in the economy and marginalisation of conservative forces in parliament.[26] The 'government of reforms' launched a wave of decrees that began to break down the old economic administrative-command system and to build up the new. Above all, from 2 January 1992 the long-awaited liberalisation of prices at last began, accompanied by enormous prise rises, inflation and falling living standards (see Chapter 12). The reforms were bitterly criticised by the majority in parliament, Khasbulatov personally, and vice-president Rutskoi. At the same time, the constitutional situation remained unclear, and it was Khasbulatov's attempts to move the pendulum back in the direction of parliamentary oversight over the government that provoked confrontation and conflict (see Chapter 3).

Yegor Gaidar: 'acting' prime minister

Fearing that popular acceptance of the reforms was reaching breaking point, Yeltsin adjusted the tiller in May–June 1992 when pressure from the conservatives and the industrial lobby forced him to undertake a government reshuffle. Industrialists had criticised Gaidar's government for failing to extend government credits to failing enterprises or to soften the social impact of reform.[27] Yeltsin appointed three former state directors to key ministries, including Chernomyrdin, who became a deputy prime minister and took over responsibility for the energy sector. Chernomyrdin had been appointed minister of the Soviet gas industry in 1985, and in 1989 he became chairman of the new state company, Gazprom. As so often with Yeltsin, a compromise in one direction was balanced by a move in the other, in this case Gaidar's appointment as acting prime minister (pending confirmation by parliament) on 15 June 1992, signalling his determination to continue on the path of radical economic reform. The radical reformer Anatolii Chubais, the head of the State Property Committee (GKI) responsible for privatisation, was promoted to become a deputy prime minister, thus strengthening Gaidar's hand in the cabinet. A 'government of deputy prime ministers' emerged as Yeltsin sought to broaden the social and political support for reform policies.

Khasbulatov continued to insist that 'the development of parliamentarianism is the path to democracy'.[28] On 13 November 1992, parliament adopted a modified version of the law giving Congress control over ministerial appointments, granting parliament the sole right to nominate ministers, and subordinating key ministers (like that of foreign affairs) to parliament. This indeed was the basis for a parliamentary republic. The struggle to control the government came to a head at the Seventh Congress in December 1992. Gaidar's uncompromising stance and the failure of Yeltsin's desperate attempt to take the confrontation between executive and legislative to the country led to Gaidar's fall on 14 December 1992.

The Chernomyrdin era

The new premier, Chernomyrdin, although committed to more state intervention in the economy, retained the majority of the liberal advocates of 'shock therapy'. Boris Fedorov at this time was given overall responsibility for financial policy, and Chernomyrdin soon retreated from attempts to regulate prices and to save industry by pouring in money, only stimulating inflation. Talk of 'an invisible *coup*' proved exaggerated.[29] Following the elections of December 1993, Chernomyrdin placed his stamp on the government. Gaidar, Fedorov and some other reformers resigned, and Agrarians and others joined, yet the government retained a broadly reformist course. In effect, a 'coalition' government was formed, but a distinctively Russian type of coalition where posts were divided not through discussions between parties but between specific individuals. The constitution does not oblige the president to appoint the prime minister from the largest party able to gain a majority in parliament; nevertheless, the president had to be sensitive to the balance of forces in the Duma to avoid his government suffering legislative defeats or votes of no-confidence. Two ministers were from the Agrarian Party, and there were even overtures towards the CPRF to contribute ministers.

The political evolution of Russian government was in full swing even before the Chechen crisis, taking on more of a conservative and nationalist colouring. The democratic internationalism that had been such a marked feature of policy since Gorbachev's time now gave way to a more assertive Russian state nationalism. This tendency was further strengthened following the strong communist showing in the December 1995 elections. Chernomyrdin remained prime minister even though his 'Russia Our Home' (NDR) party gained only 10 per cent of the vote, but the government further changed its complexion. Kozyrev resigned as foreign minister on 5 January, as did Shakhrai as a deputy prime minister, both preferring to keep their Duma seats. Chubais, the last member of the 'government of reforms' (responsible for the economy) resigned on 16 January 1996. As for the extension of coalition government, Chernomyrdin argued that 'I am in favour of a government that consists of professionals because a government is not a political body.'[30]

In August 1996, Chernomyrdin was appointed for a second term, and immediately was forced to repay in political currency the financial support that the oligarchs had given Yeltsin in his re-election campaign. The appointment of 35-year-old Vladimir Potanin as first deputy prime minister in charge of economic affairs signalled the regime's close links with the emerging banking sector. In 1993, he had become chairman of Oneksimbank, one of Russia's five largest banks, and helped create the consortium that organised controversial shares-for-loans auctions with the government. His bank took advantage of these auctions to acquire a 38 per cent stake in the world's largest nickel producer, Norilsk Nickel, and then in July 1997 was able to take control of the huge telecommunications company, Svyazinvest, in an auction that was widely considered to have been rigged. Potanin's appointment marked recognition of the role that he and other financiers, like Vladimir Gusinskii at the head of the Most Group, had played in bankrolling

Yeltsin's re-election. The political economy at the basis of regime politics in post-communist Russia represented a conflation of political and economic resources. For the new elites, the semi-marketised and heavily bureaucratised economy proved rich feeding grounds for rent-seeking behaviour. The Russian economy found itself stuck half-way between the plan and the market.

The presidential regime vested supreme power in the president, but during the Chernomyrdin years Yeltsin tended not to interfere in daily politics and thus escaped responsibility for the actions of the government while remaining the supreme political arbiter. This allowed policy drift and, indeed, elements of the old Brezhevite 'stagnation' became apparent. In response to this in March 1997 Yeltsin engineered a major government reshuffle, promoting reformers like Boris Nemtsov (brought in from the governorship of Nizhnii Novgorod) and Chubais in an attempt to kick-start the reforms. A continued sense of inertia provoked Chernomyrdin's dismissal in March 1998.

With Yeltsin's physical decline, the regime began to think of the succession. Between March 1998 and December 1999, Russia had five prime ministers. This reflected a structural weakness in the Russian political system, above all in the balance of power between the executive and legislative branches. We can now see that the parade of prime ministers reflected not simply Yeltsin's whimsy but the search for a way for the regime to perpetuate itself. In other words, the search was on for the successor. The idea of a 'succession', of course, is a term more appropriate for a monarchy than a democratic republic, and reflects the pre-eminent role of the presidency. Klyamkin and Shevtsova describe the Russian political system as an 'electoral monarchy'.[31] Yeltsin's second term can be considered as devoted mainly to ensuring a succession that would not challenge the system that he had built or threaten the personal security of himself, his family and closest associates. It is this factor that helps explain the rapid turnover of prime ministers following Chernomyrdin's dismissal at a time when he looked the prime candidate for the presidency. Chernomyrdin's increasing self-confidence and view of himself as Yeltsin's successor threatened Yeltsin's ability to control the succession process. Chernomyrdin had become a powerful politician in his own right, building alliances with the communist leadership in the Duma and corporate interests in society; he had not, however, been able to lift the economy out of its prolonged stagnation. His own convoluted words serve as the best epitaph on his period in office: 'We wanted to do things for the best, but it all turned out as usual.'

Sergei Kirienko: from technocracy to politics

Yeltsin's nomination of the 35-year old unknown, Sergei Kirienko, was equally unexpected. Kirienko had served briefly in the Chernomyrdin government as minister of fuel and energy as Nemtsov's protégé. In their shared home town, Nizhnii Novgorod, Kirienko had directed one of the most successful of the local banks. Kirienko was only accepted by the Duma at the third attempt on 24 April and only after enormous exertions by Yeltsin behind the scenes, together with open attempts to bribe deputies. The appointment of a government of technocrats headed by Kirienko appeared to signal a new resolve to find long-term economic solutions to fiscal problems. The government made the new state treasury system work more effectively, with some 75,000 budgetary organisations now funded through regular procedures rather than the old *ad hoc* system. It appeared for the first time in some four years that a government had emerged that was serious about structural economic reform focusing, above all on trying to raise federal government revenues by means other than the excessively high-interest rate-bearing treasury bonds (GKOs). Moves were taken towards shifting the tax system away from the corporate sector towards individuals and the service sector. However, within weeks of his appointment, on 27 May Kirienko was forced to triple interest rates – to 150 per cent – to defend the rouble. At that time total Russian national debt was 44 per cent of GDP, and government bonds comprised 34 per cent of national expenditure.

With its back to the wall, the government succeeded in getting the Duma to adopt an anti-crisis programme in July whose measures included changing the structure of VAT and personal income tax, and introducing a new sales tax of 5 per cent. Kirienko sought to broaden his base of support by inviting the former head of Gosplan, Yurii Maslyukov, to join the government with broad responsibilities for trade and industry. Elected a communist deputy in December 1995, the leadership of the CPRF denounced his membership of the government and moved to expel him from the party. The Kirienko government was now becoming dominated by the struggle for autonomy: of politics from economics, and of politicians from the dominance of economic oligarchs. By the end of its term in office it became clear that the office of prime minister in Russia was capable of genuine policy initiative. However, lacking a firm parliamentary base, it remained vulnerable to presidential interference.

By August 1998, the Kirienko government began to transform itself from a 'government of professionals' into a more openly political government, in the sense that it began to argue that the solution of some of the country's economic problems lay in politics. Kirienko's brief premiership became dominated by attempts to deal with the financial crisis, above all fears that the government would no longer be able to service its debts. Kirienko struggled to transform oligarchical capitalism into a more open version. His failure to deal with the legacy of nearly a decade of mismanagement led to the partial default of 17 August 1998, and his own dismissal six days later. It was at this time that Nemtsov resigned, leaving the government devoid of liberals.

The recalled Duma met on 21 August, and while sceptical of the government's actions reserved their anger for Yeltsin himself, adopting a vote of censure against him that was adopted by 248 votes to thirty-two. The economic crisis was now extreme, and it was at this time that Yeltsin transformed it into a full-scale political one by dismissing Kirienko and his government on 23 August, and nominating Chernomyrdin to return to his old post. Despite Chernomyrdin's attempts to ingratiate himself with the communist opposition, his nomination was rejected by the Duma. After being twice rejected, Chernomyrdin's candidature was withdrawn and Yevgenii Primakov, who had served as foreign minister since January 1996, was confirmed as prime minister on 11 September by a vote of 317 to sixty-three. Chernomyrdin was too closely associated with the policies of 1992–8 to win support, and he was the man held responsible for many of Russia's woes. His earlier dismissal no longer made political sense if Yeltsin was willing to reappoint him prime minister in August. Not only Chernomyrdin's prestige suffered, but what remained of Yeltsin's authority was further dissipated in this futile attempt to turn back the clock.

Yevgenii Primakov: the struggle for consensus

While Yeltsin's regime suffered a severe blow in August 1998, the political system in Russia did not collapse; the political and economic crisis did not become a constitutional one. The appointment of the ex-head of the Foreign Intelligence Service (SVR, 1991–6) Primakov as prime minister revealed, however, just how far the liberal trend had ebbed. Economic stringency under his leadership remained, although it was now more a matter of necessity than conviction in the virtues of neo-liberal economic theory, given Russia's indebtedness and inability to collect taxes. In the political field the achievements of earlier years in the spheres of press freedom, human rights and basic liberties were eroded – although not repudiated. The key point, though, was that a new type of coalition politics looked set to emerge, one where government was conducted on the basis of agreement with the majority in parliament. Although the Kirienko government had begun to curb the excesses of the oligarchs, it was only under Primakov that their privileges were openly challenged, especially since their financial resources had been drained by the financial crisis.

In his early appointments Primakov sought to please the Duma majority. Elements of a genuine coalition government emerged. Maslyukov was appointed first deputy prime minister with overall responsibility for the economy. Victor Gerashchenko, whom Jeffrey Sachs had earlier dubbed 'the world's worst central banker', was reappointed head of the Central Bank. His government, however, was not a formal coalition in the Western sense, and neither was it a party government made up of the group able to command a majority in the Duma. As so often during the Yeltsin era, Primakov claimed to represent a government composed of pragmatic professionals whose party allegiance weighed less than their expertise. Nevertheless, the government did mark a departure from the previous pattern. It was a coalition to the extent that it sought to reflect the distribution of political support in the Duma. His government included members of the CPRF and Vladimir Zhirinovskii's Liberal Democratic Party of Russia (LDPR). The finance minister, Mikhail Zadornov, was a former member of the Yabloko faction. The only group now missing was Russia Our Home (NDR), formerly the party of power; Alexander Shokhin resigned as deputy prime minister ten days after accepting the post. As for regional leaders, only Leningrad *oblast* governor Vadim Gustov was willing to give up his elected post to serve as first deputy prime minister responsible for regional affairs and the CIS.

Many of the country's most prominent politicians refused to have anything to do with Primakov's government, fearing that its failure would blight their electoral prospects. The tone of the government appeared to be retrospective rather than progressive. With Gerashchenko back at the helm of the Central Bank, it appeared that the confusions and hesitancies of the Gorbachev years had returned. Primakov himself had close historical links with the security apparatus and the power ministries (defence, interior as well as foreign affairs), and thus his focus naturally moved away from economic issues towards foreign and internal political affairs. In the event, it appeared that the best economic policy in Russia was not to have one, and the economy in 1999 staged a modest recovery based on import substitution. The four-fold devaluation of the rouble made imports prohibitively expensive, and encouraged domestic manufacturers and producers to take up the slack.

What the government lost in coherence in becoming so broadly based it did not gain in support. Even the parties represented in it, like the communists, sought to place a healthy distance between themselves and the government. Yavlinskii condemned the cabinet for not being a team of like-minded specialists but representatives of various lobbying interests, and for good measure condemned it for corruption. As for the policies pursued by the Primakov administration, he insisted that his government would not reverse the results of privatisation. Thus, the property settlement of the Yeltsin years would not be undone. The slogan of the Primakov government, like his period in office as foreign minister, was pragmatism.

Deep structural and institutional changes could only be implemented if the government could win credibility, and for that it needed a long-term developmental strategy. The depth of the immediate crisis, however, precluded this. Above all, the political and ideological basis to Primakov's government was unstable. He tried to pursue a right-wing policy with a left-wing orientation. The bankruptcy of his policy of 'pragmatism' was seen in the area that was peculiarly his own, foreign policy. The beginning of Nato's bombing campaign in Yugoslavia over Kosovo on 24 March 1999, which lasted seventy-eight days, provoked a rupture in Russia's relations with the West. By the end of his period in office, Primakov had managed to isolate Russia in a manner reminiscent of the USSR on the eve of Gorbachev's accession to power in March 1985. The country found itself surrounded by sullen neighbours and few real allies, despite much talk of a 'strategic partnership' between Russia, China and India.

The unstable basis to the Primakov government led many to suggest that it would be of short duration. Primakov's government was largely imposed on an unwilling president by an assertive Duma. Yeltsin disliked the popularity and independent power of Primakov, and hence sought to replace him with a more loyal and dependent person at the first opportunity. By early 1999, Yeltsin was openly snubbing his own prime minister, and on 12 May 1999 Primakov was dismissed. More surprisingly, the response of parliament was remarkably muted, not wanting to provoke early parliamentary elections. Months of preparation for Yeltsin's impeachment collapsed at the first vote.

Sergei Stepashin: the interim prime minister

Primakov's dismissal reflected an inexorable political logic. He had been forced on Yeltsin by a recalcitrant Duma in September 1999, and Yeltsin never made a secret of his personal distaste for the man. In his place on 19 May 1999 he nominated Sergei Stepashin, the former head of the Federal Counter-Intelligence Service (FSK) in 1994 and one of the hawks in the first Chechen war. He was dismissed from this position in June 1995 as part of the price for his failure to avert the Budennovsk hostage crisis. Stepashin later was one of the few members of the so-called 'party of war', those who had so cavalierly launched the first Chechen war in 1994, to have admitted that it had been a mistake both in conception and implementation. He was returned to office in July 1997 as justice minister, and then as minister of internal affairs (MVD) on 24 April 1998.

Stepashin turned out to be a conscientious prime minister, unwilling to subordinate the government to Yeltsin's electoral campaigning. On his nomination to the post of prime minister Stepashin hastened to both the Duma and Federation Council to outline his plans and policies. Like Primakov, it was clear that he intended to work with parliament, indicating attempts to institutionalise Russian political life and to move away from the court politics that were so typical of Yeltsin's rule. However, Stepashin's cabinet was fatally divided and was riven by the battles between the various clans surrounding the president. Roman Abramovich, one of the favoured oligarchs of the time who had gained control of Sibneft through a number of underhand deals, threw his weight behind Nikolai Aksenenko, who was made deputy prime minister despite Stepashin's resistance. Stepashin proved unwilling to find an excuse to ban the Communist Party, and thus eliminate one of the main contenders in the forthcoming Duma elections. His unsatisfactoriness from the point of view of the Kremlin was compounded by his failure to prevent the alliance between the Fatherland (*Otechestvo*) group of Yurii Luzhkov (mayor of Moscow) and the All Russia (*Vsya Rossiya*) alliance of governors to create the Fatherland All Russia (OVR) bloc, especially when the new OVR alliance succeeded in making Primakov their figurehead on 17 August. More importantly, the Stepashin government was an unstable coalescence of two groups: the financial oligarchs led by Boris Berezovskii, and the raw materials and energy lobby represented by Chubais (now head of the giant electricity monopoly United Energy Systems, UES). These groups struggled to control the country's financial and material resources, which in Russian terms meant striving for exclusive access to the political regime. Stepashin did not last long, and a more loyal and unscrupulous man was sought. On 9 August 1999, Stepashin was dismissed.

Vladimir Putin: the struggle to save Yeltsin

The fifth premier in two years, Vladimir Putin was soon transformed from a reticent official (he had worked sixteen years in the security apparatus) into a relatively independent political figure. On appointing him Yeltsin had announced Putin as his successor, but experience suggested that this was a precarious position. Putin was appointed as a Yeltsin loyalist, and it appeared at first that he would enjoy little more autonomy than his predecessors. Like all of Yeltsin's prime ministers, Putin was not given independence to form his own cabinet and instead had ministers foisted on him by the presidential adminstration. Above all, Aksenenko, as first deputy prime minister, openly pursued his own interests and those of the presidential 'family', and on several occasions (as in the displacement of the head of Transneft), ignored Putin entirely. The influence of Berezovskii and his ally Abramovich, known as the treasurer to Yeltsin's family, remained strong. The energy minister Viktor Kalyuzhnii and the interior minister Vladimir Rushailo were part of this group. Putin, however, soon transcended the limitations of his post. On any scale, Putin's metamorphosis was remarkable, and he soon emerged as the leading candidate in the presidential election. The success of his bloc, Unity, in the December 1999 parliamentary elections opened the way for the unexpected *dénouement* of the succession operation.

At least four factors help explain Putin's remarkable rise. The first is that the Kremlin put its entire weight behind him, attacking his rivals, and providing him with all sorts of open and behind the scenes support. Second, the renewed war in Chechnya turned out to be a genuinely popular war, unlike the first from 1994–6. Putin's image as an 'iron chancellor' was created and sustained by his uncompromising approach to the Chechen problem, with the second war provoked in September 1999 by four bombings of apartment blocks (Buinaksk, two in Moscow, and Volgodonsk) with the loss of over 300 lives, and the two invasions of Dagestan in August and September by Shamil Basaev. The third factor is that, unlike his predecessors, Putin soon enjoyed unprecedented powers for policy initiation. Although formally he could be sacked by Yeltsin, Putin in the last months of 1999 acted with remarkable confidence and independence. Putin was able to transform the prime ministerial office into a quasi-presidential post, eclipsing Yeltsin personally. Although the Kremlin may have acquiesced in this, the trend with the last few prime ministers had been in this direction anyway. All had seen their popularity ratings soar on appointment to the office. Fourth, Putin appeared able to restore Russia's national dignity, adopting neither an obsequiously subservient nor an impotently assertive attitude towards the West but one based on a measured understanding of Russia's real needs and capacity. In short, Putin's rise was based on a mixture of systemic and personal factors.

Mikhail Kasyanov: loyalty on the brink

As finance minister in earlier governments, Kasyanov had negotiated the restructuring of the London Club (commercial) debt twice in three years in the late 1990s. Kasyanov was formally appointed premier by Putin in May 2000, but his tenure was accompanied by endless rumours of his imminent dismissal. To be prime minister in Russia's dual executive system is one of the most uncomfortable jobs imaginable, especially when the president is a young and energetic man with ideas of his own and with an eye out for future re-election. In the Soviet era prime ministers had been merely administrative officials, whereas under Yeltsin they had become politicised. Under Putin's activist presidency, the prime minister's office returned to the Soviet pattern. The Yeltsin system continued, however, to the extent that the ministries under Kasyanov remained virtually autonomous baronies, staffed by a vast, formless and poorly trained army of bureaucrats hardly deserving the title of civil servants. The fusion of commercial and political interests reached to the very top of many ministries, with a government appointment seen as a route to personal enrichment. Kasyanov's earlier friendship with the most ruthless of the tycoons, Berezovskii, did not augur well, and he had been known as 'Mr Two Per Cent', allegedly representing his cut of various deals. Unlike Yeltsin, who sacked his prime ministers if they were becoming too popular, Putin found it hard to dismiss officials, and in personnel terms his early period in office was marked by strong continuity with the Yeltsin era.

Public administration: from *nomenklatura* to civil service?

Administrative weakness was one of the heaviest legacies that the old regime bequeathed to the new.[32] Public administration had been subordinated to the Communist Party apparatus and even lacked the basic responsibility of recruiting its own civil servants; this was managed by the Party's *nomenklatura* system. The soviets were primarily political bodies and were never designed to be effective instruments of administration. Their bloated memberships met rarely in plenary session while the actual administrative work was carried out by their executive committees (*ispolkomy*) guided by the local Party organisations, the all-powerful *obkoms* at *oblast* level and *gorkoms* in the cities and towns. Gaidar noted that 'The plenitude of power of the bureaucracy inevitably leads to the complete destruction of the organisation of the work of the state.'[33] The Soviet regime was polymorphous, with little distinction between political, social or economic institutions. T.H. Rigby coined the term 'mono-organisational socialism' to describe this system in which all levels of social activity were controlled by the Party.[34] The weakness of governance was both cause and consequence of the parallel rule of the Communist Party, which gave a semblance of unity and direction to Soviet administration while ensuring that the state (narrowly defined) did not become an autonomous political force in its own right.

Building democratic institutions must be at the heart of any democratisation process, but this was relatively neglected in the first post-communist years as attention focused on economic transformation. The state bureaucracy remained one of the least affected institutions in the transition. Compared with the other post-Soviet states, it was both easier and more difficult for Russia to establish the institutions of an independent state. Russia inherited the buildings, staff and networks of the defunct Soviet Union, but this itself caused problems because it inherited the attitudes, bureaucratism and inefficiencies of the old regime, whereas the other republics could start with a relatively clean page. Just as Lenin in the early years of Soviet power attributed the defects of the new regime to holdovers from the old system, so too the new government in Russia had a ready object on which to place responsibility for its own inadequacies. The revolution of 1991 destroyed the unity of Soviet power but its elements remained embedded in the Russian body politic. In the mid-1990s, over three-quarters of all civil servants were former *nomenklatura* officials.

A law of 31 July 1995 on state service sought to achieve two contradictory purposes: to transform the state apparatus into a modern civil service, while at the same time it sought to defend the corporate interests of the bureaucracy. The former aim was to be achieved by the introduction of examinations, competitive entry and better training. The second was achieved by inertia, with a lack of turnover leading to nearly half the personnel of some ministries being of pensionable age, while their ethical qualities appeared to have fallen since the Soviet period, marked by the growth in corruption. The establishment in 1997 of a Commission for Administrative Reform helped formulate the tasks, and some of their ideas were reflected in Yeltsin's annual address to the Federal Assembly in 1998. The Presidential Administration, however, jealous of its personnel appointment rights, proved an obstacle in the way of the fulfilment of the president's own programme.[35]

Although Russia has only half the population of the former USSR, its government bureaucracy is no smaller. Already by September 1992, Russia had 137 central ministries and departments, compared to eighty-five in the former USSR. By 1 October 1995, the seventy-three federal ministries, state committees, committees and services employed some 30,000 people (with another 5,500 vacancies); 5,000 officials (excluding technical staff) were employed by the president's office and 2,000 by the cabinet secretariat; while federal agencies in the regions employed an astonishing 364,000, double the 187,000 for the whole USSR in 1990.[36] There was considerable controversy in 2001 whether the state bureaucracy was still growing: the vice-premier and finance minister Alexei Kudrin insisted that in 2000 it had fallen by 15 per cent to 333,232 (including 24,904 employed by the central apparatus); whereas Yegor Ligachev, now a CPRF Duma deputy, argued that the number had increased by 10,000 in the previous year to 1,340,000 (*sic*) and that expenses on maintaining the army of officials had risen nine-fold since 1995.[37]

Reform of public administration is a crucial element in building a democratic state. The problem of weak administrative structures was compounded by the absence of an effective (let alone honest) civil service and professional central and local government administrators. With wages in the public sector falling relative to what could be earned in business, the administrative system either 'commercialised' its own activities through corruption, or its most active members left. Civil servants were forbidden to participate in business by a law of 22 March 1991, yet many continued their economic activities.[38] It was an open secret that many important government officials were in the pay of financial and industrial groups, allowing the oligarchs to influence government policy. Bogged down in elite conflicts and institutional turf wars, and lacking a solid professional core of modern administrators, reform in this sphere proceeded as contradictorily as in most other areas.

A professional civil service reflecting civil society rather than acting as an administrative instrument of executive authority only slowly emerged. A General Directorate to train senior cadres for the civil service (known as Roskadry) was established by a decree of 28 November 1991, accompanied by plans to introduce competitive entrance exams and the like. The Institute of Management in Moscow was transformed into a new Civil Service Academy, designed to train a new generation of professional government employees. At the same time, the material incentives for senior government service were greatly improved from 1997, including free housing allocation and seniority pay. The presidency itself became ever more active in appointments, with any personnel appointments of any significance having to be cleared first not only with the presidential administration but also, increasingly, with the security services as well. The latter was justified by the need to combat crime and corruption, yet the FSB files on officials could clearly be used for other purposes as well.

Conclusion

The 1993 constitution sought to prevent a repetition of the conflict between executive and legislative authorities that so nearly destroyed the Russian state in the early 1990s, but in so doing introduced new imbalances that themselves became the source of instability. A strong and largely irremovable president was largely freed

from parliamentary accountability and was thus able to act as the focus of a reconstituted extra-systemic political force that we have called 'the regime'. On the
plus side, the 1993 constitution did provide an effective environment for political
stabilisation, marginalising extremism and facilitating political compromise and
policy consensus. This political compromise, however, entailed a stagnatory 'neo-
corporatist' trend that tended to sacrifice the pursuit of hard policy options on the
altar of political stability. This stagnatory tendency was most in evidence during
Chernomyrdin's premiership.

One of the characteristics of Russia's democracy is the emergence of a number
of centres of political power (president, government, State Duma, Federation
Council, and regional leaders) that balance and constrain each other. Despite the
formal powers granted by the constitution, in practical terms the presidency does
not have autonomous powers outside these constraints. If a president did try to rule
autonomously, the reaction from the other centres of power would destroy the
present constitutional settlement. Although a modicum of constitutional stability
has been restored to Russia, the political system remains unstable. An effective
working relationship has been established between the various branches of the
polity, but in all areas various asymmetries provide points of tension. This is as true
in the relationship between the president and parliament as it is in the development
of 'asymmetrical federalism' itself (Chapter 10). A mixed parliamentary and presidential system as practised in Russia, where the government is simultaneously
subordinate to the president while requiring at least informal parliamentary
support, is inherently prone to conflict. Yeltsin was able to manage the relationship
by conceding ground to his opponents when they appeared strong, by adopting
many of their key positions, by co-opting important individuals, and in general by
governing through bluster, threat and inertia. He thus made the system work.
Whether a successor could do so with equal success while remaining broadly within
the existing political order is questionable, and it is for this reason that constitutional reform figured so prominently in the late 1990s.

6   The legislature

Men are in public life as in private, some good, some evil. The elevation of the one, and the depression of the other, are the first objects of all true policy.

(Edmund Burke)[1]

The birth of parliamentarianism in Russia has been tortuous. Three times in Russian history a legislature has been dissolved by force: on 9 July 1906 Nicholas II used troops to dissolve the First State Duma, only two months after its convocation; the long-awaited Constituent Assembly met for only one day on 5 January 1918 and was forcibly prevented by the Bolsheviks from reconvening the next day; and on 21 September 1993 Yeltsin ordered the dissolution of the Russian Congress of People's Deputies (CPD) and the Supreme Soviet. In addition, the Soviet CPD, established amidst so many high hopes by Gorbachev in 1988–9, was prematurely terminated in September 1991, and its Supreme Soviet followed into the dustbin of history by the end of the year. The first two pre-revolutionary State Dumas were dissolved prematurely (the First, as noted, by force, and the Second lasted only three months from February–June 1907), the Third (1907–1912) lasted its full term, the Fourth was brought to a sudden end in February 1917, and none were marked by conspicuous success in bringing executive authority under effective control. After 1993, Russia tried once again to establish a viable parliamentary system.

The 1993 constitution abolished the two-tier system of Congress and Supreme Soviet and created a bicameral Federal Assembly: the upper house, the Federation Council (FC), made up of 178 representatives from Russia's eighty-nine federal components; and the lower house, the State Duma, with 450 deputies elected for a four-year term in normal circumstances. The establishment of the Federal Assembly marked a decisive break with Soviet traditions. The constitution outlined the functions of the two chambers of parliament, with the powers granted to the Assembly balanced by countervailing powers of the executive. Although the powers granted to the Federal Assembly are relatively weak, they are far from negligible.

The State Duma

The State Duma elected in December 1993 was an interim one and lasted only two years, on the grounds that the pace of change was too rapid for a long parliamentary term. The accompanying debate over the new electoral law sought to draw on world experience. The simple first-past-the-post system, as practised in Britain, was considered unfair, and a mixed territorial and party system, as applied in Germany,

Georgia and Lithuania, was adopted for elections to the Fifth (First) Duma in 1993, to the Sixth (Second) in 1995 and to the Seventh (Third) Duma in 1999, with half the Duma elected by a proportional party-list system and half from single-member constituencies.

Organisation and role

The first task facing the Fifth Duma was to establish its own working practices. It adopted a law on the status of deputies, the Duma's budget, regulations (*reglament*) on its work and on secretarial and other support for deputies. Article 97.3 of the new constitution insists that 'Deputies to the State Duma work on a professional permanent basis' unless engaged in teaching, scientific research or work related to the arts; the transitional arrangements for the Fifth Duma, however, allowed ministers to remain MPs. The Duma meets in plenary session for only two days a week, and the other three are devoted to work in the committees.

The formation of parliamentary committees on the party principle was an attempt to kick-start the party system, as was the rule that a party group required a minimum of thirty-five deputies to be registered. According to Mikhail Mityukov, the chair of the presidential commission on legislative proposals and the main author of the regulations governing the work of the new assembly, the rules prevented the emergence of a new Khasbulatov, and by focusing on party factions promoted the development of a party system. The chair of the Duma and the vice-chairs were to belong to different factions, and instead of a Presidium there was a Conference consisting of the chairs and delegates from factions and groups with voting power in proportion to their size. The Conference's role was to be purely organisational. The rules, moreover, allowed a faction or bloc to recall a deputy and replace him or her with one further down the party list.[2]

The distinction between factions and groups is important: a faction is formed by parties crossing the 5 per cent threshold (8 in the 1993 elections, 4 in 1995 and 6 in 1999); whereas deputy groups, enjoying the same rights as factions, can be formed on an *ad hoc* basis as long as (according to rules adopted in January 1994) a minimum of thirty-five deputies join. This allowed the large number of deputies elected as independents in single-member constituencies to combine, although some joined the established factions. In January 1994, the New Regional Policy group attracted sixty-seven newly elected deputies from the constituencies (where over half were elected as independents), and even attracted deputies from established factions, in particular from Russia's Choice.

The proportional system had been introduced to tie deputies to the emerging party system by imposing an element of discipline on their behaviour. The intention had been to 'parliamentarianise' the embryonic parties and at the same time to stimulate their development.[3] These aims were only partially fulfilled. While the shifting mass of weakly differentiated factions lacking effective leadership typical of the earlier CPD may have gone, many of the new factions and groups (above all those composed largely of independent deputies) were weakly organised and susceptible to significant shifts in membership. Party factions and groups remained fluid with considerable movement between them with, for example, a quarter of Gaidar's faction deserting him in the Fifth Duma, while a quarter of the LDPR faction led by Zhirinovskii were not even members of his party. Only the CPRF faction developed a sense of cohesion, and thus contributed to the emergence of a rudimentary sense of party discipline in voting.

Duma committees (there were twenty-three in the Fifth and twenty-eight in the Sixth and Seventh Dumas) are divided among factions according to what is known as portfolio agreements. Committee chairmanships are divided not only between the factions crossing the 5 per cent threshold but also the groups formed in the new Duma. Elections are followed by an unholy scramble to gain the chairmanship of the committees, usually leaving some of the parties bruised and alienated. Following the 1995 elections, for example, the CPRF headed nine committess, the three other factions four apiece, and the rest divided among the three other groups. The seizure of the majority of committee chairs by representatives of the CPRF and Unity factions following the 1999 election aroused particular bitterness (the CPRF kept nine and Unity took twelve – five of which went to the allied People's Deputy faction). It is in the committees that acts are discussed and amendments proposed, work that is invisible to the general public until it bears fruit in legislation. While much legislation passes through on the nod in Western parliaments, in Russia each paragraph tends to be the subject of heated debate by the Duma as whole.

Learning from bitter experience, the constitution does not envisage the post of speaker as the organiser of parliament, and neither does it provide for a presidium. The presidium has been replaced by a committee that manages general organisational affairs; and the powers of the speaker were drastically reduced. The candidate from the Agrarians, Ivan Rybkin, was elected chair of the Fifth Duma, with the support of communists and the LDPR, but in contrast to his predecessor, Khasbulatov, he turned out to be a fair and non-partisan speaker. Rybkin's supple leadership played an important part in facilitating co-operation with the executive and thus restored the credibility and authority of parliament.[4] His successor in the Sixth and Seventh Dumas was Gennadii Seleznev, a deputy speaker in the Fifth Duma and from January 1995 a secretary of the CPRF's Central Committee. Like Rybkin, once in the job of speaker his political identity was largely subsumed into that derived from the post. Although he refused to suspend his Communist Party membership, he claimed he would work on behalf of the Duma as a whole and concentrate on improving the Duma's functioning.[5] From the moderate wing of the CPRF, Seleznev in 2000 went on to establish the social democratically oriented 'Rossiya' group within the CPRF. The majority of communist deputies themselves, moreover, had become 'parliamentarianised', and communists became one of the most effective parliamentary factions. The speaker is supported by a first deputy speaker and a number of other deputy speakers, representing various political currents in the Duma.

The Duma is at the heart of the legislative process, drafting and endorsing laws and issuing directives (*postanovleniya*). A number of bodies are granted the right to initiate legislation, including the government, the Federation Council and the president (Art. 104.1), who was also granted, as we have seen, the right to issue laws by decree as long as they do not contravene the constitution. Legislative acts take priority over presidential decrees; if discrepancies persist the Constitutional Court adjudicates contradictions between parliamentary legislation and presidential decrees. The Duma and the Federation Council can over-ride a presidential veto or decree if both houses can gather a two-thirds majority. For a bill to become law a simple majority of the Duma and then of the FC is required; budgetary and taxation laws also require the approval of the government. Bills are then passed to the president and, if within fourteen days he or she vetoes it, it is then sent back to parliament and can only become law if passed by two-thirds of the deputies in both chambers. In its two-year convocation the Fifth Duma passed 461 draft laws, 282 of which were signed into law by president Yeltsin. Three out of the twelve constitutional laws were adopted (On Referendums, on the Constitutional Court, and on the Supreme Arbitration Court).

The Duma's prerogatives include the initiation of impeachment proceedings against the president, endorsing the president's choice of the prime minister, declaring an amnesty (the president retains the right to issue pardons), and calling for a vote of confidence in the government as a result of which the president can either change the government or dissolve the Duma (Art. 103, and see Chapter 5). A parliamentary amendment of 14 April 1995 requires a faction to collect a minimum of ninety votes before tabling a no-confidence motion in the government. The Duma's oversight functions over the budgetary process are relatively limited, simply adopting the budget as a whole. This does prevent the adoption of the budget in the autumn session becoming traumatic. Only in December 1995 was a budget adopted before it was actually due to come into effect; and for the first time in 2000 was a budget adopted that balanced income and expenditure.

The most controversial issue is the relationship between parliament and the choice of prime minister and the cabinet. In parliamentary systems the government is chosen by parliament and held accountable to it, but other than endorsing the president's choice of prime minister the Duma has little to say in the formation of the government and cannot dismiss specific ministers, let alone the prime minister. As noted, the State Duma has the right to reject two presidential nominees for prime minister, but if it rejects them a third time then the president can dissolve the Duma, a right that cannot be exercised in the first year after parliamentary elections (Art. 109.3) or in the six months prior to presidential elections (Art. 109.5). Despite the constitution's stipulation that the head of the government is nominated by the president, the State Duma must give its consent and normal parliamentary practice, albeit in an attenuated form, has asserted itself to ensure some correspondence between the composition of the government and the political complexion of the Duma. The debate over changing the constitution to enhance the Duma's powers in the appointment of the prime minister and cabinet ministers was particularly active during Primakov's premiership, and remains a live issue. In addition, there is discussion over the need of constitutional amendments to increase the Duma's control over the budgetary process and its general oversight over the executive.

After 1993, Russia for the first time was able to create a genuine parliament. Virtually all deputies have completed higher education and work in parliament on a full-time basis. The new legislature has become an effective professional parliament and not simply a decorative adjunct to presidential politics and party struggles. The Duma proved capable of independent initiatives, but its powers were limited. In February 1994, the Duma exercised its questionable right to pardon those involved in the events of 3–4 October 1993 and in the 1991 *coup*. Despite Yeltsin's protests, Rutskoi, Khasbulatov and others were released from gaol, and an end was put to the affair. The first Chechen war (1994–6) revealed the limits of the Duma's powers, with unsuccessful attempts to bolster the legislature's control over military action within Russia, and at the same time exposed its divisions; factional differences prevented the passage of a no-confidence vote on the government. The crisis starkly revealed the changed balance of power between the executive and the legislative.

Formally, the Duma lacks the right of interpellation (the calling of ministers to account in writing) but the work of ministers has been monitored through the committee system, and the Duma devotes the last hour of every Friday to examine the work of ministries. The Duma also lacks sufficient powers to monitor the implementation and observance of the laws it passes, without which legislative activity becomes meaningless. The Duma does, however, hold parliamentary hearings, and many of the resulting recommendations have been adopted by the ministries concerned or incorporated into decrees and laws. Despite the limited rights formally granted by the constitution, parliament's oversight functions have grown. The 1993 constitution provided an effective environment for political stabilisation, marginalising extremism and facilitating compromise and consensus. In his press conference of 22 December 1993, Yeltsin committed himself to working closely with the new assembly,[6] and by and large he kept his promise. Although it was a dangerous business to be a Duma deputy in Russia, with six murdered between 1993–8 alone, politics left the streets and entered the debating chamber. Parties focused on fighting elections and working in the legislature; the virulent rejectionists have been marginalised. Deputies play a stabilising role in the regions, with many of the most influential politicians, together with representatives of social and political movements, directly involved in parliament. A core of experienced legislators have now emerged, determined to avoid the fate of earlier legislatures. In the Fifth Duma's final session on 22 December 1995 Rybkin read out a letter from Yeltsin praising the lower house for furthering Russia's transition 'to civilised parliamentarianism'.

Membership

As we can see from Table 6.1, the composition of the Duma reflects a combination of a stable core membership and a fluid periphery.

The Fifth (First) Duma (1994–5)

Elected for a two-year transitional period, this convocation was fragmented and torn between a large nationalist bloc in the form of Zhirinovskii's LDPR, a liberal group focused in Gaidar's Russia's Choice, and a communist bloc.

The Sixth (Second) Duma (1996–9)

The Sixth Duma was less fragmented than its predecessor, and the presence of only four factions dramatically altered its voting dynamics, with fewer smaller factions to mediate and moderate policy-making. The more radical deputies elected from

Table 6.1 Membership of the State Duma

	Seats in Fifth (First) Duma (%), 1994	Seats in Sixth (Second) Duma (%), 1996	Seats in Seventh (Third) Duma (%) on 21 January 2000
Party factions (crossing the 5% threshold)			
Communist Party of the Russian Federation (CPRF) (Zyuganov)	48 (10.7%)	149 (33.1%)	90 (20%)
Liberal Democratic Party of Russia (LDPR, Zhirinovskii)	64 (14.2%)	51 (11.3%)	17 (3.7%)
Yabloko (Yavlinskii)	23 (5.1%)	46 (10.2%)	21 (4.6%)
Russia's Choice (Gaidar)	70 (15.6%)		
Agrarian Party (APR, Lapshin)	33 (7.3%)		
Women of Russia	23 (5.1%)		
Party of Russian Unity and Consensus (PRES, Shakhrai)	18 (4.0%)		
Democratic Party of Russia (DPR, Travkin)	15 (3.3%)		
Russia Our Home (NDR)		65 (14.4%)	
Edinstvo (Gryzlov)			82 (18.2%)
OVR (Primakov)			45 (10%)
SPS (Kirienko–Nemtsov)			32 (7.1%)
Deputy groups (need a minimum of 35 members)			
People's Power (Ryzhkov)		37 (8.2%)	
People's Deputy (Raikov)			57 (12.6%)
Russian Regions (Morozov)		42 (9.3%)	41 (9.1%)
Agro-Industrial (Kharitonov)		35 (7.8%)	39 (8.6%)
Small parties and others	15	(65)	26
Independents (at the time of election; many later joined deputy groups)	141 (31.3%)	(77) (17%)	(105) (23.3%)
Total	450	450	450

Source: http://www.russiavotes.org/Duma_align.htm, modified.
Note: Some deputy groups were 'lent' deputies from factions that crossed the 5 % threshold, hence their totals (for example, of the CPRF) are lower than presented in the tables showing the election results.

the party lists were diluted by members elected from the constituencies, often without any clear political affiliation, but the cost was a lack of clear political orientation in the Duma itself.[7]

The Sixth Duma contained 157 members of the old Duma (35 per cent), and 49 per cent of the new convocation had been legislators at various levels before; 52 had worked in various executive branches, 15 had previously been members of the Federation Council, and 29 per cent came from Moscow.[8] Although the CPRF did remarkably well, winning 149 seats in the new Duma, the pro-communist bloc with 45 per cent of the seats failed to obtain the two-thirds required to overturn a presidential veto. The CPRF faction reflected the age profile of the party as a whole, with over one-third over fifty, and another 6.5 per cent over sixty; workers accounted for no more than 7 per cent.[9] Despite earlier fears, the CPRF-dominated Duma did not entail constitutional paralysis, although the Belovezh Accords were denounced and there were attempts to put Yeltsin on trial.

The Seventh (Third) Duma (2000–3)

From containing a majority of anti-Yeltsin communists, the Seventh Duma could muster some 280 votes as part of a broad non-communist coalition, a healthy majority in support of Putin's government. Unity, which received Putin's 'unofficial' blessing, became the core of a pro-government alliance. About a third (166) of the deputies from the previous convocation were re-elected to the new Duma.[10] The CPRF won 24.29 per cent of the party list vote, giving it sixty-seven seats, and forty-seven SMD seats.[11] In the Duma a CPRF faction with ninety members was formed, together with an allied 'Agro-Industrial' faction of thirty-nine. The loss of its former allied Agrarian and Popular Power groups reduced the left's share of the Duma from 211 (47 per cent) to 127 (28 per cent). The relatively poor showing of OVR rebounded to the benefit of the CPRF, now no longer seen as the main enemy, and indeed the communists had long proved a useful foil to the Kremlin. There was in any case a large area of agreement between the government and the left, including most security issues (above all Chechnya) and support for the military-industrial complex. For the first time a president commanded a stable majority in the Duma, even though its political composition was more fragmented than it had been in the Sixth Duma. The situation in the Seventh Duma was more like that in the Fifth (1993–5) rather than in the Sixth (1995–9), with a greater number of factions and with no hegemonic bloc like the one represented by the Communists, Agrarians and Popular Power in the Sixth Duma.[12] For the first time parliament and the government would be able to work together to adopt necessary legislation. The regime itself under Putin was reinvigorated and sought to maintain control over parliament, calling on it to focus on legislative work and not to pick quarrels with the government.

The Duma in politics

Although there is a tendency to denigrate the role of the Russian parliament, the political composition of the Duma is extremely important, although voting patterns are not always predictable. For example, Zhirinovskii's LDPR usually votes in support of the government and in the Sixth Duma supported economic austerity measures with greater enthusiasm than the supposedly liberal Yabloko party. The dominance of the left in the 1990s impeded the adoption of important legislation, especially on economic issues like foreign direct investment and the land code. The law on production sharing agreements (PSAs) in the oil industry was held up for three years and even then probably did not go far enough, the liberalisation of land ownership and sales remained a permanently vexed issue, and the rejection of important parts of the anti-crisis package in July 1998 gutted them of whatever coherence they may have had.

Yeltsin had little respect for his parliaments, being irritated by what he considered its unconstructive approach. Relations between the two branches of power after 1993 were adversarial, but, in the new institutional framework, rarely confrontational. The relationship changed as a result of the 1999 election and the change of the presidency. Instead of the Duma being dominated by an anti-presidential majority of communists and independent deputies, the Kremlin regime gained one in which no single orientation could dominate. The dynamics of presidential-parliamentary relations changed radically. The presence of the pro-presidential Unity bloc provided the Kremlin with a compliant bloc of deputies. For many this represented a decline in the Duma's role. One commentator argued that 'today the Duma plays a significantly smaller role than under Yeltsin or Nicholas II'.[13] The Duma's role as the initiator of legislation had certainly declined, and instead the Duma tended to act on bills proposed by the Kremlin.[14]

The Federation Council (FC)

In the Soviet period after 1936, the two chambers of the Supreme Soviet, the Council of the Republic and the Council of the Nationalities, were in effect two parts of a single unit, often meeting together and with a single presidium, whereas the Federal Assembly today is a genuinely bicameral body. The State Duma and the Federation Council are located in different buildings and meet separately, except for ceremonial occasions. The FC allows the direct representation of the components of the federation in the parliamentary system and acts like the Senate in the United States, with two representatives apiece from Russia's eighty-nine components, representing the executive and legislative branches (Art. 95.2). It is a body responsible for a range of national issues, but is especially concerned with ethnic issues (the 'nationalities question', in Soviet parlance), the prerogative of the old Council of Nationalities, and bears special responsibility for the monitoring of regional issues.

The question of 'forming' the Federation Council

While the constitution stipulates that the Duma is to be 'elected', it does not specify a mechanism for the 'formation' of the Council. According to the constitution (Art. 95.2), the FC 'consists of two representatives from each member of the Russian Federation; one each from the representative and executive bodies of state power', but the detailed procedure for 'forming' the FC was to be regulated by federal law (Art. 96.2). The notion of 'forming' (*formirovanie*) allows varying interpretations, including election, delegation or appointment.[15] The upper house in Germany, the Bundesrat, is appointed, but the Duma argued that this was unsuitable for Russian conditions and insisted that the Federation Council should remain an elected body. However, should the elections be open to anyone, or should the heads of administration and the legislatures be elected and then automatically made members of the FC? The majority of heads of administration at that time were not elected but appointed by the president, while about half of the local legislatures were filled by appointees of the executive authorities. From 1996, the heads of the executive and legislature in the regions were elected, but this only raised more sharply issues of conflict of interest and more practical questions of how 'senators' could manage simultaneously to be effective regional and national politicians.

The problem of how to form the upper chamber rumbled on throughout the Yeltsin years and was then a nettle grasped firmly by Putin, although doubts remain over whether his solution was the optimal one. Yeltsin's plan to convert the unelected Federation Council created in August 1993 into the upper chamber of parliament was opposed even by his own supporters, and soon after the October events he announced simultaneous elections to both houses of the Federal Assembly. The first two-year convocation of the FC was elected in open competition in the December 1993 elections. Electoral associations were largely irrelevant and the great majority of members elected (108) were independents. Dominated by elites from the regions and republics, the FC brought together many experienced and serious politicians, including many presidents of the republics and regional governors. The first convocation of the FC by and large supported the Yeltsin administration, voting for the Social Accord Treaty in April 1994 and giving critical support on other issues. The selection of Vladimir Shumeiko, a close presidential ally and a member of Russia's Choice, to the speakership helped moderate conflicts between the Duma and the president. Since the majority of deputies were employed elsewhere, however, absenteeism was high and it was often difficult to gather a quorum. Duma deputies customarily spend three weeks in four in parliament and a week in their constituencies (if elected from constituencies); it was the other way round for members of the FC, who usually had major responsibilities in their constituencies.

It took two years to establish the rules for selecting members of the FC. The delay in adopting a law threatened to undermine the validity of the 1995 Duma elections, since one house on its own cannot pass legislation. The legislative committees of both houses supported the electoral variant, which would have created a popularly elected, full-time Council, and a law to this effect was passed on 27 July but was vetoed by the president. Yeltsin sought to have regional leaders, most of whom he had appointed himself, to become Council members automatically. At that time, sixty-six out of eighty-nine regional governors and presidents of republics were presidential appointees. According to a second version adopted on 11 October 1995, taking into account Yeltsin's objections, the administrative and legislative heads of each region would become Council members *ex officio*, but the governors would be popularly elected as well. Governors who were presidential appointees would have to face the voters before the presidential election scheduled for June 1996. Yeltsin, who wanted the governors he had appointed to remain in place so that they would support him during the presidential campaign, once again vetoed the law.[16]

In concession to this the final law adopted by the Duma on 5 December 1995 allowed the postponement of gubernatorial elections for up to one year (to be held no later than December 1996, although twelve exceptions were made allowing elections in December 1995). According to the law the FC was formed from the governors (heads of administration) and legislative heads from each of Russia's eighty-nine components. Those republics with bicameral assemblies (like Karelia and Yakutia) were forced to choose between their two speakers. A candidate won if they gained 50 per cent plus one of the vote; if not, the contest went to a second round between the two leading candidates.[17] The Duma had been forced to use a two-thirds majority to over-ride the objections of the Council, since most of the members elected in 1993 were neither heads of regional executives nor chairmen of regional legislatures. The new Federation Council took office in January 1996.

The stakes in regional elections were now doubled since each of the executives elected became, *ex officio*, a member of the FC, while the chairmen chosen by the legislatures also joined the Council automatically. Only one-third of the second convocation of the FC had sat in the first, with the heads of the Moscow, Petersburg and Chechnya power bodies joining for the first time.[18] The new FC elected the former Politburo member Yegor Stroev as its chairman on 23 January 1996. He sought to strengthen Russia's federal system, above all through budgetary devolution, while improving the work of the FC itself, in particular by addressing the problem of poor attendance. Stroev had been elected governor of Orël *oblast* on 11 April 1993 and won a seat in the FC in December 1993 with 80 per cent of the vote. The Council was now in a state of permanent renewal as the regional elections took place at various times.

The system adopted in 1995 for forming the Council was clearly unsatisfactory. Direct popular elections (as applied in 1993) would have created an upper house of professional legislators who could devote their full attention to the legislation under consideration. Instead, a Council of part-time members was created, who simultaneously held high office in their home regions. Their focus, understandably, was on striking deals with the federal government to benefit their own region rather than working for the national good and fighting for an independent stance for the FC. They were able to block legislation that threatened their interests. The Council was rarely in session and was easily dominated by its own officialdom and the federal authorities.

It was for this reason that one of Putin's first acts on coming to power was to change the way that the FC was formed. The idea at first was to return to a variant of the earlier system of elections, to allow the senior figures to concentrate on the problems facing their regions. In the event, to appease the regional leaders, a system of delegation was adopted. The new 'senators' would be full-time delegates of the regional authorities, nominated by regional leaders and legislative bodies. How this would resolve the problem of the 'separation of powers' was unclear. The existing members of the FC would lose their immunity from criminal prosecution, but in compensation they would be able to control the nominees; their influence on national affairs would be little diminished.[19] The passage into law of even this rather half-boiled measure was subject to extensive bargaining, with three Duma votes in support of Putin's measure being overturned by the Council, leading to the formation of a Conciliatory Commission. The governors managed to achieve a 'soft turnover' of the membership of the Council, striving to stay until the end of their terms and only then giving way to their nominated successors. The original plan was for the new composition of the Federation Council to be in place by 1 February 2001. The governors in addition tried to maintain sole control over the nomination of the new representatives, without their nominations having to be ratified by the regional assembly. The governors, moreover, demanded the right to recall the regional representatives from the upper chamber.[20]

The measures voted on 19 July 2000 agreed that a governor's appointment of a representative could be blocked by a two-thirds majority in the regional legislative assembly within two weeks. Dismissal was also to be approved by a two-thirds majority of the local legislature. Agreement was also reached over a 'soft turnover' of Federation Council members, with governors leaving the Federation Council as their terms expired or by 1 January 2002 at the latest. A large number of governors faced election in autumn 2000, and were not able to return to the upper chamber. In all, thirteen amendments were approved. Although Putin had made some concessions, the overall package was in line with his aspiration to create a full-time working upper chamber. On 19 July 2000, the compromise bill was approved by the Duma and on 26 July it was adopted by the upper house by the surprisingly large majority of 119 votes in favour and eighteen against, with four abstentions. The vote did not so much reflect the senator's enthusiasm for the reform as resignation that any contrary vote would simply be over-ridden by the Duma.

Thus, the Federation Council was to be replaced by two permanent representatives, one nominated by each region's executive branch and one by the legislature. The new representatives were to be dismissed in the same way as they were selected. The current members of the Federation Council who were not members of local legislatures were to lose their immunity from criminal prosecution after 1 January 2002. With the regional leaders in the conciliatory commission having won the right to recall their representatives, the latter were rendered not much more than puppets. According to Andrei Ryabov, 'With this law, they [the governors] lost nothing but prestige.'[21] Luzhkov insisted that replacing the regional leaders with representatives in the Federal Assembly was the first step in abolishing the Federation Council altogether: 'After they change the make-up of the chamber, it will become clear that no one needs a branch of power with no authority and that it should be abolished.'[22] The new composition of the Federation Council was highly heterogeneous. For example, the newly elected governor of Krasnodar *krai*, Aleksandr Tkachev, in late 2000 appointed his predecessor Nikolai Kondratenko, who had become notorious for his anti-Semitic comments.

The reform of the Federation Council demonstrated Putin's peculiar mix of strength and weakness. He achieved the reform that he desired, but in doing so lost more than he gained. With the regional leaders having won the right to recall their representatives, this made the latter not much more than puppets. Luzhkov's warning that replacing the regional leaders with representatives in the Federal Assembly was the first step towards abolishing the Federation Council altogether proved percipient. The new Federation Council had to fight to regain its authority, while some even called for its abolition.

At the same time, an extra-constitutional consultative council (referred to as a State Council) under the president was created by presidential decree on 1 September 2000, made up of regional leaders, to ensure that the latter retained direct access to the national leadership.[23] Since the body would be consultative, its creation did not require amending the constitution. The State Council appeared a sop to the regional leaders displaced from membership in the Federation Council. Its presidium consists of seven regional leaders serving for six months each, one from each federal district. It meets in plenary session once every three months to discuss two main topics, usually prepared by commissions headed by a presidium member. The establishment of the consultative council, under the president and made up of regional leaders, threatened to undermine the Federal Assembly as the State Council took on functions that were the prerogative of parliament.

Role

The constitution requires an upper house for the Duma to be able to act as a law-making body. The FC shares the legislative role with the Duma, with a majority in both houses required for most bills to become law. If the president vetoes a bill, a two-thirds majority is required to override the veto. Certain legislative functions are exclusively the preserve of the upper house (Art. 102.1), above all matters affecting the republics and regions, approval of internal border changes, confirming presidential decrees, imposing a state of emergency or martial law, the use of armed forces outside the Russian Federation, scheduling presidential elections, impeachment of the president (following a complicated procedure), and certain judicial functions including (on the president's initiative) ratifying and removing from office the Procurator-General, appointing judges of the Constitutional, Supreme and Supreme Arbitration Courts, and overseeing federal laws adopted by the State Duma.

Bills are usually drafted by committees of the Duma and then, if passed by a simple majority, are sent to the FC where, if supported by half of the FC, become law when signed by the president. In case of disagreement a reconciliation committee is established. Most laws passed by the Duma are automatically forwarded to the president if the Council does not consider them within fourteen days. Certain categories of laws, however, must be approved by the Council before they are sent to the president. These include laws concerning the federal budget; federal taxes and collections; financial, currency, credit or customs regulations, as well as monetary emissions; the ratification or denunciation of international treaties; the status and defence of Russian Federation borders; and declarations of war and peace.

The question of equality of rights between them does not arise since the two bodies have different functions, a major advance in the development of constitutional order in Russia. However, certain functions that might properly be considered the prerogative of the Duma, like the right to introduce a state of emergency or the decision to send troops abroad, are granted by the constitution (Art. 102) to the FC rather than to the Duma as a result of the convulsions of 1991–3.[24]

Members of the FC between 1996 and 2001 were full-time officials in their own regions or republics and thus had little time to devote to Federation Council matters. To compensate, the FC's apparatus was strengthened to increase the throughput of legislation. The FC acts as a counterweight to the Duma and has been able to moderate conflict between the president and the lower house, especially when the latter (as with the Sixth Duma) was dominated by the communists. The Council was able to reject draft laws (for example, on social benefits or restrictive land codes) that would inevitably have been vetoed by Yeltsin, thus lowering the political temperature. The work of the upper house demonstrated the irrelevance of party labels, and appeals for support had to be couched in the language of regional interests. As the membership of the Council changed in 2001, however, a group called 'Federatsiya' was formed in support of Putin encompassing some hundred members.

The introduction of the new system of selecting delegates to the Council raised important constitutional issues. As we have seen, the upper chamber according to the 1993 constitution has the right to declare a state of emergency, to authorise the use of the military abroad, to appoint and remove the Prosecutor General, and many other important functions. With the new assembly made up of nominated figures, was it appropriate for these functions to remain with the assembly? Would it not be better for these tasks to be fulfilled by the Duma? A constitutional amendment would be required to make the change, yet Putin avoided talk of amending the constitution. The reform raised important institutional questions, as well as equally important political ones. As the president of Chuvashia, Nikolai Federov, noted at the time, 'the change destroys the system of checks and balances, and is very dangerous for democracy'.[25] At some point in the future the upper chamber could be directly elected, as it was between 1993–5.[26]

Parliamentarianism and Russian politics

In the transition from communism the articulation of interests and group concerns far exceeded the abilities of the political system to aggregate them.[27] The fate of the old parliament clearly demonstrated the difference between 'democratisation', a process in which the political and economic bases of democracy are established, and 'democracy' itself, which by and large can concern itself with the defence of rights and the formal pursuit of contestatory politics. The bracketing of the process from the purpose suggests that a different set of rules apply to each, a course fraught with danger. The Bolshevik regime itself was ostensibly nothing else but a means to an end, but ultimately its self-preservation became the end itself.

The Russian parliament between 1990 and 1993 acted as a permanently acting constituent assembly, passing hundreds of constitutional amendments, while the president in turn issued hundreds of *ukazy*, modifying Russia's legal space at will. The multi-tier legislature in Russian and Soviet history has typically been designed to limit popular sovereignty. The use of undemocratic methods to establish democracy raises many of the classical issues about the extent to which a democratic order has the right to defend itself. The Nazi Party was banned in post-war Germany, and other countries have legislated against incitement to racial hatred or the violent overthrow of the state. While there are undoubtedly dangers in the recourse to unconstitutional acts, the resolution of the crisis of dual power in September–October 1993 by forceful means represented a setback for the growth of parliamentarianism in Russia, but at the same time the removal of the Soviet-style parliament and the establishment of the Federal Assembly opened the door to the emergence of Western-style parliamentary politics and the rule of law.

After October 1993, some of the structural sources of conflict between parliament and the presidency were eliminated. The creation of a bicameral assembly represented a major advance towards democracy in Russia. The abolition of the Supreme Soviet's Presidium, which had in effect become an alternative government, now gave the concept of the separation of powers institutional form. Whereas deputies in the old Supreme Soviet veered towards irreconcilable opposition, politics in the new Duma set up a drift towards the political centre. The redistribution of powers between the branches of government established a viable political system and eliminated the source of some of the earlier conflicts. The strong presidency now had a juridical basis to it, while the emergence of a strong prime minister gave greater flexibility to executive power and allowed a separation of functions within the political system. Above all, the removal of the constitution as a weapon in political struggle allowed political stabilisation.

The adoption of the constitution inaugurated a new period in the development of parliamentarianism in Russia. Yeltsin's alleged strategy for a 'controllable democracy' in Russia was only partially successful. The new legislature, in contrast to the old Supreme Soviet, is clearly now the junior partner, but fears that the new legislature would be a 'pocket' parliament proved exaggerated. The legislature has not been converted into a branch of the executive; nor can it claim the prerogatives of the executive. The Duma was able to carve out an important role for itself *despite* the formal provisions of the constitution but *within* the constitution's framework. The constitution, moreover, does not regulate in detail the relations between the executive and the legislative branches of government, and it is these very ambiguities that potentially allow the development of a viable parliamentarianism in Russia. Primakov advocated an increase in the powers of the legislature and the creation of a government based on the 'parliamentary majority' while simultaneously increasing the powers of the government and, commensurately, decreasing those of the president. These views gained significant support in late 1998–9, but were marginalised by Putin's personal predominance of the political scene and the apparent moratorium placed on constitutional change.

Conclusion

The tragic end in October 1993 of Russia's first post-communist parliament demonstrated that it is as destabilising for legislatures to have too much power as to have too little. The 'Fifth' State Duma elected on 12 December 1993 was the first legislature in modern times to see out its full term. Although the parliament that emerged out of the turmoil of late 1993 appeared no more than a weak rubber-stamp body wholly subservient to the presidency, in practice this turned out to be far from the case. The new bicameral Federal Assembly proved to be far more authoritative than many had suspected possible. There is a separation of powers at the heart of the new constitutional order, although the separation clearly remains unbalanced. The law-making process respects classical democratic procedural principles, with legislation moving from the Duma to the Federation Council and then to the president for approval. The role played by party factions in organising the work of the Duma is much greater than in the parliament dissolved in 1993, and these groupings provide the Duma with a sharp political relief, compared to the rather amorphous mass of deputies in the old parliament. Above all, in contrast with the near civil war conditions of 1991–3, politics moved off the streets and into parliament. Parties focused on fighting elections and on legislative politics, while the militant rejectionists (those who reject marketising and liberal policies) have been marginalised.

On the political level, the Duma proved to be no one's lapdog. The Duma has asserted itself on many occasions, often passing non-binding resolutions sharply at odds with official policy, while some important legislation (for example, on land ownership) that the presidency sought to pass has been blocked. For most ordinary legislation, however, effective business-like relations have been established between the executive and legislative branches, and most business is resolved through compromise and conciliation. Overshadowed by the presidency, both houses of the Federal Assembly retain a certain autonomy and act to restrain the emergence of an overtly authoritarian presidential regime. Parliament, however, lacks the right to exercise normal legislative control over the government, in its formation and its activity. The separation of powers in Russia is now institutionalised but unbalanced.

7　Electoral politics

For forms of government let fools contest,
That which is best administered is best.
(Alexander Pope)[1]

Elections play a crucial part in the development of a democratic society, but in and of themselves they do not denote the achievement of democracy, defined as popular control over the executive through effective representation in a legislature. The years between 1989–2001 saw ten competitive national elections and three national referendums. In that time the institutional contours of Russian electoralism have become established, certain behavioural patterns have emerged that are repeated from one electoral cycle to the next, and the legitimacy of the new political order has been firmly rooted in the popular validation achieved through the ballot box. Russia's electoral politics, however, are constrained and relatively isolated from power relations. In terms of *succession*, changes of government and even the presidency appear disconnected from the outcome of elections. In terms of *accountability*, both at the federal and regional level, elections have been rather more free than fair, with the electoral process often distorted by asymmetries in financial, administrative and power resources.

The experience of elections

Despite flaws in their conception and implementation, elections have nevertheless played an important part in the development of Russian democracy. Unlike most other post-communist countries, relatively free elections were held in Russia some two years *before* the fall of communism. This gave rise to a peculiar amalgamation of the structures and elites of the old regime with a novel legitimacy derived from their partial adaptation to democratic electoral politics. This hybrid system, in which change was led largely from within the system itself, marginalised the democratic insurgency and helped insulate the regime from the usual effects of electoral politics. Below we shall briefly review the experience of elections in Russia, and then analyse some of their key features.[2]

The emergence of electoral politics

Competitive, if not yet multi-party, elections were the centrepiece of Gorbachev's liberalisation programme. Rather than re-legitimising the Soviet system, however, they acted as a powerful vector contributing to its dissolution. The first attempt at competitive elections was in the local soviet elections of 1987, where some 5 per cent of seats were fought in multi-candidate contests.[3] The elections in spring 1989 to the new USSR Congress of People's Deputies marked an important new stage in competitive elections, but the choices were limited (see Chapter 1). We have noted (Chapter 1) the role that the spring 1989 elections played in revealing popular hostility to the old regime. The actual operation of the Soviet 'parliament', moreover, revealed the limitations of *'perestroika* democracy', a legacy that also impeded the development of genuine parliamentarianism in Russia later. As noted, Gorbachev did *not* place himself before the people in March 1990, and instead was selected as president by the Soviet Congress. The 'disconnect' between electoral cycles and executive power was already evident.

Russian legislative elections, March 1990

The Russian parliamentary election of 4 March 1990 (with the second round on 18 March) marked an important moment in the 'insurgency phase' of the democratic opposition and, of greater long-term importance, the shaping of a distinctively Russian political identity. The vessel of democratic politics was no longer the USSR but 'Russia', or, as the democrats tended to put it at the time, 'the country'. Only Russia retained the two-tier legislature, and the election was to a 1,068-member CPD, which in turn selected a smaller Supreme Soviet responsible for current parliamentary matters. Constitutional and other high-policy matters were the prerogative of the full Congress.

Following widespread criticism of the 1989 elections, the electoral system was modified to remove some of the filters on the nomination of candidates, abolishing the pre-electoral district meetings and the bloc of seats reserved for 'social organisations'.[4] This allowed a wave of independent candidates to be nominated, supported by numerous voters' associations established in the wake of the disappointments of the previous year. This did not prevent numerous violations, with nominated independent candidates arbitrarily being refused registration, their names being deleted from the ballots, and with fraudulent counting in areas beyond the supervision of independent observers. The democrats' strength lay in industrial regions and cities, whereas in rural areas, where neo-feudal relations had emerged, local Party and collective farm (*kolkhoz*) officials were able to deliver the vote for their candidates.[5] There is little evidence, however, of widespread fraud, especially since the electorate had become more politicised since the previous year, partly by the spectacle of the televised Soviet CPD debates. The adaptation of communist elites to democratic procedures (and indeed, the adaptation of democratic proceduralism to the constraints of regime politics) is a characteristic feature of the transition in Russia.

The Communist Party was still the only party represented in these elections, but by then it was so divided that it would be fair to characterise the elections as non-party. The election was contested by four broad groupings: Russian nationalists and neo-Stalinists, who made relatively little impact but began to forge an alliance that would take them to the *coup*; communist traditionalists supporting Leninist politics, above all the maintenance of the one-party state and the command economy,

who would in June 1990 act as the driving force behind the creation of the fundamentalist RSFSR Communist Party; reform communists, supporting Gorbachev's
perestroika (a dwindling constituency); and self-styled 'democrats', made up of
neformaly and some prominent public figures (above all Yeltsin himself), organised
under the broad umbrella of Democratic Russia (*Demrossiya*).

The elections were semi-free, with traditional structures of Party rule still in
place and the media still largely dominated by the old regime, but the common
image that the deputies were no more than communist stooges, with a sprinkling of
democrats, is not altogether accurate. Deputies were elected if they received more
than 50 per cent of the votes cast, and for the vote to be valid there had to be at
least a 50 per cent turnout. Candidates stood unopposed in only thirty-three
constituencies (3 per cent, compared to 10 per cent – 147 out of 1,500 – the
previous year), and in 906 there were more than three candidates. Almost 80 per
cent of candidates had to go through to a second round.[6] Although 86.3 per cent of
the deputies elected were communists, the CPSU did not stand as a united party
and communists in the majority of constituencies competed against each other.
Only 1,061 deputies were elected, seven having failed to attract 50 per cent of the
electorate.[7] Deputies from the national territories were not necessarily members of
the titular ethnic group, and indeed the *nomenklatura* in 1990 found them a safe
haven from the democratic storm.[8]

The 'democrats' could count on about 400 seats in the new assembly, and it was
this cohort that went on to establish the Inter-regional Deputies Group whose effective head was Yeltsin (see Chapter 1). In elections to local soviets held at the same
time democrats won 240 out of the 400 seats available in the Leningrad soviet, and
in the Moscow soviet the Democratic Russia bloc took 280 out of the 500 seats in
the first round.

First Russian presidential election, 12 June 1991

The political context surrounding this election is discussed in Chapter 1, and the
institutional issues in Chapter 5. Here we will only briefly discuss the results themselves (see Chapter 1). The former prime minister, Nikolai Ryzhkov, was the most
serious challenger to Yeltsin, standing as the candidate of the establishment and
receiving the support of the Communist Party apparatus and the media. His
programme appealed to the stability and order of the Soviet system, a system that
was palpably unstable and disordered. Vadim Bakatin represented the more liberal
side of the communist establishment, the side represented by Gorbachev's
reformism. Though he had established his liberal credentials when minister of the
interior before being replaced by Pugo in late 1990, Bakatin's poor challenge was
yet another indication of the low esteem in which Gorbachev's reform communism
was held. Vladimir Zhirinovskii was apparently a joke candidate, with his wild
imperialist rhetoric and populist promises of instant wealth, yet his strong showing
revealed the volatility and alienation of the electorate. General Al'bert Makashov
had already made a name for himself at the founding congress of the CP RSFSR in
June 1990, when he had assailed Gorbachev's record both at home and abroad.
Aman Tuleev was the chair of the Kemerovo *oblast* soviet and posed as the
defender of local autonomy and controlled economic reform.[9]

The electoral hiatus, August 1991–December 1993

Schmitter has noted that 'what definitely is most peculiar about Russia's transition is the role that elections have (not) played in it'.[10] This is not quite accurate, since the elections to the Soviet Congress in March 1989, to the Russian Congress a year later, and the presidential elections of June 1991, were defining moments in the dissolution of the old order and the emergence of the new. Nevertheless, the absence of general elections for some two years following the *coup*, at a time of accelerated political development, is remarkable and this is one of the reasons why we call this period 'phoney democracy'. After August 1991, Yeltsin imposed a moratorium on elections in the regions and localities. The absence of elections reflected the contradictory logic of the Russian transition, above all attempts to maintain its consensual and evolutionary nature at a time of polarisation and revolution. In the by-elections that were held at this time attempts to fill vacancies failed because of the inability to reach the 50 per cent threshold against the background of popular demobilisation and disillusionment with the unseemly struggle between president and parliament.

The question remains, however, of why no elections were held after the *coup* in autumn 1991, when Yeltsin's popularity was at its peak and the 'democrats' could have been expected to cruise home. Fresh elections would no doubt have encouraged the development of a genuine multi-party system, re-legitimised the Russian state and assisted the development of state institutions. Numerous factors inhibited this strategy. First, the Russian Supreme Soviet had played an enthusiastic part in the defeat of the *coup*, and it would have been a poor reward for it to be dissolved at the first opportunity. The CPD, moreover, appeared willing to go along with Yeltsin's plans, above all with his priorities for radical economic reform and a new constitution, and at its meeting from late October 1991 granted him yet more powers to impose economic reforms by decree. Second, before elections could be held it was clear that there would have had to have been a drastic reorganisation of Russian representative institutions, above all the abolition of the unwieldy Congress and constitutional reform. Third, there was no guarantee that parliamentary elections would have resulted in a Congress that differed significantly from the previous one.

Fourth, and most importantly, the re-legitimation of Russia's representative institutions would have placed the development of the presidency at risk. Russia at this time was still a parliamentary republic and Yeltsin's powers were enjoyed only in so far as they were delegated by the legislature; and what was delegated could be revoked. Finally, elections at this time would have reinforced Yeltsin's dependency on Democratic Russia and the 'democratic' movement as a whole; and as a corollary, the deepening of the democratic revolution would have entailed an assault against the *nomenklatura* class, something Yeltsin was loathe to do since he soon came to rely precisely on these managerial and administrative elites. Yeltsin tactically marginalised Democratic Russia and the democratic movement as a whole, and they exercised little influence on appointments;[11] at times of crisis, however, he was not above calling on them as his foot soldiers in the struggle against the current enemy, as in the referendum of April 1993. The recourse to a referendum in itself suggested a failure of routine electoralism.

Federal Assembly elections, 12 December 1993

Only after the October 1993 events did Russia embark on its first genuine multi-party electoral campaign, but the circumstances were hardly propitious for a fair and honest election.[12] The referendum, as we have seen (Chapter 3), provided Russia with a constitution that, despite its many flaws, established the ground rules for a democratic political process. The results of the parliamentary election, however, revealed the profound divisions in Russian society: no clear winner emerged and the new parliament was deeply fragmented (Chapter 6).

Yeltsin's decree of 21 September 1993 dissolved the Russian CPD and the Supreme Soviet and transferred their powers to a new bicameral Federal Assembly, and simultaneously suspended the operation of the old constitution. The existing Federation Council was vested with the functions of the upper chamber of the Assembly, while elections to the new lower chamber, the State Duma, were to take place on 12 December 1993. Accompanying the decree were acts establishing the electoral system.[13] The new legislature and the rules regulating its election were thus born in a process that was both unconstitutional and anti-constitutional. This irregular procedure, while breaking the impasse in the struggle between the Supreme Soviet and the presidency, undermined the development of a legal basis to Russian government. During the course of the campaign, moreover, the rules governing the election and the referendum were modified by the president, further undermining their legitimacy.[14] The duration of the new legislature, moreover, was reduced from four to two years.

According to the new constitution (Art. 95.2), the Federation Council consists of one representative each from executive and legislative authorities in the federal components (see Chapter 6). This laid up a whole minefield of potential problems since the relationship between *ex officio* membership and changes in local adminis-tration was not clear. Was the membership of the Council to be changed each time a local leader was changed? After the October events, Yeltsin decided that the Federation Council's first convocation would be elected.[15] Two seats were available in each of Russia's eighty-nine republics, regions, federal cities and other federal areas. A total of 494 candidates fought directly for seats in the 178-seat upper house. Some 40 per cent of candidates to the Federation Council were leaders of executive authorities and 16 per cent were heads of legislatures.[16] The elections to the Federation Council were conducted almost entirely on an individual rather than a party basis.

The electoral system for the State Duma differed from Soviet practices in three main ways. First, instead of a simple first-past-the-post system, a mixed propor-tional and majoritarian system was adopted, with half the seats to the 450-member State Duma to be elected from single-member districts (SMDs) and the rest to be chosen on a proportional basis from federal party-lists (PL). This drew on German experience but was adapted to Russian conditions. The old majority elec-toral system used in Russia up to that time was unusual, with most other post-communist countries having reverted to the proportional systems prevalent before communism, and indeed the elections in November 1917 to the Russian Constituent Assembly had been proportional. Second, the method of nominating candidates was changed from the Soviet emphasis on labour collectives and gatherings of electors to a uniform system of collecting signatures. Candidates simply had to get enough signed support to be registered. Third, the subject of the electoral process changed from amorphous labour collectives to electoral associations and blocs. All three changes were intended to promote the development of a party-political system in Russia. The abolition of the second round in single-member districts was particularly criticised, but according to a study by Alexander Sobyanin it is unlikely that its retention would have made much difference to the results in December 1993.[17]

Michael Urban calls the new system 'democracy by design', whereby 'those in control of the state machinery attempt to shape the institutions and procedures of a competitive election in ways that ensure an outcome favorable to the designers themselves'.[18] The whole history of the evolution of British (and much of European) democracy is, of course, based on this principle, but in the Russian case the attempt to shape the rules to the advantage of the ruling elite had an effect opposite to that intended. The increase in the proportion of Duma deputies elected from party-lists from the earlier proposed one-third to a half, for example, was condemned as liable to exaggerate the support of certain blocs:[19] a warning borne out by events – Zhirinovskii's Liberal Democratic Party of Russia (LDPR) topped the party-list vote but won only five seats in single-member constituencies. To stand a party or bloc required at least 100,000 nominations, with no more than 15,000 signatures drawn from any one of Russia's eighty-nine regions and republics so that the bloc or party had to have demonstrable support in at least seven.[20] This provision was designed to stimulate the creation of a national party system and to avoid the dominance of Moscow, and at the same time to force the creation of larger blocs to overcome the fragmentation of Russian political life. According to Victor Sheinis, one of the main architects of the new electoral law,[21] the aim was to ensure that local leaders did not exercise an undue influence on the elections.[22]

A representation threshold was incorporated into the party-list system to prevent the proliferation of small parties. To enter parliament a party had to take at least 5 per cent of the national vote, with the whole country considered one giant constituency. It was assumed that this would give reformist candidates an advantage since their natural strength in the big cities, above all in Moscow and St Peterburg, would counteract the conservatism of rural areas. In contrast to earlier practice the elections were to be held in one round, thus abolishing run-off contests, and the old minimum turnout requirement of 50 per cent was reduced to 25 per cent. To be elected a candidate had to poll not, as before, the majority of votes (50 per cent plus one) but simply gain more votes than rivals as long as the minimum turnout requirement was met. The Central Electoral Commission (CEC) headed by Nikolai Ryabov monitored the whole process. The CEC itself became a permanent agency and was latter dubbed 'the ministry of elections'.[23]

Candidates required a minimum of 1 per cent nominations to enter the contest in single-member districts unless they had been nominated officially by one of the party blocs, in which case the necessity of obtaining what on average was 4–5,000 signatures was waived. Coming soon after the October events, the requirement that the passport number had to be included alarmed many potential signatories and made canvassing by opposition groups difficult. In the event, 1,586 candidates contested the elections in Russia's 225 single-member constituencies.[24]

The other 225 seats in the State Duma were distributed to the parties on a proportional basis as long as they cleared the 5 per cent threshold. By September 1993, thirty-seven political parties and over 2,000 public organisations had been officially registered in Russia,[25] although the CEC issued a list with only ninety-one all-Russian political and social organisations with the right to nominate candidates.[26] Electoral associations had to register with the CEC at least six weeks before the election, having provided the minimum 100,000 signatures. Groups allied to the National Salvation Front, which had played a central role in the insurgency of October 1993, were banned from participating in the election, as was Victor Anpilov's militant Russian Communist Workers' Party (RCWP); but so too initially were two more mainstream parties, the CPRF and Rutskoi's People's Party of Free Russia.[27] Subsequently the Ministry of Justice allowed the CPRF and individuals from the other banned groups to stand.

Thirty-one associations scrambled to form electoral blocs in time for the deadline, and twenty-one sought to find the required list of nominations. There are many suggestions that the authorities hindered the signature campaign, amid allegations that the police detained oppositional activists and confiscated the signatures that they had managed to collect.[28] The Russian All-people's Union (ROS), headed by Yeltsin's bitter opponents Sergei Baburin and Nikolai Pavlov, claimed that the police had raided its offices and stolen some 20,000 signatures and impeded their campaign in other ways.[29] They failed to qualify, although Baburin fought the election as an individual candidate in his native Omsk, and won. In sum, eight out of the twenty-one blocs were turned down by the CEC after the documents were checked. Thirteen 'electoral associations' (the official name given them by the CEC) were allowed to proceed, fielding a total of 1,717 candidates, giving a grand total of 3,797 candidates in all categories.[30]

If during the April 1993 referendum some 60 per cent of voters supported Yeltsin and some 40 per cent the opposition, by December 1993 the picture had changed (see Table 7.1). The two explicitly pro-government parties, Russia's Democratic Choice and the Party of Russian Unity and Consensus (PRES), jointly polled 22.2 per cent of the vote, less than the LDPR alone. The total opposition vote now reached 43.2 per cent (22.9 per cent LDPR, 12.4 per cent CPRF and 7.9 per cent APR); whereas the proportion voting for the 'democrats' (both in power and in opposition) had fallen to 33.2 per cent (15.5 per cent Russia's Choice, 7 per cent Yabloko, 6.7 per cent PRES and 4 per cent Sobchak); while the Women of Russia bloc (8 per cent) inclined towards the communists, and Travkin's DPR (5.5 per cent) and the Civic Union (1.9 per cent) sought to occupy what appeared to be a disappearing centre. Another interpretation, of course, for the weak performance of the openly centrist parties is that all the others now moved to occupy 'centrist' positions – all, that is, with the exception of Zhirinovskii's LDPR.

The failure to collect 100,000 signatures eliminated a number of important groupings from the election itself, while the establishment of a 5 per cent threshold excluded from parliament parties that together won 8.7 per cent of the total vote. There were, moreover, persistent claims that the vote was marked by widespread fraud. The main accusation is that regional administrations, which in these elections organised the local electoral commissions, exaggerated voter turnout in order to ensure that the 50 per cent threshold for the adoption of the constitution was

Table 7.1 State Duma election, 12 December 1993

Turnout and validity:
Out of a total electorate of 106,170,835, a total of 53,751,696 valid ballot papers were cast.
Of which 46,799,532 were for the eight groups passing the 5 % barrier.
The official turnout figure (58,187,755) represented 54.8 % of registered voters.
Only 25 % needed to vote for the Federal Assembly elections to be valid.

Result:

Party/bloc	Party list		Single-member seats	Total seats	
	%	Seats	seats	No.	%
Russia's Choice	15.51	40	30	70	15.6
LDPR (Zhirinovskii)	22.92	59	5	64	14.2
Communist Party	12.40	32	16	48	10.7
Agarian Party	7.99	21	12	33	7.3
Yabloko (Yavlinskii)	7.86	20	3	23	5.1
Women of Russia	8.13	21	2	23	5.1
PRES (Shakhrai)	6.76	18	1	18	4.0
DPR (Travkin)	5.52	14	1	15	3.3
Five % representation threshold in the party-list vote					
Civic Union	1.93	0	1	1	0.2
RDDR (Sobchak)	4.08	0	4	4	0.9
Dignity and Charity	0.70	0	2	2	0.4
New Names	1.25	0	1	1	0.2
Cedar	0.76	0	–	–	–
Against all	4.36	0	–	–	–
Spoiled ballots	3.10	–	–	–	–
Independents	–	–	–	141	31.3
Postponed	–	–	6	6	–
Total	–	225	225	450	100

Sources: *Rossiiskaya gazeta*, 28 December 1993, p. 1; *Byulleten Tsentral'noi izbiratel'noi kommissii Rossiiskoi Federatsii*, No. 1 (12), 1994, p. 67.
Note: The top eight percentages in column 1 refer to the latter figure, the rest to the former, hence the column exceeds 100 per cent.

exceeded.[31] Sobyanin argues that the results to the Federation Council were the most distorted, while those to the State Duma in the single-member constituencies the least, with some 9.2 million ballot papers falsified in one way or another. Local heads of administration sought to ensure victory to the Federation Council by raising their vote but were then forced to alter the tallies in the other three votes to ensure a correspondence between the turnout and votes cast, and thus they added votes to what they thought would be the less noticeable variants, above all the LDPR.[32] Changes in the number of registered electors remain unexplained.[33] The CEC finally came up with a figure of 106.17 million in its results published on 15

February, yet the figure of registered voters given earlier was 105.28 million.[34] Even the new figure fell short of the 107.31 million registered for the referendum of 25 April 1993.[35] What had happened to over a million voters? There had been no demographic dip in the birth rate a generation earlier, and, if anything, since April 1993 the Russian population had increased as refugees and migrants came in from the former Soviet republics.

The results suggest a highly discerning and sophisticated pattern of voter behaviour, able to take advantage of the multiple voting choices offered by the interweaving of the various campaigns. The case of Nizhnii Novgorod illustrates some of the processes at work. In casting their ballots for the Federation Council and single-member candidates, voters supported local reformist candidates, but in voting for the LDPR in the party-list section the electorate was clearly signalling dissatisfaction with the overall course of government policy. Support for Zhirinovskii can also be interpreted as a sign of dissatisfaction with the Moscow elite that had come to power following the August *coup*.[36] The absence of a second round, moreover, reduced further the possibility of achieving a popular mandate in single-member constituencies. In many cases (as in Novosibirsk), if the total vote cast for reformist candidates is combined this exceeds the vote cast for opposition-ists on the party-lists. Thus, the party-list vote was used as a classic instance of the 'protest' vote (dissatisfaction with national policies and so on); whereas in the single-member constituencies they voted *for* rather than *against* particular candi-dates and programmes.

The December 1993 elections revealed patterns in Russia's political geography of Russia that were to endure for a decade. The vote divided along several axes, with divisions between metropolitan areas and the countryside, and between the north/north-west and the south/south-west. The main base of communist support was in the Central Black Earth region to the south-west of Moscow (dubbed the 'red belt'), whereas the LDPR's strongest support was in the new Russian border areas (especially in the south) and those in proximity to national conflicts. While Moscow and St Petersburg were distinguished by the greatest concentration of people who benefited from the reforms and hence supported democratic platforms, the south-western part of the country, including regions like Voronezh with a strong concentration of military and engineering plants, was closer to the commu-nists. Voters above the 55th parallel (on which Moscow stands) on the whole supported reformist positions, while those below tended once again to support the repackaged *nomenklatura* elites. The European north was predominantly industrial, while the south was more rural and agricultural. The pattern, however, was not consistent, with the reformers maintaining their support in the capitals, parts of the Urals, the north (especially Arkhangel'sk *oblast*) and parts of the Far East (Khabarovsk *krai*), but lost areas that were traditionally sympathetic to them, in particular some of the industrial centres of the Urals and some regions in Siberia.[37]

Any judgement on the political culture of Russia based on these elections must be tempered by the relative arbitrariness of the results. If the elections had been held only on a proportional system, the LDPR would have been the single largest group; but if the old two-stage single-member system had been retained, the LDPR would hardly have figured. While support for reformist candidates remained strong in Moscow, St Petersburg and some other places, in the provinces their support fell sharply: by 15 per cent in Vologda *oblast*, in Vladimir *oblast* by 10 per cent, and so on. Lyubarskii argues that the riddle is easily resolved: widespread fraud by the old Soviet apparatus. He insists that support for reformist forces had not declined but had probably increased.[38] The results of the referendum adopting the constitution held at the same time have also been questioned, and the charge of vote-rigging still hangs over the December 1993 elections.[39]

In this context, only tentative conclusions can be drawn from these elections: the confused results reflected genuine confusion in the Russian political scene. A large number were seduced by the promises of easy solutions and the restoration of Russia's great-power status; but a solid bloc at the same time voted for the continuation of reforms. The populace had sent two mutually exclusive signals: in apparently accepting the constitution they were voting for stability; but in voting for the opposition they were rejecting the existing basis for order. The results can be interpreted as not only a protest vote against the 'monetarist' policies pursued by the liberals since late 1991, but perhaps above all against the political establishment that had come to power in Russia in the wake of the August 1991 *coup*. Political and social structures were separated from the realities of Russian life; the political order represented by the August regime did not reflect the inherent order of society. Aware of this, the August democrats had launched a revolution to establish their social base through rapid privatisation but they had been inhibited in carrying the revolution to its logical conclusion because the nature of their revolution was, by definition, anti-revolutionary and democratic. However, before the rejectionists could consolidate their success they had to do more than reflect the desperation of society but also to lead it, and here they failed to formulate coherent alternative policies.

State Duma elections, 17 December 1995

Granted only a two-year term, there were attempts to prolong the Fifth Duma's mandate. Ryabov, however, insisted that any delay would infringe the constitution,[40] and the view that the constitution would become meaningless if its provisions were altered at will by the political bureaucracy triumphed.[41] According to the constitution (Art. 84.a) the president sets the date for elections, an announcement that must be made at least four months before an election falls due; if the president fails to do this, then the electoral law gives the CEC the right. The elections were duly announced, although wrangling over the new electoral law continued up to the last minute, in particular over attempts to reduce the 5 per cent threshold.

The president's draft electoral law of November 1994 exempted groups already represented in the Duma from having to collect signatures to support their candidacy, a provision that was dropped later, as was the prohibition on candidates standing simultaneously in party-list and single-member elections. The presidential draft proposed reducing the proportion of those elected from party-lists from half to a third (returning to the original proposal of 1993), and while Vladimir Isakov (head of the Duma's legislative committee) admitted that there were solid grounds for this 'since the weight of parties in society is still not very high', he accepted that political realities prevented any change.[42]

The electoral law adopted in June 1995 forced party leaders to prune the number of Moscow-based politicians on the party-list to twelve, with the rest to be chosen from the regions. The law stipulated that only parties or movements registered six months before parliamentary elections could enter the campaign, thus drawing a clear cut-off point beyond which party formation would be pointless. The number of parties nevertheless proliferated to reach some 300 and engaged in frenetic bloc-making to collect signatures. The number of signatures now required for the registration of electoral associations doubled to 200,000, with no more than 7 per cent from any one of Russia's eighty-nine component units. To stand in a single-member district a candidate had to collect signatures from 1 per cent of the voters (which could count towards the 200,000 if the candidate was officially part of a bloc), and the candidate who gained a simple plurality of votes won.

The retention of the 225:225 split in the election and the unchanged minimum voter turnout threshold at 25 per cent signalled not only the strength of vested interests of the factions already in parliament but a continued commitment to the belief that a proportional system stimulates the development of parties. The retention of the 5 per cent threshold for party-list candidates to enter parliament, however, was bitterly contested on the grounds that a significant proportion of the vote might end up unrepresented in the Duma; instead, a 'representation threshold' was suggested by presidential aide Georgii Satarov whereby the threshold percentage would be gradually lowered until 75 per cent of votes cast were represented.[43] Sheinis defended the law on the grounds that tiny parties 'do not have the right to exist' and that it should encourage the creation of strong parties. He admitted that the lack of a second round in single-member districts was the electoral law's greatest flaw.[44]

Despite rhetorical allegiance to unity, splits continued among the party elites. The rule restricting central party lists to a maximum of twelve from Moscow limited the scope for coalitions, while large electoral blocs were inhibited by the rule that blocs had to re-register if one party left.[45] By the deadline of midnight on 22 October, forty-three out of the sixty-nine electoral associations that had earlier signalled their intention to stand turned in their signatures.[46] This was still not the end of their travails, and the registration of some blocs was refused by the CEC on technical grounds. For obvious reasons Ryabov was keen to reduce the number of parties standing, but despite accusations that bans on groups like Yabloko and Derzhava were politically motivated it was more likely a case of bureaucratic pedantry. The role of the courts in these elections was notable, with the Supreme Court ruling that groups, including Democratic Russia and Yabloko, were to be reinstated.

Each of the forty-three party-lists was headed by three names, which appeared on the ballot paper, with a total of 5,670 candidates registered on the party-lists. The CEC registered 2,751 candidates in the single-member districts, an average of twelve for each of the 225 constituencies, one-third of whom were independents. The candidates on both systems included stars from the arts and entertainment. Some 370 military figures were registered as candidates, some 150 of whom were serving officers, with the majority aligning themselves with the opposition although some well-known names appeared on Chernomyrdin's Russia Our Home (NDR) list and on Boris Gromov's 'My Fatherland' list.[47] Whereas General Alexander

Lebed was forced to leave the army because of his political activities, General Rokhlin on the NDR list remained on active duty. The Ministry of Defence even went so far as to create a separate unit to support military candidates – in the event to little avail.

Why did the number of groups seeking to enter parliament proliferate? We shall examine this question further in Chapter 8, but here we may note that this extreme fragmentation was not simply a result of the leaders' ambitions, ideological differences, or the increased activity of special interest groups entering politics. It was, rather, a sign of a profound crisis in Russia's multi-party system. With the decline of the democratic insurgency and waning public interest in politics, parties came to represent only a few professional politicians, concerned mainly about their own status and position on the party-list. Focused entirely on elections, parties did not require a large number of activists or regional organisations: it was enough to have a few qualified organisers and resources to collect signature and put up posters. The Communists were precisely distinguished from the others because it did not limit itself to electoral work but remained an enduring presence in politics between elections.[48]

The two-party system envisaged by Yeltsin in April 1995 had not materialised. He had sought a centre-right dominated by Chernomyrdin's NDR, while the centre-left slot was to be taken by Ivan Rybkin's Electoral Bloc; the latter went through several permutations and was challenged by a number of social democratic, trade union, and manufacturers' associations, as well as the Women of Russia bloc running with a federal list of eighty women.[49] Even more than in 1993, the 'democratic' part of the political spectrum fragmented into small groups. Party leaders calculated that by gaining access to free air time by heading a party-list group their chances in single-member districts would be enhanced; they thus placed their individual interests above those of the movement, something not restricted to the democratic camp.[50] The tactic worked for Irina Khakamada of Common Cause, returning to the Duma from a single-member district although her party failed to cross the threshold, as it did for Boris Fedorov from Forward Russia! (which sought to attract the patriotic as well as the democratic vote), for Vladimir Lysenko from the Pamfilova–Gurov–Lysenko Bloc (established in Summer 1995 on the basis of the Republican Party of Russia that had earlier been part of Yabloko), and for Konstantin Borovoi from the Party of Economic Freedom. Gaidar's Russia's Democratic Choice – United Democrats failed to reach agreement with Yabloko, although they tried to avoid candidates in single-member districts standing against each other. The Democratic Russia movement headed by Lev Ponomarev at the last moment called for its supporters to vote for Yabloko.

The left was dominated by the CPRF, the Agrarian Party of Russia headed by Mikhail Lapshin, and a number of extreme rejectionist parties, above all Victor Tyulkin's and Victor Anpilov's bloc Communists–Working Russia–For the Soviet Union. Zyuganov's CPRF came into the elections the beneficiary of the widespread discontent with the course of reforms and the victor in numerous regional elections. Gaidar, however, argued that the result of the elections would depend on the turnout and whether young people participated in the elections, insisting that communists lacked a political base among those under thirty and were very weak among those aged between thirty and forty.[51] He noted that 'If our Communist

Party were a good, charming reformist party of a social-democratic nature I would not attach any importance to the elections. But it requires enormous ignorance to confuse our Communist Party with the reformist parties of Eastern Europe.'[52] Zyuganov rejected claims that his party appealed to the aged population, but agreed that his programme would be incompatible with the existing constitutional order: he proposed 'a constitution of soviet popular power (*narodovlastie*)', which he thought could be achieved by the 'popular-patriotic' victory in the polls.[53] The CPRF's electoral manifesto was more a blend of patriotic populism than communism, avoiding a commitment to specific Soviet policies while stressing the reintegration of the USSR. Zyuganov sought to reassure Western business that the CPRF would not destroy the private sector if it came to power.

The nationalist wing was once again dominated by Zhirinovskii's LDPR. It had won almost a quarter of the vote in 1993 but was now forced to share the national-patriotic vote with numerous other groups. Patriotic centrists were represented by the Congress of Russian Communities (Kongress Russkikh Obshchin, KRO), whose leader was the former secretary of the Security Council, Yurii Skokov. Second on the list was General Lebed (retd), formerly commander of the Twelfth Army in Moldova, who made clear his presidential ambitions. The KRO had been established by Dmitrii Rogozin in 1993 but he had ceded first place later to Skokov. Lebed announced his entrance into active politics in April 1995, when he joined forces with Skokov, and he resigned his commission in May. There were tensions within the KRO, and in particular between Lebed and Skokov, who also nurtured presidential ambitions and allegedly noted that Lebed's 'education is inadequate. He is not ready yet to be president.'[54] Lebed's major advantage was that he was not tainted by association with the existing powers. His policies were more than a pale reflection of Zhirinovskii's: like the majority of candidates in these elections he promised to extirpate corruption and to resist Nato expansion; but unlike Zhirinovskii he unequivocally condemned chauvinism and refused to label himself a nationalist, calling for Russia to be a state for all its peoples without a hierarchy of 'elder' or 'younger' brothers. He rejected the *velikoderzhavnost* (great-power ambitions) of Russians and supported KRO's calls for a Union of Peoples.[55] His calls to restore order, with an 'iron fist' if necessary, appealed to the 80 per cent of Russians identified by Yurii Levada (the head of VTsIOM) as placing order above democracy,[56] but at the same time insisted that 'it is impossible to build a state according to military principles'.[57] In late October 1995, he established his own movement 'Honour and Motherland' (Chest i Rodina) whose aim was to reform the army and to 'restore a strong, peaceful and dynamically developing Russia'.[58]

One does not have to be a political scientist to note the 'farcical' elements in the December 1995 elections, hence the calls for postponement until a more sensible electoral law was adopted.[59] The law On the Status of Deputies provided extensive immunity, making Duma membership extremely attractive to criminals. The large number of parties running for seats in the Duma, according to Gaidar, demonstrated the immaturity of the Russian political system.[60] With the major exception of the CPRF, the campaign focused not so much on programmes but on personalities; with so many associations on the ballot, voters could only distinguish between them by identifying certain key individuals. Far too many associations stood and far too few entered the Sixth Duma (see Table 7.2). Fears about the steepness of the

Table 7.2 State Duma election, 17 December 1995

Turnout and scope:
Out of a total electorate of 107,496,558 million registered voters, 69,204,820 million (64.44 per cent) participated.
A total of 1,320,620 ballots were declared invalid, leaving 67,884,200 valid ballots.
Only 25 % needed to vote for the elections to be valid.
Gubernatorial elections were also held in twelve regions in which 25 % of the population live, something that helped inflate turnout figures.
Twenty-five electoral associations received less than 1 % of the vote and seven received between 1 and 2 %.

Result:

Party/bloc	Party-list		Single-member seats	Total seats	1993 seats
	%	Seats			
CPRF	22.30	99	58	157	45
LDPR	11.18	50	1	51	64
Russia Our Home	10.13	45	10	55	N/A
Yabloko	6.89	31	14	45	25
Five % representation threshold in the party-list vote					
Women of Russia	4.60	0	3	3	23
Working Russia (KTR)	4.53	0	0	0	0
KRO	4.31	0	5	5	N/A
PST	4.01	0	1	1	N/A
DVR	3.86	0	9	9	76
APR	3.78	0	20	20	55
Derzhava	2.59	0	0	0	N/A
Forward Russia!	1.94	0	3	3	N/A
VN	1.61	0	9	9	N/A
Pamfilova *et al.*	1.61	0	2	2	N/A
Rybkin bloc	1.12	0	3	3	N/A
Blocs with 1 MP	–	0	10	10	N/A
Independents	–	–	77	77	162
Total	100	225	225	450	450

Sources: *Segodnya*, 27 December 1995, p. 2; *Moscow News*, No. 51 (29 December 1995), p. 2; *Segodnya*, 30 December 1995, p. 1; *OMRI Daily Digest*, No. 1, Part 1 (2 January 1996).
Note: Although 1.3 million ballots were declared invalid the 5 per cent party-list threshold was calculated using the total number of ballots cast, not only valid ballots.
Abbreviations:
CPRF – Communist Party of the Russian Federation; LDPR – Liberal Democratic Party of Russia; Working Russia (KTR) – Communists–Working Russia–For the Soviet Union; KRO – Congress of Russian Communities; PST – Party of Workers' Self-management; DVR – Russia's Democratic Choice; APR – Agrarian Party of Russia; VN – Power to the People.

5 per cent threshold proved amply justified as only 50.5 per cent of the party-list votes were actually represented, indicating to some that the Sixth (Second) Duma was unrepresentative and illegitimate. As in 1993, the electoral system amplified the representation of the parties making it over the threshold (four in this case), and voters supporting the other thirty-nine blocs were in effect disenfranchised. With some 34 million votes in 1995 'wasted', the political tendencies that had formed in society were only partially reflected in the Duma. All of this once again raised the question of changing the electoral system; lowering the 5 per cent threshold; reducing the proportion of MPs elected from party-lists or abolishing the proportional part of the election entirely; and reintroducing a second round in single-member districts.

Gaidar had moved into opposition to the government, but his vote fell dramatically and Russia's Democratic Choice failed to cross the threshold. As for the 'democratic' opposition, Yabloko became the main standard-bearer of reformist policies in the Sixth Duma. As a newly established party, Russia Our Home did well to enter parliament at its first outing, but its weak showing in single-member constituencies revealed its inability to capitalise on its ruling status in the regions; indeed, its status as the 'party of power' was bitterly resented. In standing as the ruling party, Russia Our Home repeated the mistake of Russia's Choice in 1993, drawing on itself the protest vote against the war in Chechnya and the social injustice arising from the reforms.

While the vote in 1993 for the LDPR represented the 'soft' backlash against the government's policies,[61] the vote for the CPRF in 1995 was the 'hard' backlash. The strong showing for the CPRF not only reflected anger at the suffering imposed on the population by the reforms but also a broader disenchantment with the post-August 1991 political order. It should be noted, however, that the CPRF's 22 per cent represented only 15.2 million votes: the total oppositional vote of some 37 per cent was less than in 1993, while the vote for pro-reform parties fell to 22 per cent. The LDPR's vote halved from that in 1993, yet, contrary to many predictions, successfully crossed the party-list threshold but won only one single-member seat. The failure of patriotic organisations like KRO to enter parliament was the greatest surprise of the elections. Ethnic Russian voters in the republics had been alienated by Skokov's attempt to create a Union of Peoples uniting moderate Russian nationalists with separatists from the non-Russian regions. In contrast to 1993, the 1995 electoral law set specific limits on campaign spending for parties and candidates, although these were clearly exceeded by some of the blocs.

Did the results mean the rejection of the whole polity established since 1991, or only protest against its policies? Despite the fluidity of the party scene the elections were accompanied by an upsurge in popular political interest, with voter turnout rising to 64 per cent, although there was little confidence that voting would have much effect. However, the institutions of democratic politics began to take root, although used largely as a vehicle of protest rather than support. The 1993 elections were characterised by competition between those in power and opposition groups, the so-called 'party of power' against the 'party of society', which took on an intensely ideological form in the wake of the October events. The programmes of leading contestants by 1995 had become more focused, seeking to defend the interests of specific groups and with more defined policies. The Russian electorate had matured, with voters increasingly choosing candidates on the basis of party affiliation rather than personality. The closer alignment between votes cast for party-lists and single-member candidates (with the exception of the LDPR) indicates greater commitment to programmes, increased differentiation among the electorate and the emergence of a more stable value system. In short, divisions between policies had now come to the fore, suggesting that the post-1993 polity had begun to stabilise.

Presidential election, June–July 1996

In 1996, the first-ever elections for the head of state of a sovereign and independent Russia were held. Candidates registered with the CEC by 15 April 1996, enclosing their tax returns for the previous two years and submitting 1 million signatures (with no more than 70,000 from any one region), a way of eliminating outside candidates. No candidate obtained more than 50 per cent of the vote in the first ballot (held on 16 June 1996) so the two front-runners entered a run-off poll a fortnight later on 3 July (see Table 7.3).

Yeltsin's own chances of re-election were reduced by the horrors of the Chechen war and his own ill-health. His popularity had fallen dramatically, from 37 per cent in December 1992 to 6 per cent in June 1995.[62] The December 1995 Duma election acted as a primary for the presidential election, identifying the strongest candidates and eliminating the weakest. Several contenders announced their candidacy, including Zyuganov, Lebed, Yavlinskii, Gorbachev and, of course, Zhirinovskii, without whom no election would be complete in Russia. Neither Yeltsin's 'democratic' critics nor the left-nationalist opposition, however, could agree on a single convincing candidate, respectively, to run and thus Yeltsin remained in with a chance. It did not look like this in early 1996, however, and the hard-liners in Yeltsin's entourage, known as the 'party of war' for their advocacy of the first Chechen war in December 1994, urged Yeltsin to cancel the elections and declare a state of emergency to thwart what they insisted was the threat of a communist victory, and all that this entailed. Leading the call for the postponement of the elections was the head of Yeltsin's presidential security service, Alexander Korzhakov, but his views were defeated by an alternative group headed by Chubais. The latter, with his typical decisiveness, was able to draw on the resources of the 'oligarchs' to organise Yeltsin's successful electoral resurrection. In a notorious letter, the 'Appeal of the 13',[63] a number of the top oligarchs pledged their support for Yeltsin, and made unquantifiable sums available to his campaign.

The first round largely confirmed Russia's traditional electoral geography, with Zyuganov gaining strong support on the southern fringe and the 'red belt' to the south-west of Moscow, although Yeltsin unexpectedly defeated the opposition in the Far East. Yeltsin fought a surprisingly effective campaign, looking fitter than before and focusing on the threat posed by the communists. The media (notably Gusinskii's NTV) fell in behind his candidacy, fearing the consequences of a communist victory, as did a large proportion of the electorate. Lebed's strong showing owed something to the covert support of Yeltsin's team, but much more to his own charisma: if in December 1995 he had been an 'iron-fisted populist', by June 1996 he appeared to have become an iron-fisted democrat.

Table 7.3 Presidential election, June–July 1996

Electoral system:
Direct elections without electoral districts.
No candidate obtained over 50 % of the vote in the first round so the two top candidates went on to a second round held two weeks after the announcement of the results of the first (3 July).

First round, 16 June 1996

Turnout:

Registered voters	108,495,023	
Turnout	75,587,139	(69.81%)
Total valid ballots	74,515,019	
Total invalid ballots	1,072,120	

Results:

	Candidate	Percentage	Number of votes
1	Boris Yeltsin	35.28	26,665,495
2	Gennadii Zyuganov	32.03	24,211,686
3	Alexander Lebed	14.52	10,974,736
4	Grigorii Yavlinskii	7.34	5,550,752
5	Vladimir Zhirinovskii	5.70	4,311,479
6	Svyatoslav Fedorov	0.92	699,158
7	Mikhail Gorbachev	0.51	386,069
8	Martin Shakkum	0.37	277,068
9	Yurii Vlasov	0.20	151,282
10	Vladimir Bryntsalov	0.16	123,065

Sources: *Rossiiskaya gazeta*, 22 June 1996, p. 1; *Vestnik Tsentral'noi izbiratel'noi komissii Rossiiskoi Federatsii*, No. 14 (34) (1996).
Note: The percentages are calculated from the total vote

Second round, 3 July 1996

Turnout:
To avoid a fall in the turnout between the two rounds the day of the election was shifted from the usual Sunday to a Wednesday, which was declared a holiday. The tactic worked and turnout fell only marginally.

Registered voters	108,600,730	
Turnout	74,815,898	(68.87%)
Total valid ballots	73,926,240	
Total invalid ballots	780,405	

Results:

	Candidate	Percentage	Number of votes
1	Boris Yeltsin	53.82	40,208,384
2	Gennadii Zyuganov	40.31	30,113,306
	Against both candidates	4.83	3,604,550

Sources: *Rossiiskaya gazeta*, 10 July 1996, p. 1; *Vestnik Tsentral'noi izbiratel'noi komissii Rossiiskoi Federatsii*, No. 16 (36) (1996).

Between rounds Yeltsin sacked some of his more unpopular officials (including defence minister Pavel Grachev and Korzhakov) and appointed Lebed secretary of the Security Council and presidential national security adviser with the brief to root out corruption and crime. Yavlinskii fought a poor campaign, failing to become the candidate of a united 'third force', while Zhirinovskii was pushed into fifth place. Yeltsin secured a convincing victory in the second round from an electorate afraid that a change of president would entail a change of regime. The 30 million votes cast for Zyuganov represented a large constituency of dissatisfied citizens, but he failed to broaden his support beyond the communist and national-patriotic opposition. Despite continuing fears over his health, Yeltsin successfully exploited the slogans of continuity, stability and reform.

Throughout the 1990s, Yeltsin was able to blunt the threat posed by elections by various strategies of co-optation, manipulation and, on occasion, outright subversion. Yeltsin was remarkably successful in imposing a binary choice on the electoral process: either a return to communism or the continuation of reforms – the latter allegedly guaranteed by a vote for him.[64] Indeed, it seemed at times that Yeltsin deliberately sought to weaken liberal parties so that the presidency could remain the only representative of the 'reform' tendency. This bipolarity was seen at its starkest in 1996 presidential elections, when Yeltsin played the anti-communist card for all it was worth, and with great success. Although by the end of the campaign in very poor health, he won another four-year mandate. What he would do in his second term was less clear, and in the event for a large part of this time he was absent in his sick bed, the country drifted from crisis to crisis, and the regime became increasingly preoccupied with the succession. The executive's ability to impose a crude bipolarity on the electoral process reflected the weakness of the emerging party system.

Duma election, 19 December 1999

The parliamentary elections of 1999 once again, as in December 1995, acted as a 'primary' for the presidential elections. Those who did well in the parliamentary elections emerged as favourites, while the credibility of candidates whose electoral blocs did badly was undermined. The interweaving of parliamentary and presidential considerations is one of the most fascinating aspects of the whole process. It affected the whole development of the party system, and added multiple complications in the calculations of political leaders.

By 1999, the attempt to impose the old bipolarity on the electoral process was no longer credible: the political field in Russia was clearly becoming more complex. The CPRF itself suffered from defections in the run-up to the December 1999 elections, above all with the majority of the Agrarian Party of Russia (APR) allying itself with the powerful new grouping headed by the former prime minister, Yevgenii Primakov. This electoral association (OVR) was made up of the Otechestvo (Fatherland) organisation, led by the mayor of Moscow, Yurii Luzhkov, and Vsya Rossiya (All Russia), comprised of some of the leading regional leaders like Vladimir Yakovlev of St Petersburg and President Mintimir Shaimiev of Tatarstan. The regions and their increasingly independent leaders emerged as a crucial new force in Russian elections. The spate of regional party formation in the run-up to December 1999 demonstrated just how fragmented the political field was. The fact that no single 'party of the regions' emerged, however, once again testified to the political and economic fissures within the regional 'lobby'. The various parties of the regions lacked a coherent policy platform other than regionalism itself, whereas Fatherland under Luzhkov could at least advance a consistent economic line of 'competent capitalism' and, on the national level, of a vigorous state-centred patriotism that would defend Russia's interests both at home and abroad.[65]

In previous elections the regime had always put forward a single quasi-presidential 'party of power' (Gaidar's Russia's Choice in 1993 and Chernomyrdin's Russia Our Home in 1995). The emergence of a reconfigured but oppositional 'party of power', focused on Primakov, the national security establishment, regional elites, and industrial and financial groups, was nipped in the bud by Primakov's dismissal as prime minister in May 1999. It was to counter the destabilising threat to the succession that in September 1999 the Kremlin sponsored the creation of the Unity (Edinstvo) governors' bloc to act as the official 'party of power'. It was headed by the popular Sergei Shoigu, the long-time head of the Ministry of Emergency Situations (MChS). Unity was certainly not a modern political party, but neither was it a mass movement. It was perhaps the best example of a political association made to order by power elites, to act as the simulacrum of a competitive political organisation and to occupy the space where genuine political parties should belong.

The big question before the 1999 election was whether the liberals would be able to unite. In the wake of Galina Starovoitova's murder on 20 November 1998, there were desperate attempts to bring the various factions together, but Yavlinksii's Yabloko remained steadfastly aloof from these efforts. In the event, although formally established in November 1998 it was only over the summer of 1999 that Chubais was finally able to hammer out an alliance of most of the significant liberal groups to form the Union of Right Forces (SPS). The bloc included the groups headed by Sergei Kirienko, Boris Nemtsov and Egor Gaidar, together with the remnants of the association led by Irina Khakamada and the social democrats headed by Alexander Yakovlev.[66]

These elections marked an important formal step in democratisation, with the regime finally separated from controlling the conduct of the elections. The new chair of the CEC, Alexander Veshnyakov, had been appointed with the support of the opposition in the Duma and was a more independent figure than his predecessor, Ryabov.[67] Attempts to prevent the criminalisation of the Duma were at least partially successful, with federal laws governing election expenses requiring candidates to report their annual income, its sources and the total value of their possessions. However, many candidates obviously under-estimated their net wealth with impunity, and it appeared that the CEC was willing to disqualify some candidates (for example Zhirinovskii, whose LDPR was forced to fight the elections in the guise of the 'Zhirinovskii bloc'), while turning a blind eye to infringements by others. Despite this, the CEC sought to apply the electoral rules impartially.

Discussion of the serious issues facing the country was overshadowed by the struggle between powerful elite coalitions made up of politicians, oligarchs and regional leaders, reflected above all by the struggle between OVR and Edinstvo. The genuine political parties, like the CPRF and Yabloko, were marginalised as programmatic debate was subsumed into the struggle for the succession. The creation of a highly presidential system meant that the stakes had become extraordinarily high, since the presidency meant access to the vast financial resources of the state and its patronage. At stake was the very survival of the Yeltsinite quasi-marketised regime system where political power and economic advantage had become almost indistinguishable.

The results (see Table 7.4) indicated that Russian electors had learnt to cast their votes more strategically.[68] If in 1995 49.5 per cent of the vote was cast for the thirty-nine parties failing to cross the 5 per cent threshold, in 1999 this fell to 18.9 per cent of the vote being 'wasted' on the twenty blocs failing to make the 5 per cent threshold. With the consolidation of the vote around 'mainstream' parties, the 'multiplier' effect was far less and only 18 per cent of the party list seats were redistributed as a 'bonus' to the six successful parties. Once again the remarkable consistency of electoral affiliations was evident. This is reflected not in repeat voting for the same party (not possible in the case of the right), but in overall political orientation. Thus, the CPRF won 22 per cent of the PL vote in 1995, and noted a slight increase in 1999, although they did far worse in SMDs. The Zhirinovskii bloc saw its base further eroded (down from its 11 per cent in 1995), but contrary to most predictions overcame the 5 per cent representation barrier. The success of Unity reflected the continuing presence of a large floating centrist and power-oriented vote, given partially to Russia Our Home (NDR) in 1995. Unity almost entirely lacked an ideology other than state consolidation around the presidency, and no new ideologically based party has been able to emerge since the founding election of the present system in December 1993. Yabloko remained consistent in losing about a percentage point in each parliamentary election, but overall the position of the liberals was consolidated by the success of the SPS. In earlier elections the 'democratic' vote was split among rival groups, but this time the SPS brought the majority together to register a significant improvement in representation, although some might argue (given their support for Putin and the Chechen war) that this was at the price of giving up their liberalism.

The CPRF continued to outpace its rivals in SMD contests, but its dominance was eroded, falling from eighty-eight seats in 1995 to fifty-five in 1999. In addition, twenty-eight of the latter were already incumbents, suggesting that the CPRF was being confined to its red belt heartlands. Only eighteen new CPRF single-member deputies were elected.[69] The success of OVR in winning thirty-two SMD seats was largely due to the support of some important regional executives, above all in Moscow (ten out of fifteen seats), Tatarstan (three out of five) and Bashkortostan (four out of six). Edinstvo won only nine SMD seats, SPS five and Zhirinovskii as previously gained no constituency seats. The use of electoral associations as a vehicle for individual candidacies proved less successful an electoral strategy than in the past. While in 1995 some two dozen individuals at the top of the party lists also ran successfully in single-mandate constituencies, this time only a handful did so, including Chernomyrdin, Vladimir Ryzhkov of Russia Our Home and Rogozin of KRO.

The Duma elections marked yet another stage in the realignment of Russian politics. This was a realignment based neither on ideology nor even on general political issues, but on an appreciation of power and its privileges. One of the great

Table 7.4 Duma election, 19 December 1999

Turnout:
Out of some 108 million Russian electors, over 60 million voted, a turnout rate of 61.7%,
comfortably exceeding the minimum 25% requirement.
An additional 1.2% of the electorate cast invalid votes

Result:

Election association or bloc	Party-list (PL) vote (%)	PL seats	Single-member districts (SMD)	Total (%)
Communist Party of the Russian Federation (CPRF)	24.29	67	47	114 (25.9%)
Unity (Edinstvo) or Medved (Bear)	23.32	64	9	73 (16.6%)
Fatherland (Otechestvo)/All Russia (OVR)	13.33	37	29	66 (15.0%)
Union of Right Forces (SPS)	8.52	24	5	29 (6.6%)
Zhirinovskii bloc	5.98	17	0	17 (3.9%)
Yabloko	5.93	16	4	22 (4.5%)
5.0% threshold				
Communists, Toilers of Russia – for the Soviet Union	2.22			
Women of Russia	2.04			
Party of Pensioners	1.98		1	
Russia Our Home (NDR)	1.20		8	
Party in Defence of Women	0.81			
Bloc of Congress of Russian Communities (KRO) and the Movement of Yurii Bodyrev	0.62		1	
Movement for Civil Dignity	0.62			
Stalinist Bloc – for the USSR	0.61			
Movement in Support of the Army (DPA)	0.59		2	
Peace, Labour, May	0.57			
Bloc of General Andrei Nikolayev and Academician Svyatoslav Fyodorov	0.56		1	
Russian All-people Union (ROS)	0.37		2	
Party of Peace and Unity	0.37			
Russian Socialist Party (V. Bryntsalov)	0.24		1	
Movement of Patriotic Forces 'Russian Cause'	0.17			
Conservative Movement of Russia	0.13			
All-Russian Political Party of the People	0.11			
Spiritual Heritage	0.10		1	
Socialist Party of Russia (I. Rybkin)	0.09			
Social Democrats	0.08			
Against all	3.36			
Independents				105 (23.8%)
Total	100	225	216	

Sources: *Vestnik Tsentral'noi izbiratel'noi komissii Rossiiskoi Federatsii*, No. 1 (91), 2000, p. 231;
Nezavisimaya gazeta, 30 December 1999, p. 1; The results can also be found at the Central Electoral
Commission's website: http://www.fci.ru/gd99/vb99_int/pif_r00.htm.

paradoxes of post-communist Russian politics is that the only recognisably Western-style party, with a relatively coherent ideology and national organisation, was the CPRF. The financing of the CPRF in particular aroused considerable speculation. In the 1995 election the party received considerable infusions of cash as the banks and corporations hedged their bets on the outcome, but by 1999 the CPRF was perceived as less of a threat, and its income fell commensurately. The party was forced to find alternative sources of support. It might be noted that of the 450 intake of December 1999, sixty were businessmen, eight of whom represented the CPRF, a party that was allegedly hostile to capitalism. It was clear that the CPRF enjoyed a relatively stable electoral base. The same could be said of Yabloko, with solid support in the intelligentsia earning above average incomes. Most groupings, however, lacked a clearly defined social base and instead exploited populist slogans and the virtual world of media politics.

Presidential election, 26 March 2000

The 1999 Duma election weakened the presidential pretensions of all main opposition candidates – Luzhkov, Yavlinskii, Primakov and Zyuganov. Russia's hybrid electoral system encouraged the development of hybrid political parties: parliamentary parties concerned with winning seats in the Duma; and presidential catch-all groupings concerned to maximise support for potential contenders. The system inhibited parties from developing effectively in either direction. The overwhelming winner of the parliamentary election was someone who was not even a candidate – Vladimir Putin. The election had provided the presidency with a strong base in the Duma, it had drawn the teeth of the main opposition figures, and it had boosted the prestige of Putin. Seizing the opportunity, on 31 December 1999 Yeltsin resigned and Putin became acting president, giving him the powerful advantage of incumbency in the presidential election rescheduled for March 2000. Yeltsin saw in Putin the fulfilment of his long-term desire to ensure a smooth transition to someone who would ensure his personal security and elite continuity. The Duma elections cleared the way for the anointment of the presidential heir apparent, Putin, and thus were only the first stage in a single electoral cycle.

The political regime associated with Yeltsin proved able to reproduce itself; although the change of leader provoked modifications, the essentials of the political system established in the 1990s survived the succession. Beneath the cycle of political crises, sackings, resignations and dramatic *démarches* in Russian politics since 1995 there lay a more profound struggle for the succession. In his televised resignation speech on 31 December 1999, Yeltsin spoke of his desire to have set the precedent of the 'civilised voluntary transfer of power' after the elections scheduled for June 2000, but 'Nevertheless, I have taken another decision. I am resigning.' There was now no danger of Russia returning to the past, and thus, Yeltsin argued, 'I have achieved the main task of my life' and thus he did not want to impede the smooth transition to a new generation of politicians. There was 'No reason to hang on to power when the country had a strong person worthy of becoming president.' As Yeltsin himself admitted, his premature exit meant that Russia would not see one democratically elected leader transfer power to another in direct accordance with the expectations laid down in the constitution (see Chapter 19). Instead, there was an attempt to pre-empt the choice of the voters by transferring power to a designated successor for whom the most benign electoral environment had been established.

The 1996 presidential election had in effect been a plebiscite on the continuation of reforms or the return of elements of the old regime, but by the time of the March 2000 presidential election such a primitive (even though politically highly effective) polarisation was a thing of the past. The law on presidential elections, signed by Yeltsin before he resigned, stipulated that candidates had to collect 500,000 signatures (1 million in normal circumstances), a requirement that thinned the field somewhat. Candidates also had to provide detailed financial information about themselves, their spouses and children. If none of the eleven candidates won more than 50 per cent of the vote in the first round, then a second run-off election between the two top candidates would be held three weeks later. Given Putin's strong support right across the political spectrum, it was clear that high turnout would benefit him. The worst scenario as far as he was concerned was that complacency over the certainty of victory would keep voters at home to such an extent that the turnout would fall below 50 per cent (in which case the election would have been declared invalid and a rerun held four months later). The rather passionless campaign threatened precisely this outcome.

Putin presented himself as a symbol of confidence and stability, promising to maintain Russia's system of power and property while radically renovating the state system and developing political and legal reform. Putin committed himself to the maintenance of the existing constitution, although he argued that some institutional innovation could take place without necessarily amending the constitution itself. As acting president Putin was able to establish the terms of the debate, and present himself as a statesman while his opponents scrabbled for votes. Putin enjoyed the advantages of incumbency of not only one post but two, as acting president and prime minister, and thus he was far from an ordinary candidate.

Putin's programme, in so far as there was one, encompassed almost every conceivable shade of opinion and thus allowed no space for a coherent alternative. An open letter to the electors in late February contained no more than generalities,[70] while the head of the Centre for Strategic Studies, a think tank headed by German Gref set the task of producing a long-term programme for Russian development, was not able to produce a detailed programme before the election. While the overall result (see Table 7.5) may have been a foregone conclusion, Putin's first-round victory (although by a relatively narrow margin) emulated Yeltsin's triumph in the 1991 presidential election and endowed Putin's presidency with extra legitimacy. Like Yeltsin's 1996 election, moreover, the result was tainted by accusations of malpractice, above all in places like Dagestan where straightforward ballot-stuffing allegedly took place, and elsewhere the use of administrative pressure by officials has been documented.[71]

Zyuganov's strong showing (29.21 per cent) represented an improvement on his party's performance in the December 1999 Duma elections and confirmed his leadership of the left opposition. However, his vote did not match the 32 per cent he received in the first round of the 1996 elections, let alone the 40 per cent he won in the run off, and thus suggested a secular decline in the communist vote that condemned him forever to second place. In particular, he lost ground in traditional

Table 7.5 Presidential election, 26 March 2000

Turnout:		
Registered voters	109,372,046	
Turnout	75,181,071	(68.74 %)
Total valid ballots	75,070,776	

Results:		
Candidate	Percentage	Number of votes
1 Vladimir Putin	52.94	39,740,434
2 Gennadii Zyuganov	29.21	21,928,471
3 Grigorii Yavlinskii	5.80	4,351,452
4 Aman Tuleev	2.95	2,217,361
5 Vladimir Zhirinovskii	2.70	2,026,513
6 Konstantin Titov	1.47	1,107,269
7 Ella Pamfilova	1.01	758,966
8 Stanislav Govorukhin	0.44	328,723
9 Yurii Skuratov	0.42	319,263
10 Alexei Pokberezkin	0.13	98,175
11 Umar Dzhabrailov	0.10	78,498
Against all candidates	1.88	1,414,648

Sources: *Vestnik Tsentral'noi izbiratel'noi kommissii Rossiiskoi Federatsii*, No. 13 (103), 2000, pp. 63–5; *Rossiiskaya gazeta*, 7 April 2000, p. 3. The full results are in *Vestnik Tsentralnoi izbiratelnoi kommissii Rossiiskoi Federatsii*, No. 16 (106), 2000.
Note: The percentages are calculated from the total vote.

communist strongholds. In the second round in 1996, Zyuganov came first in thirty-two of Russia's eighty-nine regions, whereas in 2000 Putin came first in all but five regions. In Kemerovo Tuleev won handsomely, leaving Zyuganov victor in only four federal units (the republics of Adygeya, Altai and Chechnya, and Bryansk *oblast*).

Although Putin emerged in the first round with the level of support that Yeltsin had achieved in the second round in 1996 (53.8 per cent), they were drawing on somewhat different constituencies. Putin was able to win greater support from rural areas that had formerly been the bedrock of the communist vote, but he fared worse in the city of Moscow, winning only 46 per cent of the vote compared to Yeltsin's first-round 61 per cent and second-round 74 per cent in 1996.[72] In his hometown of St Petersburg, however, Putin romped to victory with 62.42 per cent of the vote. While the dichotomy between a red belt and the rest had been maintained in 1996, by 2000 it had eroded to the extent that Putin could win in the traditional heartland red belt region of Krasnodar *krai*. The relative uniformity of Putin's support across Russia reflected the success of his strategy of appealing to all classes, social forces and ends of the political spectrum. It is clear that Putin's constituency was a broad one. Surprisingly enough, in the context of the Chechen war, is the extent to which Putin drew support from the liberal wing of the electorate: the young, educated and economically successful.

The reasons for Putin's popularity derived not simply from manipulation and the creation of a benign environment for his anointment through the ballot box to the presidency. He represented the widespread yearning for stability in a society traumatised by disintegration and decline. In that context, Putin's 'anti-political' approach to the election, in which he waged a 'non-campaign', made sense.[73] A greater danger, however, lurked behind this approach, and that was the repudiation of politics itself as the mode of adjudication between interests and concerns in society. An anti-political approach can easily slip into authoritarianism, Bonapartism or populism, where the united will of society is represented by the charismatic leader without the necessity of mediating political institutions. Putin's election represented a fresh start and the reinvigoration of the presidency; it remained to be seen whether it represented the consolidation of democracy.

Elections and the Russian political system

Although overall electoral preferences have been more or less accurately reflected by the results, elections have been marred by numerous abuses. Elections in Russia reflect the hybrid nature of the political system itself. Democratic processes in the centre coexist uncomfortably with a presidential regime that is to a degree self-perpetuating and in the regions with a variety of regime types that try to subordinate electoral processes to administrative control (see Chapter 10).

Founding elections and the limits and achievements of electoralism

The notion of a founding election figures prominently in the literature on transition,[74] but in Russia the issue is by no means clear cut. The elections of 1989 to the Soviet CPD represented an enormous step towards the reconstitution of competitive politics, but the absence of party choices and the limits to campaigning hardly allow this to be reckoned Russia's 'founding' election. Much the same can be said about the Russian republican elections in March 1990, although the subject now at least was Russia proper. The absence, indeed, of a founding election immediately following the change of regime in August 1991 and the disintegration of the USSR later that year had a deep impact on the shape of Russia's struggling democracy, retarding party development and allowing a state system to consolidate itself relatively insulated from popular control. The Russian election of December 1993 was in effect the founding election; but it did not entail a change of government and was held in an atmosphere of extreme polarisation; the electoral law was imposed by decree rather than legislative consultation.

Rather than identifying any single event as the founding election, it may be best to consider all of the elections held so far as part of an extended process of democratic habituation and adaptation. The hybrid nature of Russian democracy is reflected in the absence of a founding election, and each electoral cycle has reinforced electoralism as the preferred mode of legitimating authority. Electoral politics have limited the choices of the regime and, however imperfect the procedures, determined the nature of Russia's emergence from communism. While the elections may have been flawed, the commitment to electoral politics precluded some of the harsher options. Chinese-type authoritarian modernisation was excluded once *perestroika* legalised political contestation. Gorbachev's own attempts to control the transition within the framework of 'managed democracy', retaining a leading although modified role for the Communist Party, shattered under the impact of electoral defeats and the emergence of parliamentary assemblies legitimised by the popular vote. Gorbachev's own refusal to accept the electoral challenge when taking on the post of Soviet president irremediably weakened his legitimacy, whereas Yeltsin's clear victory in the Russian presidential elections of June 1991 gave him the popular mandate to face down the *coup* attempt and ultimately to challenge Gorbachev himself.

Early votes, however, were constrained by external factors: in 1989 by the Party apparatus; in 1990 the elections were partial in that the Russian parliament was far from sovereign; in June 1991 the Russian president was formally subordinated to all-Union structures; and the December 1993 elections were held in the wake of a political cataclysm with a large swathe of the political spectrum excluded. Only in December 1995 were all the elements of a free election in place, governed by an electoral law passed by parliament and within the framework of a stable constitutional order. However, by that time the ability of elections to change the political order was constrained by the provisions of the new constitutional order. The 1996 presidential election confirmed not choice *within* the system but once again the polarised nature of the contest forced a choice *between* systems; in the context, this struggle between two versions of the polity meant choicelessness in terms of policy options. The 1999–2000 electoral cycle was dominated by the problem of the succession to Yeltsin, and, although once again apparently about choice between candidates, was subsumed into the struggle of the Yeltsin regime to perpetuate itself.

Electoral politics in Russia have therefore been a distinctive mix of quasi-elections and referendums. Votes have had a plebiscitary character in that they have focused as much on the nature of the political order as on the renewal of the personnel of an existing system; constitutional politics have not yet given way to 'normal' politics. The plebiscitary nature of Russian democracy became entrenched as public opinion was manipulated to consolidate the rule of strong leaders in Moscow and the regions. Representative democracy, in which elections lead to the transfer of power from one group or another, was thereby undermined. The institutional basis for this type of electoralism was the powerful presidency, which discounted strong parties and weakened the role of parliament.

Despite the flaws, electoral politics have had a tangible effect by becoming the main form of social contestation, reducing the typically Russian contest of ideological absolutes. In the 1990s, the old struggle between 'Westernisers' and 'Slavophiles' was echoed in the tension between 'Atlanticists' and 'Eurasianists', while the binary structure of politics was reflected at first in the struggle between 'democrats' and 'partocrats', and later between 'democrats' and 'red-browns'. Elections became one of the primary form of political mobility, bringing new people into political life; people who in one form or another reflected real social interests.[75] This was over-shadowed, however, by the ability of the presidential regime to co-opt personnel and resources in ways that by-passed the electoral process.

This did not prevent a relatively high turnout over the years (see Table 7.6), suggesting a popular commitment to the democratic process. After a decline in

Table 7.6 Electoral turnout

Election or referendum	Turnout (%)
Soviet parliamentary election, 26 March 1989	89.8
Russian parliamentary elections, 4/18 March 1990	77.0
Referendum on renewed Union, 17 March 1991	75.4
Presidential election, 12 June 1991	74.7
Referendum of 25 April 1993	64.5
Duma election and referendum, 12 December 1993	54.8
Duma election, 17 December 1995	64.4
Presidential election: 16 June 1996 (first round)	69.8
Presidential election: 3 July 1996 (second round)	68.9
Duma election, 19 December 1999	61.7
Presidential election, 26 March 2000	68.7

turnout between 1989 and 1993, turnout rose to 64.5 per cent in the December 1995 parliamentary elections and then averaged 68 per cent in the 1996 presidential elections before falling to 61 per cent in 1999. Changes in turnout are not spread equally across the political spectrum. Communist voters, who tend to be older, are the most committed voters (it having been compulsory in the Soviet period), thus a low turnout works to the advantage of the left. By contrast, the higher the turnout, the better the liberals do since the vote for the communists is relatively stable. This rule was confirmed in the 1999 Duma elections.

The electoral system and its reform

In the mixed system introduced in 1993, to recap, half the seats to the new 450-member State Duma were elected by the traditional first-past-the-post single-member districts (SMDs), but the other half were elected from party-lists (PL) according to a weighted system of proportional representation. In order to be eligible to stand a party or bloc required at least 100,000 nominations, with no more than 15,000 signatures drawn from any one of Russia's eighty-nine regions and republics; the bloc or party had to have demonstrable support in at least seven regions or republics. This provision was designed to stimulate the creation of a national party system, to overcome the proliferation of small parties, and to avoid the dominance of Moscow. To enter parliament on the PL system a party had to take at least 5 per cent of the national vote, with the whole country considered one giant constituency.

The electoral system was manipulated by reformers to promote specific goals, above all to encourage the development of a multi-party system.[76] The mixed proportional and constituency system, according to Victor Sheinis, one of its main architects, would not only foster a party system but also avoid 'an atomised parliament with factions like those we have today, representing no more than interest clubs'.[77] According to Ryabov, the proportional elections played a positive role 'in the development of the parties and movements themselves, assisting the development of multipartyism in Russia'.[78] Others, however, argued that the electoral system worked more to strengthen parliamentary factions than parties.[79] As we shall see in discussing party development (Chapter 8), while voter alignments may have remained relatively stable, the fluidity in the parties available to express their preferences forced voters to choose anew in each electoral cycle.[80]

Electoral systems are not neutral institutions but reflect society itself and the aspirations of the political elite. The dual form of the Russian electoral system reflects the divisions at the heart of the process of political transformation. A fully proportional system is usually designed to ensure the sovereignty of parliamentary representation and its pre-eminence over the power of the executive. A majoritarian system, on the other hand, prioritises governmental stability and the relative autonomy of the executive. While proportional representation tries to *represent* the plurality of needs, demands and interests in society, a first-past-the-post electoral system seeks to *constrain* them in the name of governmental stability.[81] Russia tried to achieve both in one fell swoop, but failed effectively to achieve either. A majoritarian system is intended to achieve a parliamentary majority, but in Russia such a majority was to a degree irrelevant since the government, appointed by the president, was not directly accountable to parliament and was not based on the ability to muster a stable majority in parliament. Other than confirming the president's nomination for prime minister, the Duma's role was limited to legislative activity and the adoption of the budget. Proportional systems tend to lead to the fragmentation of parliamentary representation, and it is for this reason that the 5 per cent representation was introduced in Russia.

Although in the run-up to the 1999 election there was much talk of changing the electoral system, above all by abolishing the PL system and replacing it with all 450 deputies being elected from SMDs, a reform favoured by the presidency, only relatively minor changes were made to the electoral law.[82] The main change was to ensure on a sliding scale that at least 50 per cent of the votes cast in the PL part of the ballot were represented in the Duma. The scrutiny of candidates and of signatures for the party-lists were made much more rigorous. Blocs could opt to lodge a deposit with the CEC rather than collecting the requisite 200,000 signatures, no more than 14,000 of which were permitted from any one region. Some two-thirds of parties and electoral associations, and a significant number of candidates in single-mandate constituencies, opted to pay a deposit rather than collect signatures.[83] The personal finances of candidates were to be examined in greater detail than ever before.[84]

Following the election, the eighteen blocs that fell below the 2 per cent PL threshold had to repay the Central Electoral Commission funds allocated during the campaign and compensate the print and state and private electronic media for the free media exposure granted to all blocs on the ballot. In the event of non-payment they were barred from future elections. Having gained more than 2 per cent, 'Communists, Toilers of Russia – for the Soviet Union' and 'Women of Russia' did not have to refund what amounted to considerable sums. The seventeen blocs that chose to place a monetary deposit to register for the ballot instead of collecting signatures and gained less than 3 per cent lost their deposits. The law on political parties adopted in 2001 had a profound impact on the electoral process, allowing only registered parties to stand and changing electoral finances (see Chapter 8).

Direct democracy: referendums

The direct appeal to the people is a two-edged sword. While on the one hand a referendum may be seen as a useful supplementary tool to normal elections to enhance popular participation and democratic accountability, the use of the plebiscite is also the traditional instrument used by authoritarian leaders to enhance their powers, defeat their enemies and to legitimate their rule. The referendum is often used to achieve popular support for a new constitutional order, but in the post-Soviet world it has also been used to establish authoritarian presidencies. The referendum has been used as an instrument of simple majoritarianism in the name of 'the people', prioritising the majority at a particular moment over the enduring values of the 'conceptual' people whose sovereignty is embedded in democratic constitutions. Plebiscites have a powerful authoritarian potential and have been used by dictators throughout the twentieth century, notably by Hitler. The referendum was also used by Charles de Gaulle to legitimise the adoption of a new French constitution in 1958, and then once again in October 1962 on the direct election of the president in an act that was technically unconstitutional.

The use of sovereignty referendums provided a legal and democratic means for the right of self-determination to be exercised in the disintegrating communist federations. A number of post-communist countries conducted 'sovereignty referendums' ('*pouvoir constituant*') on the core issue of independence: nine out of fifteen Union republics held these before the disintegration of the USSR in December 1991, and four of the seceding republics in Yugoslavia. In the USSR these were balanced by Gorbachev's 'anti-secession' referendum of 17 March 1991, boycotted by six of the most eager secessionists: Estonia, Latvia, Lithuania, Moldova, Armenia and Georgia – without Abkhazia. Like Tatarstan, Chechnya lacked Union republic status and was thus not considered an appropriate vessel in which to conduct a sovereignty referendum. In a referendum in 1995, 80 per cent of the Transdniestrian population voted for the region to become an independent member of the CIS. No such right exists in the Russian Federation today (or in the rump Yugoslav Federation), and thus could not be applied to regulate the Chechen (or Kosovo) crises.

The options for Chechnya, moreover, were further limited by the process of adopting the Russian constitution and then the great difficulty in introducing changes to that document. As we have seen, Russia's 'constituent referendum' on the adoption of its constitution took place on 12 December 1993 in the wake of the violent struggle between the president and parliament. In Russia modifications to the constitution are exceptionally difficult and cannot be achieved by the relatively simple mechanism of a modifying referendum. As noted, its core chapters (1, 2 and 9) require the convocation of a Constitutional Assembly, while the rest have to be approved by a super-majority of each house of the Federal Assembly and the legislatures of at least two-thirds of the regions of Russia. Special provisions govern amendments to Chapter 65, dealing with the composition of the Russian Federation; this is covered by a federal constitutional law.

Historical experience suggests that the sovereignty referendum is a poor instrument for determining the fate of a state.[85] Who are the relevant people who should be asked their opinion of the matter? A vote in the larger state on whether a small area should be allowed to secede is as problematic as a vote held only in that small area. Just as in Canada, where the question of who should decide the fate of Quebec remains unresolved, so too in Russia and other post-Soviet states the *pouvoir constituant* is precisely what is at issue. The vote for autonomy in the two Estonian cities of Narva and Sillamse in 1993, dominated by Russians, was declared invalid by the Estonian parliament. Thus, the referendum is an inadequate means for determining whether a people are entitled to self-determination. The problem, however, is that no other methods, such as adjudication by an international agency or representative body, is any better. This is indeed a circle that cannot be squared by formal normative methods but is usually resolved by political luck or force.

Russia's first experience of the referendum was in the dying days of the Soviet Union. In a desperate attempt to save the crumbling USSR, on 17 March 1991 Gorbachev appealed above the heads of the warring elites and national groupings to the people. The result of the referendum, the first and last ever held in the USSR, demonstrated strong support for the continuation of the Union (see Chapter 1), but it also revealed just how vertically segmented this support was: as we have seen, six republics refused to take part. In the post-Soviet world the referendum has repeatedly been used by incumbent presidents against hostile legislatures. The first attempts in this direction were by Yeltsin, who in the referendum of 25 March 1993 sought to go over the head of the recalcitrant CPD to the people. Although he gained renewed legitimacy, the institutional context did not allow the crisis to be resolved in this way. Following the forced dissolution of the Congress in September–October 1993, Yeltsin called a referendum on the adoption of a new constitution and achieved a contested majority for the founding document of the new state.

Other presidents have been more successful. Aleksandr Lukashenko in Belarus achieved his populist presidentialism by plebiscites on 14 May 1995 and 24 November 1996. In Kazakhstan president Nursultan Nazarbaev undermined the fragile independence of parliament by adopting a new constitution on 30 August 1995. In Moldova a referendum on 23 May 1999 called by President Lucinschi sought to transform a mixed parliamentary-presidential system into a fully presidential one. In response, parliament voted to downgrade drastically the role of the presidency, and now Moldova is effectively a parliamentary republic. President Leonid Kuchma in Ukraine referred six questions to the people on 16 April 2000 to weaken what he considered an obstructive parliament (the *Verkhovna Rada*) and transform Ukraine into a presidential republic. Thus, the referendum is a powerful instrument in the hands of presidents seeking enhanced powers, but occasionally their plans are thwarted or reversed. It should also be noted that in a number of countries (Belarus, Kazakhstan, Turkmenistan and Tajikistan) the referendum has been used to prolong the term in office of incumbent presidents, especially when there are constitutional prohibitions on being re-elected twice.

In Russia the Federal Constitutional Law on the Referendum came into force on 10 November 1995, stipulating that at least half of registered voters must participate for the referendum to be valid.[86] To initiate a referendum 2 million votes must be collected, to be verified by the CEC. In 2000, environmental groups collected 2.5 million signatures on a petition to hold a national referendum on Putin's decision to import spent nuclear fuel, but the CEC disallowed over 600,000 signatures thus leaving the total just short of what was required.

Explaining electoral behaviour

Numerous theories seek to understand elections, in post-communist societies and elsewhere.[87] The classic approach is to suggest that voting behaviour is associated with socio-economic divisions and interests, but this can hardly be applied (yet) to Russian society.[88] Simplistic rational-choice theory would suggest that governments that deliver the goods get rewarded, whereas those held responsible for poor economic performance (on a national or personal level) get punished. In Russian conditions this would mean that any government for the forseeable future would be deeply unpopular. More nuanced approaches seek to incorporate belief systems and political commitments into voting behaviour, the role of negative or 'protest' voting, as well as the problem of 'tactical' voting.

Duma elections belie the optimism of those who see post-communist Russia in terms of a unified democratisation process.[89] The already tenuous concept of parliamentary government was further discredited. The rise of nationalist senti-ments in 1993 and of neo-communist restorationism in 1995 reinforced national democracy as the predominant ideology of the regime. The brute struggle for the succession in 1999 trampled media impartiality underfoot. The presidential elec-tions, moreover, appeared to reinforce the role of charismatic authority while undermining the part that democratic institutions could play in the new polity. Ballots offered simple alternatives, reducing the political choices facing the voter: communism or democracy; Soviet power or Yeltsin's democracy; the continuation of reforms or the renewed dominance of the old managerial classes; the president or Congress; Yeltsin or Khasbulatov (or Zyuganov). With the dissolution of external threats to democratic transformation, the regime sought to contain this danger from within the democratic process itself.

Post-communist elections in Russia might well reflect the immaturity of the Russian electorate and its susceptibility to demagogic promises, but they also reflect a more profound institutional immaturity of the democratic system and of political and social processes in their entirety. Crisis appears to be the normal state of Russian politics, and institutional reorganisation typical of the system. As for society, the revolutionary implications of the fall of communist power and the change in property relations have not yet given birth to a stable new class or ordered hierarchy of elite privileges and societal values. The whole concept of 'support' appears friable and susceptible to rapid changes; and, by the same token, 'opposition' to a large degree cannot be taken as a stable political position but a reflection of temporary antipathies. Elections, nevertheless, have stabilised the political system, providing peaceful forms for ideological contestation.

Conclusion

In Chapter 3 we introduced the concept of displaced sovereignty, and in this chapter we have noted that there remains a question over the degree to which popular sovereignty has been achieved and, indeed, over the very definition of popular sovereignty in a system where the president is so powerful and where elections can be reduced to mere electoralism. In a presidential system there is no direct relationship between parliamentary elections and the formation of the government; Duma elections tended to be subsumed into the struggle for the presidency. The strong vote for the CPRF and for Zyuganov personally in June 1996 and March 2000 suggests not only disaffection with the reform process but a larger alienation from the post-August 1991 political order. Although taking full advantage of the benefits conferred by incumbency, Yeltsin's re-election in July 1996 reflected more than electoral manipulation but the emergence of a solid constituency in support of the new order – or, at least, opposed to the restoration of the old. Thus, the elections of the 1990s revealed a polarised society. It was only with the election of Putin in March 2000 that these divisions began to be transcended, although whether his victory represented democratic consolidation is unclear.

8 Party development

The stability of any constitution depends not so much on its form as on the social and economic forces that stand behind and support it; and if the form of the constitution corresponds to the balance of those forces, their support maintains it unchanged.

(James Bryce)[1]

Political parties play a fundamental role in modern representative democracy.[2] They connect civil and political society, advance the perceived interests of individuals, groups and social strata while aiming consciously to develop these constituencies, and provide a link between civil society and the state, espousing the claims of the one and enforcing the rules of the other.[3] In post-communist Russia parties only marginally fulfilled these functions. The relative independence of government from both parliamentary oversight and party control, and the emergence of a powerful presidential system based on the apparatus of the state, marginalised the political role of organised social interests. Trapped between an ill-formed state system and a rudimentary civil society, the nascent representative system was unable to assert itself against other political actors like the military and security apparatus, oligarchical financial and commercial interests, regional governors, and the government itself. Rather than parties generating the political dynamism that formed government, the regime itself tended to take the initiative in party formation. This chapter will examine the tortuous process of party development in Russia, noting that a multiplicity of parties does not of itself demonstrate the existence of a functioning party *system*. As we have seen in Chapter 7, Russia's electoral politics focused on parties, and they then provided structure to the politics of the Duma itself (Chapter 6). Despite all the odds, parties have become an essential element in the Russian political scene. This chapter will trace this development and serve as a conclusion to this part of the book.

Stages of party development

Party development in Russia evolved through four main phases. The first was the insurgency stage of movements and *neformaly* (informal) organisations accompanying the dissolution of the power of the Communist Party of the Soviet Union (CPSU) during *perestroika* (1985–91). The second stage was the period of constitutional crisis between August 1991 and October 1993, when the presidency and parliament struggled for supremacy. In the absence of elections and the fight for political power between rival elite factions, we have characterised this period as a peculiar sort of 'phoney democracy'. The third stage was inaugurated by the dissolution of the old Russian legislature and the events of 3–4 October 1993. This period, lasting up to Yeltsin's resignation in December 1999, was characterised by a contradictory dual adaptation. Political leaders and organised interests adapted themselves to constitutional and democratic mass politics, largely renouncing the street politics of the insurgency and 'phoney democracy' phases. Democratic forms and constitutional norms, however, were adapted to the needs of the political leadership (the regime), thus undermining the real impact that organised political interests could have on the conduct of government and the shaping of policy. The hybrid nature of the regime, both democratic and elitist-oligarchical, was strongly in evidence. In the fourth phase, accompanying Putin's presidency from early 2000, the role of political parties was formalised and the policy process broadened, but now popular representation was constrained by statist-governmentalism. We will examine all four phases – insurgency, 'phoney democracy', dual adaptation and formalisation – in more detail below.

The insurgency phase

The dissolution of communist power was accompanied by the emergence of movements covering social, environmental, gender and other issues, as well as the formation of the first political popular fronts and proto-parties.[4] The tumultuous proliferation of *neformaly* and an independent press reflected a distinctive type of negative popular mobilisation against the old regime, a mobilisation that proved very different to channel into positive civic endeavour. The politics spawned by the insurgency phase was untidy and anarchic yet they undermined political cultural theories stressing Russian passivity and innate authoritarianism.[5] The integration of this upsurge of civic activism into a new polity, however, remained problematical.[6] Much of this activity was united by little other than its anti-systemic character, devoted to overcoming the dominance of the CPSU. When it came to a positive programme, Russian society proved deeply fragmented, quite apart from its inability to impose accountability on the authorities and even on its own leaders.

The Leninist-Stalinist terror and decades of stifling one-party rule ruptured continuity with the past. Pre-revolutionary Russia was characterised by hundreds of societies and clubs, and this rich associational life continued into the early Soviet period but thereafter dried up to the degree that only three social organisations were created in the Brezhnev years.[7] Early studies of the *neformaly* blurred the distinction between political and social activities – and for good reason: *any* autonomous social activity represented a repudiation of the old 'administrative-command' system (to use the term of Gavriil Popov, mayor of Moscow between June 1991 and June 1992). Gorbachev's model of reform communism (which he called *perestroika*), however, sought to constrain this autonomy.[8]

The establishment of the Democratic Union (DS – *Demokraticheskii soyuz*) on 9 May 1988 can be taken as the beginning of the renewed era of multi-party politics in Russia. Rejecting Gorbachev's attempts to expand the base of the Party regime by incorporating new social forces, the party declared its outright opposition to Soviet power and its allegiance to a 'peaceful democratic revolution'.[9] The party adopted a strongly anti-communist line, favouring the introduction of Western-style liberal democracy and market economy. Many of the DS's campaigns at first appeared blasphemous but soon entered the vocabulary of the public and then became official policy. It was the DS that first raised the Russian tricolour at the Kazan Cathedral in St Petersburg and Pushkin Square in Moscow, and indeed which first launched the campaign to rename Leningrad. After the *coup*, the DS insisted that the revolution was still to come, that a change of symbols had taken place but not the revolution of democracy itself. They insisted that popular consciousness was permeated by a totalitarian mentality and had simply trans-ferred its loyalty from the Bolsheviks to the 'good Tsar' Yeltsin and had still not attained a sense of civic responsibility.[10] The problems attending the development of the party, like poor organisation, leadership splits and low membership, were to be mirrored by countless other parties later.

In the other republics the informal movement took the form of popular fronts, with Sajudis in Lithuania one of the largest representing aspirations for national autonomy and, later, independence. These popular fronts were catch-all single-issue movements and acted as the substitute for political parties. In Russia the absence of an all-encompassing national issue meant that popular fronts were weak and no single movement for the whole nation emerged. Democracy took the place of nationality politics as a mobilising force, and as mass electoral politics emerged Democratic Russia (*Demrossiya*) came the closest to covering all of Russia. *Demrossiya* was formally established in January 1990 as an umbrella organisation to fight the March elections, and at its formal inaugural congress on 20–1 October some eighteen social movements and nine political parties came together. *Demrossiya* played a leading part in maintaining the pressure on Gorbachev in the year before the *coup* and its candidate, Yeltsin, emerged triumphant in the presiden-tial elections of June 1991. After the *coup*, however, Burbulis was the only major figure from *Demrossiya* offered an important political post, and the rest had to be satisfied with jobs in the localities or in administration.

The insurgency phase in Russia was both shorter in time and more anarchic than in most of Eastern Europe.[11] The ending of the CPSU's guaranteed monopoly on power in March 1990 was followed by a wave of new parties, formalised by the Soviet Law on Public Associations passed on 9 October 1990, which placed polit-ical parties and independent trade unions on a legal footing. By late 1990, there were at least 457 political or politicised organisations in Russia, confronting analysts with major problems of classification.[12] Many of the new parties were barely distinguishable from the burgeoning mass of *neformaly*, but by early 1991 Russia had some hundred organisations that could be recognised as political parties, of which only about twenty recruited in other republics.[13] The problem soon became one not of the lack of parties but one of 'over-partification', hundreds of small groups covering every known, and some newly discovered, nook and cranny of the political and social spectrum, and some several times over. Broadly speaking, up to August 1991 Russian politics were characterised by a bipolar struggle between communist and 'democratic' movements, with the embry-onic national and patriotic movements torn between the two.

The end of the CPSU's monopoly allowed informal movements to take on more structured forms but they remained stamped by the politics of insurgency. Elections before August 1991, and in particular those in March 1990, were not fought between different social and political groups on the basis of alternative platforms and social groups defending their interests, but rather as voting alliances against a discredited regime (see Chapter 7).[14] The onset of electoral politics *preceded* the emergence of a multi-party system, something that distorted the whole process of party formation. Elections were dominated by the anti-politics of opposition to the communist regime, and movements were largely unable to make the transition from mobilisational to representational politics.[15] Practically all respondents in a survey of middle-level *Demrossiya* activists stressed that the movement prospered because of its commitment to the removal of the CPSU from power and the transition to a new social order.[16] Thus, unity in the insurgency phase was forged by the negative programme of opposition to the communist regime, in favour of greater civic freedom and a looser form of federation, but failed to define positive political and social programmes.

The informal movement was only one route of party formation in this period, with others including groups emerging from within the CPSU itself, openly anti-communist alliances and the 'revolutionary movement' represented by DS and Democratic Russia.[17] All reflected a rather simplistic bipolarity since the struggle against the CPSU (from within and beyond) facilitated the emergence of a multitude of pseudo-parties. While the term proto-parties suggests a natural evolution to full-blooded partyhood, pseudo-parties were caricatures of the conditions in which multi-party politics came to Russia. Dozens of parties emerged and scored easy victories with the minimum of organisational or intellectual resources against the debilitated CPSU and the decaying partocratic system. Who needed a defined programme when the old system provided such a vulnerable target? The new parties were marked by:

> numerical weakness, weak and amorphous organisational structures (particularly at the local level), regionalism, ideological vagueness and a negativism bordering on populism, and low-calibre leaders who, for the sake of self-affirmation, actively set themselves up against other parties, even ones that were ideologically close to them.[18]

The emerging multi-party system was highly fragmented: if the process within the CPSU can be described as from party to faction, then the larger process can be described as from faction to party, a transformation that very few groups actually achieved. There remained a gulf between insurgent political elites and the political system. This gulf was reproduced once a section of the insurgent elite, headed by Yeltsin, came to power in August 1991 in an independent Russia.

'Phoney democracy': August 1991–October 1993

The fate of parties and the structure of party politics depends on the timing of elections and the type of electoral system adopted. The electoral process is itself a major stimulus for the development of parties and a party system, and the absence of a general election up to December 1993 inhibited further democratisation. Parties in this period, quite simply, had nothing to do. In the absence of elections most political associations barely qualified to be termed parties, failing to meet Sartori's basic definition of a political party as 'any political group that presents at elections, and is capable of placing through elections, candidates for public office'.[19] In the absence of elections a peculiar sort of 'phoney democracy' emerged as the regime born of the August *coup* consolidated itself.

By 20 February 1992, thirty-eight political organisations had been registered with the Russian Ministry of Justice,[20] and by April of that year, according to Stankevich, there were 820 registered public associations, including twenty-five political parties, encompassing over 300,000 people.[21] By May 1993, the number of organisations registered with the Ministry of Justice had risen to 1,800.[22] The new parties, however, palpably failed to become the basis of the new political system, and Russia moved from being a one-party state to a non-party state, albeit accompanied by numerous pseudo-parties. The onset of pluralism in Russia was not the same thing as the establishment of a multi-party system, and instead politics focused on the struggle between institutions (above all between parliament and the president) rather than between parties in parliament. The period was characterised by a distinctive type of dual power in which a presidential apparatus was superimposed on the nascent parliamentary system, with little co-ordination between the two. Parties were left hanging in the air with little constructive purpose.

Maurice Duverger stresses the electoral and parliamentary origins of modern political parties,[23] and in the absence of either the development of a multi-party system stagnated. The elimination of the CPSU and the ensuing vacuum opened up new political spaces but failed to trigger political mobilisation. Highly fragmented political parties divided over political, economic and nationality policy. Against the background of the kaleidoscopic formation, division and reformation of *groupuscules* calling themselves parties, a broadly bipolar system emerged in which 'democrats' stood against various nationalist, patriotic and communist splinter organisations dubbed 'red-browns', the alliance of communist rejectionists and nationalist reactionaries. The ideological homogeneity of the insurgency phase now gave way to programmatic divergence over such issues as the powers of the presidency, relations with the 'near abroad' and, above all, economic reform. Programmes began to reflect the realities of contemporary Russian politics rather than idealised versions of abstract transitional processes to 'the market' or of 'rejoining world civilisation'.[24] Anti-communist unity now gave way to polarisation not only in the content of programmes, as the umbrella 'democratic' movement ceded ground to patriotic and nationalist organisations, but also in the 'irreconcilable' style of politics that came to predominate at this time.

The pseudo-parties had been sustained by the conjunctural circumstances attending the dissolution of communist power and not by their popular appeal, leadership qualities or organisational resources. The social base of the 'democratic' movement was extremely heterogeneous, including intellectuals, security officials and miners, united only, according to Popov, by their 'hatred for the bankrupt CPSU regime'.[25] The failure of social movements to 'particise' themselves, notably in the case of *Demrossiya* and also the Civic Union later (see below), is one of the distinctive features of the transition in Russia.[26] The disappearance of the CPSU removed the incentive for the 'opposition' to unite, while much of the old CPSU elite made a smooth transition and became part of the new establishment. A gulf remained between the parties emerging from below and official representation in the legislature, with parliamentary and popular organisations operating on separate levels, inhibiting the development of distinct party identities and organisations.

Attempts to create a political bloc in support of Yeltsin and his reforms repeatedly failed. A number of parties were established in 1993 in anticipation of general elections, notably Gaidar's Russia's Choice, representing the 'party of power', Sergei Shakhrai's Party of Russian Unity and Concord (PRES), which adopted a moderately critical stance even though some of its leaders were in government, and a bloc bringing together 'oppositional democrats' headed by Yavlinskii, Yurii Boldyrev and Vladimir Lukin, the Russian ambassador to the United States, to form a group based on their initials, Yabloko (Apple).

In the centre the All-Russian Union for Renewal (*Obnovlenie*) was formed in June 1992 by Arkadii Vol'skii, the chairman of the Russian Union of Industrialists and Entrepreneurs (RUIE, formerly the Scientific Industrial Union), and was soon dubbed the 'party of managers'. Renewal sought to act as a coalition of the managers of state enterprises, the new private entrepreneurs, and the chief executives of local government. On 21 June 1992, Vol'skii's Renewal joined with Alexander Rutskoi's People's Party of Free Russia (PPFR), formerly the Communists for Democracy faction formed in March 1991, and Nikolai Travkin's Democratic Party of Russia (DPR) to establish the Civic Union, a 'constructive' and 'loyal opposition' bloc against not Yeltsin but Gaidar's economics team whose policies, they insisted, could provoke a social explosion.[27] The Civic Union favoured a slower and more socially oriented approach to economic reform.[28] The group was wary of the West, favoured greater integration within the CIS and adopted what they called a broadly Eurasianist perspective.[29] The Civic Union was not an ideological alliance but a pragmatic attempt to rally the opposition of the centre. Vol'skii hoped to convert the RUIE into a fully fledged Industrial Party, but hesitated out of fear of creating 'yet another flash-in-the-pan party formed "from the top"'.[30] In the event, following a disappointing performance at the Seventh Congress of People's Deputies in December 1992, the Civic Union withered away, although the RUIE remains one of the most important interest groups in Russian politics.

The national-patriot movement covered a wide spectrum from national-socialists at one extreme to democratically minded Russian 'statists' at the other. A percipient article at the time argued, 'We should not fool ourselves: this movement will inevitably come to power, if only because it is the only political force which played no part in the crimes, mistakes and oversights of recent years.' Just as Yeltsin had overcome Gorbachev because of his intuitive understanding of the mood of Russia, so the national-patriotic forces would triumph because of their understanding that Russia was tired of humiliation and of experiments, whether of the communist sort or those copied from Western models.[31] The analysis was accurate but premature: Putin's programme of patriotic statism was precisely a response to these concerns.

The national-patriots weakened their own position by emphasising one strand of Russian statism at the expense of the other. Their stress on a greater Russia, encompassing other Slavic areas, appeared not only futile but dangerous as well, carrying within it the potential for war with Ukraine, Kazakhstan and others: the slaughter that accompanied Serbia's claims to defend the rights of Serbs in Croatia and Bosnia by incorporating them into a 'greater Serbia' stood as an awful warning of what could happen in the former USSR. From December 1991, Yeltsin began to talk of a 'red–brown' coalition between rejectionist communists and revanchist Russian nationalists. Such an anti-Yeltsin coalition did indeed begin to take shape and presented a radical challenge to the August settlement. They had a cause, the rights of Russians 'abroad', the bowing to the West, the alleged economic incompetence of Gaidar's government and the catastrophic fall in standards of living and levels of production.

They were weakened, however, by the tendency to drift towards irreconcilable extremism.[32] The leader of the Russian National Assembly (*Russkii obshchenatsionalnyi sobor*, RONS), the former KGB general Alexander Sterligov, for example argued that the seven years of *perestroika* had completed the seventy-year process of the 'total destruction of the life of the Russian people and its statehood', and sought 'by constitutional means to overthrow the present government of national betrayal'.[33] The nationalists adopted ever more extreme positions, calling not only for the overthrow of the government but by mid-1992 challenged the president himself. The creation of the National Salvation Front (NSF) signalled a deepening of political polarisation. Established at a founding congress of some 3,000 communists and nationalists on 24 October 1992, the NSF brought together some of the more irreconcilable nationalists.[34] The NSF was declared unconstitutional by Yeltsin on 28 October 1992, the first political movement to be banned in Russia since the *coup*. On 12 February 1993, the Constitutional Court lifted the ban and the NSF went on to lead the military resistance to the dissolution of parliament in September–October 1993.

A distinctive mix of great Soviet patriotism, populism and Russian nationalism was propounded by Zhirinovskii, leader of the clearly misnamed Liberal Democratic Party of Russia (LDPR). At its founding congress on 31 March 1990, Zhirinovskii, a 44-year old lawyer working in a publishing house, had been elected leader. He had been born in Alma Ata (then called Verny), the capital of Kazakhstan, and like many from the periphery was more of a nationalist than those living in the metropolis. Zhirinovskii made much of the fact that he was one of the few Russian leaders who had never been a member of the Communist Party, though he apparently worked closely with the security establishment. His programme in the presidential elections of June 1991 was a simple one: to cut the price of vodka, to restore Russia's greatness by renaming the USSR (including the Baltic republics) Russia, and to keep Soviet troops in Eastern Europe until 'Russia' was ready for their return. This programme attracted 6 million voters, some 7.8 per cent of the electorate. He went on to attack Yeltsin for pursuing an 'anti-national, anti-Russian policy', and averred that the majority of Russians were in favour of dictatorship and called for the restoration of the Russian empire, firstly within the borders of the former USSR and later to encompass the former Tsarist empire, including Poland, Finland and Alaska.[35] Zhirinovskii directed his appeal to disaffected sections of society threatened by marketisation, and part of the business community who valued stability above democracy. The LDPR kept its distance from the maelstrom of nationalist movements and was able to take advantage of the political vacuum created by the destruction of many militant nationalist movements in October 1993 to score his apparent triumph in the elections of December 1993.

Communists represented the fourth main tendency. The fall of communist power was followed by a debate over whether the CPSU had been a party at all or a 'quasi-state organisation that concentrated all the basic functions of power in its hands'?[36] A group of 36 Russian MPs appealed to the Constitutional Court to adjudicate the legality of Yeltsin's three decrees issued between 23 August and 6 November 1991, banning the CPSU in Russia and confiscating its property.[37] A counter-petition by a group of Russian MPs led by Rumyantsev claimed that the Party's activities had been subversive and illegal, 'usurping state power and undermining state sovereignty that belongs exclusively to the people', and thus that the ban had been constitutional.[38] The Court on 26 May 1992 ruled that the two petitions would be considered together, and the hearings on the legality of the three decrees opened on 7 July 1992 and soon turned into a trial of the Party's activities since October 1917. The presidential team argued that the CPSU had not been a party but a state organisation, and therefore not the courts but the president had the right to decide its fate.[39] On 30 November 1992 the Court ruled that Yeltsin had acted lawfully in banning the CPSU's ruling bodies, but not its local branches. In effect, the Party was divided into two: the local membership and the governing bodies dominated by *apparatchiki*. The latter, as Yeltsin asserted, had become entwined with the state and were illegal; but the mass of the rank-and-file membership had been perfectly legitimate members of a political organisation and were entitled to renew their activities.[40]

Following the Court's ambivalent ruling Valerii Kuptsov, the last leader of the CP RSFSR, insisted that the Party would start reorganising and called for Yeltsin's impeachment. The Communist Party of the Russian Federation (CPRF) came back to life on 13–14 February 1993 at a conference not far from Moscow. Four of the successor parties attended, including Roy Medvedev's Socialist Party of Working People (SPWP) and Alexei Prigarin's Union of Communists, and the whole session was presided over by Ivan Rybkin, organiser of the Communists of Russia parliamentary fraction. Old-style Stalinists and pensioners were well represented, but the words 'of the Russian Federation' in the party's name signalled its recognition of existing borders. Gennadii Zyuganov, long associated with the Russian nationalist wing of the movement and formerly leader of the so-called 'Committee of the National-Patriotic Forces of Russia' and author of 'A Word to the People' (the manifesto of the *coup*), was elected leader. Viktor Anpilov's militant Russian Communist Workers' Party (RCWP) refused to join, and Nina Andreeva's Stalinist All-Union Communist Party of Bolsheviks (VKPB) also kept its distance, but even without them the CPRF soon eclipsed all other parties. The CPRF transcended the politics of insurgency and drew on reserves of organisational and political experience matched by no other. It claimed to be the official successor to the CPSU, and thus hoped to have some of its property restored by the courts. Rejecting the calls of some irreconcilable oppositionists to boycott the December 1993 elections, Zyuganov led the party to a respectable third place (see table 7.2). The CPRF became Russia's largest party, with a membership of over half a million, and became the main opposition party.

In the phoney democracy phase parties neither guided the president nor formed the government, and parliament and the parties in it were marginalised. Parties fulfilled the communicative and link functions between the political elite and the people only fitfully. The failure to integrate parties into the operation of the political system undermined the stability of the new democratic institutions and forced reliance on a supra-party technocratic ideology of democratic and market reforms from above. The absence of a multi-party *system* impeded the development of serious parties, but at the same time the absence of serious *parties* inhibited the development of a multi-party system. Elements of phoney democracy were to become an enduring feature of the Russian political system.

The dual adaptation stage: December 1993–December 1999

The adaptation stage was marked by the adoption of a new constitution and the first genuine national multi-party elections of 12 December 1993. The electoral system (Chapter 7) was designed to encourage the development of a multi-party system, but did so only partially. The pseudo-parties of the earlier periods were now faced with the hard school of an election in which their inflated claims of support were finally put to the test; few withstood the challenge and most faded into the obscurity whence they had come. The adoption of the hybrid electoral system only revealed more starkly the fault lines in Russian society. Thirteen parties and electoral blocs negotiated the hurdles to stand in the election, and of these only eight cleared the 5 per cent threshold. The election contributed to the development of parties by forcing the development of organisations and alliances, while the adoption of the constitution finally provided a stable institutional framework in which parties could operate. The hasty formation of impromptu and often unprincipled electoral associations, however, can also be seen as disruptive of the process of party organisation and consolidation. The LDPR registered notable success in gaining fifty-nine of the 225 party-list seats, yet the organisation was less a party (with 40 per cent of its deputies not even members of the party) than a vehicle for Zhirinovskii's charismatic leadership.

A new generation of parties emerged, most of whom drew their provenance from earlier stages but adapted to the dramatically changed political climate. The consolidation of the party system as an integral part of Russian government proved problematical, but the characteristic feature of this period was the adaptation of political parties to the conventions of democratic electoral and parliamentary politics. The extremes of left and right were marginalised. However, the second aspect of this adaptation was less positive: to the exigencies of regime politics and the structures of power themselves.

The aim set by Popov earlier, to 'parliamentarianise' the opposition by offering them a forum away from their accustomed street politics, was only partially fulfilled.[41] The establishment of a viable parliamentary system created a forum in which party politics could flourish, but hopes that the elections would kick-start the party system, however, were only partially fulfilled. The presence of relatively small factions and groups in the Fifth Duma prevented the establishment of a stable majority, inhibited the development of parliamentary government and perpetuated the supra-party system of regime politics. Party factions were once again relatively fluid and deputies were marked by a lack of discipline. Many deputies elected on

the party-lists, moreover, were not even members of the parties they officially represented, notably in Zhirinovskii's LDPR, whose caucus in the Duma fell prey to
endless splits. The lack of correspondence between the composition of parliament
and the formation of the government, moreover, accentuated the fragmentation of
the Russian party system. The major centres of power were based on personalities,
many of whom were outside the parliamentary and party system altogether, and
within parties links between the leadership and membership were tenuous. Parties
were trapped between strong executive authority and an amorphous civil society.

To heal the wounds inflicted by the October events and to stabilise the political
situation, Yeltsin sponsored a Charter for Civic Accord, signed by 148 political,
trade union, religious and public figures on 28 April 1994.[42] The president
promised not to launch early parliamentary elections, while the signatories in return
promised not to demand early presidential elections, and a ban on strikes was to be
observed. Zhirinovskii signed up, but the opposition was notable by its absence,
with the CPRF and its close ally, the Agrarian Party, refusing to sign, while
Yavlinskii did not even attend the ceremony, regarding the whole exercise as pointless, 'imposing no obligations on anyone'.[43] The opposition, meanwhile, had
organised its own Accord for Russia, including the CPRF, the APR, Rutskoi, and
the former head of the Constitutional Court, Zor'kin. Both the oppositional
Accord for Russia and Civic Accord reflected the traditional pattern of 'supra-
party' bloc politics and harked back to the inclusive 'popular front" politics of the
insurgency phase; both were 'anti-party' in their very essence by seeking to replace
competitive multi-party politics by para-constitutional corporatist deals. By the end
of the year, in any case, Yeltsin quietly repudiated his Accord.

In the run-up to the parliamentary elections of December 1995, Russia's already
fragmented party system atomised even further. By May 1995, seventy-nine parties
had been registered by the Ministry of Justice to fight the elections, and by the time
the process was complete in late November forty-three groups were registered to
stand, making the ballot paper an extraordinarily thick document. All the familiar
features of post-communist party building were taken to new extremes: the
emphasis on personalities, amorphous and poorly drafted programmes, the de-
institutionalising influence of regional politics, the constant splitting and
sub-dividing of parties and factions, and the absence of party discipline. Although
the major players came from above, there was an enormous ferment of primary
activity in the wards, and the degree of grassroots democracy should not be
minimised. The campaign was marked by a novel professionalism, with numerous
image-making agencies at work and vigorous fund-raising activities. PR (in Russian
piar!), indeed, became one of the major growth industries and allowed many a
social scientist to prosper as they advised candidates and electoral blocs on what
they liked to call 'political technologies' and 'image making'.

It is against the background of a fragmented party scene that an attempt was
made to impose an ordered two-party system from above. The plan was to unite the
centre-right parties around a political bloc to be led by Chernomyrdin, while the
centre-left would be anchored around a movement led by Rybkin, the speaker of
the Duma. It soon became clear that Rybkin's bloc would not be much more than a
loose alliance of parties, losing even the support of his own APR, and it failed to
enter the Sixth Duma. Chernomyrdin's bloc fared rather better. At its founding

congress on 11 May 1995, the new party adopted the grand name of 'Russia Our Home' (*Nash dom Rossii*, NDR), dedicated to 'progress without shocks' and promising to lead Russia into an era of stability and strength. The energy lobby, and in particular Chernomyrdin's old fiefdom Gazprom, supported the new venture. Its key slogan was 'pragmatism', but the way the party was conceived and built suggested a new attempt at '*nomenklatura* democracy', a top-down attempt to secure the existing order.

The adaptation phase began to bring ideology, social interests and party structures into alignment. Russia remained distant from a real multi-party system, however, and as the dust settled on frenetic party formation and re-formation the country was left with only one genuine party – the Communist Party, inherited from the previous age. The CPRF under Zyuganov became one of the few genuine mass parties, with a membership of some 550,000, a strong if contradictory programme and a serious national organisation. This was reflected in its notable success in the December 1995 elections, coming top in the proportional part of the elections with 22.3 per cent of the vote, giving it ninety-nine seats in the Duma plus another fifty-eight single-member seats (see Table 7.2). The results of the 1995 election came as a surprise to many, above all the strength of the combined rejectionist vote (CPRF and LDPR). It was not clear whether the return of communists to influence in Russia was an indication of the failure of the democratic transition or evidence of its success. The 'centre' was anchored in the relatively disappointing vote for Russia Our Home, while Yabloko was the only 'democratic' party to enter the Sixth Duma.

Yavlinskii considered the victory of only four parties in the party-list contest in the December 1995 elections a sign that Russia had outgrown the 'infantile stage of multi-partyism'.[44] Popov noted that the general-democratic stage of the transformation was complete, the fundamentals of democracy had been introduced, and the first phase of privatisation was complete. More importantly, Russia's political configuration changed. The transition was based on an alliance between reformist sections of the Soviet bureaucracy and a programme drawn from liberal-Westernisers, marginalising the democratic movements born during the insurgency against communism. Now a new model began to emerge in which political regeneration from below and the regions, the emergence of a structured political space, and the fragmentation of the old elite allowed competition between formalised political programmes.

Although Yeltsin on several occasions floated the idea of establishing a presidential party, every time he fought shy of undertaking the organisational work required for such a venture. Instead he claimed to be president of all Russians. Attempts to unite the 'democratic' forces behind a single presidential candidate came to nothing, and instead in the 1996 presidential elections the organisational and financial resources of the presidency itself, allied with powerful 'oligarchs' to which the presidency then became indebted, were the key resource that ensured Yeltsin's re-election.

By the time of the December 1999 election, the situation had somewhat stabilised with twenty-six blocs standing and six entering parliament, including the newly-formed Unity (*Edinstvo*) organisation supporting Putin's presidential ambitions. Although the centre of Russian politics, rooted in marketising reforms, international integration and representative democracy, lacked convincing political representation, the adaptation phase had to a large degree universalised these policies, albeit without some of the liberal rhetoric of the earlier era. The frantic regrouping of parties in the adaptation phase, however, could not disguise the weakness of the party system and all forms of social representation.

The formalisation stage: January 2000–

Against this broad characterisation of the contemporary Russian party scene there were discernible tendencies transforming the fragmented and amorphous party scene into something approaching the emergence of a party system with effective parties, differentiated programmes and stable electorates. The formalisation phase, in which Putin sought to transcend Russia's historical contradictions and its contemporary political divisions, in the sphere of party politics was marked by differentiation, which took place in three ways.

- Frenetic party formation and re-formation continued, but the 1995 and 1999 elections distinguished a small group with representation in the Duma from the mass of pseudo-parties.
- The programmes and policies of this small group were now far more clearly differentiated along the classical political spectrum – the CPRF on the left, Unity and Luzhkov's Fatherland in the centre, Yabloko and the SPS on the centre right, and the LDPR on the nationalist right, although cross-cutting issues allowed alliances across the spectrum.
- Russian society itself began to develop a contoured political structure as class, societal and institutional interests, which in the Soviet era related to each other in non-political ways, now asserted their positions by employing the classical gamut of democratic instruments, above all parties.

Differentiation in the Russian population was reflected in more stable party alignment between demographic and economic groups. Yabloko, SPS, Women of Russia, Russia's Democratic Choice and the LDPR attracted younger people, while the Communists and Agrarians appealed to the older generation and the poor. People with little education preferred the Agrarians, LDPR and Communists, while SPS and Yabloko attracted the more highly educated. Reformist parties were more strongly represented in the capitals of Moscow and St Petersburg, while the APR dominated the villages, although the Communists had growing support, while liberals were rarely supported here. Many of the new generation of parties were now better funded and began to sink local roots, drawing on a well of consistent support with name and programme recognition. Parties began to mobilise their resources more effectively and to devise programmes that reflected Russia's genuine problems.

Although Putin's rise had been sponsored by Yeltsin, his policies and political style in many respects represented a repudiation of Yeltsinism as elitist-oligarchical rule gave way to statist-governmentalism. This was nowhere more true than in the sphere of party development. Putin came to power proclaiming the need for his government to have proper social support reflected in political organisation. On several occasions Putin argued that 'Russia needs a real multiparty system', not parties 'that represent only themselves, but rather...reflect the interests of large groups of society', which could 'shape the policies of the state'.[45] It appeared that this would take the form of a two- or three-party system, with Unity (a party that did not hide its aspiration to become the 'ruling party') possibly becoming the core of a presidential party. Putin appealed to voters across the political spectrum, but attempts to create a party system from above, however, were in danger of reducing all parties to little more than shades of a single 'party of power'. By contrast with Yeltsin, Putin was willing to identify himself with a pro-Kremlin party of power and at some point he could decide formally to establish a presidential party. The merger of Fatherland and Unity in 2001 appeared to be the first step in this direction.

A number of questions emerged as Putin reorganised Russian governance: Would his support for a more structured party system recognise and incorporate the pluralism that had emerged since the late 1980s, or would he try to reduce parties to little more than departments of state responsible for organising public politics? To what extent would a genuine system of governmental accountability to society emerge? Finally, would the environment (above all, a free media, free and fair elections, an independent judiciary and a transparent funding regime) allow parties and other social organisations effectively to participate in Russian public life? Above all, as Putin used the presidency as an instrument of political change, would the presidency itself become responsible to public and parliamentary accountability? From Putin's public utterances in his first period in power, it was clear that he himself did not know the answer to these questions.

Parties and the multi-party system

The political and social environment attending the emergence of a party system in Russia was in certain respects reminiscent of the early American experience. The American constitution from the beginning was explicitly biased against parties, termed factions by James Madison. To the present day, the two major United States parties act as loose coalitions rather than as relatively disciplined and structured parliamentary parties of the West European sort. Emerging from the suffocating tutelage of the Communist Party, such anti-party views fell on fertile ground in Russia. Anatolii Khimenko noted that the many years of communist dominance had 'discredited the very concept of "party"'.[46] In his book *Rebuilding Russia* Solzhenitsyn argued against party politics, to allow the organic fabric of community to develop. He noted that:

> Party rivalry distorts the national will. The principle of party-mindedness necessarily involves the suppression of individuality, and every party reduces and coarsens the personal element. An individual will have views, while a party offers an ideology. [47]

In the event, the Yeltsin years had provided conditions for the development of associational life and representative institutions, but of a distinctive type. The representative system and the regime operated largely independently; Putin sought to close the gap, but it was unclear whether this would take the form of genuine accountability or the establishment of a new type of statist hegemony that would incorporate parties into an expanded and revived governmental process.

The party system today

In their study of post-communist party systems Kitschelt *et al.* argue that:

> In the final analysis, whether democracy becomes the 'only game in town' depends on the *quality of democratic interactions and policy processes* [italics in original] the consequences of which affect the legitimacy of democracy in the eyes of citizens and political elites alike.[48]

The quality of democratic procedures determines democratic consolidation and not only the durability of the system. This is particularly pertinent for Russia, where the formal institutions of democracy often masked quite undemocratic practises. Already in 1911, Robert Michels had argued that political parties, whatever their programmatic aspirations, tend to succumb to the oligarchical tendencies inherent in modern social organisation.[49] Russia appears to have fallen victim to this 'iron law of oligarchy' even before party life had become routinised. Similarly, most of the larger social organisations, above all the trade unions, tended to be top-heavy bureaucratic organisations with weak links with the mass of their membership (see Chapter 13).

By early 2001, Russia had fifty-six registered parties and 150 political associations,[50] but party saturation (as in most post-communist countries) remained remarkably low. Party membership as a proportion of the adult population remained minuscule. The post-communist model of parties as electoral organisations focused on parliamentary life and party-list elections undermined the need for large constituency organisations. The large numbers involved in the demonstrations, marches and so on during the insurgent 'movement' phase of party formation was not translated into party membership later, especially since mobilisation declined dramatically once the old system fell. Most parties were marked by limited recruitment to create a mass of 'divan' parties. In 1994, only 3 per cent of adults were members of any of the parties, movements and associations,[51] and this figure thereafter fell to some 1 per cent. Only the CPRF became a mass party, with its half-million members double the membership of all other parties taken together, although in 2001 Unity claimed a membership of 350,000. Disillusioned by cross-ideological alliances, reflecting too often opportunism rather than principle, society was depoliticised. However, the persistently high turnout in elections (see Table 7.6) suggests that this withdrawal has been from party politics, narrowly defined, rather than from politics in general.

Party affiliation was rendered difficult by changes in party labels, but general political orientation remained quite consistent. Party geography mutated from one election to the next, with only four parties fighting all three Duma elections in the 1990s. Russia's 'floating party system' inhibited stable party identification as electors were forced to become 'floating voters' as parties came and went.[52] In mid-2000, some 180 parties were registered in Russia, but the vast majority were of little significance. Of the six parties that crossed the 5 per cent representation threshold in 1999, three were new: Unity as the reconstituted 'party of power'; the centre-left grouping Fatherland–All Russia (OVR); and the liberal Union of Rightist Forces (SPS). Despite the lack of continuity, however, a number of parties survived the turmoil of the 1990s to play an important part in the politics of the new century.

The organisation that most properly deserved the title of 'party' was the CPRF. With a network of regional organisations covering the entire country, some 20,000 primary cells and a membership of about half a million, and a large deputy fraction in all three post-communist State Dumas, the CPRF was potentially an important political force. The CPRF became one of the cornerstones of Russian parliamentary life and, although somewhat eclipsed in December 1999 by Unity, the CPRF remained the largest group in parliament. However, the party was unable to realise its potential and its leader, Zyuganov, appeared forever to be the runner-up and never the victor, as in the 1996 and 2000 presidential elections. The CPRF's ideology was a potent and largely incompatible mix of nationalist, imperialistic (in the Soviet sense) and communist principles; its policies were incoherent in that elements of the market were accepted as long as market *forces* were to be constrained; and its politics appeared to place its own institutional comfort (above all in the Duma) above principle. The party was the main oppositional force in the Duma, yet its policy stances too often appeared opportunistic and contradictory.

The CPRF remained riven by problems of political identity. Was it a revolutionary party intending to overthrow Russia's nascent capitalist institutions, or was it more of a social democratic party seeking to humanise the workings of the capitalist market? What would be the balance between nationalism and socialism? These questions, faced by the whole social democratic movement in the early part of the century and by the West European communist parties in the post-war era, was one that confronted post-communist communist parties in a particularly stark form. These ideological questions were far from abstract since on them hinged questions of organisation and strategy. To what degree would the party support strikes and street demonstrations?; would the emphasis be on the working class or the intelligentsia?; what would be the party's economic policy?; how would the party relate to the other former Soviet republics? On all these questions the CPRF equivocated. The absence of a clear-cut ideology and the aged profile of its membership inhibited the mobilisation of the party's resources. Above all, its nationalist ambitions, socialist aspirations and its democratic commitments were far from integrated. Following the December 1999 election, some of the tension in the CPRF came out into the open. A new political movement of the moderate left, headed by the Speaker of the State Duma, Seleznev, was formally established in September 2000. Called *Rossiya*, the new movement remained allied to the CPRF but the relationship was strained, especially since it was suspected that the movement had been inspired by the Kremlin.

Yavlinskii's Yabloko party had since its foundation in 1993 represented the anti-Yeltsin wing of the 'democratic' movement. It too, like the CPRF, lacked a clear ideological orientation: it was clearly a liberal party, but opposed some of the neo-liberal policies pursued by the reformers; but it was also a social democratic party, although one with few links to the working class. The party seemed locked in a trajectory of gentle decline, hence following the 1999 election it discussed some form of alliance with the Union of Rightist Forces. Of the other groups, only a limited number could be considered parties as such. One of these was the Liberal Democratic Party of Russia (LDPR), headed by the flamboyant Zhirinovskii. In the early 1990s, the party was rampantly nationalist and imperialist, in the sense that it sought to recreate the USSR, but by the end of the decade it had lost some of its fire and, indeed, had become a steady supporter of the government in the Duma. The most significant of the new parties that emerged out of the 1999 parliamentary elections was Unity. Party forms of representation have traditionally been over-shadowed in Russia by the predominance of conglomerate pseudo-parties like Russia Our Home (NDR), Fatherland–All Russia (OVR) and now Unity. Unity was neither a modern political party nor a mass movement but was instead a political association made to order by power elites to advance their interests. Unity (or its equivalent) could become the core of a new type of hegemonic party system in which patronage and preference would be disbursed by a neo-*nomenklatura* class of state officials loyal to Putin. Unity could become the core of a patronage system of the type that in July 2000 was voted out of office in Mexico after seventy-one years.

The type of resources available for party formation has shaped the party system. In the insurgency phase mobilisation took place largely on ideological grounds, whereas later this shifted to a variety of forms but was marked by the weakness of organised social groups in civil society coming together to seek political representation. Instead, parties drew on the organisational resources of the state itself, with various ministries providing the organisational resources for a number of parties. Above all, those groups fortunate enough to enter the Duma were able to draw on the administrative and technical resources allowed deputies (up to five advisers paid by the state, plus secretarial and other help) to promote the development of the associations to which they belonged. In party formation as elsewhere a process of territorialisation of politics was apparent, with insiders carving out areas of concern and resources to further their own political ends. The role of prominent personalities, often with access to sources of financial support, is striking. Although most parties had adapted to the conventions of parliamentary politics, they had also succumbed to the intrigue-ridden regime-dominated politics of the Yeltsin years. This dual adaptation under Putin began to give way to a rather more formalised, although some feared not necessarily more democratic, system.

Normative framework of party development

Throughout the 1990s there were attempts to adopt a law on political parties to supersede the 1990 Soviet law on public associations. Up to 2001, no overall legislation had been adopted to regulate the sphere of social organisations, and the absence of direct instructions in the constitution concerning the adoption of a law on political parties was seen by the opposition as part of the broader chaos in political relations, inhibiting effective work in the Duma and one of the reasons for abuses in regional elections. The lack of rules concerning the financing of political organisations meant that commercial organisations were given a free hand, and sought to ensure the maximum benefit from their 'investment'. In the absence of structured party politics lobbies formed their own parties, as with the Agrarian

Party. At the same time, the presidency relied on quasi-political 'parties of power', combining the organisational and financial resources of the executive branch with access to the media.

The first major attempt to adopt a law on political parties came in December 1995, when the Duma discussed a draft that sought to regulate the types of parties that could be formed, procedures for creating and registering them, their rights and responsibilities, and ways of monitoring their activity. Three types of political parties were envisaged: national, with regional organisations in at least forty-five components of the Russian Federation; inter-regional, with membership from at least two components; and regional. Party groups were prohibited from forming in executive agencies or local government, the armed forces, law enforcement agencies, or in the staffs of state or local legislative authorities. Funding for the election campaigns of national parties was to come from federal funds, although they could engage in economic activity of their own and accept donations.[53] Some of these ideas were incorporated into the law adopted in 2001, although the idea of different types of party was dropped.

The law on political parties became part of the larger package of changes to the electoral system, usually discussed with particular energy after every election. Moser notes the effects of Russia's dual electoral system, favouring parties that can combine both high name recognition with local organisation.[54] The main party that fitted this bill, as we have seen, was the CPRF, allowing it to maintain strong representation in the Duma. In a situation of party and candidate proliferation (in December 1995 an average of twelve candidates fought for every single-mandate seat) the more disciplined and organised CPRF was able to win in single-mandate seats with a small proportion of the total vote. Governors themselves favoured a revision of Russia's electoral law to increase the number of deputies elected directly from local constituencies, something that would allow them greater leverage than the party-list system.

Following the December 1999 election, discussion over the party law was resumed with greater urgency. Veshnyakov, the chair of the Central Electoral Commission, argued that a law on political parties was required to make their financing and organisation more transparent, and in return only genuine political parties would be allowed to participate in parliamentary elections. Such a reform would at a stroke eliminate the pseudo-party electoral associations. Already in the 1998 Ukrainian election, only parties were allowed to stand on the party-list. Consolidation would also be achieved by Unity's proposal to raise from 5 to 7 per cent the share of votes necessary to enter the Duma in the party-list system. Not surprisingly Yabloko, which barely crossed the 5 per cent threshold in the 1999 elections, sought to retain the existing level.[55] Attention also focused on campaign financing, the role of the media in elections and the structure of political parties. The new law on parties, after much debate and over a thousand amendments to the draft proposed by Putin in December 2000, was finally signed into law in July 2000.[56] Its main points, to come into effect after a two-year transition period, are as follows:

- Parties have to have a membership of at least 10,000 nationwide, with no fewer than a hundred members in at least half (that is, in no fewer than forty-five) of

Russia's regions and branches of at least fifty members in the others. Groups that failed to meet these conditions can be disbanded by a decision of the Supreme Court.

- Only registered political parties are allowed to participate in national polls, thus excluding the various movements and regional parties. Parties must regularly advance candidates in elections.
- No one can be a member of more than one party.
- To secure state financing, a party has to win more than 3 per cent of the vote in national elections. Federal assistance no longer comes before elections but is paid afterwards in proportion to the number of votes won.
- Parties have to present an annual financial account reporting the amount received from donors and be open to auditors to examine their financial activities.
- Private contributions to political parties are limited to 3,000 roubles ($110) a year per individual, and the maximum corporate contribution of 2 million roubles (some $70,000) had to be made by bank transfer. Foreigners and international organisations, as well as enterprises that are 30 per cent state-owned, are banned from making financial contributions. The maximum a party can collect in private campaign contributions is 2 billion roubles ($700 million).
- Changes to the role of the media tried to draw a clearer line between information and commentary in an election campaign.
- Compliance with the law is the responsibility of the justice ministry, not the Prosecutor General's office as originally intended, with the decision on banning to be made by the Supreme Court.

The key point was to try to reduce the number of parties by several orders of magnitude – the great majority of Russia's 197 parties would be de-registered leaving twenty to thirty, and some argued even fewer, to fight national and regional elections. Critics argue that regional membership requirements ignore variations in the population between regions, and thus preclude party registration for many groups. The law essentially destroyed regional political parties. The law, moreover, lacks a paragraph enunciating general principles or forbidding ideologies of supremacy based on racial, ethnic, social, religious or other grounds. Above all, the law is criticised for the vague wording of clauses allowing parties to be 'disbanded', which could open the door to political tyranny.[57]

Problems of social representation

Democratic theory speaks of representative democracy but it is party democracy that is most commonly meant, focusing above all on competition between parties to win votes and form governments. While the age of mass parties may everywhere be in decline, the political party as a representative institution remains central to any model of democratic institutionalisation. Classical analyses, notably that of Stein Rokkan, attribute the features of emerging party systems to the cleavage lines generated by the great processes of nation- and state-building: workers and capitalists, church and state, centre and periphery, giving rise to certain categories of parties (socialist, Christian, conservative, liberal and so on), although the correspondence between the cleavage and a particular party may be based on any number of independent variables.[58] In post-communist Russia the lines of such a cleavage structure are blurred to the point of illegibility. Instead, identity, ideological and interest conflicts interact in unpredictable ways and mostly do not line up to reinforce each other. In fact, the very opposite appears to be the case, with political affiliations torn by cross-cutting concerns. Identity conflicts, for example, are particularly pronounced in the ethnic republics, but they are reinforced neither by economic interests nor by ideological concerns and hence remain relatively marginal. In addition, mechanisms of patronage and political clientilism are divorced from the party system,[59] and thus one of the main factors that promotes party development elsewhere is largely absent in Russia. This may change, of course, if Putin's plans to reinforce the party dimension to Russian politics bear fruit.

In addition, according to Rokkan, there is an extraordinary continuity in the political alignments and party systems in Europe between those of the 1920s and the 1960s, suggesting that parties first in the game capture most of the resources available to support a party (voter loyalty, programmes and so on) leaving the system 'frozen' and making it very difficult for new parties to break in, irrespective of the changes that may have transformed society.[60] Rokkan suggested differing processes of political mobilisation between the establishment phase of party alignment and the continuity phase, with changes later tending to be channelled through existing parties rather than through the establishment of new ones. Russia is still far from this, and rather than being 'frozen' Russia's party scene remains excessively fluid.

Party development in Russia reflects, in an exaggerated form, processes common to most post-communist countries.[61] How can we explain the under-developed character of Russian party development? Is there something specifically post-totalitarian inhibiting the development of an effective party system, or is the problem broader, reflecting a general crisis of party systems in mature industrial democracies? We can identify ten factors that inhibit the development of an effective party and representative system in Russia: Russian history and political culture; the provenance of parties as part of the insurgency against the decaying communist regime; the character of the state; presidential patterns of politics and governance; the electoral system; parliamentary politics and government formation; the regionalisation of politics; the post-totalitarian legacy of a fragmented society; the social bases of partisan alignment; and the general crisis of parties and organised interests in modern societies. Having said this, we should immediately add the caveat that the role of parties and organised interests in post-communist Russia has been far from negligible.

History and political culture

The current fever of party formation has much in common with Russia's first attempt to establish a multi-party system between 1905 and 1917. The dominance of individuals, the relative lack of influence on government, shifting leadership alliances, poor ties with the mass membership, wild sloganeering and the tendency for abstract ideological demands to take the place of immediate political programmes, are all reminiscent of the earlier period.[62] In addition, the upsurge of party formation and hopes for a fundamental constitutionalisation of Russian politics between 1904–7 was ultimately inhibited by the reconstitution of imperial power;[63] and likewise the insurgency phase of party formation up to 1991 was eventually constrained by the emergence of regime politics. The way that the Bolsheviks, being only one among many political parties, were able to come to power and establish a one-party system, remains a warning of what might come of Russia's contemporary bacchanalia of party formation and mutation.[64] According to a survey ranging from 1917 to 1990, the central feature of Russian party formation has been the absence of a broad social basis and the effect of an archaic unity (in both Tsarist and Bolshevik guises), combined with state-dominated forms of industrial development.[65]

It is often asserted that Russian political culture is hostile to the emergence of political parties because of a popular commitment to collective values and a predilection for a single authoritative source of political authority.[66] As Stephen Welch has pointed out, however, political culture is far more malleable than sometimes suggested, and in place of the traditional static approach suggests a dynamic model stressing the evolutionary dynamics of political culture.[67] This is illustrated by the case of the United States where, as noted, the political culture was originally hostile to parties but gradually a party system became accepted.[68] In Russia, too, traditional appeals to collectivism, both of the traditional Russian sort (*sobornost*) or of the Soviet communist variety, do not necessarily undermine ideological cleavages and policy preferences taking the form of partisan alignment. The experience of over a decade of free multi-party elections suggests that the Russian voter is as sensitive to party affiliations as electors in any other country even though, as we have suggested above, this may not take the form of voting for the same party from one election to the next. The extraordinary stability of electoral preferences, with roughly a third of the vote from one election to the next supporting the left nationalist opposition, and a fifth the liberal democrats, suggests the presence of the political base for a two-party system.

The legacy of insurgency

The formative phase of a social formation is crucial, and never more so than in the case of Russia's transition from communism. As Golosov notes, the roots of the fragmented and undeveloped party system lie in its genesis.[69] Insurgency politics left its mark on Russian party formation. The manner in which the old regime dissolved gave rise to a distinctive establishment phase. The legacy of the unprecedented concentration of political power and claims to ideological predominance by the CPSU provided an inauspicious terrain for parties to claim a share in power. Post-communist Russian politics does not operate on a *tabula rasa* but where traditional social institutions and groups try to preserve their position while challenged by new social actors. The deceptive ease and the incomplete way in which the old regime finally fell masked the resilience of the former structures, both formal (e.g. the *nomenklatura* elite) and informal (mafia-type structures).

During *perestroika*, the negative connotations of the concept of 'party' led many groups to call themselves 'unions', 'movements' or 'associations'. The fluid politics associated with the insurgency phase continued into later years, with few associations imposing rigorous membership criteria, or even maintaining membership registers. Insurgency politics were characterised by the weakness of the link between parties and political representation in legislative bodies. A great mass of deputies were swept into the soviets as part of the democratic tide of 1989–90, yet once elected they lacked a structured political identity and as a mass reflected the amorphous character of the party system in its entirety. Insurgency politics were marked by the ability of small groups and leaders to achieve victories and fame with relatively small organisational, membership and, indeed, financial resources. Parties until well into the post-communist era remained stamped by the formative stage and largely remained elitist organisations with a fairly small mass base and fluid organisational structures. The major legacy of the politics of insurgency is the gulf between the elite (above all those elected to legislative bodies) and the mass membership.

The character of the state

The character of state formation following communism was crucial in establishing the context for party development. As M. Steven Fish notes of the *perestroika* period, the nature of political groups was determined largely by 'the character of state power'. Ideas and the convictions of individual politicians played a minimal role, while the critical legacy of a society thoroughly permeated by an activist state was determining.[70] Post-communist Russian state-building proved inimical to the conversion of the insurgent political formations into genuine political parties. The state did little to assist the development of parties or a party system, and little came of Yeltsin's promise to provide assistance at a meeting with the leaders of fifteen of the largest parties on 12 December 1991.[71] The institutional framework of post-communist politics, moreover, inhibited the development of a functioning party system, with the government chosen, as we have seen, on a non-party basis. Above all, the gulf between the representative system and the regime, and the thorough bureaucratisation of social relations inhibited the political organisation of sectional interests.

Presidential politics

Presidential systems in the best of circumstances tend to inhibit the emergence of party government, while Yeltsin's insistence on the non-party essence of presidential rule further reduced its potential. Yeltsin's first act on being elected chairman of the Russian Congress on 29 May 1990 was to suspend his membership of *Demrossiya*, insisting that he would defend 'the interests not of separate groups or parties or organisations but the interests of the peoples of the Russian Federation'.[72] On resigning his CPSU membership on the last day of the Twenty-eighth Congress in July 1990 Yeltsin declared that he would join no party and declared himself to be above party politics. *Demrossiya* had provided crucial support for Yeltsin's presidential victory in June 1991, yet his victory did not lead to its consolidation as the 'party of power', or, indeed, to its consolidation as a party at all. Yeltsin clearly felt more at ease working through his own 'team' free of political or social control, and his claim to be president of all Russians only strengthened the tendency towards charismatic above-party leadership. In the presidential elections of 1996, Yeltsin ran as an independent, as did Putin in 2000.

The development of a hegemonic presidency is discussed elsewhere (Chapter 5); here we shall only identify some of the implications for party development. The key point is that the representative system, epitomised by parties, is largely divorced from the process of forming governments. The very structure of government was inimical to the development of a party system, with the premier and cabinet chosen on a non-party basis and forced to resign their seats as deputies on appointment. The idea was to maintain the separation of powers, but this rather crude principle, typical of presidential systems, only divorced the power and representative systems from each other, and weakened the accountability and responsibility of both.

The electoral system

The institutional design of an electoral system lies at the heart of a new democratic system.[73] The attempt to manipulate the electoral system to encourage the consolidation of effective electoral parties proved only partially successful. The version of the electoral law presented to the Constitutional Assembly in June 1993 by a group of experts led by the deputy Victor Sheinis proposed a mixed system on the German model of direct constituency elections and party-lists, intended precisely to encourage the development of a party system.[74] The introduction of the party-list system for the election of half the deputies to the State Duma, although designed to stimulate the creation of solid political parties, in practice accelerated the fragmentation of the party system. The 1995 electoral rules, for example, allowed only twelve Moscow politicians on the party-list, encouraging those lower down the list to form their own electoral blocs.

The mixed plurality and proportional electoral system used in Russia has certain political consequences, some of which have been noted above. It has been argued that 'a proportional system in a country with an undeveloped civil society only impedes the growth of genuine multi-partyness'.[75] The establishment of electoral blocs allowed numerous small parties, which independently would not have been able to cross the 5 per cent threshold, to gain seats in the new Duma. The formation of associations to fight elections was governed by one logic – the attraction of star leaders, the search for campaign sponsors and the like – which does not correspond to the logic of genuine party formation: the patient consolidation of regional organisations, the honing of a programme and the establishment of a permanent central staff. Electoral pacts undermined the development of a normal parliamentary party system. In response to this the new electoral law from 2001 allows only registered parties to fight elections. As for the single-member districts, parties did not fight the majority of seats in the constituencies, and party affiliation made little difference to the vote. In all three Duma elections in the 1990s, a large proportion of all constituency deputies were elected as independent deputies rather than by party affiliation, and this was then reflected in the relative fluidity of factions in the Duma. This fluidity was exacerbated by the lack of continuity in the choice of parties offering themselves up for votes from one election to the next. As noted, instead of parties in search of an electorate, we appeared to have an electorate in search of parties.

Parliamentary politics and government formation

Just as the engineers of democracy sought to mould the electoral system to promote party develoment, so, too, there were attempts to shape the working arrangements of the State Duma in 1993 to create cohesive party groups. The weakness of party groups in the 1990–3 Congress of People's Deputies was widely considered to be one reason for it having been captured by radical rejectionists. In the Duma there are strict rules about the minimum number of deputies required to form a group (thirty-five), and only those parties crossing the 5 per cent threshold have the right to call themselves party factions. Parliamentary committees as we have seen are formed on the party principle. The rules governing Duma organisation are designed to support party politics, but these attempts were undermined by the nature of Russia's political system. The upper house of the Federal Assembly, the Federation Council, in the form in which it existed up to 2001, was based not on party but on regional representation.

Parties fight elections, but in Russia they do not fight elections to form the government. As we have seen, there is no direct correlation between representation in parliament and the colour of the government. Instead, a syncretic political process predominated. Extensive individual co-optation, personalised ties and a relatively fluid party system mean that the distinction between parties in government and those in opposition was unclear. Russia's Choice was established as the party of government, yet ministers in that very same government were members of opposition parties. In the 1995 elections, Russia Our Home managed the remarkable feat of presenting itself as the party of government while at the same time criticising the shortcomings of that very same government. The CPRF had tacitly supported Chernomyrdin's government on several occasions, and during Primakov's premiership in effect became part of the governing coalition. Voters, understandably, were often confused by the 'choice' offered to them, and even more so since the relationship between parties and the government, let alone the government and the presidency, was not always clear. Various extra-constitutional Accords and fora were established as part of Yeltsin's attempts to incorporate active political forces into a dynamic and mobile form of consensus politics run firmly from the top. It appeared that Yeltsin, quite simply, did not understand the principles on which a multi-party system operates.

Regionalism and party politics

The Russian party system is highly fragmented and its reach is partial. Historically, parties have emerged as the coalition of local or sectional interests that have only later been aggregated at the national level. In post-communist Russia regionally based parties are weak and have minimal impact on national politics, while parties based on ethnic politics are wholly de-legitimated. Most party formation in Russia has been top down, only reinforcing the tendency for much of politics to be conducted outside the framework of party politics, whether national or local. One of the reasons for this is the fragmentation of political space itself. Under Yeltsin a rich variety of regional political systems and regimes emerged, ranging from the democratic to the outright authoritarian, and national parties had to accommodate themselves to local circumstances. Local name recognition and political capital derived from non-partisan sources are often as important as organisation in regional elections.

Party development reflected the national fragmentation, and while regional organisations might bear the same name as the central one, there were often great differences in policies. Between 1993–7, for example, the Tatarstan republican organisation of the CPRF was effectively a separate party, disagreeing over the CPRF's centralising line on ethno-federal issues. The increasingly regional character of Russian politics suggested that conditions were lacking for the development of a mass national political party. Mndoyants and Salmin confirm that 'Russian parties are not complete formations. Sections in Moscow and organisations in the provinces can differ substantially over ideological and other matters.'[76] One and the same party label could mean very different things to people in various parts of the country. No single party could hope to encompass the regional, national, ethnic, class, group, elite and other cleavages in society, and nor could a single party mediate the multiple social forces, processes and ideologies that buffeted intellectual life. The sheer size of the country made it difficult to constitute a genuinely national party penetrating not only the major cities but also provincial towns, rural areas and the national republics.

While the centre–periphery cleavage in Russia has lost none of its force, the language of 'national-self determination' has become compromised while regional political organisations have been weak. The establishment of the 'Transformation of the Urals' bloc by Eduard Rossel, the governor of Sverdlovsk *oblast*, in 1995 was the most sustained attempt at regional party formation, but this did not break out from its Sverdlovsk heartlands into the rest of the Urals, let alone make an impact on national politics. By contrast, Catalan aspirations after Franco found a strong and self-sufficient party ready to express them. In addition, parties based on ethnic politics are wholly de-legitimated, while those in favour of new state identities are as yet weak. In Tatarstan, for example, in the forefront of the struggle for autonomy, the leading role is taken not by a party but by a social movement, the Tatarstan Social Centre (TOTs) based, like most nineteenth-century national movements, on the intelligentsia.

Gubernatorial elections demonstrate the lack of correlation between national elections and those held on the regional level. Although the CPRF enjoys the advantages of a national organisation, it is unable to dominate the political life of even 'red belt' regions. The CPRF is not the source of patronage or advancement, even where its governors identify with it. The communist former governor of Voronezh, Ivan Shabanov, for example, insisted that no party would enjoy any privileges in his administration, much to the distress of local communists who had hoped to enjoy the spoils of victory. A similar pattern was repeated elsewhere. In Volgograd *oblast* under communist governor Nikolai Maksyuta communists complained that there were too few comrades in his administration. Political parties there and elsewhere remain under-developed and out of the loop of power and patronage.

In addition, regional parties appeared unconnected with ideologies. Although proclaiming an anti-market ideology, the CPRF in the regions accepted that the triumph of capitalism was irrevocable. As one analysis noted:

Ideologies are merely a kind of political label – tools in the struggle for a place in the capitalist sun. Group identification arises not from a common system of values but from a pragmatic assessment of the advantages or disadvantages of occupying this or that niche in the political market.[77]

Regional elites had greater incentives to exploit personal connections and to cultivate local sponsors than to devote their energies to the long-term strategy of building up party organisations. In polarised national elections, moreover, like that for the presidency in 1996, regional leaderships were able to counteract any organisational advantages that the CPRF's candidate, Zyuganov, may have enjoyed. In the first round Zyuganov won in forty-five regions, but by the second round this had declined to thirty-one (with a decisive victory in only nineteen of these). This was even more accentuated in the 2000 presidential elections, where Zyuganov won in only four regions. Putin's attempts to homogenise Russia's political and legal space will in all probability create a more auspicious environment for the development of a national party system. The emergence of Unity as the putative presidential party has the potential to transform the Russian party scene by bringing together power and electoral maximisation strategies of governing elites while provoking the counter-mobilisation of oppositional parties on a national scale. A classic two-party system may emerge.

The post-totalitarian society

Whereas in most post-communist Central European and Baltic countries functioning national party systems based on the classic left–right division have consolidated themselves, in Russia, where communism lasted much longer and with greater intensity, only a glimmer of such a consolidation is evident. The legacy of the unprecedented concentration of political power and claims to ideological predominance by the CPSU provided an inauspicious terrain for parties to claim a share in power. We have noted the popular 'anti-party' mood, but the problem was deeper. Traditional social institutions, groups and practices are deeply embedded despite the formal change of political regime, and new social forces and democratic social institutions (above all political parties) remain superficial. In post-communist countries political and social structuration takes distinctive forms. Classic theories of party development connected particular interests with party alignment, but Russia's post-totalitarian social structure blurred the link between party choice and socio-economic structure. However, the correlation existed, as evidenced for example by the consistent support of the agrarian sector for the CPRF and of young upwardly mobile urbanites for Yabloko and other liberal parties. In general, though, Kulik accurately identified the emergence of a vicious circle in which parties developed but were weak because of the 'post-totalitarian condition of Russia', while society could not be democratically integrated into the state without powerful parties.[78]

The weakness of the state and Yeltsin's personalised style of rule, moreover, encouraged the development of a type of mimetic pluralism where political bargaining took informal forms and subverted institutionalised patterns of interest aggregation. Political integration tended to bypass political parties, and mecha nisms whereby parties can be integrated into the governmental process remain undeveloped. The mass mobilisation that does take place is derived not from social cleavages but from the organisational capacity of 'political machines'.[79] In short, the post-communist psychological atmosphere, social structure and political processes inhibited party development. Socio-economic and other social interests acted directly on the state without the mediation of traditional 'gatekeeper' organisations like parties. In these circumstances the running of 'party' elections in an atomised and essentially 'non-party' country could not but have perverse consequences. Few parties represented the interests of specific social groups, although gradually programmatic crystallisation has taken place and the outlines of a traditional political spectrum along which parties align is beginning to emerge.

Social interests and partisan representation

Schmitter argued that substantial changes have taken place in the role and nature of parties in established Western democracies, and that it would be anachronistic to assume 'that parties in today's neodemocracies will have to go through all the stages and perform all the functions of their predecessors'.[80] The secular–religious divide appears in a new light in post-communist conditions, although in the West, too, party alignments derived from this cleavage are waning. In Russia the Orthodox Church had acquiesced in its own subservience to the regime, and this ambiguity tended to undermine its political and moral authority in the post-communist period. Even in Poland where the Catholic Church had been unambiguous in its call for political openness, the advanced secularisation of society prevented the emergence of a serious religiously based party in the aftermath of Solidarity.

It might well appear that socialist movements, too, have had their day: a phenomenon of the late nineteenth to the late twentieth century inappropriate for the challenges facing the world in the twenty-first century. A response to modernisation, industrialisation and the onset of mass society and a reflection of resistance to the market economy and the secularisation and individualisation of social life, the apparent triumph of liberalism has left the distinctive features of alternative politics without an anchor. Attitudes do not line up with partisan alignment, as the various attempts to establish a mass social democratic party demonstrate. As Fyodor Gavrilov put it:

> The average Russia voter is a textbook social democrat. He's in favor of the market, but with broad social guarantees. He's for civil rights, but as long as they're vigorously enforced by the state. He supports the family, but he's for the right to abortion and divorce.[81]

However, the average Russian elector does not vote for the various social democratic parties on offer. Both Christian and social democracy were responses to the traumas accompanying the rise of market capitalism but have found it difficult to sustain alternative policies in mature industrial societies. The Russian voter was offered a number of social democratic parties, including Gorbachev's United Social Democratic Party, but few voted for them.

In Russia, of course, the capitalist social formation is only now emerging and the problem is inverted: if in the West capitalism has matured and, on the whole, delivers the goods, in Russia it is difficult to organise against a capitalism that is struggling to be born and that may one day deliver Western standards of prosperity. This 'ideological' inhibition against militant anti-capitalist politics (shared in part even by the CPRF) was reinforced by the numerous structural and institutional constraints discussed above. Regime autonomy was sustained by its self-proclaimed modernising mission; allegedly fulfilling tasks that were too important to be threatened by the vagaries of electoral politics. The monolithic character of the CPSU was reproduced in an inverted form by the emerging opposition movements, united only in their desire to destroy the communist monopoly. This negative unity was perpetuated after the fall of the regime by a commitment to the broad principle of creating a market system in Russia, and even those movements that criticised capitalism were unable to sustain an effective alternative programme. Post-communist party formation was inhibited by the 'post-historical' period in which it was born, where the great ideologies associated with modernity have given way to an individualised politics of identity, self-satisfaction and, in the case of the CPRF, by a retrogressive vision of Russian nationalism.

The absence of a recognisable social base to the new political parties was perhaps the single most important factor inhibiting the development of party politics.[82] Parties in Russia suffered a two-fold estrangement: from the social and political interests that they claimed to represent; and from the coherent formulation of a forward-looking policy taking into account actually existing realities rather than an ideologised version of what should be. This double disassociation inhibited the consolidation of a coherent governing coalition or an effective opposition. The disjuncture between marrying an ideology to an organisation and a social group was stark, weakening the institutions of political society. The absence of social subjects able to express their interests reinforced the role of leadership and personalities. Ludmilla Alekseeva, for example, notes that 'The role of political parties among workers is extremely small'.[83] In an ironic version of 'catching up and overtaking', and indeed of 'combined and uneven development', post-communist Russia displayed the symptoms of an advanced 'post-modern' social structure in a society whose 'modernity' remained archaic. It is this 'modernisation without modernity' that we label mismodernisation (see Chapter 18).

The actual structure of the Russian social terrain, however, is extraordinarily complex. Post-communist political life is even more fractured than the 'post-modern' and 'post-industrial' societies of the West. The extreme pluralism that emerged in these conditions gave rise to a permanently fragmented party system and an unstable democratic politics.[84] While numerous groups existed, it is probably premature to talk of interest group politics: few generated a homogeneous 'interest' and politics was not as yet 'sub-system dominant'. The weakness of the state did not necessarily mean the strength of society but indicated a general crisis of political institutions and civil associations in post-communist Russia.

The general crisis of parties and partisan representation

Party development in Russia reflects only in more extreme form what some have identified as the 'unfreezing', if not general crisis, of parties in European politics.[85]

The shift from materialist to post-materialist preferences in the value system of voters and the apparent decline in the role of parties as such, eclipsed by new forms of participation such as social movements and alternative forms of political communication (such as television), have given rise to a new volatility in established party systems.[86] Although there is much evidence to suggest overall stability in party systems,[87] the end of the Cold War has promoted increased fluidity in some party systems. The 'end of ideology', the thesis advanced by Daniel Bell in the late 1950s[88] and taken up by Francis Fukuyama in the form of the 'end of history',[89] promoted a more managerial approach to social development, while ideology itself, as reflected in party programmes and manifestos, became more symbolic rather than a guide to action.

Everywhere the old cleavage between left and right is blurred, the left itself has taken on new forms, and the era of mass parties appears over.[90] The fusion of information and communications technology has accelerated the creation of 'virtual' communities in which politics has become even more spectral, reduced to the level of images and attractions that have little relation to the realities of public life. Jacques Derrida argues that the media has rendered the professional politician 'structurally incompetent' by generating a set of demands associated with performance on air and image projection that displaces parties and parliaments.[91] Parties in general, from this perspective, appear obsolete as vehicles of popular mobilisation, regional and national identity, individual development, and, in the Russian context, even as instruments of power. In contrast to the 'golden age' of parties from the late nineteenth century to the 1970s, the contemporary era is marked by a plurality of competing forms of political representation (in particular, single-issue pressure groups), and the space in which parties operate has changed dramatically. The electronic media acts as the functional equivalent of political parties, able to mobilise an electorate and substitute for a network of party committees. The traditional baggage of political organisation and nationally organised political parties appears dispensable when an effective performance and advertisements on the silver screen count for so much – as American politicians long ago realised.

Conclusion

Competitive elections embedded the nascent party system in the new order. With the country on the verge of civil war in 1993 the role of elections in stabilising the political situation should not be under-estimated. However, while elections may be necessary, they are not a sufficient condition for democracy, and the very weakness of Russia's party system allowed executives partially to co-opt the electoral process for their own ends. Parties are an expression of the attempt to institutionalise the diverse interests of civil society, but parties may no longer be the predominant political vehicle for this process. Parties are only one aspect of the representative structure of complex democratic societies. The formation of a structured party system in Russia is inhibited by the intrinsic weakness of civil society, the rise of new forms of representing social interests, the fragmentation of 'interests' themselves, and the dissolution of the art of representative politics. The 'American exception' – the absence of ideologically defined mass parties of the socialist sort – has now become the norm.

An open political 'market' emerged in Russia, not monopolised by any single party or category of parties, but the potential market finds very strong 'consumer' resistance to joining parties and political activism. Two sets of reasons can be postulated to explain this resistance. The first looks to the emerging parties, which have been fractious and incompetent in achieving mass appeal; while the second suggests that, however effective parties might be, in existing post-communist conditions there are few takers, explained by such factors as alienation because of the Bolshevik experience, the struggle to survive, and the charismatic type of politics that has emerged focused on presidential politics. Social cleavages characteristic of the early part of the century, based on class, religious and regional politics, have largely been superseded. The traditional class structure had been overturned, organisations and associations destroyed, and quasi-political forms of mobilisation instituted that tend to weaken political participation. Politics remain focused on private, top-level intrigues and lack transparency, while political organisations are only slowly sinking roots into society itself.

Part III

Federalism, regionalism and nationalism

For the republics in Russia, sovereignty came to be equated with federal non-interference in their internal affairs and a degree of economic autonomy. Instead of developing a sustained legal framework for federalism, under Yeltsin a segmented regionalism emerged reflecting not so much the spatial separation of powers but the fragmentation of political authority. Sovereignty claims by regional leaders, including in the republics, gained little support among the non-titular peoples, and even titular groups were divided. Putin sought to achieve the reconstitution of the citizen as the subject of Russian political space by giving substance to the idea of *Rossiiskii* citizenship – an aim that has been explicit effectively since the end of the nineteenth century. The degree to which the Russian state can serve as a framework for articulating multinational aspirations is as unclear now as it was then. The First World War 'revealed the incapacity of the weakly integrated and underinstitutionalized Tsarist state to stretch – in Benedict Anderson's neat formulation – "the short, tight skin of the nation over the gigantic body of the empire" (p. 84)'.[1]

The existence of Russia in its present borders is questioned. Gorbachev, who perhaps did more than anyone to make possible the break-up of the USSR even though he did all that he could to avert the disintegration of the state that he had committed himself to reform, questioned the viability of Russia on its own. As he put it:

> increasingly, the Russian people understand they were deceived…the press and television in Russia try to convince people that what is needed today, above all, is to think about 'how to live in Russia'. *But in fact the very question of 'how to live in Russia' involves the question of what to do about integration, how to arrange relations with other member states of the CIS.*[2]

These are the problems that we shall begin to explore in this Part.

9   Federalism and the state

A multitude is strong while it holds together, but so soon as each of those who compose it begins to think of his own private danger, it becomes weak and contemptible.

(Niccolo Machiavelli)[1]

The Russian Empire grew through a process of overland expansion: rather like the United States, it occupied territories across a vast continental mass, a type of colonisation that is largely irreversible. The emergence of these two continental states overshadowed the traditional nation-state and each, as De Tocqueville foresaw, seemed 'called by some secret design of Providence one day to hold in its hands the destinies of half the world'.[2] The major difference, however, between the two is that whereas the United States some 200 years ago devised an effective political system and a sturdy relationship between individual states and the federal authorities, Russia is still in the process of building a viable relationship between the centre and the regions. Although the 1993 constitution establishes the framework of Russian federalism, its ambiguous formulations and provision for further laws de-limiting powers between the centre and the regions stimulated a repeated although more muted version of the 'war of the laws' that had brought down the USSR.

Ethno-federalism and its legacy

The concept of path dependency argues that earlier institutional choices foreclose options later. This is nowhere more true than in the area of Russia's federal relations. The Soviet state had been federal-unitary; federal in form, but in effect unitary. The heart of the old state system, the CPSU, had never pretended to be federal and instead had been a centralised body governed by its Central Committee and Politburo in Moscow. The fourteen republican Party organisations had been no more than a single unit governed by the principles of democratic centralism. Within Russia only certain autonomous areas populated by national minorities were the subjects of ethno-federalism, whereas regions populated by the titular nationality (Russians) were part of the unitary and centralised state. Russia was bequeathed a complex ethno-federal system in which its eighty-nine regions were divided into a number of status groups, each jealously defended by its local elites.

The Soviet ethno-federal system

Defeats in war and the fall of Tsarism in 1917 allowed several nations to leave the Russian empire. The aspirations of Poland and Finland to independence went largely unopposed; whereas Ukrainian independence was precarious and was undermined as soon as the Bolsheviks won the Civil War of 1918–20. Earlier declarations in favour of 'the right of nations to self-determination', notably in Lenin's 1916 pamphlet of that name, was modified in January 1918 by Stalin, the people's commissar of nationalities, to be 'a right not of the bourgeoisie, but of the working masses of the given nation'.[3] National liberation was subordinated to the class struggle. The Bolsheviks once again 'gathered the lands' of the historical Russian state, but based on the new principle of 'socialist internationalism'. Autonomous national independence movements were crushed, as were varieties of 'national communism'. Ultimately a state was recreated that reflected Lenin's views of national self-determination, enshrining the principle of territorial autonomy for specified ethnic groups with the formal right to 'self-determination up to and including secession'. In practice, of course, in keeping with the Marxist view that economic modernisation would make national differences redundant, national aspirations were firmly subordinated to the imperatives of socialist construction, as defined by the Bolsheviks themselves.

The principle of federalism was only grudgingly acknowledged, and then only partially implemented. While Lenin, in his 'Declaration of the Rights of the Toiling and Exploited People', prepared for the Constituent Assembly in January 1918, called for 'a federation of the Soviet Republics of Russia', the RSFSR constitution adopted in mid-1918 contained no effective federal elements. The consolidation of Bolshevik rule over Ukraine and the conquest of Armenia, Azerbaijan and Georgia in 1920–1 necessarily intensified the debate over the structure of the state. Stalin proposed the 'autonomisation' plan to reduce the newly conquered states to the status of Russia's existing autonomous republics (Tataria, Bashkiria, Kazakhstan and Turkestan). Lenin, however, concerned by the chauvinist and arrogant behaviour of Bolshevik officials in Transcaucasia, on 26 September 1922 rejected the autonomisation plan in favour of the creation of a new federation, and as a first step the three Transcaucasian republics were federated into one.

The Union Treaty of 30 December 1922 creating the USSR brought together four union republics: the RSFSR, Ukraine, Belarus and the Transcaucasian Soviet Federative Socialist Republic; together with twenty-six autonomous areas, twenty-two of which were in Russia. The first Soviet constitution of January 1924 was marked by a centralising ethos, with Russia's governing institutions mostly converted into the corresponding USSR body. The policy of *korenizatsiya* (indigenisation), however, adopted by the Twelfth Party Congress in 1923, sought to root Soviet power in native elites and encouraged the use of indigenous languages, but by the early 1930s state policy had changed to renewed Russianisation. The Soviet Union that died in December 1991 was a very different one from that born in 1922. By 1991, the number of Union republics had risen to fifteen: three emerged as a result of the disintegration of the Transcaucasian Federation (Armenia, Azerbaijan and Georgia); five Central Asian republics as a result of carving up the territory of the RSFSR (Kazakhstan, Kyrgyzstan, Tajikistan, Turkmenistan and

Uzbekistan); and four had been incorporated into the USSR during the Second World War (Estonia, Latvia, Lithuania and Moldova). That some of the autonomous areas became Union republics and others not remains a source of bitterness for areas such as Tatarstan to this day.

Russia, too, had changed, and the country that in 1991 became the 'continuer' state to the USSR was far smaller than in 1922, having donated territory to Ukraine and the Central Asian republics.[4] The geographical area of the RSFSR under Soviet power had decreased both in absolute and in comparative terms: if in 1922 the RSFSR comprised 94.7 per cent of the territory of the USSR, by 1991 this had fallen to 76.2 per cent. In terms of size, the USSR had become rather more a Union of equals, divided up into fifty-three different types of national-territorial units: fifteen union republics and thirty-eight autonomous republics, *oblasts* and *okrugs*. Russia replicated the federal-unitary structure of the USSR (see Fig. 9.1); in 1990 it consisted of eighty-eight administrative units, seventy-three of which were primary and fifteen were secondary (i.e. subordinated to one of the former), reflecting the hierarchical *matryeshka* doll-like construction of Soviet government.[5] There was, moreover, a considerable disparity between the historical and the actual ethnic borders between the peoples.

This distinctive form of national-territorial federation was intended neither to promote the emergence of ethnically pure nation-states nor, on the contrary, to allow the emergence of multinational "nations' within the framework of the ethno-federal areas: they were seen as no more than a transitional stage in the long-term goal of complete state unity, passing through an initial stage of 'coming closer' (*sblizhenie*) to result ultimately in complete fusion (*sliyanie*), on a world scale if possible. In the mean time, however, rather than being a Union of equal and sovereign peoples, Soviet federal policy was based on a strict hierarchy of nations, with some privileged to have a state in their name, while other ethnic groups failed to qualify for the honorific of 'nation' and instead were called 'nationalities' (*narodnosti*). While the 1989 census listed 128 nationalities, only sixty-eight formally made up the fifty-three ethno-federal units. Ethnic Russians made up just over half (50.78 per cent) of the Soviet Union's population of 290,938,469 in July 1990. They were followed by Ukrainians at 15.45 per cent, Uzbeks at 5.84, Belarusians at 3.51 and Kazakhs at 2.85 per cent (see Table 2.1). The official language was Russian, but the country was host to over 200 languages and dialects, at least eighteen of which had more than 1 million speakers.[6]

As the USSR disintegrated the ethno-federal republics were drawn into the struggle between the Union and the republics. In the Law on the De-limitation of Powers between the USSR and the Subjects of the Federation of April 1990, Gorbachev gave Russia's autonomous republics the right to join any new Union Treaty on terms equal with the Union republics. The elevation of the political status of the republics was later rejected by Yeltsin as a threat to Russia's territorial integrity.[7] Instead he sought to rebuild Russia on the basis of a civic identity and loyalty to a democratic Russian state. As we shall see, he was willing to renegotiate the relationship between Russia and its republics and championed the achievement of sovereignty from below on condition that they remained loyal to the Russian state.

For most of the period, the Soviet national-state system maintained a precarious balance and survived because the CPSU exercised real power. Declarations of

Figure 9.1 Russia and its republics

republican sovereignty and the Russian Decree on Power of June 1990 unwittingly accelerated the destruction of the Soviet state, although their main target had been the communist regime that had sat uncomfortably above them all as some sort of sixteenth republic. While a viable post-communist federation or confederation might have been feasible,[8] in the event, the destruction of communism was accompanied by the disintegration of the USSR (see Part I). The August *coup* destroyed the final shreds of legitimacy of attempts to 'renew' the communist system and at the same time delivered a devastating blow against Gorbachev's attempts to save the Union.

Ethno-federal structure and composition

Sovereignty declarations in 1990–1 were accompanied by the 'republicanisation' of Russia; the constitution was amended on 15 December 1990 to delete the word 'autonomous' in the title of Russia's sixteen republics, and they simply became 'republics forming part of the Russian Federation'. On 3 July 1991, the Supreme Soviet elevated four of the five autonomous *oblasts* (Adygeya, Gorno-Altai, Karachai-Cherkessia and Khakassia) to the status of republics and they were removed from the jurisdiction of the *krais* to which they were formerly subordinate.[9] This brought the number of republics to twenty, leaving only the Jewish autonomous *oblast*. The number of republics rose to twenty-one when on 4 June 1992 the Supreme Soviet split the Chechen-Ingush republic into two. The twenty-one national republics comprise 15.2 per cent of the population and 28.6 per cent of Russia's territory. Most of the autonomous *okrugs* declared themselves sovereign, trying to free themselves from the control of the corresponding *oblast* or *krai* to become subjects of federation in their own right.

Russia's eighty-nine federal components and their status is listed in the constitution (Art. 65.1), and prima facie any change to their status would require a constitutional amendment. Russia's territory is organised on two principles: territorial and ethno-territorial. The territorial principle alone applies to the two federal cities (Moscow and St Petersburg), the forty-nine *oblasts* and the six *krais* (the latter differ little from *oblasts* except that they once stood on the edge of the country). The remaining thirty-two units of the Federation are defined by unstable ethno-territorial characteristics: twenty-one republics (with the Chechen-Ingush counting as two) (see Table 9.2), one autonomous *oblast* (Birobijan) and ten autonomous *okrugs* (see Table 9.3). The ethno-federal territories occupy 53.3 per cent of Russia's territory but only (in 1989) 16.7 per cent of the population.[10]

Ethnic Russians make up the overwhelming majority of the country's population but find themselves in the anomalous position of not having an ethno-federal area of their own – hence the calls by some nationalists either for its establishment or for the abolition of the territories of ethnic minorities. Out of a total RSFSR population of 147.02 million in 1989, 119.87 million (81.53 per cent) were ethnic Russians: of these 108.06 million (90.2 per cent, or 73.5 per cent of the total RF population) lived outside ethno-federal units; while 11.8 million (9.8 per cent, 8.02 per cent of total RF population) lived within the national-state territory of some other nationality. The nearly 12 million ethnic Russians living in the ethno-federal territories of others comprise 45.7 per cent of the population of these areas (see Table 9.1) and constitute a source of potential Russian nationalist mobilisation.

Table 9.1 National composition of Russian Federation, 1989

Ethnic group	Total number	% of RF pop.	Living on the territory of their own ethno-federal unit	
			Number	% of national group
Total population	147,021,869	100		
Of whom:				
Russians:	119,865,946	81.53		
– living outside ethno-federal areas	108,063,409	73.50		
– living in others' ethno-federal areas	11,802,537	8.03		
Tatars	5,521,096	3.75	1,765,404	31.97
Ukrainians	4,362,872	2.96		
Chuvash	1,773,645	1.21	906,922	51.10
Bashkirs	1,345,273	0.91	863,808	64.21
Belarusians	1,206,222	0.82		
Mordvinians	1,072,939	0.72	313,420	29.21
Chechens	898,999	0.61	734,501	81.71
Germans	842,000	0.57		
Udmurts	714,833	0.49	496,522	69.46
Maris	643,698	0.44	324,349	50.39
Kazakhs	635,865	0.43		
Avars	544,016	0.37	496,077	91.19
Jews	536,846	0.36	8,886	1.65
Armenians	532,390	0.36		
Buryats	417,425	0.28	341,185	81.74
Ossets	402,275	0.27	334,876	83.24
Kabards	386,055	0.26	363,492	94.15
Yakuts	380,242	0.26	365,236	96.05
Dargins	353,348	0.24	280,431	79.36
Azerbaijanis	335,889	0.23		
Komis	336,309	0.23	291,541	86.69
Kumyks	277,163	0.19	231,805	83.63
Lezgins	257,270	0.17	204,370	79.43
Ingush	215,068	0.15	163,762	76.14
Tuvans	206,160	0.14	198,448	96.26
Peoples of the North	182,000	0.12		
Moldovans	172,671	0.12		
Kalmyks	165,821	0.11	146,316	88.28
Gypsies	153,000	0.10		
Karachais	150,332	0.10	129,449	86.11
Komi-Permyaks	147,269	0.09	95,215	64.65
Georgians	130,688	0.09		
Uzbeks	126,899	0.09		
Karelians	124,921	0.08	78,928	63.18
Adygeis	122,908	0.08	95,439	77.65
Koreans	107,000	0.07		
Laks	106,245	0.07	91,682	86.29
Poles	95,000	0.06		
Tabasarans	93,587	0.06	78,196	83.55
Greeks	92,000	0.05		
Balkars	78,341	0.05	70,793	90.36
Khakas	78,500	0.05	62,859	80.07

cont.

Nogais	73,703	0.05	28,294	38.39
Lithuanians	70,000			
Altaians	69,409	0.05	59,130	85.19
Cherkess	50,764	0.03	40,241	79.27
Nenets	34,190	0.02	29,786	87.12
Evenks	29,901	0.02	3,480	11.64
Khants	22,283	0.01	11,892	53.37
Rutuls	19,503	0.01	14,955	76.68
Aguls	17,728	0.01	13,791	77.79
Chukchis	15,107	0.01	11,914	78.86
Koryaks	8,942		6,572	73.49
Mansis	8,279		6,562	79.26
Dolgans	6,584		4,939	75.01
Tsakhurs	6,492		5,194	80.00

Source: *RSFSR v tsifrakh v 1989g* (Moscow, Financy i statistika, 1990), pp. 23–5, modified.

Table 9.2 The republics of Russia

Name of republic	Capital	Population	Titular nationality (%)	Russians %	Russians Number
Adygeya	Maikop	446,800	22.0	68.0	303,825
Altai	Gorno-Altaisk	196,700	31.0	60.4	118,807
Bashktostan	Ufa	4,042,000	22.0	40.0	1,616,800
Buryatia	Ulan-Ude	1,056,600	24.0	69.0	729,054
Chechen-Ingush	Grozny	1,235,000	70.7[1]	23.1	306,075
Chuvashia	Cheboksary	1,359,000	67.8	26.7	362,853
Dagestan	Makhachkala	1,925,000	80.2[2]	12.0	231,000
Kabardino-Balaria	Nalchik	785,900	58.6[3]	32.0	251,488
Kalmykia	Elista	321,700	45.4	37.7	121,281
Karachai-Cherkessia	Cherkessk	434,000	41.0[4]	42.0	182,280
Karelia	Petrozavodsk	799,600	11.0	72.0	575,712
Khakassia	Abakan	583,000	11.5	80.0	466,400
Komi	Syktyvkar	1,246,000	23.3	57.5	716,450
Marii El	Ioshkar-Ola	764,000	43.0	48.0	366,720
Mordovia	Saransk	963,800	32.5	60.8	585,990
North Ossetia	Vladikavkaz	651,000	53.0	29.9	194,649
Sakha (Yakutia)	Yakutsk	1,074,000	33.4	50.3	537,000
Tatarstan	Kazan	3,723,000	48.5	43.3	1,612,059
Tyva	Kyzyl	306,000	64.3	32.0	97,920
Udmurtia	Izhevsk	1,642,800	30.9	58.9	967,609
Total		21,161,000	48.7	51.3	10,864,073

Source: *Novaya Rossiya: informatsionno-statisticheskii almanakh* (Moscow, Mezhdunarodnaya akademiya informatizatsii, 1994), pp. 137–45, modified.
Notes:
1. Chechens comprised 57.8% and Ingush 12.9% of the total population.
2. This percentage represents the sum for all the indigenous peoples of Dagestan made up of the following peoples: Agul 0.8%; Avar 27.5%; Dargin 15.6%; Kumyk 12.9%; Lak 5.1%; Lezgin 11.3%; Nogai 1.6%; Rutul 0.8%; Tabasaran 4.3%; Tsakhur 0.3%.
3. Kabards 49% and Balkars 9.6% of the population.
4. Karachai 31% and Cherkess 10% of the population.
Population figures are for 1 January 1993; no separate figures are available for the Chechen and Ingush republics.

Table 9.3 Autonomous *oblasts* and *okrugs*

Names of component	Titular nationality (%)	Russians (%)
Jewish autonomous *oblast* (Birobijan)	4.2	83.2
Agin-Buryat autonomous *okrug*	54.9	40.8
Chukchi autonomous *okrug*	7.3	66.1
Evenk autonomous *okrug*	14.0	67.5
Khanty-Mansi autonomous *okrug*	1.4	66.3
Komi-Permyak autonomous *okrug*	60.2	36.1
Koryak autonomous *okrug*	16.5	62.0
Nenets autonomous *okrug*	11.9	65.8
Taimyr (Dolgan-Nenets) autonomous *okrug*	13.7	67.1
Ust-Orda Buryat autonomous *okrug*	36.3	56.5
Yamalo-Nenets autonomous *okrug*	4.2	59.2

Source: *Argumenty i fakty*, No. 13 (March 1991), p. 1, where the administrative divisions are those of 1989, but the figures are updated 1989 census returns reflecting the situation of early 1991.

Some peoples have a 'republic' and others not: thirty-three national groups have some sort of territorial home (though some live in great communal dwellings like Dagestan) and sixty-three do not. The have-nots include Russians and some of the less numerous peoples. Equity would suggest that all should be on an equal footing, irrespective of whether they have a republic in the 'near abroad' – 7.8 million compatriots of the titular nationalities in the fourteen former Union republics live in Russia, including 4.4 million Ukrainians (see Table 9.1); or in the 'far abroad' – Germans (821,000), Koreans (107,000), Poles (95,000), Greeks (92,000), Finns (47,000) and a few other peoples; or Jews who have a nominal homeland abroad (Israel) and one in Russia, Birobijan (the Jewish autonomous *oblast*).

At the time of the 1989 census, the titular nationality comprised an absolute majority of the population in eight of the thirty-one ethno-federal units of that time,[11] a comparative majority in three,[12] and in the other twenty ethnic Russians were in the majority (Tables 9.1–9.3). In the sixteen autonomous republics the titular nationalities comprised only 42 per cent of the total population; in the autonomous *oblasts* 22 per cent; and in the autonomous *okrugs* only 10.5 per cent, largely as a result of the heavy in-migration of Russians and other peoples. The total population of the forty-one nationalities with their own or sharing ethno-federal areas is 17.71 million (12.05 per cent of the total population of the RSFSR), but of these only 10.32 million (58.3 per cent, or 7.02 per cent of total RF population) live in their own titular federal unit (Table 9.1).[13] As for the twenty-one republics in Russia today:

- The titular population comprises over 50 per cent of the population in only seven: Chechnya, Chuvashia, Dagestan (where Avars, Dargins, Kumyks, Lezgins and Laks make up 73 per cent of the population), Ingushetia, Kabardino-Balkaria, North Ossetia and Tyva.

- In eight of the republics Russians comprise the majority: Adygeya, Buryatia, Gorno-Altai, Karelia, Khakassia, Komi, Mordovia and Udmurtia.
- In the other six republics (Bashkortostan, Kalmykia, Karachaevo-Cherkessia, Marii El, Sakha (Yakutia) and Tatarstan) no group has an absolute majority.
- The dispersion quotient is also marked by great variations: over 90 per cent of Yakuts, Tyvans, Kabards and Balkars live in their republics, while at the other extreme two-thirds of Tatars and Mordvins and nearly half of Chuvashis and Maris live outside their titular republic. A total of 9.7 million people live outside their nominal republic (see Table 9.2).[14]

The status of the ten autonomous *okrugs* remains ambiguous. Article 5 of the constitution asserts that they are equal to the other eighty-nine units of the Federation, while article 66 subordinates them to the *oblast* or *krai* in which they are located. In addition, some of the *okrugs* are extremely rich in natural resources (oil and gas), like Khanty-Mansi and Yamal-Nenets in West Siberia, while others are very poor. Not surprisingly, the rich *okrugs* have sought absolute independence from the *oblasts* of which they form part, but so far only Chukotka has achieved this goal, separating from Magadan *oblast* in June 1992. Like the republics, the autonomous *okrugs* were established in the name of titular ethnic groups, but the eponymous nationality makes up over 50 per cent only in Komi-Permyak and Agin-Buryatia, while Russians make up the majority elsewhere (Table 9.3). Under Putin there was considerable debate over the fate of the autonomous *okrugs*, with views divided over whether they should be fully subordinated to the host *oblast*, or whether they should become separate units. The status of the last remaining autonomous *oblast* was equally perplexing. Birobijan was established in the inhospitable Far East by Stalin as a homeland for the Jews, but today they comprise only 4.2 per cent of the population and represent only 1.7 per cent of Russia's Jews. The *oblast* separated from Khabarovsk *krai* on 25 March 1991, and under Putin discussion centred on it becoming an integrated part of its former host.

The potential for conflict

The complexity of minority issues in Russia is daunting. The rich diversity of Russian ethnic composition means that much of the population has multiple identities with overlapping ethnicity, religion, culture and language. As noted, the 1989 census identified 128 ethnic groups, although sixteen had a population of fewer than 5,000. There are twenty-six groups among the peoples of the north alone, ranging from the Nentsy numbering 34,200 to the Entsy at 200. Table 9.1 demonstrates the overwhelming predominance of the ethnic Russians at 81.5 per cent of the population, followed a long way behind by the second largest group, the Tatars at 3.75 per cent. Soviet statistics probably under-estimated the number of Jews, and probably the number of ethnic Germans and Poles as well.

While there remains a devastating potential for Russia to split up, the figures above suggest a picture that differs in several respect from the nationality problems of the USSR. The majority of Russia's republics lack a clear demographic basis to aspirations for independence, and to date a trigger mechanism for disintegration has been lacking. However, territories where the titular nationalities are the strongest can be found on the borders: in the North Caucasus the Islamic bloc of Dagestan, Chechnya, Ingushetia and Kabardino-Balkaria, together with Buddhist Kalmykia and Christian North Ossetia; and in the Far East Tyva on the borders of Mongolia, and Agin *okrug*. The Volga and Kama republics form a single contiguous territory in the centre of Russia (see Figure 9.1), but in Chuvashia and Marii El Russians make up a clear majority. In Tatarstan Tatars comprise 48.5 per cent of the population and Russians 43.3 per cent, but only a third of all Volga Tatars live in Tatarstan. The independence of some of the republics at the margins of the Federation, like Chechnya or Tyva, might not destabilise the fragile unity of the country; whereas the secession of a republic in the heartlands, like Tatarstan, could stimulate a snowball effect tearing the unity of the Federation apart.

Woodrow Wilson was asked during the Paris peace conference in 1919, 'Does every little language have to have a state all its own?' The answer for the USSR in 1991, as in Eastern Europe in 1919, appeared to be 'yes'; whereas in Russia today a somewhat different dynamic operates – or so the leadership believes. In the United States Theodore Roosevelt had tried to transcend ethnic identities – Italian-Americans, Hispanic-Americans, Anglo-Americans – to forge a nation of *Americans*, whereas the current trend towards multiculturalism has reversed assimilationist policies. For historical reasons the question in Russia cannot be posed in quite the same way. The Bashkirs, Tatars and others were long established, and in many cases predated the arrival of the Russians themselves; but at the same time the existence of Tatar-Russians, Bashkir-Russians and so on is an established fact. This is reflected in the two terms used to denote 'Russian' in the language: *Rossiiskoe* means 'of Russia', used adjectivally, giving rise to the noun *Rossiyanin*, a citizen of Russia of whatever ethnicity; whereas *Russkii*, the noun, denotes those who are ethnically Russian.

The *korenizatsiya* policy of the 1920s had contributed much to the development of the national consciousness of the peoples of Russia, and in particular had consolidated national cultures and scripts. From the 1930s onwards, however, schooling in native languages was reduced and the policy of national development reversed. With the collapse of the Soviet regime policy returned to that of the 1920s, with the difference that the earlier nation-building was now accompanied by state-building; for many peoples in the republics the restoration of cultural symbols and culture was not enough and they now sought full statehood. The former communist regime had always been able to invoke the concept of class to denigrate 'nationalism', but Russia lacked such a safety net. In Russia the defence of the integrity of the state has lacked any such ideological subterfuge and has been direct and unmediated – as the Chechens found to their cost.

The Russian leadership from 1990 sought to prevent the 'Balkanisation' of Russia. The central question was to define a new relationship between the many peoples of Russia and the state. The ethno-federal legacy left a heavy burden, with political inequalities not only between regions and national areas, but between the autonomies themselves. The sixteen autonomous republics in the RSFSR had had their own constitutions but (in contrast to the fifteen Union republics) no right of secession, whereas the five autonomous *oblasts* and the ten autonomous *okrugs*, quite apart from the mass of ordinary *oblasts*, had no constitutions and even fewer rights to self-government. This legacy of inequality in national relations represented the single most urgent problem facing the new government. Some peoples (like the Chechens and Tatarstan) sought to become nations in their own right, and tried to do this within the framework of traditional ideas of statehood. Not all of the 128 peoples in the Russian Federation, however, could or even wanted to achieve statehood. The emphasis for the majority moved from 'national self-determination', taking the form of state-building, towards forms of national-cultural self-development. The rediscovery of national identity is at the same time the remaking of this identity in post-Soviet conditions where *all* societies face a crisis of values and viability.

The division of Russia into national areas did not 'solve' the national question but exacerbated it. The question of national development, instruction in native languages and so on cannot be reduced to the question of statehood since so many people live outside 'their' state (an argument the rejectionists make about the USSR as a whole). Not only do a large proportion of people with their own titular republic live outside their nominal area, but the national areas themselves are home to many other peoples (primarily Russians). Russians, however passively they behave, by the mere fact of their presence are perceived as a threat to native languages and traditions, representing an ever-present danger of cultural assimilation. In most areas, however, Russians never considered themselves the bearers of an imperial creed but sought to escape hardship at home, to find work and better wages, or were deported involuntarily. The absence of counter-mobilisation to the nationalism of some of the titular nationalities is striking. The strong vote for Zhirinovskii in some of the national areas in December 1993, however, revealed ethnic Russian fears.[15] Just as in the elections to the First and Second Dumas in 1906 and 1907, where the greatest support for Russian nationalist parties came in the fifteen *gubernii* of the Pale of Settlement and border areas with mixed populations, so too in the elections for the Fifth Duma in December 1993 strong support for Zhirinovskii's nationalism came from areas of mixed settlement. However, in later elections opposition to the ethnocratic territorial organisation of the country was not a significant factor.

Russia is now an entire borderland, the distinguishing feature of post-imperial identities. The very existence of Russia as a state has been questioned. Ryszard Kapuscinski in his book *Imperium* formulates the problem succinctly:

> In short, following the disintegration of the USSR, we are now facing the prospect of the disintegration of the Russian Federation, or, to put it differently; after the first phase of decolonization (that of the former Soviet Union) the second phase begins – the decolonization of the Russian Federation.[16]

The strongest exponent of this view is Rafael Khakimov, one of Tatarstan president Mintimir Shaimiev's chief advisers in the early 1990s and still an influential figure. He espoused the 'decolonisation' model, contrasting a Moscow-based officialdom and 'a provincial, colonial nation living in another world'.[17] In his view, as the regions struggled for greater cultural and economic autonomy and achieved ever more legal sovereignty, Russia itself would gradually disappear:

Russia will increasingly become an ephemeral notion limited to rather vague emotional slogans. There is no hope of preserving Russia in its earlier condition. Russia's borders have lost their legitimacy. There are no legal norms whereby its approximate borders could be defined....Regional interests and the idea of regionalisation offer a way out of the impasse for Russia.[18]

For Khakimov Russia as a geopolitical reality was destined to disappear. This is certainly not the way that things look from the perspective of Moscow. The attitude identified by Kapuscinski remains strong:

For in such a state as the former USSR (today, CIS, tomorrow...?) there exists a certain class of people whose calling is to think exclusively on an imperial scale, and even more – on a global one. One cannot ask them questions like 'What's happening in Vorkuta?' for they are utterly unable to answer them. They will even be surprised: And what is the significance of it? The Imperium will not fall because of anything that is happening there!...Between the Russian and his Imperium a strong and vital symbiosis exists: the fortunes of the super-power truly and deeply move him. Even today.[19]

As we shall see when we discuss foreign and security policy (Part 5) a great-power mentality is pervasive in Russia. Yet, on the basis of our discussion above, we argue that the decolonisation model is not an appropriate one for Russia. Russia may have displayed aspects of an imperial state, but its mix of nationalities suggests that some sort of multinational nation had emerged.[20]

The constitution now recognises all territories as multinational, guaranteeing equal rights for all of Russia's citizens irrespective of where they find themselves. The problem, however, arises when it comes to the question of collective rights. While all the peoples of Russia have the right to national and cultural development, the political form in which this can be expressed remains ambiguous. Russia is considered a state of all of its citizens, irrespective of their nationality, but the ethno-federal legacy of the Soviet period is difficult to reconcile with this civic conception of citizenship (an issue we shall return to in Chapter 11). The fragmentation of citizenship was particularly resented. A survey in Komi republic revealed that 60 per cent of the ethnic Russians considered themselves primarily citizens of Russia rather than of the republic.[21] The ethno-federal system itself remains a potent element stoking the fires of inter-ethnic conflict (although it is neither a sufficient nor a necessary condition for such conflicts). Attempts, however, to separate the national question from the problem of territorial autonomy would in the short run only precipitate conflict. Of all the chalices bequeathed by the Soviet regime, ethno-federalism was perhaps the most poisoned.

Russian federalism

Russia's federal character in the Soviet period was derived not from the regions where the majority of the population lived, which effectively lacked federal representation, but from the national republics. The system was a mixed ethno-federal and unitary one, and thus very different, say, from the United States, where representation is uniformly federal-territorial. How was Russia to move from an ethno-federal system to a genuine federal-territorial system in which *all* of Russia's territories were subjects of federation? Opinion divided between those who sought to make all the components of Russia equal subjects of federation, and those who tried to maintain a hierarchy in the relationship between the republics and the rest. The debate over the new federal treaties reflected the struggle between two different visions, one focusing on individual rights in a democratic state, while the other prioritised national rights loosely identified with the existing ethno-federal regions. The debate is one familiar to France where exponents of the Jacobin tradition, for example, opposed the granting of autonomy to Corsica on the grounds that this would subvert the principle of republican equality.

Towards the Federal Treaty

Learning from the fate of the USSR, which had responded too late to the problem of nationalism, the First Russian CPD in May 1990 decided that the Russian federal system should be renewed; the Declaration of State Sovereignty of 12 June 1990 recognised 'the need for a significant extension of the rights of the autonomous republics...and regions of the RSFSR'; and the Supreme Soviet Presidium on 17 July proposed a timetable for a Federal Treaty. A draft was ready for the Third CPD to adopt in March 1991, but the vigorous anti-federalist lobbying of a group of deputies forced it to be redrafted. The fourth draft of the USSR Union Treaty, published three days before the *coup*, made provision for a Russian treaty to regulate its own inter-national relations. The disintegration of the USSR and the problems encountered in adopting the new Russian constitution placed even more of a premium on achieving an agreement to prevent the disintegration of the Russian Federation.

The debate focused on what was to be the subject of the Russian federal system? If only national-territorial areas, then what role would the regions play, and, even more, what about peoples without territory? Sakharov had suggested making all fifty-three Soviet national-territorial units subjects of federalism in his draft constitution for the Union of Soviet Republics of Europe and Asia. It was not clear why fifty-three republics should represent the 128 census nationalities, especially when ethnic boundaries did not coincide with the national ones and where the titular nationalities were often in a minority in the republic that bore their name. To counter the threat of secession by Lithuania and other republics Gorbachev responded by getting the USSR Supreme Soviet in April 1990 to adopt a law on the 'De-limitation of Powers' between the USSR and the subjects of the Federation equalising the rights of autonomous republics with those of Union republics. This meant that autonomous republics could now negotiate on equal terms with the republics of which they formed part. The idea was to hang a sword of Damocles over republics that threatened to secede; if they tried to leave the union, then they could be faced by secession within the secession.

It was in part to counter Gorbachev's threat that Russia declared its own state sovereignty while at the same time promising extensive sovereignty for its own autonomous republics. Russia's declaration of state sovereignty *vis-à-vis* the USSR was thus accompanied by declarations of sovereignty by its own national areas. On

20 July, North Ossetia declared itself a Union republic, albeit as part of Russia. Karelia on 9 August declared its sovereignty but did not change its status, while Khakassia on 15 August unilaterally raised its status to an autonomous republic. On 29 August Komi and on 30 August Tatarstan declared themselves sovereign, followed by Udmurtia on 20 September and Yakutia on 27 September.[22] What these declarations meant in practice remained to be discovered, but it soon became clear that a declaration of sovereignty by no means signalled its achievement. Russia's autonomous republics sought to join Gorbachev's Union Treaty process in their own right, an idea at first supported by Gorbachev to undermine Yeltsin's power base – even if it meant the destruction of the Russian Federation. Resentment over this lingered throughout the 1990s. It is for this reason that the autonomous republics most active in seeking sovereignty were also those that most actively supported the putschists in August 1991, with the leaderships in Tatarstan, Kabardino-Balkaria and Chechen-Ingushetia actively supporting the *coup*. In Chechnya a lingering Sovietism persisted until well into the 1990s; president Johar Dudaev always argued that he would be happy for Chechnya to become a Union republic in the USSR but not a republic of Russia (*mutatis mutandis*, this is the position of Abkhazia *vis-à-vis* Georgia, and for the same reason). What is often forgotten is that later, in his enthusiasm to achieve a renewal of the Soviet Union through the Novo-Ogarevo process in the spring and summer of 1991, Gorbachev simply confirmed the rights of the fifteen existing Soviet Union republics as the subjects of the proposed Union Treaty, and in effect washed his hands of their own internal secessionist problems.

It was as part of the attempt to out-bid Gorbachev, however, that on a visit to Tatarstan in August 1990, following his election as chairman of the Russian parliament, that Yeltsin declared 'Take as much independence as you can', and he went on to suggest that if this meant secession from Russia, then 'your decision will be final'.[23] In Bashkortostan soon after he once again urged the local authorities to 'take as much power as you can swallow'.[24] In his speech to the Fifth CPD on 28 October 1991, Yeltsin argued that:

> The process of self-determination of peoples, which began even before the revolution of 1917 but which was interrupted by crude force for many decades, is now entering its decisive phase. A new national consciousness is forming in the Russian people that is democratic in its very essence.[25]

It was all very well to urge local sovereignty in a bid to counter Gorbachev's overtures to Russia's republics, but how was this 'freedom' and 'self-determination' to be institutionalised, and would it be democratic and compatible with the unity of the state? Yeltsin was to find that the nations of Russia, which under the Soviet system had enjoyed various degrees of formal autonomy, now tried to convert their rights into genuine powers. While the Karelians, the Dagestanis, the Buryats and the Yakuts sought to extend their autonomy to control resources on their territory, the Chechens and certain groups in Tatarstan sought outright independence.

One of the concrete manifestations of sovereignty was the 'presidentification' of Russia's republics, once again following the example set by Yeltsin himself. Tatarstan led the way, electing a president on the same day as Russia (12 June

1991). By the end of 1991, presidents had been chosen in Kabardino-Balkaria, Marii El, Mordovia, Chechnya and Tyva, and with other republics moving in the same direction. Tatarstan had moved the furthest in translating its declaration of sovereignty into practice, having chosen not only a president but also a new name (formerly Tataria) and a coat of arms, and sought economic sovereignty by establishing its own bank and bringing former Union enterprises under its own jurisdiction. The only other republic to have set on the same path was Chechnya. The key issue everywhere was control over local property, natural resources and budgetary matters, especially taxation.

In the struggle to shape a new post-Soviet federalism 'democrats' like Yelena Bonner (Sakharov's widow) argued that 'The choice is either the creation of a democratic state with guarantees to all the peoples of the federation of the right to self-determination, and protection of this right, or disintegration in accordance with the same former USSR scenario.'[26] They insisted that Russia could avoid the fate that had befallen the USSR only by granting full autonomy to the republics, whereas statists responded that it was this logic that had led to the break-up of the USSR. Instead, they insisted that since the ethnic borders of Russia only roughly corresponded to the existing borders, and because every single region of Russia was multi-ethnic to one degree or another, rights should be individual rather than national. While some Russian nationalists revived the Whites' Civil War slogan of Russia 'united and indivisible' (*edinaya i nedelimaya*), the principle was shared by most of Russia's new leaders, although they were divided over how this could be achieved.

Official policy in the early period was criticised for constantly reacting to crises rather than developing consistent principles. Galina Starovoitova, Yeltsin's adviser on nationality issues until October 1992, placed her hopes on the development of an effective federal system, but in the mean time argued in favour of giving the republics a free rein so as not to provoke conflict. The State Committee for Federalism and Nationalities under Shakhrai took a harder line, insisting that national self-determination was to be dependent on two other principles of international law, human rights and the inviolability of borders. The Committee's policy was based on a number of principles: the equality of all peoples living in the Federation; the genuine development of federalism in Russia; the de-politicisation of nationality policy; reliance on the legally formed authorities in the components of the Federation, whether the centre liked them or not; the indisputable priority of political methods in resolving national conflicts; accepting the link between economic and nationality policy; and consistency in nationality policy.[27] According to Vladimir Lysenko, the state was to ensure the neutrality of the federal centre in inter-ethnic conflicts, hold a moratorium on border changes, ban the creation of new federal components through the division of existing units, assist the stabilisation of political elites in the republics by advancing moderate nationalists, managers and entrepreneurs to leadership positions, and prevent the fusion of state and mafia-criminal structures in the national areas.[28] By contrast, Ramazan Abdulatipov, the chair of the Supreme Soviet's Council of Nationalities, insisted that the revival of the national life of the peoples of Russia was an essential part of the formation of civil society and the establishment of a legal state: 'We consider national rebirth as the combination of the national idea with general human interests and democratic principles.' He insisted that in a multinational society the state should not stand above the various ethnic groups, and he condemned those who sought to replace the national principle with the territorial one. He agreed that the priority was individual human rights, but this should not infringe national rights.[29] The points made above indicate the range of issues discussed at this time.

Federalism has a long history in Russia. It has been argued that the treaties signed between the Tsar and the governments of peoples entering the empire, like the Caucasian khans and Central Asian emirs, contained provision for a division of powers between the centre and the locality, the hallmark of federalism. Various national areas of the old empire had certain rights and privileges, allowing local self-government and limiting the prerogatives of Tsarist *chinovniki*. These early elements of federalism were undermined during the centralising and unitarist period of the second half of the nineteenth century, as the supranational principles of Tsarist imperial statehood began to give way to a nation-building statism, yet did not disappear entirely. The Bolsheviks had at first condemned the concept of federalism, but were soon forced to incorporate it in their state-building. However, as we have seen, federal forms were undermined by a unitary practice. In drafting Russia's new constitution Yeltsin insisted on three key principles: that human rights were to be guaranteed throughout Russia, including the republics; the unity of Russia must be maintained; and the constitutions of the republics should not contradict the Russian constitution.[30]

The major obstacle to adopting the constitution was disagreement over what was to be the subject of Federation. The draft of October 1991 weakened the old ethno-territorial division of Russia by proposing two forms of representation: ethno-federal from the *republics*, which would not necessarily be the same as the existing autonomous republics; and federal-territorial, as in the United States or Germany, from *zemli* (lands, or in German *Länder*). A highly regionalised Russia was to emerge with some forty units, the republics and the *zemli* (whose relative status remained to be determined). All of Russia for the first time would become a subject of the Federation and not just specified ethnic parts.[31] Trying to steer a course between those who argued for the re-establishment of a unitary state (in the form of the restoration of the Tsarist *gubernii*) and extreme ethno-federalists, encompassing not only secessionists in Tatarstan or Chechnya but also Russian nationalists who called for the creation of an ethnic Russian republic, the draft appeared to satisfy neither. On the one hand, it was attacked for undermining the unity of the country by conferring extensive rights on the titular republics, and indeed for infringing the rights of Russians living in them. On the other hand, the attempt to equalise the rights of republics and lands was interpreted as an attack on the privileges of the former. The draft represented a move away from the traditional Soviet absolutisation of the ethnic dimension in state-building, which had granted statehood to all sorts of ethnic groups to whom the principle was often alien and pointless; but having tasted statehood the ethno-federal territories would not give it up without a struggle.

The October 1991 draft constitution asserted that Russia existed as a multinational state that had come into being over the centuries. The draft reflected the view that Russia was a *constitutional* rather than a *treaty* Federation: the state sovereignty of Russia only needed to find a constitutional and federal form; it was not formed by contracts between its members. This did not exclude the signing of a

Federal Treaty between the republics of Russia and the state as a whole, but did not give the republics the right of secession since they were already part of a pre-existing Russian state. Thus, the draft condemned the treaty path to a new constitution, which would have given all the subjects of the new Federation the choice whether to join or not. According to Rumyantsev, this would not only have caused endless conflicts but it would also have denied that Russia was a priori already a 'sovereign state created by the peoples historically living in it'.[32] Russia had never been a treaty Federation (unlike the USSR) and therefore none had the right to secede; and neither would they be given a choice of whether to join. Tatarstan, Tyva and Chechen-Ingushetia had never formally signed to join the RSFSR or the USSR, and were now bitter that they would not be given the option of choosing to enter the Russian Federation as signatories of a new treaty.[33]

Post-communist Russian state-building was thus torn between three principles:

- The first suggested that all national-territorial formations should be abolished in their entirety, and that Russia should become a unitary state and be divided into simple administrative regions like the Tsarist *gubernii*, a view advanced by patriots and even more vigorously by nationalists like Zhirinovskii. Advocates of 'gubernisation' insist that a unitary state is not necessarily a centralised one, and point to the example of France where regional devolution has eroded Napoleonic centralism. In Spain since the death of Franco in 1975, a hybrid type of federalism has emerged with the devolution of authority to seventeen self-governing provinces; but the lack of historical identity of some of the regions suggests elements of 'false federalism'.
- The second view absolutised the federal principle and sought to divide Russia into fully fledged republics and *zemli* with equal rights.
- The third view, advanced by the leaders of Russia's republics, sought to maintain the existing hierarchy of federalism, with the ethno-federal units at the top.

The 1991 draft constitution took the second path and weakened the ethno-federal principle in favour of a de-ethnicised federalism. This led to protests in the republics by advocates of the third path, and later versions of the constitution made concessions in form to the national elites in the titular republics while equalising the content of the new federalism. The special status of national republics was retained but the rights of Russia's regions were enhanced.

This balance between privileges and rights was enshrined in the three federal treaties (known collectively as the Federal Treaty), signed on 31 March 1992 and ratified by an overwhelming majority by the Sixth CPD on 10 April.[34] The Treaty allowed a significant degree of de-centralisation, providing for joint jurisdiction over education, environmental protection and conservation, health care and natural resources, while recognising certain areas as the sole prerogative of the subjects. The Treaty recognised three types of federal subjects:

- Twenty (now twenty-one) national-state formations (formerly autonomous republics) as sovereign republics within the Russian Federation.
- Fifty-seven administrative territorial areas (*krais*, *oblasts*, as well as the cities of Moscow and St Petersburg).

- Eleven national-territorial areas (autonomous *oblasts* and autonomous *okrugs*).

All had equal rights and obligations, but the republics were allowed the attributes of statehood: constitutions and laws, elected Supreme Soviets (parliaments), supreme courts, and, if they so wished (which most did), presidents.[35] With the elevation in 1991 of four autonomous *oblasts* to the status of republics the total had risen to twenty, and, of these, eighteen signed the Treaty. Tatarstan, which had earlier voted for self-rule, and the Chechen Republic, which had declared independence from Russia in November 1991, refused to sign. Tatarstan insisted on a separate bilateral treaty between itself and Russia as equal sovereign states. Bashkortostan had threatened not to participate but at the last moment agreed to sign when granted additional budgetary rights.[36]

The Federal Treaty did not signify the creation of a new state since such a state had existed already for centuries, and neither did it denote the transformation of the state into a federation, since Russian statehood had long contained elements of federalism, but was an attempt to define the powers of the Federation and its subjects.[37] The Treaty rendered the subjects of Federation equal in a juridical sense, yet the republics were granted more of the attributes of statehood and more economic powers than the regions.[38] In contrast to the old Soviet constitution, the Treaty did not grant the republics the right to secede but bound them together while granting greater powers and freedoms. The Treaty was not intended to act as a substitute for the constitution, and instead was incorporated, with some amendments, into the constitution of the time as a special section. Moscow retained the right to control defence and security and to set federal taxes, while the signatories now gained some control over natural resources and formalised their borders. They could now also conduct foreign trade on their own. The extent of their control over natural resources and the right to levy taxes remained unclear and caused endless conflicts later – including a joint declaration by the presidents of Bashkortostan, Tatarstan and Sakha (Yakutia) that the federal authorities ignored the legitimate rights and interests of the republics.[39]

Once again a form of ethno-federalism was confirmed in Russia despite hopes to avoid this route. The new Russian federalism now developed on a constitutional-treaty basis, though much remained to be done. The local and national constitutions had to be amended to take into account the new agreements, numerous national laws had to be changed and the rights of the non-national areas had to be given a juridicial foundation. It appeared absurd to retain three different types of subjects of federation, yet 'asymmetrical federalism' appeared to be the only basis on which the Russian Federation could survive. Under asymmetrical federalism components of the Federation have different competencies and status, whereas in a symmetrical federation they are equal.[40] There are well-grounded fears, however, that asymmetrical state structures give rise to conflicts, since not all components are willing to accept the disparities in status and prerogatives. It may even provoke the emergence of dual federalism, with one or more states becoming entirely distinct from the others. This was the process that engendered the division of Czechoslovakia, provoked regional conflicts in Spain between the so-called nationalities and provinces, and which placed the Belgian state (divided into three separate language communities) under enormous pressure as Flanders gained many of the attributes of statehood.

Yeltsin had earlier favoured the division of Russia into some eight to ten large regions to avoid nationality clashes and separatism, and Rumyantsev had favoured the division of Russia into *zemli* and republics with equal rights. This had been opposed by the national republics who wanted more rights in *comparison* with the Russian *oblasts*, even though they were gaining extensive rights in comparison with the past. The national republics were united on this, irrespective of their ethnic composition. Karelia, a republic in which the titular nationality made up only 10 per cent of the population, sought exactly the same rights as Tatarstan or Tyva with much larger proportions of the titular nationality. Behaviour was defined by status rather than ethnic composition. The rise of regional separatism later added to this leapfrogging battle of relative sovereignties.

The Federal Treaty did not put an end to debates in Russia about the form of its federalism. Questions of property and taxation remained vexed, the fundamental question over whether Russia should be a regional rather than an ethno-national federation had not been resolved, and an unstable hierarchy of federalism had been established. The twenty-one republics were endowed with the appurtenances of a state, but the others were not. Tatarstan's constitution affirmed that it was a state 'associated with Russia',[41] and the constitutions of some of the other republics (namely Tyva, Karelia and Yakutia-Sakha) declared the primacy of local laws over Russian ones.[42] The struggle between executive and legislative power in Moscow allowed the regions to ignore presidential decrees and legislative acts and weakened economic links. In 1993, for example, Moscow collected only 40 per cent of the tax revenues due to it from the regions and republics,[43] and over two dozen refused to pay the centre their federal tax obligations. The confusion allowed considerations of short-term advantage to predominate over juridical principles of unified and equal state-building for all of Russia.

The constitutional basis of the new federalism

Drafts of the constitution had both encouraged the aspirations of Russia's republics for sovereignty while at the same time limiting these aspirations, a tension still not satisfactorily resolved. Strengthened by his victory in October 1993, Yeltsin took a more assertive line towards the regions and republics of Russia and in effect reneged on what he had been forced to concede during the struggle with Gorbachev and parliament. In particular, the word 'sovereign', incorporated into the Federal Treaty and which a number of republics had adopted to describe themselves, was struck from the constitution on the grounds that one state could not have two sources of sovereignty. The constitution adopted on 12 December 1993 finally gave legal form to Russia's federal system.

The Federal Treaty was excluded from the constitution, although the basic principles of de-centralisation, joint and sole jurisdictions, remained. The new constitution, which took precedence over the Federal Treaty, took a more restrictive view of these rights. Although the definition of the republics as 'sovereign states' was dropped from the new text, the federation structure continued to apply different criteria to various units despite the formal claim that all federal components are equal (Art. 5.1). The rights of Russia's federal units were significantly equalised and made subject to the laws and decisions of federal authorities. The principle of 'asymmetrical federalism', the keystone of the Federal Treaty, was in principle abandoned (although as we shall see in Chapter 10, it was very much alive in practice). No longer were some subjects of the Federation 'more equal' than others – at least in theory. While the provisions of the Treaty were reflected in the new constitution, the text itself was no longer bodily incorporated to underline the principle that Russia is a Federation based on a constitution and not on a treaty. The constitution regularised the hybrid federalism that had been emerging in Russia based partly on national areas (like Belgium and India) and partly on areas lacking any national significance (as in Brazil, Germany and the United States). This mix of national and territorial federalism was accompanied by declarations (Art. 5) on the equality of all the subjects of the Federation, when in fact they had greatly differing rights. The republics, for example, have their own constitutions, governments, parliaments, presidents and other attributes of statehood denied the territorial formations; the latter, however, have the right to issue their own charters. The constitution tried to move away from the old Soviet primacy given to the ethno-federal organisation of the state, a principle that was largely meaningless under communist rule. The new document sought to prioritise civil over collective ethnic rights, and at the same time tried to prevent ethnic differences becoming the foundation of local or central statehood, a development that could only exacerbate centrifugal tendencies.

Regions and republics were now guaranteed significant areas of autonomy as long as their legislative acts did not contradict the Russian constitution or federal laws. Articles 71–3 of the constitution lay out the respective powers of the federal authorities and the regions. Article 71 subordinates civil law, the court system and the procuracy to the federal authorities; Article 72 outlines the elements of joint jurisdiction, including the control and use of natural resources; and Article 73 ascribes all that is not specified in the previous two articles to regional jurisdiction, although this is vague and does not specify what these are. Putin's struggle against non-compliance has been waged within the terms of reinstating the primacy of Article 71, but the danger arose that the provisions of Articles 72 and 73 would be undermined.

The long-standing dispute between republics, on the one hand, and between regions and territories, on the other, was not resolved, and debates over Russia's state structure continue. In contrast to the republics, the powers of the remaining sixty-eight subjects of the federation appeared residual, sharing certain listed powers and enjoying other unspecified prerogatives not conflicting with the national state (Art. 76.6), but there was no mention of any detailed regulatory or financial powers that they could exercise independently. Republics can elect presidents and adopt constitutions, while regions often have governors and adopt 'charters'. Regions sought to narrow the difference, while republics fought jealously to preserve the differential.

Conclusion

All three federal communist systems disintegrated: the USSR, Yugoslavia and Czechoslovakia. In the early 1990s, many expected the Russian Federation to go the same way, yet this did not take place. With the exception of Chechnya, new ways were found of voluntarily binding together the new state. Russia replicated the federal-unitary structure of the USSR. Its eighty-nine regions and republics are ordered in a complex hierarchy, with the main division between the twenty-one ethno-federal republics that seek many of the attributes of sovereign statehood, and the rest who lack these attributes. The lack of support for separatism in the 1993 and subsequent elections suggests that reports of the imminent demise of the Russian Federation are exaggerated. The comparison with the USSR is misleading because the dynamics of Russian politics are very different; there are powerful centripetal trends that check the tendency towards disintegration.

The Kremlin leadership was well aware that any attempt to abolish the ethno-federal republics would provoke massive resistance and probably precipitate the break-up of Russia. Moscow instead sought accommodation with the republics and enshrined the principle of asymmetrical federalism in a series of treaties with republics (see Chapter 10). The struggle over the constitution and Federal Treaty was only one aspect of finding a new political framework for the conduct of relations between the peoples of the Russian Federation. While fears about the disintegration of the Russian Federation might have abated, they have not disappeared. The 1993 constitution limited the sovereignty of Russia's republics, but the power-sharing treaties then enhanced their status. Meanwhile, support for a return to the *guberniya* principle, whereby Russia would be converted into a unitary state and divided into administrative units and the principle of ethno-federalism abolished, remains strong.[44] Opinion remains divided between those who want to make the components of Russia equal subjects of federation, and those who try to maintain a hierarchy in the relationship between the republics and the rest. The 1993 constitution, however, provides a viable framework for the development of a federal state, but there remain many points of tension and the management of regional relations is one of the main concerns of the government, and it is to this that we now turn.

10 Regional and local politics

> In every age justice has been called the keystone of the social edifice. By acting towards each other justly, the citizens maintain the condition of trustfulness and friendship which is the basis of an unforced and fruitful co-operation; by acting with justice towards each and all, the public authority wins the confidence and respect which render it effective.
>
> (Bertrand De Jouvenal)[1]

Regional politics are extremely diverse, both in type of governmental system and in regime characteristics. Most republics have a president, whereas most *oblasts* have a governor. The legislative bodies in each region (the collective term we shall use to describe Russia's eighty-nine federal units) are also composed in diverse ways and have different powers, stipulated by regional constitutions and charters. As for the political characteristics, some regions are relatively democratic, whereas in others authoritarian regimes have emerged. All took advantage of the weakness of the centre under Yeltsin to seize powers and a degree of sovereignty that in certain cases posed a threat to the continued existence of the Russian state. Instead of an effectively integrated federal system, a type of segmented regionalism emerged. Yeltsin managed regional affairs by a mix of concessions and personal contacts, whereas under Putin regional laws and statutes were made to conform with the Russian constitution, and normative acts and powers of regional actors in national politics were curbed. The debate continues over whether Putin's reforms represented the development of federalism or its repudiation in favour of traditional Russian centralism. Local government, meanwhile, remained a relatively neglected area, over-shadowed by the powerful regional bosses and limited by inadequate funding.

The organisation of power

Yeltsin-style authoritarianism never quite developed into full-blown dictatorship but equally never quite submitted itself to popular accountability and constitutional and legal restraints. The phenomenon was replicated at the regional level. An extremely heterogeneous pattern of regime types emerged, ranging from the relatively democratic in Novgorod, Arkhangel'sk, Samara and St Petersburg, to the outright authoritarian in Primorskii (Maritime) *krai* under Yevgenii Nazdratenko and Kalmykia under president Kirsan Ilyumzhinov. There was also diversity in types of state-political structure. Udmurtia was a parliamentary republic (until a referendum in early 2000), Tatarstan was a fully fledged presidential republic,

Dagestan was governed by a form of consociational democracy in which a State Council sought to balance and represent the ethnic diversity of the republic, while Moscow city replicated the 'super-presidentialism' of the central government itself. This diversity in part reflected local traditions, the dynamic of elite relations, and the ethnic and social composition of a particular republic, and in turn affected policy outcomes.[2]

Regional government remains part of the state system, whereas local self-government is separate from the state. The struggle between executive and legislative authority at the centre between 1991–3 was reflected locally. The regions duplicated the national power system, with the heads of administration appointed by Yeltsin and the regional soviets subordinated to parliament. Only after the events of 3–4 October was the old system of soviets abolished, and new regional legislative bodies created. Below we will briefly discuss the main instruments of power in the regions.

Regional executives and their election

The vacuum created by the fall of the CPSU and its once mighty network of *obkom* first secretaries was filled by the appointment of heads of administration in each region, who soon became known as governors (*gubernator*). Governors up to 1995 were directly appointed rather than locally elected, and most were former *oblast* Party leaders, provoking Yeltsin's democratic allies to talk of 'the revolution betrayed'.[3] Regional governors in turn appointed heads of administration in cities and districts, replacing the old Soviet executive committees (*ispolkomy*) headed by chairmen, who hitherto had been the senior executive figures in the districts. The appointment of governors was intended to be an interim measure until the regional elections due in December 1991, but these were repeatedly postponed.[4] On 17 September 1995, Yeltsin once again suspended the local electoral process, decreeing that regional governors be elected in December 1996 (that is, after the presidential elections due in June 1996) and legislatures only in December 1997. Later, twelve exceptions were made to allow regional elections in December 1995 and Moscow's mayoral election on 16 June 1996. The number of presidentially appointed administrative heads gradually decreased. In the autumn of 1996, fifty-two executives faced election, joining the handful who had already been elected.

Regional elections not only affected individual areas but also had implications for national politics; each of the executives elected became, as noted in Chapter 6, members of the Federation Council, as did the chairmen chosen by the newly elected legislatures. It is for this reason that the centre took great pains to influence regional elections. Pro-Yeltsin sitting governors used all the powers of incumbency to retain their jobs, and even successful opposition candidates became more co-operative with the federal government to gain privileges for their regions. The classic case was Sverdlovsk governor Eduard Rossel, who was elected in August 1995 as a defender of the idea of a semi-autonomous 'Urals Republic', yet went on to become a staunch supporter of Yeltsin's re-election as president.

As at the federal level the electoral process was distorted by power and resource asymmetries between the candidates, above all between sitting governors and their challengers. Incumbents clearly enjoyed numerous advantages, including influence over the local media, and financial resources, and were in most cases better known to the public than their opponents. The typical campaign strategy pursued by incumbent governors, and in some cases by challengers, was to present themselves as competent non-partisan economic managers untainted by corruption – the 'strong manager' (*krepkii khozyaistvennik*) syndrome. A number of pro-Yeltsin incumbents were defeated, but once in office oppositionists were forced to come to terms with Moscow's power, especially over the purse-strings, and mend their fences with the presidential administration. Although the great majority of governors are drawn from the Soviet elite, there have been notable exceptions. Perhaps best known are Boris Nemtsov, governor of Nizhnii Novgorod in the early 1990s until called to Moscow in 1997, Mikhail Prusak in Novgorod and Alexander Lebed in Krasnoyarsk. From 2000, the trend for businessmen to take power directly was strengthened, notably with the election of former Sibneft head Roman Abramovich as governor of Chukotka and Norilsk Nickel boss to the governorship of Taimyr autonomous *okrug* in January 2001.

Regional elections illustrated the flaws of Russia's democracy. According to the CEC, electoral laws in twenty-seven regions in the late 1990s contravened federal legislation, restricting voting to those permanently residing in the region or including residency or language requirements for candidates. Most regional election laws required only a 25 per cent turnout for the elections to be valid, allowing the victor in heavily contested regions to win with as little as 6 per cent of the vote. Low voter turnout encouraged local electoral commissions to inflate the figures they reported. In case of disputes local courts, lacking resources and independence, were easily pressured either by the administration or by the communists. There were initially few provisions for public monitoring of the elections, allowing one side or the other to influence the results. In some republics (like Bashkortostan and Kalmykia) mass-media laws violated the federal constitution by limiting the individual's right to information.

All the advantages of incumbency are sometimes not enough to guarantee re-election. Controlling the media was not always foolproof and was liable to backfire: it had to be used effectively. Voters were alienated by excessively ideological campaigning or by home-grown mini personality cults and instead favoured professionalism (the 'good manager' factor) and judged candidates on their moral character. The significant turnover of regional executives suggests that Russian electoralism does have a certain bite. Out of the total of 148 elections of regional executives between 1995 and 2000, sixty-five (44 per cent) lost (see Table 10.1). The trend, however, was for incumbent governors to marshal their resources to greater effect in electoral races, and the chances of incumbents winning improved.[5] One technique used to good effect was bringing forward the date of electoral contests, thus wrong-footing opponents, even though Russian electoral legislation bans the arbitrary extension or curtailment of the terms of elected officials or bodies of state power.

The replacement of leaders through elections is the key test of democracy, and at the regional level has been working only fitfully. The dynamics of regional economic dependency on Moscow meant that even though the opposition strengthened its presence in the Federation Council (although falling far short of the two-thirds majority required to overcome the presidential veto on legislation), the

Table 10.1 Gubernatorial elections

Year	Number of elections	Incumbent wins (%)	Incumbent loses (%)
1995	14	10 (71.4)	4 (28.6)
1996	46	22 (47.8)	24 (52.2)
1997	17	7 (41.2)	10 (58.8)
1998	10	4 (40)	6 (60)
1999	17	12 (70.2)	5 (11.8)
2000	44	28 (63.6)	16 (36.4)

Sources: http//:www.fci.ru/elections/isp_99.htm for results up to October 1999; Robert Orttung, 'Resourceful Governors Able to Counter the Kremlin', EastWest Institute, *Russian Regional Report*, Vol. 5, No. 10 (15 March 2000); *Moscow Times*, 24 January 2001.

FC continued to work with the presidential administration. The elected governors (unlike presidential appointees) could no longer be dismissed by the federal authorities; once elected, they enjoyed a power base separate from the president. This deprived the Yeltsin administration of a powerful instrument that had helped regulate relations with the provinces. Governors usually had a say in appointing the heads of federal agencies to be found in every federal subject. Under Putin long-formulated plans to deprive them of this right were activated (see below).

The law limiting governors to a maximum of two terms was passed on 19 October 1999, to come into effect on 19 October 2001, giving the governors a two-year grace period.[6] By early 2000, there were thirty-two governors serving their second terms, with the first of the putative third-term governors coming up for election being Shaimiev in Tatarstan. Regional leaders hoped to win a third term before the deadline, forcing some to plan to move up their elections before the fateful date. In the event, on 25 January 2001 the Duma adopted a generous amendment to the law. The first term of the governor was to be counted as the one starting after 19 October 1999, allowing sixty-nine regional executives to run for a third, and in seventeen cases a fourth, term. Luzhkov, who was re-elected in December 1999, could stand for one more term, while Shaimiev could seek two more terms. This represented a major capitulation to the regional lobby, although some pressure remained to remove restrictive electoral conditions (like that in Tatarstan specifying that a candidate had to speak both Russian and Tatar). Further amendments banned governors from forcing pre-term elections by resigning and then standing again; resignees would not be allowed to stand in the subsequent election.

The vicissitudes of electoralism encouraged some governors to contemplate giving up whatever legitimacy they may have gained through the electoral process and return to the old system of appointment from the centre. In return, governors sought greater powers of appointment over mayors of regional centres and heads of districts, thus re-establishing what was called the 'presidential (or executive) vertical' all the way from the Kremlin to the local level. A notable expression of this trend was the letter of three governors to Putin in February 2000 calling for such a reform, with the necessary constitutional amendments to be enacted through a Constitutional Assembly, spiced with the call for the presidential term of office to be extended to seven years.[7] Quite apart from instrumental considerations, as far as they were concerned electoralism fostered regional particularism, something in their view that could only be overcome by re-centralisation.[8] For others, like Konstantin Titov of Samara, such a change represented 'a detailed plan for the liquidation of democratic achievements in Russia', undermining the emergent democratic political links in the federal system and once again reasserting administrative ties.[9]

The 'presidential vertical'

From 1991, presidential envoys (*predstaviteli prezidenta*) were appointed to the regions to monitor the work of the newly appointed governors.[10] In a few cases, as in Nizhnii Novgorod, Moscow and St Petersburg, the presidential envoy was also the governor. The envoys were likened to the Bolshevik system of commissars, who monitored the political reliability of former Tsarist officers in the Red Army during the Civil War. This embryonic pro-consular system alarmed Yeltsin's erstwhile supporters, if only because he did not appoint more of them to these positions.[11] The decree of 22 August 1991 stated that envoys were to ensure that local legislation was compatible with national laws, and could recommend the dismissal of local officials who undermined national policy, and they were to report back to the president.[12] Their basic task was to ensure local compliance with central policies. Envoys could impose presidential decrees directly, avoiding the local bureaucracies. Rather contradictorily, they were enjoined not to interfere in local administration or to issue orders covering the given territory.[13] Separate instructions limited the powers of the presidential envoys in the national republics of Russia.[14] The state inspector was to oversee the work of the representatives as well as co-ordinate the work of local executive bodies.

Yeltsin clearly hoped that the presidential envoys would be able to work in harmony with local administrations while at the same time relying on the support of local democratic movements to place pressure on recalcitrant administrations. They were ordered to 'facilitate' the observance of federal laws, decrees and presidential instructions.[15] The aim was to establish a supervisory authority that could act as an autonomous presidential vertical chain of authority. They were present in some eighty regions by the time that they were subsumed into Putin's reform of the 'presidential vertical' in 2000 (see below). The vague formulation of their powers, the lack of financial resources that often rendered them dependent on the very governor on whom they were meant to check, and the lack of consistent policy from the centre soon rendered them largely ineffective. The process of elite consolidation in any case meant that many came to terms with the existing establishment.

Regional government remained marked by chaos and corruption. The GKU, as we saw in Chapter 6, became the Main Territorial Administration (GTU), monitoring the work of administrations both ideologically, to ensure loyalty to the president, and technically, above all to ensure probity and financial order. The second head of the GKU, Yurii Boldyrev, noted that many abuses stemmed from officials combining administrative posts with entrepreneurial activities. He insisted that corruption could not be justified by arguments about the necessary evils of the primary accumulation of capital, because that way would lie the Latin American path of development.[16] The prevailing criminalisation of the regions stifled entrepreneurs and invaded the sphere of politics as representatives of the mafia fought to win electoral office. Boldyrev himself fell foul of intrigues among the presidential staff, having secured the dismissal, for corruption, of some regional heads of administration who happened to be presidential allies, and, when in March 1993 his attempts to investigate the corruption in the Western Group of Forces in Germany was blocked by the president, he was forced to resign.[17]

With the establishment of the seven federal districts (FDs) by Putin in May 2000 (see below), the role of the GTU and its relationship with the seven presidential envoys were much debated. In February 2001, with the dismissal of the long-time head of the GTU, Sergei Samoilov, some of the central staff were transferred to the FDs, whose own staff by this time was about 230 each. The relationship between the presidential administration and the envoys remained tense, with some in the former accusing the envoys of trying to usurp power.

The Security Council was another instrument occasionally used to monitor regional affairs. In 1992, its secretary, Yurii Skokov, was invested with powers to establish local commissions of the SC in the regions to monitor the work of local administration. Under Putin the role of the Security Council in regional affairs was once again enhanced, but its role in managing the seven federal districts that were the cornerstone of Putin's attempts to re-establish the presidential vertical was unclear. We shall discuss Putin's regional reforms later in this chapter.

Regional legislatures

Between 1991–3, regional administrations and soviets appeared to operate according to two sets of laws: presidential decrees for the mayors and administrative bodies; and executive orders of the Russian Supreme Soviet for the soviets. From July 1991, regional and local soviets were required to form a 'small soviet' one-fifth the size of the full complement of deputies, thus duplicating the national pattern of the CPD electing a smaller Supreme Soviet. The presidiums of the soviets, which had co-ordinated their work, were made redundant and in most places abolished.[18] Following the October events, Yeltsin issued a number of decrees dissolving local soviets and stipulating that new elections should be held to reconstituted regional assemblies. The decree of 9 October 1993 proposed radical changes to local assemblies.[19] They were to be reduced in size from the old 2–400 to some 15–50 deputies, who were to be full-time legislators. The legislatures in the republics, however, tend to be larger with some 100–130 deputies. On 22 October 1993, Yeltsin called for local and regional elections to be held between December 1993 and the following spring, but his decree established only the broadest of 'basic guidelines', allowing the regional authorities (in most cases the governor) to establish detailed electoral arrangements. The balance of power between the regional legislative bodies and governors remained unclear. The decree of 22 October 1993 gave the new regional assemblies (usually called assemblies or *dumas*, with a few at first sticking with the traditional name of 'soviet') the right to pass laws, something denied the old regional soviets. At the same time, however, the decree gave local governors, many of whom were appointed by Yeltsin, a great deal of authority over the new regional parliaments. Local laws were not to contradict federal laws, presidential decrees or governmental instructions, a stipulation that was widely flouted until Putin began his campaign to establish a 'single legal space' throughout Russia.

Regions are allowed wide discretion in their electoral systems, and republican leaderships have taken full advantage of this (by districting in favour of rural areas and so on) to ensure compliant assemblies. Many regions abolished minimum turnout because of the difficulty of exceeding the 25 per cent threshold. In some regions residence and occupational restrictions have been imposed on voting rights, while elsewhere governors simplified procedures to the extent that they simply appointed deputies to regional assemblies. Although two-fifths of deputies have to be full-time legislators, this rule has not been enforced. Local administrative officials often became members of regional legislatures, to the degree that in Tatarstan the republican legislature was dominated by district bosses, who themselves had been appointed by the republic's president. Political parties in such systems were rendered totally redundant. Similarly, managers of local enterprises and farms tended to dominate regional assemblies.

De-centralisation on its own did not enhance democracy, and indeed allowed regional authoritarian regimes to thrive, and thus Putin's reassertion of central authority was welcomed by many. Regional legislatures were traditionally overshadowed by the executive authorities and enjoyed little legislative autonomy. Some, however, had been in opposition to the local executive, a trend that increased in the 2000s. Already the regional parliaments in St Petersburg, Krasnoyarsk, Irkutsk, Tver and Sakha had asserted themselves against the local governor, a trend that the Kremlin sought to encourage. Under Putin there were vigorous attempts to ensure that those working for the executive branch were not allowed to sit in regional legislatures on the grounds that the practice violated the division of powers. Reform plans included the requirement that regional legislatures would be required to elect some of their members on the basis of party-lists. This would deprive governors of the full control that they typically enjoyed over the selection of members. Various schemes were suggested, including the idea that a certain proportion (figures between 15 and 50 per cent were suggested) of deputies should be elected from party-lists. Such mixed systems were already in operation in Kaliningrad, Krasnoyarsk and Sverdlovsk. The new law on parties adopted in 2001 (see Chapter 8) prevented regional parties (usually under the control of the governor) from participating in regional legislative elections while encouraging national parties to play a more active part in regional politics.

Federalism and regional politics

Weakening central power under Brezhnev had been accompanied by the commensurate growth of the power of regional elites. Even before the *coup*, the CPSU was losing power, but the more far-sighted communist officials were already shifting over to posts in the local state system and later reinvented themselves as democratic leaders. The end of the communist regime allowed these regional elites, in particular in the republics, to consolidate their authority, albeit now in a democratic guise. Traditional elites, in alliance with some of the new social forces, underwent a dual adaptation comparable to that experienced by political parties: they adapted to the new market and political conditions; and at the same time ensured a convergence between elite interests and the uncertainty engendered by the new electoral politics. Neither project met with uniform success, yet regional elites showed remarkable ingenuity in subverting democratic forms and ensuring that elections were robbed off their sting.

Segmented regionalism and asymmetrical federalism

While no federation can be completely symmetrical (for example, in terms of population and area), very few give political form to asymmetries. In Russia there is a formal power asymmetry enshrined in the differing prerogatives granted republics and regions, and further codified in power-sharing agreements.[20] In the 1990s, the old hyper-centralised Soviet state gave way to the fragmentation of political authority and contesting definitions of sovereignty. A complex and unstable balance was drawn between the claimed prerogatives of the centre and the normative and *de facto* powers of the regions. The tension between central and regional claims not only concerned practical issues of governance and finances, but also focused on fundamental competing sovereignty claims. The evolving practice of 'asymmetrical federalism' affected the very definition of the state. A distinctive type of 'segmented regionalism' emerged, whereby Russia in effect had ninety governments. The federal authorities at the centre entered into asymmetrical bargaining relations with the other eighty-nine 'subjects of the federation', one of which (Chechnya) claimed outright independence. Some went so far as to argue that under Yeltsin Russia had turned into a federation of mini-dictatorships in which press freedom and human rights were abused by regional leaders, who in some cases were little more than representatives of organised crime.

The federal separation of authority was undermined by spontaneous processes of segmented regionalism.[21] The development of asymmetrical federalism may well have provided a framework for the flexible negotiation of individual tailor-made solutions to Russia's diverse ethnic and political composition,[22] but it failed to do this within the framework of universal norms of citizenship or republican notions of equality. Instead, segmented regionalism fragmented the country juridically, economically and, implicitly, in terms of sovereignty. By the end of Yeltsin's term in office, Russia was beginning to become not only a multinational state, but also a multi-state state, with numerous proto-state formations making sovereignty claims *vis-à-vis* Moscow.[23] The country was increasingly divided into segments, not only spatially but also in terms of the fragmentation of political authority. Overlapping jurisdictions and fragmented administrative and legal practices led some to suggest that Russian politics had become 'medievalised'. The emergence of a national party system was stunted by the proto-state claims made by regional executives, their ability to control patronage resources and to influence electoral outcomes. The Federation Council, moreover, gave regional elites a powerful hold on the national decision-making process and, while providing a focus for a common political discourse, ensured a regional veto on national issues.

This was the situation facing the incoming president, Putin, on coming to office in 2000. His response was to appeal to the principle of 'the dictatorship of law', and in particular the unimpeded flow of constitutional and juridical authority throughout the territory of the Russian Federation. Sub-national sovereignty claims were thereby rendered illegitimate, even though federalism as a principle is all about shared sovereignty. Fundamental issues were occluded by Putin's attempts to reconstitute the state, above all the question of the form of state sovereignty. Was Russia to become a genuine federation, in which law would be defined in accordance with the normative spatial division of sovereignty; or would it take the form of *de facto* regionalism, where an effectively unitary state grants rights to devolved units, in which case a very different definition of sovereignty would operate?

Under Yeltsin regional regimes came to exert considerable autonomous authority over their 'fiefdoms'. Putin's reassertion of central authority in defence of the writ of the constitution represented the defence of a particular vision of democracy. His aim was to place the constitution at the centre of the political process in regional relations. For some this was no more than a new form of Russia's traditional centralism; others argued that it offered an opportunity to move away from asymmetrical federalism towards a more balanced form. Asymmetrical federalism not only granted differential rights to regional leaderships, but effectively established different gradations of democratic citizenship to those living in different parts of the country. The attempt to achieve a universal and homogeneous type of citizenship lay at the heart of Putin's attempt to reconstitute the state.

Attempts in the 1990s to build federalism from the top down were countered by the regions which managed, *de facto* if not yet *de jure*, to ensure a significant bottom-up devolution of power.[24] All federations are designed to constrain central political power, but not all do so with equal effect. In Russia, whatever the nature of the local regimes themselves, regions acted as a check on the central authorities; a type of spatial separation of powers emerged that to a degree compensated for the inadequacy of the vertical separation of power in the new constitutional order. In this context, however democratic the reconstitution of the Russian state may be, the weakening, if not the removal, of this 'fourth pivot' in Russian government (in addition to the classical trinity of the executive, legislative and judiciary), could weaken the overall democratism of the Russian constitutional order. Segmented regionalism and asymmetrical federalism provided more effective checks, if not democratic balance, on executive authority than the relatively weak legislature and judiciary.

Patterns of regional politics

Mikhail Alexseev notes that 'The specter of regional separatism has haunted Russian politics since the collapse of the Soviet Union in 1991.'[25] Segmented regionalism was underpinned by competing sovereignty claims. The crisis of the state and the economy allowed some of the republics to expand their *de facto* sovereignty by adopting laws that created a legal space which became increasingly distinct from that established by Moscow. In the vanguard of this process, dubbed 'disassociation by default', were Tatarstan, Bashkortostan, Khakassia and Yakutia. The unifying role of the military was lost, and, indeed, the army became increasingly dependent on the regional authorities. The federal authorities were unable to guarantee basic civil rights in the regions, and even lost control over regional branches of state agencies. The local offices of the procuracy, the MVD (internal ministry) and other ministries fell into the hands of governors and local presidents.

Only the KGB's successor, the Federal Security Service (FSB), appeared able to withstand 'capture' by regional authorities. Segmented regionalism was generated by historical, material and social factors, and not simply by the strategic choices of post-communist central and regional elites. However, while federal asymmetry reflected the diversity of the country, it did not explain the legal and juridical disparities between the country's regions. In the 1990s, federal relations developed largely as a function of the immediate political needs of the presidency. The lack of genuine reciprocal and transparent relations between the centre and the localities was one of the most significant failures of Yeltsin's presidency. As his regime gave way to Putin's, a whole series of issues remained problematical. We examine some of them below.

Subject-level constitutions and charters

By the late 1990s, at least fifty of the eighty-nine local constitutions and charters contradicted the federal one, while a third of local legislation violated in one way or another federal legislation. The constitutions of Bashkortostan, Tatarstan and the regional charter of Tula *oblast* were exemplary cases of subjects claiming rights not allowed for in the national constitution, derogating from the principle of equality between subjects of the federation. Article 1 of Bashkortostan's constitution, adopted in December 1993, stated:

> The Republic of Bashkortostan has supreme authority on its territory, inde-
> pendently defining and conducting domestic and foreign policies, adopting the
> Bashkortostan constitution and its laws, which have supremacy on its entire
> territory.

Komi's constitution granted special rights to citizens of the republic who were ethnic Komi, stipulating that the head of the republic and deputies to the legislative assembly had to be citizens of Komi, while its citizenship laws themselves contravened the national constitution. One of Putin's immediate concerns was to bring the republican constitutions and regional charters into line with the Russian constitution. Bashkortostan proved the most resistant to bringing its constitution into line with that of Russia, fearing that doing so would reduce Russia once again to a unitary state.

The fragmentation of legal space

According to the Justice Ministry, an examination in 1997 of 44,000 regional legal acts, including laws, gubernatorial orders and similar documents, found that nearly half did not conform with the constitution or federal legislation.[26] Sergei Stepashin, at the time Minister of Justice, in December 1997 noted that his ministry had analysed 9,000 laws adopted in the regions, and claimed that a third contradicted either the Russian constitution or federal legislation. On the same theme, the Prosecutor General, Yurii Skuratov, noted that nearly 2,000 regional laws had been revoked for contradicting the constitution, but warned that Russia lacked sufficient 'levers' to ensure compliance at the regional level with the rulings of the Constitutional

Court.[27] In addition, subjects of the Federation signed agreements among themselves, bypassing the centre, which further fragmented Russian economic and political space.

It was under the premiership of Stepashin (May–August 1999) that the long-awaited law 'On the Principles of Dividing Power between the Russian Federation Government and the Regions' was finally adopted,[28] stipulating that all new federal and regional laws had to be adopted in conformity with this law, and that all previously adopted legislation and treaties had to be brought into line within set periods. The law reinforced attempts to establish a unified national system of the administration of justice. The role of the Constitutional Court in interpreting the writ of the constitution in disputes between regional and federal prerogatives has increased. The national judicial system acted as a barrier, however weak in some places, to the emergence of regional despotisms. It was this obstacle to the fragmentation of law that Putin sought to strengthen. By mid-2001, according to justice minister Yurii Chaika, 94 per cent of regional laws had been brought into conformity with federal legislation.[29] A meeting of the Security Council in June 2001 chaired by its new secretary, Vladimir Rushailo, however, noted that legislation in Tatarstan, North Ossetia, Kabardino-Balkariya, Komi and Pskov still diverged significantly from federal norms, while fifty-seven articles of the constitution of Sakha (Yakutia), which specifies Russian, Yakut and English as state languages, contradicted the national constitution.[30]

Power-sharing bilateral treaties

In a departure from the principle enunciated in the constitution (see Chapter 9), the signing of the treaty between Tatarstan and Russia on 15 February 1994 suggested that Russia was indeed a treaty rather than a constitutional federation. The treaty affirmed Tatarstan's right to have a constitution, tax system, foreign policy and foreign trade policy. During Yeltsin's presidency forty-six power-sharing treaties were signed between the leaders (not, it should be noted, by the subjects as a whole) of forty-two individual regions and the federal authorities, accompanied by 260 specific agreements. The treaties formalised the emergence of asymmetrical federalism where the rights of separate regions were negotiated on an *ad hoc* and often conjunctural basis. The terms of many of these treaties, included in various annexes and annual supplements, were not made public, and their net result was to accentuate the asymmetries in federal relations. The bilateral treaties allowed customised deals between the centre and the subjects, and to that degree Yeltsin had a case in arguing that they 'strengthened Russian statehood',[31] yet they could not but undermine basic principles of constitutional equality and political transparency.

The federal authorities insisted that these were not international treaties, but their precise juridical status was not specified. Did these various treaties take priority over federal laws, supplement them, or trump them? The law 'On the Principles of Dividing Power' of June 1999, mentioned above, formalised the procedures for the adoption of power-sharing treaties, stressing above all that everything was to be done openly, thus forbidding secret clauses and sub-treaties. This law, together with the one adopted in October 1999, substantially changed the legal environment and rendered power-sharing treaties redundant as a way of managing federal relations. Although treaties with Tatarstan and other regions later were renewed, bilateral treaties had become an outmoded way of managing federal relations and no more were signed after 1998. On 26 June 2001, Putin established a commission to examine federal relations as a whole, and the role of the treaties in particular, under the leadership of his close colleague, Kozak. He made no secret of his view that most of the treaties contradicted federal law and would have to be changed to establish a 'single legal space' in Russia. In anticipation of negative findings, a number of regions repudiated their treaties (for example, Perm, Ulyanovsk, Nizhnii Novgorod and Marii El in July 2001) to ensure, in their words, 'the superiority of the constitution and federal law'.[32] It was unlikely, however, that Tatarstan, Bashkortostan or Sakha would follow suit, since their treaties gave them considerable privileges in keeping taxes and over the natural resources in their regions, while Sverdlovsk governor Eduard Rossel noisily defended his treaty.

Supra-regionalism and regional development

The fragmentation of Russia into eighty-nine regions is considered by many to be excessive, prompting repeated plans to merge them into larger (supra-regional) units while at the same time prompting the creation of inter-regional associations. In his presidential campaign of June 1991, Yeltsin had argued for the division of the country into some eight to ten large economic regions, and the idea had been incorporated, as we have seen, into the October 1991 draft constitution in the form of *zemli*. It was at this time that Moscow, and Yeltsin personally,[33] supported the creation of regional associations, in part to counter-balance the sovereignty movement of republics and regions.[34] Dating from the Soviet period, Russia had eleven economic regions, each closely tied to the national administrative system,[35] but from 1990 they were effectively superseded by the creation from below of eight Inter-regional Economic Co-operation Associations.

The most effective associations were those most distant from the centre – the Far East, Siberia and the Urals – where regionalism was infused with the separatist spirit that had already been evident at the time of Russia's earlier disintegration during the Civil War. The Siberian Association (*Sibirskoe soglashenie*) was established on 2 October 1990 and brought together all nineteen administrative regions of East and West Siberia (see Figure 10.1). It was the most effective in integrating regional and nationality politics. The borders of some of the associations changed in order to correspond more closely with the local definition of the region rather than the economic definition taken from the Soviet state planners. In Siberia there was even talk of the need to 'decolonise',[36] accompanied by demands for greater control over Siberia's rich natural resources, the right to conduct foreign trade directly, and an end to what was called colonial exploitation by Moscow.[37]

They had a point. The traditional Soviet system of planning had given priority to vertically integrated branches of the economy run by ministries, and had paid very little attention to questions of regional development (or, indeed, environmental issues). In Siberia the emphasis had been on extractive industries and energy supplies, at the expense of developing a local manufacturing base, infrastructural development or food supplies. In exchange for the 'export' of industrial raw materials, either to the rest of the country for processing or abroad for hard currency,

Figure 10.1 The regions and republics of European Russia

Key to abbreviated names
K   Kaliningrad Oblast
N   Nakhichevan
RI   Republic of Ingushetia
K-C   Republic of Karachai-Cherkessia
K-B   Republic of Kabardino-Balkaria
NO   North Ossetian Republic

Siberia had to import most of its food, machinery and consumer goods. In the long-running 'East–West' debate the advantages of developing regional industrial complexes in Siberia were contrasted with the availability of skilled workforces, good transport and closeness to markets in European USSR, and indeed the bulk of investments went to republics like Ukraine and Belarus. The collapse of the centralised supply system threw Siberia's dependency into sharp relief, and various regions were forced to resort to barter, such as coal for machinery between Moscow and Kemerovo. While the prices of raw materials remained depressed, the price of producer and consumer goods rose many-fold. Thus, there were powerful economic factors, generated by the distorted pattern of Soviet development, fuelling demands for supra-regional autonomy and organisation in the post-Soviet era.

Rossel, in 1995 the exponent of the creation of a 'Urals Republic', in the run-up to the 2000 presidential election advocated the consolidation of Russia's eighty-nine regions into larger macro-regions; the existing eight regional associations could become the organisational base for the future federation.[38] Putin ultimately adopted a variant of such an approach in the creation of the seven federal super-regions. The associations had been established to co-ordinate the actions of their members, and thus to increase their leverage, but they failed to act as cohesive bargaining agencies. During Primakov's premiership (September 1998–May 1999), the heads of the associations joined the presidium of the government, and Stepashin continued the practice, which was of enormous symbolic significance but little practical consequence. With Putin's reorganisation of the country into seven federal districts the existing inter-regional associations, including the most active like Siberian Accord, Great Volga and Great Urals (*Bolshoi Ural*), were marginalised and lost much of their *raison d'être*. This was exacerbated by the lack of coincidence between the borders of the federal districts and the inter-regional associations. Several regions, for example, that had traditionally been considered part of the Urals (Bashkortostan, Udmurtiya, Perm and Orenburg) ended up in the Volga federal district, while Volgograd became part of the Southern FD.

Fiscal federalism

The asymmetry in federal relations was reflected most sharply in budgetary matters. Although fiscal matters can never be fully symmetrical, there is a long way for Russia to go before the procedure for distributing transfers among regions becomes both transparent and accurate, with the clear enunciation of the formulae whereby budget revenues are collected and distributed. The struggle over the allocation of tax revenues at the point of collection and from the federal budget became the defining indicator of Russia's failure to establish itself as a genuine federation.

The principles underlying inter-regional transfers have been the subject of considerable debate.[39] The whole notion of 'donor' or 'subsidised' region depends to a large degree on definitions, on what is included and what is left out in making these calculations. By May 1999, only thirteen regions were calculated to be donors,[40] but this did not mean that all the others were recipients: about a third received nothing from the centre. In addition, the various bilateral agreements discussed above allowed differences to emerge in the amounts of tax revenue transferred to the centre. Tatarstan, for example, passed on only 50 per cent of its VAT revenues to the federal budget, while other regions transferred 75 per cent of what is the most effectively collected tax in Russia.

The fundamental fact of fiscal dependency for most remained, although the degree to which the centre used the system of transfer payments for overtly political purposes has been questioned.[41] The leading exponent of the 'politicisation' thesis regarding fiscal flows is Daniel Treisman, who has argued that during Yeltsin's rule transfers were used as 'bribes' to encourage subordination among the more fractious regions rather than as 'rewards' for those who demonstrated loyalty.[42] Treisman argued that the central authorities operated a policy of 'fiscal appeasement' to gain the loyalty of regional leaders. Potential separatist ambitions were bought off in a policy that, paradoxically, rewarded not loyalty but rebelliousness. Although not efficient in economic terms, political stability was thereby achieved.[43] Treisman's approach, while raising important issues, suggests a competence in Moscow in managing regional affairs that is probably exaggerated. Budgetary transfers were only one part of the story of fiscal flows between the centre and the regions.

Others have argued that transfers were more de-politicised and reflected relatively objective criteria of need, rather than acting as a mechanism of punishment and rewards.[44] Lavrov and his 'Fiscal Transparency' team in 1999 examined the allocation of federal and public financial resources, analysing not only budgetary distribution (the focus of Triesman's work) but also off-budget outlays (e.g. for social insurance and pensions). The team quantified federal expenditure in the regions and the aggregate tax burden, and above all the proportion of public spending in the unit that was derived from the inter-regional allocation of funds. Contrary to the traditional view that only between ten and twelve regions were 'donors', Lavrov's team suggested that there were more self-sufficient regions than conventionally believed; about twenty-five of the eighty-nine regions contributed more to the federal budget than they received in state spending. Examination of the scale and nature of extra-budgetary flows began to fill in one of the largest 'blank spots' in Russian politics, with enormous implications for the development of regional policy. The debate shifted from how to squeeze money out of the handful of allegedly super-rich regions, to placate the vast majority of the supposedly indigent, to how to formulate a balanced policy of regional economic development and political sustainability.[45]

It was Moscow's enduring control over the allocation and disbursement of funds to the regions that was often considered the main cement holding the federation together. Regions dependent on the centre for subsidies, whatever their political complexion, were forced to establish good relations with the Kremlin to ensure the continued flow of funds. The adoption of the budget provided an annual spectacle of bargaining and deals. The lack of transparency of financial flows under Yeltsin encouraged corruption and barter. The development of the Federal Treasury system contributed to the gradual improvement of the management of federal finances; by 1998, over 60 per cent of all expenditures were channelled through the Treasury. Monetary flows were centralised and instead of the federal government transferring money to regional administrations, who often took a cut and exercised discretion in allocating funds, the Treasury now makes payments direct to agencies disbursing, for example, payments to veterans.

Putin's reforms signalled a shift of economic power in the regions. Income tax revenue at the close of Yeltsin's term was divided 51:49 between the federal government and the regions, but this now changed to 55 per cent of all tax revenues going to federal government, leaving 45 per cent for the regions. The Tax Code adopted in July 2001 shifted the entire revenue from VAT to the centre, depriving regions of the 15 per cent that they had kept earlier. The 4 per cent turnover tax, mostly spent in the regions, was to be abolished. The new Tax Code was designed to be easier to understand, as well as to implement. The reform provided for much greater centralisation of collection and redistribution of tax revenues between the regions than had hitherto existed. Not surprisingly, the poorer regions (the great majority) supported the reform. All regions apart from Moscow benefited from another change operating from 2002: firms are now to pay taxes in the region where they actually work rather than where they are registered. The establishment of a social programme co-financing fund means that every rouble spent by regions on social issues is matched by one from the federal authorities, irrespective of the level of income in the region. At the same time, the practice of 'unfunded mandates', costs that are imposed on regional administrations without sufficient resources to cover them, will be phased out. By some estimates, such mandates amounted to some 8 per cent of GDP (600 billion roubles) in 2001. [46]

Economic differentiation and the fragmentation of the national market

Since 1991, the economic independence of Russia's regions has increased considerably: regional and republican governments now account for 50 per cent of tax raising and 70 per cent of government spending. Despite the Soviet regime's commitment to regional equalisation, there were marked disparities in the level of economic development and standards of living, with the national areas tending to be at the bottom of both scales. The 1990s saw increased differentiation between regions in the speed and scale of reform, but this only exacerbated existing differences.[47] Regions able to exploit raw materials (like oil- and gas-rich Tyumen) or which act as gateways for Russia's booming trade with the world economy (like Moscow) are doing well, while those dominated by agriculture were locked in deep depression throughout the 1990s. The development of a genuine capitalist national market would encourage a type of unity from below, whereas the regions that pursued a slow model of economic reform tended towards economic autarchy and, often, political separatism.

The growing economic divergence between regions provided an economic basis to federal asymmetries. Some regions have access to world markets through the sale of energy, raw materials or basic finished industrial goods, giving them an independent resource in the federal bargaining game. Central to the development of segmented regionalism is the political economy of the post-Soviet period. Economic 'reform' in the 1990s was not so much a transition from the Soviet forms of economic planning to the market but rather endless exploitation of the opportunities opened up by the transition process itself. Martin Nicholson notes:

> From heady beginnings, when they acquired control over the wealth-creating assets of the former Soviet Union, regional leaders have become locked into an

economic system that is neither 'socialist' nor 'capitalist', but a battle of vested interests in which normal economic indicators, including money, play little part.[48]

As in politics, the political economy of Yeltsinism looked both forwards (towards the effective liberalisation of the economy and its integration into the global economy) and backwards (towards bureaucratic regulation and arbitrary state interventions). This tension helps in part to explain why regions like Primorskii *krai*, bordering on China, Korea and Japan, failed to take advantage of the opportunities to integrate into the Pacific Rim market but instead focused on an *oblastnichestvo* ('regionalism') that sparred with Moscow but which ultimately remained dependent on Moscow.[49] The regional leadership concentrated on the expanded opportunities for rent-seeking and other pathologies of a semi-marketised economy, termed a 'partial reform equilibrium' by Hellman (see Chapter 12). At the heart of regional politics here, as in many other regions, was the coalition of political and business interests that proved resistant to federal interference.

Non-governmental actors were an increasingly important element framing Russia's political and economic space. Above all, the large energy producers and primary materials exporters negotiated directly with subject-level leaderships, and indeed appeared to conduct their own foreign policies. The sectoral fragmentation of Russia, with powerful lobbies enjoying direct access to government at all levels, was reminiscent of the old Soviet economic ministries.[50]

Throughout the 1990s, regions tried to impose restrictions on the movement of goods and foodstuffs. The August 1998 financial crisis stimulated further the 'economisation' of regional politics. Regions and republics, forced back on to their own resources, saw themselves increasingly as autonomous economic subjects and less as part of a single national market.[51] Regional responses fell into two categories: measures designed to take control of financial flows, including the refusal to pay taxes to the central budget; and laws that tried to control the market by regulating prices and the movement of goods. Many regions stopped remitting tax revenues to Moscow, and a number introduced price and other controls over their economies. Krasnoyarsk *krai* governor Alexander Lebed and Kemerovo *oblast* governor Aman Tuleev, and some others, placed limits on food price rises and imposed restrictions on the movement of foodstuffs, something explicitly banned by federal law, while in Pskov protectionist barriers were established against goods from other regions or neighbouring countries.[52] The national market appeared to be breaking down. Many other non-market responses were implemented as regions took advantage of the crisis in the payments system to increase their autonomy. Some of these measures were temporary and primarily defensive in character as the inter-dependence of central and regional economies became clear. Nevertheless, an underlying trend towards the imposition of regional administrative controls remained. On 24 June 1999, for example, Kirov *oblast* became the third region in Russia, after Khabarovsk *krai* and Tyumen *oblast*, to impose price controls on selected food products, industrial goods and services like rented housing, heating and public transport.[53]

The attempt to recreate a national market became one of the central planks of Putin's regional policy. The general weakening of the power of individual regions during his presidency had important economic consequences, in particular in the struggle against Russia's 'virtual economy' (the network of barter and non-payments) that was very much regionally based. At the same time, the federal government began to revoke many of the tax concessions that it had granted under Yeltsin.

The regionalisation of foreign policy

Regions began to emerge as international actors. Between 1991–5 alone, Russian regions signed over 300 agreements on trade, economic and humanitarian co-operation with foreign countries, undermining Moscow's monopoly on foreign relations and shifting attention away from high diplomacy to the pressing needs of Russia's regions. Some republics, like Tatarstan, pursued their own foreign policies, while the views of regions on international questions cannot be ignored. In the Far East, for example, the Primorskii *krai* Duma, supported by the assertive governor Yevgenii Nazdratenko, in March 1996 requested that the Constitutional Court review the May 1991 Soviet–Chinese border agreement that resulted in the transfer to China of about 1,500 hectares of disputed territory. Other Far Eastern regions have categorically refused to contemplate the possible return to Japan of the four contested Kurile Islands (called by Japan the Northern Territories, see Chapter 15). While some regions inhibited problem solving, particularly those in the Far East, others like Karelia and Pskov acted to stabilise their regional foreign relations by establishing warm relations with their neighbours (in the case of Karelia in the framework of the EU's 'Northern Dimension'). Over half of Russia's regions are borderlands, and need the support of the federal authorities in dealing with their neighbours. The exclave of Kaliningrad, indeed, could not be more of a border-land, separated from the rest of Russia by Lithuania and Belarus.

Regions on occasions effectively exercised a veto on foreign policy. This was particularly in evidence during the Kosovo war of 1999, when Shaimiev of Tatarstan threatened to send Tatar volunteers to support the Moslem Kosovars if Russian nationalists sent volunteers to assist the Serbs. The prospect of Russian fighting Russian in the Balkans, in the context where some 30 million Russian citizens had some Islamic heritage, brought the government and public opinion back from the brink of ethnicising Russian foreign policy.[54] The preferences of Russia's regional leaders became part of the complex tapestry of Russia's foreign relations.

The long-term trend was for regions to try to enter the global market directly, bypassing Moscow. Despite the rhetoric of globalisation, however, there are limits to the ability of a region to enter the world market. The conventions of the international financial system, for example, do not allow regions to have a higher credit rating than that of the country as a whole. Thus, when Moscow sneezes, the regions catch a cold. Nevertheless, regions actively seek foreign direct investment (FDI); particularly successful in this respect was Novgorod, although naturally Moscow and St Petersburg were way ahead. By 2000, Tatarstan had twenty offices abroad, dealing mainly with economic issues, and the republic had signed fifty-six agreements with foreign institutions. Of course, neither Tatarstan nor Chechnya had achieved anything like external recognition since, as Alan James stresses, 'the concept of state sovereignty – in the sense of constitutional independence – is of fundamental importance for the maintenance of international order'.[55] No country wants to be seen supporting the break-up of an existing state – if only out of fear that such an action might boomerang back on itself.

To co-ordinate regional and federal foreign policy, in October 1997 the Duma adopted a law ensuring that regional authorities liaised with the Foreign Ministry over any negotiations with a foreign government.[56] A special department was established by the ministry dealing with inter-regional affairs, with branch offices in regions and republics that were particularly active in foreign affairs. A Council of Regions for International and Foreign Economic Ties was established; a forum used by the foreign minister, Igor Ivanov, on 30 January 2001 to warn governors that the government planned to improve its oversight of their foreign political and economic policies.[57] The principle that only the federal government had the right to sign international treaties (*dogovory*) was jealously guarded, and upheld by numerous judgements of the Constitutional Court.[58]

Putin's reform of the federal system

Segmented regionalism undermined state-building and the emergence of a unified national market, legal space and Russia's coherence as an international actor. The ambiguities in the federal system were exploited by actors in the regions to enhance their privileges and powers, while the central leadership was more concerned with political advantage than the coherence of the state. It was against this segmentation of political, economic and juridical development that Putin set his face.

The Yeltsinite regional bargain provided the regions and republics a free hand as long as they did not threaten secession.[59] As in the Ottoman and Habsburg empires, local privileges were granted in return for loyalty. The development of civil society was inhibited since these were privileges granted not to individuals but to corporate groups. The free hand extended to the manipulation of elections (until the abrogation of the results of the elections for the head of Karachaevo-Cherkessia in May 1999, no election result had been rescinded), allowed the political elites of titular ethnic groups to consolidate their dominance, and permitted various types of authoritarian regimes elsewhere. Even in Novgorod under Mikhail Prusak, typically contrasted favourably with neighbouring Pskov, Dinello argued that consensus there was 'vested in an authoritarian political model in which rigidities are moderated by a charismatic and enlightened governor'.[60] She argued that it was this model that was being applied to the rest of Russia by Putin. In the context of the segmentation of regional politics, the individual had few recourses.[61] Segmented regionalism threatened the rights of minorities and of individuals. It was in response to this that the countervailing republican (in the Jacobin state-building sense) agenda represented by the national state was asserted. Yeltsin's traditional style of managing the regions, where relative independence and selective privileges had been granted in return for support for the Kremlin at the federal level, now gave way to a period of federal activism. In his book *First Person*, Putin had stressed the importance of an independent judiciary together with greater federal control over the regions,[62] and now he implemented this programme. This activism initially combined four strands.

Federal districts

The reconstitution of the state became the central theme of Putin's programme, interpreted as the reassertion of presidential authority. The centrepiece of the new 'state-gathering' policy was Putin's decree of 13 May 2000 dividing Russia's eighty-nine regions into seven larger federal districts (see Figure 10.2).[63] Russia's existing territorial-administrative divisions were left intact, but an administrative layer was inserted between the federal centre and the regions. The new FDs are headed by presidential appointees, thus undermining the principle of regional democracy, and are directly subordinate to the president. Although intended to restore the 'executive vertical', it appears to have established a 'triangle' with the FD capitals intervening in relations between the regions and Moscow.

The seven new representatives were responsible for organising the work of federal agencies in the regions (with particular attention to the law enforcement bodies), monitoring the implementation of federal policy, providing the federal authorities with information on what was going on in the regions, and were to advise and make recommendations on federal appointments in the region. They were also to work with the eight inter-regional associations to devise social and economic policies. The system of presidential representatives was abolished. As we have seen, they had not been notably successful in restoring presidential authority; indeed, many had been 'co-opted' by the very regional authorities that they had been intended to monitor. The new system would make the emergence of these regional 'policy communities' much more difficult since each of the new presidential representatives would be responsible for a dozen-odd regions.

The new federal districts largely coincided with the military districts, suggesting a certain 'militarisation' of federal relations. With only two exceptions (Nizhnii Novgorod instead of Samara, and Novosibirsk instead of Chita), the new federal centres coincided with the headquarters of the military districts.[64] It was, moreover, noteworthy that no ethnic republic was made the centre of a federal district. The seven presidential representatives appointed on 18 May, moreover, reinforced the military/security tone to the measure. Only two were fully civilian figures: Sergei Kirienko and Leonid Drachevskii.[65] On 30 January 2001, Putin issued a decree that placed the seven presidential representatives directly under chief of staff Alexander Voloshin, ensuring that the Main Territorial Administration (GTU) retained its role. The representatives were now to be guided in their work by the constitution, federal laws, presidential orders and the instructions of the chief of staff. The degree to which they would become political actors and economic managers in their own right rather than simply overseers remained open. The representatives sought expanded powers to control budgetary flows and even to establish their own governments.

The measure tried to ensure regional conformity to national laws, but in addition the reform had a straightforward administrative rationale: to stop the 'capture' of federal agencies by regional executives, who had often supplied the former with offices, transport and other facilities. They co-ordinated the work of federal agencies in the regions, of which there were between thirty-six and fifty-three (ranging from the MVD to the State Property Committee) employing a total staff of 380,000. At last the giant army of federal employees and federal agencies in the

Figure 10.2 The seven federal districts

Figure 10.3 Siberia and the Russian Far East

regions were re-subordinated to Moscow. The seven Federal Districts gradually took on a range of functions. The Ministry of the Interior (MVD) reorganised its key departments along the lines of the seven super-regions, with new offices established in each of the regions in charge of preliminary investigations. Similarly, the Procurator General set up office in each of the new Federal Districts, as did the Justice Ministry and the judicial system as a whole. Federal District branches of the Justice Ministry not only examined regional legislation but also ensured that it complied with federal norms. Important federal-level agencies like the treasury and the tax ministry all adapted themselves to the new structure of government. The influence of vested regional interests was diluted as the supremacy of federal legislation was asserted throughout Russia.

The aim was clearly to reassert central control over its own agencies. The new representatives would report directly to the president, with deputies in the regions within their jurisdiction. It was unclear how the new system would be an improvement on the old. The Presidential Representatives set up their own staffs and administrations. The representative in the Central Region, Georgii Poltavchenko, for example, established a staff with forty people in Moscow and three to four in each of the other eighteen regions in his federal district. He drew up an inventory of regional laws to check their conformity with federal norms, and noted that, while the situation was generally positive, some 140 regional laws and acts did not correspond with federal legislation.[66] In addition, he condemned the Moscow authorities for failing to end the registration (*propiska*) system, imposing restrictions on movement that had already been judged illegal by the Constitutional Court.[67] The Representative in the North-west Federal District, Viktor Cherkesov, argued that his main concern was the reform of the economy and establishing an opposition to the regional elite.[68]

The reform was enacted through a presidential decree rather than through a law or constitutional amendment, and thus the juridical basis for the new system remained precarious. Any attempt to 'constitutionalise' the change would be fraught with difficulties. In principle, since the change affected only the president's own administration and did not alter the powers of the governors or restructure the Russian federation itself, the constitutional question was avoided. The measure appeared to be a halfway house on the way towards the fulfilment of Solzhenitsyn's (and indeed Zhirinovskii's) plan for the 'gubernisation' of Russia and a functioning federal system. It appeared that little more had been achieved than establishing another layer in the bureaucracy with unclear responsibilities and disputed prerogatives over financial flows, and almost non-existent democratic accountability. While the reform signalled that Yeltsin's tolerance of diversity and asymmetry in federal relations was over, above all in establishing a single legal and economic space, it did not yet indicate that a way had been found of ensuring effective national governance, federal devolution or the subordination of the whole country to the constitution.

Re-forming the Federation Council and the State Council

Soon after the announcement of the creation of the federal districts, in a televised address on 17 May 2000, Putin submitted a package of laws to the State Duma designed 'to strengthen and cement Russian statehood'.[69] 'The common task of all these acts,' according to Putin, was 'to make both the executive branch and the legislative branch truly working, and to fill the constitutional principles of the separation of powers and the unity of the executive vertical with absolutely real content.'[70] At the heart of the package was reform of the Federation Council. As we have seen (Chapter 6), the first convocation of the FC in 1993 had been formed by direct election in the regions, but later the heads of the regional executive and legislative branches had been made *ex officio* members of the upper house. Now Putin sought to allow the senior figures to 'concentrate on the specific problems facing their territories'.[71] Although Putin was forced to make concessions, the overall package was in line with his aspiration to create a full-time working upper chamber. The Federation Council, as we saw earlier, is formed by two permanent representatives, one nominated by each region's executive branch and one by the legislature. The new 'senators' would be delegates of the regional authorities rather than popular representatives. The new representatives were to be dismissed in the same way as they were selected. A governor's appointment of a representative can be blocked by a two-thirds majority in the regional legislative assembly within two weeks. Dismissal is also to be approved by a two-thirds majority of the local legislature. Regional leaders and heads of regional legislatures retain a determining voice in choosing the full-time representatives. How this resolves the problem of the 'separation of powers' is unclear. The creation of the State Council, moreover, while giving regional executives direct access to the presidency, only confused lines of authority.

The dismissal and dissolution mechanism

Another of the package of bills provided a mechanism whereby the heads of regions could be removed and regional legislatures dissolved if they adopted laws that contradicted federal legislation. Although in principle the courts already enjoyed the power to dismiss governors, two court decisions were required stating that the governor had violated federal law. In introducing the new law to the Duma, the presidential representative there, Aleksandr Kotenkov, warned that 'at least 16 governors' faced the prospect of criminal prosecution.[72] In the event, the Duma on 19 July 2000 adopted the bill allowing the president to dismiss regional leaders and to disband local parliaments. The law allows Russia's president to dismiss regional leaders, including governors of *oblasts* and presidents of republics, for violating federal laws. A court ruling that the official had broken the law and a letter from the Prosecutor General that a case had been opened against a regional leader regarding a serious crime was required to confirm that a regional leader was facing criminal charges. To dissolve a regional legislature, the president had to submit a bill to the State Duma.[73] Nazdratenko was the first victim of the new presidential powers (which came into effect on 1 February 2001), resigning from the post of governor of Primorskii *krai* on 5 February 2001 after nearly a decade of misrule. Although the full power of the new law was not applied against him, the threat (in the form of repeated inspections by the GKU, headed at this time by Yevgenii Lisov) apparently was enough for him to step down.

Delineation of powers and functions

The presidential commission headed by Kozak, mentioned above, sought to develop the legislative basis for the division of power between the federal, regional and local levels of government. The constitution's assignment of a number of responsibilities to joint jurisdiction had proved to be a recipe for confusion, and now the idea was to draw up a list of functions and designate them to specific levels. As noted, the role of the bilateral treaties would be reduced and would be subordinate to the constitution, federal law, presidential decrees and federal government directives. The aim was to establish a common set of rules for all regions and to provide them with equal rights. The twenty-two-member commission included a number of governors, and sought to proceed, in a manner typical of Putin, by consensus. Putin's decree even agreed that some of Shaimiev's ideas on federal reform placed before the State Council in autumn 2000, which at the time were condemned by Kozak as 'threatening the destruction of the country's legal system', were to be taken into account, and indeed Shaimiev was made a member of the commission. The seven federal districts were each to establish their own mini-commissions, to report back to the main commission by the end of the year.

The net effect of these measures was to reduce the influence of regional leaders on federal policy, but in return their control over regional politics was confirmed. Conflicts between the federal centre and the regions were now to a degree displaced to the level of relations between the federal districts and individual regions. Centre–regional conflicts were no longer so politicised, and instead the courts played a more active role in managing federal relations. The writ of the constitution was now to run unimpeded throughout the territory of Russia. This legal offensive against segmented regionalism brought regional charters, republican constitutions and all other normative acts into conformity with the constitution and federal law. Regional authorities had long been condemned for transforming their territories into separate fiefdoms where they ruled like the boyars of old, apparently insulated from the writ of federal laws and the constitution. The vote for Putin in March 2000 had been for strong authority that could defend people from the arbitrariness of bureaucrats and ensure the supremacy of law at all levels. Putin's attempts to rein in the regions were not only about the reassertion of federal authority but about the defence of the rights of citizens. The country now was to live according to one constitution and one set of laws regardless of the region where one lived. The era of special privileges for territorial entities was over.

Local self-government

Local self-government refers to the political and managerial activities of local authorities in municipalities and *raions* below the level of *oblast* government. Amendments to Article 138 of the old constitution on 24 May 1991 introduced the concept of 'local self-government' for districts, towns, boroughs and villages, replacing the soviet *ispolkom* responsible for local administrative services with a 'local administration' and its 'head of administration' responsible to the soviet.

Local soviets would now monitor the work of the head of administration and other officials in the local administration (Art. 147).

These provisions were incorporated into the 'Law on Local Self-Government in the RSFSR' of 6 July 1991. In a crucial departure from Soviet practice (which postulated the unity of the state from top to bottom), local self-government was defined as an autonomous entity and not part of the state system (in contrast to regional government). The law provided for the popular election of a head of administration for a five-year term who was to provide leadership in local administration but who would be responsible to a soviet, also popularly elected for five years. The respective functions of mayors and councils (which were to have no more than a hundred deputies) were spelt out in detail but in places overlapped, creating a permanent source of conflict. The law, which applied to city soviets and below, extended the autonomy of local authorities in setting budgets and taxation, control over land use and the local economy, and gave them greater powers over municipal property in the transition to the market economy. The provisions of the law were to be implemented following the election of mayors and local councils on 6 December 1991, but, as we have seen, following the *coup* local elections were postponed and the law was modified.[74] In particular, heads of administration were appointed rather than elected, and further changes in 1993 modified the whole basis on which budgets were organised.

The tendency to strengthen executive power at the national level was duplicated in the localities. On 12 June 1991, Popov (in June 1992 replaced by Luzhkov) and Sobchak were elected mayors of Moscow and St Petersburg, respectively. The introduction of an elected chief executive represented a radical innovation in Russian politics. The creation of the mayoralty in Moscow was accompanied by the establishment of a system of prefects who represented the mayor in ten newly established prefectures that were superimposed on the thirty-three old boroughs (*raions*); the boroughs themselves were broken up into 124 new 'municipal districts' based on district housing boundaries.[75] The buildings and property of the old *raion* soviets and their executive committees were taken over by the prefects. In a departure from Soviet practice, executive authority separated itself from the legislative, not only institutionally but also physically.

Following the October 1993 events, the whole structure of local soviets was swept away. Yeltsin on 7 October ordered the dissolution of rebel soviets and soon afterwards all village and town soviets, but not regional or republican ones.[76] On 27 October 1993, Yeltsin ordered elections to reorganised local councils in Moscow, St Petersburg and the other sixty-six regions and areas.[77] Thus, Yeltsin fulfilled his promise to put an end to the Soviet era. However, Yeltsin did not order elections in Russia's twenty-one 'ethnic' republics, although the decree recommended that these republics reorganise their legislatures and hold elections, and the majority agreed to do so. The new legislative bodies were to be much reduced in size and to become professional bodies made up of full-time deputies. The new councils, now often called *dumas*, were to be elected for two years and to have between fifteen and fifty deputies.[78] They were to be purely representative bodies, losing their earlier administrative-executive character. In Moscow the elections on 12 December 1993 were for a new thirty-five-member Duma, now displaced from its grandiose building on Tverskaya Street (taken over by the mayor's office). As with the national legislature, so too the Duma's new charter, devised by Luzhkov, emasculated the new assembly in an attempt to avoid the old conflicts, giving the mayor the power to veto its decisions and even to dissolve it. The Duma was to be largely non-political and to concern itself with the administration of the city.[79]

The actual number of sub-national governments in Russia ranges from two to four, and there remains significant confusion over the budgetary and legitimate legal rights of the various levels. There is no precise correspondence between levels of government and levels of the intra-regional budgetary system.[80] The reform of local government was particularly divisive and ultimately the constitution allowed scope for considerable local variations. As Article 131.1 puts it:

> Local self-government in urban and rural settlements and other territories is exercised with due consideration for historical and other local traditions. The structure of local self-government bodies is autonomously determined by the population.

Among the rights of local authorities were the management of municipal property and local budgets, the levying of local taxes and duties, the protection of public order, and also the resolution of 'other questions of local importance' (Art. 132.1).

In August 1995, a new Law on Local Self-Government was adopted by the State Duma, part of the continuing attempt to structure political space in Russia. The debate over the law was influenced by the Council of Europe's Charter on Local Government, and the text was amended to take into account Western standards. The constitutional right to devise local government bodies was confirmed, thus surrendering the principle of uniformity, as was a degree of control over local resources and taxation. Relations between local legislatures and executive authorities were clearly defined, as were the functions of the local authorities, including ensuring the implementation of laws and social policy. Municipal charters were to be adopted by local assemblies, but these were to conform to the broad rights allowed by the regional authorities over local government. Regions themselves, as earlier established by the constitution, were to adopt their own charters. Local elections were to have been held within six months of the adoption of the law, but as usual they were postponed. While regional agencies were jealous of the powers granted local government, the latter were also faced by encroachments on their prerogatives by federal institutions. Central government ministries in post-communist Russia appeared as difficult to bring under local control as their Soviet predecessors had been.[81]

The federal authorities has frequently proclaimed the need to strengthen local self-government, long considered to be 'at the bottom of the heap',[82] as a counter-weight to the power of the governors. On 29 May 1997, the establishment of a Council on Local Government gave the president direct access to the country's mayors. A law of 25 September 1997 on local government financing was designed to foster greater independence for local authorities, who found themselves in competition with regional governments for scarce funds. The usual pattern is for cities and districts (*raiony*) to be financed out of the *oblast* budget, to whom the bulk of taxes and transfer payments from the centre are made. Local self-government has the potential to become a powerful third tier, something fostered by the central authorities as a way of undermining the trend towards the regionalisation of Russia. In a number of cases, however, governors and presidents reduced local government to no more than top-down executive management. In Bashkortostan, Tatarstan and North Ossetia local officials were in effect appointed from above, while regions like Kursk and Voronezh moved in this direction. The tension between the regions and the municipalities was easily exploited by the centre, but it was the failure of the centre consistently to uphold the principles of local self-government and federalism that allowed both to decay.

Local authorities are torn between the increasing demands made of them and their limited resources. Traditional Soviet patterns still exist in that local government remains responsible for a far wider range of activities than is typical in the West; responsibility for the whole local 'communal economy' includes not just housing, trading standards and the like, but also production and ensuring supplies of food and consumer goods. Amid the general economic collapse, local mayors tried to maintain services not properly within their domain, and have levied local taxes to maintain them. Since the local finance base remains so weak local authorities have been driven to desperate stratagems to fund their activities, including the seizure of resources intended for the centre or to appeal for subsidies from the government. Whether out of traditional commitments to local welfare or as acts of political survival, local authorities have tended to subsidise local services and supplies. This not only impeded the marketisation of social relations but also undermined attempts at effective central fiscal management.

Federal law established three levels of government, federal, regional and local, and each had the right to create their own budgets. In practice, only about half of Russia's 29,000 local self-government units hold their own budgets. As part of Putin's plans to reform the system of budgetary federalism there were plans to modify the Budget Code to clarify the definition of what local government is, their budgetary rights and how local governments could raise revenue. Local revenues traditionally came primarily from sales taxes rather than any system of rates or local taxes on individuals and enterprises, although this now changed. Cutbacks in central funding disrupted city services, and as enterprises became more independent from their parent ministries from the late 1980s their parlous finances and growing concern for profits meant that they were less inclined to subsidise local services, and thus the local authorities found themselves even shorter of money.[83] Today, each level of local government negotiates with the level above it for the share of revenues it can keep, with the regions responsible for collecting taxes and then passing the money upwards – if they are so minded. As the federal tax inspectorate became more organised many of the loopholes were closed. One of the major possible sources of funds, the privatisation of housing and trade, was not always exploited to maximum effect; although Luzhkov in Moscow showed a very profitable way this could be done, with the city itself taking a stake in a vast range of enterprises. The adoption of the second part of the Russian tax code in 2000 sharply reduced the tax income of Russian cities. They no longer received housing taxes, VAT or revenues from the sales tax. Municipalities were forced to squeeze greater income from the property that they owned and from the services (e.g. heating and hot water) that they provided, forcing consumers to pay more. Reform plans included the idea that instead of dividing various taxes between the various levels of government, specific taxes should be entirely dedicated to each level.

Solzhenitsyn and other patriots have advanced the *zemstvo* alternative.[84] This advocates the 'gubernisation' of local government, becoming part of a single unitary state system but with a great degree of local decentralisation. They argue that this would overcome the tangled skein of overlapping authority and encourage participation in local affairs. In the event, Putin began his administration with a direct threat to the autonomy of local self-government. As part of his package of federal reforms, a third measure acted as a compensatory mechanism: granting the regional leaders the right to dismiss local authorities subordinate to them. Regional executives had long sought greater control over local self-government, including the power to fire mayors and dissolve legislatures in towns and cities on their territory. As noted above, local self-government is not part of the state system, and thus the proposal ran directly contrary to the attempt to democratise local government that had been one of the main aspirations of social movements since the late 1980s, quite apart from violating the principle enshrined by the constitution.[85] It appeared that Putin was willing to contemplate the destruction of local self-government to allow the implementation of his broader reorganisation of regional affairs in Russia. The amendment to the law on local government was significantly modified in its passage through the Duma, but the struggle continued to defend the election of administration heads and mayors against attempts of the regional governors to gain the power to appoint them.

Local self-government remains in a limbo. In financial affairs, for example, the situation at first deteriorated under Putin. A declining percentage of revenue, as we have seen, goes to regions, while the proportion designated for local government remains no more than 15 per cent of a declining regional share, even though the budgetary commitments of local government comprise 30 per cent of regional expenditures. Since local government provides a range of welfare goods, the chronic under-funding, exacerbated by Putin's reforms, may provoke some sort of social crisis. In response, Putin sought to reform the 'communal-housing complex' (*kommunal'no-zhilishchnoe kompleks*, KZhK), whose annual budget never exceeds 50–70 per cent of need,[86] to try to raise more money locally, but all such reforms are directed towards ensuring that people pay more for local services. In his interview on the anniversary of his first year in power Putin argued that rent support should be more targeted; old Soviet traditions of subsidies for all are to be abolished.[87]

Conclusion

Regional politics are dominated by at least five key institutions or groups: the regional governor or president; the regional legislatures; the heads of local self-government, above all the mayor of the provincial capital; the presidential envoy, formerly based in the majority of regions but since 2000 co-ordinated by the seven governors-general; and the heads of the largest economic interests in the region. Relations between the centre and the localities in Russia are in a state of unstable equilibrium and undergoing significant change. Policy under Yeltsin allowed a rich variety of different regional regimes to emerge, many of which were more authoritarian than the federal regime. In exchange for loyalty, the federal authorities refrained from interfering in the 'internal' affairs of the regions. Under Putin there was at first an attempt to impose a single regional policy, and, although registering significant success in ensuring regional compliance with federal norms, the powers of regional leaders appeared little diminished. Although repudiating the *laissez-faire* approach of his predecessor by developing a whole range of instruments of federal intervention, the style of federal reforms under Putin in their early stages perpetuated the secretive and personalised approach.

Regional and local government remain in a state of flux, although certain patterns emerge. In particular, these are: the trend towards strengthening executive authorities in the localities; the emerging alliance between regional leaders and economic elites; increased differentiation between regions with respect to the speed of economic reform; and the striving for regional autonomy. The attempt to re-establish vertical structures between the centre and the localities has been accompanied by the growth of numerous horizontal structures between the regions.

Attempts to maintain the unity of the state primarily by administrative means, and even less by outright violence as in Chechnya, were counter-productive. Russia could only be kept together by political means, by a constant process of political negotiation and accommodation. Such a policy appeared to work in Tatarstan, and was the only viable approach to Russia's regions and localities. This does not mean that Russia has to retain precisely the same borders as today: some territories might leave (Chechnya), and some aspire to join (Abkhazia, South Ossetia, Transdniester), but if these changes are achieved by political means they will not threaten the unity of the state. Neither does it assume that Russia has to remain a relatively centralised state; federalism provides a mechanism to balance regional and central interests. The fate of the democratic experiment in Russia will be settled as much in the regions as in the central institutions of the state.

11 National identity and state-building

States are not given by some supranatural dispensation. They are the result of purposeful activities exercised through forced projects or political contracts. States are not eternal – especially not as to size and shape – and they are perceived differently by members of the society, designated by state borders as well as by the outside world. States are constituted not only by territories, by citizenship, and by a legal-constitutional framework....Only shared values, symbols, and a mutually accepted legal-political order can provide the necessary broad popular legitimization: top-level agreements and even international recognition are insufficient to build or uphold a state.

(Valery Tishkov)[1]

One of the unique features of West European civilisation was the emergence fairly early on of territorially sovereign states whose relations were regulated, at least since the Treaty of Westphalia in 1648, by a rudimentary system of international law. These sovereign states in time evolved into nations based on principles of popular sovereignty in which the nation was considered to consist of a broad political community expressing the political will of all the people. In the eastern half of the continent, however, dominated by empires until the First World War, the concept of nation retained a primordial ethnicised content whereby an individual was a member of an ethnic community irrespective of their will. The nation was a community relatively independent of politics, allowing several culturally based nations to coexist within a multinational state. Kohn drew the famous distinction between the alleged 'Western' form of nationalism, which was 'civic' and 'rational', and the 'Eastern' type that was 'organic'.[2] Such a distinction is inappropriate for contemporary Russia, although the distinction does help structure debate. Russia offers a third approach to the idea of nationhood where ethnicity and democratic inclusion is entwined with the ethics of state survival itself. It is the tension between these three currents – national (ethnic) self-affirmation, civic participation (building a democratic political community) and (imperial) statism – that has shaped post-communist Russian national identity and state-building.

From empire to state

The natural corollary of the question 'What is Russia?' is the question 'Who are the Russians?' The population of Russia at the time of the 1989 census was 147.02 million, 51.4 per cent of the USSR's population of 286.72 million. The proportion of ethnic Russians in the Soviet population was 50.78 per cent, and in Russia itself 81.5 per cent (119.86 million).[3] Thus, 18.5 per cent of the population of the Russian Federation (some 27 million people) are ethnically non-Russian (*Rossiyane* rather than *Russkie*); and slightly fewer, some 25 million, ethnic Russians in 1989 lived beyond its borders. The fundamental ambiguity over the definition and status of Russians abroad (described by terms like 'compatriots' or 'Russian speakers') reflects ambiguity over the identity of Russia itself.

Sovietisation was no less intense in Russia than in the other republics, but the largely Russian face to the Soviet regime masked the devastation that Russian culture and society also suffered. While political representation was denied Russia, the opportunities for social advancement in the Soviet regime were enhanced and the cultural prestige of Russia was augmented. It is for this reason that Russian nationalism was to stand in a far more complex relationship to the communist regime and democratic revolution than elsewhere.

Empire and nation

Neither the Russian empire nor the USSR had been nation-states in the conventional sense, but neither were they, according to patriots and others, empires in the colonialist sense. Beissinger stresses the ambiguity in the distinction between states and empires, with the Tsarist empire in particular representing 'a confused mix of empire and state-building'.[4]

Russia did not have an empire; it was an empire. For much of its history Russia did not have a nation as such.[5] In 1721, Peter the Great had declared Russia an empire to elevate the grandeur of the country and his throne, but even before that the country had not had stable institutions of nationhood. The very existence of Muscovy was bound up with dynastic politics, and its sense of nationhood was only embryonic. Occupied by the Mongols from 1240 to 1480, Russia had been torn away from Europe and ever since preoccupied with national defence. The state had become the central element in Russian national identity in the struggle against the Mongols and then in the drive to 'gather the Russian lands' around Muscovy. Migration, colonisation and state expansion were the rhyme, if not the reason, of Russian history. Russian identity and the Russian state became bound up with the idea of the Russia empire. As Sergei Witte put it, 'ever since the time of Peter the Great and Catherine the Great there has been no such thing as Russia; only a Russian empire'.[6]

Russia had lived as an empire, but a distinctive one since it lacked the characteristic division between a metropolis and a periphery. The development of the Russian state thoroughly confused the concepts of empire and nation: many different nations lived together within the framework of imperial institutions and law, and it was far from being the 'prison-house of peoples', as Marx had inadequately dubbed the Russian multinational empire. Only under Alexander III in the 1880s had there begun a serious retreat from imperial supranational policies to build a Russian nation through the Russification and assimilation of peoples. Russia at this time moved away from being an 'empire-state' based, like the Habsburg empire, not on the colonial model of the subjugation of peoples but a system in which all came under the tutelage of an abstract supra-ethnic ruler (the emperor) to become a 'state-nation'. Russia had never been (and still is not) a nation-state but remains a 'state-nation' – a multinational entity focused on the institutions of the state.[7]

The USSR, too, had been an empire-state, incarnated no longer in the form of an individual but in the guise of the collective emperor, the Party. Lenin had been hostile to Russian nationalism, considering it almost by definition as chauvinistic. Within months of the Bolshevik revolution, Lenin began a ruthless attack on the cradle of Russian national identity, the Russian Orthodox Church, and by the late 1920s the official church had compromised with the atheist state in what was called Sergianism, after the capitulation of Patriarch Sergei to the secular authorities in 1927. The policy of indigenisation (*korenizatsiya*) during the 1920s, which sought to redress some of the imbalances of Tsarist nationality policy by advancing national elites to positions of power in the non-Russian areas, was inherently anti-Russian. Stalin's collectivisation destroyed the peasantry, the backbone of the Russian nation and the source of its most profound spiritual and cultural traditions, and the purges destroyed the old intelligentsia, the source of the brilliant age of cultural achievement from the middle of the nineteenth century.

A new Soviet intelligentsia was born, and at the same time concessions were made to the form if not the content of Russian identity and history. Stalin increasingly used Russian nationalism as a way of re-legitimising the Soviet system, especially during the Second World War (known as the Great Patriotic War, to distinguish it from the Patriotic War of 1812 against Napoleon) but at the same time gutted it of any cultural or historical dynamism. The complaints of the other republics against the Union centre were often directed against Russia, with whom the union was understandably and often deliberately confused. To the other republics (and to a certain extent to Russians as well), Soviet power was synonymous with Russian power. Russians predominated in positions of authority, especially in the central apparatus of government and party, and the Russian language and culture buttressed their position. The USSR appeared a 'Russian' empire in a new guise.

Russia's identity was dissolved in that of the USSR, and not only the peripheral republics but Russia also was ruled by Soviet Moscow in a neo-colonialist manner. The development of Russian national consciousness and statehood was inhibited. Russia itself was less shielded against central policies than perhaps any of the other republics, and its social and economic welfare was neglected. Its educational level was among the worst of any of the republics, and its standard of living was in the middle range. The physical decay of Russia's towns and countryside was evidence enough for Russia's 'village writers', like Valentin Rasputin and Vasilii Shukshin, of its lack of economic and social privileges. Unlike the 'national liberation' movements in the other republics of the USSR, Russian anti-communist movements were not necessarily anti-imperialist or ethnically based. Russia had never achieved a developed sense of itself as a nation-state and no distinction between empire and nation was considered necessary in Russian thought, since Russia by destiny was considered to be an imperial nation. Even the Slavophiles of the nineteenth century did not advocate a retreat from empire, although they recognised the burden that it imposed.

Only from the 1960s, as part of so-called dissent, did a rediscovered sense of anti-Soviet and anti-imperial Russian national identity and consciousness begin to take shape.[8] The new Russian nationalists were sustained by a profound sense of the crisis in which the Russian nation found itself, a crisis marked by the weakening sense of Russian identity, the loss of Russian national traditions, the destruction of the countryside, and Russia's lack of status within the USSR. Solzhenitsyn was one of the first to argue that Russia was paying too high a price for empire, an empire moreover that was only pseudo-Russian, insisting that Russia was squandering the resources it needed for its own regeneration. He stressed that the heart of the Soviet system was an ideology based not on a people but on an abstract utopianism interpreted by a political party, and warned against the destruction of the Russian people while arguing that minority groups should be allowed to secede from the USSR.[9] He urged the regime to abandon communist ideology, insisting that only if it did so could it save the people, and probably itself too. For his pains, in 1974 he was sent into exile. Igor Shafarevich argued that in their attempts to undermine so-called 'great Russian chauvinism', the old regime had generated and sustained an innate Russophobia.[10]

During the 'stagnation' period under Brezhnev an *official* Russian nationalism flourished to buttress the decaying regime, but this nationalism was used to support Soviet colonialist imperialism both in relation to the non-Russian Soviet republics and abroad. Early on in Brezhnev's regime, two members of the Politburo, Dmitrii Polyanskii and Alexander Shelepin, were dismissed for allegedly promoting the Russian nationalist cause and defending Russian national interests. Only a few years later, however, Alexander Yakovlev, later to be one of the architects of *perestroika*, was punished for his denunciation of renascent Russian nationalism. In a long article in the November 1971 issue of *Literaturnaya gazeta*, Yakovlev, then acting head of the Propaganda Department of the CPSU's Central Committee, condemned the anti-Leninist stance adopted by various nationalists and neo-Stalinists in some official publications. In response, he was dismissed from his post and sent into 'exile' in Canada to serve as Soviet ambassador until recalled by Gorbachev. The incident revealed the extent to which communist ideology was being eroded by an incipient great Russian nationalism long before the fall of the USSR. The regime tolerated a Russified Soviet nationalism to compensate for the declining appeal of Marxism–Leninism.

From Soviet to Russian

When the long-awaited revolt of the nationalities against the Soviet state came, it was led by Russia, something few had anticipated. The disintegration of the USSR was accompanied by some unanticipated political dynamics. Who could have predicted, for example, that in the final period of the Soviet Union an alliance would have formed between Russian radicals and nationalists in the other republics;[11] or between Russian nationalists and communist hard-liners? Communist internationalism now gave way to a 're-nationalisation' of politics, and some strange patterns emerged. Russian radicals after the *coup* were astonished to find themselves denounced as 'democratic imperialists'. Although in the Soviet system power relations to some extent coincided with ethnicity, with Slavs (rather than Russians narrowly defined) predominant, the struggle against communism was only tangentially a struggle against the dominance of ethnic Russians, especially since under Brezhnev national elites had thoroughly consolidated their positions in the ethno-federal republics.

Already towards the end of the Soviet regime the distinctive features of patriotic and nationalist tendencies in Russian national thought emerged. The *patriotic* trend stressed Russia's spiritual traditions, the revival of Orthodoxy, and the need to act as stewards of Russia's environment in harmony with the many peoples who share the Eurasian land mass. The *nationalists* espoused a far more aggressive view, stressing Russia's imperial role as the 'gatherer of the lands' and drew on the national Bolshevik tradition of Nikolai Ustryalov in the 1920s and the Eurasianist thinking of the time to proclaim Russia's separateness from the West and its destiny to dominate the Eurasian landmass. They emphasised the need for military power, rule over the non-Russian peoples and contempt for the decadent West.[12] The Soviet regime could make common cause with the second but was profoundly at odds with the first.

In the union republics the awakening of political consciousness during *perestroika* took on national forms: the struggle against Sovietisation was accompanied by the attempt to separate from the 'centre' in Moscow, thus implicitly taking on an anti-Russian hue. The rebirth of Russia, however, was a struggle not only against the communist centre but also against elements of Russia's own history. Here it was not only the story of the imposition of a foreign ideology borne by an alien culture, but of destroying a system that in a peculiar form had made Russia great. Rejecting the Soviet and communist past meant rejecting not only the tragedies but also the triumphs of the past: the gleaming hydro-electric installation on the Dnieper, Stalingrad, the Soviet flag over Berlin in May 1945, the first cosmonaut in space (Yurii Gagarin in 1961) and superpower parity. While nationalism and anti-communism marched hand in hand in the non-Russian republics, in Russia there could be no such simple equation. Thus, in the *coup*, hard-line Russian nationalists allied with hard-line communists to save the (imperial) state.

The contradiction between the *nationalist* and *patriotic* faces of Russian national thinking (the term nationalism here is misleading) became evident during *perestroika*. The regime sought to use the nationalists against patriots and democrats, who were irreconcilable opponents of the communist (if not Soviet) regime. Russia's patriotic rebirth was perceived as one of the main enemies of communism and thus the authorities tried to discredit it. The extremist Pamyat nationalist organisation, peddling a hysterical concoction of anti-Semitism with assaults against freemasons, foreigners and democrats, was probably sponsored (and certainly tolerated) by the KGB to discredit the independent movement in general and Russian patriotism in particular. The influence of Pamyat, however, was over-estimated and they never gained more than a handful of votes in all the elections in which they stood. In a typically ambiguous way Gorbachev sought to co-opt some elements of Russian national rebirth to buttress the regime. The Orthodox Church in 1988 was allowed to celebrate the millennium of Christianity in Russia with great pomp, the representation of non-Russians in the Politburo was decreased to one (Shevardnadze), republican Party leaderships were purged to eliminate some of the corruption, and Russians given a greater role in Kazakhstan, Turkmenistan and Uzbekistan, and the 'project of the century', the scheme (opposed by Russian patriots) to divert Siberian rivers to Central Asia, was cancelled.

Following the elections in March 1989, the struggle intensified for Russia to become a fully fledged republic within the USSR, with the full range of republican institutions and social organisations. Between the patriots and the nationalists the democrats now emerged as advocates of a distinctive form of de-nationalised (civic) political community in an independent Russian state. These 'democratic statists' sought to reassert Russia's political institutions and sovereignty in the struggle against the communist regime and the Soviet centre. The Russian nationalists now became alarmed, since while they supported the rebirth of Russia they considered that this should take place only within the framework of a (de-communised) union, insisting that Russia was the historic core of a multinational community. The nationalists, and indeed some of the patriots, soon realised that the struggle for state sovereignty by the many peoples that made up the USSR threatened the existence not only of the larger community but of Russia itself.

A tacit alliance between Russian nationalists and conservatives within the communist regime itself was forged to preserve the union. The nationalists condemned the Union Treaty on the eve of the *coup*, as in Zyuganov's 'A Word to the People', the manifesto of the *coup*, and fought the hardest for a renewed union afterwards. Zyuganov's brand of communist nationalism later became one of the dominant trends in the CPRF.

Nationalism and patriotism

Russia's 'nationalism' is of a peculiar sort. The country's struggle for sovereignty in the late Soviet years was both national *and* democratic; Russia's rebirth as an independent state took a national form but did not adopt the classic exclusive forms of nationalism. 'Nationalism' as such is something largely alien to the Russian tradition, where the focus has historically been on maintaining the state. Klyamkin noted that 'Nationalism has not taken root in the Russian mentality, and contrary to the West, is perceived by Russians with suspicion.'[13] Patriots in the Slavophile tradition consider nationalism yet another Western invention, like Marxism, come to snare the poor Russians.

The distinction between patriots and nationalists is one drawn by patriots themselves. Patriots draw on the 'soil-bound' (*pochvennik*) tradition of Slavophilism and stress the existence of a historically constituted supranational community on the Eurasian land mass in which all the various peoples had broadly been able to pursue their own destinies, even when incorporated into the Russian empire. While Russians might be an 'elder brother' to some of the peoples, with a particularly rich culture and destiny, all the various cultures had an equal right to their development. This 'imperial' approach is supranational and stresses the rights of individuals and communities rather than nations. The Eurasianist Elgiz Pozdnyakov insists that patriotism, love of the motherland and one's people, has nothing in common with nationalism.[14] In his view 'Nationalism is the last stage of communism, the last attempt of an outdated ideology to find in society support for dictatorship.'[15] The nationalists, however, stress precisely the development of state structures exalting the ethnic Russian nation and defend a type of colonialist relationship with other peoples and its neighbours. Nationalists consider the Soviet regime, with its crude 'Russification' policies and its power politics, in a more favourable light than the patriots, and hence are more willing to ally with Soviet nationalists and rejectionists.

The tension that was apparent throughout the Soviet era, and which divided the 'dissident' Russian national movement in the Brezhnev years, continues to this day. On the one hand, the *gosudarstvenniki* (statists or state-builders) argue that a strong Russian state is the central feature of the very existence of the Russian people, and thus draw on the tradition of the 'national Bolsheviks' who from the 1920s made their peace with the Soviet system as the recreator of the Russian empire. Today, this tradition is reflected most vigorously in the pages of Prokhanov's paper *Zavtra* (before October 1993 *Den'*), arguing that for centuries the Russian multinational state has been engaged in a struggle to defend 'the Russian idea' against cosmopolitanism, freemasonry and Zionism, and, as Dostoevsky had suggested earlier, Russia should turn its back on the decadent and insidious West and seek its destiny in the East (the Eurasian option). On the other hand, the *vozrozhdentsy* (a term that can loosely be translated as 'revivalists') condemned the Soviet state and Marxist ideology for having subverted the true nature of Russian statehood and culture, and insist that only the cultural and moral revival of the Russian people, based on the values of Orthodoxy, can save Russia. Solzhenitsyn is firmly in this tradition, insisting unequivocally: 'The time has come for an uncompromising *choice* between an empire of which we ourselves are the primary victims, and the spiritual and physical salvation of our own people.'[16]

Yeltsin's own approach was unabashedly that of a civic nationalist. He had exploited the power of Russian patriotism in the struggle against communism, and later sought to find a way of incorporating patriotic demands within the democratic political order, a balancing act that was not always successful and appeared at times to concede too much to more irreconcilable nationalists. Ultimately, however, he did not compromise with exclusive forms of ethnicised nationalism and refused to exploit the grievances of Russians abroad to broaden his political base. While Hitler had exploited the grievances of the *Volksdeutsche* (Germans after the First World War who ended up as minorities in the newly independent national states), Yeltsin refused to exploit the concerns of a comparable group of '*Volksrussen*' in the former USSR. Excoriated by the national-patriots for allegedly betraying their compatriots, Yeltsin remained the president of all citizens in Russia and refused to proclaim himself the militant defender of Russians abroad, as Slobodan Milosevic had done in Serbia.

In the post-communist world Milosevic was an extreme form of a general type: the *nomenklatura* nationalist. In the Russian republics there was no shortage of *nomenklatura* nationalists, in particular in the North Caucasus and the Volga. Numerous studies have demonstrated how the political establishments existing at the end of communism successfully maintained themselves in power, often in the guise of nationalists. However, instead of taking a virulently expansionist form, as in the quest to create a 'greater Serbia', *nomenklatura* nationalists in post-communist Russia precisely focused on drawing the sting from ethnic mobilisation. In Tatarstan, for example, Shaimiev exploited the power of Tatar national feelings but managed to incorporate the large non-Tatar communities into the expanded definition of Tatarstani sovereignty.[17] Where the fall of communism was accompanied by a revolution against the *nomenklatura*, as in Chechnya, events took on a more violent turn. *Nomenklatura* nationalists held on to power in other post-Soviet republics, too. In Turkmenistan the old party boss Saparmurad Niyazov transformed himself into a post-communist nationalist leader, as did Islam Karimov in Uzbekistan. The most spectacular transformation was of Leonid Kravchuk in Ukraine, who changed from being the persecutor of national aspirations in the communist system to the proponent of state-building as the old regime crumbled.

Although Yeltsin was a scion of the *nomenklatura* himself, retaining many of the habits of mind of that class, he personified all the contradictions of Russian national rebirth. A post-imperial civic identity began to emerge but it was challenged. The civic approach was found wanting because of its failure effectively to incorporate patriotic concerns about the loss of Russia's status and the failure to defend its interests. Calls for the restoration of empire, territory, prestige and order were reflected in the vote consistently given to the 'neo-imperial' part of the political spectrum (the communists and nationalists). The weakness of organised liberal blocs left a profound political vacuum that various nationalist and patriotic groups sought to fill. The anti-Soviet democrats appeared to have believed that the destruction of the old system would be enough to create a new one, and thus lacked a serious programme of political and economic reforms for Russian conditions. The patriots advanced a set of alternative conservative values that were perhaps more in keeping with Russian traditions: nationality (*narodnost*), fairness (*spravedlivost*), patriotism and statehood (*gosudarstvennost*), accompanied by such notions as spirituality (*dukhovnost*) and morality (*nravstvennost*) as part of the reinterpretation of

Figure 11.1 North Caucasus

the 'Russian idea' that rejected the liberal emphasis on materialism, the democratic emphasis on individualism and the reformers' emphasis on Westernisation. Post-communist Russian patriotic movements, however, found themselves locked into a dialectics of extremism. The excesses and hysteria that marked much of the thinking of the national-patriots during the transition period inhibited the development of constitutional patriotic conservatism – until Putin gave voice to this constituency.

A distinctive 'national democratic' tendency began to take shape in the early 1990s, joined in the early period by such figures as Rumyantsev, Lukin, Stankevich, Boris Fedorov and many more. The new liberal patriots insisted that they could provide an alternative to the 'vulgarised version of the "Russian idea"', which stressed the cult of the state and of Russia as a great power, and which associated the idea of empire and state. They insisted that 'only a democratic Russia could be great', a greatness which lay 'not in force but in truth, not in material power but in nobility of spirit'. The growth of chauvinism would only provoke the persecution of Russians in other CIS states, and then turn back on Russia itself in the form of refugees and migration.[18] Liberal patriots tried to prove that not all manifestations of Russian identity were right-wing and sought to retrieve the national idea from the domination of the nationalist rejectionists, with their inability to understand the aspirations of the peoples of Russia for elements of sovereignty, their crude threats to the other former Soviet republics and their hankering for the restoration of the old USSR. It was this tendency that came into its own under Putin.

Russian national identity

The fall of the USSR forced a redefinition of Russian identity: Russia had never been a nation-state, and it was now not a question of appealing to tradition but of creating a new national identity. One of the issues dividing patriots, nationalists and democrats was the question of how much of the Russian past was 'usable' in the present. Tsipko asked 'if the formation of a new Russian statehood is unavoidable, on which historical foundations should it be built?'[19] The choice between 'empire' and 'nation' was far from clear cut, since by its very nature there would be imperial elements in Russian national identity derived not necessarily from any aggressive tendencies but from its sheer size, history and demography. The patriots sought to maintain the union (by democratic means), and even sections of the reborn democracy could not reconcile themselves to the smaller nation-state form of Russia, while the nationalists openly espoused the reintegration of the former Soviet Union, denouncing the creation of the CIS.

Russia after the empire

From the perspective of power politics, Russia was the greatest loser at the end of the Cold War. The fall of the USSR undermined the principles on which Russians had defined themselves as a state for centuries. The Bolshevik experience had lasted a mere seventy-four years, but its fall shattered the statehood (*gosudarstvennost*) that had emerged in the course of a millennium. Russia had lost territory before when, in 1918, Poland and Finland gained their independence, although some of their territory was regained by Stalin during the Second World War. The separation of the Central Asian republics also did not affect Russia's core perception of itself, having only conquered the area in the late nineteenth century and then bound it loosely to Russia. However, the alienation of Ukraine, and to a lesser degree Belarus, struck at the very heart of Russian self-identity. It was in Ukraine that the Russian state emerged and here were born many of Russia's greatest writers: Nikolai Gogol in Poltava, Anna Akhmatova in Odessa and Mikhail Bulgakov in Kiev. The former editor of *Moscow News*, Len Karpinskii, observed that 'Millions of Russians are convinced that, without Ukraine, it is impossible to speak not only of a great Russia but of any kind of Russia at all.'[20] It came as a shock for Russians to have to start thinking about Ukraine as a separate country: a shock that the English survived when most of Ireland and the homeland of some of the greatest 'English' writers such as Jonathan Swift and George Bernard Shaw achieved independence.

Ukrainians, however, argue that the contemporary Russian state draws its provenance not from Kiev but had developed as a new state separate and distinct from the earlier Kievan Rus following the Mongol conquest.[21] As the French discovered during the decolonisation of Algeria, it is not always easy to determine what is the core and what is the periphery. On the Eurasian landmass, with weak natural frontiers, historically shifting borders and centuries of migration and intermarriage, this is an even more intractable problem. The separation of Algeria or Ireland did not strike at the very heart of the identities of France or Britain, but Russia appeared to lose part of its soul. Those on the wrong side of borders after 1991 were liable to develop a form of *pieds noirs* nationalism, and those on the 'right' side could become prey to revanchism and neo-imperialism.

After the Soviet collapse Russia lost access to nearly half of its traditional ports, retaining only 600 kilometres of the Black Sea coast and the same length of the Caspian shore. Half of the merchant fleet went to Russia while the Black Sea Fleet became the subject of acrimonious disputes with Ukraine. Sentiments of defeat, retreat, loss and humiliation placed enormous strains on the fragile democratic institutions. Democracy and the attempts to rejoin Western civilisation in the popular mind began to be equated not only with economic hardship but the destruction of the state itself. The writer Alexander Zinoviev had already argued that *perestroika* was an unmitigated disaster.[22] Now others began to argue that democracy itself was a comparable disaster for Russia.[23] The USSR had reformed itself out of existence, and now there was a danger that Russia would go the same way.

Defining the national community

In this context, where historical and territorial narratives are contested, it is not surprising to find that Russian national identity is fluid and multi-layered. This is reflected in the rich but confusing language used to define Russians living in the RF and in the former Soviet states. Russians can define themselves in many different ways.

• To call oneself an ethnic *Russkii* signifies membership of the Russian people and a proprietorial right of access to the Russian state, including protection by the Russian Federation.

- To be a *Rossiyanin*, on the other hand, emphasises membership of a non-ethnically defined community of citizens of many different ethnicities in the Russian Federation and beyond. The main desired polital status for those living outside the RF is dual citizenship, something that none of the other republics have been willing to grant.
- A third definition is *Russkoyazychnye*, Russian-speakers. This suggests a broader community than that encompassed by the RF and includes Russian-speaking titulars and minority groups. In Ukraine this would broaden the 11 million-strong body of ethnic Russians to some 20 million, including some 7 million Russian-speaking Ukrainians.
- A rather weaker category are *sootechestvenniki*, or compatriots, encompassing former citizens of the Soviet Union who seek to affiliate themselves in one way or another with the RF, but towards whom the RF itself bears no legal responsibility and towards whom political obligations are usually instrumental and mostly ignored unless suiting some broader purpose of the Russian political elite.
- Similarly, the notion of citizens (*grazhdane*) abroad lacks legal or political definition but remains a vague category that suggests the possibility of Russian diplomatic or political protection.

Brubaker stresses that the three corners in his triadic relationship between the nationalising *state*, the national *minority* and the external *homeland* are fundamentally dynamic and relational concepts.[24] This is reflected in the debate over terms to be used to describe groups in the republics within the RF and beyond: indigenous population, titular nationality or premier groups. The idea of a 'titular nationality' is a very Soviet term and occludes the rights of titularity that can be endowed by civic mechanisms. It is clear, moreover, that Russians outside the RF lack a single identity and are far from comprising a single category. Many non-Russian minorities who speak Russian consider themselves 'Russians'; while about 40 per cent of Russians 'abroad' were born in their republic of residence,[25] and many feel that they belong in that republic.

So, what is the Russian nation and how can it be identified?

- It can be associated with the Russian language and therefore with Russian speakers (*Russkoyazychnye* or *Russofony*). This immediately raises a number of problems. What about the large number of Russian speakers (many of whom are ethnically non-Russian) in the former Soviet republics outside Russia? Are they part of the Russian nation; and if so, what relationship should they have with the Russian state?
- Alternatively, the Russian nation could be determined by ethnicity, with only ethnic Russians (*Russkie*) considered part of the Russian nation. But what about the 19 per cent of the inhabitants of Russia who are not ethnic Russians?; and how is one to establish the difference, for example, between an ethnic Russian and an ethnic Belarusian? How does one define ethnicity? Is the Soviet definition of ethnic Russians as 'having Russian parents' acceptable? What about those of mixed parentage?
- The Russian nation can be identified through religion. For some scholars, like

Edward Keenan, the Orthodox Church stands as the 'only authentically Russian national institution'.[26] However, Russia since the sixteenth century has contained significant numbers of Muslims, and today a number of the Federation's republics (in particular on the middle Volga and the North Caucasus) are reviving Islamic culture and institutions. What about the Buddhists, Jews and pagans?; what is their nationality? In addition, in a secular society, how many Russians today are practising Orthodox Christians?

- The Russian nation can be identified more broadly with its culture, but this again raises a number of problems. For example, Gogol is quintessentially part of Russian culture yet he was, as mentioned, of Ukrainian provenance.
- Finally, the Russian nation can be defined through its common history. This is the path taken by the Eurasianists who argue that 'the peoples of the old empire possess a common past that preceded both Tsarism and Soviet communism'. For them the Russian nation encompasses 'that vast stretch of continental land from the Carpathians to the Pacific'.[27] This is probably too broad a category to be of much operational significance since reliance on a single definition blurs precisely the problems in establishing the contours of the national community.

The contours of national identity

While it is hard enough to define the Russian nation, the associated question of national identity is even more intractable.[28] The new identity is torn between four distinct approaches, which while not exclusive define the nature of the new polity.

Return to empire

The first is the restoration of an imperial role and the recreation of some sort of union. The debate over Russian national identity is overlain and complicated by the problem of Tsarist imperialism and the Soviet Union. While most neo-communist movements (like the CPRF) use the language of militant Russian nationalism, their relationship with 'genuine' Russian national thinking is ambivalent: Russian statism is not necessarily the same as neo-Soviet imperialism. Movements like Zhirinovskii's LDPR are essentially imperialist and openly display their irredentism, adopting an avowedly 'imperial' stance on the disintegration of the old union. The solid vote for the LDPR in parliamentary elections reflects the disenchantment of those who equate democracy with disintegration and loss of national prestige. Henry Kissinger has repeatedly warned that Russian nationalism could be translated into a desire to return to a position of dominance over the other republics.[29]

Ethnicity and state

Another focuses on ethnicity, on loyalty to ties of blood and kinship. The nation (defined here as an ethnic community) is not necessarily coterminous with state: the Russian (like the Hungarian) state today is smaller than the Russian nation, whereas in most of the other fourteen post-Soviet republics the state is larger than the nation. The ethnic definition is opposed by democrats, patriots and nationalists alike (the latter appealing to imperial supranational traditions), although claims to defend Russians 'abroad' contains elements of ethnicised nationalism. The Slavic identity has rather more resonance, focusing on Russia as a nation of the Eastern Slavs (Russia, Belarus and Ukraine). The *nomenklatura* nationalists in places like Tatarstan or South Ossetia are careful to check claims to ethnic exclusivity made by the titular nationality. Thus, the dynamics of post-communist Russian politics differ from those in Yugoslavia, but there remains a devastating potential for ethnic conflict.

Culture and state

The third approach stresses the development of a cultural community, the view that the core of Russian national identity lies not so much in its imperial traditions but in religio-cultural features. One of the most sophisticated exponents of this view is Dmitrii Likhachev. Born in 1907, Likhachev was a witness to the revolution and its sufferings. Arrested in 1928, he spent six years in the notorious Solovki camp, a former monastery on an island in the White Sea that Lenin in 1920 converted into a prison.[30] Likhachev survived and pursued a life of scholarship in his chosen field of philology until his death in 1999. He traced the interaction between Russia and Europe, and stressed that Russian culture was part of European culture in general, opposing the myth of Russian exceptionalism and supporting pan-European development. At the same time, Likhachev extolled the elements that make Russia Russia, and above all the Orthodox Church and its liturgy, though he opposed theocratic versions of Russian destiny. Contrary to much writing in the political culture vein, he insisted that an ethos of individualism had been growing since at least the seventeenth century to temper the traditional collectivism of Russian society. Respect for tradition, he insisted, should not entail the 'mechanical imitation of what has ceased to exist'. Praising patriotism, he condemned nationalism as a pathology parasitic on genuine love of one's motherland, and in particular he denounced Great Russian nationalism and anti-Semitism.[31]

The cultural definition of Russian statehood is also fraught with dangers; it is not clear how any version of cultural homogeneity, defined even in weak terms of a dominant tradition, is possible in a country marked by such ethnic diversity. In relation to other groups the old messianism about Russia's leading role and the cultural mission of Orthodoxy, formulated at the end of the nineteenth century by V. Solovyev and others, can appear threatening. An inverted form of this messianism was used by the Bolsheviks to sustain the idea of the universal proletarian revolution emerging out of Russia, and the struggle for democracy on occasion became a new form of traditional messianism.

'Civis Rusanis sum'

The fourth approach argues precisely that the loss of Russia's imperial role and the fragmented sense of Russian nationality can be compensated by the establishment of a new identity based on the civic institutions of revived statehood. The major obstacle to the development of a civic national identity is the emergence and consolidation of national elites in the autonomous republics and regions of Russia, and the persistence of the 'greater Russia' idea. Nevertheless, Russia has a unique chance of forging a new national identity, not despite but because of the catastrophic failure of the old system: there appeared to be no choice but to start again. The civic approach to Russian national identity and the democratic statist approach to rebuilding the country became the dominant ideology of the government after August 1991. This stressed civic responsibility, the rebirth of Russian statehood governed by law, a democratic and inclusive form of nationalism, and good relations with all the other resurgent nationalisms both within and beyond Russia.

The rediscovery of national identities, language and culture is an essential element of democratic state-building. Often, the discovery of one's own culture only enhances respect for others; as Friedrich Engels long ago observed, 'The Poles are never more internationalist than when they are at their most national.' Nationalism in the anti-communist revolution therefore has a dual character: both integrative and supportive of state-building and political order (with or without democracy); and divisive, when ethnicised or exclusive nationalism is used by elites or oppositional forces to gain power and to preserve what they see as threatened national identities.

State-building

Post-communist Russia embarked on a distinctive type of nation-building on the foundations of a fragmented sense of the political community and an unclear definition of national identity. Nation-building in Russia faces some of the problems that had brought down the USSR. The aspirations of some of Russia's republics (Chechnya and Tatarstan in particular) replicated those of the Baltic and Transcaucasian republics earlier, threatening to tear the federation apart. There are major differences, however, and these will be examined below.

Building the political community

Soviet policy had simultaneously maintained separate national identities, above all through the notorious point 5 of Soviet passports where individuals had to state their ethnic identity (chosen from either the maternal or paternal line, but once entered largely irrevocable), and crushed any but the most formal political expression of that identity. The Soviet regime had been shockingly careless about generating a substantive sense of *Soviet* nationality, limiting itself to abstractions about 'eternal friendship' between peoples united in an 'indivisible union'.[32] Like the USSR, the Russian Federation is also a multinational state, with some 27 million non-ethnic Russians living in a state consisting of 128 recognised nationalities. In three crucial respects, however, Russia is a very different multinational state from the USSR: the absolute predominance of ethnic Russians (81 per cent in the RF compared to about half in the USSR); the very large proportion of ethnic Russians in many of the potential secessionist states (in nine of the twenty-one republics Russians are a majority, see Table 9.2), and Russians make up 10.4 million (45.1 per cent) out of a total population of 23.1 million people living in the republics; and Russian identity as the relatively unmediated core of the new state.

The place of ethnic Russians themselves in the new order, and the juridical form that the cultural and historical differences of other ethnic groups should take, however, remains contested. The great majority of peoples and federal units were agreed that a distinctively *Russian* political community should emerge, but this was contested by a few. One group that did contest this proposition was the Chechens, launching what became a violent bid for secession because of the failure (one shared to different degrees by both sides) to exploit the new political opportunities, opened up by Russia's democratisation, to renegotiate the relationship (up to a politically negotiated separation). Tatarstan also questioned its relationship with the nascent Russian political community, but did so politically – taking skilful advantage of the new circumstances to extend the boundaries of its own sovereignty. In international affairs sovereignty is an absolute (either a state is recognised as autonomously empowered to enter foreign relations or it is not), whereas in domestic politics sovereignty is a far more malleable notion.

Federalism itself (as we saw in Chapters 9 and 10) is one way of sharing sovereignty, but the 'asymmetry' in Russia's federal relations itself reflected a painful process of negotiation in the early stages of establishing a new political community. In his attempt to iron out the asymmetries in Russian federalism Putin was in danger of blocking one of the sources of innovation that had allowed a relative equilibrium to emerge in inter-national relations in Russia. At the same time, however, Putin's aim – to ensure equality of citizenship rights across Russia – represented a vision of the political community that found considerable support, not only among ethnic Russians but others as well. Universal citizenship not only sought to undermine segmented regionalism but also challenged the emergence of ethnocratic states in some of the republics, where the titular populations were privileged over the rest.

We suggested above that Russian nation-building is torn between three forms: ethnic self-affirmation, supranational statism, and the attempt to establish a democratic *political* community. In practice, the three are not mutually exclusive and Russian nation-building contains elements of all three. However, the three represent quite different visions of what Russia should look like. We shall explore some of these tensions below.

Setting the borders

The borders of the USSR were predicated on an expanding communist world system and in a sense, as Strada points out, they only formally ran across space: essentially, they ran across time.[33] Under Stalin, however, border policy took on a far more instrumental role, and while often formally arbitrary they were part of a conscious design to foster ethnic conflict as part of his *divide et impera* policy, to make all nationalities dependent on Moscow. The current borders established by the communist regime reflect neither the historical legacy nor demographic realities, but neither would any others – hence the Russian national-patriotic argument that there should be no borders at all. The Russian government rejected the ethnic principle of state-building and sought to find a balance between collective and individual rights while trying to ensure through the CIS that the administrative borders that had now become state frontiers should be 'transparent', allowing free passage for citizens of CIS states. Ukraine, however, objected to the distinction between 'internal' and 'external' borders, and insisted that they all should be considered state borders. There was a gradual hardening of these frontiers, exacerbating problems of citizenship.

There appeared no logical reason why the fifteen union republics should be the best state form for the emerging post-communist national communities, and the fall of the old regime was followed by tension as territories sought to make adjustments to the Soviet legacy. There were conflicts in the Transdniester and the Gagauz area of Moldova, the Crimea and Transcarpathia in Ukraine, Abkhazia and South Ossetia in Georgia, civil war in Tajikistan, and many more. The disintegration of the USSR and Yugoslavia revealed the contradiction between the two central principles of the OSCE: the immutability of borders and individual human rights. What if a group of people wished to change the borders and live in a different state? There are no mechanisms available to facilitate the transfer of territory, and history would suggest that border changes are almost always the result of *force majeure*. In addition, there was no clear answer to the problem of reconciling individual rights with the rights of minority groups in any particular territory, the struggle between civic and ethnic identities.[34] The border question became perhaps the single most important symbolic issue in the former Soviet Union. The question acted as a mirror to post-communist politics, testing the readiness of states for democratic and peaceful solutions to intractable problems involving not only territory but questions of national identity and competing truths, if not myths, about the past and present. The issue questioned the very substance of the modern nation-state form of political-territorial organisation.

Soviet borders were intended to be purely administrative divisions and not state frontiers. For this reason, among others, the regime could move the borders arbitrarily and take so little account of ethnic and other factors. When in 1991 these arbitrary lines became state borders, the scene was set for endless conflicts. By late 1991, there were some 168 territorial-ethnic disputes in the former USSR, four times as many as in 1990, and of that figure seventy-three directly concerned Russia.[35] In Central Asia borders were artificial and the states within them may well not survive in their present form. Nearly a quarter of Russia's 61,000 km of border was not 'formally recognized and specified in any international legal acts'.[36] Rutskoi insisted that the real Russia could not be contained within the borders of the current Russian Federation, though he failed to specify where precisely they should lie or how they could be changed.[37] At the same time, the separation of the peripheral republics exposed what had been the Russian heartlands, and now only thirty rather than the earlier forty-seven of Russia's seventy-six primary components lacked external borders. Attempts to strengthen borders, moreover, were fraught with problems. The Russo-Azerbaijani frontier, for example, is straddled by the Lezgin people living in both republics, and for long it did not become a policed state border. With its millions of compatriots abroad, Russia favoured the transparency of borders, though was concerned about the security risk posed by its open frontiers to the south. Drugs and arms smugglers, and other criminals took advantage of weak frontier controls. Russia increasingly assisted the CIS republics to police their external frontiers rather than establishing stronger controls on its 'internal' borders.

As soon as a line is drawn on a map the question of secession arises focusing on four main problems: borders and the allocation of territories; the rights of minorities (and in some cases majorities) in the territory that has seceded; the rights of secessionist nationals in the country from which the territory has seceded; and the problem of procedures – how do we know that the leadership of the secessionist territory genuinely reflects the stable wishes of the majority of the population in the territory concerned? All these issues were manifestly present in the case of Chechnya's bid to secede from Russia, but to a lesser extent in some other regions.

Unlike the Soviet constitutions, the Russian constitution does not grant the right of secession. One of the few guarantees of stability in Africa had been the declaration by the Organisation of African Unity in 1964 that the colonial borders, however unfair and divisive of 'tribes', should be retained. This principle, despite all the wars, has held to this day, and a similar status was enacted in Latin America. One of the basic principles of the OSCE is the recognition by member states of the inviolability of each others' borders, a stance that did not help attempts to resolve the Nagorno-Karabakh crisis. During *perestroika* the principle was extended to the USSR in the affirmation that internal borders were unchangeable, a stance that strengthened the legitimacy of the Union and autonomous republics, even though Article 78 of the USSR constitution made provision for changes. It was perhaps less Helsinki and more Karabakh that had confirmed the sanctity of intra-Soviet borders.

However, the border question would not go away. The announcement by Yeltsin's press secretary, Pavel Voshchanov, on 26 August 1991 that borders were negotiable if republics became independent drew accusations of Russian chauvinism. Nazarbaev condemned the raising of the question on the grounds that it would make keeping the USSR together much more difficult, but both the border incident, and the earlier threat of sharply raising the price of Russia's oil, were raised out of a 'unifying' impulse, to warn of the consequences of secession. However, the means had undermined the aim, and set alarm bells ringing in the capitals of the other republics. Yeltsin had hoped to make the other republics aware of the price and dangers of seeking full independence, but the plan backfired and accelerated the disintegration of the USSR. Those previously uncommitted now perceived a threat of Russian revanchism, and this helps explain the overwhelming vote for Ukrainian independence on 1 December 1991. Instead of a clear principle becoming the 'guarantor of stability',[38] it became the source of destabilisation.

The Russo-Japanese frontier between the Kurile Islands was the only Russian border not to be recognised in international law, but there were at least twenty frontier disputes that could explode into conflict. Japan made territorial claims on Russia over the Kurile islands, while some revanchist groups in Germany sought the return of the Kaliningrad region. Areas of Karelia and Pechenga were forcibly incorporated into the USSR during the war, but Finland agreed that the borders would only be changed through legal processes and according to OSCE principles. The major border dispute was with Estonia over lands that had been granted to it by the Treaty of Tartu of 1920, but which had been excluded from Estonia by the Molotov–Ribbentrop Pact of 1939 and after the war incorporated into the Pskov and Leningrad regions of Russia. To many Russians it seemed illogical for Estonia to deny the validity of any Soviet acts, and yet to lay claim to territory on the basis of an act of the discredited Soviet regime, whose arbitrariness in drawing boundaries was well-known. The disputed territory covered only a total of 1,924 sq km

(750 sq miles) and contained no major towns and was populated by Russians. Russia was fearful of establishing a precedent, itself having renounced any territorial claims against any of its neighbours. It was not clear why nationalists in Estonia wished to incorporate a Russian area when the country already had problems with the Narva region, the great majority of whose population were Russians. In 1995, the conflict was regularised and Estonia officially renounced claims to the area.

In Russia the possibility of border changes was much debated. Travkin noted that 'The frontiers problem has always been at its most acute when an empire falls to pieces.'[39] He opposed the revision of borders, and denied that Russia was interested in grabbing land but was 'struggling for national and state survival'. In particular, he insisted that Russia had a duty to defend its nationals living outside its borders, such as in the Transdniester republic, though in democratic ways. Other patriotic groups, like Popular Accord and the Russian National Union, argued that borders could be changed, and recommended a version of the system used to demarcate the border between Poland and Germany in Upper Silesia in 1920–1 where plebiscites were held district by district. The precedent did not augur well since in Silesia most districts voted to return to Germany, yet the region remained with Poland.[40] Hard-liners insisted that 'At the present time, relations between CIS states do not lend themselves to regulation by diplomatic means alone.'[41] Kozyrev warned that the demands by the national-patriots to resolve border conflicts by imperial methods, including the use of armed force, would lead to the collapse of the CIS and the emergence of a ring of hostile states around Russia.[42]

Solzhenitsyn in 1991 recommended the retreat of Russian power to defensible borders around the Slavic heartlands (Russia, Ukraine, Belarus and North Kazakhstan). He insisted:

> *We don't have the strength* for the peripheries either economically or morally. *We don't have the strength* for sustaining an empire – and it is just as well. Let this burden fall from our shoulders: it is crushing us, sapping our energy, and hastening our demise.[43]

He noted 'with alarm that the awakening Russian self-awareness has to a large extent been unable to free itself of great-power thinking and of imperial delusions'.[44] The USSR had disintegrated along lines of fracture that did not correspond to those that would be recognised by Solzhenitsyn and others as somehow 'natural', reflecting the ethnic and historical core of a post-imperial Russian state. Solzhenitsyn's belief that the 'irresponsible' and 'haphazard' Soviet demarcation of borders could be corrected by 'panels of experts' and local plebiscites was impractical.[45] The view that Russia could become a genuinely post-imperial state following the adjustment of borders was considered by its neighbours as a typically Russian imperialist approach.

However much borders are moved, there cannot be an exact fit between state boundaries and nationalities. Furman notes that the right of states to inviolable borders contradicts the rights of nations to self-determination. The present borders of Russia and the other republics are absurd, yet, he warned, referring to the tragic precedents of Versailles Germany and 1990s Serbia, while accepting the present line of the borders means acquiescing in the repugnant acts that had made them so, democrats had no choice but to accept them. Russia found itself in the position of inter-war Germany:

> A large country surrounded by weaker countries with national minorities representing the large country, especially if these national minorities are oppressed (and any national minority may well be oppressed, to a certain extent), is virtually unable to withstand the temptation to use its strength.

He urged that Russia as the most powerful country in the CIS should set an example of a peaceful and humane resolution of border and national issues, up to providing a legal framework for the secession of the Tatars and Chechens, which would then give it the moral right to back minorities in other republics.[46] But what about the rights of the minorities in the secessionist territories? Borders demarcate not only territories but competing truths: they cut across both time and morality.

Citizenship and nationality

Up to December 1991, almost all the inhabitants of the USSR had been Soviet citizens; with the demise of the USSR in theory they all became stateless until each republic adopted its own citizenship laws. Russia's first citizenship law of 28 November 1991 granted citizenship to all those resident in Russia or the USSR as long as they registered with the Russian authorities and did not take the citizenship of another state. Dual citizenship was allowed only to those who opted to keep Soviet citizenship. The Russian government declared itself the protector of Russian citizens at home and abroad, and banned the typically Soviet practice of depriving people of their citizenship. With the collapse of the USSR a modified version of the law on 6 February 1992 removed the reference to dual Soviet citizenship and allowed any Soviet citizen resident in the USSR on 1 September 1991 to take out Russian citizenship within three years, as long as they had not adopted the citizenship of the republic in which they were residing.[47] A further amendment of 17 June 1993 removed the ambiguities surrounding the Baltic republics and Georgia which had declared independence before 1 September 1991, and allowed residents in other republics to keep their local citizenship while taking out Russian citizenship.[48] From 1 January 2001, the old simplified system for Soviet passport holders to gain citizenship through simple registration procedures was abolished, and instead a complex set of documentation and residence permits had to be provided. This built on Putin's decree of 17 May 2000 that made it harder for residents in the CIS and the Baltic states to gain a Russian passport.[49] The president had spoken of encouraging labour migration from the CIS, and these moves were hardly likely to encourage this.

Thus, Russia adopted an inclusive citizenship policy (although becoming slightly more restrictive), recognising Russian citizenship for millions living outside its borders. Russia, moreover, sought through bilateral treaties to ensure that other states granted the right to dual citizenship. Russia, fearing a flood of refugees, reasoned that its compatriots would be more likely to stay in the other republic if they knew that they could move to Russia at any time. Attempts to introduce dual citizenship in the other former Soviet republics were not pursued consistently.[50] For the other republics the adoption of citizenship laws was a crucial element in state-building, but at the same time proved bitterly divisive. All the republics, with the exception of Estonia and Latvia (who adopted exclusive citizenship laws), offered citizenship to all those resident on their territory on the day the citizenship law came into effect. Russia's attempt to convince the other republics to allow dual citizenship was resisted for fear that divided loyalties might create a potential fifth column. In Ukraine dual citizenship was regarded as the first step towards renewed union with Russia, and even republics like Kazakhstan and Kyrgyzstan, which favoured closer relations with Russia, feared that it would undermine new national and civic identities. The struggle continues to turn Soviet citizens into Kazakhstanis, Ukrainians and Russians.

There is a similar struggle within Russia itself. The 1996 law on 'National Cultural Autonomy' gave ethnic groups either lacking a defined territory, or living outside the area in which they were nominally titular, the right to create cultural institutions such as schools or social support institutions. This law marked a radical departure from Stalinist practices, which had tied national development very much to a specific territory, and with few opportunities for those living elsewhere to express their cultural identity. This particularly affected the Tatars, three-quarters of whom, as we have seen, live outside Tatarstan. They have been among the most active groups taking advantage of the opportunities offered by the 1996 act. The law sets strict registration procedures, and forbids ethnic communities established in this way from engaging in politics. Although transcending Soviet practices, the law reflected Soviet thinking in still talking of 'nationality', rather than the Western concept of ethnic group, and suggesting, for example, that Tatars were part of a 'diaspora' even though they had been living in Moscow and across the Volga region (outside what is now Tatarstan) for as long as Russians had. The legal restrictions placed on their activities and the traditional concepts used to describe the process indicated the distance that Russia still had to go to achieve an autonomous civil society.[51]

Putin sought to undermine the emerging elements of an 'inner abroad' by claiming to assert the undisputed priority of Russian law. Russian citizenship was to become universal throughout the country, undermining attempts to impose various types of 'quasi-citizenship' in some of the republics. In particular, in Tatarstan and Bashkortostan the Russian passport was to be introduced even though, against the objections of the local authorities, it did not specify the holder's nationality or use the local languages. A government order of 8 July 1997 had ordered all Soviet passports to be replaced with the new ones, but instead local identity documents had been issued. This made it difficult for their citizens to enter universities elsewhere in Russia or to travel abroad. The distribution of the new Russian passports provoked protests in Kazan and elsewhere. The Tatar Public Centre, for example, on 2 January 2001 condemned Moscow's 'colonialist' policy that sought to restrict the rights of Russia's national republics. They condemned in particular the new passports, which allegedly contained numerous Orthodox symbols and which failed to specify the holder's ethnicity.[52] In the event, the passports were issued with an insert in the native language. It was at this time that Tatarstan planned to switch back to using the Latin alphabet.

Much of the discussion over citizenship focuses on the tension between ethnic and civic definitions. An ethnic definition of citizenship bestows citizenship rights only to titulars; a civic definition grants all those born in a given territory or permanently resident there for a certain period of time the same civil rights as citizens. The situation is far from straightforward, however. For example, laws making the language of the titular nationality the state language privilege native speakers, fluent in job applications and favoured in appointments to the new state administration. More broadly, the Russian nationalist cry of 'Russia for Russians' is, as Kapuscinski notes, torn by an irreconcilable contradiction

> between the criterion of blood and the criterion of land....According to the criterion of blood, the point is to maintain the ethnic purity of the Russian nation. But such an ethnically pure Russia is only part of today's Imperium. And what about the rest? According to the criterion of land, the point is to maintain the full extent of the Imperium. But then there can be no hope of maintaining the ethnic purity of the Russians.[53]

The tension between blood and land, the ethnic and the imperial agendas, is here vividly portrayed, but it leaves out of account the third option, the democratic political community.

Conclusion

Russian national thinking contains various strands, and even those antagonistic to the West are not necessarily incompatible with some form of democratic law-based state. In contrast to most of the states of Eastern Europe, in Russia the national issue only rose to prominence on the political agenda *after* the democratic revolution, whereas elsewhere the struggle against communism had simultaneously been *sui generis* forms of decolonising national liberation struggles. Public opinion was therefore democratic before it became nationalistic. At the same time, the 'nationalism' of the dominant nationality is a much more amorphous phenomenon than that of the smaller nations, torn between patriotism, nationalism and imperialism of various stripes. While Russians did not become Soviets in quite the same way that the English became British, the challenge facing Russia (and Britain and France earlier) was to achieve self-liberation from imperial ambitions and messianism.

A post-imperial Russian patriotism emerged in the late Soviet years, and after the *coup* focused on remaking a Russian nation-state based on economic liberalism, democratic constitutionalism and oriented towards partnership with the West and integrated into the global economy. This, however, was challenged by a more introspective form of hybrid nationalism drawing on Russian and Soviet traditions and extolling Russia's dominance in Eurasia and its separateness from the West. The aspirations of some of Russia's republics (Chechnya and Tatarstan in particular) reflect those of the Baltic and Transcaucasian republics earlier, threatening to tear the federation apart. There are major differences, however, and no simple parallel can be drawn between the fate of the USSR (or Yugoslavia) earlier and Russia today. The majority of Russia's republics lack a clear demographic basis to aspirations for independence, and to date a trigger mechanism for disintegration has been absent. The outlines of a democratic political state and a post-imperial national identity have begun to take shape.

Part IV
Economy and society

12 Marketising the economy

Gaidar's reform secured macroeconomic change, namely the destruction of the old economy. It was a wildly painful break, surgically crude, with the rusty grinding sound of pieces of old parts and mechanisms being ripped out together with the flesh, but the break occurred. Most likely, it simply could not have happened any other way. We had virtually nothing to work with apart from Stalin's industry, Stalin's economy, adapted to the present day. And its make-up dictated precisely that sort of a break: over the knee. The system was destroyed in the same way that it was created.

(Boris Yeltsin)[1]

The divergent trajectories of post-communist economies, where countries like Poland by 1994 appeared set on the path of sustained growth whereas Russia languished in depression, raised the question of explanation. In his last work Mancur Olson stressed the role played by the state in the development of markets, identifying what he called 'market-augmenting governments'.[2] In Russia in the 1990s, there was, to put it mildly, tension between market-augmentation and economic destruction. By the end of Yeltsin's presidency Russia did have a functioning market economy, but a heavily distorted and criminalised one. Putin's government sought to reconcile market development with state reassertion to achieve economic growth.

The road to the market

The fall of the Berlin Wall ended the political division of Europe, but it exposed the economic one. Two Europes still faced each other, one relatively prosperous, the other confronted with the legacy of a failed economic experiment. By some reckonings the Soviet Union in 1991 was comparatively as far, if not further, behind the leading Western countries as Russia had been in 1913. The Soviet system stormed into the industrial age but failed to respond to the challenges of post-industrialism. Only under Gorbachev was the assault against the market tempered but the search for a distinctive socialist economics was not abandoned. Only after the August 1991 *coup* did economic reform give way to the marketising transformation of the entire system. There is no single optimal path of transition, and the question of sequencing – the relative priority between liberalisation, stabilisation, privatisation and restructuring – had to be determined in the course of the reforms themselves.[3]

The pre-history of economic reform

Russia contributed 61 per cent of the USSR's GNP, and even before the *coup* Russia had begun to disengage itself from the Soviet economy. Already on 3 September 1990, the prime minister, Silaev, outlined the Russian government's programme, which envisaged a speedy transition to the market, but recognised that this would be impossible without co-ordination among all the republics. The programme, which ran to over a thousand pages, advocated a new structure to replace the ministries for separate industries, an inter-republican economic council. Despite its length, the programme was marked by the absence of governmental unity, personal conflicts and the lack of clear criteria for implementation. By November 1990, the Russian parliament had passed laws on agriculture and began devising its own economic reforms. The Russian government unilaterally cut by 80 per cent its 1991 budget contribution to the Soviet treasury. However, the period up to August 1991 was marked by frustration as Russian programmes came into conflict with Soviet ones, and the economic crisis only worsened. With the fall of the Soviet government the Russian economics team inherited a yawning budget deficit, a mountain of roubles accumulated as a result of years of monetary and fiscal laxity, and a debilitating system of price controls. The result was empty shops, low labour productivity and rampant inflation.

The lack of clarity over what exactly was the subject of economic reform, Russia or the Soviet Union, continued to impede progress after the *coup*. The Inter-Republican Economic Committee headed by Silaev, with Yavlinskii one of its key advisers, sought to maintain an integrated economy. Their efforts led to the signing of an economic treaty on 8 October 1991 in Almaty by eight republics.[4] The treaty stressed private ownership, free enterprise and competition, and committed the republics to marketisation and restricted government interference. They were forbidden unilaterally to take control of shared property or to put up trade barriers between themselves. The rouble was to be the common currency, but members were allowed to have their own currencies if it did not harm the rouble.[5] The treaty in essence repeated the provisions of the rejected Shatalin–Yavlinskii 500-day plan of August 1990, but in the new circumstances of independent states it did not really offer viable measures to deal with the economic crisis. The main problem was that it dealt with the external aspects and not with the root causes of crisis in each of the republics. Hopes for a federal reserve banking system, an economic arbitration court and all the other trappings of a federal union were probably unrealistic given the obstacles to maintaining political union. The independent republics, led by the Baltic republics, instead began putting up customs posts. Ukraine declared that it would establish its own currency and other republics considered taking similar measures.

The break-up of the Union dislocated regional patterns of economic specialisation and destroyed the national market.[6] The vertically integrated Stalinist economy had encouraged the manufacture of goods in gigantic plants in an attempt to benefit from economies of scale, and the production of key items for the whole USSR were concentrated in a limited number of plants. When some pharmaceutical plants were closed in 1989–90 because of their high pollution levels, they soon had to be reopened because they were sole suppliers of items necessary for medicines. However, a debate continues over the extent of economic dependency between the republics, with suggestions that this was exaggerated by Gorbachev and his associates in their attempt to prove the desirability of the Union.[7] A study of the Baltic republics, for example, argued that their dependence on the rest of the Union was not as critical as had been thought, and certainly nothing that normal economic contracts could not cover.[8] It has been estimated that the disruption of trade with CIS countries contributed 10 per cent to Russia's overall economic decline in the early 1990s.[9]

The CIS documents signed in Minsk and Almaty in December 1991 were vague on economic integration. The paradox emerged that the republic with the greatest potential for independent economic development, Russia, remained the most committed to a larger economic unit. Russia provided nearly 67 billion roubles in subsidy to the other republics in 1989, and in 1988 was the least dependent on trade with the other republics. Russia sold its energy and raw materials relatively cheaply, and paid for consumer goods at inflated prices. Russia stood to gain most from a shift to the use of the dollar in inter-republican trade. The desire of the other republics for economic separation was politically motivated, though in the long term they were probably right to believe that they could manage their own resources and enterprises better than distant Moscow could under the old regime. They feared Moscow's domination in whatever shape it came, benign or malign, subsidy or exploitation. Only the Central Asian republics sought to maintain the old links since they were clear net beneficiaries of subsidies from Moscow, but even they soon sought to forge new links with their regional neighbours.

The Soviet legacy to Russia was a heavy one indeed. The structural reorganisation of the Russian economy took place against the background of a sharp decline in real incomes and production, the latter falling in the USSR as a whole by 17 per cent in 1991, and in light industry, hit hardest by the cuts in imports, output fell by 40 per cent.[10] In comparison, in 1932, the hardest year of the Great Depression in the USA, GNP fell by only 14 per cent. In Russia national income fell by about 5 per cent in 1990 and 9 per cent in 1991.[11] Pavlov's government had been marked by fiscal and budgetary anarchy and rising budget deficits. This was made worse by local authorities refusing to contribute to republican funds, and republics reneging on commitments to the Union budget, in particular the central stabilisation, pension and social security funds. Credits were received from the State Bank, which in turn only encouraged the printing presses to work faster. The problem of the USSR foreign debt burdened the transition, having risen under Gorbachev to $77 billion ($60 billion to Western creditors and $17 billion to Asian and East European countries) by late 1991.[12]

The Soviet economic crisis had been exacerbated by *perestroika* but had long been evident. There had been a sharp decline in growth rates since the mid-1970s, the growth of debt money and budget deficits. The anti-alcohol campaign of 1986–7 and its attendant revenue losses were only one element in a larger crisis in which enterprises and ministries took advantage of the weakening centre to obtain cheap investment funds from the central budget. The problems, in the words of Chubais, were 'only the summit of a prolonged socioeconomic structural crisis connected with the decay of the centrally planned economy'.[13] The decay, however, had not been terminal and many studies suggest that the Soviet economy could have limped on for a good few years until destabilised by reform projects themselves.[14]

In the early 1990s, the structural crisis turned from a latent to an actual one. The financial crisis reached catastrophic proportions, and this more than anything else hastened the demise of the USSR. The Soviet inflation rate quadrupled in 1991, reaching some 700 per cent by the end of the year. The chairman of the State Bank, Victor Geraschenko, warned in early December that only enough funds remained for a few days of expenditure, a crisis precipitated by the Russian parliament's objections to the Bank's policy of printing money to meet commitments. Yeltsin agreed to bail out the Union government, but at the price of a tough budget strategy and the transfer of the Soviet Ministry of Finance to Russian jurisdiction. On 20 November, the process was accelerated when Yeltsin in effect took over all the remaining Union economic ministries, disbanding several of them, and imposing Russian control over all strategic natural resources. Thus, Russia, despite itself, was forced to take over Soviet economic institutions, but was in danger of finding itself in the position of responsibility without power since little positive could be done until there were new budget laws, effective taxation, credit and monetary policies.

Facets of economic reform

As the USSR moved towards oblivion Russia drew up a fully fledged independent economic policy. Yeltsin outlined his programme to the Russian CPD on 28 October 1991.

- Economic stabilisation based on tight monetary and credit policy, strengthening of the rouble (although one of the major problems was the influx of roubles from the former Union republics) up to the creation of a separate Russian currency to protect the economy.
- Price liberalisation.
- Privatisation and the introduction of a mixed economy with a growing private sector, accelerated land reform.
- Reorganisation of the financial system, tight control of budget expenditure, reform of the tax and banking systems.[15]

Yeltsin's proposals promised 'to stabilise the situation' and then to 'begin the process of rejuvenation', although he admitted that the measures would be unpopular but expected there to be an improvement by autumn 1992. This was a programme for radical changes in both ownership and management of the Russian economy that drew much on the Polish experience of shock therapy.

On 1 November, the CPD granted Yeltsin wide powers (valid until 1 December 1992) to be used to promote reform. Presidential decrees on such matters as banks, property and land reform, taxation, currency and so on were to be submitted to parliament, and if not rejected within seven days they became effective; otherwise they were to be discussed by parliament within ten days.[16] On 6 November, Yeltsin reorganised the government, stating that for the duration of radical economic reforms the president would also act as head of the 'government of reforms' himself. A new Russian Council of Ministers with twenty-three ministers was appointed, and the country prepared itself for yet another grand attempt at social engineering.

Liberalisation (shock therapy)

The many different approaches reduce to two different philosophies of the transition to the market. One urged the need for 'shock therapy' and a 'big bang' on the Polish model and insisted that only in this way would vital Western assistance be forthcoming. They drew the conclusion from Gorbachev's reforms that half-measures are often worse than none. The other line, advocated by Yavlinskii at the head of Yabloko and the left, proposed a slower route with controlled price rises, de-monopolisation, gradual privatisation and assistance to enterprises. Russia's road to the market began with a vigorous 'big bang', but then began to draw on elements from the second school.

The idea behind 'shock therapy' is that countries plagued by years of planning, state ownership and bureaucracy have to be jerked into the mainstream of market reforms. This is to be achieved by the rapid liberalisation of prices, removal of subsidies, expenditure cuts and severe reductions in money supply. To use Kornai's term, the aim is to overcome 'soft budget constraints'.[17] The result in Bolivia, Poland, Russia and elsewhere has been an immediate explosion in prices, a rapid rise in unemployment and a steep fall in production. The aim was for goods that had previously been hoarded to find their way back to the shops and for queues to decrease, deterred by the high prices if not eliminated by the sufficiency of goods. Higher prices would encourage production, and a revived private sector would gradually bring supply and demand into line. Price rises would then stabilise, and the economy would begin to move out of recession.

The theory was condemned by the veteran economist John Kenneth Galbraith as 'simplistic ideology'. He argued that the neo-liberal reliance on the market to the exclusion of any major role of the state was primitive economics.[18] Shock therapy places intolerable strains on the economy and society, and companies that in other conditions might have fought their way to viability are forced to close for lack of liquidity. The fall in production is matched by spiralling prices and the population sees its savings disappear and endures yet more suffering. Living standards, already low, plummet, and tight budgetary constraints mean that there is a lack of funds to provide adequate social security for the growing army of the unemployed and needy. The sheer speed of the transition intensifies the suffering and the whole fragile tissue of democratic institutions is placed under almost intolerable strain. It took Germany ten years to move to a market economy after the war, and Britain retained price and other controls into the 1950s.

In defence of his strategy, Gaidar stressed the initial disastrous conditions in autumn 1991: grain reserves down to four months supply, foreign currency and gold reserves exhausted, and a lack of credit-worthiness. The old system was completely paralysed and the new one did not work. In these conditions, he insisted, all talk about a soft, evolutionary approach to reform was meaningless. His strategy was based on a three-year programme, but in the event he was out of government within thirteen months. Those countries that had three years of consistent reform, like Poland, Estonia, the Czech Republic, Latvia and Lithuania, saw rises in production, whereas in Russia the premature relaxation of policy undermined any immediate benefits. According to Gaidar, the problem was not that

Russian reforms were pursued too dogmatically, but that they were pursued without consistency and firmness.[19]

Gaidar's political position was always exceptionally weak; appointed deputy prime minister in charge of economic policy on 7 November 1991, he became first deputy prime minister on 2 March 1992, acting prime minister on 15 June 1992, and was dismissed on 14 December 1992 (returning briefly to the economics portfolio in late 1993). Nevertheless, he was the architect of the first stage of Russia's economic reforms. His policy was marked by a commitment to traditional International Monetary Fund (IMF) precepts including a balanced budget, the reduction of inflation, cutting back subsidies, exposing the domestic economy to the world market and raising energy prices. He and his neo-liberal allies tended to idealise neo-classical economic theory and denigrated the role of the state and other regulatory institutions of contemporary capitalism.[20]

In late 1991, wage limits were lifted, restrictions on foreign economic activities eased, minimum wages set, all customs barriers introduced by individual regions of Russia banned, VAT set at 28 per cent, guidelines for privatisation in 1992 adopted, and much else besides. Then, on 2 January 1992, came comprehensive price liberalisation, with prices freed from administrative control on about 90 per cent of retail prices and 80 per cent of wholesale prices. On 29 January, the restrictions on trading, imposed in the 1920s, were lifted and soon kiosks sprouted on streets everywhere. Ambitious targets were set to reduce the budget deficit, which by some estimates reached a fifth of GDP in 1991, and to achieve a balanced budget by the end of the year. Monetary policy was tightened, and attempts made to bring the flood of roubles under control. Bread, milk, vodka, medicines, rents, public transport and the price of some utilities remained controlled, and from March 1992, local councils had the right to impose local controls as long as they paid for any subsidies. From May 1992, energy prices were increased, but, because of political fears, not up to anything demanded by the IMF, and as late as 2001 energy prices in Russia were still only a third of world prices.

The January measures were a mixture of price liberalisation and price reform, raising prices rather than letting the market find a natural level balancing supply and demand. Demand was damped down by what for most Russians were exorbitant prices, but too little was done to free the supply side of the economy, with only desultory moves towards privatising the retail sector and breaking the stranglehold of monopolies. Reforms to price structures appear to have operated mainly in one direction – price increases. Consumer price inflation rose sharply, by 245 per cent in the month of January alone before falling back to 10 per cent in August;[21] at which point the government's attempt to resolve the problem of inter-enterprise arrears stimulated a new wave of inflation, rising to a monthly 25 per cent by the end of the year. By November 1992, prices had risen twenty-two-fold, whereas wages had only increased ten-fold.[22] An incomes policy had been an essential element of shock therapy in Poland, but in Russia the government considered wage controls politically unfeasible and unnecessary since the wage–price spiral was not the central element fuelling inflation. The impact of the price rises was cushioned by savings and accumulated goods, but these were soon exhausted; the wiping out of savings, indeed, became one of the most bitter charges against Gaidar's economics.

Shock therapy leads to a sharp drop in manufacturing production. In Poland industrial output fell by 37 per cent from 1990 before beginning to pick up in late 1992, but was worse in Russia because shock therapy was applied to an economy already in very deep recession. Industrial output in Russia plummeted by 20 per cent in 1992, compared with a fall of 11 per cent in 1991. Production was hit by the tight squeeze on investment: the aim was to destroy the old inefficient system rather than to construct anything new.[23] In Russian conditions of extreme monopolisation, instead of firms cutting prices to compensate for falling demand they cut output and raised prices. Between 1990 and 1995, GDP fell by some 50 per cent, compared to a cumulative fall of some 31 per cent in United States GNP during the Depression.[24] Despite the temptation to blame shock therapy for this fall, countries (like Ukraine) that tried a 'soft landing' into economic reform fared even worse.

Stabilisation and crash

Already from mid-1992, political pressures forced a shift from liberalisation towards stabilisation. Fears of a social backlash meant that energy prices were raised only five-fold in April 1992, despite the demand of the IMF to raise them to world levels. Tight monetary and fiscal policies were pursued to restrain inflation and to stabilise the value of the rouble against international currencies. The Russian budget deficit, nevertheless, tended to rise as the government eased its public sector spending restrictions and raised state sector wages. The management of the economy was reorganised, with the new Ministry of the Economy absorbing the old general ministries like Gosplan and Gossnab, the state supply system abolished in January 1992. The Ministry of Industry took over some two dozen branch industrial ministries, while others were turned into concerns, trusts, associations and so on, but still closely tied to ministerial departments. Large debts were run up between companies, primarily between the old state industries and the military industrial complex, because they could not sell goods to consumers, who had no spare cash. This was because they had been unwilling to sack workers or to cut down on overheads, but above all because they in effect gained credit by not paying for goods received. The economy for most of the 1990s appeared paralysed, with factories waiting for orders from ministries in Moscow that no longer existed. Lax fiscal and political controls encouraged 'rent-seeking', defined as 'any activity designed to exploit a monopoly position or to gain access to government subsidies, as opposed to profit-seeking in a market with competitive firms'.[25] The whole system, moreover, was permeated by corruption as managers looked to their own interests rather than those of their enterprises, and sought ways of profiting from the crisis by transferring ownership to themselves and associates on the cheap, by purloining foreign currency income, intercepting cash flows and in general by exploiting the opportunities of a system stuck between the plan and the market, neither 'socialist' nor 'capitalist'. Joel Hellman characterised this as a 'partial reform equilibrium' where the winners of the first phase of reform seek to protect their gains by obstructing further change.[26]

One source of opposition to Gaidar's liberal policies came from the industrialists, represented above all by the Russian Union of Industrialists and Entrepreneurs (RUIE), largely made up of the directors of the large state enterprises who favoured a slower pace of reform and more government subsidies. Another came from opposition democrats like Yavlinskii, who insisted that it was a mistake for the government to liberalise prices before privatisation and competition had been introduced. His warnings were correct in that monopolies took advantage of the liberalisation to raise prices and cut production, the opposite of what the reform policies were meant to achieve. A third source of opposition came from parliament, who had demanded the replacement of the young academics in government with 'professionals'. The appointment on 30 May 1992 of Chernomyrdin, chairman of Gazprom, as energy minister was a response to these demands, reflecting the reforms' lack of a solid parliamentary base. The government reshuffle of June 1992 led to concessions to the industrial lobby in the form of writing off debts and increased monetary emissions.

The challenge to neo-liberal policies finally succeeded when, on 14 December 1992, Chernomyrdin replaced Gaidar as prime minister. While most of the radical 'government of reforms' remained, a change of tack was promised with more credits for state industry, and on 5 January 1993 limits on profits on some consumer goods and services were announced in an attempt to keep prices down.In the event, Chernomyrdin's economic policy did not differ all that much from Gaidar's. The policy of tight credit and monetary policy was restored, and financial stabilisation and the strengthening of the rouble became his priorities. The Fifth Duma from 1994 proved receptive to the logic of centrist economic reform, and in December 1995, as noted, for the first time since 1991 a budget was adopted before it was due to come into operation.

The 1993 constitution grants the Central Bank of Russia (CBR), previously subordinated to the Supreme Soviet, a degree of independence from the legislature. It is allowed to determine the money supply within the framework of a commitment to the stability of the rouble. Its director is hired or fired by the State Duma, but only on the president's recommendation. Thus, the CBR gained some room for manœuvre, above all from parliament, but enjoys nothing like the degree of independence enjoyed by the Bundesbank or the Federal Reserve Bank in the United States. Few restrictions were placed on capital flows in and out of the country. The final demise of the rouble zone followed the CBR's currency reform of July 1993, giving Russia effective monetary and credit control, and by 1995 almost all the other republics had introduced their own currency.

Stabilisation was marked by a roller-coaster of booms and busts. A notable low point was 'black Tuesday', 11 October 1994, when the rouble lost over 20 per cent of its value, largely as a consequence of an earlier loosening of monetary policy and, it was suspected, because of machinations by bankers. The rouble swiftly recovered its value but its vulnerability was exposed and between September 1994 and January 1995 it lost half its value. By 1998, the rouble was effectively stabilised within a dollar corridor, with inflation reduced to tolerable limits. The major problem, however, was to achieve full rouble convertibility, without which Russia would attract little foreign investment because of difficulties in repatriating earnings, given the natural limits to barter or counter-trade.

The whole policy depended on the West in the form of debt restructuring and stabilisation funds. Debt relief released valuable foreign currency to finance imports and stabilise the currency, while standby loans are a crucial element in providing a source of non-inflationary financing. Russia gained full membership of the IMF and the World Bank on 27 April 1992, after some debate over the size of Russia's quota in the IMF, which sets its capacity to borrow, and thus became eligible for loans. In the 1990s, IMF assistance totalled some $24 (£13.5) billion, tied to a set of conditions including tight monetary and fiscal policies, reductions in the budget deficit, cutting credits to loss-making enterprises, establishing the legal framework for private ownership, reforming the farm and energy sectors, servicing debts to the West and establishing a unified exchange rate for the rouble. Although direct credits to state firms had been phased out from 1994, subsidies continued to flow to agriculture while high tariffs (for example, on imported automobiles) protected domestic car makers.

Between mid-1995 and mid-1998, money supply and exchange rates remained stable, but ultimately severe fiscal imbalances undermined monetary stability and led to the end of the rouble–dollar anchor. In the 1990s, direct state subsidies to enterprises were largely replaced by debts. Tax shortfalls led to budget deficits (including the deficits of the federal budget, the regional budgets and social security) that the government tried to finance in a bacchanalia of bond issues (GKOs) whose ever higher-interest rates could not be sustained indefinitely, provoking the crash of August 1998. The devaluation provoked by the financial crisis of 1998 improved the competitiveness of the Russian economy and allowed significant growth to take place from 2000 (see Table 12.1) as import substitution gave a boost to domestic manufacturers and suppliers. The benefits lasted some two years.

Privatisation

The main purpose of privatisation is to break the dependence of enterprises on the state budget. Subsidies and relatively easy access to bank credits fuelled inflation and undermined the credibility of the whole reform programme. However, privatisation is as much a political act as economically expedient. The destruction

Table 12.1 Russian economic performance since 1990

Year	GDP change (%) against preceding year	Industrial production change (%) against preceding year
1990	-3.0	-0.1
1991	-5.0	-8.0
1992	-14.5	-18.0
1993	-8.7	-14.1
1994	-12.7	-20.9
1995	-4.1	-3.3
1996	-3.5	-4.0
1997	0.9	1.9
1998	-4.6	-5.5
1999	3.2	8.1
2000	7.6	9.3
2001	5.5	5.2

Source: Ruslan Grinberg, 'Desyat let sistemnoi transformatsii', *Nezavismaya gazeta*, 22 December 1999, p. 4; *RFE/RL Newsline*, 3 January 2001.

of the old monopolies and their corporate dependence on the state not only begins to create a capitalist market but also entails the destruction of the associated bureaucracy. For Chubais, the deputy prime minister at the head of the State Committee for the Administration of State Property (*Goskomimushchestvo*, GKI) responsible for privatisation, the programme was designed to create a new class with a stake in property and thus make society less susceptible to political demagogy. In his address to the nation on 19 August 1992, Yeltsin described privatisation as the 'ticket to a free economy'. Private property was considered the basis of a civilised society and the foundation on which democracy could be built.

The Soviet economy was the most monopolised in the world. Up to a third of all industrial enterprises were absolute monopolies, producing goods that no other company in the USSR produced. The system was characterised by 'the "super-monopolism" of state power' in production, in the sphere of management, in trade and supply and in research and development.[27] De-nationalisation would have to be accompanied by de-monopolisation to stop privatisation simply transforming state monopolies into private ones. As in Britain, however, privatisation tended to precede the break-up of monopolies, and in most cases simply achieved the transfer of a state monopoly into the private sector where they could impose punitive charges on captive customers. The state committee for anti-monopoly policy, a body independent of the government, vetted all company registrations valued at more than 50 million roubles. The anti-monopoly legislation, however, was relatively ineffective and pursued with a singular lack of vigour, and de-monopolisation tended to take spontaneous rather than planned forms.[28] Monopolies, however, affected only certain industries, and overall the concentration of industry was not that much greater in Russia than in the United States. The problem in Russia was 'the missing fringe of small firms', the source of technical innovation, competition and job creation.[29]

The aim of privatisation is to overcome the amorphous nature of state property; allegedly belonging to all, it belongs to no one. The intention is to personify it in the form of concrete owners or known corporate agencies while creating a new class of property owners (in our case, 'new Russians' and oligarchs). The presidential decree on the Privatisation of State and Municipal Enterprises in the RSFSR of 29 December 1991 set ambitious targets for privatisation, but little was said about de-monopolisation.[30] The Government Programme of Privatisation of June 1992 was the main document outlining Russia's privatisation programme.[31] Strategic and defence enterprises, utilities and those with over 10,000 employees could only be privatised, if at all, with the government's approval. All small enterprises (the 200,000 enterprises with up to 200 employees, most of which were owned by local or municipal authorities) were to be sold through competitive auctions, commercial tender competitions or lease buy-outs. Large enterprises (with 1,000 to 10,000 employees) were to be transformed into joint-stock companies (corporatised), after which their shares were to be sold or distributed according to the provisions of the mass privatisation programme. Medium-sized enterprises could adopt either the direct sale or corporatisation method. Three main approaches were available for disbursing the assets of joint-stock companies, while a fourth sought to involve the mass of the population.

- The first was for collectives to receive up to 25 per cent of non-voting shares free, and another 10 per cent of voting shares at a discount, while managers could buy up to a fifth of voting shares for a nominal sum.
- The second was for workers and managers to purchase 51 per cent of normal shares in closed sales. This was the preferred option for most companies, but since the workers' shares could not be held collectively they were easily over-shadowed by management, allowing the enterprises effectively to be taken over by their own administrations.
- The third option applied only to medium-sized enterprises and allowed a managing group to privatise an enterprise while ensuring solvency and employ-ment for at least one year; the managing group could buy 30 per cent of voting shares, while 20 per cent was sold to workers and managers at preferential terms.[32]
- In addition, in August 1992 the government began to issue privatisation vouchers with a nominal value of 10,000 roubles. Citizens were given invest-ment coupons, that is, registered securities enabling them to buy shares or management shares at preferential rates of the 6,000 medium and large compa-nies earmarked for corporatisation in 1992 and privatisation in 1993. The coupon method does not create additional capital or strengthen the manage-ment of companies, but instead was meant to symbolise the advent of 'popular capitalism'. In the event, instead of creating a new class of shareholders, voucher privatisation turned into a disaster as the management companies set up to manage the popular shareholdings simply stole the shares; very few ever paid out any dividends.

Much of the debate over privatisation focuses on the issue of equity. If state enterprises had earlier belonged to the people, then how was their formal ownership now to be translated into real ownership? The argument that enterprises should be given to their workers was flawed since those in viable enterprises would benefit far more than those in the service sector or bankrupt plants. The debate was often couched in terms of equity versus efficiency, though some argued that giving away shares combined both efficacy and equity, and would at the same time build up popular support for the reforms.[33] Others favoured the most rapid disbursement of state assets to establish a critical mass early on in the reform process.[34] Milton Friedman, however, insisted that ownership meant not only assets but also liabilities, and that old illusions would be perpetuated if the first step on the road to the market was giving people something for nothing instead of having to provide something in return.[35] The giving away of state property to workers might well undermine both efficiency and equity since those who did not work in a state enterprise or had retired would be at a disadvantage, and the value of enterprises in any case varied sharply.[36]

Privatisation turned out to be a highly complex affair in which genuine problems were compounded by an almost obsessive fear of foreign penetration of the economy, allied with the attempt to avoid the Soviet mafia buying up land and enterprises with their ill-gotten gains. The latter consideration failed in the most spectacular way, and privatisation was accompanied by massive insider dealing and the 'grabbing' (*prikhvatizatsiya*, a pun on the Russian word for privatisation) of public wealth by what were to become 'oligarchs' as a result of the process. In one respect, however, privatisation was easier in Russia than elsewhere since the process was little affected by reprivatisation, the restitution of property. Russia's former owners were for the most part dead, and their heirs scattered to the four corners of the earth. Changes in property relations took a number of forms, of which outright privatisation was only one. The other options were leasing arrangements, worker-management schemes, the so-called '*nomenklatura* privatisation' whereby managers and former political officials took the best of the state enterprises, and the creation of new businesses. Leasing, holding companies and the like appeared to be at best a half-way stage, a type of pseudo-privatisation.

Privatisation always has a directly political purpose. The aim here was to make the transition to the market economy irreversible by creating a class of property owners while at the same time making firms more efficient and market-oriented. In addition, rapid state-sponsored privatisation sought (unsuccessfully) to pre-empt factory directors from appropriating choice parts of the state economy. The majority of privatised enterprises were not sold to the public but in workforce elections; staff, encouraged by their managers, voted for the option that allowed them to buy 51 per cent of the stock at a fixed price. Rather than outside owners coming in and shaking out factories and sacking staff and managers, control remained within the factory gates. Voucher privatisation was followed from mid-1994 by a second stage focusing on key aspects of enterprise restructuring and with more emphasis on private sector development, including the transition to cash privatisation, the attempt to achieve more efficient corporate management, and the accelerated development of securities markets and legal reforms. Enterprises were now encouraged to raise investment resources on the open capital market, and at the same time cash auctions and investment tenders for stakes in the newly privatised companies and for blocks of shares held by the state in privatised enterprises accelerated. Attempts were made to attract foreign investment, but continuing capital flight depressed investment.

Local authorities played a key role in the privatisation process, especially in the housing and retail areas. Moscow insisted on control over privatisation in the city, and even safeguarded for itself the right to renationalise enterprises in the capital. Enterprises had traditionally provided a range of social facilities such as subsidised canteens, crèches, housing and hospitals, which they considered a form of hidden taxation on their enterprises and thus refused to pay taxes to the state. These non-productive social services were gradually transferred to the local authorities, but the latter usually lacked the resources to maintain them (Chapter 10).

By early 2001, 130,180 enterprises formerly owned by the state had been privatised, representing exactly two-thirds of the total. The attempt to conduct privatisation without strict controls by the executive and judicial authorities allowed a small group of economic managers and new capitalists to seize the lion's share of state property. The 'loans-for-shares' scandal, as we saw in Chapter 4, allowed the oligarchs to consolidate themselves as a class. It was clear that not enough had been charged for the assets that had been privatised. If in Russia privatisation revenues per capita are $56.40, in Hungary they stand at $1,252.80.[37] Russian capitalism took on carpet-bagging forms, interested in short-term gains, rent seeking and asset-stripping. A distinctive type of 'comprador capitalism' emerged.[38] Putin, however, set his face against renationalisation and insisted that there would be no redistribution of property. He did, however, ensure that privatisation took place more fairly and that the state received its due share by holding competitive auctions. He also tried to ensure cross-subsidy. For example, in 1999–2000, Oleg Deripaska and his associates at the head of Russian Aluminium were allowed to take control of 70 per cent of Russia's highly lucrative aluminium industry in exchange, it appears, for a commitment to support the Russian automobile industry. Russian Aluminium went on to buy enterprises such as the massively loss-making GAZ car plant in Nizhnii Novgorod, with its 100,000 workers, corrupt management, outdated product lines and huge burden of social expenses, and began its modernisation.[39]

Putin's administration began to change the way in which the government functioned, above all strengthening the power of the federal government at the expense of the regions. The measures, as we have seen above, included the creation of the seven new federal districts, the strengthening of the federal treasury and the federal prosecutors, and changes in the management of the natural monopolies (including Gazprom and RAO UES, the electricity monopoly). The government's control over the management of these companies was strengthened. The new push for reform suggested that the 'partial reform equilibrium' identified by Hellman could be overcome by an outside force, in this case a rejuvenated presidency.

Problems of the Russian economy

As a result of liberalisation, stabilisation and privatisation, the basic legal framework of a market economy has now been established. Within not much more than a decade after the fall of communism the achievement is impressive, yet major problems remain. The rights of creditors are poorly defended, above all because of the cumbersome procedure whereby the courts take the assets of debtors and only after an auction provide some of the returns to the creditor; this made debt financing (which is part of investment) highly problematic. In addition, the rights of minority shareholders over management are too weak to prevent asset-stripping or to exercise a hold over corporate governance at all; majority shareholders ride roughshod over minority shareholders, encouraging 100 per cent investment. There remain major gaps in the law, for example over intellectual property rights and the land code. The main problems facing Putin in the economic sphere were enterprise restructuring, public finance, the banking system and corporate governance. The development of an operational market economy in Russia required the strengthening of the rule of law, the development of legislative standards and frameworks, and attention to the social aspects of a modern Western economy.

On 28 June 2000, the plan devised by German Gref's centre was adopted by the government and represented an integrated plan for the modernisation of the Russian economy and society. It sought to make social benefits more targeted, with pensions linked to contributions. A more benign business environment was to be created by reducing licensing, streamlining investment decisions and introducing international accounting standards for the corporate sector. The plan committed the country to global integration, although its aspirations for accelerated World Trade Organization (WTO) membership proved rather premature. Echoes of the plan resound in the following policy areas.

Finances

Tax policy and collection

The state's punitive exercise of *its* property rights through taxation, which in some cases exceeded 100 per cent of what was being taxed and thus encouraging barter, was compounded by selective enforcement. This was remedied by the introduction of international standards reflected in Part I of the new Tax Code, establishing the basic relationship between tax payers and the authorities. On 26 July 2000, the second part of the new tax code was overwhelmingly approved by the Federation Council, despite the fact that it would cause an immediate fall in regional tax revenue. The main features of the tax package were a flat rate 13 per cent income tax (the lowest in Europe), a minimum 5 per cent unified social tax, a 2 per cent social charge on wages, the raising of some excise taxes, and the amending of the law on VAT.

The failure to collect taxes in the 1990s undermined the basic sinews of the state and forced the government to resort to high-interest short-term borrowing, precipitating the crash of August 1998. Tax evasion (or avoidance) is always a problem in federal states, where the very structure of politics engenders suspicion of the centre. The tax service itself was chronically under-funded, with only 200,000 ill-equipped tax inspectors. Above all, the high level of distrust between the state and its citizenry encouraged tax avoidance since there was no confidence that the monies collected would go to public benefit. The new Tax Code improved matters, liberalising and simplifying the tax system. Tax collection in 2000 increased by 60 per cent to reach 20.7 per cent of GDP.[40]

The banking system

Up to August 1998, Russia had some 1,800 banks, but the twenty largest banks alone controlled 57.8 per cent of the total assets in the banking system.[41] Russian commercial banks did not engage in the normal financing of economic enterprises but instead focused on the speculative pursuit of short-term interest. In 2000, the Central Bank withdrew the licences of thirty-six banks, reducing the number to 1,316.[42] Gradually confidence in the banking sector was restored, demonstrated by the growth in retail deposits in real terms. Yet banks played very little part in financing investment, and banks still operated largely as the financial arms of enterprises or FIGs. The Gref plan called for the restructuring of the banking system, consolidation into a smaller number, the establishment of a more robust regulatory system and easing restrictions on the participation of foreign banks and a system of deposit insurance.

Bankruptcy

De-nationalisation is usually accompanied by bankruptcy laws allowing previously subsidised but unprofitable companies to go to the wall. In September 1991, for the first time a mine in Donetsk was declared bankrupt, unable to pay its debts and the banks unwilling to extend further credits.[43] Thus began the process of hardening the budget, but the various bankruptcy laws remain open to abuse, above all because creditors have little incentive to recover their claims. Bankruptcy proceedings have turned into another form of asset-stripping.

Inflation

Inflation was the bugbear of the reforms of the 1990s, approaching hyper-inflation at certain times, but as a result of stabilisation policies was brought under some sort of control. By 2000, inflation had fallen to 20.2 per cent for the year. Part of the reason for the fall was the increasingly tight control over the banking system.

Investment

The decline in the rate of investment far exceeded the decline in output during the early years of radical reform. The absolute level of investment between 1990 and 2000 fell by 75 per cent. The great deficit of investment resulted in an exhausted capital stock and massive cumulative productivity shortfalls that will cast a long shadow into the future. The inadequacy of the banks meant that most investment came from the enterprises themselves. The investment climate, however, began to improve under Putin. In 2000, investment in fixed capital reached 17.7 per cent, up from 5.3 per cent in 1999.[44] One of the reasons for this is that it was clear that there would be no grand redistribution of property and therefore owners could now turn to running their businesses for long-run profitability, rather than short-term asset-stripping.

Capital flight

Corporate capital flight took place through export and import contracts involving transfer pricing, the non-repatriation of export revenues and the distortion of information. Capital flight was stimulated by weak property rights, the lack of domestic investment opportunities and tax evasion. No accurate figures are available, but it is estimated that at least US$20–30 billion of corporate capital left before August 1998. There were other types of capital flight as well, above all in cash, amounting in total to several hundred billion dollars. Annual losses to Russia in illegal capital flight are estimated to be $25–30 billion. The weakness of the rouble and the fragility of the banking system encouraged people to hoard dollars, often kept in accounts abroad. Small businesses would try to avoid paying taxes by buying cash dollars as a means of payment. As a result Russia's stock of cash dollars is estimated to be $60 billion, equalling the $50–70 billion that the US Treasury estimates is held in cash dollars in the United States itself. Among the other positive economic indicators of Putin's early rule, capital flight in relative terms (as a proportion of export earnings) began to decline, suggesting that there could be a reversal of capital flight. An early indication of this was the growth in domestic investment. At the same time, cash flows at the federal level were now much more tightly controlled, above all through the establishment of the Federal Treasury and a more effective tax system. A new law against money laundering adopted in mid-2001 tightened supervision over financial transactions, to some degree in response to Western concerns. The permissive environment towards corruption typical of the Yeltsin years now gave way to the struggle for a new probity in public affairs encouraging some 'return flight', above all from Russian accounts in places like Cyprus.

Budget deficits

For most of the 1990s, Russia ran severe budget deficits, and sought ever more creative ways of covering the gap between spending commitments and income. Only in 2000 did Russia finally achieve a budget surplus (some $6 billion), compared with the enormous deficits of earlier years. The government refused the demands of the left in the Duma to divert funds in the 2001 budget to provide state support for the manufacturing sector or for increased social spending, provoking the ire of the communist opposition.

Foreign debt

In 1991, Russia's foreign debt totalled $120 billion, one-third of which was held by the nineteen-strong Paris Club of state-to-state creditors and the rest with the London Club of commercial creditors. By 2001, Russian sovereign debt (excluding private foreign debt by Russian enterprises and banks, and the foreign debt of regional and local governments) had risen to some $150 billion. In 1990, Russia's sovereign debt represented 10.4 per cent of the country's GDP; by July 1998, this figure had risen to 31 per cent; only to rise to 113 per cent in December 1998, then falling back sharply. The debt carried over from Soviet times was $103 billion, and it was this component that particularly angered those in Russia who argued that the debt burden prevented productive investment and the maintenance of services. Others argued that, although Russia's foreign debt looked high, compared to other countries it was not so bad, amounting to only 21 per cent of GDP or 140 per cent of total export earnings. By comparison, Poland's $43 billion foreign debt represented 32 per cent of its GDP or 144 per cent of its export earnings; Brazil's $190 billion debt was 25 per cent of its GDP and 330 per cent of its export income. In terms of GDP, Russia's debt had become an burden, although somewhat alleviated by high energy prices in 1999–2001.

The total of Paris Club debts was $48 billion, of which some $19 billion was owed to Germany, its single largest creditor. Moscow was forced to roll over its debt in a series of humiliating annual negotiations. An agreement was reached with the London Club in 2000 that wrote off some debt and restructured the rest, but no similar agreement was reached with the Paris Club. Russia, as a member of the Paris Club of government creditors, sought to recover Soviet-era debts from former allied countries such as Vietnam. To service its debt in 1999 Russia required $17.5 billion, at a time when its entire domestic budget was not much more than $20 billion. The country's total budget in 2001 was $42 billion, and even with anticipated growth debt servicing would take at least a third of all government spending in 2003. The crunch year was indeed 2003, when Russia would owe $17 billion to Paris Club creditors. Only by emergency restructuring and rescheduling of the debt could Russia scrape through. Putin rejected all talk of a default.

External economic assistance

The European Bank for Reconstruction and Development (EBRD) was established in May 1990 to provide risk capital for the transition economies, and over the years supported specific sectors and enterprises in Russia. The main source of economic assistance, however, came from the IMF, while the World Bank invested significantly to restructure strategic industries such as coal mining. External official assistance to Russia has been small in relation to Russia's GNP (0.3 per cent in 1996, and declining thereafter). However, in 1997, one-sixth of the federal budget deficit was financed from external official sources. By 2000, however, this source of deficit coverage had almost dried up.

Foreign direct investment (FDI)

At first wary of foreign direct investment (FDI), especially in larger firms, the Russian government later sought to attract foreign investors. For this a strong legal and financial system was required, as well as a reasonably stable political environment. In 2000, FDI rose to $12 billion, a growth of 20–25 per cent over the previous year. However, like the foreign investment boom of 1997–8, this includes investments in Russian stocks, including Russian-owned companies quoted on non-Russian stock markets. The share of FDI comprised by direct investment in new plant and equipment still fell below $5 billion. This is far less than the FDI in much smaller countries like Poland and Hungary, and Russia's FDI totalled less than 5 per cent of the total FDI that has flowed into China. Most foreign investment went into trade and public catering as well as into the food industry, while the fuel industry received a relatively small proportion because of problems protecting minority shareholder rights and repatriating profits.

Foreign bond issues

Russia's unexpectedly successful bond issue in November 1996 raised a billion dollars on the global market. Moscow's first international issue since the 1917 Bolshevik revolution was heavily oversubscribed, with bids totalling two billion on an offering that had originally been expected to be pitched at a cautious $300 million. The issue boosted the financial credibility of the country, struggling in its negotiations with the IMF over Moscow's failure to meet its structural adjustment terms on a three year $10.2 billion loan package. It appeared to give Russia a new source of budget finance, and opened the way for Russia's city authorities and major industries to issue their own bonds, raising the infrastructure investment they could not get from the state or on the domestic money market. In the event, the August 1998 crash disappointed hopes that this was the way to unblock the investment logjam in the country, which was holding up industrial and infrastructure development at all levels.

Accounting standards

The Soviet system enjoyed a highly developed system of book-keeping, but this was directed towards the planned economy and was not sensitive to issues of market accounting and accountability. Considerable progress has now been made towards meeting international standards of accounting. For a company to be listed in international exchanges three years of audited accounts are required. Who would do this auditing remains contentious, although many international accounting companies have set up offices in Russia.

Trade and enterprise

Foreign trade

A presidential decree of 15 November 1991 and later measures decisively broke with the old state monopoly on foreign trade by liberalising foreign economic relations, and regulating flows by tariffs rather than quantitative restrictions. Trade patterns changed dramatically, with a shift away from the former Soviet markets towards Western Europe. By 1994, Russian trade with the EU was worth almost double that with the CIS and by 2001 represented 40 per cent of its exports. The formation of the Eurasian Economic Community (see Chapter 16) and other integrative initiatives boosted Russia's trade with the former Soviet republics, especially Belarus. Russia's trade surplus in 2000 reached $69 billion, the best performance since Gorbachev's first year in power in 1985. The trade structure, however, was unbalanced, consisting mainly of energy and raw material exports and the import of consumer goods. Every $1 fall in the price of a barrel of oil represents a $1 billion fall in government receipts. High energy and commodity prices, however, are only part of the story. Imports in early 2001 were still 40 per cent lower than pre-August 1998 levels, reflecting the enormous amount of import substitution that had taken place after the devaluation.

The fuel and energy complex and the Dutch disease

A large proportion of Russia's budgetary and national income came from the fuel and energy complex (FEC; in Russian TEK). Total Russian energy reserves, in oil and gas, are second only to those of Saudi Arabia, and as a major energy exporter Russia benefits from price rises of a commodity that traditionally provides over half of Russian export earnings. Over half of exports (54.7 per cent) are in the petroleum sector, providing just under half of the trade surplus noted above, boosted by the rise in world oil prices, climbing from the low of $12 a barrel in 1998 to $33 a barrel in autumn 2000. The managers of Russia's oil industry sought to protect their dominance by excluding external actors, even though well aware of the need for foreign investment to raise the technological level of the Russian oil industry. The Production Sharing Agreement of 1995 proved inadequate and was revised in January 1999, but still did not prove attractive enough to encourage significant foreign investment into the minefields of the Russian economy.

The large role played by the export of energy and other natural resources threatened the country with the 'Dutch disease'. The term describes the situation when large trade and current account surpluses cause a country's exchange rate to rise in real terms, either because the price of foreign exchange is forced down by the surplus or because inflows of foreign currency produce inflation. The strong currency and inflationary pressures make the export of the country's other goods uncompetitive, and render imports cheaper than domestically produced goods. Thus, what apparently look like healthy trade surpluses strangle domestic manufacturing and achieve industrial stagnation. There were elements of this Dutch disease in Russia before the devaluation of 1998, and it is an ever-present threat. Putin's attempts to achieve structural reform of the economy, however, combined with fiscal discipline and political stability, began to produce results. The decision to ease foreign exchange surrender requirements in mid-2001, for example, eased real appreciation pressures.

Information and communications technology

Russia has an obsolescent communications infrastructure, but the Russian Internet is one of the fastest growing in the world. Russian software services are among the most technically innovative, based on a traditionally high level of programming culture and habituation to levels of virtual reality.

Entrepreneurialism and small business

Following the adoption of the Law on Co-operatives of 26 May 1988, the number at first increased rapidly, but their contribution to the economy did not meet the expectations of some of their most ardent partisans. Some turned into other types of businesses, and most worked closely with state enterprises, and indeed many were formed by these enterprises to supply and sell their goods more effectively than the unwieldy state firms. Relatively few co-operatives were genuinely commercial businesses started from scratch by entrepreneurs to meet the needs of the market.[45] Joint ventures had been the great hope of the Gorbachev years, yet they, too, failed to live up to expectations. By the end of 1991, there were some 2,600 joint ventures registered in Russia, employing some 135,000 people, the great majority of whom were Russians.[46] They were producing over 7 per cent of all computers, 10 per cent of the telephones and a growing proportion of shoes.[47]

The creation of new businesses began to change the shape of Russian ownership, although the roots of many in the shadow economy perpetuated the links between business and crime. Some 80,000 businesses were created in 1991, though not all were new in the strict sense but represented the privatisation or changes in the legal status of existing enterprises.[48] The first commodity exchange was formed on 4 April 1990,[49] and by early 1992 there were some 400 in Russia dealing with everything from metals to money, acting as a substitute for the old centrally controlled distribution system bringing buyers and sellers together. The largest was the Moscow-based Russian Commodity and Raw Materials Exchange, dealing in goods ranging from electronics to aircraft. The business ethics of some of the commodity exchanges, however, were on occasion questionable.

The greatest failure of Russian economic reform, in the event, was the inability to sustain the growth of small businesses. Whereas in Poland and other Central European countries new businesses had fuelled economic growth for a decade (there were 2 million registered small businesses in Poland in 2000, in a country whose population was a quarter that of Russia's), in Russia the number actually fell: there were around 910,000 in 1994 but only 875,000 in late 2000. Punitive and arbitrary taxation, excessive regulation and the pressure from criminals combined to stifle the development of a thriving small business sector.

De-bureaucratisation

Under the leadership of Gref, the Ministry of Economic Development and Trade sought to reduce the number of activities requiring licences. The multitude of permissions required to undertake even the most minor of economic activities was one of the main factors inhibiting the development of small businesses and fostering rampant corruption. According to one estimate, up to a tenth of the prices paid by consumers went towards paying for these 'administrative barriers'.[50] Gref had initially hoped to reduce the number of licensed activities from 341 at the federal level (if regional licences are included, the number would reach at least 500) to 50. After extensive lobbying, however, this figure rose to 102 activities requiring licensing, and a number of powerful agencies were exempted from the new regulations.

Free economic zones

Thirteen free economic zones had been established in Russia by the end of 1991, encompassing some 18 million people, 12 per cent of the total population of Russia.[51] Later, the concept of these zones was questioned, and their status was weakened.

Agriculture

The legacy of the Soviet regime was particularly heavy in agriculture. Since Stalin's decision to launch forced collectivisation in 1929, Soviet agriculture had suffered a 'permanent crisis'.[52] This crisis was marked by low productivity of land and workers, gross wastage, and food shortages that on occasion reached famine levels, as in Ukraine in the early 1930s and again in 1946. Average crop yields between 1975–90 were a third of those typical in the United States, and much of what was grown was squandered since it could neither be harvested nor stored correctly. Some 80 per cent of potatoes spoil during harvesting, and then over a half of what is left rots in storage; the USSR lost as much grain as it was later forced to purchase from abroad, 30–40 million tonnes. The lack of good farm machinery meant that 66 per cent of work was carried out by hand. The shortage of housing and socio-cultural facilities in the villages gave rise to an extraordinary internal migration in which 27 million people left the villages for towns in the twenty years from 1965. Thousands of villages lie deserted, and others are populated only by the old, drunk and infirm. The agrarian sector of the economy had been 'treated as a type of internal colony out of which resources were pumped for the development of towns and industry'.[53] Agrarian relations had been re-feudalised and a distinctive type of new serfdom emerged.

Agrarian reform was therefore high on the agenda in the transition from communism and is an essential element in the restoration of private property and market forms of economic co-ordination.[54] However, the concept of agrarian reform is ambiguous, and can mean a simple redivision of land between different proprietors and users with the emphasis on the development of private ownership (land reform in the narrow sense); or it can mean the reorganisation of agrarian relations in their entirety, affecting not only land ownership but the whole structure of the agro-industrial complex. Both would be long and hard. The international trend is towards larger farms, so a radical shift to small farms in Russia could well reduce its comparative advantages. One of the options for the collective and state farms, commonly practised in Hungary and the Baltic, was to transform themselves into joint stock companies, and for some to be reorganised into something like the Danish and Dutch producers' co-operatives. Marketing for smaller concerns could be assisted by processing and distribution co-operatives, popular in both France and Italy. Above all, a land bank like the Credit Agricole in France is essential. Little of this has yet been achieved.

The attempt to transform peasants into farmers, as under Stolypin, faced numerous obstacles, not least of which was the reluctance of the mass of the peasantry to lose the traditional support of the collective farm. Land is but one component of agriculture, and the private farmers, lacking seeds, equipment and credit, faced an uphill struggle for survival. The absence of a land market giving farmers the right to buy and sell land inhibited the development of private farms. The Law on the Land passed by the Soviet CPD in March 1990 refused explicitly to endorse the concept of private property in land, but it marked a considerable advance in accepting 'lifelong ownership, with the right of bequeathal' (Art. 3) as long as the land was used 'for family smallholdings, personal cultivation' and so on (Art. 20).[55] Yeltsin's government went further and committed itself to the break-up of the collective and state farms, and the creation of a system of small private farms.

Land remained outside the purview of the privatisation programme outlined above. The ban on the resale of land and limitations on land entitlement remained in place until the early 2000s, despite attempts to force the issue by holding a referendum. Only in 2001 was a new and relatively liberal land code adopted by the Duma; despite the desperate warnings of its communist opponents, the new code allowed the buying and selling of no more than 10 per cent of the country's land. By that time, state support for agriculture had fallen some twenty-fold since 1991, representing only 1.7 per cent of budgetary expenditure.[56] The Federal Land Registry announced on 3 January 2001 that some 130 million hectares of land in Russia had become privately owned in the previous decade. At that time, there were 43 million landowners who owned some 8 per cent of the country's total land surface.[57] Most of these were not private farms but small peasant holdings and cottage (*dacha*) plots. In contrast to the Baltic republics and the Western marches of the Soviet Union, the great mass of Russia had never known a system of consolidated family farming. Before 1929, peasants in effect owned land, but in the form of strips governed by the commune and subject to periodic redistribution. After 1991, the aim was not to reprivatise or reconstitute the family farm system, but to build it from scratch and thus to complete what Stolypin had tried to achieve when he was prime minister between 1906 and his assassination in 1911.

The obstacles facing the independent farmer are formidable. Not only do they lack tools, seeds, fodder, breeding stock and so on, but they also face hostility from the collective farms and in many cases from the villagers themselves. Furthermore, they probably number no more than a quarter of a million, mostly in European Russia and particularly in the Volga and North Caucasus regions. Agrarian reform entails a revolution in the countryside, and is resisted not only by the agricultural bureaucracy but also by a rural population accustomed to the security provided by the traditional neo-feudal agrarian system. The most active people had long ago been killed or moved to the cities. The collective and state farms were the centre of local life and the population: pensioners, agrarian specialists, local schools, and much else, all depended on the network of social and economic relations that centred on them. Without the farm, village society and economy are in danger of collapse.

Evaluation of market reform

After a decade of nearly unbroken economic decline (see Table 12.1) Russian GDP per capita fell from 39 per cent of the EU average in 1990 to only one-fifth (22 per cent) in 1997.[58] By 1998, industrial production had fallen to 45.8 per cent of the 1989 level. By comparison, at that time the Czech Republic was 80.4 of the 1998 level.[59] Russia had fallen out of the top forty in the table of countries listed by GDP at PPP per capita (see Table 12.2). Economic reform staggered forward in response to short-term crises and needs. The notion of shock therapy strictly speaking applies only to the first months of 1992, and thereafter lax money supply undermined economic stabilisation until the tight money supply policy of 1994–5 forced down inflation – and living standards. Despite the tendency to view develop-

Table 12.2 The Russian economy in world context (1997)

	GNP in billion dollars in purchasing-power parity (PPP)	Population (millions)	Military expenditure in billion dollars	Armed forces (thousands)
United States	6,920	263.8	263.5	1,523
China	3,205	1,203.6	56.2	3,031
Japan	2,595	125.5	41.7	212
Germany	1,380	81.3	36.6	398
India	1,320	936.5	8.5	1,265
France	1,109	58.1	42.69	506
Italy	1,034	58.3	20.6	450
UK	994	58.3	34.0	273
Brazil	916	160.7	5.8	296
Indonesia	666	203.6	2.0	271
Mexico	634	94.0	1.6	175
Russia	627	149.9	10.0	1,700
Canada	579	28.4	10.3	80
S. Korea	547	45.6	11.9	750
Turkey	322	63.4	7.1	811

Source: Sergei Rogov, 'Rossiya i SShA na poroge XXI veka', *Svobodnaya mysl*, No. 4 (1997), p.34.

ments through apocalyptic spectacles, and given the appalling starting conditions and the lack of a coherent reform programme, this is understandable, Russia had nevertheless made significant advances on the road to a market-based economy. As one survey put it:

> The role of the state in controlling the economy has been vastly reduced, domestic prices and foreign trade have been extensively liberalised, and monetary and fiscal policy is increasingly moving towards operational standards typical of market economies.[60]

Yeltsin insisted that the great achievement had been the change in popular attitudes, the weakening of the dependency syndrome and an awareness that the transition to the market was now, after so many false starts, for real and that new opportunities existed.[61] Attitudes had indeed changed, and even the CPRF no longer supported a return to the command economy and accepted a role for foreign investment. There has been little public protest, and the level of strikes throughout the 1990s never rose above that of 1991. Russia began to be reintegrated into the world economy, hosting the 'G8' summit in spring 1996 and later becoming a fully fledged member of the group. A structural transformation of the economy has taken place, with cuts in defence spending, the rise of a vigorous financial services industry and the growth of the service sector, rising from 33 per cent of GDP in 1990 to 50 per cent in 1994; for the first time since Stalin's industrialisation, production of services exceeded production of goods. The reforms have gained a self-sustaining character, having learnt some of the rudiments of the operation of a market economy. Powerful interests are now bound up with the continued marketisation of the economy. The process, however, requires political stability, a clear legal framework and the development of self-regulatory mechanisms to avoid the endless repetition of the scandals and excesses of the early reform years.

The success of economic reform is measured by the stimulation of economic activity, the modernisation of the structure of industry, competitiveness on world markets, rising living standards, a stable and convertible currency, and budgetary stability. The bill for inefficiency should no longer be paid by the consumer but shifted back to the monopolist industrial structures, forcing them to reduce excessive costs and increase production. This remains to be achieved, giving rise to no shortage of critical analysis. Marshall Goldman, for example, explains 'why economic reforms in Russia have not worked'. Shock therapy in his view failed to stimulate the supply side of the Russian economy and instead sucked in imports.[62] Economic growth requires an institutional setting that allows 'low-cost transacting' and the enforcement of property and contractual rights and obligations.[63] An effective state in economic terms would collaborate with business elites but would remain relatively insulated from particularistic societal pressures.[64]

Much was made of the insalubrious 'primary accumulation of capital' phase of early Western capitalism; Russia, it is argued, is only experiencing a delayed version. If this is the case, the best policy would be sound money, minimal and simple laws, straightforward regulation and basic taxes to unfetter Russian entrepreneurialism and allow it to race 'ahead of our Western form of corporate capitalism, which has grown flabby and slow. It is possible to imagine a future of

Russian capitalism that asserts itself in the early 21st century as the envy of the world.'[65] However, the law of uneven development would suggest that stages are not repeated but jumped, and, while capitalism was new to Russia, it was not the early stages of capitalism that Russia needed. The structure of modern capitalism as a world system has changed radically.

Russia may find itself locked into a type of comprador capitalism in which small elites with external links exploit resources to the benefit of foreign capital rather than developing a solid indigenous industrial and commercial structure. Russia had great difficulties in establishing an adequate market environment because of structural and cultural factors. In conditions of high transaction costs in a market plagued by corruption, banditry, political opportunism and fiscal instability, entrepreneurs sought to maximise immediate returns to the detriment of long-term investment. Rather than trading acting as the nucleus and source of capital for a productive market economy, it might end up as the substitute for a genuine market system. Rather than acting as a motor of development, the system may become endemically corrupt in the manner of some Third World countries, and find it very difficult to break out of the cycle of misdevelopment.

The modernisation of Russian industry involves not only the creation of a national market and regional specialisation to overcome the vertical centralisation of Soviet planning, but also overcoming the problem endemic to mature industrial powers, that of old 'rustbelt' industries. Even if Russian economic reforms were successful, the problem of the old coal and steel industries would remain, affecting in particular Kuzbas in Siberia (Kemerovo region) and the Urals. In the short term, regional fragmentation accelerated, exacerbated by the uneven embrace of market relations. Existing regional imbalances in standards of living and incomes were exaggerated, and prices varied greatly even between neighbouring towns. Land reform was most effective in the south, whereas in the north and the non-Black Earth regions they marked time. The great majority of new businesses and joint enterprises are found in Moscow, St Petersburg and Nizhnii Novgorod, whereas traditional industrial areas, quite apart from the political complexion of the regional leadership, found it difficult to adjust to competitive market conditions. An area like Udmurtia, with three-quarters of its workforce employed in military enterprises, could not survive without state orders and subsidies, and a rapid transition to the market was out of the question.

For most of the 1990s IFIs encouraged Russia to reduce the role of the state in the economy through deregulation and liberalisation, but by the end of the period the opinion had shifted towards a greater appreciation of the role of the state in economic development, including more state intervention in areas like foreign exchange controls and, possibly, protective tariffs. Above all, Western advice had focused on macro-economic stabilisation, while micro-economic management issues had been neglected. No one was suggesting that the state should return to the role of direct economic manager, and, indeed, despite the headline figure that 60 per cent of Russia's economy had been transferred into private hands in the 1990s, the state's role in the economy remained large (nearly 100 per cent in agriculture, mining and defence, 60 per cent in banking and 50 per cent in health). While liberalisation was achieved relatively swiftly, the economy still remained heavily monopolised. Nevertheless, by early 2001, a precarious growth had resumed. A

Swiss study in 2001 placed Russia 45th in the world in terms of competitiveness, above countries like Poland and Indonesia. The problems identified, however, included the foreign debt burden, representing 86 per cent of GDP, high energy consumption per dollar of GDP, absence of protection for foreign investment, and high alcohol and drug abuse.[66] Russia's economic growth at this time was no longer fuelled by the export of natural resources alone but was increasingly led by domestic demand, both investment and consumer.

Russia was faced by an awesome legacy of economic mismanagement, mismodernisation and decay. The question of economic transformation was a question of what sort of Russia was to emerge from the shell of communism. No longer did Russia set itself up as an alternative model; it sought to join global processes of economic interdependence, but found that there was no single model of the market economy. Russia and the other post-communist societies had to feel their way forwards on the edge of a precipice in the dark. The cold rationalism of shock therapy imposed enormous strains on the economy and society, and its benefits, like a stable currency and improved productivity, appeared elusive. However, no other economic programme provided a coherent alternative. The political system survived the various crises, and indeed gradually socialised the population into acceptance of the market. The lesson of the reform experience in Eastern Europe, however, appeared to be that, while drastic economic liberalism might be necessary in the first stage, it has to give way to strategies aimed at stimulating growth and combining macro-economic stabilisation with micro-economic enterprise viability and national development. Amid the endless debates, however, one thing was clear: the fate of democracy in Russia and the stability of the international system depended on the successful economic transformation of Russia.

Conclusion

Russia's economic transformation in the 1990s was accompanied by largely negative economic indicators: living standards were falling; goods faced problems of demand rather than supply; inflation was on a roller-coaster of rises and falls; the budget deficit remained large but was gradually brought under control when it stopped being funded by monetary emissions; some foreign capital was invested in Russia but was dwarfed by capital flight; industrial production fell by unprecedented percentages but gradually bottomed out; the fall in overall GDP also slowed down and returned to growth in 1999; inequalities increased sharply but income differentials had stabilised by late 1995, with the richest 10 per cent earning thirteen times more than the poorest 10 per cent; unemployment rose (although not as fast as predicted); and the rouble continued to depreciate, although after 1998 stabilised. Critics point to the large black economy and the associated difficulty of collecting taxes, the emergence of rentier capitalism and the priority of merchant capital over industrial production, and the problem of monopolies. In agriculture there is only a limited development of competitive market forms, and the state continues to pour in subsidies, although at a reduced rate compared to Soviet times. In industry privatisation tended to change the form but not the content of enterprise behaviour and failed to stimulate consistent enterprise restructuring. Privatisation allowed an already privileged class to consolidate its position by the transformation of public goods into private wealth, and allowed a small group of oligarchs to plunder the national economy. Whole sectors of the economy were criminalised, often with the connivance if not the participation of the government agencies designed to regulate them.

By 2001, the World Bank had taken Russia off the 'crisis list'. Russia had become a market economy. By 1998, Russia was ranked tenth in the world in terms of purchasing-power parity (PPP), below Brazil but above Mexico.[67] Russia's integration into the world economy was 'shallow', mostly accounted for by a rise in trade with the developed economies and focused primarily on primary materials and energy exports. Nationalists argued that Russia's economy had become 'Kuwait-ised'. Deeper integration would be accompanied by more FDI and structural changes in the economy. As the millennium began, there was some evidence that production was becoming more profitable than asset-stripping, especially in the context of high commodity prices. The 'initial accumulation of capital' phase appeared over as enterprise managers sought to add value rather than seize cash flows and export commodities. The great challenge facing Russia was to restore the micro-economic tissues of an entrepreneurial and active society combined with market-enhancing macro-economic policies. The absence of an effective banking system and contract law, and the presence everywhere of street hawkers and market hustlers, robber taxi drivers and organised crime, gave birth to the image of the 'Wild East', a riotous free-for-all on the fringes of the emerging market. The fear remained, however, that the fully fledged market would not emerge, and that this anarchic hustling and criminalised market operating in the interstices of the bureaucratised system would actually *be* the market in Russia.

13 Society and social movements

No society can surely be flourishing and happy, of which the far greater part of the members are poor and miserable.

(Adam Smith)[1]

Democracy is as much a social and cultural project as a political one: it cannot be built in the air, in the minds of intellectuals and politicians, but needs to be rooted in society itself. As Solzhenitsyn put it: 'Stolypin believed that it is impossible to create a state governed by laws without first having an independent citizen: social structure precedes any political programme and is a more fundamental entity.'[2] After seventy-four years of the Soviet regime, the social basis for democracy in Russia was at best ambiguous. As Shakhrai, the state legal adviser at the time, put it:

> We have no middle class of property owners upon which to build a stable government. If I have something to lose: my work, my apartment, my family, my dacha, my car, my savings, then I will be a support for the state and of a stable social stratum. Unfortunately, our society has not progressed to that stage yet.[3]

The basic principle of the reformers was, to quote Solzhenitsyn again, that 'there can be no independent citizen without private property'.[4] As we saw in the previous chapter, private property has been established in Russia, however tenuous its legal guarantees, but the citizen of democratic Russia (whose views we shall examine in the next chapter) has had a decidedly tough time since 1991.

Social structure and dynamics

In Russia democracy came before the development of a bourgeoisie, and as Barrington Moore long ago observed, 'No bourgeois, no democracy.'[5] The existence of a substantial middle class is no guarantee of democracy, as Germany discovered in the inter-war years, but to date there has been no liberal democracy without a capitalist social structure. A traumatised and unequal society jeopardised the building of democracy in Russia, while the weakness of social organisations, like trade unions and professional bodies, undermined political pluralism. While the concept of transition refers properly to political change, Russia entered a period of accelerated social transformation affecting all aspects of class and elite relations, the family and social groups. The marketisation of social relations not only undermined the achievements, however rudimentary, of the Soviet welfare state, but also challenged the whole network of existing social relations and cultural values.

Demography

Russia suffers from a severe demographic crisis (see Table 13.1). Natural population increase has been falling for at least a quarter of a century, reflecting the pattern common to most developed industrial societies where planned parenting and affluence has seen a dramatic decrease in the size of families. In Russia the fall in the number of women in the primary childbearing age group, the lack of confidence in the future, increased levels of stress in a changing society and declining living standards provoked a sharp decrease in the fertility rate (the average number of children born to a woman between the ages of fifteen and fifty), falling from around two between the 1960s and the late 1980s to 1.17 in 2001, well below the replacement level of 2.14.[6] The average family has but one child, thus falling below the level of natural population replacement. Russia still has a very high abortion rate, rendering up to one-third of Russia women infertile. In 1960, the RSFSR had seen natural population growth of 2 million,[7] in 1985 749,500, whereas in 1992, for the first time since the war, there was a natural population decline as deaths outnumbered births by 190,000 (Table 13.2).[8] In

Table 13.1 Size of resident population of USSR and Russia

Year	Total population (millions)	Of whom			
		Urban		Rural	
		Million	%	Million	%
USSR					
1979	262.4	162.9	62	99.5	38
1989	286.7	189.2	66	97.5	34
Russia					
1979	137.4	94.9	69	42.5	31
1989	147.0	108.0	73	39.0	27
1990	148.0	109.2	74	38.8	26
1993	148.3	108.5	73	39.8	27
1994	148.0	108.0	73	40.0	27
1995	147.9	107.9	73	40.0	27
1996	147.6	107.7	73	39.9	27
1997	147.1	107.3	73	39.8	27
1998	146.7	107.1	73	39.6	27
1999	146.3	106.8	73	39.5	27
2000	145.6	106.1	73	39.5	27

Source: *Rossiya v tsifrakh* (Moscow, Goskomstat, 2000), p. 67.

Table 13.2 Births, deaths and natural movement of Russian population

Year	Births	Deaths	Change
1960	2,782,000	886,000	+1,896,000
1970	1,904,000	1,131,000	+773,000
1980	2,203,000	1,526,000	+677,000
1985	2,375,000	1,625,000	+750,000
1990	1,989,000	1,656,000	+333,000
1993	1,379,000	2,129,300	-750,300
1994	1,408,200	2,301,400	-893,200
1995	1,363,800	2,203,800	-840,000
1996	1,304,600	2,082,200	-777,600
1997	1,259,900	2,015,800	-755,900
1998	1,283,300	1,988,700	-705,400
1999	1,215,800	2,140,300	-924,500

Source: *Naselenie SSSR, 1988* (Moscow, 1989), p. 40; *Demograficheskii ezhegodnik 1991* (Moscow, Goskomstat, 1992), p. 55; *Rossiya v tsifrakh* (Moscow, Goskomstat, 2000), p. 70.

1994, the population declined by 920,000,[9] a fall that was offset by in-migration from the former Soviet republics (see below), but the total population still fell by 124,000. Once again, in 2000, deaths exceeded births by 930,000, accompanied by declining in-migration. Between 1989–2001, Russia's adult population declined by over 3 million from 148 to 144.5 million on 1 May 2001, accompanied by a 6 million fall in the number of children. Projections suggest that Russia's population will fall to 133 million by 2015 and to only 85 million in 2050 if present tends continue. If the estimate for 2015 is correct, Russia will fall from being the world's seventh most populous state to fifteenth.[10] The decline has not only economic but also security implications, threatening the country's ability to maintain a large conscript army.

The decline in the birth rate, falling by 13 per cent in 1992 alone, was accompanied by a dramatic rise in the mortality rate; the death rate from unnatural causes alone rose in that year by 8 per cent.[11] The infant mortality rate (for children up to the age of one) peaked at 19.9 per thousand in 1993, much higher than the average for developed countries.[12] By 2000, the infant mortality rate had begun to fall to reach 15.3. Infant mortality was highest in Ingushetia, with 34.7 children dying before the age of one, and lowest in Samara *oblast* with 10.1 dying in that period.[13] It was these sort of figures that provoked the national-patriots to argue that Russia was victim of planned genocide, that democracy was no more than a Western plot to undermine the very genetic basis for Russian life.[14] By 2000, the birth rate had begun to rise for the first time in many years, to 8.7 per thousand population, compared to 8.4 in 1999.[15]

The starkest symptom of the social crisis was the declining life expectancy of Soviet men, ranked fifty-fourth out of fifty-six countries that supplied data in 1989. Average male life expectancy fell from the peak of 65 in 1986[16] to the trough of 57.6 in 1994, to stabilise at about 60 by 2001.[17] The State Statistics Committee (Goskomstat) in 2001 forecast that, if current trends continue, only 58 per cent of men aged 16 at that time will reach 60. The committee's experts noted that this was little better than life expectancy in 1897 when 56 per cent were expected to reach 60. Russian life expectancy had peaked in 1985–6 at 64.91 for men and 74.55 for women.[18] Female life expectancy compared to men was higher but had also declined from 75 in 1986 to 71.2 in 1994, rising to 72 by the end of the decade. Average life expectancy in Russia in 1992 was 68, falling to 64 in 1994, before rising to 66 by 1999 compared to 75.5 in the United States (72 for men and 69 for women). There is a marked variation within Russia, with life expectancy in rural areas in general lower, and with regional disparities, with the situation worst in the Far East and Eastern Siberia, and best in the North Caucasus and the Volga region. There are also differences between the old Soviet republics, with the highest life expectancy in 1990 in Armenia at 68.4 years for urban dwellers, and the lowest in Turkmenistan at 60.6.

There are many reasons for high Russian male mortality rates, ranging from workplace and traffic accidents, the prevalence of heart disease, a high suicide rate (rising from 39,150 in 1990 to 61,886 in 1994),[19] and violent deaths (rising from 16,000 to 26,000 over the same period). In 1999 alone, 580,000 Russians died of non-natural causes (accidents, poisonings, murder and suicide), 27 per cent of all deaths. High rates of tobacco addiction and the instability of family structures play their part. One of the main factors, however, is alcohol abuse, with *per capita* consumption in Russia for the first time exceeding that of France in 1993. Between 1986 and 2000, alcohol consumption rose from 11 litres per head of population to 14.5, while deaths directly caused by alcohol (per 100,000 of population) over the same period rose from 9.3 to 37.8.[20] Gorbachev's anti-alcohol campaign had dramatically misfired, encouraging the production of low-grade moonshine liquor (*samogon*), and the abolition of the centuries-old state monopoly on vodka production in 1992 (as part of Russia's commitment to economic liberalisation) saw prices fall dramatically.[21] Since 1995, there have been numerous attempts to reimpose the vodka monopoly, both for fiscal and health reasons. The deeper causes of Russia's alcohol dependence, however, still have to be treated, with some arguing that it was a response to the authoritarianism of society and its profound inequalities, and others, like the sociologist Igor Bestuzhev-Lada, insisting that the system itself was responsible for alcoholism, and that the only cure was the democratisation of society and the development of a citizenry responsible for its own actions.[22]

The higher death rate for men led to a sharp gender imbalance, with 9.1 million more women than men in Russia's population of 146.3 million by 2000. The age structure was also unbalanced, with the proportion of the population above working age rising from 29.1 per cent in 1993 to 38 per cent by 2001. There are some 37 million pensioners in Russia today, but many are forced to continue to work. Plans to raise the retirement age, currently 60 years for men and 55 for women, have been delayed since such a small proportion of men survive to pensionable age. For every 1,000 people of working age, there are 770 non-working (pensioners and children under 16). The nearly two-fifths of Russia's population who are pensioners are an important factor in electoral politics, tending to be more keen on casting their votes on election day and allegedly taking a more conservative approach than the rest of the population, which in Russian conditions means voting communist.

Migration and refugees

The late twentieth century has been dubbed 'the age of migration', and indeed the Soviet and post-Soviet experience confirms the view that processes of global change have stimulated a new wave of population displacement.[23] Population movement in the post-Soviet area is marked by the following processes.[24]

Returnees

Those returning to their homelands from which they had been expelled by Stalin. The category of returnees includes Germans expelled from the Volga at the beginning of the Second World War, Crimean Tatars expelled to Central Asia, and a number of North Caucasian peoples. In their home regions there were few jobs or houses for them, and the new populations typically were hostile.

Ingathering

A broad phenomenon of 'ingathering', the consolidation of ethnic and national groups. Many Ukrainians and Belarusians left Russia to help rebuild their own countries, while Kazakhs left the war in Tajikistan to return to their homeland. However much the idea is now denigrated, in a feeble and distorted form the Soviet Union had created a new community of peoples, where a Georgian could freely study in Moscow and then go to work in Kiev, and the failure of the CIS to establish common citizenship forced every ethnic group back into the laager of national myth-making and imagined identities.[25]

Russian out-migration

Since the 1970s, there had been a drift of Russians away from the other Soviet republics, and in the 1990s this accelerated. In that decade, over 8 million people moved to the RF from the former Soviet republics, significantly reducing the total of 25 million Russians who found themselves outside Russia in 1991. In Kazakhstan before the disintegration of the USSR Russians occupied half of the top positions in agencies and ministries, but this had fallen to less than a quarter. According to incomplete official figures, 600,000 Russians moved to Russia in 1992, 560,000 in 1993 and over 700,000 in 1995. In the mid-1990s, it was estimated that some 10 out of the 25 million Russians abroad wanted to migrate to Russia, but were prevented by lack of funds.[26] Nowhere are Russians and Russian speakers recognised as ethnic minorities.

Anti-Sovietism had often tended to take the form of anti-Russianism, and now this inglorious tradition took on a new intensity. Russians in Uzbekistan, for example, were now categorised as *pieds noirs* even though many had lived there for generations. The structure of the old relationship between the metropolis and the periphery meant that few had learnt Uzbek; Russian had been the language of higher schools, factories and top-level politics. Russians made up a growing number of internal migrants between the former Union republics. By late 1992, half the Russians of Tajikistan had left, together with a third from Azerbaijan. Some 3 million ethnic Russians had left the former Soviet republics since 1991, one of the largest migratory movements since the Second World War. While there was undoubtedly some discrimination against them, a survey by the Russian Minorities Research Centre found that only 9 per cent of ethnic Russians abroad expressed concern about their ethnic rights. Economic worries appeared to be a far more potent source of concern.[27] The CIS agreement on pensions provoked an estimated migration of 2 million people to Russia to take advantage of the more generous benefits.[28]

The flow, however, declined and in 2000 it compensated by only 17 per cent the decline in Russia's population from excess deaths over births, a proportion that had fallen to 6.3 per cent in the first four months of 2001, reflecting the lowest in-migration for the period 1992–2000. Russian in-migration into Russia, which in 2000 numbered 200,000, is the main reason why Russia's overall population had only declined by 2 per cent since the fall of communism. For the donor countries, however, the natural demographic losses were compounded by this out-migration. Kazakhstan suffered the most, losing about a million Russians since independence (about 8 per cent of its population). The migrants tended to be more urban and better educated, and now the rural population in Kazakhstan's 14 million population is a greater proportion of the total than it was in 1991. Belarus was the least affected by migration, where Slavs are a larger majority than in Russia itself, and the population remained stable at about 10 million. Ukraine's population had fallen about 5 per cent since independence where, in 2000, deaths outnumbered births by two to one accompanied, as in Russia, by a declining birth rate.

In a speech in Novosibirsk on 17 November 2000, Putin had argued that Russia's demographic shortfall could be compensated by labour immigration from the former USSR. He had in mind some of the 20 million-odd ethnic Russians in the CIS and the Baltic states and not non-Slavic ethnic groups, above all 'persons of Caucasian nationality'. By inviting Russians in neighbouring states to migrate to Russia the economic and military security of those states was challenged and their own state-building endeavours undermined. Russia's ability to manage in-migration in any case was questionable, lacking housing and jobs for those already resident. The speech did, however, signal a shift in emphasis as Russia's 'compatriots' in the former Soviet states were now perceived less as a political lever against those states than as an economic resource for Russia.

Economic migration

Economic migration, including a drift from the harsh Siberian North to more temperate climes. Economic migration took place both within countries and between them in the former Soviet space. In Russia alone by mid-1994 there were some 2 million economic migrants forced to move by lack of work and the decline of areas of marginal economic activity. In the six months to May 1994 alone some 500,000–600,000 people moved out of the Russian Far North and the Far East,[29] and between 1992–9 the population of the Far East declined by 10.9 per cent, with Chukotka *okrug* alone registering a fall of 48 per cent. A growing number of foreigners arrived to work in Russia; 213,000 in 2000 alone.

Illegal immigrants

By 2001, there were an estimated 1.5 million illegal immigrants in Russia.[30] The bulk of these were Chinese in the Far East.

Urban/rural drift

We have noted above that the long-term migration from rural areas to the towns has now moved in reverse as city dwellers head for the countryside.

Refugees from wars and other disasters

Refugees became a mass phenomenon in the former USSR, with numbers rising from an estimated 422,000 in 1988 to some 2 million by 1994 alone from the former Soviet republics, mainly from areas of inter-ethnic conflict,[31] most of whom settled in South European Russia. The category of those fleeing actual or implied threats of war and other catastrophes includes so-called ecological refugees, in particular those fleeing the contaminated areas around Chernobyl. Armenians and Azerbaijanis fled the other's territory, and people sought to escape the wars in South Ossetia, Abkhazia, Trans-Dniester and Central Asia. By February 1992, there were officially 220,000 refugees (overwhelmingly Russians) in Russia, with some 15 per cent of the 300,000 Russians in Chechnya leaving in the year after the *coup*,[32] and the rest soon after. Russians also left neighbouring Dagestan, with their proportion in the total population falling from 9.21 per cent in 1989 to 5.6 per cent in January 2001.[33] The number of Russian refugees from the other republics reached 460,000 by September 1992, with 50,000 arriving in August alone as Russians fled the fighting in Abkhazia, while some 30,000 of the total came from Kazakhstan and 13,000 from Kyrgyzstan.[34] By May 1994, there were 860,000 registered refugees in Russia.[35] Attempts by Russia to sign treaties with other republics regulating the status of Russians were resisted. There were few arrangements for the payment of compensation and so, for example, the Russians who left in a mass exodus from Baku in 1991 received nothing from the Azerbaijani authorities.

Yeltsin had promised refuge for all Russians who wanted to live in Russia, but in fact Russia was in no position to offer jobs, homes or even passports to the Russians who suddenly found themselves living abroad. Some 9.5 million of Russia's own native citizens were waiting for housing already. The status of 'refugee' in Russia remained ambiguous. Only the disabled, pensioners, women and children received food coupons and housing while most refugees were treated as strangers in their own land. They increasingly encountered the hostility of local populations, in particular Cossacks, in the struggle for scarce housing, food and jobs.

Emigration out of the former USSR altogether

Some took the 'exit' option and emigrated from the former Soviet Union, although the number taking this route was lower than anticipated. A total of 2.5 million had left in the four decades after the war, but between 1987–90 alone over a million left.[36] Soviet emigration rose from 39,000 in 1987 to almost 500,000 in 1990, and in 1991 the figure reached 700,000. A study in March 1991, however, found that 75 per cent of the population had no intention of emigrating, and of the rest 15 per cent thought in terms of a short visit abroad and only 2 per cent firmly considered emigration, which, although a relatively high proportion of the population, in the circumstances is not that high.[37] Apart from Jews and Germans, Russians did not leave in great numbers. The liberal foreign travel law (initially passed for the USSR on 20 May 1991 and then adopted by Russia) came into effect on 1 January 1993 and entitled all Russian citizens to a foreign passport, provided they were not on trial, doing military service or privy to state secrets. The new passports were valid for a fixed term, rather than the old documents which necessitated a fresh exit visa for each trip. Despite fears about a flood of Russian economic migrants, the expected mass tide of emigration did not take place. Most former Soviet Bloc countries in Eastern Europe had no visa requirements (until membership of the EU forced them to put up barriers) but tightened restrictions against the hundreds of thousands of Russians who came officially on tourist visits but failed to leave on time.

Occupational structure

While the events of August 1991 were dramatic and came to symbolise the fall of the old regime, the Soviet system had already undergone a long decay since at least the death of Stalin in 1953. The old authority system underwent significant evolution, and at the same time an embryonic new pattern of social relations began to emerge. The protracted degeneration of the old system itself became a factor in shaping the new order as features like patronage networks, corruption and clientilism became endemic. The long transition allowed morbid systems of social irresponsibility to become firmly lodged in the body social as a pseudo-civil society, regulated not by law but by the anti-law of customary practices, took shape. The emergence of powerful criminal networks in the lee of decaying Party authority, the evolution of the political *nomenklatura* appointments mechanism into a corrupt social phenomenon, the development of a shadow economy preyed on by protection rackets and living off the inefficiencies of the state economy, all this and more shaped the social subject of the transition.

The seventy-four years of the Soviet regime had churned society as if it had gone through a concrete mixer. Tatyana Zaslavskaya argued that instead of the social structure having become simpler, it had in fact become more complex than comparable capitalist societies. Groups, classes, elites, workers, peasants, and indeed whole peoples, were displaced, mixed up and thrown down. Instead of the organic growth of social complexity and differentiation over a more or less steady pattern of development, the USSR had telescoped decades of modernisation (and an ideologically driven pattern of mismodernisation at that) into just a few years. The alleged *lumpenisation* of the Soviet population was accompanied by a type of negative egalitarianism in which society was levelled down to the lowest common denominator, distinguished not by equality of opportunity but by an equality in poverty impatient of complex solutions.[38] Social ties today show great signs of instability; the very fabric of society has been torn and the process of healing will take decades.

Table 13.3 Employment structure in 1989

Occupation	Millions	Percentages
Total employed	70.0	100
Of whom:		
Workers	45.0	64.3
Employees	21.0	30.0
Collective farmers	4.0	5.71

Source: *RSFSR v tsifrakh v 1989g* (Moscow, Finansy i statistika, 1990), p. 21.

The old regime recognised three great groups in society depending on their relationship to property and the means of production: the two classes of workers and peasants and the stratum of the intelligentsia. The ranks of the working class had increased rapidly, rising from some 1.7 million in Soviet Russia in 1920 to 45 million in 1989 (see Table 13.3). Stalinist industrialisation had seen the growth of the working class, the accompanying cultural revolution the emergence of a Soviet technical intelligentsia, while collectivisation destroyed the peasantry as a class and encouraged a mass exodus to the towns. From the 1950s to the 1970s, an average each year of some 1.7 million people fled the devastated countryside to seek new opportunities in towns.[39] In the early 1990s, 26 per cent of the population lived in rural areas, a proportion that rose as life in the cities became tougher for certain sections of the population, above all pensioners. By 1989, out of a total Soviet population of 284.5 million there were 117.24 million (41.21 per cent) workers and employees, 19 per cent of whom were employed in agriculture and forestry.[40]

Russia began its post-communist journey with a higher proportion of its workforce in state employment than in most other republics. Post-communist Russia underwent a rapid change in occupational structure (Table 13.4). The USSR had been an 'over-industrialised' economy, and now in the 1990s the proportion of GDP coming from the production of goods fell from 60 to 40 per cent, while the service sector, including trade and transport, rose sharply. Total employment in the same period fell from 72 million to 64.5 million, with the fall sharpest in the industrial sector, falling a third from 21 to 14 million (Table 13.4). At the same time, a middle class appeared to have emerged. An article in early 2001 argued that 20–25 per cent of Russians had three of the five characteristics of being middle class: a certain income level, ownership of some property, some savings, a certain educational level, and a perception that they were 'successful and worthy members of society'.[41]

Welfare and incomes

Advocates of the 'strong hand' argued that democracy might have to be sacrificed to allow market liberalism to develop; a more accurate formulation suggests that it was the welfarism of social democracy rather than democracy *per se* that was sacrificed in the transition to a market economy. Budgetary constraints forced a retreat of the frontiers of welfarism, but in the long run the aim was to divert resources to

Table 13.4 Employment in the state and non-state sectors

	1992	1993	1994	1995	1996	1997	1998	1999
Total employed, millions (%)	72.07 (100)	70.85 (100)	68.48 (100)	66.44 (100)	65.95 (100)	64.64 (100)	63.64 (100)	64.50 (100)
State and municipal	49.66 (68.9)	37.52 (53.0)	30.61 (44.7)	27.98 (42.1)	27.73 (42.0)	25.90 (40.1)	24.26 (38.1)	23.86 (37.0)
Social organisations	0.58 (0.8)	0.59 (0.9)	0.52 (0.7)	0.47 (0.7)	0.40 (0.6)	0.41 (0.6)	0.44 (0.7)	0.45 (0.7)
Private	14.07 (19.5)	19.93 (28.1)	22.59 (33.0)	22.89 (34.4)	23.45 (35.6)	25.75 (39.9)	27.46 (43.2)	29.25 (45.3)
Mixed Russian (without foreign participation)	7.57 (10.5)	12.50 (17.6)	14.42 (21.1)	14.73 (22.2)	13.84 (21.0)	11.84 (18.3)	10.47 (16.4)	9.67 (15.0)
Mixed with joint Russian and foreign participation	0.19 (0.3)	0.30 (0.4)	0.34 (0.5)	0.43 (0.6)	0.54 (0.8)	0.74 (1.1)	1.00 (1.6)	1.26 (2.0)

Source: *Rossiya v tsifrakh* (Moscow, Goskomstat, 2000), p.77.

productive investment and industrial modernisation. The reformers were divided over the degree to which the inevitable hardship resulting from economic reform should be compensated: how generous should the system of social provision be to protect the weaker sectors of society? At one extreme were the neo-liberals who accepted that economic reforms would inevitably entail a high social cost. They advocated complete deregulation and minimal controls on the free market, and condemned rationing systems as distorting the operation of the market. On the other side, the left insisted that full-scale free market economic policies could not be applied to Russia in its fragile state. In the event, a middle course was adopted, seeking to maintain a minimum threshold of welfare benefits but imposing cuts in the general level of social provision. Repeated promises to inject a 'greater social content' into the reforms were defeated by the equally harsh imperative of financial stabilisation. Only under Putin were there attempts to ensure the payment of wages and pensions on time. The outcome of over a decade of post-communist development was a mixed one, and while certain groups saw their working conditions and living conditions deteriorate, for some professional groups standards improved.[42] In terms of the United Nations' Index of Human Potential, Russia by 2001 had put an end to its long decline and moved up from 62nd to 55th place.[43]

Health

Soviet health care had always been lamentably under funded, despite attempts during *perestroika* to improve the situation. The USSR spent only about 3.6 per cent of its GNP on health care, half that of most West European countries and a third of the sum spent in the United States. The reforms had undermined already low wages, and the provision of medicines and equipment became even more sporadic. Following the fall of communism funds devoted to health fell to 1.8 per cent of the Russian budget in 1994, and traditional shortfalls and inequalities in the standard of provision were exacerbated.[44] Standard facilities had never been very high but now deteriorated further, while staff were demoralised by low pay and lack of resources and medicines. For all but the richest, standards of health care fell sharply, a decline dramatically illustrated by the outbreak of cholera and diphtheria across Russia.

Cases of infectious diseases increased sharply, with tuberculosis once again prevalent in the majority of Russia's regions. The breakdown of mass immunisation was one of the main factors allowing diphtheria to return, while the spread of cholera was facilitated by antiquated water and sewage systems. According to official statistics, the number of drug addicts rose twelve-fold following the collapse of the USSR, with 300,000 registered addicts in 2001. International experience suggests that the real number is ten times the number registered, which in Russia would make the figure 3 million or 5 per cent of the population.[45] The rising incidence of HIV infection, reaching 53,000 according to official figures in late 2000 (the real figure could be up to a hundred times more), was for a long time ignored. By 2001, it was clear that Russia was facing a major crisis, exacerbated by the shared use of needles by drug addicts but soon moving far beyond this community.

Housing

The onset of market relations exacerbated the housing crisis inherited from the Soviet Union. According to official statistics, in Moscow alone in 1994 there were 30,000 homeless people, but the actual figure may well have exceeded 100,000, while in Russia as a whole some 4 million were estimated to be homeless.[46] Out of a population of some 8 million in Moscow, some 8 per cent still live in communal flats – *kommunalki* – in which numerous tenants share the kitchen and bathroom. Their number is declining, however, as tenants are moved out and the apartments converted into large and highly desirable flats.

Social security

The USSR's highly developed system of social security benefits was gradually eroded. Budgetary constraints forced a radical overhaul of the social security system to target it towards low-income groups and to improve the social safety net. While 'Benefit programs must provide security but at the same time discourage dependence on the state', the optimum balance is something that eludes most developed societies let alone the former communist states.[47] The main thrust of reform was to lessen direct dependence on the state budget by developing employer insurance schemes with employee contributions for health, pensions and unemployment benefits.[48]

Wages, incomes and poverty

The transition to the market economy meant changing the whole social landscape. Enterprises under the old system were more than production units offering only pay but also provided food, housing, holidays, medical and child care. Local authorities, short of money themselves, could take over only a fraction of these responsibilities. The economic reforms challenged what the Chinese called the 'three irons' of the Maoist era: the lifelong job, lifelong wage and lifelong position. This was balanced by the 'iron ricebowl', a minimal but secure standard of living. Marketisation now challenged the traditional pattern of work, wages and job security.

Money wages in the Soviet Union by 1991 had fallen far below even the miserly rate of neighbouring countries. Khasbulatov stressed that the Soviet state had been a super-exploiter, giving only 7 to 15 per cent of the labour value back to the worker in the form of wages, whereas under capitalism workers received 60–70 per cent.[49] The economist Matlin argued that the Soviet government had long been waging an economic war against its own people, a war which had intensified during *perestroika*. By 1991, surplus value reached 210 per cent of wages, rising from 126 per cent in 1985 and 102 per cent in 1908 under the allegedly exploitative Tsarist regime. The methodology on which these figures are based can be disputed, but the trend is clear: late communism was twice as exploitative as late Tsarism. Matlin argued that 'The political revolution of August [1991] should be followed by an economic revolution, dismantling the state monopoly of the means of production.'[50]

Economic reform imposed new hardships and provoked the further pauperisation of society. The prices of goods, including basic foodstuffs, began to approximate world levels, yet the average monthly pay remained at absurdly low levels. As the economic reforms began to bite, money wages tended to fall even lower in relative terms and wage differentials increased sharply as the transition to the market sharply exacerbated social inequalities. Economic reform was accompanied by growing inequality. In 1992, at the beginning of the reforms, the incomes of the lowest 10 per cent of the population represented 6 per cent of overall monetary income of the population, while the top 10 per cent received 40 per cent (6.6 times more); in 2000, the share of the poorest 10 per cent had fallen to 2.4 per cent, while that of the richest accounted for 32 per cent of income (a difference of 13.3).[51] Income stratification increased sharply, with the richest 10 per cent of the population gaining 27 per cent of the country's total income, while the poorest 10 per cent had only 2.5 per cent, with 63 per cent of the population earning below average incomes.[52] Those with access to foreign currency and goods, or employed by a successful enterprise, could become relatively rich very quickly, while those tied to a state wage and pension saw their position further eroded. The economic reforms initially depressed standards of living and made the monetary measure of household wealth even more arbitrary than before.

The old system of subsidised housing, transport, child care and much else had rendered the money wage part of income relatively less important,[53] but now the end of generalised subsidies meant that money wages had to cover far more of individual needs. Access to quality health care, pre-school facilities and even education now increasingly had to be paid for. The government found itself trapped since wage rises could only be met by increasing budget expenses in the form of subsidies, and this would only return the whole process to square one. The government negotiated a tortuous path between the pressures of the IMF for financial stabilisation, on the one hand, and the ability of the Russian people to endure yet more hardship, on the other. The dash for the market was tempered by attempts to cushion some of the painful effects of the transition for vulnerable groups by ensuring at least a survival income.[54] Miners in the Kuzbass region of Siberia and elsewhere engaged in industrial action at various times (for example, in the 'rail war' of 1998), and fear of working-class protest clearly influenced budgetary priorities. This was to a degree self-defeating since increased wages without commensurate rises in productivity only fuelled inflation.

Only a relatively small proportion were the 'winners' in the transition, while the vast majority in the short term saw their incomes shrink and their job security eroded. Millions lived below the poverty line throughout the 1990s, but the whole notion and the appropriate level of such a 'line' has been much debated. In Russia it is based on level of household income required to maintain a minimum level of consumption, but the actual income in many families is often hidden from the authorities and as the tax system began to bite was usually under-stated, quite apart from wide regional variations. Real income did not fall dramatically in the first years of liberalisation because of inflationary budgetary emissions, but the imposition of a tight money policy saw real incomes fall in 1995 before gradually rising until 1998, and thereafter they plunged as a result of the financial crisis, and in 2000 still remained 20 per cent lower than in 1998 despite rises in wages and welfare payments under Putin.

Poverty and inequality increased markedly. Some 40 per cent of the Russian population live in poverty (according to the UNDP criterion for the transition countries of $4 per person per day). The poor are concentrated in particular groups (families with more than two children, female single-earner families) and in particular regions (lowest in Moscow and St Petersburg and highest in the North Caucasus, Siberia and the Far East). While Muscovites enjoyed incomes 3.3 times higher than the average in other regions, and only eight other regions exceeded the average, residents in Ingushetiya and Ust-Orda Buryat Autonomous *okrug* had average incomes that were only a quarter of the national average.[55] Employment is not necessarily the antidote to poverty, especially when there are long delays in wage payments and their level can be minimal. Two-thirds of the adult poor were working in 1996. As a result of the improvement in Russia's overall economic performance in 2000 the number of 'utterly destitute' declined from 60 million to 46 million, but still one-third of Russia's population were left below the poverty level.[56]

Unemployment

Despite claims that the USSR had beaten the problem of unemployment in the 1930s, and concerns over labour shortages in the 1980s, unemployment had in fact been disguised by endemic overstaffing in Soviet enterprises leading to the low labour productivity typical of the extensive model of economic development. The structure of the Soviet labour force, while broadly corresponding to trends elsewhere, nevertheless revealed a high proportion engaged in manual labour, some 50 million out of a 133 million-strong labour force (with another 7 million involved with the armed forces). Until the RSFSR Law on Employment of 19 April 1991 it was a crime not to work.[57] For most of the Soviet years there had been a relatively free movement of workers, but there had not been a labour market as such.

Unemployment increased but its scale was less than some of the more apocalyptic predictions had suggested, although for a society unaccustomed to any
official unemployment the phenomenon itself was shocking. On 1 January 1996,
2.3 million people (3.1 per cent of the working population) were registered as
unemployed, an increase of 690,000 over the previous year, while some 5.9 million
people (8.1 per cent) were jobless.[58] After a surge of unemployment following the
financial crisis of 1998, official unemployment fell from 7.4 million in June 2000 to
6.6 million a year later.[59] The scale of 'hidden unemployment', however, is difficult
to estimate but probably affected another 10 million. The official unemployment
figures, moreover, have been much criticised by bodies like the International Labour
Organisation who condemned the bureaucracy involved in registering with the
Federal Employment Service.[60] Unemployment was worst in Ivanovo *oblast*, dominated by the crisis-ridden textile industry predominantly employing women, where
joblessness is five to six times higher than the national average. Unemployment was
also particularly high in Ingushetia, Norilsk in the Far North, timber and logging
towns, and previously secret defence industry towns.[61] Long-term unemployment
also rose, with those without a job for over a year trebling in 1994 to 7 per cent.
Women and young people were particularly affected by long-term joblessness.

While the conventional view attributes the lack of mass unemployment to the
lack of restructuring, changes in the structure of employment, the shift to new and
more dynamic sectors of the economy may well have absorbed labour surpluses.
The anticipated catastrophic rise in unemployment, moreover, was averted by weak
or non-existent bankruptcy laws and the reluctance with which enterprises shed
staff, especially in small towns with only one enterprise. Wages ultimately were paid
by state subsidies, acting as a huge form of hidden unemployment benefit. With the
end of the Soviet regime it might have been thought that the army of bureaucrats,
some 80 per cent of whom were women, would become redundant, but the Russian
administrative apparatus continued to burgeon.

New placement and retraining schemes were launched, the benefits system
simplified, and Russia's 2,300 employment exchanges run by the Federal
Employment Service (itself only established in April 1991) began to be modernised
and the 10,000 staff retrained to cope with the influx of 'customers'. The emphasis
was on developing an effective placement service, retraining for displaced workers,
and financial incentives to employers to take on hard-to-place workers.[62] Thirty-
seven million people had passed through its doors by 2001, half of whom had been
found jobs.[63] Many of those who lost their jobs felt no need to go to a labour
exchange since they could find jobs on their own, but as the traditionally taut
labour market became much slacker demand increased for the range of specialist
services provided by such centres.[64] In the long term, in the light of the demographic changes discussed above, it was anticipated that by 2015 Russia would
experience a labour shortage of some 10 million.

Social movements

One of the key questions of the democratic transition in Russia was how society
was to be integrated into the post-communist political order. The old gulf between
workers and intellectuals had been partially bridged as the new Soviet technical

intelligentsia had emerged, but independent labour politics had been de-legitimised and incorporated, like the women's and youth movements, as part of Soviet 'transmission belt' politics in a monstrously bureaucratised trade union movement. In the post-communist era the whole notion of class politics was in bad odour because of its association with the discredited Soviet regime, and the new pluralism was highly segmented.

Labour and trade unions

The trade union movement, organised in the form of the All-Union Central Council of Trade Unions (VTsSPS), in the Soviet period was a vast bureaucratic organisation whose leadership was appointed by the Party and whose role was reduced to little more than provider of rest homes, holiday vouchers, pensions and welfare entitlements. The VTsSPS administered a large part of the social security budget, but this only served to underline the administrative nature of the organisation: functions that in most countries are undertaken by special ministries in the USSR were fulfilled by a body nominally representing workers' interests.[65] Lenin in 1920 had talked of trade unions and other mass organisations acting as 'transmission belts', relaying Party policy to the people, and under Stalin this was achieved with a vengeance for all social organisations, including the youth movement (Komsomol) and women's organisations. Although under the post-Stalin leadership mass organisations became a little more responsive to the needs of their members, they remained heavily bureaucratised organisations with a relatively low status in the Soviet pecking border.

On 11 July 1989, the first major strike of the Kuzbass and other miners demonstrated that *perestroika* was no longer simply a revolution from above but had now to accommodate itself to worker activism from below.[66] The miners' strike, moreover, swept away any residual belief that the CPSU was in any serious way a party of the working class. A year later these same miners staged an avowedly political strike calling for the resignation of Ryzhkov's government and for radical reforms. These strikes demonstrated that the nascent workers' movement, at least in this area, were fighting not for any renewed form of 'the dictatorship of the proletariat' but for a broad democratic programme.

In the 'phoney democracy' phase the official trade union movement was reformed and de-étatised, while the new trade unions were subject to the factionalism and splits typical of the pseudo-parties. An independent trade union movement emerged and numerous new unions were established.[67] The first was the Independent Miners' Union (NPG) established in Donetsk in October 1990, but later it was plagued by divisions and financial scandals. One of the largest trade union organisations was the Moscow Federation of Trade Unions (MFPS), claiming the affiliation of thirty-nine unions with 5.7 million workers. Another active union was Sotsprof, which originally called itself socialist but later simply called itself a 'social' trade union and supported Yeltsin's dash for the market. The General Confederation of Trade Unions (VKP) sought to act as an umbrella organisation throughout the CIS but remained embryonic. The main process, however, was for old unions to rename themselves and to try to adapt to new conditions, now without state subsidies, compulsory membership and stripped of some of their social functions. The leadership of the new unions were often the same as the old Soviet ones.

Although a number of independent new unions were formed, the vast majority remained under the umbrella of what was now called the Federation of Independent Trade Unions of Russia (FITUR; in Russian FNPR), the successor of VTsSPS, created in March 1990, with some 60 million affiliated members out of a total Russian labour force of some 70 million organised in forty All-Russian unions. The FNPR perpetuated the traditions of the old union movement, including collective membership of whole industries, covering managers as well as workers. The FNPR, at first chaired by Igor Klochkov, protested against Gaidar's neo-liberal policies and attempts to impose a wage freeze, insisting on 'market wages for market prices'.[68] Klochkov was replaced by Mikhail Shmakov, the head of the MFPS, at the time of the October 1993 events. While broadly supportive of the Russian government's attempts to transform the economy, he insisted that this should not primarily be at the expense of working people.

Old Soviet practices, when trade unions were part of the *troika* of management and party bosses to ensure the fulfilment of the five-year plan, lingered on.[69] The defence of workers' interests played little part, but in return workers could not be sacked, however poorly they worked. This neo-Stalinist bargain, where 'the workers pretend to work and the state pretends to pay them', is today reflected in relatively low official unemployment rates. Under-employment rather than unemployment became chronic as workers and management often presented a common front against outsiders, and workers became ever more dependent on management, acting as a barrier to collective action.[70] Reflecting the under-development of Russian parties, in the 1995 and 1999 parliamentary elections trade unions sought directly (albeit in loose electoral alliances) to achieve representation in the Duma.

In keeping with his corporatist instincts Yeltsin sought to work with the labour unions, and effectively integrated the FNPR into the regime. The idea of social partnership was formalised by the establishment in January 1992 of the Tripartite Commission on the Regulation of Social and Labour Relations, bringing together organised labour, management and the state, with the brief to review and set wage levels and to mediate in labour disputes, and helped establish the system of quarterly indexing of minimum wages and pensions.[71] Russian welfare payments and salaries in the state sector are calculated as multiples of the minimum wage, set by the Tripartite Commission and influenced by the Duma. In the face of labour activism and wage demands the government usually capitulated, but the price of labour peace was a strained budget. The new Labour Code adopted in July 2001 sought to modernise labour policy by relaxing some of the restrictions inherited from the Soviet period to create a more flexible labour market. Employers would be granted the right to sack workers without the approval of the unions, as well as hiring workers on fixed contracts without granting them social benefits. Not surprisingly, this neo-liberal approach to labour issues raised considerable controversy, although there were compensatory features: the minimum wage must be no lower than the subsistence level; workers should receive two-thirds of their wages if the enterprise stops as a result of the actions of employers; and employers pay penalties if there are delays in wage payments.

Soviet trade unions had traditionally distributed social security benefits and payments for medical treatment. The government now took over many of these functions, including the crucial Social Insurance Fund, and only the wealthiest of the unions could continue to provide subsidised holidays or nursery and other facilities for working parents. Much of this now became marketised, often priced beyond the reach of a large part of the population. Unions no longer received subsidies from the government or employers. One problem was the unclear juridical position, with antiquated Soviet legislation on the statute books and unclear Russian laws to regulate their status. A far more profound problem facing unions, however, was their shifting social and political role, lacking credibility in the workplace and in society at large.[72]

In conditions where membership was no longer compulsory, union numbers fell sharply. In 1992, FITUR boasted that it represented 60 million Russian workers, but even then that claim was doubted and now no more than 40 million are union members. At the same time, their role changed. In free-market conditions, strikes are one of the main weapons of the labour movement, yet the number of workers involved in a strike in any one year remained remarkably low, hovering at the half million mark except for a peak of nearly a million in 1997.[73] The opposition had long threatened that the government would be swept away by a tide of popular dissatisfaction led by organised labour. Although these apocalyptic predictions were mistaken, there was nevertheless an undercurrent of economic strikes, conducted primarily by miners, teachers and health workers. Miners, once Yeltsin's strongest supporters, repeatedly took industrial action against arrears in wage payments, caused largely by delays in delivering state subsidies. Much of Russia's coal industry, employing 800,000 workers and in many places the main support of the local community, is inefficient and unprofitable, necessitating subsidies to the tune of 40–5 per cent.[74] Plans to close some eighty mines by the year 2000 provoked a new round of protests. Economic liberalisation severely weakened the bargaining position of workers and relative wages fell sharply. Despite the hardships, however, popular opinion did not harden against Yeltsin's reforms, partly because unemployment had not yet taken on a mass character. Remarkably, in May 2000, no strikes at all were recorded. In conditions of dramatic economic decline, huge wage inequality and mass impoverishment the persistence of social peace is surprising.[75]

Trade unions were transformed from instruments of the state to instruments of collective bargaining, facing the employers in the form of the RUIE. The major challenge facing the union movement was to transform itself from a bureaucratic state agency to the organisational core of the labour movement.[76] The FNPR to many represented no more than part of the political *nomenklatura*, allied to the enterprise directorate and more interested in elite-level intrigues than the membership. The FNPR moderated its criticisms of the government out of fear that it could lose its extensive network of sanatoria, rest homes and hotels worth a fortune at market prices. It is for this reason that a number of unions, often calling themselves 'free' to distinguish themselves from the old-style unions, were established, and in contrast to the old unions did not allow members of management to join.[77]

Classic struggles emerged in workplaces, with employers sacking workers for attempting to establish independent trade unions, arguing that the existing FNPR network was sufficient, although the latter more often than not sided with the management against the workers they claimed to represent. Not surprisingly, trade unions did not figure significantly in workplace life and according to polls are one of the least trusted social organisations.[78] The intelligentsia on the whole kept itself well apart from the struggle for free trade unions, while political parties at first had almost no role to play in labour struggles. The new Labour Code places restrictions on the right of workers to strike, while newly privatised enterprises often try to eliminate organised labour altogether from the workplace. In short, the labour struggles that had accompanied the rise of Western industrial society are once again being re-enacted in Russia.

Gender politics

The functionalist analysis of women in three roles, as workers, mothers and home-makers, is standard when studying Soviet society. The Bolsheviks considered that gender inequality would be overcome if women were absorbed into social produc-tion, children's upbringing and daily life socialised, and a socialist cam-araderie established in relations between the sexes. In the early 1930s, the separate women's departments (*zhenotdely*) in the Party were closed and the 'women's question' was declared resolved. The 'thaw' of the 1950s and 1960s revealed that the question was far from over, and later analysis revealed that on all the main indices of social achievement and psychological freedom women were at a disadvantage compared to men.[79]

The participation rate of women in paid employment was one of the highest in the world at around 90 per cent. In the period of extensive economic growth the proportion of women in the Russian workforce peaked in the 1970s at 53 per cent, but as the economy began to shift to a more intensive form of development the proportion fell to 52 per cent in 1987[80] and by 1990 was down to 48 per cent and continued to fall as reform increased female unemployment. Women made up 60 per cent of Soviet specialists with higher and secondary special education, consti-tuting 58 per cent of all engineers, 67 per cent of doctors, and up to 91 per cent of librarians. Even though half a million women in the USSR were directors of enter-prises, institutions and organisations,[81] there was both vertical and horizontal professional segregation. Within the workplace the usual 'glass ceiling' on promo-tion was in place; the higher one went in an administrative or professional hierarchy, the lower the proportion of women. Women predominated in less qualified work and nurturing professions, and received on average a third lower wages than men. Women are barred from some 500 jobs, from coal mining and senior positions in the Navy, and there are quotas on the number of female police officers allowed.

Women are the losers of Russia's new transformation. As workers, women are made redundant before men and often with worse benefit rights. The average unem-ployed person in Russia is a woman with higher or specialised education in the 35–40 age group with one child.[82] Women, who had traditionally made up half of the Russian workforce, account for 75 per cent of the officially unemployed; three out of every four people who lost their job in the early years of reform were women.[83] Wages in the highly 'feminised' professions, moreover, fell below the living minimum leading to strikes by teachers, health care workers and textile workers. Post-war Soviet economic development drew on women instrumentally, as the last great reserve army of labour (together with the peasantry), but as soon as labour shortages gave way to labour surpluses, the alleged emancipatory benefits of paid employment were soon forgotten and the other two roles of women, as mothers and homemakers, were once again stressed. The low birth rate had already prompted Gorbachev to argue that the Soviet regime's attempt 'to make women equal with men in everything' by putting them to work on construction sites and in offices and factories had been at the cost of 'their everyday duties at home – house-work, the upbringing of children and the creation of a good family atmosphere'. The strategy therefore was 'to make it possible for women to return to their purely womanly mission'.[84]

However, as homemakers, too, women are under enormous pressure.[85] The lack of housing, alcoholism, the high incidence of male violence against women, and the stultifying social atmosphere place the family at risk, with a high divorce rate, but whether the appeal to the traditional values of the patriarchal family is an adequate response may be doubted. The level of domestic violence is shocking. According to official statistics, some 12,000–16,000 women die each year from domestic violence, comparable to the total deaths in the Afghan war.[86] The average Russian family itself is changing: it increasingly lacks the clear predominance of either the male or female side; it is increasingly nuclear as the tradition of living with parents and grandparents wanes; it is often childless or one-child; and it is increasingly single parent as, typically, the woman struggles to bring up a child as the man (especially in the villages) lies drunk in a ditch. Children tend to be economically dependent on their parents for longer than in the West because of housing shortages, low wages and other labour market inflexibilities. Changing perceptions of morality have given rise to an exceptionally large proportion of marriages being provoked by the pregnancy of the bride, and it is these marriages that prove to be the most unstable, with the child almost always staying with the mother. If in 1960 twelve out of every hundred marriages ended in divorce, by 1990 an extraordinary forty-two out of every hundred marriages failed.[87] Fewer than a quarter of divorced women enter into a second marriage within ten years of divorcing, thus millions of children live in one-parent families without the benefit of the father's influence, and usually without any male role models at all.[88]

The division of labour in homes remains traditional, with women doing most of the domestic chores and taking primary care of children.[89] Hence the well-known phenomenon of the 'double burden': a full shift at paid work and then several more hours of unpaid work looking after the home and (in the old days) queuing for goods. Loss of a job at least reduces one of the burdens, but in the transition to the market this was accompanied by a profound reorientation of women's identities in the mass media, suggesting that it was somehow 'unfeminine' to be active profes-sionally and politically.

It was also accompanied by a rapid deterioration of the social facilities used by women. The fall of communism led to the destruction of social services like child care and pre-school nurseries or their commercialisation, placing them far beyond the reach of average families. While women had earlier been forced to work, the birth of a child now usually means giving up paid work altogether. The electoral bloc Women of Russia noted that 3 million single women in Russia had to rely on their earnings alone. Their wages had declined relative to men's: if earlier women's wages were nearly 70 per cent men's, by December 1993 they had declined to about 40 per cent. They were also concerned about maternal and infant mortality, and high levels of illness.[90]

As citizens, too, women have largely disappeared from national leadership. Under the old regime, quotas were reserved for women, and they comprised from a third of the total deputies (in national) to half (in local) soviets. A third of the deputies elected to the eleventh convocation of the USSR Supreme Soviet (1984–9) were women, and the partial removal of quotas led the proportion elected to the USSR CPD in March 1989 to fall to 15.7 per cent.[91] With the complete abolition of quotas in the March 1990 elections to the Russian Congress the proportion of women fell to just 5.5 per cent.[92] However, the trend was reversed in the December 1993 elections, largely due to the efforts of the Women of Russia electoral association, which won 8.13 per cent of the party-list vote.[93] The proportion of women in the Federal Assembly rose to 10.8 per cent, but this figure masks the disparity between the Fifth Duma, where women comprised 13.1 per cent of the total (58), and the Federation Council, elected on a first-past-the-post system where women appeared to be at a disadvantage, resulting in only 5.1 per cent of women members.[94] The Women of Russia bloc was a unique attempt in Russia for a women's party to appeal directly to women as a specific constituency.[95] The bloc, however, failed to breach the 5 per cent threshold in 1995, leading to a fall in women's representation in the Sixth Duma to 46 (10.2 per cent).[96] In the 1999 Duma election, only nine of the twenty-six electoral associations had women in the top three of their party lists and there were no women in seventy-four of the 225 single-mandate districts. As a result, only twenty women were elected in SMDs and only fifteen became deputies through the list system, giving a total of thirty-five (7.7 per cent).[97] The problem is not that there are any legal obstacles to women entering political decision-making arenas; it lies in the realm of attitudes and multiple obligations.

It would be misleading to suggest that women were simply passive victims of the transformation. Opportunities for women to participate in the rich socio-political life of post-communist Russia, in the new political parties, trade unions, business life, protest movements and human rights groups, increased as much as for anyone else.[98] Even here, though, women were under-represented, especially in leading bodies. A strictly numerical approach does not always reflect reality, and there is no doubt that qualitatively women played an important part in the democratic movement. However, as in the West, women tended to be absent at the point where decisions are taken: 'Where there is power there are no women; where there are women, there is no power.'[99] Some women, like Ekaterina Lakhova, the head of the Women of Russia Duma faction, took an active part in issues like renewing Russia's Family Code (regulating marriage and family matters) and the former Yabloko deputy Elena Mizulina played an outstanding part in the life of the Duma as deputy chair of its legislative committee, drafting, for example, amendments to the Criminal Code. In government Valentina Matvienko was a long-serving minister for social welfare. In December 2000, the only female governor of a Russian region, Valentina Bronevich of the tiny Koryak autonomous *okrug*, lost her seat.

Women's interests are weakly articulated in the political system because, among other things, women's organisations are weak. The fall of the Soviet regime led to the dissolution of some of the old bureaucratic women's organisations. The Soviet Women's Committee, however, survived with the new name of the Russian Union of Women and kept its lavish headquarters, but without subsidies it was forced to take up commercial activities. It was one of the main sponsors of the Women of Russia bloc. A women's movement began to take shape at the grassroots, but there were numerous social and political factors inhibiting a strong separate women's movement in Russia. If the social democrats of the past had argued that 'the women's question' was just one aspect of the emancipation of labour as a whole, so in the post-communist transition the emphasis has been on the achievement of democratic and citizenship rights for all. Women's activity was channelled into the struggle for democracy, just as once before it had been subordinated to the struggle for socialism. Rather than building strong collective organisations, women in post-communist Russia have tended to adopt individual strategies. This may well reflect what has been called the 'escape from forced emancipation' typical of Soviet-type systems, marked by an allergy to public engagement.[100]

The problem of gender differentiation did, however, generate three main forms of women's political activity. The first was the development of numerous local associations and pressure groups that campaigned for various measures or focused on particular issues. Brutal conditions for conscripts and the horrors of the Chechen war stimulated the creation of the Union of Committees of Soldiers' Mothers and similar organisations. The second form was involvement in some of the existing women's organisations to try to turn them from bureaucratic structures of Soviet power into genuinely responsive organisations not only *for* women but also *of* women. The third was the attempt to create genuinely independent new structures. One of these was the Centre of Gender Studies of the Academy of Science, established in early 1990 and directed by Anastasiya Posadskaya, which analysed demographic and social problems of women in Russia and acted as a link between Russian and Western feminists. However, despite the direct threat posed by marketisation to women (in economic, social and identity terms), there was no upsurge in a politicised women's movement in Russia. Posadskaya noted that state policies were still designed *for women* and not programmes of *women themselves*.

As in other spheres, the question remained whether the 'modernisation' of Soviet women would necessarily repeat Western patterns, or whether Russian modernity might differ in significant ways from that prevalent in the West. Why should sexual identity become gender identity?[101] The question is often raised of Russian women's own consciousness of their own interests in the three spheres mentioned above (work, motherhood, family) and as individuals or part of a feminine community. In refusing to adopt Western criteria of feminism, had they in some way internalised their own subjection; or was their refusal to adopt Western ways of thinking a reflection of a deeper cultural difference between Russia and the West?

Environmentalism

Marxists traditionally looked upon nature as a resource to be plundered in the service of humanity. Holloway notes that 'Land, air, and water were as much victims of Stalin's ruthless policies as the people of the Soviet Union were. "We cannot expect charity from nature," Stalin said. "We must tear it from her."'[102] The environmental movement had played a central role in popular mobilisation during *perestroika*, and indeed throughout the communist era environmentalists had acted as a residual source of social consciousness and responsibility. The outstanding plant biologist Academician Nikolai Vavilov, for example, had tried to defend the autonomy of science against the depredations of Trofim Lysenko, but had failed and was arrested in June 1940 and died of starvation soon after.[103] He was not alone, and the courage of the earth scientists prompted Douglas Weiner to describe the discipline as 'the Gulag of freedom'.[104] In a certain sense the biologists and allied disciplines of the Soviet period can be described as the kernel of civil society waiting for more propitious circumstances to germinate.

These better times proved to be Gorbachev's *perestroika*. A multitude of environmental groups emerged who insisted that communism had been as much an environmental disaster as it had been a political and economic one.[105] A study by Goskomstat revealed that an average of nearly 100 million tons of pollutants were discharged into the environment annually in the five years to 1991.[106] Commercial felling of forests at some 2 million hectares a year far exceeded the replacement rate, which in *taiga* conditions in any case is very slow. The indiscriminate use of chemical fertilisers and pesticides laid waste great tracts and contaminated rivers and ground waters; the deserts of Dagestan and Kalmykia had increased from 15,000 to a million hectares in a generation; in the Arctic tundra overgrazing had led to the loss of 40 million hectares of pasture (an area larger than Germany); the wildlife of Eastern Siberia has been devastated by factory pollution; the level of the Aral Sea is falling by one metre a year; the closed Caspian Sea is filling with poisons; Lake Ladoga (Europe's largest lake near St Petersburg) is dying from nitrate and phosphate poisoning; on the high seas the USSR had systematically lied about slaughter of a large part of the world's protected whale population, dumped nuclear waste into the Sea of Japan, and discarded seven nuclear submarines and an ice-breaker, six of them in the shallow sea around Novaya Zemlya between the Barents and Kara Seas, north-east of Murmansk; and the sad list could go on.[107] The cumulative effect of these disasters has a devastating effect on public health.

Nikolai Vorontsov had been the first non-communist Soviet minister, given responsibility for the environment in 1989, and he increased spending on environmental protection to 1.3 per cent of GNP. However, this had little impact on the gross pollution of most industrial cities, with the worst affected like Kemerovo, Bratsk and Norilsk exceeding by ten times permitted levels of air pollution.[108] Alexei Yablokov became the Minister for the Environment in the new Russian government, a man who had long fought for environmental causes and had been the first chair of the Soviet branch of Greenpeace. Russia faced a daunting task in overcoming the disastrous environmental legacy of the old regime. The loss of biodiversity was matched by the human health hazard posed by the crisis, and Yablokov calculated that 20 per cent of the country's population lived in ecological disaster zones and another 35–40 per cent in ecologically damaged conditions.[109]

It was clear that the money required to deal with this ecological catastrophe was not available. Even more tragically, Russia faced the dilemma shared by other post-communist countries, namely the balance to be drawn between environmental policies and the costs in economic and job terms. It was all very well to advocate the closure of environmentally hazardous plants and industries, but how would the economic losses be covered, and where would the new jobs for those made redundant come from? Who would pay for the closure of the giant pulp and paper mills threatening Laka Baikal in southern Siberia, the deepest freshwater lake on earth containing one-fifth of the world's freshwater and home to 1,500 plant and animal species, 1,200 of them found nowhere else in the world? The main form of industrialisation in Siberia was resource extraction, and with the acute pressure for foreign-currency logging of the fragile *taiga* forests, half of the world's coniferous forest and over one-fifth of all forest (being twice as large as the Amazon rainforests), was set to increase. Korean, Japanese and American firms increased their presence despite the resistance of local authorities and the native peoples, and who would police environmental laws, prevent the erosion of soils and silting of rivers, prevent the loss of animal habitat and make up the losses in hard currency earnings for raw timber exports?[110]

The disintegration of the USSR jeopardised Soviet environmental and conservation legislation as each republic sought maximum advantage for itself, leading, for example, to the return of sea fishing of sturgeon in the Caspian, banned in 1962 by the Soviet Ministry of Fisheries.[111] The collapse of the Soviet economy, however, also had a beneficial environmental impact, as plants closed and industrial activity declined, but de-industrialisation is hardly a long-term solution to the crisis. The tension between environmental security and economic well-being is an acute one in countries in economic crisis..

In his drive for administrative rationalisation, one of Putin's first acts on coming to power was the abolition of the State Committee for Environmental Protection, dissolved on 17 May 2000. The task of environmental protection was transferred to the Ministry of Natural Resources, a move that many considered akin to placing the fox in charge of the hen coop. The old Committee, it must be stressed, had been criticised for its sometimes intrusive (some argued exploitative) interference in business, for example the development of the energy resources on Sakhalin, motivated (it was claimed by its opponents) by the opportunities afforded by the need to receive its approval for bribery. At the same time, the State Committee on Forestry was also eliminated. The appointment of Alexander Gavrin, who had close links with Lukoil, the country's biggest oil producer, as energy minister added further to the impression that business had captured government.

Above all, the weakness of regulatory oversight over Russia's nuclear industry was notorious. None of Russia's twenty-eight nuclear power plants had a full safety certificate, yet the minister for economic energy, Evgenii Adamov, planned to build another twenty-three nuclear power stations, as well as forty advanced 'fast breeder' reactors. While the Chernobyl nuclear catastrophe of 26 April 1986 is well-known, the contamination caused by three disasters in 1946, 1957 and 1967 sparked off by the nuclear waste produced by the Mayak plant fifty miles north of Chelyabinsk, the centre of the Soviet nuclear weapons production system, was if anything worse than that caused by Chernobyl. The Soviet Northern fleet was based on the Kola peninsula, near the border with Norway, and dumped submarine reactors, spent fuel and other nuclear waste into the sea. It was in connection with this that Alexander Nikitin, the former naval captain mentioned in Chapter 4, produced a report for the Norwegian environmental group, Bellona. As a result he was arrested by the FSB in 1996, and Putin, at the head of the FSB in 1998 and 1999, defended the action on the grounds that environmental groups provided a cover for foreign spies. Nikitin was finally cleared in September 2000, but the result could hardly be claimed as a resounding victory for freedom of speech or social activism in Russia.

The issue was particularly acute concerning nuclear power. The explosion at Chernobyl was dreadful proof of the dangers of nuclear technology in the hands of an irresponsible state.[112] The USSR had fifty-three nuclear power stations operating in 1991, most of a primitive design lacking concrete container systems. The presence of such a dome at the RBMK-type Chernobyl power plant might have contained much of the radiation released following the explosion. In republics like Russia, Ukraine, Lithuania and Armenia nuclear power played a crucial part in the energy balance. Russia's twenty-eight nuclear power stations supply 11.8 per cent of the country's energy needs (18.9 GWe – gigawatts electric), while Ukraine's fifteen supplied 25 per cent (13 GWe). Ukraine suffered from chronic energy shortages, amassing enormous debts to Russia for oil and gas deliveries, and insisted it could not close the remaining two working reactors at Chernobyl (which supplied 7 per cent of Ukraine's electricity) until the West helped pay for alternatives, like a gas-fired power station. In Armenia the Metzamor station was taken off line in March 1989 in the wake of the December 1988 earthquake, but returned to active service in 1995. Thus, while many reactors should close on environmental grounds, to do so would leave cities cold in the harsh winters. The energy shortage, exacerbated by falling output of oil, gas and coal, led Russia's powerful 'Minatom' agency in December 1992 to propose an increase in nuclear power output to 37 GWe by 2010 by completing unfinished plants and constructing new ones.[113] Yablokov called the plan 'unacceptable from the legal, ecological, economic and political points of view',[114] but the severity of the energy shortfall was such that there was no guarantee that his warning would be heard, especially since nuclear power was a smaller component of Russia's energy balance than in many developed Western states.[115]

The legacy of past nuclear irresponsibility, however, was one that could not be avoided. The problem of radioactivity was the greatest single catastrophe afflicting the country. Some 8,000 people had died as a result of the Chernobyl explosion, and contamination affected large parts of Ukraine and 40 per cent of Belarus – provoking movements for national independence – as well as sixteen regions of Russia. The sarcophagus containing the damaged Reactor 4 at Chernobyl, moreover, is in danger of disintegrating.[116] In Moscow itself, leakage from nuclear plants and research institutes made certain parts of the city extremely dangerous. Some 600 miles of the Yenisei downriver from Krasnoyarsk-26 are heavily contaminated since in the past water from the cooling towers in a military plant producing plutonium went straight into the river. The legacy of atmospheric nuclear tests still affected parts of Siberia downwind of the Semipalatinsk test site in Kazakhstan. An explosion in tanks containing nuclear waste in 1957 at the Chelyabinsk-40 installation cast radioactive materials over a wide area, and another explosion at Kyshtym near Chelyabinsk in 1976, kept secret for twenty years, contaminated a large part of the Urals. And everywhere there were Chernobyls waiting to happen, in old nuclear power stations and secret nuclear factory towns like Chelyabinsk-65.

In this context, Putin's plans to import spent nuclear fuel for reprocessing (approved by parliament in July 2001) sparked bitter controversy.

The fall of communist power did not resolve the environmental crisis but made possible analysis of its scale. At the same time, a whole series of new problems arose in conditions of marketisation, weak state power and energy shortages.[117] The Russian government was conscious of the relationship between economic transformation and environmental factors, adopting a Law on Protecting the Environment on 19 December 1991,[118] and sought to develop co-operation with the other CIS states on environmental policy.[119] The Law on Specially Protected Natural Areas, finally signed into law by Yeltsin on 14 March 1995, was the corner-stone of measures to regulate the protection and use of specially protected areas. Russia already had strictly protected Nature Reserves (*Zapovedniki*), established some seventy years ago, National Parks (set up in 1983), Special Purpose Reserves (*Zakazniki*), Nature Monuments, and some others, and the Act now introduced a new type of protected area, Regional Natural Parks (analogous to State Parks in the United States). The Act drew a clear distinction between the federal and regional level of protected areas, a particularly important delineation at a time of privatisation, with the *Zapovedniki* and National Parks to remain federal property, while the *Zakazniki* were under regional control.[120] The *Zapovedniki* were the heart of Russia's conservation policy and biological diversity, whereas some of the other areas were virtually 'paper parks', encroached upon by the increasing number of small landowners, farmers and herders, quite apart from the pressure of mining, logging and other business interests.

The constitutional provision (Art. 42) that 'Each person has the right to a decent environment' is far from being fulfilled. Democratisation thus acts as a two-edged sword in the field of environmental politics. On the one hand, it makes possible the relatively honest appraisal of environmental problems, allows the mobilisation of lobbies and groups, and promotes public participation in legislative acts. On the other hand, powerful new corporations and business lobbies emerge to exploit natural resources, private entrepreneurs encroach on protected areas, the capacity of the state to regulate and implement environmental programmes weakens, and the resources available for conservation and rehabilitation decline. The Russian case demonstrates clearly, however, that environmentalism is not the preserve of affluent Westerners[121] but is a global concern.

Conclusion

While the old regime had lacked freedom, it did at least ensure a degree of security. The new freedoms after the fall of communism were accompanied by a high degree of job and physical insecurity, to the extent that many yearned for the old days. Social and psychological stress is revealed in high rates of crime, suicide, divorce, alcoholism and ill health. Men in particular are coping poorly, with life expectancy falling below that of India. Russia witnessed an upsurge in communicable diseases such as malaria, TB and sexually transmitted diseases. Poverty and inequality have increased markedly. The official trade union movement was reformed and de-étatised, while the new trade unions were subject to the factionalism and splits typical of parties. The old Soviet women's organisation also dissolved and a number of independent women's organisations were created, but women as a group have been a negligible force in politics. Russia faces an environmental crisis of the first order, but in conditions of weakening state capacity, liberal economic policies and international integration, it has failed to devise a coherent response.

14 Cultural transformation

> I think that Russia can only be Russia. It is neither Asian nor European. It is just Russia.
>
> (Alexei Podberezkin)[1]

Accompanying the political, social and economic revolutions was a no less profound transformation of the cultural sphere. Instead of the closed, introspective and heavily administered Soviet system, a more open, pluralistic and free society began to emerge. The financial and institutional basis for this freedom, however, remained tenuous. The censorship of the communist years was abolished, but new constraints emerged, above all financial. The press may have cast off one form of oppression, but reliance on wealthy benefactors or subsidies imposed new limitations. The role of the intelligentsia as the 'conscience of the nation' also gave way to attempts to find new ways to survive in a free but relatively impoverished society. Religious freedom was restored, but here, too, fears that Russia was becoming exposed to excessive foreign evangelism led to the imposition of new restrictions. While the old political order may have changed in 1991, the people remained the same although their attitudes and views evolved. How can democratic institutions function democratically if societal values remain in some way antithetical to Western democratic values? The old forced ideology had gone, but the country appeared to experience a crisis of values.

The media

Glasnost had been the defining characteristic of Gorbachev's *perestroika*; society came to know itself and its own past, and in so doing appeared to lose itself.[2] Revelations about Soviet crimes and follies undermined faith in the regime; *glasnost* acted as a profoundly disintegrative force. The revelatory aspect of *glasnost* continued into the post-Soviet era, but its impact was reduced since the new facts were now part of history rather than politics. Nevertheless, some of the details revealed following the fall of the old regime retained their power to shock, especially when the executioners spoke out. A former NKVD chief Vladimir Tokarev described in chilling detail how it took a month for NKVD troops in Kalinin (Tver) to shoot 6,295 Polish officers one by one. He revealed that 3,897 had died in a similar fashion in Katyn and 4,403 near Kharkov, a total of 14,595.[3] It was only in 1990, and then without a hint of repentance, that the Soviet regime had admitted that they, and not the Nazis, were guilty of the murders in April 1940.

Glasnost gave way to freedom of speech and the press, confirmed by the liberal Law on Press Freedom of 12 June 1990. *Glasnost* had been subversive of the old regime and had undermined social consensus, or at least made vivid the absence of consensus. Now, the new freedom contributed towards the creation of a distinctively Russian public sphere and focus for social discourse. Freed from censorship, the new quality papers acted as a forum for debate of public issues. Freedom of the press acts as a major form of control over executive power, and papers now took great pride in calling themselves the 'fourth estate'. Papers like *Nezavisimaya gazeta* (The Independent), for example, gloried in the freedom to act as a forum for debate. Its own position was a liberal patriotic one, acting as the mouthpiece for the democratic intelligentsia. The new Russian Law on the Press debated in autumn 1991 was in certain respects less liberal than the Soviet one, allowing the ministry to close a newspaper down if it had been 'warned' twice, but after protests the law that came into effect on 6 February 1992 extended press freedoms and now included provisions against monopoly ownership.[4] The freedoms that had begun during *glasnost* now blossomed into genuine freedom of speech and the press, and the variety of publications and the openness of their content was unparalleled in Russia's history.

The press struggled to adjust to post-communist conditions. If earlier they had been subject to political restrictions, they had at least been subsidised and shielded from market forces. The media moved from peddling lies to pursuing profits, with an intervening stage of the enthusiastic half-truths of *glasnost*. In the first period after the *coup*, the press still faced the monopoly distributor of newspapers and journals, *Soyuzpechat*, and later distribution remained a problem, with the major central papers rarely available for purchase in the regions. The supplier of newsprint enjoyed a monopoly, and did not hesitate to take advantage of it by raising prices. Higher prices sharply reduced subscriptions, a trend that was only reversed in the late 1990s. In March 1992, *Pravda*, the flagship of the Bolshevik movement since Lenin founded it in 1912, ceased publication until it reappeared with the help of a loan from a Greek millionaire. The other of the two great Soviet newspapers, *Izvestiya*, the paper of the USSR parliament, came out of the *coup* with an enhanced reputation but was later taken over by the 'oligarch' Potanin.

The price of freedom was economic hardship, and papers were forced to enter the marketplace and take on advertising, while some in addition sought to attract readers by dropping the high-minded asceticism (however hypocritical) typical of the communist press and moved resolutely downmarket with a diet of sex and scandals. The government found ways of subsidising sympathetic papers, while in the regions governors created their own subservient media groups. This was particularly threatening to freedom of expression, since 70 per cent of subscriptions are now to local newspapers. The ideal would be press freedom and government subsidies that would shield the papers from commercial pressures and the ensuing compromises, but, as in the West, this was not to be. The dissemination of propaganda gave way to the pursuit of profits, and the prestige of the press fell accordingly. The fall of communism allowed the media to escape from state ownership, but the difficult economic situation has meant that few remained genuinely independent. One by one the oligarchs snapped up media outlets. Following a financial crisis in August 1996, for example, *Nezavisimaya gazeta*, whose very name proclaims its independence, was taken over by one of the most predatory of

Russia's post-communist tycoons, Berezovskii. The under-developed condition of the advertising industry and its concentration in just a few hands means that it is difficult to retain commercial independence. Only *Moskovskie novosti* (Moscow News) was able to maintain its independence by a mix of income from sponsorship and advertising. While some moguls bought up existing media outlets, others established new ones, while bodies like Gazprom set up its own voice in the form of Gazprom-Media. It was this media conglomerate that bought a large stake in Vladimir Gusinskii's NTV, and later under Putin took a controlling interest in the television company. Berezovskii never made any secret of the fact that he 'never in the course of the decade viewed the mass media as a business', instead considering it 'a powerful lever of political influence'.[5] This was something that Putin, too, understood.

The electronic media followed the same trajectory as the press: first a renaissance during *glasnost'* and the early post-communist years, the latter marked by the development of independent television and radio, followed by financial crises, commercialisation and oligarchical control, although here the paths diverged. Unlike the press, television re-entered a phase of state 'influence', if not control. Under a deal agreed between the Soviet and Russian presidents, Channel 2 became a purely Russian channel (RTR), and later the first channel (Ostankino) became the basis for an inter-state television network for the CIS (ORT). Television lost some of its Reithian earnestness and desire to educate that it had gained in the years of *perestroika*; in market conditions, it now sought to entertain as much as to enlighten. The creation of Gusinskii's NTV marked a radical departure from Soviet traditions. The station was marked by its fearless reporting of the first Chechen war, although in Yeltsin's 1996 re-election campaign it threw in its lot (temporarily) with the regime. NTV was particularly critical of Putin and all his doings in 1999–2000, until finally subordinated to Gazprom in April 2001. It was never clear whether the struggle over control of NTV was primarily about finances or politics.

The news agencies also underwent a radical reorganisation after the *coup*. The Novosti Information Agency was brought under the wing of the Russian Information Agency to form RIA-Novosti, which sought to become a non-political news-gathering organisation like other world press agencies such as Reuters or Agence France Presse. The major problem was that Novosti had been an unprofitable organisation, having been subsidised by the Soviet state and other organisations including the KGB, and in order to become profitable many foreign publications were closed, including *Soviet Weekly* in Britain, whose last issue came out on 5 December 1991. The new head of Tass was Vitalii Ignatenko, formerly Gorbachev's press secretary, who pledged to turn Tass into a normal press agency, and it was later merged with RIA-Novosti to form a single agency ITAR-TASS. The field was beginning to get rather crowded, since the independent agencies Interfax and Postfactum also served much the same market. However, the vigorous growth of these agencies was testimony to the stress now placed on accurate and de-ideologised news.

'Thick journals', periodicals that enjoyed a long history in Russia as the forum for the intelligentsia but which had died out in Britain in the early twentieth century, enjoyed a renaissance in the heady days of *glasnost* in 1988 and 1989 but now once again fell upon hard times. They were forced to put up cover rates and the number of subscribers fell. Subscriptions to *Novyi mir* (New World) fell from 2.5 million to 250,000 in 1992, *Znamya* from 1 million to 250,000, and *Druzhba narodov* from 1.2 million to 90,000. At the thin end of the thick publications, numerous political and social journals were transformed by the fall of the regime. After the *coup*, some of the former communist periodicals engaged in some astonishing breast beating. *Partiinaya zhizn* (Party Life), for example, distanced itself from the Central Committee, whose mouthpiece it had long been, or at least, of its '*nomenklatura* core'. The editorial insisted that this small group of 'impostors' had claimed to speak on behalf of the whole party, hence the journal had often published the 'hypocrisy, banalities and malicious conceits of the parto-cratic jargon'. The journal, now under the control of its workers, exclaimed, 'thank God, that this excrescence (*narost*) on the body of society has been removed'.[6] The journal went on to rename itself *Delovaya zhizn* (Business Life), and thus completed one of the more astonishing transformations of the transition to post-communism in Russia. Even more breathtaking for its sheer audacity, however, was the transformation of *Kommunist* into *Svobodnaya mysl* (Free Thought), though under the auspices of the Gorbachev Foundation it lived up to its name.

In the 2000s, the persecution of the Radio Liberty reporter Andrei Babitskii, of the retired Navy captain and environmental reporter Alexander Nikitin, of the popular muckraking reporter Alexander Khinstein and others, all appeared to signal the end of the luxuriant but dirty profusion of press liberties that had emerged in the late 1980s and somehow survived under Yeltsin, although much of it had become bent to the will of the oligarchs. Babitskii had been arrested in Chechnya and then held incommunicado for a month before being exchanged for some Russian prisoners to the Chechen insurgents. On his release in Dagestan, he was accused of having false documents and was banned from leaving the country. The information regime imposed on reportage of the second Chechen war took contemporary Western informational practices in times of warfare to new extremes. It appeared that any non-official reporting of the war could be construed as 'anti-state activity'. The raid by masked tax police on the offices of NTV, the only national independent TV station, on 11 May 2000, followed by Gusinskii's impris-onment for four days (and thereafter he feared for his life), suggested a sustained assault against press freedom. It was unlikely that Gusinskii was any more corrupt than other oligarchs, but he was the head of an independent media company that was critical of Putin and 'the family'.

It may be noted that the integrity of the media in the West has also been ques-tioned. As Stjepan Mestrovic notes, 'postmodernist journalism has abandoned the notion of seeking truth in reporting'.[7] A study of the state of media freedom in Russia concluded that 'each region violates media freedom differently but each of them does so'. According to the survey, Moscow and St Petersburg were rated to be most free, with the ethno-federal republics at the bottom.[8] Media freedoms remained fragile in the centre as well, with threats that the government would be given the powers to licence publications, a power that could easily be used to limit freedom of speech. The Information Security Doctrine of 9 September 2000, devel-oped by the Security Council, revealed a defensive and security-dominated approach to media freedoms, listing a whole range of 'threats to the informational security' of the country,[9] and was followed by a renewed spy scare and increasing attempts by security agencies to control the informational sphere.

Culture and the intelligentsia

The lifting of censorship and the other controls during *perestroika* raised expectations that society would enjoy an explosion of long-repressed creativity. While the flood of hitherto suppressed facts about the Soviet past and discussion of previously taboo subjects raised the circulation of the 'thick journals' and the press, by 1989 interest was waning. *Perestroika* was not accompanied by a cultural renaissance, and indeed by 1991 some critics began to talk in terms of the 'death' of Soviet and Russian literature.[10] The Soviet regime in its heyday had produced works of more universal value than a literature that veered between obsessively grimy and introspect works, on the one hand, and escapist writings, on the other.

The political revolution and the market posed dramatic challenges to the whole intellectual and cultural life of society. The USSR Academy of Sciences had long been criticised not only for being an elite establishment, absorbing almost all research funds and thus starving universities and colleges, but also for being a grossly inefficient body. Whole institutes had produced little in the way of worthwhile research for years, and yet took their wages, bonuses, housing and rations. Attempts by the USSR Academy of Sciences to become independent of Russia were scotched soon after August. As Yeltsin noted, 'Then, the USSR Academy of Sciences, 96 per cent of whose institutions and scholars are in Russia, tried to become an organisation independent of Russia. Now the situation has changed dramatically.'[11] In a decree of 21 November 1991, Yeltsin created a Russian Academy of Sciences (RAS), and all members of the old academy joined automatically. The new academy faced a severe financial crisis and its institutes were forced to find alternative income to supplement state subsidies. As with the press, freedom was gained at the price of financial security.

Russia's educational system also suffered from a crisis of financing and reorientation. The fabric of schools had decayed in the last Soviet years, and they remain unmodernised. Only about a quarter have a computer, and less than 1 per cent are connected to the Internet. Once again, as in the early 1980s, the educational system in the early 2000s faced a major reorganisation.[12] Universities are now allowed to take a certain proportion of paying students to help subsidise the rest. A particularly acute problem is the gulf between higher education and the economy, with universities turning out over a million graduates every year whose skills often fail to meet the requirements of a modern economy, and who thus find difficulties in finding jobs. University libraries lacked resources to update their collections, and it was only with the help of the Soros Foundation that 56 per cent of higher education establishments had been endowed with Internet centres.

In the last years of *perestroika*, the two streams of Russian culture, in exile and at home, began to come together, and in the post-communist era they fused as the divisions of the revolution and the Civil War healed. Yeltsin began his visit to the United States in June 1992 by telephoning Solzhenitsyn and asking him to return home after seventeen years of exile. Solzhenitsyn had resolutely refused to have anything to do with *perestroika*, but now that the communist regime had fallen he returned home in 1994. Vladimir Voinovich, Andrei Sinyavsky and many other *émigrés* visited the motherland, and Russian cultural figures could now travel freely abroad. The magazine *Kontinent*, edited in Paris since 1974 by Vladimir Maximov, moved to Moscow and sought to reflect religious concerns and the problems of the intelligentsia. Its new editor, Igor Vinogradov, noted that the magazine would discuss problems of Russian national consciousness in the new conditions and whether indeed there could be a 'special path' for Russia, avoiding 'the real dangers of Western civilisation'.[13]

The disintegration of the USSR was reflected in the Byzantine manœuvrings within the organised writers' movements. The liberal Union of Russian (*Rossiiskie*) Writers was bitterly opposed to the RSFSR Writers' Union, dominated by extreme nationalists, while the old USSR Writers' Union gave way to a new Commonwealth of Unions of Writers, which itself later split. The struggles reflected the extreme politicisation of writers and literature as a whole, but the farcical plots and counter-plots within the cultural establishment discredited them all. The intrigues surrounding the Russian Booker Prize perpetuated old conflicts in new form. While the views of writers were sought after and valued during *perestroika*, the fall of the old regime was accompanied by their marginalisation and indeed the devaluation of culture as a whole. Crude commercialisation, the shortage of paper for journals and books, the high prices, all played their part in the alleged decline of literature. However, the displacement of ideological constraints by the demands of the market was only one aspect of the problem. By 1991, much of the suppressed or exiled literature had been published, but the new wave of writers at first proved decidedly thin. This gradually gave way to a vibrant new literature in whose vanguard were writers like Victor Pelevin, whose *Babylon* (in Russian *Generation P*) is a satire on Western influences on contemporary Russia, and the Yukio Mishima-like figure of Eduard Limonov, whose nationalism ultimately led him to the Lefortovo gaol in 2001. A socio-cultural revolution was in the making.

In Eastern Europe the intelligentsia had by and large survived, though the old bourgeoisie had been destroyed, and thus an invaluable link with the past and with the West remained.[14] In Russia the old middle classes had been destroyed, but a multi-layered intelligentsia had emerged from the debris of the old system. The core of the cultural intelligentsia maintained traditional values of scholarship throughout the Soviet period, and indeed took on some of the hegemonic functions of the bourgeoisie. However, in a way traditional for Russia, its values were isolated from society and because of the peculiarities of the Russian state formation they were unable to combine a programme of democratic reforms, state modernisation and national aspirations. The intelligentsia had played a leading role during *perestroika*, but at the same time as a group had become irrevocably split. The divisions of the Russian intelligentsia reflected the contradictions of the Russian state system in its entirety.

The Russian intelligentsia changed as *perestroika* progressed, and became increasingly engaged with the political life of the country to the extent that a large number of the former intelligentsia became leading members of the new elite. However, as a class the intelligentsia suffered during the transition to more marke-tised forms of social life. The enormous number of institutes and network of privileges of the old USSR Academy of Sciences were cut back as budget cuts took their toll. The intelligentsia had enjoyed a brilliant swansong during *perestroika*, when for the last time the Soviet regime courted them and Gorbachev sought to enlist them as allies in the struggle against the bureaucracy, but this was only the flicker of a star in its death throes.

In democratic societies the intelligentsia as such is fractured between academic, media, and other groups in the diverse patterns of modern life. The old Soviet middle class had been unique in that it was not so much based on property but on occupation and strategic location in the reproduction of cultural values, above all the creative and scientific intelligentsia. Against the background of hyper-inflation and falling incomes Boris Saltykov, the Deputy Prime Minister in charge of science and education, talked of the 'disintegration of the middle class', a process Khasbulatov called 'the lumpenisation of society'.[15] The old Russian *esprit de corps* of the intelligentsia waned. Its economic security eroded and its cultural superiority undermined, the liberal intelligentsia began to adopt nationalist positions.[16] The transition to the market was accompanied by the decline of the traditional Russian intelligentsia and the erosion of middle-class life styles; the crisis affected both the producers and consumers of culture.

Religion and the state

In his appeal to Russians living abroad Yeltsin stressed the religious basis to Russia's national tradition. He spoke of 'reviving all the good things that were lost after [the Bolshevik revolution of October 1917], all that which made Russia Russia'. These included 'the Russian spiritual heritage, ravaged by the senseless and pitiless ideological struggle'.[17] Already in June 1988, church and state had achieved what was in effect a new concordat when Gorbachev allowed the celebrations of the millennium of the Russian Orthodox Church (ROC), and the authorities thereafter sought the assistance of the Church in establishing the moral basis for a new order. In the elections of March 1990, 300 priests of various denominations were elected to soviets at all levels. *Perestroika* allowed a revival of the organisational life of the ROC and by late 1990 11,940 parishes came under the jurisdiction of the Moscow Patriarchate, 1,830 of which had been registered in the first nine months of that year alone.[18] The reconsecration of churches was often accompanied by moving acts of social reintegration, and in Kazan 10,000 joined in the first service at the returned cathedral. The USSR Council for Religious Affairs, which had exercised harsh supervision over the Church for decades, was finally disbanded in December 1991.

As the Soviet Union disintegrated, so did the territorial unity of Orthodoxy as Moscow's pastoral authority was challenged by numerous movements. The Uniate or Ukrainian Greek Catholic Church in Western Ukraine practised Orthodox rites but acknowledged the authority of the Roman Pope. By mid-1990, the Uniates, headed by Cardinal Libichevskii since 1984, claimed jurisdiction over some 1,400 parishes and had taken over all of the Moscow Patriarchate's churches in Ivanovo-Frankovsk and all but one in Lvov. The Pope's visit to Ukraine in June 2001 for the Uniate church represented the culmination of the hopes of many generations, whereas for Moscow it appeared to aggravate old sores. The Ukrainian Autocephalus Orthodox Church (UAOC) also grew rapidly and by mid-1990 claimed 300 parishes, some 200 of which were in the Ivanovo-Frankovsk region. With the independence of Ukraine, Metropolitan Filaret of Kiev, representing the Moscow Patriarchate's Ukrainian Orthodox Church (UOC), was placed in an increasingly difficult situation until finally his alleged earlier collaboration with the KGB made his position untenable. Under a cloud of nationalistic rhetoric, supported by Kravchuk, he made the UOC autocephalus and thus beyond Moscow's jurisdiction. The Ukrainian government supported a division that even the French revolutionaries had not contemplated by trying to establish a separate Catholic Church in France. In Russia itself Suzdal and other communities transferred their allegiance to the Free Russian Orthodox Church (under the jurisdiction of the New York-based Russian Orthodox Church Abroad, ROCA), while the True Orthodox Church (the part of the Catacomb Church that did not join the Free Orthodox Church) enjoyed a significant revival. While Patriarch Aleksi called for reconciliation with ROCA, the leaders of ROCA insisted that the Moscow Patriarchate had for too long been the tool of a godless regime and should publicly repent.

One of the gravest problems facing ROC was coming to terms with its compromised relationship with the Soviet state and its penetration by the KGB. For decades, ROC had been ruled by an ecclesiastical *nomenklatura*, and the election of Patriarch Aleksi, a man considered reliable by the old regime, to replace Patriarch Pimen in June 1990 appeared a continuation of old ways. The collapse of the USSR finally made possible the revelation of the names of the KGB 'agents in cassocks' in the Orthodox hierarchy (which included Metropolitan Filaret of Kiev), and the way that the KGB had tried to influence the World Council of Churches.[19] The ROC, however, had survived one of the cruellest onslaughts against religion in history, and in the 1990s it was consistently the most trusted public body in Russia.[20]

The opening of the borders made Russia fertile ground for missionaries and representatives of organised religion. Roman Catholic and Protestant churches developed their organisations, while the big cities were host to numerous fringe groups ranging from Hare Krishna, old Russian paganism (banned since 1552) and Freemasonry. The Hasidic community successfully campaigned for the return of the collection of manuscripts known as the Shneerson books, kept in the Lenin Library since being illegally confiscated in the 1920s. The wealth of the Unification Church of Sun Myung Moon, established in Korea in 1954, against the background of Russian poverty allowed it to exert a strong influence, as did various American Baptist and evangelical organisations. Post-communist religious life was marked by

> the amazingly ready credulity of the general public in the face of any self-styled preacher of 'spirituality' which is quite understandable in a country where the extermination of several generations of religious philosophers and theologians led to the oblivion of the fact that Reason has its own rules not only in the secular world, but also in the domain of religion.[21]

It was the fear of foreign penetration that provoked the Law on Freedom of Conscience and Religion, adopted in September 1997, which sought to place barriers in the way of foreign proselytism. A distinction was drawn between 'traditional' and 'non-traditional' religions, with Orthodoxy, Islam, Buddhism and

Judaism in the former category, while various 'cults' and 'sects' were in the latter. Religious *organisations* were granted certain privileges (such as the right to own property, employ people, conduct charity work and maintain formal international relations) that were denied religious *groups*. All religious bodies were to be registered, with particular stipulations concerning groups that had been in Russia for less than fifteen years. Some groups, above all Jehovah's Witnesses and some Baptist churches, claimed that regional authorities have placed obstacles in the way of registration, while attempts to block the registration of the Salvation Army on the grounds of its 'obvious militarism' were later reversed by the courts. Despite extensions to the deadline for registration, by 31 December 2000, 13,922 congregations had been approved, while 3,000 had failed to register (mostly because they had ceased to exist or failed to present the necessary documentation) and were disbanded.[22] It is clear that the need to re-register was not as discriminatory as some had feared. Indeed, a study found that by mid-2001 there were over 20,000 congregations, compared to fewer than 5,000 in 1990, suggesting a religious flowering in Russia both in number and diversity.[23]

The influence of the Church on society was significantly extended. Thousands of Sunday schools have been established, and numerous religious, philanthropic and charitable organisations visited hospitals, cared for the old, the indigent and the unemployed, looked after orphans and distributed food aid. Over a hundred Russian Orthodox brotherhoods were established, reviving a tradition dating back to the Middle Ages, concerned with religious and philanthropic work. The Orthodox priesthood also played its part in the development of a new business class. In the prevalent conditions of lawlessness and rudimentary business ethics, enterprises managed or monitored by priests were among the few that could be trusted. This was a rather literal application of Weber's and Tawney's views on the role of the 'Protestant work ethic' in the rise of capitalism,[24] though the part played by the Orthodox priesthood in the restoration of the cultural values and motivations of capitalist accumulation might be considered anomalous.

According to the constitution (Art. 14.1), 'The Russian Federation is a secular state. No religion may be established as the state religion or a compulsory religion.' In the 1990s, however, it was clear that four 'traditional' religions were favoured (Orthodoxy, Islam, Buddhism and Judaism), with representatives of the four given prominence on state occasions, such as Yeltsin's inauguration for his second term in August 1996. Of the four, Orthodoxy was clearly given primacy. This was reflected in the Preamble to the September 1997 federal law On Freedom of Conscience and on Religious Associations, which acknowledged that Russia was a secular state but recognised the special role of Orthodoxy in Russian history and culture. Similar formulations were adopted in Georgia (for Georgian Orthodoxy) and Mongolia (for Buddhism), and implicitly followed in Poland (for Roman Catholicism). These churches were not 'established' in the British sense, yet their pre-eminence was recognised.

Political culture and public opinion

The attitudes and values engendered by the political socialisation of the earlier era, both official and unofficial, cast a long shadow over the new politics. While a type of democratic politics is formalised at the level of the state, the question focuses on whether it is adequately integrated into the patterns of daily life. Eckstein had spent his academic life examining the problem of 'congruence' between social attitudes and state institutions, and post-communist Russia proved a particularly complex case study.[25] The question whether Russia enjoys the prerequisites (and indeed, the nature of the prerequisites themselves) for democracy remains open.

One of the more popular approaches of the earlier age was the notion of political culture, and in particular the question of the civic culture, the ideas and attitudes that sustain a political system.[26] Political culture refers to the values, perceptions of tradition and history, and beliefs about politics held by individuals. Seven decades of communist dominance, a period that itself followed only the briefest of political openings in the first years of the twentieth century, inevitably raises the question whether the Russian people themselves have the appropriate mental approach and attitudes to sustain the democratic experiment. One view stresses that, given Russia's background, the Russian people could hardly be ready for democracy, having experienced collectivist socialisation and a manipulated political system. For Biryukov and Sergeev, the key to Russia's political culture is the concept of *sobornost*, a pre-political attachment to collectivism, anti-individualism and hostility to pluralistic representative institutions.[27] Lukin takes this argument further, suggesting that the political culture of Russia's 'democrats' was little more than an inverted form of that held by the communists, hoping to replace one form of monolithic power with another (their own), failing to understand the deeper meaning of democratic pluralism. Although the anti-communist insurgency used the language of democracy, it did not really understand the deeper meaning of the terms that it so glibly threw around.[28] An opposed view argues that even within the old order, whose legitimation was democratic if in practice it fell far short of classical liberal democratic practices, a democratic consciousness had been maturing, fostered by the modernisation advanced by the regime itself. The shift from a predominantly peasant and rural society to an urban, literate and highly educated one could not but transform public values.

Political culture can be used in several different senses, including popular attitudes towards government and questions of political behaviour, but one of the most common ways of applying the term is to compare the degree to which historical factors determine present behaviour both at the elite and the popular levels.[29] In all communist countries, however, there were a choice of pasts, and it was easy to find elements that confirmed the historical continuity of the regimes then current rather than stressing the ways that they had repudiated the past. The past, like facts, is created in the eyes of the beholder. There are many Russian pasts reflecting its Asiatic and European identities. In the nineteenth century, Russia was torn between Slavophiles like Alexei Khomyakov and Ivan Kireevsky who stressed Russia's communal, Orthodox and traditional ways against Westernisers like Konstantin Kavelin, Boris Chicherin and, on the socialistically inclined wing, Alexander Herzen and Vissarion Belinsky, who rejected appeals to Russia's uniqueness and insisted that the only road to the future lay through Europe. In the twentieth century, the country once again was divided between liberals espousing the development of individualism, the rule of law and the market, and socialists of various stripes espousing collectivism, egalitarianism and constraints on the market, if not its abolition in its entirety.

Putnam demonstrated that beneath apparently similar political institutions, deeper social structures and behavioural patterns can differ sharply, even in a country as small as Italy.[30] Although Russia is many times larger, the Soviet regime imposed a relatively similar experience of industrialisation and modernisation across the country, although in regions like the North Caucasus traditional patterns remain a living presence. Russia's past is multi-layered, and faced with the current challenge of modernisation and democratisation its history is once again being trawled to find elements that can sustain the new democratic experiment. The view of Russia as eternally autocratic has now given way to one which suggests that there were popular and philosophical constraints on autocratic rule.[31] Nicolai N. Petro stresses that

> before Peter the Great the Russian ideal of 'good government' was not abso-lutism, as the political culture approach suggests, but a strong (autocratic) government constrained by religious and national tradition to serve the will of the people. Peter weakened these traditional constraints, but the populace never forgot them. The rift between the popular ideal of good government and the political reality of Imperial Russia was just beginning to heal when the October 1917 revolution seemed to dash popular aspirations for democratic govern-ment.[32]

From this perspective, advocates of the view that there is profound continuity from the pre-Soviet period to the present have to identify precisely which strand of the past they have in mind. There is also a fatalistic element to the continuity thesis, in that Russia's twentieth century was certainly not a period of the glorious triumph of democracy but a succession of social cataclysms and political breakdowns.

The contrasting views of Russia's past were reflected in the many dimensions of Russian popular thought as reflected in public opinion polls. It was clear long before the end that the Soviet regime had lost the confidence of the 'brightest and the best'.[33] A large-scale poll in March 1991 found engineering-technical workers the most dissatisfied social group with conditions of daily life, but reasonably satis-fied with their work.[34] This may well explain why the majority (58.4 per cent) at the time favoured the market though only a small minority (12 per cent) thought that it would have a positive effect on their enterprise.[35] Public opinion and values have been much analysed in the 1990s (see Bibliography on the web). The upsurge in public confidence following the *coup* soon evaporated. In a broad survey of public opinion in April 1992, only 13 per cent responded that their life was shaping up well in the new conditions, 63 per cent said tolerably, while the rest ranged from bad to very bad. At the same time, 33 per cent insisted that the situation in the country was alarming or close to a crisis, 60 per cent called it a crisis or disastrous, while only 3 per cent considered the situation normal. Thus, there was a gulf between people's perceptions of their own tolerable circumstances and the disastrous state of the country.[36] By the time of the first anniversary of the *coup*, 55 per cent of Muscovite supporters of the White House accepted that their hopes had been disappointed, 19 per cent were unable to answer, while only 26 per cent considered that their hopes had been fulfilled. There had been a shift in sympathies, and now only 42 per cent (compared to 62 per cent a year earlier) supported the democratic forces, though still only 7 per cent (compared to 4 per cent earlier) supported the putschists, while just over 50 per cent were indifferent or could not answer.[37] The early period of post-communism in Russia was therefore marked by a sharp rise in disillusionment with the new political system and the market.[38]

Society was left disoriented and alienated by the changes, yet it appeared that they did not threaten the market or democracy. The informal networks that had sustained people during the turmoil of *perestroika* helped people adjust to the collapse of the USSR and the emergence of a new order. Above all, public attitudes were permeated by a thorough democratism, for the institutions of democracy if not for the democrats themselves. A study in Yaroslavl examined whether Russian political culture was compatible with the establishment of democratic institutions and discovered substantial support for democratic values and institutions.[39] Support for Yeltsin can be interpreted as support for economic reforms, if not always for the specific policies implemented by his governments. There appeared to be a high degree of social consensus on basic values like non-violence, the democratic resolution of conflict, and economic reform. This might suggest that there was little chance for a nationalist or neo-communist government coming to power, and the desire for strong government did not entail support for authoritarianism.[40]

Popular attitudes to private enterprise, private employment (long considered to be tantamount to 'exploitation'), and the transition to the market as a whole were far more favourable than stereotypes would allow.[41] The standard image was one of hostility, though it soon became clear that this had been much exaggerated. Yakovlev in October 1991 argued that 'Equality in poverty is the major obstacle to any social progress; it was the great invention of the ruling class, cementing its unlimited powers.'[42] A widespread popular passivity was identified, but this was not so much apathy as demobilisation, a calculated response to circumstances. The problem appeared to be that 'Many wanted to live in a market-democratic society, but rejected the steps, means and methods required to create such a society.'[43] A persistent theme was support for some sort of reconstituted USSR. Any number of polls demonstrated a sense that some sort of natural community had been destroyed in 1991, but at the same time there was no agreement over the nature of a possible reconstituted state. Just as in 1990–1, the majority had been in favour of retaining some sort of union of republics, but few had favoured the existing structure,[44] and it was Gorbachev's inability to reconcile these two positions that led to disintegration, so later integrationists like Zyuganov could not find an adequate formula in which to frame aspirations for unity. A nation-wide survey in February 1992 found that over 40 per cent preferred a reformed or even a restored USSR. Freedom of speech was considered by 71 per cent as the greatest achievement of the new system, but a significant proportion thought that within five years these freedoms would be curtailed. The concept of 'social justice' changed its meaning and was now used not as it had been by the democrats, to condemn the privileges of the elite, but by the conservatives to justify slowing down the reforms to avoid the development of excessive inequality. So, from a revolutionary slogan, the term was converted into a conservative one.[45]

Political demobilisation served the reformers well, and the political emancipation of society was not accompanied by popular activism which might have jeopardised the policies that were considered to be in the people's long-term interests. The new political system, despite its many problems, was more stable than many had anticipated, especially in the absence of any serious alternative. Clearly, age, gender, geographical location and occupation all affected views. A poll in May 1992 revealed that 40 per cent of the respondents had a positive attitude to the West and 36 per cent a more negative approach, but perhaps more significant was the very strong correlation between age and attitudes, with the young far more open than the older generation.[46] One finding from opinion surveys was the rejection of force as a method to solve political disputes. Between 45–50 per cent of the population strongly rejected the use of extraordinary measures, and 80 per cent opposed the use of military force even in the most critical situations.[47] The strength of democratic commitment, however, was another matter.[48] Under Putin support for building up the power and might of Russia tempered the desire to integrate with the West.[49] On this issue, and on most others, there was no evidence of a gulf between elite and popular values; in fact, there was a remarkable coincidence.[50]

The detailed empirical study by Miller *et al.* suggested that political values and support for democratic political systems differ little between East and West Europe. Although there are numerous minor differences, there was no sustained East/West division correlating to different historical experiences and contemporary political values. In terms of attitudes to liberal values, the rule of law, tolerance for minorities, multi-party elections, the state's role in the economy, socialist values, nationalism and cultural conformity, there was little to choose between Britain and states emerging out of Tsarist, Ottoman or Habsburg rule. A large majority in all the states surveyed, including Russia, supported liberal and democratic values as well as the institutions embodying these values, and this was reflected in structured voting patterns. All this suggested that

> there was no evidence that the people of the former Soviet Union and East Central Europe were not ready for democracy…the lines of division that have excited so many theorists and historians seem remarkably faint in terms of contemporary political values.[51]

The traumas following the fall of communism provoked a return of former communists, but this in itself did not suggest opposition to democracy as such. Of course, those social groups and regions who lost the most in the transition, above all the aged and workers (especially agricultural workers, working in a sector locked in almost permanent recession) were the most deeply alienated from market reforms, and proved the most consistent supporters of revived communist parties. By contrast, those who benefited the most, the young, the urban and those employed in the private sector, repudiated socialism most strongly and were the bedrock of support for the new democratic order. Thus, it was not historical legacies that determined political values, but the experience of the transition itself.

Similar findings are reported by Colton and McFaul. They take issue with the popular view that Russians prefer order above democracy, although there is plenty of polling evidence (which they cite) that could support such a view. However, while they demonstrate that Russians are dissatisfied with the actual operation of Russia's democratic institutions, this does not betoken a repudiation of democracy itself. Asked in broad terms whether they support democracy or not, 64 per cent came out in support.[52] More detailed examination of attitudes towards core elements of democracy like freedom to elect the country's leaders and freedom of speech revealed high levels of support (87 per cent).[53] When it came to a choice between order and liberty, Russians were not enthusiastic once again to discard their freedoms.[54] In confirmation of the findings of other research, there was a strong correlation between age and attitudes, with the older generation, not surprisingly, more attached to the Soviet system (and its values) than younger people. Putin's supporters, moreover, were not in any way more authoritarian than voters for any of the other candidates in the 2000 presidential election. In sum, there was a 'chasm between democratic attitudes and inadequately democratised institutions',[55] but not a repudiation of democracy itself.

The crisis of values

Values became disoriented as all the old certainties and articles of faith were undermined. The crisis affects far more than the collapse of the aspirations of the communist project and the social life support systems of the socialist regime. By the time the old system expired in 1991, the number of true believers had been sharply reduced, and communism had became more a way of life than an attractive goal, and indeed the more that communism receded as a goal, the more attractive it became as a way of life. The relatively cheap housing, energy and transport, the almost free telephones for local calls, the subsidised crèches and nurseries and holidays, the stable irrationality of the economic system and the strongly ordered social and cultural life, all provided a relatively congenial environment for the citizens of late communism – as long as they kept their mouths shut in public. Alexander Zinoviev argued that:

> Ibanskian [i.e. Soviet] society is one which, in practice, has no effective institution of political rights. The reason is that it does not produce or reproduce on a large scale individuals capable of becoming the subjects of political law....The few political individuals who appear from time to time are subjected to persecution not because of a bad political law, but because of the absence of any political law.[56]

Under communism people were absolved of responsibility since the party-state was responsible for, and guilty of, everything. People were thus in a distinctive way free of personal responsibility, a form of infantilism. While Zinoviev was right in asserting that the laws of the Soviet regime had nothing to do with daily life, he was mistaken to suggest that the system reflected the social characteristics of the psychological types inhabiting its universe. In other words, the system was not derived from the existence of a particular character type, but *homo sovieticus* was a morbid symptom of the system itself. Change the system, and *homo sovieticus* would soon die out.

The real Soviet citizen lived according to a self-evident counter-rationality which generated a stable pattern of counter-values that did not so much oppose the Soviet system as ignore it. The counter-values came to predominate after August 1991, but these forms of resistance reflected the subject of resistance and reproduced some of its values in an inverted form. It was this network of counter-values, rather than the Soviet values in which few believed, that was shaken during the hard transitional period following the fall of the old system. The belief in democracy as a universal panacea, faith in the West, trust in international institutions and guarantees of human rights, belief in the value of the word and rational argument to avoid conflict, were undermined by the economic collapse, the inadequacy of the West's response and by the bush wars that erupted across the former Soviet Union.

The communist regime engendered a peculiar paradox whereby it created millions of people who were bourgeois in culture and aspirations but who were locked into a socio-economic system that denied these aspirations. They were proletarian in economic terms, largely propertyless and with only their labour as assets. These people resolutely refused to adopt the proletarian consciousness that the regime espoused, and instead tried to achieve the rudiments of a bourgeois existence insulated from the rest of society. Their energies built up not the national economy but a private semi-legal economy. This was an intermediate class in all senses, prey to ultranationalism, authoritarianism and indeed fascism if their aspirations to property were not satisfied. The Bolsheviks were only too successful in reducing the bourgeoisie to the proletariat, but the proletariat itself became imbued with the aspirations of the bourgeoisie.

The dissolution of the old order necessarily meant the partial dissolution of the subject of society, 'man', since the self is to a degree shaped by the relationship to society. The reordering of society meant a reshaping of its subjects. As far as the national-patriots were concerned, the liberal experiment in Russia in fact meant the dissolution of the subject as they scrabbled to join the grazing herd of Nietzsche's 'Last Men', a fate which they did not even develop themselves but borrowed from abroad. If there is anything worse than slavery, it is to borrow the slavery of others (Marxian socialism earlier, and now market liberalism), they argued.

A new festal system replaced the festivals of the Bolshevik regime. The holiday of 7–8 November, to mark the Bolshevik revolution, was last celebrated in 1991, and two extra days were added to the New Year holiday until suitable new holidays could be found. In 1996, Yeltsin issued a decree renaming the 7 November holiday the Day of Accord and Reconciliation, although this did not stop the holiday becoming a day of leftist protests. In 1992, the Russian Orthodox Christmas, celebrated on 7 January according to the Julian rather than the Gregorian calendar, was for the first time a public holiday. The May Day holiday was de-politicised, although thousands of old communists still demonstrate on that day. One of the new public holidays, first celebrated in 1992, was 12 June and became known as Independence Day, the day when in 1990 the Russian declaration of state sovereignty was adopted. Finally, 12 December is celebrated as Constitution Day.

Without Gorbachev to defend him, Lenin soon joined the grisly pantheon of Bolshevik leaders. During *perestroika* there had been a vigorous debate over what was to be done with the Lenin Mausoleum on Red Square, and soon after the *coup* Sobchak urged that Lenin should be removed and given a decent burial near his mother's grave in St Petersburg, as Lenin himself allegedly had wished on his death bed.[57] Following the October events, Yeltsin removed the honour guard from the Mausoleum and placed them at the eternal flame in memory of Russia's dead in the Great Patriotic War (1941–5). Lenin was not without his defenders, however, and no decision was taken about what to do with his embalmed corpse.

Underlying much of the unease about the accelerated integration into world society and the market economy was the fear that Russia's 'uniqueness' might be lost. This is a fear shared by the Japanese, Chinese and other major civilisations faced with the apparently relentless tide of Americanisation. Some of these fears were articulated by Solzhenitsyn and the patriots. New forms of resistance to Western capitalist modernity will no doubt emerge in Russia as they have in the West with the development of the 'anti-capitalist movement'. In Russia, however, capitalism has first to be built before a coherent opposition can be sustained.

Conclusion

While the rapid creation of a market economy posed unprecedented challenges, the transformation of society was no less dramatic. The elite structure was reformed and traditional cultural and social values were undermined as commercial relations affected the media, education and the very identity of individuals. While the *homo economicus* gradually squeezed out the *homo sovieticus*, it was not clear what would be the scope for the broader political and social community. The citizen and the bourgeois both now emerged, but what would be the relationship between the two?[58]

Part V

Foreign policies

Russia is different not only from the other former Soviet states, but also from countries comparable in size and population. It is different not only because of its geopolitical role in Europe and Eurasia and being by far the dominant state in the CIS, or because of its strategic significance as the world's second largest nuclear power, or because of its political weight associated with its status as a permanent member of the UN Security Council. These are important factors, but above all Russia is different because it perceives itself to be different. For some policy-makers in the West, above all in the corridors of the hyper-power, the gulf between Russia's ambitions and its weakened realities became increasingly irksome. Russia's pretensions to be a 'Great Power' were derided and the country was urged to reduce its attitudes and policies commensurate with its decreased territorial space, economic resources and comparative military potential. Russia, however, was more than just another European state, a view reflected in any number of comments and official documents. For example, Anatolii Utkin at the USA and Canada Institute argued that Western advice that Russia should 'forget about our past greatness and become another Brazil' ignores the fact that '150 million don't perceive themselves as Brazilians'.[1] The Russian government's Medium-Term Strategy argued:

> As a world power situated on two continents, Russia should retain its freedom to determine and implement its domestic and foreign policies, its status and advantages as an Euro-Asian state and the largest country of the CIS, and independence of its positions and activities at international organisations.[2]

15 Foreign policy

Russia's misfortune lies in this: Russia and Europe live in different historical times.
(G.P. Fedotov)[1]

The fall of communism overshadowed perhaps an even more epoch-making event, the disintegration of a geopolitical unit that had lasted some 500 years, and in comparison with which the reign of communism had been a mere interregnum. The whole geopolitical and strategic balance not only of the post-Second World War era but of the whole epoch since the Congress of Vienna in 1815 came to an end. Russia's long climb from local, regional, continental and then to global power was suddenly dramatically reversed. The dissolution of communism ended one set of problems associated with global confrontation in the Cold War, but the disintegration of the Soviet Union raised no less epochal issues. Would the inherent instability of Russo-European relations for the last 400 years give way to a new partnership? Would the new Russia be able to define a post-imperial and post-communist national identity and integrate into global economic and political processes? What sort of 'normality' was normal for Russia?

The evolution of foreign policy

The definition of foreign policy to a large degree depends on the self-definition of a country itself; Russia had to find itself and come to terms with its evolving national identity before any coherent foreign policy based on 'national interest' could be defined. The interdependence of foreign and domestic policy under Yeltsin was closer than ever before as Russia sought a favourable international climate to assist economic reform and to facilitate its reintegration into the international system. In the first period Russian foreign policy was thoroughly 'domesticated', with domestic reform taking priority over any remaining global ambitions, but gradually the outlines of a more 'balanced', or as others would put it, a more assertive if not aggressive, policy took shape.

Russian foreign policy has passed through six main stages. Each was marked by contradictory goals that imbued policy with what we shall call an 'essential ambiguity', often reflected in what appeared to be irresolution and muddle. We use the term 'essential' because the conflicting aims were structured into the very situation and could hardly be avoided if a complex policy was to be pursued; and 'ambiguous' because they reflected the profound and unresolved (and probably insoluble) civilisational and geopolitical choices facing Russia. The bases on which choices would be made were themselves contested: Would economic development be the priority? Or would it be the struggle to restore Russian dominance in Eurasia? Or would the attempt to maintain good relations with the West predominate? Russia's size, location, and history generated multifaceted if not contradictory foreign policies.

The emergence phase: before the coup

Even before the *coup*, the outlines of an independent policy had emerged, yet the problem of defining Russia's separate interests distinct from those of the USSR had not been resolved. Yeltsin's election to chair the Russian CPD on 29 May 1990 and the Declaration of Russian State Sovereignty on 12 June set the scene for a debate over Russia's national interests and over the shape of its foreign policy. Already by October, two central principles had emerged: that Russia would seek friendly relations with the other Soviet republics in a renewed union; and that Russia wished to return as an autonomous force in world politics, defending its status as a great power but at the same time seeking 'to occupy a worthy (*dostoinoe*) place in the community of civilised peoples of Eurasia and America'.[2]

A separate Russian diplomatic service was re-established in October 1990, and in November Andrei Kozyrev was appointed foreign minister. From 1974 to 1990, Kozyrev had worked in the Directorate of International Organisations in the Soviet Ministry of Foreign Affairs (MFA), and thus it is not surprising that he later placed so much emphasis on international institutions. He argued that Russian policy would no longer be based on ideology or messianic ambitions but on common-sense and the realistic evaluation of concrete needs. He developed new approaches to international issues, even though policy, in this area as in most others, remained in Yeltsin's hands. Russia's first independent acts reflected the blurred distinction between foreign and domestic policy, namely the signing of treaties with Ukraine on 19 November, Kazakhstan on 21 November and with Belarus on 18 December 1990. The treaties recognised the signatories as sovereign states and declared that their relations would be based on principles of equality, non-interference and the renunciation of the use of force, and that they would establish diplomatic relations with each other. Soviet and Russian foreign policy began to diverge as Russian diplomacy sought to facilitate the radical transformation of society and to defend what came to be seen as Russian national interests separate and distinct from those of the Soviet Union. During Gorbachev's visit to Japan in April 1991, for example, Yeltsin made it clear that the USSR could not negotiate a return of the four disputed Kurile Islands without consulting Russia.

Yeltsin's defence of the concept of a sovereign and independent Russia, presented so eloquently during his presidential campaign in June 1991, however, was conceived within the framework of a renewed Union. Russia sought not the disintegration of the Union but its transformation on the basis of a renegotiated treaty, retaining a system of collective security, a co-ordinated foreign policy, and the maintenance of a common economic, transport and migrational space. To this end Russia took an active part in the nine-plus-one negotiations for a new Union treaty and was committed to signing the documents on 20 August when the *coup* intervened. Russia's assertion of an independent foreign policy, therefore, was considered compatible with a renewed Union with its own federal government. This is a clear example of the 'essential ambiguity' of Russian policy since it was difficult to see how mutually exclusive claims to sovereignty could be reconciled within a single state.

The establishment phase: August–December 1991

The nine-plus-one Union renewal process was derailed by the events of August 1991 and never gained momentum thereafter, despite Gorbachev's last-ditch attempts to transform the USSR into a Union of Sovereign States (see Chapter 2). The tension between decaying Soviet and embryonic Russian foreign policies provoked only confusion and frustration.

Following Eduard Shevardnadze's resignation as Soviet foreign minister on 20 December 1990, Alexander Bessmertnykh had been appointed in his place, but during the *coup* he had wavered. He in turn was replaced by Boris Pankin, the former ambassador to Prague and one of a handful of Soviet envoys who denounced the putschists without hesitation. Pankin notes the atmosphere:

> In those days the common obsession that gripped our entire leadership was with the idea of becoming a 'civilised state'. The issue of being patronized or humbled did not arise. In fact giving advice to the Soviet Union was a pastime that had been positively encouraged by the highly sociable Shevardnadze, who in all his contacts with the West seemed more ready to be polite and accommodating than to stand firm.[3]

Pankin, however, proved to be only a temporary appointment, and although he fought to defend the Soviet MFA and modified some of the cuts imposed on its personnel, he was accepted neither by the Soviet foreign policy establishment nor by the emerging Russian MFA. The Soviet MFA began to wither away, despite attempts to 'democratise' its ruling collegium and its reorganisation into a Ministry of External Relations after merger with the Ministry of Foreign Trade. The reappointment of Shevardnadze on 19 November 1991 as Minister of External Relations represented Gorbachev's last desperate attempt to restore his crumbling authority.

Conflicts between the USSR and Russia were provoked not only by institutional rivalries but also over policy issues. Russia influenced the decision in September 1991 to remove the Soviet training brigade from Cuba, the decision to halt arms sales to Afghanistan on 13 September, and the restoration of diplomatic relations with Israel on 24 October 1991, twenty-four years after they had been broken off after the Six Day War of June 1967. Yeltsin's state visit to Germany, hitherto Gorbachev's keenest supporter, in November 1991 sought to secure economic assistance for Russia's own promised reforms, and at the same time was a clear signal that Russia had returned to the international community as a nation in its own right.

By the end of the year, Russia had swallowed up the Soviet state. On 18 December 1991, Yeltsin brought the Soviet diplomatic service under Russian control, and on 22 December the Soviet foreign and defence ministries were abolished. The Soviet Ministry of External Relations was merged with Russia's, and Shevardnadze once again left political office until he entered the political fray in his native Georgia, where he became president of the independent republic. Yeltsin placed himself at the head of the Russian MFA, and Burbulis took over routine operations.[4] Russia inherited the mantle of responsibility and sought international recognition for its new role. Russia was recognised as the 'continuer' state to the USSR, taking over responsibility for Soviet treaties and obligations, and above all for the Soviet strategic arsenal (see Chapter 17). Russia became the residual legatee of all the authority that was not devolved to the other republics. A vivid manifestation of Russia's dissolution in the Union was that, whereas Ukraine and Belorussia as well as the USSR took seats in the UN as founding members (according to a deal agreed with Stalin in 1945), Russia had been left firmly in the cold. Now Russia took over the USSR's seat as one of the five permanent members of the UN Security Council, giving it a right of veto.

The 'romantic' phase: January 1992–February 1993

Freed from the burden of the Union, Russia re-entered the world stage and by January 1992 had already been recognised by 131 states. Addressing the Russian MFA on 27 October 1991, Yeltsin set two main aims for Russian policy: to secure favourable external conditions for domestic political and economic reforms; and to overcome the legacy of the Cold War and to dismantle confrontational structures.[5] Both policies were laced with ambiguities: To what degree would economics (reform at home and global integration) be placed above national interests, however defined? How would this Atlanticist orientation be compatible with Russia's great power status? Why was nothing said about forging a new relationship with the former Soviet states? Questions such as these have led to this period of Russian foreign policy being dubbed 'romantic', allegedly excessively pro-Western at the expense of Russia's own interests and at the price of the neglect of its own 'backyard' in the CIS.

National-patriots, centrists and democratic statists alike were to varying degrees sceptical about the viability of the Soviet successor states, and insisted that Russia should direct its policy far more actively towards them. Post-communist Russian nation-building was profoundly influenced by the problem of the 25 million Russians (however defined) who had suddenly found themselves 'abroad', and the claimed defence of their rights and status permeated domestic politics. The Russian leadership were hesitant to adopt ethnicity as a factor in inter-state relations and thus allegedly abandoned their compatriots abroad; by the same token the sanctity of the new international borders and the sovereignty of the new states was acknowledged. This did not, however, prevent the blurring of the distinction between domestic and foreign policy when discussing relations with the former Soviet states, especially when Russian strategic interests were concerned. The widespread use of the term *blizhnee zarubezh'e* (near abroad) for the former Soviet republics suggested that these countries were somehow in a different category from genuinely foreign countries.

Kozyrev noted that 'the second Russian Revolution unfolded in a favorable foreign policy setting',[6] and proceeded on the assumption that military force was no longer relevant as an instrument of policy. This view was immediately contradicted by the dominant role that the Russian military played in shaping policy in the near abroad as the foreign ministry all but abdicated responsibility in the area. Kozyrev on several occasions condemned the military and the 'party of war'.[7] With the onset of a deep Western economic recession in the early 1990s and Germany's preoccupation with absorbing its new eastern territories, the international environment deteriorated. Western funds became more limited, and in any case the bulk went to the 'old' Eastern Europe (above all Hungary, Poland and the Czech Republic). Whether justified or not, there was a palpable sense of disappointment in Russia as early hopes of a rapid transformation with Western help evaporated. This period has been dubbed 'romantic' but it might better be characterised as idealistic, in the sense that it sought indeed to base policy on a set of universal ideals. Soviet ideology had given way to a democratic idealism, but structurally it could be argued that policy remained abstracted from the realitities of Russia's new position and challenges.

The reassertion phase: March 1993–December 1995

Post-communist Russian foreign policy is marked by continuity in strategic goals, but a turning point in tone and to a lesser degree in substance took place towards the end of 1992 and into early 1993. The opposition condemned Kozyrev's alleged servility and 'romantic' obsession with the West and his failure to formulate an effective policy towards the former Soviet republics. As far as the national-patriots and centrists were concerned, allegiance to the principles of a cosmopolitan liberal universalism threatened Russia's very existence as a state. Russian policy began explicitly to assert a hegemonic concept of its 'vital national interests' in the near abroad, coupled with a reassertion of Russia's great power status in the world at large. It was at this time, Pavel Baev notes, that 'geopolitics successfully replaced communist ideology as the conceptual basis for Russia's foreign policy'.[8] This brought the concept of *realpolitik* firmly back into the lexicon of foreign-policy discourse, displacing the idealistic universalism of the Gorbachev years. Russia had become a post-imperial state, but this did not mean that it had no interests to defend.

Already in March 1992, Stankevich and other proponents of an active post-imperial Russian foreign policy sponsored a Russian Monroe Doctrine, defining the whole area of the former Soviet Union as one vital to Russian national interests.[9] This approach was further developed in August 1992 in the first 'Strategy for Russia' report of the Council for Foreign and Defence Policy (CFDP), established by Sergei Karaganov, the deputy director of the Institute of Europe. The document argued that Russia's interests were not necessarily the same as the West's, and, indeed, that the gap between the two would probably increase; and as a corollary, the focus of Russian policy should shift from the West to the near abroad from whence the main challenges to Russian security would come. Thus, the document advocated an 'enlightened post-imperial course' that could balance the relationship with the West and Russia's concerns in the near abroad.[10] In a speech to the Civic

Union conference on 28 February 1993, Yeltsin for the first time made explicit Russia's claim to have a 'vital interest in the cessation of all armed conflicts on the territory of the former USSR', and appealed to the UN 'to grant Russia special powers as the guarantor of peace and stability in this region'.[11] In 1993, the new line was formalised in the 'Foreign Policy Concept' drafted by the Security Council, which once again declared Russia to be the guarantor of stability in the former Soviet Union. While the international community was reluctant to endorse Russia's special role, it was unwilling to intervene itself and thus *de facto* Russia was granted a free hand to impose its own order in the post-Soviet space – with the important exception of the Baltic states.

Kozyrev's own position evolved, with his enemies accusing him of a chameleon-like opportunism to maintain his post, usually involving uncritical support for Yeltsin. Kozyrev sought to combine two principles that according to some were mutually exclusive. On the one hand, he sought to 'guarantee the rights of citizens and the dynamic socio-economic development of society'; on the other, he insisted that Russia was 'a normal great power, achieving its interests not through confrontation but through co-operation'.[12] By late 1993, Kozyrev had adopted a more sharply defined empire-saving strategy, insisting that Russia had the right to intervene to prevent the country 'losing geopolitical positions that took centuries to achieve'.[13] Alarmed by the apparent appeal of Zhirinovskii's nationalistic rhetoric in the December 1993 elections, much of the Russian political elite incorporated some of his ideas into their own programmes. The attempt to make Russia a democracy *and* a great power became the central principle of Russian policy from early 1993, but these aims (typical of the essential ambiguity characteristic of Russian policy) were not entirely compatible. As far as Kozyrev was concerned, Russia could be a democratic post-Cold War great power pursuing a non-ideological definition of national interests that might sometimes entail elements of competition with the West. This tough approach was vividly manifested in Kozyrev's refusal in November 1994 to sign documents already agreed with Nato concerning the Partnership for Peace (PfP) programme in Brussels. Attempts by the West to de-legitimate the pursuit of Russia's 'normal' great power interests by forever raising the spectre of a revival of the Cold War, according to Yeltsin a month later at the Budapest summit of the OSCE in December 1994, threatened precisely to lead to the emergence of a 'cold peace'.[14] It was at this time that Kozyrev left the Russia's Choice faction in the Duma when they condemned the war in Chechnya. Kozyrev became a proponent of the reconstituted ideology of power, but this did not mean the abandonment of all of his earlier views and he remained committed to a viable relationship with the West. Despite his partial conversion to a great-power ideology, his critics continued to characterise his foreign policy as confused and amateur.[15]

Kozyrev's new-found statism not only undermined his credibility as a liberal but also damaged his ability to function as foreign minister. At home his stand was widely interpreted as yet another manœuvre to stay in power, while abroad his cred-ibility, already undermined by the indeterminacy of Russian policy in the Bosnian war (1992–5), imbued Russia's foreign policy with a damaging unpredictability.[16] National-patriots' and neo-communists' denunciations were roused to fever pitch by his weak response to the threat of Nato expansion and the bombing of Serb positions in Bosnia in August 1995. Despite his alignment with 'pragmatic national-ists' Kozyrev remained committed to a constructive relationship with the West, refusing to accept that the latter remained the threat it had been during the Cold War. In the December 1995 elections, Kozyrev retained his single-member seat in Murmansk; faced with the choice of leaving the foreign ministry or giving up his seat, he chose the former and on 5 January 1996 resigned. Thus, a distinctive era in Russian foreign policy came to an end.

The new pragmatism: January 1996–1999

His replacement as foreign minister was the head of the Foreign Intelligence Service, Yevgenii Primakov. A specialist on Middle Eastern affairs, Primakov had risen high in the former regime, holding senior positions in the academic world and becoming a candidate member of the Politburo. He had been Gorbachev's envoy to the Gulf in 1990–1 charged with averting war with Iraq. Although foreign policy is a presidential prerogative, the change of ministers inevitably changed the tone and modified the substance of policy. While seeking to maintain good relations with the West, Russia would now reassert its position in China, the Far East and with its traditional allies in the Middle East. A pragmatic politician, Primakov nevertheless took a substantive view of Russia's national interests and insisted that the country was a great power.[17] His four priority tasks for Russian foreign policy were to create the external conditions to strengthen Russia's territorial integrity; to support inte-grative tendencies within the CIS; to stabilise regional conflicts (above all in the former USSR and Yugoslavia); and to prevent the spread of weapons of mass destruction.[18] Primakov had been highly critical of the West, and thus his appoint-ment was welcomed by the communists and nationalists in the Duma.

As prime minister between September 1998 and May 1999, Primakov remained a guiding influence on foreign policy, although the new foreign minister, Igor Ivanov, had views of his own. During the Kosovo crisis of 1999, Ivanov was willing to employ some harsh anti-Western rhetoric, yet was careful not to back Russia into a corner. While expressing support for the Serbs in general and Milosevic in partic-ular, the Russian leadership retained its freedom of manœuvre and did little to help Milosevic, refusing to commit itself militarily, or even materially. Russian foreign-policy pragmatism remained even after Primakov's forced retirement from government.

The new realism: 2000–

On coming to power Putin retained Ivanov as foreign minister, yet an appreciable change took place in foreign policy. Although elements of Primakovian 'pragma-tism' remained, policy now lacked the groundless assurance that Russia was a great power, and that it was the West's misfortune not to recognise this. Following a meeting of the Security Council on 24 March 2000 devoted to Russia's new Foreign Policy Concept, Ivanov commented that the document was 'more realistic' than its 1993 predecessor.[19] The Concept was adopted on 28 June 2000 and combined a commitment to international integration with assertions about Russia's great power status.[20] Although almost all the elements were there before, Putin's foreign policy was marked by a more sober appreciation of reality and of Russia's real as opposed to idealised interpretations of its interests. In a keynote speech to the MFA on 26 January 2001, Putin urged that Russian diplomacy had to focus more on promoting the country's economic interests abroad, while at the same time improving its image.[21] The new realism was no less ambitious in its own evaluation of Russia's role, but was marked by a realisation that the means were lacking to maintain what was considered Russia's rightful place in the world. Putin stressed the need to rebuild the domestic economy, while at the same time sought to achieve by diplomacy what was lacking materially. He engaged in a round of high-profile visits (some thirty in his first year as president) as he took the management of foreign affairs into his own hands. However, the tangible benefits of his globe-trotting appeared slender, and ultimately only accentuated not Russia's global role but its difficulty in sustaining that role.

The phases discussed above were marked by excesses: in asserting Russian autonomy the first undermined the viability of the USSR; the second precipitated the collapse of the USSR by reducing Gorbachev to little more than a figurehead; the third exaggerated dependence on the West; the fourth in reaction failed to build a stable and predictable relationship with the world at large; the fifth endangered the very real achievements of Kozyrev's foreign policy in normalising relations with the world at large; while the sixth was based on the dangerous illusion that economic weakness could be compensated by diplomatic virtuosity.

The structure of policy-making

Soviet diplomacy had traditionally had two faces: one focused on the professional diplomats in the Soviet MFA, characterised by traditional expertise in negotiation techniques, conflict management and the like; the other, inspired by the residual internationalism of the socialist system, was organised by the Communist Party's International and other departments. Shevardnadze had limited the prerogatives of the latter and by the end of *perestroika* foreign policy had firmly shifted from the Party to the state and was concentrated in the hands of the specialists in the Soviet MFA. Already by August 1991, the Party organisation had been abolished in the Russian MFA, and the merging of the Russian and Soviet MFAs in late 1991 was accompanied by the 'de-ideologisation' of the new ministry. This was designed above all to improve its professionalism and to ensure that the ministry worked to defend Russia's national-state interests. The cause of international revolution was officially pronounced dead.

The Russian MFA inherited the buildings and diplomatic staff from the old regime. Kozyrev moved into the luxurious offices in the foreign ministry building on Smolensk Boulevard and set about rebuilding the Russian diplomatic service. Up to 1991, about two-thirds of Soviet embassy staff abroad were also on the payroll of the KGB.[22] The Russian MFA was restructured to reflect the new priorities of foreign policy. The traditional confused system of administrations (*upravleniya*) and sections (*otdely*) was replaced by a more ordered system. Thirteen departments (*departamenty*), overseen by deputy ministers, nine functional administrations (*upravleniya*) and three services (*otdely*) were initially established. The old regional administrations were transformed into seven departments: Europe, North

America, Central and South America, Africa, the Near East, the Asia-Pacific region, and South West Asia. There were also departments for International Organisations and Global Problems of International Humanitarian Assistance, and Cultural Co-operation. The departments dealing with information and the press were significantly upgraded. Of particular significance was the creation in April–May 1992 of a department for relations with CIS countries, a belated recognition of the importance of this area of what had now become foreign policy.

In February 1992, Yeltsin subordinated the 'power' and 'political' ministries to the presidency, bringing the MFA and the ministries of defence, internal affairs, security, justice and some others firmly under his control.[23] Numerous presidential agencies and advisory groups were spawned to formulate the main lines of foreign and security policy, and to supervise the current work of the ministries, reducing the foreign ministry to not much more than a specialist executive agency. Even though Yeltsin in November 1992 made the MFA responsible for co-ordinating Russia's foreign policy, confusion remained as individuals and institutions, above all the Supreme Soviet under Khasbulatov, sought to pursue their own foreign-policy agendas. Under Putin elements of this confusion remained as the Security Council took on an enhanced role, while the MFA (in the eyes of critics) appeared to become little more than a glorified travel agency organising Putin's many trips abroad.

The adoption of the 1993 constitution confirmed the president's pre-eminent role. Article 80.3 baldly states that the president 'determines the basic guidelines of the state's domestic and foreign policy', Article 80.4 stipulates that he or she 'represents the Russian Federation within the country and in international relations', and Article 86 specifies that the president 'exercises leadership of the foreign policy of the Russian Federation' (Art. 86a), conducts negotiations, signs international treaties (Art. 86b) and instruments of ratification (Art. 86c), and accepts letters of diplomatic accreditation (Art. 86d). The president decides membership of the Security Council, chairs its sessions and is the final arbiter of Russia's military doctrine. The president, in consultation with parliament, nominates ambassadors, and has the right to appoint and dismiss members of the government, including those responsible for foreign policy. The government's powers over foreign policy are limited, authorised only to implement measures for 'the realisation of the foreign policy of the Russian Federation' (Art. 114.1e). In other words, it is intended to do little more than to implement policies coming from the presidency. The work of the MFA in the new conditions was formulated by a presidential statute of 14 March 1995, subordinating it to the president but delegating to it 'the development of the general strategy for Russian foreign policy'.[24]

This was reflected in the reduced foreign-policy role assigned to parliament. Formally, the State Duma's functions are restricted to approving or rejecting international treaties (Art. 106d), while the Federation Council authorises the use of Russian troops abroad (Art. 102.1d). Both issues could prove controversial. Parliament's foreign-policy role, however, is broader than the above would suggest. Above all, the committee system ensures that foreign-policy issues remain firmly within the purview of deputies. The FC's committees for foreign affairs, CIS affairs, and security and defence policy are complemented by the Duma committees for foreign affairs, defence, security, CIS affairs and links with compatriots. The anti-

Western majority in the Fifth Duma, and even more in the Sixth, forced foreign policy to adopt the language of 'struggle' between Russian and Western interests. The resulting espousal of Russia as a 'great power' meant that 'ideological dogma had priority over common sense'.[25] With a supportive majority in the Seventh Duma, the president's foreign-policy initiatives were now secured by a solid legislative base.

Many other organisations play their part in the foreign-policy process. In addition to the domestic security agencies and the Foreign Intelligence Service, the Security Council at various times has taken an active foreign-policy role. The SC under Sergei Ivanov became one of Putin's main institutional supports, until Ivanov moved on to become defence minister, at which point the SC once again went into decline. With the creation of the Russian Ministry of Defence in May 1992, older Soviet patterns of rivalry between the foreign and defence ministries re-emerged. Kozyrev insisted on the primacy of the foreign ministry, and warned (unsuccessfully) against the military becoming an autonomous force in areas such Transdniester.[26] On several occasions, as in Abkhazia and elsewhere, it appeared that Russia had two foreign policies, an official presidential one and another pursued by the military. Yeltsin's debt to the military following the October events only increased their scope for independent initiatives.

The country was marked by the proliferation of non-governmental 'think tanks', lobbying pressure groups, pseudo-academic research institutes established by retired or dismissed politicians, and money-making ventures launched by institutes of the Academy of Sciences to augment the meagre funds available from the state. By far the most important, however, was the CFDP, founded in June 1992 'as a public organisation of politicians, entrepreneurs, civil servants, media figures and academics whose purpose is to support the development and implementation of strategic conceptions for the development of Russia, its foreign and defence policies'.[27] In the words of its director, Karaganov, its task was to co-ordinate the contending proposals to create 'a stable political centre in the country'.[28] Membership ranged across the political spectrum, encompassing academics, Duma deputies and politicians. Its first report (noted above), called 'A Strategy for Russia',[29] strongly influenced the evolving debate over Russia's foreign policy and place in the world, while its second report in May 1994 had even greater resonance (see below).[30]

In contrast to the Soviet era, and indeed even under Gorbachev, policy-making was now a much more open and pluralistic process. Some regional and republican leaders (in particular Tatarstan) also sought to sustain foreign-policy initiatives, but the scope for this was limited by the Federal Treaty of 31 March 1992, which unequivocally reserved to the federal government responsibility for foreign policy, and by the 1993 constitution (although as we saw in Chapter 10, this did not stop some regions trying to develop autonomous foreign policies of their own). The MFA in December 1994 established a Consultative Council of Russian Federation Subjects on International and Foreign Economic Relations to co-ordinate local initiatives. Primakov sought to curb international freelancing by regional elites. Institutions and social forces sought to influence policy through lobbying, press campaigns and other normal features of pluralistic politics. However, the politicisation of foreign policy had some negative consequences as crude representations of complex foreign-policy decisions became part of domestic political struggles, adding yet another layer of unpredictability to Russian foreign policy. Foreign and security policy became part of an intensive public debate reflected in the print and electronic media. The emergence of active domestic constituencies concerned with foreign policy limited the range of options available to the leadership. Foreign policy became the object of domestic political conflict, further undermining the coherence and consistency of Russian foreign policies.

Despite the new pluralism, post-communist Russia reproduced aspects of Soviet, if not Tsarist, patterns of foreign policy-making. Once again the government was reduced to executing policies taken by the Tsar, Politburo or president, with its functions largely focused on economic issues. Decision-making in the Soviet system might have been cumbersome, with foreign-policy decisions co-ordinated between the relevant ministries, Central Committee departments and the KGB, but at least policy was marked by consistency. Russian policy, however, was characterised by lack of co-ordination and often contradictory purposes. In its second policy statement 'A Strategy for Russia', the CFDP was bitterly critical of the fragmentation of foreign policy-making:

> None, even the most elementary strategy for the defence and realisation of the national interests of the country, can be implemented under the present condition of the institutions intended to formulate and implement it....Each official enjoys the freedom to have his own policy. This situation not only weakens the position of the country but also disgraces it. This is one of the most difficult challenges for Russian foreign policy.[31]

Although foreign-policy prerogatives were concentrated in the hands of the presidency, the presidential apparatus itself was divided into competing factions seeking to influence Yeltsin.[32] The presidential system included a number of analytical centres and presidential assistants for foreign policy. Whatever their merits, these advisers could not substitute for a solid bureaucratic structure combining expertise with the ability to control decision-making and implementation. The 'presidential' foreign-policy structure could not effectively replace the role of the MFA and other ministries in the formulation and implementation of policy. The foreign, defence and intelligence ministries represented concentrations of information, expertise and experience, and with their own policy agendas. Thus, the erratic jerks in Russian foreign policy reflected not only conceptual shifts but changes in the relative weight of various governmental agencies.

The ambiguities that we have identified in policy were exacerbated by the fragmentation of the policy process itself. It often appeared that Russia was pursuing several different policies simultaneously. On the one hand, the official line sought integration into the Western system on the basis of a commitment to 'Western values', but at the same time the Ministry of Defence and other security agencies appeared to pursue an independent 'neo-imperial' line in the near abroad and at home. Thus, Russia appeared to have one foreign policy run by civilians, what Furman called the 'dinner jacket policy', and another conducted by the military, dubbed by him the 'camouflage suit policy', as seen in Georgia (Abkhazia), Moldova (Transdniester) and Tajikistan.[33] These contradictions, and the insecurity that they generated, in part explain the enthusiasm with which Russia's Western neighbours sought membership in Nato. Russia's foreign policy was marked by a gulf between rhetoric and capacity, reflecting the struggle between national-patriots and internationalists at the heart of policy-making. The great-power policy demonstrated that Russian thinking remained rooted in the past and that it had only been partially demilitarised. As Eggert puts it, 'The Russian military bureaucracy, which is not controlled by civil society and has a vague notion of the outer world, is incompatible with the Western one, which is subordinated to a civil society and is well educated'. In its relations with the 'near abroad', too, Russian policy was coloured by the belief that the independence of countries like Ukraine was only a temporary phenomenon, provoking the West to view Kiev as a counter-balance to Russia and inhibiting the establishment of normal relations with Ukraine. While focusing its attention on minor issues, Russian foreign policy often neglected problems of primary importance: 'Instead of pretending to be a great power, Russia should rather open its frontiers to ideas and capital.'[34] The development of an aggressive post-democratic foreign policy could not be excluded. Russia is still far from being a 'normal' great power.

The debate over foreign policy

By late 1991, Russia had lost much of the territory for which it had fought for centuries. Peter the Great's defeat of the Swedes at Poltava in 1709 gave Russia access to the Baltic ports, and in particular Riga. Catherine the Great's defeat of the Ottoman Turks gave Russia access to the ports of the Black Sea, above all Sevastopol in the Crimea. Victory in the Second World War gave the USSR an extended security zone reaching as far as Berlin. Russia's military-strategic expansion now not only ended but collapsed, and the 'gathering of the lands' went into reverse as the rump Russian state in the west was reduced to not much more than Muscovy under Ivan the Terrible in the sixteenth century. From an imperial point of view, the collapse of communism and the disintegration of the USSR was a defeat for Russia. It lost its warm-water ports in the Baltic republics, and now had to rely on Kaliningrad, separated from Russia by Belarus and Lithuania, St Petersburg, not really a natural harbour, and the ice-bound ports of Murmansk and Arkhangel. The retreat from the Baltic and the Black Sea pushed Russia eastwards away from Europe and the Middle East, and back into the Eurasian heartlands. It is against this background that the debate over Russian foreign policy unfolded.

Ideology and interests

Empires have fallen before, but never one armed with nuclear weapons. While a strong Soviet Union had been a threat to the rest of the world, a weak Russia was equally dangerous because of the damage it could do itself and its neighbours. It has indeed been argued that Russian foreign policy took on the characteristics of the 'tyranny of the weak', threatening economic and military anarchy if it did not receive substantial assistance from the West and was not accepted into global economic structures.[35] From the Russian perspective, however, things looked very different. Sergei Rogov, the Deputy Director of the Institute of the USA and

Canada, noted that 'Today the country has no enemies, but neither does it have reliable allies capable of and prepared to render support in trying times.'[36] As far as he was concerned, Russia had failed to achieve a 'civilised' divorce with the former Soviet states, giving rise to a zone of instability around Russia, and neither had it been able to defend its status as a great power.

From 1990, a separate Russian foreign policy emerged, but as time passed it appeared that more and more elements were borrowed not only from the Soviet Union but also from the pre-revolutionary era. The question of continuity was posed in ever sharper forms as foreign policy evolved away from the so-called 'liberal universalism' of the early period towards a more vigorous assertion of Russian great-power national interests. There was no consensus, however, on what precisely constituted Russia's national security and other interests. The liberals saw them as lying in close ties with the West and peace with its neighbours; the centrist groupings sought greater reliance on indigenous economic and military resources to buttress a rather broader vision of Russia as a great power; the national-patriots envisioned Russia as a type of superpower in regard to its neighbours and in the world at large, to be achieved by restoring aspects of the old administrative command system; the neo-communists more explicitly sought to re-establish the Soviet system and the Soviet geopolitical space; while Zhirinovskii's crude nationalism promised easy solutions to a disappointed people but threatened Russia's neighbours and provoked once again the image of Russia, whether communist or not, as the permanent enemy. Each vision of Russia's national security interests reflected profound differences in thinking about what it means to be a Russian and what Russia itself means. As Ivanov noted, 'The rethinking and definition of the country's national interests continued throughout the 1990s.'[37]An instability lay at the heart of Russian foreign policy as long as no new orthodoxy could emerge or be imposed.

Post-communist Russian foreign policy is predicated on a post-imperial and democratic relationship with the world at large and with the successor states, while asserting its proper status. However, what were Russia's national interests, and what form would their espousal take in the international system? Would Russian foreign policy indeed become something new or would traditional great power and Russian imperial traditions reassert themselves? Gorbachev's foreign policy, adroitly managed by Shevardnadze, was conducted within the framework of what was called the New Political Thinking (NPT). Russian foreign policy continued some of its concerns, such as ending political and military divisions, reintegration into the world community and the demilitarisation of foreign policy, but at the same time qualitatively new issues emerged. It no longer made sense to talk of the de-ideologisation of foreign policy, of a world divided into 'two camps', however interdependent, or of the conflict between the social systems of capitalism and socialism; but at the same time the idea of 'multipolarity' sought to impose new lines of division.

Now, more than ever before, there was a blurred distinction between domestic and 'foreign' policy. Foreign policy was a field over which domestic politics was fought, but while various interests sought to exert their influence policy remained firmly in the hands of the president and his ministers. The challenge now was to redefine Russian national interest in the new geopolitical circumstances of the post-Cold War world and the disintegration of the USSR. However, before national interest could be established, the nature of Russia itself had to be defined. The interests of a national democratic state would be very different from a neo-imperial Russia, and it would hardly be appropriate to talk of the national interests of a Russia dissolving once again into the principalities of the fourteenth and fifteenth centuries. Did Russia have constant geostrategic, political or ideological interests, and what social groups could mould a new Russian national interest?[38] Pre-revolutionary imperial messianism, whereby Russia had not only a military but also a spiritual mission to bring enlightenment to neighbouring peoples and the world, and the Soviet Union's self-definition as the harbinger of international socialism, were repudiated. Russia's national identity began to be reformulated as a state rather than as an empire. However, even some of those who accepted the birth of a nation insisted on the retention of Russian universal values, threatened allegedly by the rush to embrace the West, and that Russia retained a 'mission' if not a messianic purpose.[39] The debate in essence was over a new ideology of foreign policy for Russia.

A distinction should be drawn between national and state interests, and indeed national interests may well be opposed to those of the state.[40] In contemporary foreign policy, it is state interests that predominate over those of the nation, yet in post-communist countries the distinction remained blurred. Estonian nationalists and extreme Russian patriots sought to identify the interests of the state with those of a particular national group. Talk of the 'national interest' in a multinational state could be misleading and some suggested that the term 'fundamental interests' might be more appropriate.[41] Mythical ideas of the homogeneity of national interests overlook the conflicting interests of contemporary civil society, and indeed the ability of nationalists and communists to subsume conflicting social interests into a single plane of national struggle testifies to the relative under-development of civil society in Russia. Pozdnyakov goes so far as to argue that national interest and state interest are identical.[42]

At the centre of the debate over Russian foreign policy was the attempt to define Russia's relationship with Western civilisation and strategic concerns. Failure to deal with this question in 1917 led to the fall of the Provisional Government. Russia's subservience to the West, above all in honouring its commitments in the Great War, allowed it to be pressured by the French into launching the disastrous Galician offensive in June 1917. The national-patriots from 1991 accused Yeltsin's government, too, of selling Russia's interests short by kowtowing to the West, begging for assistance and alienating Russian lands and islands. A new Russian isolationism emerged, warning against 'over-Westernisation' and the 'Americanisation' of foreign policy. They stressed the need for native (*samobytnyi*) traditions and questioned the need for Russia's 'return' to Europe and reintegration into the world economy. The dominant centrist view, however, can be formulated as 'the road to our future passes through the West but does not stop there': joining the world but on Russia's terms, not as a supplicant but as an equal, retaining Russia's own identity and defending its interests.

Eurasianism and the world

Opinion is divided over whether Russia constitutes a separate civilisation or whether it is no more than a variant of 'world civilisation', usually considered synonymous with the West. The emergence of a 'new Eastern Europe' of Ukraine and Belarus separating Russia from the rest of Europe stimulated the 'Eurasian' tradition in Russian philosophy, and indeed the tension in Russian national identity can be interpreted in the light of a struggle between Atlanticists and Eurasianists.[43] The latter shared Dostoevsky's view that Russia should concern itself with dominance in Asia rather than dreams of European integration: 'In Europe we are hangers-on and slaves, but in Asia we walk as masters.' The old debate resurfaced between the Westernisers, oriented towards Western values and Russia's integration into European processes, and the Slavophiles, stressing Russia's native traditions and distinct culture. Tibor Szamuely argues that before the revolution and again today Russian thinkers

> would not have accepted the idea of the Russian past having been just a part of a single, uniform, homogenized European experience....Whether they gloried in this difference and strove to perpetuate it, like the Slavophiles, or yearned for a decisive break with tradition, like the 'Westernisers', all alike recognised that Russia had merely been in Europe, but not of it.[44]

Likhachev takes issue with Szamuely's view that Russia is the only European country that 'owed virtually nothing to the common cultural and spiritual heritage of the West'.[45] He insists that Russia was part of European development, owing its religion and much of its culture to Orthodox Christianity and borrowing early concepts of statehood from the Scandinavians.[46]

Eurasianists argue that Russia is not part of European civilisation but represents a separate and distinct civilisation of its own, acting as the 'balance holder' between Europe and Asia.[47] They deny the need for Russia to integrate into Europe, civilisationally part of which, they argue, it had never been.[48] The Eurasianists revived the geopolitical school of thinking, developed by Halford Mackinder in the early part of the century, according to which Russia encompasses most of the 'geographical pivot of history', acting as the balance holder in the World Island.[49] As far as they were concerned, Russia was a bridge between Western and Eastern civilisations. The modern Eurasianists, drawing on the thinking of their predecessors in emigration of the early 1920s, question uncritical pro-Westernism and advocate a reorientation of policy towards the countries of the former Soviet Union. Stalinist xenophobia, in their view, had given way to a condition that Krizhanich had already diagnosed in Russia three centuries earlier. 'Xenomania (*chuzhbesie* in our language) is an obsessive love of foreign people.'[50] Sergei Goncharov, a researcher at the Far East Institute, noted that

> today, we are moving away from total confrontation with the West toward an equally total fraternisation. In the process, we sometimes overstep the bounds of reason in our desire for alliance....The idea of the primacy of human rights is being turned into an absolute as zealously as the earlier concept of 'class interests' was.

He advocated a policy of 'rational egoism' that placed the success of domestic reforms over any other considerations, even though this might lead to measures that displeased the West.[51] Eurasianism thus represented the moderate face of the Russian rejection of the West.

Of all the Slavophiles Peter Chaadayev was the most pro-European, a sympathy accompanied by a denigration of Russia. In his first *Philosophical Letter* he wrote 'We do not belong to any of the great families of humanity, to either the West or the East, and have no traditions of either. We exist outside time.'[52] It was this attempt to emulate the West by vilifying Russia that so incensed sections of society following the fall of communism. Pozdnyakov, one of the leading exponents of Eurasianism, pointed out that no sooner had the socialist utopia died out than a host of new ones sprang up to replace it, including '*mondialiste* Westernisers whom Russian national traditions tell nothing whatever – are pushing Russia into Europe', and he insisted that 'it would be very wrong and, in fact, dangerous to forget that Russia's history, the history of the formation of our society and state, differs *entirely* from that of Western Europe'.[53]

The debate over Eurasianism is essentially a debate over paths of development and the principles of political and economic reform. Zagorskii stresses, however, that the concept of the West is no longer confined to Europe or America but includes Japan, South Korea and other newly industrialised countries, none of whom had renounced their own civilisations but had become part of the synthesis of global civilisation. The concept of Russia as a bridge is therefore meaningless, since links between Germany and Japan could quite happily by-pass Russia. Eurasianism is a bridge leading nowhere.[54] The debate, however, clearly signalled, as Mark Frankland has observed, 'that the natural relationship between Russia and Europe is more likely one of rivalry than of unbroken cooperation'.[55]

Drawing the line

Russia's attempt to formulate a new international doctrine took place in a relatively benign international environment, with no direct threats to its integrity and no global threat of the sort that had derailed the democracies in the 1930s.[56] This did not, however, prevent the emergence of a movement in both domestic and foreign policy challenging the liberal-democratic view dominant in the first post-communist period that was firmly oriented towards the West and the global institutions of the post-war world. This provided fuel for those who argue against the 'democratic peace' hypothesis,[57] and in particular those, like Jack Snyder, who suggest that democratising states pose a threat to peace.[58]

Russian foreign policy developed against the background of a debate over the structure of international relations itself in the late twentieth century. The democrats espoused a normative approach, insisting that ethical and moral considerations had an important part to play in international affairs. They were attracted by the concept of world society, and sought to integrate Russia into the existing system of international institutions. The national-patriots held to a more traditional view, stressing the primacy of the national interest in a 'realist' world in which foreign policy was determined by the power of states. The neo-communists incorporated patriotic themes into a programme that sought not only to reconstitute the Soviet Union but to reassert its superpower status. The realities of power rather than the pursuit of justice dominated the thinking of the centrists. But whose power? The realist pursuit of alleged national interests in an international system dominated by nation-states now had to be tempered by a world covered by a multitude of international non-governmental and governmental international organisations. The unravelling of Stalin's 'hyper-realist' foreign policy ultimately led to the collapse of the USSR as the Baltic and other forcibly incorporated republics took their revenge. The lesson appears clear: there is nothing more unrealistic than brute realism.

Russia was torn between remaining a *status quo* power or becoming a revisionist power. Russia had been the greatest loser of the territorial settlements of the Soviet years and was thus potentially a revisionist power. In addition, a type of 'Versailles syndrome' emerged whereby the democrats were alleged to have betrayed Russia's national interests in the exit from communism, above all in signing the Belovezh Accords that consigned the USSR to the dustbin of history. As with Britain earlier, the loss of empire is accompanied by the search for a new role.

The view that Russia should be a great power did not go unchallenged. The journalist Oleg Moroz argued that earlier attempts to become a superpower had given Russia nothing except futile wars in Korea, Vietnam and Afghanistan. He argued:

> It is time for us to give up our primitive habit of puffing up our cheeks and making a first-rank power of ourselves....Whether we want to or not, we are now forced to admit that by all criteria Russia is a second-rank power....In terms of importance, we should take our place somewhere between Egypt and Colombia, and sit there quietly.[59]

Not many were prepared to accept such a radically minimalist view of Russia's status, especially when armed with nuclear weapons. Under Primakov the concept of a multi-polar world was developed to symbolise the need to move away from the allegedly excessive unidirectional (American-centred) foreign policy of earlier years. Multi-polarity became the central concept of Putin's foreign policy and was expressed in the June 2000 Foreign Policy Concept. While stressing the need to extend co-operation with Nato, the document insisted that the alliance limited the security role of any other pan-European institution. The whole concept of multi-polarity, however, was ambiguous, looking for new principles of division in a world that was objectively unifying. Russia's share in global GNP in 2001 was 1.6 per cent and falling, and it lay in 62nd place in terms of per capita GNP. Was this a position from which to base its claims to represent a separate and distinctive pole in world politics?[60]

Russia and the world

Russia sought to find its place in the world at a time when, unfrozen from the Cold War, international relations is in an unprecedented state of flux. Above all, long-term processes have come to fruition whereby economic strength is a more accurate measurement of power than narrowly defined military power. Economic weakness undermined Russia's aspirations to become a great power. While Moscow was invited as a guest to G7 meetings and was later invited to become part of what became G8, in matters concerning the management of the global economy the group operated as 'seven-plus-one'. The financial collapse of August 1998 fundamentally weakened Russia's weight in international politics, although its own perception of its proper role did not commensurately diminish. The gulf between Russian aspirations and capabilities yawned ever larger, and would get wider if Russian economic power declined further. Russian foreign policy is determined by the tension between its ambition to remain a major regional and world power and its economic weakness. The ambition itself became the driving force for policy, but as long as the gulf remained between Russia's aspirations and capacities Russia's role in the world would remain characterised by 'essential ambiguity'.

Russia's foreign policy is constrained by geopolitical factors. The sheer size of Russia means that it is faced with a multiplicity of regional issues, and in certain respects it has as many foreign policies as it has neighbours. In particular, Russia was forced to define a new relationship not only with the world at large but also with the former members of the 'indissoluble' USSR (see Chapter 16). The emergence of fifteen independent republics onto the world stage ranks as an event of unparalleled historical importance, shifting the balance of power on the Eurasian landmass and altering the global system of international relations. The very concept of the 'near abroad', as noted, suggested some sort of intermediate status between sovereign statehood and traditional dependence. Russia was linked by centuries of political and human contacts with these new states but now had to find new forms of interaction. We will examine Russia's relations with the former Soviet states in the following chapter, while here we will look at some of the key issues in Russia's relations with the world at large.

The United States

The fall of Soviet communism made possible the global hegemony of the single remaining superpower, but at the same time it removed any over-riding purpose to this predominance. The Soviet MFA had long been torn between 'Americanist' and 'Europeanist' tendencies, and while during *perestroika* European policy had been revived the concentration on the United States in the old game of superpower politics remained. Reflecting the shrinkage in Russia's global weight, it was only natural that Russia focused more on the European aspects of its foreign policy, although care was taken not to neglect other spheres and the relationship with the United States remained crucial. The meeting in Vancouver in April 1992 between Yeltsin and Clinton was the first ever 'superpower' summit devoted not to overcoming confrontation but to economic issues. Yeltsin's visit to Washington in June 1992 dispelled the lingering reservations that characterised Soviet–American relations even at their best and marked the confirmation of Russia's status as a partner in world affairs. In his address to Congress on 17 June, Yeltsin drew a thick line under the past, insisting that communism, 'which spread everywhere social strife and brutality, which instilled fear in humanity', had collapsed never to rise again. Yeltsin insisted that Russia had made 'its final choice in favour of a civilised way of life, common sense and the universal human heritage'. For good measure, he stressed that 'The freedom of America is now being upheld in Russia.'[61]

Points of tension, however, remained in Russia's relations with the United States. The lack of co-ordination between Russia's aggressive arms sales and foreign policy led on several occasions to conflict, as over the proposed sale of submarines and nuclear power technology to Iran and cryogenic engines to India. The economic depression in the final period of Bush senior's term in office and his weak leadership meant that the euphoria of the end of the Cold War was not translated into effective policies to assist the rehabilitation of Russia and other post-communist states. The Clinton presidency pursued a 'Russia first' policy, but this was not translated into much more than support for Yeltsin personally. The role of American assistance and support for Yeltsin's version of reform has been much criticised.[62] Plans to expand Nato to Eastern Europe (see Chapter 17), the war over Kosovo and American plans for (National) Missile Defence (NMD), which led to the American repudiation of the 1972 Anti-Ballistic Missile (ABM) treaty in December 2001, brought Russia's apparent national interests into confrontation with those of America. According to Georgii Arbatov:

> Towards the end of the Soviet Union there was virtually no anti-American sentiment in Russia. But then these rosy expectations changed into doubts, disappointment, and suspicion. What was actually inevitable has now become clear: that the political interests of Russia and America are different and rarely coincide in reality.[63]

Events in Iraq and Yugoslavia, combined with the eastward enlargement of Nato, appeared to place Russia and the West in opposed camps once again.

Europe and the EU

The primacy of superpower dialogue over specifically European policy towards Russia gradually faded. However, Europe itself was divided, with tensions between the French ambition to create a European presence on the world stage, German concerns about insecurity on its eastern borders, and Britain's insistence on the primacy of Nato and support for the expansion of the EU to CEE in the hope that 'widening' would undermine the 'deepening' of EU integration. The EU's concentration on deepening integration through the Maastricht process, a treaty that significantly raised the threshold of the *acquis communautaire* (the body of Union law), made it more difficult for the Eastern European countries to meet membership criteria and postponed their accession to the EU into the 2000s.

The European direction of Russian foreign policy was repeatedly stressed by the Yeltsin administration, but was only fitfully implemented. At a press conference in Paris on 17 April 1991, Yeltsin stressed that Russia could 'play a unique role as a bridge between Europe and Asia and that it can contribute towards extending the area of European co-operation, particularly in the economic field, from the Atlantic to the Pacific'.[64] Russia's economic weakness inhibited the development of this programme, but its openness to the international economy gradually bore tangible fruit. Russia's links with the EU were strengthened, but this was to be a long and hard road. Although Russia signed a Partnership and Co-operation Agreement (PCA) with the EU on 24 June 1994, it only came into effect in 1997 and would take many years for its potential to be fulfilled. Rather than imposing sanctions the West signalled its displeasure with the conduct of the Chechen war by putting pressure on the political elite by suspending moves towards Russian integration into Western institutions. The EU delayed the signature of a trade and co-operation agreement, while the Parliamentary Assembly of the Council of Europe suspended membership procedures.[65] The head of the Council of Europe, Daniel Tarschys, insisted that as long as Russia ignored 'basic rules and standards' of human rights it would be inappropriate for Russia to join.[66] However, following the elections of December 1995, Russian membership was approved on the grounds that 'integration is preferable to isolation'. Russia on 28 February 1996 became the 39th member of the Council of Europe.

A dramatic reorientation in Russia's trade patterns took place, shifting from Eastern to Western Europe, with the EU by 1993 becoming Russia's biggest export market. It was understood, however, that Russia's entry into the EU would not be considered in the immediate future, although it was not inconceivable. Kasyanov insisted that at some point Russia could become a member as part of its general effort to promote a common European space.[67] The *Common Strategy of the EU on Russia,* adopted at the Cologne summit in June 1999, was intended to guide EU policy-makers for an initial period of four years, although its implications would last far longer than that and the document was to be periodically reviewed by the European Council.[68] The *Common Strategy* identified four 'principal objectives' facing Russia:

- The 'consolidation of democracy, the rule of law, and public institutions', together with 'the emergence of civil society'.
- The 'integration of Russia into a common European economic and social space', which required the development in Russia of an 'operational market economy'.
- The third element was the establishment of 'co-operation to develop stability and security in Europe and beyond', based on the recognition that Russia and the EU had a common interest in achieving this.
- And finally, a number of issues were considered 'common challenges on the European continent', including a common energy policy, the management of resources, nuclear safety, environmental problems, organised crime, money-laundering, and trafficking in human beings and drugs.[69]

The Russian government formulated its own views on Russian–EU relations, in part as a response to the EU's *Common Strategy*, in the document *Medium Term Strategy for the Development of Relations Between the RF and the EU (2000–2010)*. As the EU's most important neighbour, there were a range of issues that required common management: minority problems, migration, border and customs issues, and perhaps above all the consequences of EU enlargement itself.[70]

Russia took a deliberately benign view of Europe, in part as a challenge to the near-permanent edge of rivalry and competing aspirations that characterised Russo-American relations. Russia was mostly positive about EU enlargement, while at the same time condemning Nato expansion (see Chapter 17). Policy towards what had formerly been known as 'Eastern' Europe was now subsumed into larger European policy, as indicated by the single department for Europe in the MFA. In 1989–90, these countries shrugged off their Sovietisation, and relations between them and Russia began on a new footing. Even as the USSR declined, Russia had been pursuing a distinct East European policy of its own marked by common democratic aspirations. Yeltsin's first official visit to the region was to Czechoslovakia in May 1991 in which he moved far beyond Gorbachev's 'regret' over the invasion of the country in 1968 and instead called it a 'gross mistake and interference in Czechoslovakia's internal affairs'. On 29 August 1991, Kozyrev condemned the armed intervention in Hungary in 1956 in equally harsh terms. By appealing to common values and laying to rest some of the ghosts of the past, some of the traditional Russophobia of the region began to dissipate.

Relations had to be rebuilt with the former bloc countries (sometimes called the 'middle abroad'), but once the immediate question of the withdrawal had been resolved relations, both economic and politics, languished. After forty-two years of a less than glorious career, the Council for Mutual Economic Assistance (Comecon) formally ended its mortal existence on 28 June 1991. In 1989, Comecon countries accounted for nearly half of Soviet trade, but from 1 January 1991 mutual trade was conducted in hard currencies at world prices, leading to a collapse of economic relations. New forms of economic interaction had to be found since Russia was the main provider of much of the oil, almost all the natural gas and the greater part of other natural resources to the region. Russia accepted the sovereignty of these states, but the legacy of mistrust remained and as long as the outcome of democratic reforms in Russia hung in the balance, the nervousness of the former satellite countries was understandable. As far as the Central European and Balkan countries were concerned, the security vacuum that had opened up from the Baltic to the Black Sea should be filled by the rapid expansion of Nato to the east, but this, as we shall see in Chapter 17, threatened precisely to alienate Russia and provoke the security crisis that it was designed to overcome.

The 'northern dimension' to European development was sponsored by the EU and espoused with particular enthusiasm by Finland. Having joined the EU in 1996, Finland's long border with Russia now became the outer face of the European community. Rather than allowing the frontier to become a barrier, Finland joined with Russia in numerous cross-border associations and ventures. The Barents–Arctic Ocean region included some Russian regions. In addition, the Council of Baltic Sea States (CBSS) – bringing together Denmark, Estonia, Finland, Germany, Iceland, Latvia, Lithuania, Norway, Poland, Russia and Sweden – encouraged regional co-operation with the support of the EU.

One of the greatest challenges to Russia's liberal foreign policy arose over policy towards the conflict in the former Yugoslavia. Russia followed UN policy in Bosnia despite the condemnation by the opposition who insisted that Yeltsin had 'betrayed' its traditional ally by failing to use its veto in the Security Council to block anti-Serbian resolutions. Nato intervention over Kosovo in 1999 by-passed the UN precisely because of the anticipated exercise of the Russian veto. The Yugoslav wars forcefully raised the dilemma in Russian foreign policy: Would alliance with the West (the Atlanticist approach) take precedence over Russia's traditional great-power interests in the Balkans based on notions of pan-Slavism and commonality of religion and ethnicity? Kozyrev vigorously defended his policies, rejecting the notion of the 'Slavic factor' in its approach to the Yugoslav crisis, and warned that the division of Europe into Slavic, Germanic or Francophone

Figure 15.1 Central and Eastern Europe

areas would return Europe to before 1914 in which yet another Serbian crisis could threaten war. The pursuit of a foreign policy based on ethnic or religious considerations could destroy Russia where millions of Orthodox Slavs lived with millions of Muslims and other faiths.[71]

Russia's political support for the Serbs, however, reflected the pressure from the national-patriots at home, and endowed Russian policy in the Balkans with a fatal incoherence: not only did Russia gain no benefit from its Balkans policy, but exposed its weakness. Russia had simply been bluffing in its Balkan policy, a ruse soon exposed as its limited influence over Serbia was revealed and thereafter Moscow was no longer considered a key player in peacemaking, although it was not altogether ignored. Russia helped broker the Sarajevo cease-fire in February 1994, and then played a crucial role in bringing the Nato bombing campaign to an end in June 1999 by brokering (through the good offices of Chernomyrdin) the Kumanovo accords that stipulated the withdrawal of Serb forces from Kosovo and the establishment of an international peacekeeping force in the region. In broad terms, it was not just the fate of former Yugoslavia that was being resolved but the future world diplomatic order, and it became clear that Russia's role in the latter would be marginal.

Asia

Following the fall of communism the 'Asianist' orientation of Russian policy gained in importance, with Russia attaining the status of a full ASEAN dialogue partner in July 1997 and joining the Asia-Pacific Economic Co-operation (APEC) forum in 1998. The problem, however, was that Russia tended to use Asia and the East as little more than a 'crowbar for relations with the West'.[72] Although two-thirds of Russia lies beyond the Urals its economic and demographic centre of gravity lies firmly in the West. Policy appeared to reflect Brzezinski's view that Russia's only serious geostrategic opportunity to play an important international role and to modernise itself lay in Europe.[73] Russia's self-image, moreover, was European and global, and only marginally Asian. The economic and demographic gap between the Russian Far East and Asia was large and growing, particularly since Russia's potential as a supplier of energy resources, above all oil and natural gas, was difficult to realise. Russia is clearly a potential major player in Asia Pacific, but its role there lacked definition. Russia remained a subaltern player in the emerging Asia–Eurasia community, although the energy resources of Central Asia and the Caucasus and the establishment of an East–West transport corridor connecting Asia and Europe could make Russia an essential part of this Asian-led community. As the late Akino Yutaka put it:

> The old corridor of the Trans-Siberian Railway runs between fifty and sixty degrees latitude, while the new corridor, tracing the ancient Silk Road, will run between forty and fifty degrees latitude.[74]

While Lenin may have argued that 'geographically, economically and historically, Russia is not only a European country but an Asian one as well',[75] it was unclear what form this dual identity would take.[76] Russian power was asymmetrical, with its strategic position secure as long as it had nuclear weapons but a marginal force in economic terms.

Fear over the fate of the under-populated and isolated Eastern regions of the country, sharing a 4,300 km-long border with China, remained a top concern. The population of the Russian Far East is 8 million and that of Siberia 25 million, and both are decreasing, whereas northeast China's population is approaching 300 million. The three provinces closest to Russia (Heilongjiang, Jilin and Liaoning) have a combined population of 80 million, provoking Russian concern about massive inflows of people from China. The major obstacle to Russia's integration in the affairs of the Asia–Pacific region, now that the fear of communism was lifted, was its own weakness and economic disintegration, ethnic unrest and separatist tendencies. In contrast to the rapid development of the Pacific region as a whole, the Soviet Far East remained backward and under-developed. Under Gorbachev, economic and political ties with China and other Pacific countries had begun to improve and mutual trade grew rapidly. The Chinese road of authoritarian modernisation combining political conservatism and economic radicalism attracted many in Russia. Russian and Chinese views on international relations converged in condemning residual Cold War thinking, the threat posed to world peace by 'hegemonism' and power politics, in opposition to the strengthening of the military blocs and alliances of the Cold War era, and the inequitable international economic order that harmed the interests of developing countries. Both claimed to defend a universal concept of security that abandoned Cold War mentalities and group politics in favour of multi-polarism. Numerous military and technology agreements were signed on arms sales, military co-operation and the modernisation of some of the 256 factories built by the Soviet Union in the 1950s. Sino-Russian relations did not quite bloom into the 'strategic partnership' mooted by Primakov and others in Russia, for the simple reason that China's economic predominance (its GNP was five times that of Russia's by 2000), demographic weight and potential military power were perceived as posing a potential threat to Russia. Bilateral relations, however, became the closest ever in their history. The establishment of the Shanghai Co-operation Organisation (SCO) at a summit in Shanghai on 14–15 June 2001 as a regional mechanism for security and co-operation, comprising Russia, China, Kazakhstan, Kyrgyzstan and Uzbekistan, brought China into Central Asian politics and under-scored the 'strategic partnership' between Russia and China.

The conflict over the Kurile Islands, called by Japan the Northern Territories (Habomai Islands, Iturup (Etorofu), Kunashiri and Shikotan Islands), occupied by the USSR since 1945, weakened Japan's participation in international funding for Russia's reforms, though Japan remained Russia's third largest trading partner. The Russo-Japanese Treaty of 1855 placed Sakhalin Island under joint control, but in 1875 Russia gained control over the whole island in exchange for the Kurile Islands. The Treaty of Portsmouth in 1905 ceded Southern Sakhalin to Japan in exchange for Russia gaining the southern Kurile Islands. Southern Sakhalin was known as Karafuto until it was annexed by the USSR at the end of the Second World War, and at the same time in September 1945 the USSR reoccupied the southern Kurile Islands after Japan had surrendered, and in violation of the Neutrality Pact, leaving Japan with nothing except an abiding sense of injustice. The Joint Declaration of 1956 stipulated that the USSR would return Shikotan and Habomai Islands to Japan and diplomatic relations were re-established, but in response to the revision of Japan's security treaty with the United States in 1960 the USSR reneged and denied the very existence of a territorial problem with Japan. For Japan the question was motivated neither by economic nor security concerns but by the very principle of territorial integrity; similar feelings informed Russia's refusal to give up territory.

Public opinion in the islands themselves suggested that at least a third would be willing to come under Japanese sovereignty if the terms were right, but public opinion in Russia opposed any territorial concessions. In 1991, Yeltsin proposed a five-stage approach to the question: a recognition that the problem existed; then Russia would declare the islands a free economic zone, where the Japanese would be given preferential treatment; the demilitarisation of the islands, entailing the closure of the many Russian bases; and, fourth, agreements would be reached between Japan and Russia on economic, trade, social and cultural issues. These four stages would take some twenty years, and by the fifth stage new leaders would appear who would be able to cut the Gordian knot.[77] At the 'no-neckties' summit between Yeltsin and the Japanese prime minister Ryuataro Hashimoto in Krasnoyarsk in November 1997, both sides committed themselves to signing a peace treaty by 2000. However, this was not achieved and the problem remained active into the Putin era.

The 'Third World' and the rest

In contrast to difficult relations with Japan, Russia inherited and maintained India as the main partner and ally in Asia. A treaty on friendship and co-operation signed in January 1993 sought to build on Soviet–Indian ties but at the same time to make them mutually beneficial by discarding the old logic of exclusive geopolitical alliances. Russia remained India's main supplier of arms, including advanced tanks and warplanes. Relations with the Third World starkly posed the question of how to define the 'national interest'. The 'burden of achievement' in Central Europe, the costs of supporting 'client states' from Cuba to Vietnam, and the disastrous war in Afghanistan, all undermined the Soviet consensus on foreign policy that had underlain its drive to become a global superpower. During *perestroika* the NPT allowed universal humanistic concerns to challenge the old view that international relations was the class struggle on a global scale. The theoretical basis for Soviet support for Third World revolutionary states was undermined by the view that development was now seen as having to precede socialism, rather than socialism being the key to unlocking development. The vigorous debate over Soviet Third World policy resulted in Soviet disengagement under Gorbachev.[78] Soviet troops were withdrawn from Afghanistan in February 1989, and the traditional relationship with Cuba became much more strained. Solzhenitsyn called these countries 'insatiable squanderers of our wealth',[79] and Soviet aid to Afghanistan, Angola, Cuba, Ethiopia, Kampuchea and Mozambique was cut. Disengagement became a rout, but as its own policy became more assertive Russia once again sought to reforge old alliances. Russia's reduced weight in world affairs was vividly in evidence in the Middle East conflict. Although one of the sponsors of the Madrid peace process, it was squeezed out of attempts to regulate the Palestinian war in the 2000s.

Conclusion

As the 'continuer' state Russia assumed not only the treaty, financial and other responsibilities of the USSR, but also many of the attitudes and ambiguities of the former superpower. Russia inherited the institutions of the Soviet Union together with uncertainty about its proper place and role in the world. Kozyrev stressed the distinction between 'the normalisation of relations with other countries and normal relations with them', noting that Gorbachev had begun the first task but it was up to Russia to complete the second. At the heart of the new foreign policy was the idea of Russia as a 'normal great power', one 'that does not rely on threats (like the USSR) but at the same time knows how to live in a world that is not conflict-free'.[80] The notion of 'great power' is itself contentious, and Russia's claims to be one inevitably alarmed its neighbours. While the idea of 'normality' in this context acted as a normative acknowledgement of acceptable forms of behaviour, it could not be anything but ambiguous.

Different conceptions of Russian national interest were reflected in contradictory foreign policies. Policy was torn between, on the one hand, an approach that stressed great power rivalries and its associated concept of the balance of power and, on the other hand, a view based on the concept of interdependence, global economic integration and mutual security regimes. Although liberals insisted that Russia's identity and national interests would be forged not in global struggle with the West but in developing a new political and economic order at home, those of a more nationalist disposition insisted that Russia should not shirk its historical responsibilities as the core of an alternative order to that of the West, as the obstacle to the allegedly hegemonic ambitions of the sole remaining superpower and its allies, and as the protector of smaller nations (Serbia, Iraq, Cuba). These fundamental policy divergences were exacerbated by the difficulty in setting priorities in a confused and weakly accountable institutional setting. The government pursued not so much a multi-polar as a multi-directional, if not outright amorphous, foreign policy. There were positive aspects to this, however, in the sense that the aggressive rhetoric of certain nationalist and neo-communist groups was tempered by public opinion, conflicts between elites and interest groups, and tensions between institutions. The Russian case seems to demonstrate that democratisation does not necessarily provoke aggressive foreign policies. The redefinition of national interest proved to be an open-ended process in which the struggle between liberal and national-patriotic approaches reflected the larger struggle over Russia's own identity and place in the world. Putin's liberal patriotic approach sought to finesse these differences if not to overcome the contradictions.

16 Commonwealth, community and fragmentation

> The disappearance of the Soviet superpower, oppressive to its subjects as it was, has created a dangerous imbalance of power among its former components and between them and their neighbours. Possibility of serious conflicts arise. Russia, which by any definition is a Great Power in the classical sense, is bordered by the much weaker states which have broken away from the Soviet structure. As with water, power will find its level.
>
> (Elie Kedourie)[1]

While the USSR might have collapsed with relatively little violence, the disintegration of the great empires of the past suggests that the greatest danger comes from conflicts between successor states and the threat of outside powers seeking to take advantage of the power vacuum. The arbitrariness of the borders, the intermingling of populations, and a host of unresolved problems provided fertile ground for conflict. The ambiguities in Russian policy towards the successor states, twelve of which including Russia came to be members of the Commonwealth of Independent States (CIS), was one of the main charges against the liberal foreign policy of the early post-communist years. The nature and purpose of the CIS was contested. The CIS was not itself a state in the conventional sense and neither was it a subject of international law. Its member states actively pursued their own independent foreign policies, intended often to distance themselves from their former partners, above all Russia. This distancing tendency by the late 1990s took the form of the establishment of the GUUAM group of states (Georgia, Ukraine, Uzbekistan, Azerbaijan and Moldova), while Russia itself sought 'ever closer union' with Belarus. Russian policy sought to incorporate the former Soviet states (excluding the three Baltic republics) into an expanded security zone and sphere of vital interests, while the other states sought to defend their sovereignty and independence. (See Table 16.1 for data on area and populations of the former Soviet states.) This chapter briefly examines the evolution of the CIS, Russia's relations with the successor states, and analyses the problem of borders and the vexed question of individual and collective rights in nation- and state-building.

The Commonwealth of Independent States (CIS)

The CIS did not become the successor state to the USSR, and there is no CIS foreign policy and no CIS 'national interest'. Instead, there are divergent foreign policies in constant uncomfortable interaction with each other. The CIS is not a

Table 16.1 Territory and population of former Soviet republics, 1 January 1990

	Territory in thousand km²	% of USSR	Pop. (thousands)	% of USSR	% urbanised
Former USSR	22,403	100.0	288,624	100.0	66
Russia	17,075	76.2	148,041	51.3	74
Baltic:	175	0.7	7,993	2.8	70
Estonia	45	0.2	1,583	0.5	72
Latvia	65	0.3	2,687	0.9	71
Lithuania	65	0.3	3,723	1.3	68
West:	846	3.8	66,460	23.1	65
Moldova	34	0.2	4,362	1.5	47
Belarus	208	0.9	10,259	3.6	66
Ukraine	604	2.7	51,839	18.0	67
South Caucasus:	186	0.8	15,880	5.5	56
Armenia	30	0.1	3,293	1.1	68
Azerbaijan	87	0.4	7,131	2.5	54
Georgia	70	0.3	5,456	1.9	56
Central Asia:	3,994	17.8	50,250	17.4	49
Kazakhstan	2,717	12.1	16,691	5.8	57
Kyrgyzstan	199	0.9	4,367	1.5	38
Tajikistan	143	0.6	5,248	1.8	32
Turkmenistan	488	2.2	3,622	1.3	45
Uzbekistan	447	2.0	20,322	7.0	41

Source: Economist Intelligence Unit, *CIS: Country Report*, No. 2 (1992), p. 11, modified.

state in international law, and each member regards economic and foreign policy, and increasingly security policy as well, as its own preserve. The CIS has been a success to the limited extent that the states have not come into violent conflict with each other, but the area has been characterised by the diversification of economic dependencies, the development of regional alliances and associations in line with traditional cultural affiliations, and the search for protectors and sponsors abroad.[2]

Organisation and development

Attempts to create a Union of Sovereign States in the post-*coup* period soon came to nothing. The draft treaty of November 1991 still provided for some form of power-sharing between a reconstituted centre and the republics,[3] but the other republics feared that the new centre would recreate patterns of domination; Russia appeared to be assuming the mantle of leadership cast off by the old Union. As we saw in Chapter 2, the Ukrainian vote for independence on 1 December 1991 sealed the death warrant for the Union treaty process, and on 8 December the leaders of the three Slavic republics announced the creation of the CIS (see Figure 16.1).

The CIS played a critical role in managing the transition to independent statehood, yet few of the objectives proclaimed in the CIS treaty of December 1991 were achieved. Commitments to co-ordinate their foreign policy, to maintain a common economic space, to co-ordinate transport and communications system, and to retain open frontiers and guarantee freedom of movement for all CIS

Figure 16.1 Member states of the CIS

citizens were only partially fulfilled.[4] Two opposing views took shape: the first, supported by Gorbachev, argued that the CIS should create supranational executive bodies and accelerate integration;[5] while the second defined the CIS as a temporary inter-governmental co-ordinating and consultative body designed only to provide a civilised mechanism for the 'divorce' of the former Soviet republics.[6] While the CIS registered a 'negative' success in preventing a total collapse of former ties, positive achievements were meagre but nevertheless real. A significant body of CIS law has been developed, establishing basic normative standards across the region.

Russia became the 'continuer' state of the USSR in diplomatic terms and in international law, but for the other 'successor' states the term suggested that Russia expected to become the dominant partner. The disintegration of the USSR posed endless questions about the division of assets, capital, institutions and the armed forces. Above all, there was the problem of determining the citizenship of the heterogeneous populations of the new republics. The division of resources proved less of a problem than had been anticipated, and operated on the principle that what was in the republics belonged to them, and what was in Russia belonged to Russia even though both sides might have contributed to its development. As for the division of foreign assets, all the CIS states agreed to exchange their share in return for Russia assuming their part of the USSR's foreign debt.

The provisional accords of 8 December 1991 stipulated that the CIS headquarters was to be in Minsk, the capital of Belarus. The CIS was to co-ordinate policy through a Council of Heads of State (CHS) and a Council of Heads of Government (CHG), both of which were to meet at least twice a year and the presidency of both councils was to rotate. Individual member states had the right to veto decisions of the councils. In 1992, the councils each met eight times and signed some 275 agreements, though most were of a declaratory nature and lacked implementation mechanisms, and about half dealt with military matters. These agreements and later ones did not formalise the deepening of relations between states but regulated their separation. Although in December 1991 it was agreed that decisions would be taken by consensus, in practice delegations could easily opt out. The Tashkent summit of 15 May 1992 adopted the formula 'consensus-minus-one', and simple majority voting for procedural issues. Even that proved too restrictive, and any state could simply declare that it was not interested in a particular decision and was thus exempted. Selective participation in signing agreements became standard practice, with only seven out of eleven member states signing the relevant document on the establishment of the CIS Interparliamentary Assembly at the March 1992 Kiev summit, only six signing the Collective Security Treaty in Tashkent in May 1992, eight delegations approving the 6 July 1992 Moscow Agreement on the status of the Economic Court, and the same with most other accords.[7] No agreement was achieved on the imposition of sanctions for the non-observance of treaty commitments.

Documents adopted by the CIS were primarily of two types.[8] The great majority fell into the category of *modus vivendi* agreements designed to prevent a total collapse of the infrastructure of the old Union. They dealt with such issues as energy, transport, payment of pensions, border forces, customs regulations and so on, and were signed by most members. While possibly contributing in the long term to integration, in the short term these agreements did little to promote the development of a common space but merely regulated the assertion of national sovereignty and tried to avoid a complete collapse of the old economic area. The second category consisted of agreements establishing co-ordinating bodies such as the Collective Security Council, a Council of Defence Ministers, a Customs Council and some two dozen others. Most tried to regulate inter-state economic relations, dealing with such issues as rail transport, statistics, energy, science and technology, and the like. Azerbaijan refused to sign agreements in the defence sphere, and from March 1992 opted out of agreements on co-ordinating bodies in socio-economic affairs as well. Ukraine was little more enthusiastic about the common institutions of the CIS and, together with Moldova and Turkmenistan, these four states were the most opposed to the institutionalisation of the CIS. They insisted that the CIS was not a suprastate institution.

Negotiations in late 1992 over a revised CIS Charter defining the rights and obligations of member states were riven by disputes over human rights, economic and other issues. At the Minsk summit on 22 January 1993, seven out of ten members approved the CIS Charter providing for a 'multispeed' CIS, allowing those countries that wished to achieve deeper integration to do so without excluding those who favoured a slower pace. While the CIS remained under-institutionalised, a rudimentary permanent executive body was established in the form of a Co-ordinating and Consultative Committee assisted by over thirty inter-state, inter-governmental and inter-departmental co-ordinating agencies covering such issues as foreign policy and the environment. It was clear, however, that a two-tier CIS was emerging. The establishment of the CIS Interparliamentary Assembly on 27 March 1992 had been intended to address this problem. Given final shape by a Convention signed on 26 May 1995, the Assembly makes no attempt to reflect the political views of its members, and is not a statutory body of the CIS but an autonomous international organisation. Although the CIS has a range of institutions, most lack formal and substantive authority. Typical is the post of Executive Secretary, who has minimal powers and cannot be compared to an executive general secretary of an international organisation.

Diversification

The CIS was marked by a differentiation process in which three groups of states emerged. The first was a core comprising Russia, Kazakhstan, Kyrgyzstan, Uzbekistan and, until engulfed by civil war, Tajikistan. These countries had been most willing to sign the Union treaty in 1991 and now signed most agreements, and appeared most devoted to the concept of the CIS evolving into a closer community of nations. Nazarbaev, indeed, urged the creation of a new Union, and after the August *coup* lamented the failure 'to unify the economy while giving all the states complete independence in matters of foreign and domestic policy'.[9] Nazarbaev's idea of a confederal Union was supported by Gorbachev.[10] The emergence of this core group led some to suggest that the CIS would become no more than a Russian–Central Asian bloc. Indeed, the Eurasianists argued that since Ukraine had driven a wedge between Russia and Europe, Russia should pursue a less Western-oriented policy and concentrate on links with the Central Asian states to ensure Russian predominance in Eurasia. In contrast to the Atlanticists, who considered that Russia should aim to join the core states of the industrialised north as quickly as possible, the Eurasians considered that Russia's natural allies were to be found in the south.[11]

The second group was made up of Armenia and Belarus; they began by being sceptical members of the CIS but became its most ardent supporters. Both at first were selective in signing agreements and were wary of the creation of supranational CIS bodies; they supported co-operation within the CIS, but sought to avoid being caught up in a political and military alliance. Belarus at first tried to reduce its Eurasian ties but under president Alexander Lukashenko from 1994 became committed to closer ties with Russia, signing a bilateral treaty on 2 April 1996 (the first of a series) committing both states to closer integration. Armenia found itself isolated from the heartlands of the CIS by Georgia and Azerbaijan, and was aggrieved that the CIS was powerless to resolve the Nagorno-Karabakh conflict or to ameliorate its own grievous economic hardship. Its very isolation later rendered Armenia one of Russia's strongest allies, and in return it received arms (some of the supply clandestine) and other forms of support.

The third group was made up of Ukraine, Turkmenistan, Azerbaijan and Moldova. Ukraine made no secret of its desire to become a 'normal' European state, and behaved as though it was embarrassed by Russia's Asian tail dragging it back in geography and time. Ukraine unequivocally opposed attempts to strengthen CIS institutions and fought hard against Russian dominance in the organisation but offered little in the way of a positive programme. Just as Austria and Bavaria had opposed Prussian domination of the German Confederation in the nineteenth century, so too today Ukraine is determined to resist the hegemony of the stronger power and opposes Russian domination in Eurasia. Ukraine thus sought to make the CIS as weak as possible, with no permanent status and a minimal staff, rejected outright the idea of a unified armed force, and objected to the CIS Charter that envisaged suprastate Commonwealth structures.

Turkmenistan adopted an independent stance secure in the enjoyment of its income from its gas fields, its eccentric leader-dominated political system, and its distance from the conflict in Tajikistan. Azerbaijan and Moldova at first appeared to be temporary members of the CIS, waiting only for an appropriate moment to leave. The 6 July 1992 Moscow summit warned that if they did not ratify the CIS Treaty they would not be admitted to the next summit. On the eve of the Bishkek summit of 9 October 1992, the Azerbaijan parliament voted unanimously against ratification and thus left the organisation.[12] Moldova, too, failed to ratify the Almaty accords, but left some room for manœuvre and continued to participate selectively in the work of the CIS. Moldova's relations with the CIS and Russia are filtered through the prism of the Transdniester conflict. At the time of the August 1991 *coup*, a group seized power in this sliver of land on the east bank of the Dniester, one-third of whose population were Russians, and then for the next decade challenged Moldovan sovereignty over the breakaway territory.

Despite fears that the whole CIS project might collapse, it soon became clear that it performed certain important functions. Russia, certainly, found it a useful foreign-policy instrument, and sought to ensure membership in the organisation. Following the overthrow of Elchibei's nationalist government in 1993, Azerbaijan agreed to rejoin the organisation. Hard on the heels of the debacle in Abkhazia in 1993, Georgia finally agreed to join the CIS. This brought membership to twelve,

Figure 16.2 Ukraine

with only the three Baltic states outside. Lacking an effective institutional framework, the CIS was an inter-governmental rather than a supranational body. There was no consensus among the member states over the way that the CIS should evolve. The debate over the CIS Charter revealed basic conceptual differences in attitudes, with one view expressed most forcefully by Kazakhstan stressing the need to establish a more coherent community, while others equally firmly argued that it should be little more than a forum for inter-governmental consultation on specific issues. Policy represented less a coherent vision of development than the lowest common denominator of agreement between groups of countries with radically different views on its evolution and future.

The development of the CIS was marked by the bilateralisation of relations between member states, undermining multilateral attempts to solve problems on a Commonwealth-wide basis.[13] Turkmenistan from the first was sceptical about the value of the CIS, refusing to sign agreements on economic, collective security, financial and other issues, and instead Niyazov relied on bilateral rather than collective agreements. Kravchuk and Kuchma on several occasions insisted that Russo-Ukrainian relations would develop on a purely bilateral basis, while the numerous agreements between Belarus and Russia allowed the former to steer clear of any political or military bloc. Bilateralisation was not altogether incompatible with the existence of the CIS, but this would be a CIS limited to the orderly management of transition to nation-states rather than one committed to finding multilateral solutions to common problems, let alone the attempt to establish a new community on confederal principles. Those (like Turkmenistan, Kazakhstan and Azerbaijan) with oil and/or gas sought to buttress their political independence by links with Western partners to exploit reserves, but the sheer enormity of the stakes in the geopolitics of energy policy served in some cases to undermine the room for manœuvre, faced by Russia's refusal to be cut out of either the exploitation or transportation of Caspian energy.

The bilateralisation of relations reflected the absence of effective multilateral organisations to mediate between CIS countries. The Collective Security Treaty of May 1992 was the only serious attempt to establish a genuinely multilateral security system, but, despite its aspirations to become some sort of eastern Nato, performance fell far short of this. Instead, a number of regional bodies emerged within the CIS that undermined its role as a multilateral organisation. The Customs Union of 1994, the successor to a much weaker agreement of 14 March 1992, promised free trade between Russia, Kazakhstan, Belarus and Kyrgyzstan, with Tajikistan joining in January 1999. At the Minsk summit in 2001, the Customs Union was transformed into the Eurasian Economic Community (EAEC). Elsewhere customs barriers began to be established, but the permeability of intra-CIS borders remained and elements of a free-trade zone remained within the CIS. Evidence of this, according to Yurii Yarov, the CIS Executive Secretary, was the growth in trade by a third in 2000 between CIS member states.[14]

While bilateralisation was encouraged by countries like Ukraine, which sought a weak CIS, in practice the process was double-edged and raised the danger of the creation of a new Union dominated by Russia. Reflecting the highly centralised nature of the old USSR, bilateral relations between the peripheral countries developed slowly and the great bulk of agreements focused on Russia. Links were closest between the core members of the CIS, and agreements on friendship, co-operation and mutual assistance were signed with Kazakhstan, Uzbekistan and Kyrgyzstan. Russia became the centre of a dense web of relationships, which rather than enhancing the authority of the CIS began to act as a substitute for it. Russia became the military, economic and political core of a new Union that might at one stage dispense with the CIS altogether. Although Putin began his leadership by repeating standard nostrums about the importance of the CIS, it was clear that as part of his 'realist' review of foreign policy, in the words of Sergei Ivanov, the 'accelerated development of the Commonwealth into a fully fledged international association is not possible in the near future', and as a consequence Russia would pursue its interests 'first of all through the development of bilateral relations with CIS countries'.[15]

The development of the GUUAM grouping of states (Georgia, Ukraine, Uzbekistan, Azerbaijan and Moldova) acted as a counter-weight to what its members suspected were Russia's hegemonic ambitions within the CIS. Established as a loose alliance in 1998, at its meeting in June 2001 in Yalta it was formally established as an institution with a Charter outlining its goals as the development of reciprocal trade, the creation of a GUUAM free-trade zone, and support for transit routes between Europe and Central Asia. The top decision-making body was the conference of heads of state, to meet annually in Yalta, the permanent site of

GUUAM summits. Ukraine, the main mover behind the organisation, would provide organisational support for the body. Partially in response to the development of GUUAM, the Russian Duma in July 2001 adopted a law that would allow parts of foreign states to join the Russian Federation. Any state or territory that is part of a state could accede to the RF on terms negotiated by authorised authorities of both parties. At issue was the possibility of Abkhazia, South Ossetia and Transdniester joining Russia, while Karabakh would be encouraged in its bid to join Armenia. The law would also make possible the incorporation of Belarus as a state.

Russia and the CIS

The Commonwealth was fundamentally lopsided by Russia's sheer size and cultural predominance, with Russian becoming the *lingua franca*, and the fears that this raised in its neighbours. The experience of seventy years of Soviet power, using Russification for its own purposes, was hardly a strong basis on which to build a community based on trust. The absence of strong co-ordinating institutions engendered an atmosphere of constant crisis. Russia tended to view Soviet property and institutions as its own; the other republics had to build theirs from scratch. In the army, the diplomatic corps and the foreign-trade offices of the USSR Russians had predominated, and with the end of the USSR they transferred their loyalties to Russia. For the other nationalities there could be no such easy transition, and loyalty to an amorphous CIS was no substitute for their own nationhood. Naturally, this gave rise to resentment, leading to fears that the CIS would be abandoned altogether.

Russia in 1992 had been hesitant to take the lead in pursuing the integration of CIS states, fearing accusations of neo-imperialism and concentrating on political and economic links with the West, but for the rest of the decade and into Putin's presidency became the main champion of integration within the CIS framework. Industrialists sought closer union between the CIS countries, and the Civic Union indeed called for the establishment of a collective organ to unify economic, cultural and scientific policy.[16] Under pressure at home and goaded by enthusiastic integrationists like Nazarbaev in Central Asia, Yeltsin became increasingly aware that there was no escaping close links with the former Soviet republics. In February 1993, Yeltsin called on the international community to grant Russia special powers as the guarantor of peace and stability in the former USSR, and the Security Council's adoption of the document 'Basic Directions of Foreign Policy' in April 1993 reaffirmed Russia's commitment to the unity of the area. Russian foreign policy towards the successor states advanced on three fronts at the same time: the attempt to preserve and strengthen the CIS; the consolidation of relations with the core states in a type of 'Eurasian union'; and the bilateralisation of relations. For a period in the late 1990s, Russia's prioritisation of the CIS was given physical shape in the form of a separate ministry for CIS affairs. It proved unable to install coherence in Russia's relations with its neighbours, and one of Putin's first acts was to abolish it and return responsibility to the foreign ministry.

Russian domestic opinion was fundamentally divided over the CIS. National-patriots and some neo-communists regarded the CIS as a fundamentally illegitimate creation. Discussion of the CIS often served as a cover to condemn the disintegration of the USSR: 'Masquerading as a foreign policy issue, it is actually a vehicle for deploring Russia's loss of empire.'[17] By endorsing the CIS Russia accepted restraints on its freedom of manœuvre in its relations with the other republics, limitations which enraged the opposition who felt that the interests of Russia as a whole and the rights of Russians abroad were being neglected. They viewed the creation of the CIS as the denial of Russia's status as a great power, evidence of Russia's 'withdrawal into Asia' and alienation of primordial Russian lands. While denouncing the 1991 Minsk Accords, the CPRF favoured the recreation of the Soviet Union and barely mentioned the CIS in its electoral programmes. Nato expansion prompted efforts to transform the CIS into a counteralliance to Nato. In his decree on CIS strategy of September 1995 Yeltsin stressed that the CIS was a 'priority area' for Russia, although he noted that this should be based on mutually beneficial economic co-operation.[18] The decree called for the transformation of the CIS into a fully fledged collective security alliance, much to the alarm of other members, especially the provision that no CIS state would be allowed to join any military alliances aimed at another CIS state.

Kuchma's election as Ukraine's second post-communist president in 1994 was in part a reaction to Kravchuk's anti-Russian rhetoric, although Kuchma in practice found his pro-Russian options limited. His election did, however, lead to improved relations and in May 1997 Russia signed a ten-year Treaty on Co-operation and Friendship with Ukraine, accompanied the following February by a Treaty on Economic Co-operation. Many of the stipulations, particularly of the latter, were not fulfilled, but the treaties placed the bilateral relations, symbolically at least, on a firm footing. Ukraine's agreement to allow Russia basing rights for the Black Sea Fleet in Sevastopol until 2017 also helped put to one side one of the thorniest issues in their relations.

The August 1998 crisis accelerated trends in relations within the CIS that were already evident. Trade within the CIS, for example, had fallen sharply after 1991 and now declined further. Trade was hampered by payments arrears, and the prevalence of barter arrangements, above all to pay for Russian natural gas deliveries to Belarus and Ukraine. By the end of the decade, none of the former Soviet states had regained their 1990 output levels, whereas countries like Poland and Hungary in Central Europe surged forwards. However, it would be an exaggeration to say that the economic transitions in the former Soviet countries had failed. Since 1997, there had been a noticeable, although far from spectacular, turn towards economic recovery, something that had been interrupted by Russia's financial crisis of August 1998 but resumed thereafter. The worst years for most CIS states had been in the early 1990s, but by 1997 ten out of the twelve CIS states enjoyed varying degrees of GDP growth, reaching double digits in Belarus, Georgia and Kyrgyzstan, with even Russia posting growth.

Although the CIS was unlikely to act as the motor of reintegration, an increasing proportion of the Russian population regretted the break-up of the Soviet Union. If, in 1992, 69 per cent were in this category, by the time of the tenth anniversary of Gorbachev's referendum on renewing the Union, which had been overwhelmingly supported (see Chapter 1), 79 per cent in 2001 spoke in favour of the Union. Over the same period, the percentage not regretting the end of the Union fell from 32 to 15 per cent. If a new referendum had been held on the tenth anniversary of the first, then 72 per cent would have voted for the unification of the former Soviet republics, although it must be stressed that 58 per cent did not believe in the possibility of such a re-unification, while 30 per cent did.[19]

Russia was the only state involved in every CIS regional grouping (except GUUAM): the Collective Security treaty (Russia, Belarus, Armenia, Kazakhstan, Kyrgyzstan and Tajikistan); the 'Caucasus Four' (Russia, Armenia, Azerbaijan and Georgia, an informal body established by Russia to prise Georgia and Azerbaijan out of the orbit of Nato and Turkey); the EAEC (Russia, Belarus, Kazakhstan, Kyrgyzstan and Tajikistan); and the Russia–Belarus Union. The former Soviet states can be arranged along a spectrum, with the Baltic option at one end signifying a complete break with the past, refusal to have anything to do with the CIS, accompanied by the vigorous attempt to join Western European institutions like Nato and the EU, and the Belarus variant at the other end, denoting the attempt to recreate some sort of post-Soviet political community with Russia at its core. As the Baltic option became increasingly attractive (and possible) for a number of countries, so their interest in the continuation of the CIS as anything more than a very loose umbrella organisation declined. The Belarusian variant, too, in its own way undermined the multilateralism inherent in the CIS in favour of strengthened bilateral ties. The creation of separate groupings, like the Russo-Belarusian state, undermined the CIS as effectively as did the partisans of the Baltic line.

Russia became one of the strongest supporters of the CIS because, among other things, it fulfils a number of essential tasks. It limits the damage caused by the

Figure 16.3 South Caucasus

disintegration, and through *modus vivendi* agreements helped avoid the total collapse of economic, infrastructural and human ties. The CIS also legitimates Russia's presence, including the deployment of military forces, in Commonwealth countries. Through the CIS Russia regulates the conflicts in South Ossetia and Transdniester, though it must be admitted that bilateral approaches predominated. According to the alternative foreign-policy programme of the CFDP, the CIS allowed 'the commonality of interests of millions of people who inhabit the space of the former USSR' to be identified. The programme stressed that the CIS contained the potential for the creation of future structures of co-operation between areas 'that were once united in a single Russian state', and in particular they argued that Russia should maintain close relations with Belarus and Kazakhstan, as well as Georgia (at the time not a member of the CIS), because of geopolitical factors and traditional ties as allies of Russia.[20]

Russia was indeed torn over whether it was simply an equal member of the Commonwealth, or whether because of its size and traditions it should act as *primus inter pares*. Ukraine in particular was determined that there would be no new centre, whether one created by the CIS itself, and even less if Russia were to claim the honour. Once again the question focused on Russia's foreign-policy priorities. If Russia's key foreign-policy objective was to prepare to move from the periphery to the core of the world economy, this could only be achieved through natural economic processes and not by diverting scarce resources to unrealistic plans to make Russia the centre of a reconstituted Eurasian union.[21] The definition of Russia's foreign policy depended on the understanding of global processes in their entirety. If one were to accept that the post-Cold War world was defined by the marketisation of world power, in which military and nuclear power had declined in importance relative to economic achievements, then Russia should abandon its military-industrial complex and concentrate on advanced economic modernisation and globalisation, and turn its back on the CIS. This was the view of the Atlanticists, but was contested by the Eurasianists.

Prospects for reintegration and the CIS

Without a government or its own armed forces, and with no mechanism to ensure that its decisions are implemented, the CIS was an unloved child of the break-up of the Soviet Union. Created hurriedly in December 1991 without prior negotiations over the division of assets, questions of citizenship or the fate of the army, the CIS has survived but not prospered. Ukraine continues to see the CIS as little more than a way of achieving a 'civilised divorce'. The CIS remains a hybrid stranger on the international scene. Created in large measure to satisfy Ukraine's desire for sovereignty, Ukraine paradoxically was the most reluctant of CIS partners. The CIS had been formed to keep Russia and Ukraine in a single political space when the attempt to create a new Union had failed, but those in favour of greater integration might one day decide to move forward without Ukraine.

Despite the lack of clarity over the role of the CIS, certain achievements can be credited to it. As Yeltsin pointed out, the CIS was a form of relations between states fated to live together. Many frontiers have only gradually become full state borders, and a visa-free regime is still in operation (with the exception of Georgia because of the Chechen war). The CIS as an institution has moved neither in the direction of closer economic integration, in contrast to the EU to which it was sometimes compared, nor to tighter security co-operation on the model of Nato. Rather than facing external threats, the main danger came from internal conflicts. The co-ordination of foreign policy and the maintenance of a common economic space were soon forgotten, a common currency zone did not survive, and attempts to maintain a single juridical space throughout the CIS were undermined. Comparison with the short-lived French Commonwealth, created on the basis of a referendum in 1958 and dissolved two years later, is instructive. However, the independent Francophone countries retain a deep affinity with France, and Russia could hope that it, too, could play a hegemonic cultural role in Eurasia, though it was precisely such aspirations that so alienated countries like Ukraine.

The debate over the future of the CIS is at the same time a debate over the past, and in particular whether the disintegration of the USSR had been inevitable. If the USSR had always been an illegitimate construct, then its dissolution was final and irrevocable; but if the USSR did represent, in however attenuated a form, some primordial unity of the Eurasian land mass, then attempts to recreate some sort of successor body were legitimate and not simply an expression of Russian neo-imperialism. While the CIS consisted of countries with very different cultures and levels of economic development, the main splits did not occur on these lines but because of conflicting elite strategies. Integration entails giving up sovereignty, but before being given up it has to be achieved, and this is the phase through which the former Soviet republics are now passing.

Security and peacekeeping

The final years of *perestroika* had been marked by increasingly bitter ethnic clashes: in Nagorno-Karabakh from March 1988 followed by the Sumgait massacres in April; in the Fergana Valley in June 1989, Azerbaijan in January 1990, Dushanbe in February 1990 and Osh in June 1990, to name only a few. The retreat of governance allowed local and regional elites to exploit ethnic grievances, eroding often fragile patterns of coexistence. Once disrupted, especially if accompanied by violence, mutual fears and hostilities fed on each other and made it extremely difficult, even with outside intervention, to restore intercommunal equilibrium. Ethnic disputes usually lie beyond the realm of rational politics and are often marked by mutually exclusive claims to historical, territorial or religious justice where compromise is seen as threatening to the very existence of the people in question. In these circumstances adjudication is a hazardous business, especially when outside forces seek to exploit conflicts for their own ends. Macartney in any case long ago noted that the welfare of minorities in these conflicts came third, after concern over general European peace and the stability of states in the European order.[22] The championing of the rights of minorities, in interwar Europe and today, is often no more than an instrument for revisionist ambitions. The human costs of the break-up of the USSR have been estimated at some 100,000 dead (although estimates in the Duma have ranged up to 600,000), with damage totalling some $15 billion, largely as a result of inter-ethnic conflicts. There have been five extended regional wars in the former USSR (Karabakh, Tajikistan, South Ossetia, Transdniester and

Chechnya, the last in a category of its own), and some twenty short military operations.[23]

A thin line separated security-building along Russia's borders and the revival of neo-imperial ambitions. Kozyrev insisted that Russia had no choice but to involve itself here in conflict-management, including the use of force for peacekeeping: 'For Russia this kind of "isolationism" would entail millions of refugees and chaos along the perimeter of the southern borders.'[24] The problem, however, was that peacekeeping effectively became privatised by Russia, and reflected less the multilateral policy of the CIS than a projection of Russian state interests.

The CIS at first provided some form of centralised control over the USSR armed forces but the republics soon formed their own armies (Chapter 17). The Joint Command structure gave way to national armies and the CIS Council of Ministers of Defence took over a co-ordinating role. The 20 March 1992 Kiev CIS summit recognised the demise of an integrated military structure and took the first steps towards a system of collective security, with joint forces to be established on a case-by-case basis.[25] Acrimony flared at the Minsk summit of January 1993 over the control of strategic nuclear weapons, with Kiev and Almaty reluctant to transfer control to Russia even though all agreed that Russia would become the only CIS nuclear power in the future.

At the CIS summit in Tashkent on 15 May 1992, the Collective Security Treaty (CST) was signed by Armenia, Kazakhstan, Kyrgyzstan, Russia, Tajikistan and Uzbekistan, but the failure of Ukraine and other countries to sign once again revealed the deep divisions. The Tashkent Treaty stipulated that aggression against one of the signatory parties would be considered aggression against them all, but it was less a multilateral military and political alliance than a way of legitimating Russian military assistance to the signatory states.[26] The Tashkent meeting also agreed on the distribution of CFE Treaty limits among the newly independent states. The CST by 2001 had established a 2,500-strong Rapid Deployment Force.

The danger of Russia being drawn into a war against its will was vividly illustrated by Armenia's threats to resign from the Tashkent agreement because of CIS inactivity over Nagorno-Karabakh. In security policy, as in other areas, there was a strong tendency towards bilateralisation, and numerous agreements were signed between Russia and other countries regulating the stationing of troops outside Russia and other issues. The Russian Ministry of Defence increasingly supplanted the Joint Command on security issues that affected not only Russia but the CIS as a whole. Indeed, it was Russia's attempts to maintain its freedom of manœuvre, and frustration at the clumsy multilateralism of earlier agreements, that prompted Russia's decision in July 1993 to dissolve the Joint Command.[27] Thus, hopes for military integration within the framework of the CIS were dashed, as were plans for standing joint peacekeeping forces. In contrast to Russia's draft Military Doctrine of May 1992, which placed a heavy emphasis on military co-operation within the CIS, the Doctrine approved in November 1993 made only one brief mention of the CIS.

At the CIS summit in Ashgabat in December 1993, a new military co-ordinating body was established directly subordinate to the CIS Council of Defence Ministers, though the definition of collective security proved contentious. While Russia defined collective security in terms of external threats, Azerbaijan insisted that it should cover threats from one CIS member state against another – obviously directed against Armenia – and in the event the Russian version was adopted and a Council of Collective Security was established. Yet again, documents were adopted at the summit in favour of developing co-operation and strengthening trust between CIS members, stressing respect for the sovereignty and territorial integrity of Commonwealth countries.[28] This theme runs as a common thread in CIS meetings and regional groupings of the CIS. The establishment of Collective Peacekeeping Forces in effect authorised Russia in the name of the CIS to intervene not only in Tajikistan but also in the Transcaucasian conflicts. The CIS legitimised Russia's military operations in the former Soviet space, but was unable to establish anything but token collective institutions to control them or collective forces to implement them. Russia increasingly relied on a few key strategic allies (Armenia, Belarus and Kazakhstan, with Uzbekistan rather more hesitant), and the very notion of common security interests for the whole Commonwealth area was soon abandoned.[29] As a *quid pro quo* for Russia's predominant role in stabilising regional conflicts in the CIS within a broadly collective framework, the other Commonwealth states maintained a nervous silence during the Chechen wars.

The diminished threat of nuclear war or inter-state conventional war is today balanced by the rise of regional conflicts.[30] Russia took an active role in 'peace-making' operations, notably in Moldova, Georgia and Tajikistan. Despite the decision to create a CIS peacekeeping force in Tajikistan, Russia's 201st Motorised Rifle Division here acted rather more forcefully than would be expected of mere peacekeepers, patrolling the frontier with Afghanistan and in effect acting as the armed forces of the regime. Tajikistan's southern border effectively became Russia's too, even though the 'Russians abroad' question did not operate here – since 1989 most of the 400,000-strong Russian community had fled. Despite attempts to regionalise the peacekeeping forces, with the agreement of 24 September 1993 providing for Collective Peacekeeping Forces to be supplied by Russia and the Central Asian states (excluding Turkmenistan), the latter proved reluctant to provide troops. In Transdniester General Lebed had stabilised the situation but was unable to provide a solution, and Russia's military presence in the region aggravated international relations into the 2000s.

The CIS proved an inadequate forum for conflict resolution. It could do little to end the conflict between Armenia and Azerbaijan over Nagorno-Karabakh, the war in Tajikistan or the conflict in Moldova. The crises in CIS states forced Russia to undertake a peacekeeping role, but that role retained a strong neo-imperial flavour. By 1996, Russia had some 30,000 troops deployed in various 'peacekeeping' operations in Tajikistan, Moldova (Transdniester) and Georgia (South Ossetia and Abkhazia). The methods used by Russian forces were unusual for UN operations, but in broad terms they remained true to the UN Charter, everywhere having been invited in by the legal governments and with the agreement of all parties concerned. Russian interventions, however, blurred the distinction often drawn between 'peacekeeping' and 'peacemaking' (or peace-enforcement); activities that require radically different approaches – or so it is argued: in the post-communist context the distinction cannot be drawn so forcefully. Nato forces in Bosnia and Kosovo, and Russian forces in Abkhazia and Tajikistan, were both making and keeping the uneasy truces. In its peacekeeping operations, moreover,

Figure 16.4 Central Asia

Russia was never a neutral third party but pursued its own perceived geostrategic interests. This did not mean, however, that under the cover of peacekeeping operations Russia actually sought to seize territory. Its aims were simply to secure for Russia a pre-eminent position and to insulate itself from local conflicts, goals that were radically undermined by the Chechen war. Liberals in Moscow, indeed, asserted that Russia's coercive 'peacekeeping' tactics led 'quite logically to the first bloody war on Russia's territory – Chechnya'.[31] Russia's reluctance, moreover, to withdraw probably inhibited conflict resolution. The November 1999 OSCE summit gave Russia until 1 July 2001 to close down its Gudauta military base in Abkhazia, and, while most combat equipment had been withdrawn, Russia sought to make the base the home of its peacekeeping operations there. The same OSCE meeting had stipulated that Russia leave Transdniester in two phases: the combat hardware by December 2001 and the personnel by December 2002. It was clear that the Putin leadership was reluctant to fulfil Yeltsin's promises at the OSCE summit.

The CIS thus emerged as a framework for collective security, under the aegis of which Russia pursued its own strategic interests and used the conflicts as a way of exerting leverage over states. In the lee of the CIS Russia restored its position in countries like Georgia and consolidated its position in areas of vital concern to itself (like Central Asia). Attempts by Russia, notably at the 48th session of the UN General Assembly, to get the international community to support these operations failed. However, it would be an exaggeration to argue that the CIS and its peacekeeping operations provided a 'fig leaf' under which Russia sought to re-establish imperial control over previously subordinated regions. Russia's ambitions were more modest and went little beyond the attempt to secure a sphere of influence, to dampen down conflicts if not to secure solutions, and to prevent others from entering the former Soviet area. This was an aim pursued both by the foreign and defence ministries, and provided coherence to Russian policy in this field while retaining the essential ambiguity of Russian foreign policy in general.

Minorities and Russians abroad

The disintegration of the USSR did not replace the idea of a historical and national core with a multinational state centred on the territories of the former USSR. This was a view shared not only by the most irreconcilable Soviet and Russian nationalists, but also by a broad swathe of democratic opinion and Gorbachev himself.[32] Russian attempts to imbue the CIS with some content were interpreted as a sign of neo-imperialism by some, but for others they reflected no more than the plain fact that the political community to which they wished to belong was larger than the Russian Federation. It is for this reason that the project to create a joint state of Russia and Belarus enjoyed support across the Russian political spectrum, although there was no agreement over the form that such a union should take.

While a common language, together with a shared history and heritage, is usually considered to lie at the core of a nation, this definition is inadequate when applied to the post-Soviet area. What is the status of Russian-speakers outside Russia? According to the 1989 census, 32.8 per cent of the non-Russian ethnic population in Ukraine use Russian as their primary language, in Belarus 31.9 per cent, in Kazakhstan 47.4 per cent, in Latvia 42.1 per cent, and significant proportions in other republics.[33] Table 16.2 shows that the titular nationality comprises approximately half of the population in Kyrgyzstan, Latvia and Kazakhstan, and between 60–70 per cent in Ukraine, Turkmenistan, Georgia, Uzbekistan, Moldova, Tajikistan and Estonia, and only in Armenia, Azerbaijan, Russia, Lithuania and Belarus approaches or exceeds 80 per cent. At the same time, significant populations live outside their nominal republic: a third of all Armenians, a quarter of Tajiks, a fifth of Kazakhs and a sixth of Russians. Within Russia as well, as we have seen, there is only a loose correspondence between the republics and ethnic composition.

The natural corollary would be to suggest that in the core areas of the Tsarist empire and the Soviet Union a new nation had in fact emerged, of mixed ethnicity but which on a number of parameters (language, history, cultural orientation and so on) constituted a recognisable community. It is precisely this conclusion that is drawn by the national-patriots and neo-communists in Russia, while liberals at home and abroad have not yet come up with an adequate intellectual response to the problems posed by the sudden disintegration of this community.

The Fifth State Duma established a Committee on CIS Affairs and Ties with Compatriots Abroad, chaired by Konstantin Zatulin. He noted that the Russian language was being ousted from the cultural life of the former Soviet republics. Only in Belarus was Russian given the status of a state language (via a referendum),

Table 16.2 Nationalities in the republics, 1989

Republic	Population (thousands)	Titular nationality in republic	Russians (%)	Minor nationalities	(%)	Other (%)
Russia	147,386	–	82.5	Tatar	3.8	15
Estonia	1,573	61.5	30.3	Ukrainian	3.1	5
Latvia	2,681	52.0	34.0	Belarusian	4.5	9
Lithuania	3,690	79.6	9.4	Polish	7.0	4
Moldova	4,341	64.5	13.0	Ukrainian	13.8	9
Belarus	10,200	77.9	13.2	Polish	4.0	5
Ukraine	51,704	72.7	22.1	Jewish	0.9	4
Armenia	3,283	93.3	1.6	Azeri	2.6	2
Azerbaijan	7,029	82.7	5.6	Armenian	5.6	5
Georgia	5,449	70.1	6.3	Armenian	8.1	16
Kazakhstan	16,538	39.7	37.8	German	5.8	16
Kyrgyzstan	4,291	52.4	21.5	Uzbek	12.9	14
Tajikistan	5,112	62.3	7.6	Uzbek	23.5	6
Turkmenistan	3,534	72.0	9.5	Uzbek	9.0	10
Uzbekistan	19,906	71.4	8.3	Tajik	4.7	16
Total	286,717					

Source: *USSR: Facts and Figures Annual*, ed. Alan P. Pollard, Vol. 15 (Gulf Breeze, FL, Academic International Press, 1991), pp. 499–502.

while in some other republics (in particular in Central Asia) Russian speakers were in effect prohibited from taking up certain professions. Article 10 of the Ukrainian constitution adopted on 28 June 1996 stressed that 'The state language of Ukraine is the Ukrainian language', but grudgingly conceded that 'In Ukraine, the free development, use and protection of Russian, and other languages of national minorities of Ukraine, is guaranteed.'[34]

The problem of national minorities in the newly independent republics became a critical one as millions of citizens suddenly found themselves 'abroad'. Some 60 million former Soviet citizens lived outside their nominal republics, 25 million of whom were Russians and 35 million of other nationalities. The sad history of the inter-war years, when large populations of Germans in the Sudetenland, Hungarians in Romania (a problem remaining to this day), Poles in Lithuania (also a current problem), and Ukrainians in Poland, all embittered the triumph of restored statehood after the First World War. The failure satisfactorily to address the question led to the wars in Yugoslavia. In the USSR the idea of a titular nationality in the union and autonomous republics inevitably gave rise to notions of ethnically pure territories. The new states have been called 'ethnocratic' because of the advantages, if only linguistic, enjoyed by the titular nationality.[35] The relationship between national rights and individual human rights was once again posed in the sharpest possible terms. The very definition of nationality is questioned, and while much is made of the contingency of ethnic identity, it is real enough for those on the ground when the issue becomes politicised.

The diaspora problem affects many peoples, including 7 million Ukrainians and 5 million Tatars. The lack of correspondence between Russia and the borders of the post-Soviet Russian Federation, however, means that by far the largest problem in this respect are ethnic Russians (see Table 16.3). Some 17.4 per cent (25.3 million people) of the total Russian population of the former USSR found themselves in the 'near abroad'.[36] Of these, 11.3 million were in Ukraine, 6.2 million in Kazakhstan, 1.7 million in Uzbekistan, 1.3 million in Belarus, and nearly half a million in Estonia.[37] How were these people to be classified? They were ethnically Russians, but many were willing to take on the citizenship (if offered) of their host republic. Already in his speech of 28 October 1991 to the Fifth CPD, Yeltsin was careful to talk of the plight of 'Russian-speakers' in the neighbouring republics, but the patriots insisted on using the term 'Russian citizens'.[38] One way or the other, the idea of a larger Russian community, transcending the apparently arbitrary state borders of 1991, remains a central factor in Russian politics.[39]

There remained the genuine dilemma of how to handle the question of Russians abroad. The OSCE sought to ensure minimum standards in the treatment of ethnic minorities by creating, in summer 1992, an office of High Commissioner on National Minorities, and appointed Max van der Stoel to the post. The aim was to achieve early intervention in ethnic disputes, but effective action was inhibited by cumbersome decision-making procedures. The United Nations appeared as ineffective as the old League of Nations in restraining the dictatorships and ethnic terror of the interwar years. The failure of pan-European institutions in the post-Cold War era is nowhere more apparent than in the failure to internationalise inter-ethnic conflicts or to establish by international treaty a supervision mechanism to uphold at least a minimal definition of human and civic rights.

Table 16.3 Ethnic Russians and Russian-speakers in Soviet republics outside Russia, 1989

Republic	Ethnic Russians		Russian-speaking	
	Estimated total	As % of population	Estimated total	As % of population
Estonia	474,000	30.3	544,000	34.8
Latvia	905,000	34.0	1,122,000	42.1
Lithuania	344,000	9.4	429,000	11.7
Moldova	562,000	13.0	1,003,000	23.1
Belarus	1,342,000	13.2	3,243,000	31.9
Ukraine	11,355,000	22.1	16,898,000	32.8
Azerbaijan	391,000	5.6	528,000	7.5
Armenia	51,000	1.6	66,000	2.0
Georgia	341,000	6.3	479,000	8.9
Kazakhstan	6,227,000	37.8	7,797,000	47.4
Kyrgyzstan	916,000	21.5	1,090,000	25.6
Tajikistan	388,000	7.6	495,000	9.7
Turkmenistan	333,000	9.5	421,000	12.0
Uzbekistan	1,653,000	8.3	2,151,000	10.9

Source: *Naselenie Rossii: ezhegodnyi demograficheskii doklad* (Moscow, the Centre for the Demography and Ecology of Man, 1993), p. 15.

Note: The category of Russian-speakers includes non-ethnic Russians regarding Russian as their native language. Since 1989, there has been considerable out-migration of Russians from these republics and thus the figures given above have decreased.

Russian policy lacked consistency and reflected the problems of developing a post-imperial foreign policy. Russian policy tended to be reactive. If indeed the issue of 'Russians abroad' was primary and Solzhenitsyn's idea of a Slavic union had any resonance, then one would have anticipated that Russian policy would have concentrated on areas where Russians were concentrated, notably eastern Ukraine, Crimea and northern Kazakhstan, whereas in fact Russia made no attempt to use the issue of Russians' right to split the countries and absorb contested areas. Any attempt to do so, as Emil Pain (a member of the Presidential Council) warned, would provoke a permanently destabilising legacy of hatred in the residual states.[40]

While continuing to reject the use of force and even economic pressure as a means to protect Russian, Russian-speaking and other minorites in the near abroad, Kozyrev noted that the principle of 'non-interference' in the domestic affairs of other states did not apply to the protection of the rights of minorities, and he insisted that Russia would continue to act to protect the rights of Russians abroad.[41] Addressing the Council of Foreign Policy, Kozyrev in early 1995 for the first time accepted that military force might join diplomatic, political and economic pressure as legitimate means of defending Russians abroad. Although Russian forces had been used in Moldova, Tajikistan and Abkhazia, the enunciation of force as an explicit policy option marked a new stage in the evolution of a more nationally centred foreign policy. Kozyrev, however, was careful to distance himself from militant nationalists, condemning their attempts to exploit the issue of Russians living abroad as liable to provoke even greater Russophobia and noting that this 'is the direct path to Russia's isolation or the Yugoslav scenario'.[42]

Conclusion

Historians will long debate whether the disintegration of the USSR was inevitable. With more effective leadership in 1989–91 could some form of confederation have been established? If Gorbachev had focused less on saving socialism and more on rooting a reformed social democratic regime in a renegotiated state, could the community that for good or ill had taken a thousand years to build have been saved? In the short term the attempt to create a new Union of Sovereign States failed because the elites in the republics did not trust the centre in Moscow and were not ready to give up their own power or to compromise the sovereignty of their republics to form a new Union. Yeltsin and his government always argued that they had had no intention of destroying the old Union, but their actions precipitated the latent disintegrative tendencies.

At the same time, although the traditional geopolitical organisation of Eurasia had failed, there remain powerful integrative tendencies. Gorbachev's argument, that it would be unwise to dissolve the Union at a time when the European Union was accelerating its own integration, was premature. Whereas the EU states began with stable subjects of union, the Eurasian unit Gorbachev was advocating would have been based on shards that had splintered from what had been in effect a unitary USSR. The republics were convinced that only after the full reconstitution of statehood could reintegrative processes begin. The creation of a customs union between Russia, Belarus and Kazakhstan is a powerful reminder of these centripetal trends.

For fourteen of the republics separation from the former USSR was a relatively straightforward process; for Russia, however, the question of withdrawing from the USSR was far more complex since in certain respects the two were one and the same; at least, this was the way that it looked to the other republics and to many in Russia as well. Thus, Soviet troops withdrawing from the Baltic suddenly became Russian troops and returned not to an abstract USSR but to a concrete Russia. Separation from the USSR and its legacy for many republics took the form of weakening their traditional links with Russia. Russia, however, did not go away and the new republics soon discovered that the diversification of economic and foreign-policy concerns had to be accompanied by a new relationship with Russia.

How were the post-communist societies and states to interact with each other, and how was their mutual interdependence to become constructive and the legacy of mistrust overcome? The CIS played a valuable part in this, yet its inadequacies reflected the larger problem of establishing national identities and structuring a post-imperial community. A fundamental instability lay at the heart of post-Soviet relations between the republics. Most had gained territory at Russia's expense, and were therefore *status quo* states, whereas Russia had been the net loser out of Soviet administrative reorganisations, and was therefore potentially a revisionist power. The national-patriots in Russia sought to exploit these latent revisionist sentiments, alarming the other republics. The mix of instability in Russian domestic politics, the problem of Russians 'abroad', the presence of what had become Russian garrisons in neighbouring states, and the insecure nationalism of the new states, all made a potentially lethal cocktail of irredentism, ethnic conflicts and war.

17 Defence and security policy

The wolfhound century leaps at my shoulders,
But I am no wolf by blood.
(Osip Mandelstam)[1]

The USSR was one of the world's most militarised states, with 5 million men under arms in 1988 and another 4 million employed in defence industries, and with some 15–20 per cent of Soviet GDP devoted to the upkeep of this vast 'state within a state'.[2] The well-known saying that 'The USSR did not *have* a military-industrial complex, it *was* one' reflected a frightening truth. Not only were the country's economic resources diverted towards supporting the country's enormous military establishment, but also the system of conscription and patriotic education made the military the cornerstone of national identity. *Perestroika* represented the repudiation of the logic of Cold War, and by rejecting a security-dominated foreign policy suggested that domestic politics and the economy would also be demilitarised. The disintegration of the USSR was soon followed by the division of the Soviet armed forces as the newly independent republics created their own military establishments. Russia was burdened with the legacy of Soviet imperial expansion, a bloated defence sector and, perhaps most significantly, a military establishment accustomed to getting its own way. Could a new model of civil–military relations be forged in post-communist Russia, and with it a demilitarised sense of national purpose?

The end of the Soviet armed forces

With the fall of communism the Soviet Armed Forces were no longer a military threat but a source of social and political instability to the countries that had sacrificed so much to give them birth. Attempts to maintain a single CIS command after 1991 were soon undermined by the aspirations of republics like Ukraine to create their own armed forces, fuelled by fears that a Russianised Soviet Army could be used to reimpose Moscow's rule. Odom, indeed, in his study of the end of the Soviet armed forces calls his chapter dealing with these events 'The Illusion of the CIS Armed Forces'.[3] Russia itself had been reluctant to create its own armed forces, yet by early 1992 was forced to embark on this path. Russia was now required to disengage its forces from neighbouring countries, maintain control over the huge nuclear arsenal, and at the same time to reconstruct its own armed forces for new tasks.

What was to be done with the Soviet Army, most of it deployed in Russia and which in ethos and tradition appeared antithetical to the principles of the new democracy? After the *coup*, the General Staff in Moscow was left virtually without a master; there was an army, but no state.[4] Yeltsin at that time sought to gain the allegiance of the high command by promising to keep the army intact, but following the disintegration of the USSR this proved both meaningless and counter-productive as morale and discipline plummeted. Some long-term solution to the problem had to be found; by necessity rather than choice because of the creation of national armies in other republics and the weakness of CIS military structures. Russia ultimately simply renamed the Soviet Army the Russian Army, and thus incorporated the best as well as the worst of the old traditions. The great majority of its officers (80 per cent) were Russian and some 90 per cent, including almost all senior officers, were members of the Communist Party. Russia was left to deal with the problems bequeathed by the old regime, with forces stationed not only in the former Soviet republics but also in Germany and Poland.

The former Soviet defence minister, Dmitrii Yazov, was implicated in the *coup*, and his replacement, Yevgenii Shaposhnikov, immediately launched a purge in the ministry.[5] He later became the commander-in-chief of what became known as the Joint Command, formally accountable to the CIS Council of Heads of State, but in practice the absence of any effective CIS command mechanism meant that he worked closely with Yeltsin.[6] The Joint Command was responsible for control over strategic nuclear arms, the co-ordination of military doctrines and reforms of CIS states, and the resolution of armed conflicts both within the CIS and along its borders.[7] The Bishkek summit in October 1992 agreed to develop a joint military security concept as well as a new command structure for CIS forces.[8] Ukraine, however, sought to escape from the old security system centred on Moscow, and attempts to maintain the CIS Joint Command as the core of a common security system soon foundered, and on 15 June 1993 it was abolished. Thus, the Soviet armed forces, victorious over Nazi Germany but also destroyer of hope in Budapest and Prague, finally died.

Already in December 1991, Ukraine, Azerbaijan and Moldova had announced plans to create their own armed forces. Kravchuk in December 1991 declared himself commander-in-chief of all forces on Ukrainian territory, some half a million men. Instead of seeking the removal of Soviet forces (the policy pursued by the Baltic states), Ukraine assimilated the Soviet Army (including some of the best equipped front-line forces and aviation) to its own purposes. In January 1992, all forces on its territory were required to take an oath of allegiance to the republic, something done with surprising alacrity by soldiers in the Kiev, Odessa and Carpathian Military Districts (MDs). Some 40 per cent were Russian, and they were faced with the choice of pledging allegiance to Ukraine or returning to an uncertain but in most cases hard future in Russia. Ukraine's decision in June 1992 to deport military officers who refused to take the oath of loyalty demonstrated the irrevocable breakdown of the concept of CIS forces.[9] Ukraine now had Europe's second largest army, with ground forces of 308,000 in 1994.[10]

The Conventional Forces in Europe (CFE) treaty was signed in Paris on 19 November 1990 by the twenty-two Nato and former Warsaw Treaty Organisation (WTO) nations (the number of signatories later rose to twenty-nine). The treaty, ratified by the Russian parliament on 8 July 1992, stipulated that the Russian Army and Navy had to be reduced from 2.8 million men to 2.1 million by 1995 and placed restrictions on the number, type and deployment of weapons and forces; indeed, of all the signatories only Russia (and Ukraine) faced restrictions on where weapons could be stationed on their own territory. Germany is allowed a maximum of 375,000 soldiers by the CFE Treaty, and Ukraine's ratification of the CFE Treaty in July 1992 limited its forces to 250,000.[11] In the event, Russia redeployed significant forces beyond the Urals, outside the scope of the CFE treaty.

The CFE treaty set strict limits to the number of conventional forces west of the Urals, and placed a ceiling on the number of forces Russia could have on its northern (St Petersburg MD) and southern (North Caucasus MD) flanks.[12] Much Treaty Limited Equipment (TLE) was eliminated by the time the treaty came into force in November 1992, and even more was destroyed in advance of the full implementation of the Treaty in July 1996. Russia was limited to 1,700 tanks in European Russia, a sixth of the Soviet total.[13] Moscow sought to revise the treaty, in particular the northern and southern flank limits, on the grounds that what had been negotiated for the USSR was inappropriate for an independent Russia, whose security and geostrategic problems had changed so dramatically. Russia hoped to replace the treaty with a more general European arms-control agreement that would limit military research and development expenditure. Above all, Russia requested greater flexibility in the deployment of its forces to meet its new security needs, in particular in the North Caucasus (including Chechnya), transformed from a rear MD in the Soviet era to a front-line zone of conflict covering Russia's only access to the Black Sea and the Caspian.[14] The West conceded that the CFE treaty placed particularly severe restrictions on Russia, and the limits were slightly revised in late 1995, and the full review in May 1996 granted Russia three extra years to comply.

The successor republics gradually took over their own security and foreign policy. In Russia the problem of ethnicity and divided allegiances played little role since the officer corps was overwhelmingly Russian. The emergence of a Russian national army, however, was retarded by the role played by the Joint Command and by a residual belief that Russia would be the centre of some larger unit. Instead, the republics created their own armed forces and the CIS failed to establish a security structure similar to Nato. The Collective Security Treaty signed in Tashkent on 15 May 1992 was limited both in scope and in terms of the countries involved (see Chapter 16). The CIS was reduced to dividing Soviet military assets between the former republics, within the terms of the CFE treaty.

Russia was one of the last CIS states to have its own army. Yeltsin's decree on the formation of a Russian Ministry of Defence on 16 March 1992 named himself acting defence minister, and on 7 May he finally ordered the creation of a Russian Army with himself as commander-in-chief.[15] On 18 May, General Pavel Grachev was appointed minister of defence. As commander of the Soviet Airborne Forces he had obstructed the plotters in August 1991, and was appointed a deputy USSR defence minister and head of Russia's Defence Committee, having operational command of Russian forces when Yeltsin was acting defence minister. In the event, Grachev proved to lack any strategic sense of how to conduct military reform, as well as demonstrating himself to be an incompetent tactician, as shown by the repeated blunders he committed in the first Chechen war.

Hopes that a civilian defence minister would be appointed and that the defence ministry would become a civilian department were disappointed.[16] The Law on Defence adopted by parliament after long debate in September 1992 defined the scope of military activity and imposed a strict system of state control over the military, but attempts to enshrine the principle that only a civilian could occupy the post of minister of defence were defeated at the last minute. The first deputy minister, Andrei Kokoshin (responsible for relations with the defence industries and scientific-military policy), was a first-rate academic defence specialist, and indeed the first civilian to be appointed to a leadership position in the armed forces since the 1920s. The majority of appointments to senior posts, however, reflected the predominance of traditionalists. The appointment of Boris Gromov, formerly commander of the Soviet Army in Afghanistan, as deputy defence minister was widely interpreted as a concession to hard-liners. It was only under Putin in 2001 that a civilian defence minister, Sergei Ivanov, was appointed, albeit a man with a security background.

The leadership of the Ministry of Defence pledged to maintain Russia as a military 'great power' and to call a halt to the strategic retreat begun by Gorbachev. The transformation of the Soviet Army into a Russian one was not accompanied by the sort of reforms in organisation and mentality that affected the rest of society. Instead, the Russian Army remained a monument to traditional Russian and Soviet values, including a strongly developed sense of self-preservation, a culture of secrecy (as demonstrated over its handling of the sinking of the Kursk nuclear submarine in August 2000), its self-ascription as the enshrinement of the highest values of society, its commitment to maintaining Russia as a 'great power', and above all a sense of its own superiority *vis-à-vis* the civil authorities. The weakening of civil control over the military was demonstrated by the remarkable freedom with which Russian armed forces appeared to conduct their own foreign policy in regions such as Abkhazia, Transdniester and Central Asia.

The great retreat

The dissolution of the WTO in June 1991 and the disintegration of the USSR accelerated the retreat of what had now become Russian forces not only from Central Europe but also from large parts of what had formerly been home territory. In the former East Germany, covering 22 per cent of contemporary Germany, 375,000 troops of the Western Group of Forces (WGF) remained. By June 1991, all Soviet forces had left Hungary and Czechoslovakia, and the last Russian combat troops left Poland in October 1992; in 1993, however, 250,000 remained to be repatriated from Germany, Poland, the Baltic and Transcaucasia.[17] Finally, forty-nine years after the Soviet flag had been hoisted over the Reichstag, the last Russian troops left Berlin on 31 August 1994. The date symbolises the end of an epoch: the Cold War, the division of Europe and superpower 'overlay' over the destiny of European states.

Russia became the successor not only to the Soviet Union, but also to the geopolitical realities that had created the Russian empire earlier. Russia *de facto* became a neo-imperial power not by choice but by history. How could Russia shed this burden while maintaining its long-term strategic interests? The definition of these interests, as we have seen, was contested, but Russia's role as a regional power was to some degree thrust upon it by the escalation of regional conflicts. The removal of forces from Moldova, for example, was complicated by the insurgency in Transdniester. An agreement was reached on 10 August 1994 for the removal of all Russian forces from Moldova within three years, but Moscow on this occasion as in the future dragged its feet over fulfilling its commitments. The vast stockpile of equipment and weapons was only slowly removed.

The Baltic republics asserted that the enforced stationing of troops on foreign soil was a violation of international law; as long as 'foreign' troops remained, the three republics could not feel fully independent. In late 1991, there were some 25,000 former Soviet troops in Estonia, 60,000 in Latvia and 40,000 in Lithuania. Negotiations on their removal embittered relations between the new democracies. Grachev in June 1992 argued that the troops could not be withdrawn until housing had been provided for them in Russia, a process that would take several years. Neither was it clear who would pay the pensions of the former military personnel living in these republics. The negotiators were caught between extremists on both flanks: in Russia the national-patriots and neo-communists urged Yeltsin to take a firmer line against the Baltic states; whereas nationalists there insisted that Russia remove the forces immediately. Up to mid-1992, Russia treated the Baltic forces as a single unit, but at that point indicated that it would be willing to contemplate the speedier withdrawal from Lithuania because of its more amenable approach to citizenship issues.[18] Despite attempts to link military withdrawal to civic rights, the number of Russian troops continued to decline because falling conscription meant that soldiers who had completed their tour of duty were not replaced; by the end of 1992, all but 50,000 of the troops had gone. The removal of troops was completed in Lithuania by the end of August 1993, and the last Russian troops withdrew from Estonia and Latvia by 31 August 1994. Thus, the North-West Group of Forces ceased to exist, and Russian troops in Kaliningrad (the Eleventh Army) now came directly under the command of GHQ Land Forces. By August 1994, some 1.5 million troops had been redeployed to Russian territory from Eastern Europe and the former USSR; no significant Russian forces were stationed outside the former Soviet Union.

The 'great retreat' affected parts of the Russian Federation proper. Following the abortive intervention in Chechnya in November 1991, when some 500 troops were sent and then summarily withdrawn, Russia removed its forces from the republic but left behind enormous quantities of *matériel* and arms, to be used by the insurgents in the war from December 1994. Russia removed its forces from Nagorno-Karabakh, and in May 1992 an agreement was signed with Azerbaijan on the withdrawal of all Russian forces within two years. The relocated troops faced a hard fate in Russia, competing for housing, jobs and pensions with those released by earlier cuts. Many of the 30,000 officers and their dependants withdrawn from Hungary and Czechoslovakia lived in converted barracks while the troops lived under canvas, with many junior officers being below the poverty line. The pitiful plight of forces from CIS countries was graphically illustrated by the case of the 104th Airborne Division, relocated from Ganja in Azerbaijan to

Ulyanovsk in 1993. In their 'home' country, the troops were treated almost as invaders and faced difficulties in finding housing and integrating into the local community.[19]

The retreat encompassed not only the physical return of troops but also a decline in the prestige and morale of the armed forces in their entirety. The military profession was no longer an attractive one, and many officers left for better-paid jobs in the growing private sector. The retreat was accompanied by the erosion of discipline, with many officers taking up entrepreneurial activities to create 'military-commercial clans' specialising in the sale of weapons and equipment. By 2001, there were some 10 million unlicensed weapons in private hands. Corruption in the Russian Army was accompanied by the illegal sale of military property through underhand deals between the military supply service and commercial interests.[20] It was while investigating corruption in the WGF that the journalist Dmitrii Kholodov was murdered in Moscow in 1994 by a suitcase bomb, planted it is alleged by officers trying to cover up massive illicit arms sales. Mass demobilisation and desertion, moreover, threatened stability throughout former Soviet territory.

The increased assertiveness of Russian foreign policy from 1994 was accompanied by attempts to put an end to the retreat. Russia's redefined security policy now sought to keep some military bases in the 'near' and 'far' abroad. Overseas, USSR/Russia since 1979 had enjoyed the rent-free lease of Cam Ranh Bay naval base in Vietnam, but following the failure to reach an advantageous deal once the lease expired in 2004 Russia pulled out, signalling the end of its aspirations to maintain a blue-water navy in the Indian and Pacific Oceans. Russia in 2001 announced the closure of the Lourdes listening post in Cuba. Nearer to home, the Skrunda radar station in Latvia was closed in 1998 and replaced by the new strategic radar site 'Volga' in Barnaovichy in Belarus. Twenty-eight Russian bases proper remained in the CIS. In Belarus an Air Force regiment remained at Zyabrouka;[21] the Russian military presence was indeed strengthened as the joint Belarus–Russia state began to take shape. There are two bases in Armenia (Erevan and Gyumri), but none in Azerbaijan, although Russia leases the Lyaki early-warning radar installation. It was clear that the Russian high command had decided against a repetition of the precipitate retreat from Eastern Europe.

The four bases in Georgia were the most contentious. At the Istanbul summit on 19 November 1999, Russia agreed to close two of the four by 1 July 2001. Russia fulfilled its obligations concerning the Vaziani base near Tbilisi (the former headquarters of the Transcaucasus Group of Forces), but at Gudauta in the breakaway Abkhaz region the local population allegedly insisted on Russia remaining at the base as the headquarters for peacekeeping operations. Georgia also sought Russia's withdrawal within four years from the bases at Akhalkalaki and Batumi, used for motor rifle divisions, while Russia insisted that for economic reasons this could only take place in thirteen to fourteen years. In the late 1990s, some 100,000 men remained in the near abroad, engaged in various peacekeeping operations and in the bases. Some 24,000 soldiers were in Tajikistan alone, policing the border with Afghanistan and maintaining the fragile regime. As the president, Imomali Rakhmonov, put it, for Tajikistan 'Russia is our chief strategic ally.'[22] The great retreat was finally over.

Defence conversion and arms sales

Soviet defence industries had absorbed about a fifth of national income every year since the Second World War. By the last year of *perestroika* in 1991, nothing much was left of the old Soviet centrally planned economy, but what did remain was over-whelming state ownership and a bloated defence sector. Despite Gorbachev's announcement at the UN in December 1988 of a conversion programme diverting resources to consumer goods,[23] little positive had been achieved. In 1991, the Russian economy was one of the most militarised in the world with some 5.5 million industrial and research workers directly employed in defence plants, 24 per cent of industrial employees.[24] According to Mikhail Malei, responsible at the time for the conversion programme, some 35 million people, including families, lived off the military or military-related industries.[25] One-third of St Petersburg's workforce were employed in defence plants, and in some other major industrial regions like Saratov or Novosibirsk the proportion was even higher. The huge scale of Russian defence industries and the large proportion of GNP that it represented, the concentration in 'company towns', the regional concentration and the isolation of the defence sector from the civilian economy with little technological spillover all inhibited attempts to demilitarise the economy.

The term 'military-industrial complex' in fact denoted the most effective part of the Russian economy in which its most technologically sophisticated enterprises were to be found. Defence factories produced not only guns and tanks, but also televisions and high-technology consumer goods.[26] The Law on Conversion of Defence Industries of 20 March 1992 provided a programme for conversion, but left the details for later legislation. Conversion from guns to butter, however, entailed large investment costs, which could only be earned by arms sales to customers paying in convertible currencies.

Controls on arms sales were relaxed to provide foreign currency for the hard-pressed exchequer. Throughout the 1980s, the USSR sold (or transferred) annually some $12 billion worth of arms, but in 1992 this fell to only $1.5 billion, a figure that rose to $2.7 billion in 1995, 13.6 per cent of the world's arms market. Russia launched an aggressive campaign of arms sales on the world market not only to gain foreign currency but also to use factories and skills to maximum advantage. An increasingly sharp rivalry developed between Russia and the United States for a share of the coveted arms market, and became a factor in Russian foreign policy. The United States had legitimate fears that Russia's desperation for foreign currency encouraged sales to unstable areas, such as submarines to Iran and Sukhoi-30Mk1 fighters to China and India, yet at the same time there was an element of commercial cupidity in the United States' calculations, as in its apparent attempt to dislodge Russia from its traditional arms market in India and elsewhere. This worked the other way as well, and with the end of the Cold War Russia moved into new markets in Malaysia, Pakistan, South Africa and Turkey. Russia fought hard to retain its status as the world's third largest arms seller, in 2000 selling $4.3 billion of arms abroad, $400,000 more than in 1999. Only the United States and Great Britain sold more.

Government policy was caught between its desire for conversion, on the one hand, and the attempt to maintain the defence capacity of the country, arms sales and employment, on the other. Although military spending in Russia fell to 7.2 per cent of GNP in 1991[27] and below 5 per cent thereafter, state arms orders and development funding fell even more dramatically. Millions of defence workers became unemployed and the rest suffered from low wages and loss of morale. Resources devoted to military scientific research fell sharply, while electronic and high-technology industries operated at sharply reduced levels. Investment in military enterprises also fell sharply, and factories making military equipment survived only by drawing on government credits, which in turn threatened macro-economic stabilisation. The Russian Army suffered from increasing technological backwardness because of cuts in research and procurements. On coming to power Putin promised extra investment in the defence industries, and intensified the programme of foreign arms sales. The conversion programme was marked by uncertainties over strategy, a lack of funds except from sources (arms sales) that perpetuated the imbalances of Russian industry which they were designed to overcome, and an unclear definition of Russia's own defence needs.

Nuclear politics and non-proliferation

With the fall of communism the instruments of the Cold War became a greater threat to world peace than the systems that had given them birth. Nuclear weapons lost much of their strategic significance but the race to possess them and the difficulty of disposing of them provoked regional rivalries and international concern. India and Pakistan in 2000 became confirmed nuclear states, while Israel, South Africa and some others were 'threshold' states, ready to join the five permanent members of the UN Security Council as nuclear states. A number of 'rogue' states, above all Iraq and North Korea, had demonstrated missile capacity, against which the United States sought to develop Missile Defence. The proliferation of nuclear technologies threatened global security, and in the former USSR they became a source of political instability.[28]

The modest cuts envisaged by the Start-1 Treaty of 31 July 1991 were surpassed by a number of proposals later that year. While nuclear weaponry lost some of its political value in East–West relations, among the successor states nuclear issues involved delicate power plays and the management of symbolic relationships. The four nuclear successor republics (Russia, Ukraine, Belarus and Kazakhstan) and the West were agreed that nuclear proliferation should be avoided and that Russia should emerge as the only successor nuclear state, but, as usual, the devil is in the details. The Almaty inaugural meeting of the CIS on 21 December 1991 vowed to maintain unified control over nuclear weapons: the president of Russia was granted the exclusive right to use them but only with the approval of the other three nuclear states. Shaposhnikov, as supreme commander of CIS forces, took over control, sharing the firing codes with Yeltsin. This arrangement did not last long, and, the day after the decision by the CIS defence ministers on 15 June 1993 to disband the Joint Command, Shaposhnikov was relieved of the 'nuclear suitcase'.

Even if the security of most of the former USSR's 27,000 nuclear weapons, about two-thirds of which were strategic and the rest tactical, were guaranteed, it would take only one to cause a major catastrophe.[29] There were fears that weapons could find their way to what were then nuclear 'threshold' states like Pakistan, Iran,

Iraq and Libya. In addition, some 900,000 people were involved in the maintenance of the USSR's thermonuclear arsenal, with perhaps 2,000 people with knowledge of nuclear weapons design and some 3–5,000 with experience in plutonium production or uranium enrichment.[30] Defeat in 1945 had allowed the United States to attract German experts in missile technology, so too now there were fears that the collapse of the USSR would lead to the proliferation of nuclear technology. The only consolation was that the medium-range weapons had already been destroyed under the terms of the 1987 Intermediate Nuclear Forces (INF) Treaty.

At the December 1991 Almaty meeting, Ukraine and Belarus agreed to join the 1968 Non Proliferation Treaty (NPT) as non-nuclear states, and only Kazakhstan hesitated in agreeing to the withdrawal of nuclear weapons from its territory. However, under pressure from a vociferous pro-nuclear lobby Ukraine later modified its approach. Ukraine regarded military policy as part of the overall struggle for independence, and thus had second thoughts about unilaterally undermining its bargaining position by renouncing nuclear weapons.[31] The prime minister and from June 1994 president, Leonid Kuchma, had for ten years been the manager of the world's largest missile plant (Yuzhmash) and insisted that Ukraine had the technical means to maintain its missiles. Ukraine sought political control over the 176 missiles with some 1,200 warheads 'temporarily' on its territory.[32] Kazakhstan and Ukraine suspected, probably correctly, that while they had nuclear weapons Russia would negotiate more respectfully with them. By mid-1992, all tactical nuclear weapons had been moved to Russia, but Ukraine and Kazakhstan equivocated over the removal of strategic nuclear weapons. The pro-nuclear lobby insisted that in exchange for surrendering its arsenal Ukraine should receive certain security guarantees. What form these guarantees could take was unclear, and the issue damaged Ukraine's international standing. The Lisbon Protocol of 23 May 1992 made Belarus, Kazakhstan and Ukraine partners to the Start-1 Treaty, together with Russia and the United States, and all three pledged to join the NPT as non-nuclear states.[33] Despite misgivings Kazakhstan finally joined the NPT, and Ukraine, too, joined as a non-nuclear weapon state on 5 December 1994.

Despite much opposition, the Russian parliament ratified the Start-1 Treaty on 4 November 1992, but already a more radical version was being prepared. Yeltsin described the Start-2 Treaty signed in Moscow on 3 January 1993 as 'surpassing all other disarmament treaties in its scale and importance', while Bush Snr, taking his final bow on the world stage, saw the treaty as marking the definitive end to the Cold War and the start of a 'new world of hope' in which 'parents and children would have a future far more free from fear'. A total of some 17,000 nuclear warheads were to be destroyed, and the American and Russian strategic arsenals were to be cut to between 3–3,500 warheads each by 1 January 2003, less than half the total agreed by the Start-1 Treaty. These cuts of a combined total of some 21,000 strategic weapons would take place in two stages and would include the elimination of all land-based intercontinental ballistic missiles with multiple and independently targeted warheads (MIRVs), notably Russia's ten-warhead SS-18s, either through straightforward scrapping or through conversion to a single warhead (to a maximum of ninety) by adapting the launching pads. Within ten years the number of submarine-based missiles (SLBMs), the main American deterrent, was to be capped at 1,750. This committed the United States to destroying about half of its 432 Trident I and II missiles with their eight warheads apiece. Several Russian demands, largely motivated by considerations of economy, were taken into account in formulating the treaty, such as its plan to adapt ninety SS-18 launch pads to take SS-25s, and to convert 105 of its six-warhead SS-19s into single-warhead weapons.

The agreement signalled that the Cold War was truly over, and that arms control had entered a qualitatively new phase with deep cuts reducing the number of super-power ballistic warheads from the peak of 26,331 agreed by the Salt Agreement of 1988 to a little over 6,000 in 2003. Russia broke with the fundamental principle of Soviet military doctrine, namely the need to maintain nuclear parity with the United States. Deterrence as such had ended in 1991 when most missiles had stopped being targeted on each other. It would be a long path, however, from signing to implementing Start-2; not only was there significant opposition in the Duma, which sought to link the issue to Nato enlargement, but the sheer cost of decommissioning placed yet more strain on an over-stretched budget. In a strange reversal of roles some of the funds were provided by the United States. In the event, one of the first acts of Putin's presidency was to convince the newly compliant Duma to ratify the Start-2 treaty, which it did in early 2000. By then there was talk of a further Start-3 process, but negotiations were compromised by American plans for the 'son of Star Wars' (National) Missile Defence (NMD) shield, enthusiasti-cally supported by president George W. Bush. Russia's fear was that Missile Defence would provide the Americans with unilateral strategic invulnerability, while the United States' European allies were concerned that the scrapping of the 1972 ABM treaty (announced in December 2001) would provoke a new arms race.

Russia and the United States have a common interest in preventing nuclear proliferation because, apart from the dangers involved, the more countries with nuclear weapons, the less influence for them. The optimum level of their nuclear arsenals, however, remains a matter of debate. Despite the awesome dismantlement costs involved, it was Russia that in 1995 had suggested negotiations for a Start-3 treaty to reduce nuclear arsenals to some thousand warheads each; sufficient for retaliation, but not enough for a disabling first strike. Faced by the deterioration of its conventional forces, however, Russia became more rather than less dependent on nuclear weapons. In the late 1990s, Russia successfully tested the Topol-M nuclear missile and began its deployment. The Soviet commitment to no first use of nuclear weapons was dropped in the National Security Doctrine adopted in 2000, and the debate over whether conventional or nuclear weapons should take priority paral-ysed military reform. While the possession of nuclear weapons on its own does not guarantee a state 'great-power' status, Russia's position as the world's second nuclear power did add a certain authority to its foreign policy.

Military reform

The Chechen wars raised in the sharpest possible form the need for military reform, revealing low morale, confused lines of subordination, weak political control and confused tactics. The first war was poorly planned and led to enor-mous civilian and military losses, the city of Grozny was pulverised, and the resort to a military solution when negotiations had not been exhausted suggested a political establishment out of control. The war was marked by staff and planning chaos, with at least three armies involved, often competing (and even firing) against each other: the regular Russian Army, interior ministry (MVD) forces, and security ministry (FSK/B) troops. Above all, the shocking brutality of the war affected public opinion profoundly, and despite the alleged support for Zhirinovskii's plans for a 'Last Push to the South',[34] polls revealed a strong rejection of neo-imperialist schemes. A survey in April 1995 revealed that 74 per cent were opposed to retaining the Chechen Republic as part of the Russian Federation.[35]

The army as such was only a reluctant accomplice to the war. The Chechen campaign was nominally an internal security affair so the MVD should have taken charge, but on its own was clearly unable to subdue a whole republic. The regular army, however, accepted responsibility only with reluctance, with Major-General Ivan Babichev arguing that the assault was unconstitutional (a view which the Constitutional Court later rejected), but finally took part in the assault on Grozny. The Defence Ministry Collegium was completely excluded from managing the operation, while the General Staff played only a limited part in the operational planning of the intervention, one of the reasons for the confused objectives and the eclectic composition of the assault forces. On 25 January 1995, the MVD's General Alexander Romanov took over operational command but inter-service conflicts continued. While the second war from a military point of view was more effective (at least, at first), the autonomy granted the military was worrying, as were the repeated human rights abuses. The transfer of responsibility to the FSB in February 2001 and the withdrawal of some troops could not mask the second failure of trying to impose a military solution on the region. The Chechen wars drained an already exhausted army, diverting reserves from other peacekeeping operations and devoured resources that could have been used to rebuild a professional military force.

Military reform focuses on two key issues: *professionalisation*, above all devising a new relationship with personnel; and *modernisation*, covering command structures, technical organisation and equipment. We shall examine other aspects of reform, such as developing a new military doctrine and forging a new relationship with the civil authorities, in separate sections below.

Professionalisation

In 1991, Russia had 196 divisions, but of the thirty-odd remaining today no more than ten are combat-ready. The precise number of Russian military personnel is difficult to establish because actual presence often diverges considerably from authorised strengths. Grachev was initially in favour of a reduced force of some 1.5 million, down from 3 million in 1991, no longer a conscript but a mobile, professional army. By 2001, the number in the regular army (Ground Forces) had fallen to some 1.2 million, accompanied by another 300,000 Interior Troops (VV) organised in twenty-nine interior divisions and fifteen brigades, while numbers in the police had grown 1.5 times to some 333,000. The functions of the VV had also changed, with fewer engaged in protecting objects and people's security, and more devoted to preventing mass unrest – a change that gave rise to the view that Russia had once again become a police state.

The shortage of personnel was a constant refrain. As an army made up largely of conscripts, the military authorities vigorously oppose attempts to limit the length of military service from the existing two years or to extend exempted categories. Under pressure from the military, Yeltsin in May 1995 extended the period of compulsory military service from eighteen months to two years, and ended certain student exemptions. Putin once again limited student exemptions and reintroduced military education into the educational system. Reformers seek the abolition of conscription and the creation of a wholly professional army, an aim conceded by Yeltsin during his re-election campaign in May 1996 but then deferred. The Soviet armed forces had always been designed as a mass army, with millions of reservists to be called up when required, and this tradition remains strong today. This is one reason why the law on alternatives to military service, a right guaranteed by the constitution, was so long delayed. There could be no serious military reform until such a law was adopted. Debates in the Duma over various drafts of the law in 2001 focused on the length of alternative service for those without higher education; international practice is for it to last twice as long as service in the army.

Personnel shortages are caused not only by the high percentage of those due for conscription who are automatically granted deferment (such as those in higher education) or exempted on health or social grounds, but above all by the low number of those actually answering conscription orders – not much more than a quarter annually (falling to 13 per cent in Autumn 2000).[36] The quality of those drafted was often low, with little education, poor health and, not infrequently, criminal records. Quite apart from low pay and conditions, the Soviet Army suffered a dreadful record of bullying (hazing) known as *dedovshchina*. In the second half of the 1980s, some 15–20,000 conscripts died 'noncombat' deaths,[37] and, in 1991 alone, according to official figures, 5,500 CIS servicemen (mostly conscripts) died through suicide, beatings or accidents, while 98,700 were wounded.[38] About a thousand conscripts committed suicide annually throughout the 1990s as a result of various barbaric initiation ceremonies and *dedovshchina*. It was in response to this that in June 1989 the first committees of soldiers' mothers were established to exert pressure on the authorities to enforce a decree allowing students to defer military service.[39] In the 1990s, the Union of Committees of Soldiers' Mothers became one of the most active pressure groups in society, exposing the barbaric way that the authorities dealt with conscripts and casualties in the Chechen wars. In addition, the demographic trends that we noted in Chapter 13, in particular the extremely low Russian birth rate, make it increasingly difficult to maintain a large conscript army, with ever fewer males reaching recruiting age annually. As a result most units are at best half-manned and the number of officers sometimes exceeds the number of conscripts. By 2001, there were more senior officers than junior officers, and one officer for every two soldiers.

Some saw the solution in the creation of ethnic and regional units, which were traditional for the Russian Army, while others sought to combine this with a purely professional force. A professional army, however, requires higher spending on improved salaries and the like.[40] The introduction of contract service in late 1992 represented a move towards the transition, with the 270,000 contract soldiers by 1996 making up an estimated one-third of Land Forces, concentrated primarily in technical and logistic units, while combat units, including those designated for peacekeeping operations, remained severely under-staffed.[41] In a typical reversal of policy, Grachev decided by early 1996 to cut the number of army personnel on service contracts by 80,000 as part of the State Duma's decision to reduce the armed forces to 1.7 million. The cost of a contract serviceman is much higher than a conscript. Military reform was once again reduced to troop cuts. This was reflected in the view of the outgoing defence minister, Igor Sergeev, in February 2001 that the basic guidelines for military reform would involve cutting the armed forces by 365,000 and defence ministry employees by 120,000 over the next five years,[42] a commitment reaffirmed by Sergei Ivanov.[43]

Modernisation

Sergeev's views reflected the larger stalemate in devising a coherent reform strategy. As the former head of the Strategic Rocket Forces, Sergeev favoured a reliance on nuclear weapons, but was opposed by chief of the General Staff, Anatolii Kvashnin. At the heart of discussion over reform was a fundamental disagreement over the requisite structure of Russia's armed forces. By 2000, Russia had four services: the three common to most countries, the Air Force, the Navy and Ground Forces, plus the Strategic Rocket Forces (SRF) that had earlier incorporated the Air Defence Forces (ADF). The SRF remained an independent unit for so long because of the extreme danger posed by unsanctioned actions, requiring exceptionally high skills and discipline in its personnel. The military insisted that the experience of other countries could not be blindly copied since Russia faced distinctive geostrategic challenges in the context of its own history and traditions.[44] Putin re-established the Chief Command of Ground Forces, disbanded in 1998, and planned to reduce the number of services to three by merging the SRF into the traditional air, land and sea structure.

Military reform (and defence conversion, as noted above) was conducted against the background of a severe economic crisis and tight budgets, with sharply reduced defence spending (halving in real terms by 1995, although in money terms the defence budget in 2001 rose by 150 per cent). In 2001, defence spending was $7 billion, or 3 per cent of GDP. Such relatively low expenditure meant reduced procurement of new weapons and equipment, shortages of fuel and spare parts, and inability to conduct training and exercises. In 1992, for the first time since the reign of Peter the Great, Russia failed to begin the construction of a single warship.[45] Speaking to the State Duma in November 1994, Grachev claimed that only 40 per cent of the Russian Army's armaments could be classified as modern,[46] a percentage that fell to some 10 per cent by the year 2000. Putin promised great increases in the procurement budget, something that would be delivered, according to Ivanov, by deep cuts in personnel. In 2001, arms procurement represented only 6 per cent of total defence expenditure, contrasted to the minimum of 20 per cent in Nato countries. The loss of technological edge and financial muscle barred Russia from genuine great-power status for at least a generation.

Civil–military relations

Civilian control of the military has been crucial in all previous transitions, notably in Latin America and Southern Europe. Even in Spain, with its much-admired democratic transition, everything was put in jeopardy in 1981 when some army officers seized parliament. In the post-communist world a decade after the fall of communism Chris Donnelly noted that 'there is not a single Central and Eastern European country today which has a civil–military relationship and a reorganized armed forces which it can consider satisfactory'.[47] In Russia civilian control over the military sphere was at best partial. The Soviet regime had created a military machine whose scope was unprecedented in peacetime but had always been careful to ensure Party and state control over the ambitions of the generals. Marxism-Leninism asserted the primacy of the Party over the military but at the same time its view of permanent conflict with capitalism served to justify the maintenance of the huge military establishment and imbued it with prestige. With the dissolution of the communist regime traditional forms of control disappeared, and at the same time the prestige and morale of the armed forces plummeted. In the apparently 'post-military' post-Cold War world, the very basis of citizenship has changed: in the past, involvement in the military through conscription and civil defence was a token of citizenship; now, economic citizenship has taken on a much higher profile. Military intervention in politics can take different forms. For some it means resolute action against the civilian leadership, something that has not yet taken place in Russia. However, there are softer forms of intervention, primarily taking the form of undue influence over the budget and policy process, visible above all in foreign relations.

According to the Russian constitution, defence, like foreign policy, is a prerogative of the president. The president is commander-in-chief of the armed forces of Russia, operating through the General Staff. The Security Council is the main military and political body controlling Russia's defence establishment, while the Ministry of Defence is responsible for developing and implementing military, technical and personnel policy. Russia's Defence Ministry liaises through the CIS Defence Council of Ministers where appropriate. The prime minister and parliament can exert considerable practical influence over defence policy through control of budgets and the Duma's defence committee. The status of the armed forces is regulated by the Law on Defence of 24 September 1992 and with a revised version signed into law on 1 June 1996. A major problem remains oversight over unit commanders; the weakening of the Soviet system of Party and instructor oversight has left lower-level officers as virtual tyrants over their fiefdoms. Another problem is the great autonomy enjoyed by the system of military justice, headed by the Chief Military Prosecutor, a post that is formally part of the national judiciary yet in practice virtually independent.

Civil–military relations in the Yeltsin years were managed by Yeltsin himself, although he never took a great deal of interest in military affairs, unlike his successor who was a career security officer. Yeltsin effectively retained control over the armed forces and denied access to any other politicians, but their subordination to his authority was not unquestioned, as demonstrated in October 1993. The power ministries are directly responsible to the president and not the prime minister. The power ministries include the Ministry of Defence, the Border Guards, the internal troops of the MVD, as well as some fifteen other services including FAPSI (communications and listening), the SVR (the foreign successor to the KGB), Railway Troops, Construction Troops, and the domestic successor to the KGB, the FSB. Yeltsin retained the power of appointment to these services that did not require the Duma's approval. The president tries to ensure that the Security Council, bringing together the heads of the leading power ministries, is headed by a loyalist – hence Lebed's rather short tenure as head between August and October 1996. The appointment of the loyal Vladimir Putin as its head at a time when the government was headed by Primakov, who had a tense relationship with Yeltsin, was a case in point. The appointment of the civilian Sergei Ivanov as defence minister in 2001 broke with tradition (although under Brezhnev the civilian CC secretary Dmitrii Ustinov had been defence minister, this made not the slightest difference in approach), but the fact that he was a Putin loyalist perpetuated another tradition. The appointment of Lyubov Kudelina as deputy defence minister in charge of the defence ministry's budget and finance department reinforced the attempt to civilianise military affairs, an appointment that is particularly important since defence consumes one-fifth of the state budget.

Defeat in the Second World War had destroyed the military establishments and militarist traditions in Germany and Japan, leaving the civilian state to concentrate on domestic economic development. In Russia the Soviet military establishment remained largely intact at independence in 1991, and it fell to the new state itself to begin the arduous task of civilianising politics. The state itself, however, was in certain respects weaker than the military; as Donnelly points out, 'large bureaucratic institutions continue to function irrespective of the lack of government...the armed forces hierarchy was increasingly determining its own agenda'.[48] The military definition of state security and the militaristic ethos of the ruling class remained to be challenged. The functional equivalent of defeat in war is humiliation in peace (the Versailles syndrome). As if the great retreat was not enough, the military discovered that involvement in domestic conflicts was extremely damaging. Every intervention acted as a self-inflicted blow on prestige and morale: the Tbilisi massacre of 9 April 1989; the brutal occupation of Baku in January 1990; and the seizure of the television tower in Vilnius and other events in the Baltic in January 1991. The civilian leadership usually retreated behind a cloud of obfuscation and equivocation, while the army was left to explain the corpses. The army's half-hearted involvement in the *coup* of August 1991 salvaged its pride, but all these events demonstrated once again the dangers of trying to solve the political agendas of others by military means. The military adopted a policy of 'neutrality' in domestic political struggle. General Lobov argued that 'people in uniforms should not engage in party activities, nor in political battles in parliament at any level'.[49] The Law on Defence, moreover, restricts the army to external defence only.

This explains why in October 1993 the army was so reluctant to become involved, and it took several hours of pleading by Yeltsin at the Ministry of Defence to get the military to suspend the formula 'the army is outside politics' and to agree to an assault on the White House.[50] The October events revealed the desperately debilitated condition of the Russian Army. The force of just 1,700 was drawn from five separate divisions in the Moscow MD. To ensure loyalty tank crews were made up almost entirely of officers, and at least half the infantry were officers or senior NCOs.[51] The military's involvement in resolving the October 1993 crisis led to much speculation that they would thereafter enjoy a disproportionate influence in policy, whereas in fact the effect was short-lived. The military gained few of the anticipated rewards like increased budgets, an end to personnel cuts and a harder line in the near abroad. Already low morale was further undermined by the Chechen campaign, which did little to enhance Grachev's personal standing. A poll of 615 generals and colonels in August 1994 revealed that less than 30 per cent trusted Yeltsin, and fewer than 20 per cent had any faith in Grachev, while half said they trusted Generals Lebed and Gromov. As far as their political attitudes were concerned, 80 per cent of these top-ranking officers favoured an authoritarian form of government and 64 per cent dismissed Western-type democracy as unsuitable for Russia.[52] Andrei Nikolaev, the former head of the border guards and then a Duma deputy, is typical of the forthright way that military personnel in Russia, both active and retired, voice their views; in his case, in a book that condemned the United States' and Nato's 'pretensions for world dominance'.[53]

During *perestroika*, the military had become increasingly politicised as the old unity gave way to the dissonance of *glasnost* and the rise of republican separatism. The demise of the old Soviet political organs (above all the Main Political Administration) left officers prey to influences from beyond the military. Organisations like the All-Russian Officers' Union, registered in February 1992, headed by Vladislav Achalov and Stanislav Terekhov were anti-government, accusing it of indifference towards corruption, dismissing officers for political reasons (above all for criticism of Grachev himself), and presiding over Russia's military decline.[54] While claiming a membership of 30,000 officers, in fact Terekhov's organisation was minuscule but the armed forces were rife with anti-government sentiments. According to military sociologists in November 1992, only 19 per cent of servicemen supported the government, while its policies were opposed by 56 per cent.[55] The reconstituted Russian military authorities fought to reverse the politicisation of the army, including a ban on party activity in the ranks, the forced resignation of those actively involved in political life (a dispensation that appears to have been dropped in the December 1995 elections) and the prohibition on army trade unions.[56]

The political views of servicemen are an important factor in electoral politics.[57] In the mid-1990s, there were 1.8 million military personnel; about 7 million members and relatives of service families with the right to vote; some 7–9 million employed in military-industrial enterprises, military research institutes and agencies, with families; some 20–21 million service pensioners and the families of veterans of the Great Patriotic and other wars; and some 2 million Russian Cossacks.[58] Thus, the armed forces and related groups make up to 40 million people out of a total electorate of just under 110 million, and this is leaving out of account those employed in security agencies, which could well add another 10–15 million people. In broad terms, the voting pattern of the military was oppositional in the 1993 and 1995 electoral cycles, but swung round in conformity with broader patterns to support Putin and his allies in 1999–2000. Voting patterns were distorted in 1993 because ballot boxes were placed directly in barracks, whereas in later elections soldiers joined with the mass of citizens in general polling stations.

Rather than riding in on a white horse the military vigorously entered the December 1995 electoral race. Having resigned his commission, Lebed joined Skokov's KRO and was placed second on their party list. Skokov had forged strong links with the military when secretary of the Security Council in 1993, and now hoped to capitalise on the revulsion among the officer corps against the venality of political life. General-Lieutenant Lev Rokhlin, commander of forces in Volgograd and veteran of the Afghan and Chechen wars, was placed third on the Our Home is Russia list. Rokhlin became an ardent oppositionist in parliament until murdered (allegedly by his wife) in 1998. He headed the Duma's defence committee, which became the virtual headquarters of the virulently anti-Yeltsin 'Movement in Support of the Army'.

The establishment of parliamentary committees overseeing security policy and monitoring the budget (and with it military expenditure) marked important stages in the development of civilian control over the military. However, the establishment of political controls primarily requires effective political institutions, and Russia has not yet reached that stage. The other side of the equation, the professionalisation of the military, also requires competent state structures. The absence of the latter encouraged the military itself to enter politics, as witnessed by the large number of soldiers participating in the December 1995 elections. Divided between parties and tendencies, however, 'the military' as such lacked a single voice, and thus diminished the incentive to enter the political arena by forceful means. Civil–military relations depend to a large degree on relations within the military itself. Like much of Russian life, this proved to be signally faction-ridden. The military 'opposition' to Yeltsin, if it can be called that, took two main forms: 'the professionals' (Gromov, Lebed, Rokhlin); and the 'irreconcilables', mainly consisting of retired oficers (including generals Makashov and Achalov, and the ex-KGB officer Sterligov). The appointment of General Igor Rodionov, formerly head of the General Staff Academy, as defence minister in July 1996 brought the professionals into the centre of military and security affairs, as did Sergeev's appointment later. Both, however, could not forgive Yeltsin for the defeat in Chechnya in 1996 and the declining role of the military in society. The second Chechen war, according to Baev, in this context should be seen

> not just as an attempt by the top brass to take revenge for the defeat of three years earlier, but as part of their larger effort to restore the 'proper' place of the army in society and check further degradation of the military structures.[59]

Harmonious civil–military relations reflect stable social relations, while social crisis gives rise to tension. The emergence of a Russian Bonaparte would be the natural conclusion of over a decade of political chaos. Military dictatorship was openly canvassed by senior army officers. The aim would be not to re-establish communism but to 'restore order' in fulfilment of the 'Pinochet option' for Russia. According to some liberal newspapers, Lebed enjoyed 'a simply unique authority among officers' and was 'in great political demand' in Russian society.[60] In the event, the role of the military in Russian politics remained marginal under Yeltsin. Under Putin, however, there was a clear pattern to rely on the security establishment, marginalising career military officers. Under both Yeltsin and Putin it was clear that the presidency and the military had interests in common, but the mere fact that the military could sustain a policy of their own suggests that Russia still has a long way to go before the military can be considered under complete civilian control. It will not be easy to shake off Tsarism's militaristic ethos or the USSR's fundamental belief that the central purpose of the state was to prepare for war with the capitalist exploiters. If the military had been considered by some a 'sixteenth republic' in the old USSR, the Russian military is not quite a state within the state but it nevertheless exhibits a dangerous degree of independence.

Military and security doctrine

The former chief of the general staff and a noted reformer, General Vladimir Lobov, argued that a 'military doctrine does not exist by itself [but] is part of the overall state doctrine' affecting the economy, science, politics and foreign policy.[61] As Scott McMichael puts it, 'Soviet military doctrine functioned as a virtual surrogate for what the West would call national security policy.'[62] Russia's military doctrine has been in a constant process of evolution. The first draft of May 1992 built on the changes introduced into the USSR's doctrine (last revised in 1987), above all in its overwhelmingly defensive orientation, the absence of residual notions of class struggle, and its rehabilitation of the concept of 'national security' and 'national interests'. Some of the old concerns, however, remained, albeit in a new guise, particularly in the notion of 'some states and coalitions' (i.e. the United States and Nato) who still seek to dominate the world. The deployment of foreign troops into countries bordering Russia was considered a direct military threat, while attacks on Russian-speaking populations in other CIS countries would give Russia the right to intervene on their behalf.[63] The struggle between parliament and president prevented this draft being adopted.

A revised version, called 'The Main Provisions of the Military Doctrine of the RF', was adopted on 2 November 1993,[64] a modified version of which was adopted in 1997. The 1993 document stressed that Russia's vital interests 'in no way involved the security of other states'. The doctrine stressed the need for conflict prevention, the territorial integrity of states, respect for their sovereignty and non-interference in their internal affairs.[65] Learning from the October events, 'separate' military units could now be deployed to support interior troops in internal conflicts or to support border troops in particular cases, provisions utilised to allow Russian forces to intervene in Chechnya. The key change from the earlier draft was the shift in threat perception, now identified as coming from local wars. The Russian Army was to defend Russia's 'territorial integrity', but it was not clear where the borders lay. The doctrine formalised the view of the former Soviet republics as part of Russia's extended security zone and tried to endow the CIS with a military dimension, with Russia acting as a type of garrison state on behalf of the other members. The army, however, could only move in with the consent of the government involved, but Russia's 'peacekeeping' operations, as we have seen (Chapter 16), blurred the principle of impartiality or neutrality in disputes. The doctrine made no mention of civil or parliamentary control over the military, and had little to say about the role of the army in Russian society. The doctrine, even though it had moderated some of the postulates of the earlier draft, reflected the 'great-power' thinking of the Defence Ministry. While declaring Russia's peaceful intentions, the doctrine nevertheless revealed an underlying bloc mentality and a deep sense of insecurity.

The focus in the 1997 version was on internal and local conflicts as the main threat to the state. The involvement of Nato in the Balkans crisis in 1999 raised the profile of the Russian military and there were signs that it was able to increase its leverage over politicians. During the bombing campaign against Serbia Russia announced that it would be reviewing its military doctrine to take into account the possibility of large-scale ground warfare, something that had been discounted earlier. A stronger role for nuclear deterrence was also suggested, the need for forces abroad (above all in Belarus) was argued and there was greater support for the demands of the generals for an increased military budget. Anti-Western sentiments among the population were mobilised to achieve promises for greater military spending. Russia's militaristic response to the Kosovo crisis, however, alarmed its allies in the CIS and only six renewed the Tashkent Collective Security Treaty when it came up for renewal in 1999. Despite Russia's attempts to lead a boycott of Nato's fiftieth-anniversary celebrations in Washington, DC, in April 1999, only Russia and Belarus stayed away while all the other countries appeared even more eager to attend. The Kosovo crisis was for Russia a domestic crisis of the first order, revealing the limits of its authority on the world and regional stage while at the same time exposing the way that nearly a decade of reform had provoked anti-Western sentiments, something that the Soviet regime with its huge propaganda apparatus had been unable to do. Russian policy and public sentiment was motivated less by sympathy for the Serbs than by fear that the power imbalance in the post-Cold War order threatened the autonomy of less powerful states, among which Russia (together with China) now found itself.

Russia's new Security Concept had been prepared by the Security Council under Putin's leadership, and was approved by presidential decree on 10 January 2000, while the Military Doctrine was prepared by the General Staff and was signed into effect by Putin on 21 April 2000.[66] There are plenty of incompatibilities between the two documents, but both failed to develop a coherent programme of military reform. It was this gap that allowed the very public clash between the defence minister Sergeev and chief of General Staff Kvashnin in July 2000 over the relative priority of strategic forces (defended by Sergeev) or whether they should be cut to provide extra resources for conventional forces (Kvashnin's view).

Security policy and Nato enlargement

In a speech in Berlin on 12 December 1989, James Baker had spoken of 'a new architecture for a new era', a new structure for European and international security. This rather inflexible imagery foreshadowed one of the abiding features of post-communist Europe, namely the crisis of the institutions created during the Cold War to conduct and regulate that conflict. While communist Cold War organisations dissolved, those in the West not only survived but sought to expand their roles. The largely unnegotiated nature of the post-Cold War peace (noted in Chapter 15) was reflected in an institutional conservativism that sought to keep existing organisations while imbuing them with a new content. Russia, however, became the champion of institutional revisionism, seeking to renegotiate the European security system by enhancing the role of the OSCE – as long as the OSCE remained constrained by rules of consensus.

In line with its reinvigorated European policy, Russia was an active participant in the web of institutions once labelled by Soviet writers as the 'all-European process'. This included the CSCE, established in Helsinki in 1975, which with the end of the Cold War entered a period both of deepening and widening. Following the Paris Conference in November 1990, it acquired a headquarters and secretariat in Vienna, a Secretary General (supporting the work of the Chairman-in-Office), a Senior Council, a Permanent Council, a centre for the prevention of conflicts, a human rights commissioner, and an office for free elections (which later became the Office for Democratic Institutions and Human Rights based in Warsaw, specialising in constitution-making), and in May 1992 the CSCE Parliamentary Assembly was established. The body itself was renamed the *Organisation* for Security and Co-operation in Europe (OSCE) at the Budapest Review Conference in December 1994 to reflect its greater institutionalisation. Russia took over the Soviet seat, and total membership rose dramatically to fifty-three with the accession of the Baltic states in September 1991, all of the former Soviet states in January 1992 (except Georgia, which joined a few months later), and the post-Yugoslav states. The accession of the Central Asian states imbued the OSCE with the Eurasian character of Russia itself. It was far from clear, however, whether the OSCE was capable of dealing with the complexity of Eurasian politics.

Expectations that the OSCE would play a growing role in the post-communist world, expressed in the lofty language of the 'Charter of Paris for a New Europe' of 21 November 1990, were disappointed. Despite greater institutionalisation, including a modification of decision-making to allow 'consensus minus one', the OSCE remained but one among many competing institutions. The Americans favoured Nato, whereas the Maastricht Treaty of 1992 envisaged a strengthened role for the defence arm of the EU, the Western European Union (WEU), as the European Security and Defence Identity (ESDI) began to take form. The OSCE played little part in conflict resolution in Nagorno-Karabakh (although its Minsk group sought to act as a mediator). Many argued that the hasty widening of the OSCE allowed membership to some former Soviet (and Yugoslav) states that did not meet accepted human rights standards and thus diluted the OSCE's human rights role. Contrary to the high hopes of 1990, the OSCE failed to become a community for the civilisational integration of Europe. However, as Zagorskii points out, in so far as the division of Europe was not yet over but had only taken on new forms,[67] the CSCE remained an important forum for the regulation of relations between the eastern and western parts of the Eurasian landmass. In gaining a stronger institutional framework the OSCE seems to have lost some of its original spirit of flexibility and consensus.

Russia's calls for a comprehensive system of collective security based on the OSCE, proposed formally in July 1994, were clearly designed in part to oppose plans for Nato expansion. If the OSCE were indeed to become the main vehicle for post-communist European security, then Nato enlargement would become meaningless. While perhaps never seriously believing that it could become an effective pan-European security organisation, Russia sought to expand the OSCE's political responsibilities and thus diminish Nato's influence and consolidate Russia's influence in European affairs. Despite Russia's equivocations and attempts to play the OSCE 'card', the fundamental question remains unanswered: If there is no longer a security threat from any European power, then why should Nato expand?[68] The subtext to the whole question of Nato enlargement is whether the West was now to be a genuine partner or whether it still represented a threat to Russia – and vice versa.

The relationship between Russia and Nato, and the question of the latter's expansion to the east (and in particular to the 'middle abroad', the states of Central and Eastern Europe) became one of the most thorny issues in Russia's post-Cold War relationship with the West.[69] With the demise of its old adversary, what was now the point of Nato, and was it possible for Russia to join? While Nato remained the only effective co-ordinating body for the defence policies of its members, and inhibited the revival of the old balance-of-power politics that had brought war to Europe so often, its future role remained a matter of discussion.[70] Nato had always been a defensive alliance, but the problem lay in the definition of the security risks facing Europe. Was Russia part of the problem or part of the solution to European security? And as for Russian membership, a long-term commitment to this end would echo the visionary statesmanship that had brought the EEC into being after the Second World War, as a way forever of preventing war between European powers, but it would effectively reduce Nato to little more than the OSCE. The very existence of an expanded Nato would create a permanent source of tension in the centre of Europe; as Kozyrev put it, 'Nato's advance toward Russia's borders cannot but be seen as a continuation, though by inertia, of a policy aimed at containment of Russia.'[71] The renegotiation of European security, with perhaps the launching of a European Treaty Organisation (involving the United States, Canada and perhaps Japan), would prevent Nato itself becoming a threat to European security; but without Nato, the paralysis in European security that had allowed the First and Second World Wars would be repeated. For good or ill and however ineptly, it was Nato that finally halted Milosevic's killing machine in Yugoslavia. The creation of the EU's 60,000-strong Rapid Reaction Force by 2003, designed to act separately but in alliance with Nato, began to remedy Europe's lack of security coherence, much to Washington's alarm. It was clear that Nato enlargement has to be seen in the context of the EU's emerging defence identity, as well as broader issues like missile defence, and arms control and non-proliferation agreements.

Twice before the USSR had sought, admittedly half-heartedly, to join Nato (Malenkov in the 1950s and Gorbachev in the 1980s), but now the question could be realistically posed. On a visit to Nato headquarters in Brussels in late October 1991, General Alexander Tsalko, deputy chair of Russia's Defence Committee, went so far as to suggest that Russia might join the organisation, initially at consultative level.[72] In late 1994, Boris Fedorov insisted that 'Russia must join Nato', arguing that membership would mean the end of United States dominance in the organisation and would counter Germany's growing power. Russian membership, moreover, would signal the genuine end of the Cold War and further guarantee democratic development in Russia.[73] In an interview with the BBC on 5 March 2000, Putin once again entertained the possibility that one day Russia could join Nato, albeit on 'equal terms'. The sentiment was reiterated by Vladimir Lukin, the former head of the Duma's foreign-affairs committee, who argued that the optimal solution would be 'the widening of Nato to Vladivostok'.[74] Even if the principle of Russian membership were to be conceded, numerous economic, military and technical problems would have to be resolved before membership could be taken seriously. Nato itself veered between the outright rejection of the notion of Russian membership and a cautious welcome of the idea.

Even if the necessity for Nato is demonstrated, did it need to expand? For many in Russia enlargement represented a breach of faith by the West since it appears that assurances were given to Gorbachev during talks over German unification that there would be no expansion. Enlargement, moreover, could be represented as Germany's traditional *Drang nach Osten* in a new form.[75] Faced with the resolute wish to join by the Eastern European states themselves, Yeltsin equivocated. During his visit to Warsaw in August 1993, Yeltsin had said 'go ahead' when asked about Poland's prospects for membership of Nato. This stance was rapidly modified on his return to Moscow. Despite some initial uncertainty about its attitude, Russia finally insisted that any expansion would have to meet tough conditions. Russia's objections were not so much a way of keeping Eastern Europe within Russia's security orbit but arose out of the obvious geopolitical consequences of expansion without commensurate commitments. In the event, the Czech Republic, Hungary and Poland did join in April 1999, although celebrations at the same time of Nato's fiftieth anniversary were rather muted as a result of the war in Kosovo. Russia's objections to the integration of the new members into the alliance's military structure were not accepted; of Nato's nineteen members, only France is not part of the unified military command and Spain is only partly integrated. In the event, the three new members did not change their relationship with Russia, just as Norway's or Turkey's membership (two other of Russia's neighbours) had not done earlier.

The question then shifted to the problem of second-wave enlargement. The ten potential members between the Baltic and the Balkans in May 2000 met in Vilnius and urged Nato to enlarge further in a single fell swoop. The 'Vilnius Ten' sought to pool information and resources, to avoid mutually destructive competition, and to lobby together for swift accession. President George W. Bush in a speech in Warsaw on 15 June 2001 held out the vision of a rapidly expanding Nato 'from the Baltic to the Black Sea'. At a second meeting of the Vilnius Ten in Estonia on 10 July 2001, they insisted that aspirant countries should be judged on their qualifications and not on their 'geography or history'. Potential members were in various stages of fulfilling their Membership Action Plans (MAPs), with the three Baltic countries in the lead.

The further advance of a powerful military alliance to its borders could not but be unsettling. From Russia's perspective, Nato expansion would jeopardise its attempts to have good relations with both East and West Europe, and would in effect signal its exclusion from Europe. Russia's concerns can be summarised as follows:

- The extension of Nato to the east would undermine the role of universal organisations like the UN and the OSCE.
- Enlargement was accompanied by a redefined role for the alliance that increased emphasis on missions outside the geographical zone of responsibility of the alliance.

- Nato enlargement would weaken the security of the alliance itself by re-establishing lines of division within Europe that could not but be directed against Russia.
- It would undercut the existing arms control regimes, above all the European disarmament architecture and its fundamental unit, the adapted CFE treaty.
- Regional security tensions would be exacerbated, above all with the entrance of the Baltic states, 30 per cent of whose population are ethnic Russians. Would the Kaliningrad region become a 'bridge' between east and west or a 'military bridgehead'?
- Enlargement would increase Russia's isolation, and risk excluding it from decision-making in Europe, possibly precipitating a post-ideological Cold War, the 'cold peace' that Yeltsin had warned of at the OSCE Budapest Summit in December 1994.
- Instead of deepening the demilitarisation of foreign policy promised by the end of the Cold War on the basis of common civilisational values, Nato enlargement insists on its members making an 'adequate contribution' to collective defence in accordance with Article V of the 1949 Washington Treaty establishing Nato, and thus risks squandering the peace dividend.

In response to these concerns, Nato sought to manage enlargement in a way that achieved the goal but did not alienate Russia entirely. The Rome summit of Nato in November 1991 established a North Atlantic Co-operation Council (NACC), and on 20 December 1991 it held its inaugural meeting. NACC's membership included thirty-six countries stretching from Vancouver to Vladivostok, including all the members of Nato and the former Soviet republics. The idea was to extend a 'shadow of security' over the region without offering concrete defence guarantees. The body remained more shadow than substance, however, and NACC in 1997 was transformed into the Euro-Atlantic Partnership Council (EAPC) as a consultative forum for crisis management, proliferation issues and much more.[76] Attempts by the EAPC to encroach on the OSCE's (and indeed, the UN's and the CIS's) prerogatives in peacekeeping and post-conflict rehabilitation were firmly rebuffed by Russia, although it welcomed attempts to enhance the EAPC's role in the field of civil emergency planning (CEP).

Committed to expansion, the dilemma for Nato was how to do so without driving Russia back into hostility. A temporary solution was the Partnership for Peace (PfP) initiative, launched by Nato on 10 January 1994, considered a prerequisite for membership although participation did not guarantee membership. Whereas EAPC is a multilateral body, operating like the OSCE largely by consensus, PfP represented a series of bilateral agreements. By April 1995, twenty-six countries had signed up to the programme, ranging from Albania to Uzbekistan,[77] but although all members were formally equal some were clearly on the fast track for membership, above all some CEE countries. Thus, PfP was simultaneously a way of managing Nato enlargement and delaying it. It was not clear whether PfP could indeed become a bridge rather than a barrier across Europe. Russia signed the Partnership Framework Document on 22 June 1994, when Kozyrev conceded that Russia 'had no fundamental objections' to Nato enlargement, but delayed signing the associated Individual Partnership Programme.

As the price for expansion Moscow sought a formal expression to the much-touted post-Cold War idea of a 'strategic partnership' between the West and Russia, a permanent forum for consultation with Nato and a voice in security developments in Central Europe, something that in any case had been emerging within the framework of the OSCE and in the form of bilateral meetings. Russia, moreover, sought guarantees that prevented the forward positioning of nuclear weapons or the stationing of alliance forces in these countries, arrangements that already existed for Norway. The Western powers, however, firmly rejected Russia's attempt to achieve a special relationship with Nato that might allow it to veto eastward expansion, but accepted that it should spring no surprises on Russia. This sparring finally resulted in the signature of the Russia–Nato Founding Act on 27 May 1997,[78] followed on 9 July by the signing of the Charter on Distinctive Partnership between Nato and Ukraine. The Founding Act established a Permanent Joint Council (PJC) as a forum for Russian–Nato discussions, typically meeting at the level of foreign ministers or at ambassadorial level, discussing issues like those associated with the continuing crisis in former Yugoslavia. The PJC in the short-term was seen as a damage-limitation exercise – to make Nato expansion more palatable to Russia by allaying its fears about the forward deployment of nuclear weapons and Nato troops in the new member states – but its scope was more ambitious: to

> provide a mechanism for consultation, coordination and, to the maximum extent possible, where appropriate, for joint decisions and joint action with respect to security issues of common concern.[79]

Tensions over Nato intervention over Kosovo in 1999, indeed, had derailed the work of the PJC for a period. As a sign of improving relations, in February 2001 Nato opened an information office in Moscow, the counterpart to Russia's rather large mission to Nato headquarters at Mons.

Nato enlargement became the defining issue in Russian foreign policy and did much to shift Russian public opinion away from the democratic and internationalist values that had informed the early period of independence.[80] Nato involvement in former Yugoslavia vividly illustrated Russia's marginalisation and raised fears that Russia itself might anticipate the same treatment if it stepped too far out of line. The Nato alliance was formed to counter a danger that had disappeared, but its continued existence appeared to run counter to Russia's long-term strategic interests. The issue of Nato expansion served to forge an almost unique consensus among all wings of Russian politics. According to Karaganov, 'Nato's plans for expansion mean a potential new Yalta....By accepting the rules of the game that are being forced on her...Russia will lose.'[81] Some in Moscow responded by insisting that if Nato expanded, then Russia should create its own new military bloc made up of the former Soviet republics and other countries that objected to an aggressive Nato on their borders – but there were few takers (except Belarus) to the invitation. Russia's attempts to renegotiate the post-Cold War order met with little success. Quite apart from the institutional conservatism of the West, Russia's initiatives were often poorly prepared and ill thought out. The prospect of a post-communist Cold War threatened to erode the fragile peace achieved with the fall of the communist regimes in 1989–91.

Conclusion

The army had traditionally been the backbone of the Russian state and thus civil–military relations would always be ambivalent. While some saw the Chechen war as the outcome of the militarisation of the Russian state (allied with the security apparatus), the war in practice revealed the enormous divisions within the security, military and foreign-policy establishments. The executive's dominance over security is enshrined in the constitution, making the president commander-in-chief, granting him/her the right to appoint and dismiss ministers and military commanders, to lead the Security Council, to declare states of emergency and war, and in addition placing them in overall control of the Ministry of the Interior and other security services. The greater problem, however, is that the military is not subordinated to the state as such but civilian control has come to mean simply bringing the military under the command of the presidency. The Chechen war showed just how dangerous this could be, and there were few checks on the use of the military in domestic conflicts.

The attempt to sculpt a lean and professional Russian army out of the bloated Soviet defence establishment at a time of economic crisis would inevitably be a long and arduous process. The Russian military was no more immune to the general degradation of public life than any other group. The task now was to forge a modern professional army, a process impeded by Russia's involvement in CIS and domestic conflicts. The more politicised an army, the less professional it will be, as evidenced by the dismissal of the arch-professionals Gromov *et al.* during the Chechen war. The course of military reform, moreover, was strongly resisted from within. The abolition of the old political officers gave the military much greater scope for autonomy than before. According to Vladimir Smirnov, a member of the co-ordinating committee of the 'Soldiers for Democracy' organisation, Yeltsin made a fateful strategic mistake in allowing the army to drift out of control and in delaying the reform of the army and the military industrial complex. This 'empire within an empire' quickly destroyed all that was good in it and degenerated: illegally selling arms and military equipment, and conducting huge financial machinations.[82]

For understandable reasons, the military favoured the preservation of the defence industries and Russia's great-power status. The military establishment continued to act as an important player in foreign policy, and in particular in relations with the 'near abroad' (as in Transdniester and Abkhazia) and also over relations with Japan. The weakness of central authority meant that the reconstituted Russian military enjoyed considerable autonomy, and allied with the still powerful military-industrial officials, tried to shape policies. The military at times appeared to be making its own policy. The Far Eastern MD, for example, had its own agenda in relations with China, while some regional commanders appeared intent on pursuing their own interests, often associated with the development of various enterprises. This was not so much warlordism as a distinctive form of military capitalism. However, by a mixture of inducements and turning a blind eye, the post-communist authorities were able to keep the military out of politics, except when called upon in moments of crisis. Despite its involvement in heavy-handed 'peacekeeping' operations abroad and a radical intervention in domestic politics in Moscow and Chechnya, Lambeth argues that 'The military nonetheless remains a responsible and stabilizing force in Russian society.'[83]

This was accompanied, significantly, by an important theoretical shift. Post-communist state-building has returned to Prussian notions whereby 'military force is increasingly considered not only as a necessary attribute of independence, but as a legitimate instrument of policy'.[84] War in Abkhazia, Tajikistan and Chechnya, *pace* Clausewitz, has become a continuation of the policy of national self-affirmation. The first 'Strategy for Russia' report noted that 'The territory of the former USSR will probably become a zone in which military power will play an essential role', and for this the Russian armed forces had to prepare themselves.[85] The age of militarised inter-state relations has not ended. Nato enlargement appeared to be proof of this, although the very nature of the Nato alliance simultaneously denies it. The two halves of Europe live in separate historical times: the western half in the recent past has waged the greatest wars in humanity's history on a global scale, yet appears complacently to have occupied the moral high ground and de-legitimised war as an instrument of policy until provoked into intervention in Afghanistan after the destruction of the World Trade Center on 11 September 2001; while the east is still racked by the volcanic pressures of state- and nation-building.

Part VI

Dilemmas of democratisation

The adoption of the constitution in December 1993 furnished Russia with the normative framework for the development of a liberal and democratic society. The genesis of the constitution, however, in a bloody struggle between representatives of the legislative and executive branches of government, stamped the new order with a political mark of Cain. The new constitutional system, nevertheless, provided Russia with the main institutions of a modern representative democracy and established the parameters within which democratic politics could be conducted. The constitution allowed the development of genuine parliamentarianism while defending liberal principles of human rights and the separation of powers. The principle of popular sovereignty, at the heart of the democratic insurgency against the communist regime, was reaffirmed, although its representation was partial and the ability of society to hold the authorities accountable was tenuous. In this part we will stand back from the detailed analysis of institutions and policy, and examine some of the larger issues and processes affecting Russia's struggle for democracy.

— Constitution December 1993

— normative framework: liberal + democratic society

— Struggle between legislative + executive reps.

— genuine parliamentarianism
— liberal principles human rights
— separation of power
— popular sovereignty.

18 Problems of transition

A weak state is a threat to democracy in no less a degree than a despotic power.

(Vladimir Putin)[1]

Gogol ends his satire on Tsarist Russia, *The Government Inspector*, with the image of a careering troika (three-horse carriage) dragging the country no one knew whither: 'And where do you fly to, Russia?' This troika has still not yet been tamed, yet a sense of direction has been at the heart of post-communist Russian developments. In this chapter we examine the historical and theoretical problems associated with the concept of democratic transition, and in the next and final chapters analyse the tribulations of democracy in Russia. As we shall see, approaches focusing on modernisation and development are misleading in suggesting an inevitability in outcomes that can by no means be assumed. The view that Soviet-style politics could be cast off to expose a nascent capitalist democracy was misleading, but not entirely erroneous. There *are* profound continuities between the Tsarist, Soviet and post-Soviet eras in Russia, but at the same time there are enormous discontinuities and innovations. It is precisely the analysis of the dynamics of change and continuity that can reveal the sources of Russian political evolution. A democratic Russia could not emerge fully formed like Minerva from the brow of Zeus; but neither was the country forever in thrall to its tragic yet glorious past.

The challenge of history

It is often argued that Russia's failure to come to terms with its past is the greatest obstacle to the development of a consolidated democracy. According to the historian Yurii Afanas'ev, 'The public consciousness has not yet reached the required level. That there existed a certain regime and that a return to it is out of the question is acknowledged only by individuals, not as yet by the society.'[2] A certain nostalgia for the past was entertained not only by the communists but also by the great mass of the people. The memory of the past, however, was selective: both in terms of choosing the particular period that suited present tastes, and in reinterpreting the significance of each particular epoch. In adopting the Tsarist double-headed eagle as the state emblem, the Soviet national anthem (with new words) as Russia's official hymn, and the 'democratic' tricolour as the national flag, Putin sought to achieve the reconciliation of the various national myths. The past, its selection, interpretation and dynamics, however, remains a problem for contemporary Russian politics.[3]

The speed of the collapse of the communist system took most observers by surprise, as happened with Tsarism earlier. When in 1913 the Romanov dynasty celebrated its 300th anniversary, the throne and empire appeared solidly in place; yet a mere four years later both lay shattered. When Gorbachev came to power in 1985 the Communist Party and the Soviet system appeared firmly ensconced; and once again just six years later communist rule had dissolved and the Soviet Union itself had disintegrated. Tsarism had been unable to survive the strains inflicted by the Great War, but in the Soviet case the absence of war made the collapse all the more astonishing. In a time of peace one of the world's greatest geopolitical powers dissolved politically and disintegrated territorially. The strains of the Cold War played their part: the attempt to challenge the capitalist democracies for world leadership and to match their combined military potential led to a severe case of 'imperial overstretch', to use Paul Kennedy's phrase.[4] However, the dissolution of the Soviet regime owed as much to its fundamental internal incoherence as to external factors. From a neo-institutional perspective, a strong case can be made that the structures of accountability and policy-making became so narrow that ultimately they lost contact with the society that they sought to manage. Political power became responsible to a narrow 'selectorate' and was unable to respond to the enormous social changes that it had itself provoked through industrialisation and the broad programme of post-Stalin modernisation.

The stability that was at the heart of Brezhnev's rule undermined the system's ability itself to adapt to the changes that it had itself set in motion. Isaac Deutscher had long argued that Stalinism would be its own gravedigger. According to Roeder, the Bolshevik 'constitution' (the rules that governed the Soviet system from the early revolutionary years into the post-Stalin era; not to be confused with the official constitutions adopted in 1924, 1936 and 1977) imposed severe institutional constraints on the USSR's adaptability and ability to reform.[5] The debate continues whether we can still call the late Soviet regime totalitarian.[6] In social terms, *perestroika* exposed the contradictions between the attempt to transcend the market and the realities of the command economy in which informal economic activity and corruption were rife; between the abolition of private property that condemned the mass of the population to a universal 'equality in poverty' and the luxuriating privileges of the political elite; between the progressive claims to political leadership by the Communist Party and its own crude manipulations of political decision-making; and above all between the regime's claims to a monopoly of truth and the mountain of lies on which it rested.

The Soviet regime, like the Romanov dynasty earlier, fell, but what was to replace it? Max Weber in the early years of the twentieth century had been sceptical about the possibility of democracy in Russia, and many today are equally doubtful given Russia's past. The history of reform in Russia provides 'many examples of opportunities missed and reform initiatives wrecked on the rocks of popular indifference or hostility or the resistance of powerful groups in society to the loss of their privileges'.[7] Equally pertinent, given the apparent adaptation of contemporary reforms to traditional patterns, is Crummey's observation about 'the ease with which initiatives for change can be sucked into the morass of traditional administrative habits and ways of thinking'.[8] The hopes of the era of 'great reforms' of the 1860s under Alexander II, under pressure from the terrorism that culminated in the

Tsar's own assassination in 1881, gave way to the reaction of the 1880s under Alexander III. The aspirations vested in the February 1917 'bourgeois democratic' revolution soon gave way to the disappointment of the Provisional Government and the calculated brutality of the Bolsheviks from October of that year. The three main reform periods of the Soviet regime itself, the New Economic Policy of the 1920s, Khrushchev's thaw of the 1950s, and Gorbachev's *perestroika*, all dissolved into disappointment.

Russia is not the only European country where the passage to political modernity has been traumatic: Weber had been as sceptical about the prospects for democracy in Germany as he was for Russia. Studies of the origins and dynamics of the Nazi regime offer a useful comparative perspective on Soviet developments.[9] Recent studies have rejected orthodox Marxist interpretations of Nazism as an instrument of monopoly capital, but at the same time the standard liberal view of Nazism as a temporary archaic regression in the onward march of modernisation is equally untenable. Like the Lenin–Stalin regime in Russia, the Nazi state was propelled towards ever more radical measures by its inherent instability.[10] Structural and institutional factors complement approaches based on political culture or social psychology. In post-war Germany the alleged 'totalitarian personality' appears to have adapted remarkably swiftly to democratic mores after 1945, although as late as 1968 Ralf Dahrendorf argued that high rates of political participation masked a qualitatively flawed political socialisation: 'Democratic institutions are accepted; but they remain external, distant, ultimately irrelevant....Democratic behaviour becomes ritualised, a mere observance of external demands, a "duty" of citizenship.'[11] The 'unpolitical German', as Dahrendorf put it, at least made a show of political participation whereas in post-communist Russia reform was thrown onto 'the rocks of popular indifference'. It is usually assumed that the unpolitical character of the German people facilitated authoritarian rule; what then will Russian 'anti-political' tendencies yield?[12]

While most other post-communist countries could aspire to return to some indigenous model of development, however mythologised, Russia's own pre-communist past was both more distant in time and more ambivalent.[13] P. Pestel, one of the leaders of the Decembrist uprising of 1825 (often considered the first blow in the revolutionary struggle for democracy in Russia), advocated a type of 'autocratic modernisation' in which 'Modernisation seemed a far more urgent goal than democracy or human rights.'[14] Russian history demonstrated that every attempt to achieve a 'leap' into modernity in fact only delayed the achievement of the desired modernisation, and, indeed, the whole history of Russia from 1825 can be seen as a struggle between the opposed principles of revolutionism and gradualism – and only gradualism has provided tangible and enduring achievements, such as the legal and *zemstvo* (local government) reforms of the 1860s. In Russia's last great opening to the West, between 1885 and 1913, industrial production grew at an overall annual rate of 5.7 per cent, and in the four years before the Great War growth reached 8 per cent per annum. In those years Russian wheat exports represented 24.4 per cent of the world market, and rye 34.3 per cent.[15] In politics, too, the standard image of the Tsarist regime as brutal and stifling has been tempered by the idea of the role of 'constrained autocracy' in Russian history.[16]

This was a period of enormous achievements in art and literature, the silver age of Russian poetry, a period of brilliant social analysis by religious philosophers like Nikolai Berdyaev, Sergei Bulgakov and Semyon Frank, thinkers who ultimately provided the most sustained rejection of the revolutionism typical of the Russian intelligentsia of that time in the *Landmarks* (*Vekhi*) collection of 1909.[17] Schools of jurisprudence developed and a law-based although not democratic state emerged. A modest form of parliamentarianism emerged, legal reforms established elements of a law-based state, and economic growth brought Russia to the forefront of the European states.[18] It was these achievements that were lauded by Stanislav Govorukhin in his film *The Russia that We Have Lost*, which played to packed houses in the early 1990s and helped launch his political career. While it was natural to portray the Tsarist era as some sort of golden age in contrast to the age of mass murder that followed, and undoubtedly represented a necessary corrective to the tendentious picture of Tsarism presented by the Soviet regime, the new representation, however, once again failed to explore the tensions in the old society. Eighty per cent of the population, for example, were peasants governed by customary law and relatively insulated from the modernising processes that were transforming the rest of society.

These tensions led to the fall of Tsarism in February 1917 and allowed the Bolsheviks to seize power in October of that year. Instead of moving from autocracy to democracy the 'transition' in 1917 was from Tsarism to communism. Peter the Great's revolution had stimulated the development of what Richard Pipes calls the 'patrimonial' state, where the whole country is an appenage of the monarch.[19] This pattern was reinforced by the communist revolution, and even more than under Tsarism the autonomy of civil associations like trade unions, political parties and public organisations was undermined. The Russian Orthodox Church was humbled and market relations and private property as economic institutions were abolished. Thus, in the late twentieth century, when democratisation and economic modernisation were once again on the agenda, their social and institutional bases were even more tenuous than in 1917. In these circumstances, the conflict between ends and means would once again inevitably come to the fore. Yeltsin from the late 1980s many times stressed that it would be impossible to reform the socialist system. In the wake of the October 1993 events, not without some irony, Yeltsin argued that 'we have said farewell to the illusion of giving socialism a human face'.[20] This may well have been true, but the corollary of abandoning an evolutionary exit from communism, of the sort proclaimed but only equivocally implemented by Gorbachev, was a return to the revolutionism that had played such a devastating role in Russian history before. It is no accident that the sub-title of Reddaway and Glinski's magisterial study of the Yeltsin era is 'Market Bolshevism against Democracy'.[21] the market, like communism earlier, was to be imposed by authoritarian means. Like the socialist revolution of the earlier age, the democratic project was built from the roof down.

Russia's past is multi-layered, and in the 1990s faced with the challenge of modernisation and democratisation its history was once again trawled to find elements that could sustain the democratic experiment.[22] Obolenskii argues that Russia's conservatism has deep roots in certain psychological constants of mass consciousness, including anti-personal social attitudes, a social inferiority complex, the lack of moral regulators of social behaviour, and the weak development of a normal work ethic, although even he concedes that there is a countervailing 'syndrome of modernisation'.[23] The view of Russia as eternally reactionary has been challenged by the argument that there were popular and philosophical constraints on autocratic rule. The political culture approach might suggest that democracy and civil society are somehow alien to Russia. This would be unduly deterministic, and Petro indeed writes of two competing political cultures in the Russian tradition whereby 'democracy, or *narodovlastie* in Russian, had deep roots in Russian history'.[24] Nevertheless, the historical failure of liberalism and democracy to strike institutional and social roots has many later parallels. The two themes that dominate today, the absence of a social basis for democracy and the need for authoritarian government in the transition, were common already in 1917.[25] On several occasions Yeltsin drew the analogy:

> If you are looking for historical parallels, I would compare the present time with the period in which the Provisional Government was in power, especially after June 1917. Despite its many mistakes and faults it sought to establish a democratic republic in Russia. Then the Bolsheviks prevented this and led the country into a bloody civil war. Now, 76 years later, the Russian people has the first real possibility of a free choice of the way forward. [26]

Yakovlev warned of the parallels between the renewed attempt at democracy in Russia and the catastrophe of 1917, arguing that the new leaders were repeating the mistakes of the February revolution. Gorbachev had failed to use presidential power to secure a de-ideologised politics during *perestroika*, and once again the 'democratic forces', in Yakovlev's view, 'do not have any extensive programme of civil transformations to withstand the possibilities of authoritarianism'. The new democrats failed to build on and advance the achievements of *perestroika*, which, in Yakovlev's view, 'managed to overthrow Bolshevism's autocracy, abandon the permanent war against our own people and the war with the people of Afghanistan, and step back from constant nuclear confrontation with the whole world'. Land reform had been delayed and economic mismanagement had plagued both the democracy of 1917 and post-1991. A mere eight months after the overthrow of the autocracy a new and more dreadful enslavement was imposed, a failure according to Yakovlev that sprang from the inability to develop the foundations of democracy. A civic culture based on compromise and dialogue had not emerged, and instead the mass-meeting democracy only reinforced intolerance and 'the bacillus of moral decay'. In the 1990s as in 1917 'the only path left is to overthrow ourselves, our infinite intolerance towards others, and our pitiful slobbering. Oh, how we hate others for our own laziness, foolishness and ignorance.'[27]

Is post-communist democracy in Russia in danger of going the way of the Provisional Government in 1917? Quite apart from the absence of war and a wholly different external environment, internally the country has changed. When the Russian imperial state collapsed in 1917 it left a semi-industrialised peasant economy, weak civic institutions, a society prey to a disintegrating army, an alienated working class and an intelligentsia tempted by utopian promises of a thorough reordering of society on a non-capitalist basis.[28] By contrast, the collapse of the

Soviet state in 1991 revealed a rich network of civic and public associations and a counter-culture, although lacking the legal and social bases of civil society, oriented towards liberal democratic forms of political representation and the restoration of the market. When Soviet authority crumbled there was not the anarchic vacuum that characterised events in 1917 but a shadow society (admittedly, heavily deformed) and republican governments ready to take the place of the old system.

While all countries are prisoners of their history, the history itself usually contains numerous seeds for the future, some of which may lie dormant for centuries. The Russian historical record is not wholly negative, and precedents can be found for the separation of powers and the principles of responsive governance. Russian history is not simply a story of a 'strong state' and 'weak society', but of unique attempts to find a synthesis of the two on the snow-bound and indefensible Eurasian landmass. There were elements of a 'usable past' in Russian traditions that could generate and sustain liberal and democratic forms of interaction between state and society.

Transitional justice

The 'Nuremberg question' has haunted all post-communist states. To what degree were the perpetrators of the mass murders and other crimes of the communist regime to be brought to account, as some of the Nazis were in the Nuremberg trials in 1945–6? To what extent was the plea 'only obeying orders' to be admissible? How deep should the purging of the past go? The fundamental question is whether the choices are to be framed in absolute moral terms, with justice to be sought on behalf of the victims, or whether the problems of one regime sitting in judgement on another would distort both equity and legitimacy. Russia's hybrid transition makes the question of transitional justice particularly acute; although the old regime was overthrown, in personnel terms it was at the same time perpetuated.[29] For Solzhenitsyn 'A public admission by the Party of its guilt, its crimes, and its helplessness would at least be the first step towards alleviating the oppressiveness of our moral atmosphere.'[30] Shortly after the *coup*, A. Yakovlev argued that 'Democracy is not thirsty for revenge',[31] and Gorbachev also insisted that there should be no witch hunt.[32] Some democrats, however, insisted that there should be a public trial of the leading bodies of the CPSU, which 'had for decades imposed a terroristic regime on the country', and called for lustration laws (from the Latin *lustratio*, purification by sacrifice) against top Party and KGB officials to prevent them occupying responsible posts.[33] In early 1993, Democratic Russia proposed its version of a lustration law, based on Japanese experience, to ban former *apparatchiks* from jobs in certain sensitive occupations, a policy, they argued, that would allow a new administrative class to emerge.[34]

There have been fourteen Truth Commissions of various sorts, notably in South Africa and El Salvador, as part of the development of 'restorative justice'.[35] There have been none, however, in the post-communist world. Neither truth nor reconciliation could be achieved through the mechanism of a special agency. Any serious de-communisation process, accompanied by dismissals and in certain cases trials, would involve unimaginable numbers and was liable to tear society, and indeed family and friends, apart, and sow misery and discord. Prosecutions for war crimes are always of the defeated by the victors, thus rendering judicial equity questionable.[36] In Poland the first post-communist government led by Mazowiecki drew a 'thick line' under the past, but the line did not hold and in May 1992 legislation allowed the exposure of the names of politicians and state officials who had collaborated with the communist regime.[37] The lustration law of October 1991 in Czechoslovakia affected more than 250,000 top officials and allowed the past of journalists and others to be exposed in a merciless process that judged people guilty until proven innocent and which led many, including president Vaclav Havel, to regret that the law had been adopted at all.[38] In the court of public opinion innocence is almost impossible to prove. Instead of 'drawing a line under the past', in the former East Germany the new authorities pursued collaborators of the Stasi (secret police) with unparalleled vigour.[39] The law from 1 January 1992 gave all citizens access to their Stasi dossiers, some 6 million of which were in the archives covering half the adult population. Many former dissidents and respected individuals (including the writer Christa Wolf) were accused of collaboration and many lost their jobs despite protestations of innocence. Legal and administrative mechanisms to enable people to defend themselves were inadequate.[40]

The long shadow of the secret police poisoned post-communist politics. As the Poles discovered, Party officials and state functionaries who did not need to be pressed into its service would not have secret police records, and neither would the millions who kept silent and thus acquiesced in what Solzhenitsyn called 'the lie'. Only those tried to resist were the subject of police pressure; and now their sufferings were to be prolonged by the moral crusade of the new leaders, most of whom had not fought against the regime when it had been dangerous to do so. During the '*épuration*' (purification) following the liberation of France in 1944, some 11,000 people accused of collaboration were executed, usually without trial. If popular vengeance were to be unleashed against the perpetrators of the Bolshevik crimes a new bloodbath would sweep Russia. Demands by the democrats for lustration laws were resisted by the Russian authorities, perhaps fearful of their own pasts. Yeltsin took the view that former communists had to be employed (unless they had committed a specific crime) since they represented the largest pool of professionalism.

The political uses of de-communisation campaigns was vividly illustrated by the timing of the report issued by the 'Commission for the Rehabilitation of the Victims of Political Repression', established by Yeltsin and headed by Alexander Yakovlev. Issued 'coincidentally' two weeks before the December 1995 Duma elections, the report called for the rehabilitation of those who suffered in the communist anti-religious persecutions. The report estimated that some 200,000 religious figures had been murdered by the Soviet regime for their beliefs, 40,000 churches had been destroyed, half the country's mosques and over half of the Jewish synagogues.[41] The timing suggested that the aim was to discredit the communists, and Yakovlev made no secret of his hopes that the report would undermine their prospects.[42]

In Russia the problem of identifying who was guilty for the years of suffering inflicted on the population was even more acute than in Germany. With the disintegration of the USSR the moral question arose, as it did in Germany: If the state and system on whose behalf the crimes were committed no longer exists, to what extent is the guilt transferred to the successor state that has repudiated the principles in whose name the crimes were committed? The guilt, shame and responsibility of a society that on the whole had condoned the crimes, if only by silence, etched themselves onto the post-communist national consciousness. Perhaps less ethically correct, but probably the only practical option, was to behave as the Germans did once the Cold War came into full swing in the late 1940s; ending the prosecution of Nazis and stopping the '*épuration*'. This approach was based not only on pragmatic considerations, but also on the moral revulsion against Bolshevik absolutism. Sergei Kovalev, the former head of the parliamentary and then the presidential human rights committees, opposed all attempts to divide society into the 'clean' and 'unclean', arguing 'There are no judges among us, not a single one. Everyone is to blame.'[43] The ethical rejection of the Bolshevik cause was no longer accompanied by the denial of the humanity of Bolshevism's servants. In his film *The Inner Circle* Andrei Konchalovsky raised the issue of the degree to which the sources of Stalinism were to be found in the people themselves. Did not the ordinary people play a part in creating the conditions that made their victimisation possible?

Models of transition

The Czechoslovak reform communist Zdenek Mlynar had argued that the process of change in what was the Soviet Union should be incremental: any sudden destruction of the existing system would be extremely dangerous.[44] However, the system did collapse and reform gave way to transition. The changes that had begun during *perestroika* in relations between the individual, social groups, the state and society were intensified. Market relations and democratic institutions were to be built in parallel.

The notion of 'transition' suggests the almost inevitable achievement of the desired end, something that in Russian conditions can by no means be guaranteed. The idea of 'transition to democracy' reinterpreted in a liberal guise the old communist view that history has a meaning and purpose, and that the end point is intelligible to observers. It was this historicism that Francis Fukuyama reinterpreted in a liberal guise.[45] Russia is in a transitional period, but there can be no certainty about the shape of the new polity that will emerge. While the collapse of Soviet socialism demonstrated the futility of trying to abolish the market and the inadequacies of central planning, and indeed discredited the whole notion of the socialist transcendence of the capitalist social system, the larger question of the new social and political order that would replace it in Russia remains open. While post-modernism, according to Jean-Francois Lyotard, is about the end of 'meta-narratives', then the post-communist era is still firmly located in the modern epoch since developments after the fall of communism are interpreted through at least three such narratives: modernisation theory, transitology and globalisation.

Modernisation and mismodernisation

The relationship between economic and social structures, and political authority and rulers, a subject that preoccupied Max Weber, is still not clear. Modernisation theorists would suggest that the Soviet system had been its own gravedigger, modernising society to the extent that it could no longer be constrained by the authoritarian carapace of the Soviet regime. The maturation of Soviet society now led on to the democratic revolution, but the nature of Soviet modernisation was highly ambivalent and so too was its relationship to democracy. Whereas in nineteenth-century Britain democracy was grafted onto a liberal system of property and law, in Russia political democracy was in search of a social base. Soviet-style modernisation was of a distinctive sort that I have dubbed 'mismodernisation', not to suggest that there is necessarily only one correct form of modernisation but to reflect the widespread view of Russia's own post-communist leaders that the Soviet economy was an inappropriate one in the contemporary world.[46] In his speech of 28 October 1991, Yeltsin observed that the economic basis for statehood had to be sought through land reform, privatisation and the market: 'We have defended political freedom; now we have to give economic freedom.'[47] The democratic revolution came before the bourgeois revolution; political changes preceded the economic and social basis on which they could be rooted. The state itself not only had to maintain order but to take upon itself 'the organisation of enrichment'.[48] This it did in a grand way under Yeltsin – for some.

Modernisation theory was at its most popular in the 1950s and 1960s and suggested two things: echoing Marx, that the more developed societies only showed the less developed ones their own future (the unilinear thesis); and that the social effects of modernisation have certain ineluctable political consequences (the spillover thesis). Over the years Lipset has advanced a cautious version of the spillover thesis.[49] In later years modernisation theory appeared discredited: societies showed a variety of developmental trajectories, and some failed to develop at all; and the effect of socio-economic development on politics was far from clear. After years on the margins, however, modernisation theory was defended by one of its leading exponents, Lucian Pye, who insisted that it was one of the most effective ways of studying the transition from authoritarian regimes. He did warn, however, that democratic outcomes were by no means assured but depended on the outcome of the struggle between national political cultures and the 'world culture' of modernisation.[50] Pye's warning is a necessary corrective to the assumption, so common in 1989, that the fall of the communist regimes would lead to the triumph of liberal values based on economic and political freedom.

Post-communist modernisation theory sought to take into account national peculiarities and distinctive types of modernisation.[51] This is not the place for an extended discussion of the concept of modernisation, but it should be stressed that the whole notion of modernity is ambivalent, and the features that distinguish being 'modern' from being 'non-modern' or traditional have been much contested.[52] Modernity takes many different shapes and forms, and although there may well be a growing underlying convergence (the 'evolutionary universal' noted in the literature) towards the creation of a 'world society', there are plenty of pockets of exceptionalism. Fukuyama argued that there were no sustained universal alternatives to liberal democracy, and Rustow argued that 'A tide of democratic change is sweeping the world',[53] but in many countries the tension between universalism and particularism remains unresolved.

Since Peter the Great, Russia has sought to achieve comparability with the West, but in its own way. Under Sergei Witte and Stalin, Russia pursued an early industrial pattern of modernisation based on factories and the extensive exploitation of resources and labour. This continued until the fall of the communist regime despite much talk of the 'scientific-technological revolution'. Some sectors like aerospace and parts of the military-industrial complex did make the transition to late industrial patterns, but on the whole the Soviet economy remained locked into an outmoded pattern of industrial activity based on iron and coal technologies. The post-industrial modernisation current in the West is based on the application of information and bio-technologies, the development of service and knowledge-based industries, the shift to the conservation of resources and nature, and the predominance of the consumer over the producer. The overall lack of modernisation of the Soviet economy and polity gave rise to the systemic crisis at the end of the 1980s: enough modernisation had taken place to provoke the systemic crisis identified by Roeder; but this modernisation was of a stunted and distorted type that left the Soviet economy lagging ever further behind the complex modernisation taking place in the West.

Rather than being 'under-developed' in the classic 'Third World' pattern, the Soviet industrialisation drive resulted in a distinctive 'Second World' form of 'misdevelopment'. Extraordinary economic achievements coexisted not only with grotesque waste and catastrophic environmental damage but with distinctly inappropriate technologies for the general level of development of the society. Space missions were launched from the Baikonur cosmodrome, for example, among a people brutalised beyond all measure in Kazakhstan: a third of whom had died during collectivisation in the 1930s and then whole nations, like the Chechens, were dumped in their midst in the 1940s. Factories were built in the wrong place producing goods that people did not want, while the queues lengthened for goods that people did want. Post-communist Russia was faced with the problem not of development as such but of redirecting an already recognisably modern economy from a Second into a First World path. Authors like Ickes and Gaddy suggest that in certain respects it would be easier to allow the old industrial economy to decay and to start from scratch instead of squandering yet more resources on trying to save 'value-subtracting' enterprises.[54]

Attempts at modernisation under Tsarism and the Soviet regime endowed Russia with a relatively developed economic and social infrastructure. The real task from 1991, it appeared, was the *remodernisation* of the economy to make it compatible with world standards. Remodernisation, moreover, was more than just an economic project but also entailed the radical reconstitution of society and the values on which it was based. As Karl Polanyi had long ago argued, the shift to the disciplines of a modern industrial economy from the late eighteenth century in Britain had required a fundamental cultural revolution to market-oriented values, what he called 'the great transformation' – and this is what now faced Russia. Polanyi argued that the 'free market' was an artefact created and sustained by laws that defended private-property rights, the law of contract and the rules of market competition, restraining monopolies while advancing the culture of capitalism.[55] For Russia, this meant that the focus of the state's activity was to shift from war and security to market regulation and social arbitration. For patriots, this was seen as part of Russia's Westernisation, but the transformation was deeper than that and could take specifically Russian forms, just as capitalism in the Far East took on Asian characteristics.

Russia's mismodernisation affected not only the economy but also politics and society. As far as society was concerned, Russia lived simultaneously in the modern world and in a world of pre-industrial mentalities that survived perhaps more there than elsewhere, shielded from the restless change and reinventions of modern capitalism by statist and autarkic forms of development. Russia appeared to live in several time-worlds simultaneously: traditional family patterns, clan relationships and ethnic affiliations coexisted with the modern world of contractual relationships and individualism. In Russia the peasantry, the great repository of national traditions and culture, was destroyed during collectivisation, but just as ethnic communities were sustained by the Soviet form of ethno-federalism and the passport regime, so traditional relations were reinvented in apparently modern forms of social interaction. The Communist Party itself was a modern invention, yet its structures of rule harked back to early modern patterns of political dominance,[56] and the collective farm appeared post-capitalist yet operated according to the all-embracing rules of a distinctive type of primitive feudalism. Social structures had a dual signification: modernising, yet at the same time adapting to a new type of traditionalism.

Modernisation theorists suggested a strong relationship between socio-economic development and political pluralism. O'Donnell and Schmitter, however, deny the view that a higher level of socio-economic development is a necessary or sufficient condition for the establishment of a pluralistic political system. For them questions of leadership and the political conditions necessary for the stabilisation of democratic processes were in the final analysis decisive. The more developed Latin American countries like Argentina had until recently failed to establish stable democratic systems, whereas a less developed country like Peru had, once again until recently, been more successful. The reverse thesis is no more accurate, that political pluralism is a necessary or a sufficient condition for socio-economic development.[57] Thus, one of the more cherished illusions of the *perestroika* years, that Gorbachev's reforms represented the maturation of the USSR's socio-economic development, were placed in doubt.[58] Few generalisations can be made about the relationship between socio-economic structures and political institutions and behaviour; specific historical and cultural factors have to be taken into account.

The transformation in Russia was predicated on the view that not all capitalist countries were democratic, as the experience of Franco's Spain or Hitler's Germany demonstrated, but all democratic countries were capitalist or at least based on some form of market system.[59] Moore agreed with 'the Marxist thesis that a vigorous and independent class of town dwellers has been an indispensable element in the growth of parliamentary democracy', although as we noted in Chapter 13 it may be a necessary but is not a sufficient condition.[60] Numerous American political scientists have stressed the connection between democracy and economic growth.[61] In a perverse way, they reiterated Marx's argument that liberalism and private property were two sides of the same coin. The debate on political development of the post-communist countries stressed the need to restore private property to anchor liberal democratic development in a network of social relationships, and above all in the self-interest of a property-owning class. An economic view of liberalism took precedence over political liberalism.[62] Classical American social science suggests that a substantial middle class is the bastion of stability, progress and democracy;

handwritten: 16 v/demo

and post-communist policy was designed to build up such a middle class. Privatisation was intended to overcome amorphous social ownership and to create a class of shareholder capitalists, but this was far from making a nation of stakeholder citizens. Privatisers assumed that in Russia the new class of property-owners would behave as in post-war Western Europe and North America. There was no guarantee, however, that privatised property would generate a new bourgeoisie; instead, it appeared to sustain the old elites and line the coffers of the criminal bourgeoisie, the mafia and comprador capitalists acting as agents for Western capital. The liberal-Lockean assumption that the Russian middle class would act with moderation, pragmatism and responsibility may prove unfounded.

handwritten margin note: priv)

On the political level misdevelopment meant that Russia's political stage was populated with bodies that carried the same name as those in the West, like political parties, trade unions and so on, but had a very different content. Parliament, too, had to cast off the primitive unanimity imposed by the communist regime, but conflict for the sake of conflict was an equally corrupt expression of political life.[63] The rebirth of politics in the 1990s, therefore, necessitated new bases of political consensus. The alternative modernity represented by communism had been demonstrated to be internally incoherent and only sustainable by coercion, and Russia's economic and social misdevelopment was now accompanied by a painful process of remodernisation. The speed of the collapse of communist power, however, left the society unprepared and thus borrowing from the West became the norm. However, civilisations cannot be borrowed from abroad or transplanted wholesale into existing societies. Putinism in this context represented the indigenisation of reform.

Political transition and democratisation

Samuel Huntington has described the current period as the third great democratisation wave in the modern era, each followed by a reverse wave: with the first lasting from 1828 until about 1922, when Mussolini's march on Rome set the trend for a decrease in the number of countries that could be considered democratic; the second phase began with the Allied victory in 1945 and encompassed decolonisation but ran out of steam in the early 1960s, with military takeovers in Latin America and authoritarian regimes coming to power in Africa and Asia; and the current wave began in 1974 with the Southern European transitions, continued with re-democratisation in Latin America, and was accelerated by the fall of the communist regimes in 1989–91 and the appearance of the concept of 'good government' throughout the world.[64] Experience would suggest that most seeds of democracy fall on stony ground and that democracy cannot be established without some degree of societal acceptance.[65] Regime change in Latin America has followed a cyclical pattern, and the fall of a regime like the Shah's in Iran did not open the door to democracy.

A large literature has emerged concerning transitions in Latin America, Southern Europe and elsewhere, and we can do no more than indicate some of the salient issues.[66] O'Donnell and Schmitter demonstrated that no transition to democracy has taken place without major cleavages within the authoritarian regime itself, in particular between 'hard-liners' and moderates.[67] Gorbachev's *perestroika* had indeed been torn by numerous cleavages, with reactionaries, conservatives, reform communists led by Gorbachev himself, and a growing band of radicals, all proposing divergent visions of the future. By 1990, reform communism had exhausted itself and Gorbachev found himself hopelessly exposed and hostage to the conservatives as he sought to shield himself from the reactionaries. The room for 'pacts' and other negotiated strategies of regime transition disappeared. The political cleavages of the final Soviet period were not replicated in the sovereign Russian state, and instead a dangerous unanimity appeared to reign, reflected in the overwhelming votes for Russian sovereignty on 12 June 1990 and for the dissolution of the Soviet Union on 12 December 1991. Yeltsin was able to place himself at the head of a relatively formless broad popular movement rather than a political party, and out of this emerged the problem of the lack of accountability that still plagues Russia's democracy. Yeltsin was able to use the radicals and the popular aspirations for a democratic society, but once he had achieved power neither his former colleagues in the democratic movement nor the representatives of mobilised civil society were able to exert control over him.

The Soviet transition did, however, share certain characteristics with the one analysed by Alfred Stepan where the success of the 'liberal' line depended on the presence of a moderate and intelligent opposition, giving critical support to the within-system reformers. This is to the advantage of both, since the moderate opposition can gain at the expense of more radical oppositionists, and the 'liberals' can ward off the assaults of the hard-liners.[68] There were major differences, however, since such a model can only work where the regime has a modicum of viability and is able to evolve, whereas the Soviet regime was in an advanced condition of decomposition and the state itself divided between the centre and the republics. While the leverage exerted by the liberals with the support of the conservatives was sufficient to neutralise the reactionaries for a time, the whole struggle within the Soviet system was outflanked by the new political pivot based on the republics. The August *coup* meant the defeat not only of the conservatives but also of the moderate within-system reformers, above all Gorbachev himself. The initiative passed to those outside the system who had launched an insurgency against it. The dialectic between 'republicanisation', the emergence of sovereign and later independent republics in the last years of the USSR, and 'democratisation', the struggle for popular inclusive sovereignty and accountable government to replace the Communist Party, led to the overshadowing of the latter. Independence for many (and this was even stronger in republics like Georgia and Ukraine) became a higher immediate political priority than democracy.

A political transition is about building democratic institutions, but it is about much more than this. The Weimar constitution in inter-war Germany had been a model of democratic institution-building, yet by the early 1930s had palpably failed either to root itself in the affections of the German public and political elite or to provide an effective framework for the solution of social and political problems. Hitler's rise to power in 1933 reflected the devastating role of the irrational in politics and the vulnerability of new democracies to demagogic ideologies. As decolonisation gathered pace, Western social scientists examined the problem of change in authoritarian regimes, the establishment of political order and how democracies achieve stability, questions which have a renewed relevance today with the fall of communist regimes.[69] Several models have been employed that trace the sequence of events which allowed democracies to emerge, notably the study of Northern Europe by Dankwart Rustow. State boundaries were established early on in the process but not without numerous wars. The struggle then shifted for dominance within the states, marked by civil wars, *coups* and internecine warfare until at last, exhausted, the political elites agreed on rules for choosing leaders. It required a few more decades for these rules to be internalised. In what Rustow calls the 'preparatory phase' competing parties are organised on the basis of unresolved class conflict and struggle inconclusively over issues of meaning to them, but generally abide by the rules of the game. In the 'decision phase' compromises on political participation and procedures are reached, and in the 'habituation phase' politicians and citizens come to accept these procedures.[70]

In post-communist countries the preparatory and decision phases have been reversed, with no prolonged period of struggle and compromise to prepare for democratic means of conflict-resolution. Seven decades of communism in Russia denied the people any experience of competitive, multi-party politics. In certain respects, however, Russia is going through both phases simultaneously, and the country remains in the 'preparatory phase' where the struggles between the centre and localities, and between the executive and legislative branches, involving profound issues of constitutional structure, have to date been waged by groups who have, broadly speaking, abided by basic democratic norms (with the exception of the events of October 1993 and the Chechen wars). Whereas in the 1930s both the left and right condemned what they considered were the discredited and degenerate rules of parliamentarianism and readily took to the streets, in Russia today the only legitimate source of authority is the law and the constitution, and, however much honoured in the breach, the great majority of political actors claim allegiance to these principles.

According to Claus Offe, post-communist countries faced a 'triple transition': the first concerned the definition of citizenship, deciding on who would be 'in' or 'out' of the nation-state and the extent of the borders of that state; the second focuses on the constitution (in the broadest sense) of the polity, the system of governance and administrative practices; while the third is concerned with distributional issues, the parameters of the welfare state and the struggle for resources by organised interests. The decisional logic and the time-scales of the three levels differ: the first is long drawn-out and involves passions and emotions; the second should be governed by reason and takes decades; while the third is immediate and is determined by power and ego.[71] Although Offe was talking of East Central Europe, these issues are no less central for Russia. However, in addition to establishing a bounded nation, a constitutional polity and deciding on the parameters of welfarism and the distribution of public goods, Russia faced some additional and more intense challenges: the struggle for a civil society; the transition to a market economy; and the reconstitution of national consciousness to overcome both the legacy of imperial thinking at one extreme, and the problem of minority separatism at the other. The rebuilding of political, economic and administrative structures in Russia would inevitably be long drawn-out and attended by national, social and political upheavals. The modernisation of the economy involves the separation of the economy and the polity, and the establishment of a new relationship between the two.[72] In the event, the simultaneous transformation of the economy and polity was partial and allowed enclaves of late modernity to coexist with more traditional areas.

There has been a lively debate over the relevance of classical third-wave 'transitology' to the post-communist states. Valerie Bunce has argued that in the latter the scale of the tasks is so much greater and the depth of the transition so much more intense, that to compare the earlier transitions in Southern Europe and Latin America with those in Eastern Europe is fundamentally misleading.[73] Rather than the post-communist transitions representing a continuation of the 'third wave', they constitute a fourth wave of their own.[74] The exit from authoritarianism and the struggle for democracy in the post-communist states, it is suggested, is very different from that found elsewhere.[75] Logically, the argument could be taken even further and the post-Soviet transitions (with the possible exception of the Baltic republics, which were only conclusively incorporated into the Soviet Union in 1944) should perhaps be distinguished from the Central European countries as distinctive 'fifth-wave' transitions. The length and depth of the communist experience in the USSR meant that civil society and entrepreneurialism were rooted out far more thoroughly than in the countries that had only relatively recently become communist. In addition, as suggested above, the dialectic between state-building and democratisation in the exit from authoritarianism was distinctive. Indeed, it could be argued that the Soviet Union in its last days under Gorbachev was *more* democratic than the majority of the successor regimes. From 1991, the logic of the national revolutions appeared to run contrary to the dynamism of democratisation. The degree to which this is true of Russia itself is a matter of considerable controversy.

Rustow's question remains valid: 'What conditions make democracy possible and what conditions make it thrive?'[76] One condition is a stable national and territorial identity, something still lacking in Russia. The delineation of borders precedes the establishment of democracy, but with continuing plans for a union with Belarus, rhetorical commitment to the deepening of integration within the CIS, and dreams of the reconstitution of the USSR, Russia's borders remain negotiable. With the disintegration of the USSR it became clear that the vessel for democracy would be the fifteen national states, but in Georgia, Russia and some other republics the debate over borders (both internal and external) is by no means over. Chechnya refuses to accept its status as a republic within Russia, and some other republics (notably Tatarstan) seek expanded sovereignty. The very nature and scope of Russian federalism remains contested.

Studies of transitions suggest that the struggle between well-entrenched forces can either lead to stalemate or force the creation of institutional arrangements to regulate the struggle.[77] This assumes agreement about the basic 'rules of the game', and it also assumes the presence of autonomous actors with defined social constituencies. The relative amorphousness of the Russian social formation, however, undermines this autonomy and promotes neo-corporatist statism. For example, press freedom is not just a matter of good press laws but also requires an independent financial base for media syndicates. In the West this is derived from advertising revenue, but in Russia the 'oligarchs' have stepped in where the market has failed. It would take years for democratic rules and conventions to find their expression in organised social interests and in society at large.[78]

Globalisation versus nativisation

The transition in Russia is often considered part of a global democratic revolution in which dictatorships have found it increasingly difficult to isolate themselves from 'the global trend of intensifying communication and economic integration'.[79] The theory (if that is what it can be called) of globalisation represents little more than a variant of modernisation theory, suggesting the irresistible spread of a global capitalist culture forged by ever greater and faster financial and information flows, with nation-states reduced to little more than providing a propitious environment for investment, a trained and docile workforce, and political stability.[80] The fate for a large part of the world is not globalisation but marginalisation. The share of world trade of the forty-nine least developed countries (LDCs) fell in the 1990s from a measly 0.48 per cent to an even more pathetic 0.4 per cent.[81]

The tension between global and national cultures is increasingly becoming the main line of political confrontation in the post-Cold War world, and takes distinctive forms in post-communist countries. Jadwiga Staniszkis has identified two main tendencies in the transition: the 'globalists' who favour Westernisation and marketisation; and 'populists' who seek to keep the changes within the bounds of what they perceive to be domestic traditions and national interests, retaining a large degree of state control.[82] The question of when a democrat, responsive to popular demands, becomes a populist is a moot one. Russian presidential policy under Yeltsin at first fell firmly within the globalist framework but was gradually forced from 1994 to make concessions to the 'populists' at home. One of the dynamic contradictions of Putin's leadership is that he appealed simultaneously to patriotic sentiments while committed to liberal marketisation and openness to the West.

Underlying much of the unease about the accelerated integration into world society and to the market economy was the fear that Russia's 'uniqueness' (*samobytnost*) might be lost. This is a concern shared by the Japanese, Chinese and other major civilisations faced with the apparently relentless tide of globalisation, a phenomenon that to many is no more than another name for Americanisation. These fears in Russia were articulated by patriots, the Communist Party and many others who considered 'democracy' little more than a cover for the loss of national identity and subordination to an amorphous cosmopolitanism. Zyuganov explicitly drew on Samuel Huntington's notion of the 'clash of civilisations' superseding the Cold War ideological struggle to justify his defence of 'the Russian idea'.[83] If Bolshevism in Russia was one form of resistance to Western modernity, then his national communism is another.

Post-communist Russian politics was marked by the struggle between contrasting policies of globalisation and nativisation, although in many instances these views were complementary. For some nativists Russian identity was bound up with notions of a strong state, giving rise to the *derzhavnik* (great-power) tendency, but for other nativists (like Solzhenitsyn and Likhachev) Russian identity was more closely bound up with cultural and social values. Support for native traditions, therefore, did not necessarily exclude integration into global economic and social processes. Staniszkis takes a more irreconcilable line, however, taking it as axiomatic that Russian problems of identity and state formation throughout history were resolved through external expansion. In her view, the end of the Soviet

Union meant that 'real' expansion (military and political conquest) was replaced by symbolic forms (posturing and manœuvring to defend Russia's status) until the Chechen war meant that this mimicry was abandoned and traditional forms of state-building were restored. Power allegedly shifted from the Atlanticist to the Eurasianist faction.[84] The argument fails to take into account the powerful countervailing currents in Russian political life. Russian policy often looked confused and contradictory because it *was* confused and torn by contradictory pressures. It is true that Russia's political elites at the centre adopted expansive concepts of military and economic security that encompassed much of the former Soviet territory, but at the same time this policy was pursued on the whole within the formal diplomatic channels available to any power. Russia was notably hesitant about embracing the attempts by Belarus to return to the fold, and Ukraine's suspension of Crimea's constitution in 1995 met with a remarkably muted response consistent with the view that the question was Ukraine's internal affair.

The very balance between security and democratisation appears to have changed. Russia's history since the Mongol conquest has indeed been marked by a dialectic between external security and internal repression, the fear that domestic divisions could lead to external subjugation. While the end of the Cold War has reduced the external threat, the sense of a society under siege has not altogether disappeared. Those in favour of authoritarian solutions at home have a vested interest in exaggerating the dangers from abroad. Unlike the earlier Time of Troubles between 1605 and 1613, when foreign powers took advantage of the dissolution of the regime to seize Moscow, the West has been broadly supportive of the Russian regime since 1991. However, a satisfactory balance in Russia's relations with the West has not yet been found. While claims that Russia has unconditionally capitulated to the West and ceded its diplomatic and trading (above all arms) positions are exaggerated, there remains a perceived lack of balance in the relationship that might well provoke the post-ideological Cold War discussed earlier.

International factors indeed play a crucial role in democratising transitions. Laurence Whitehead observes that the most successful transitions are those that do not challenge the existing alliance system, and which reinforce existing political and economic links.[85] Events in Eastern Europe, and even more so in the USSR, not only forced the establishment of new security structures and a new balance of power in the region and in the world as a whole, but even questioned existing borders and gave rise to the birth of new states. The transition in Eastern Europe and Russia entailed a total transformation of their socio-economic systems and network of international relations. As we have seen, the extension of Nato to include some of the USSR's former allies provoked an extended and profound debate in Russia. There was no inevitability that geopolitical competition would undermine Russian democratisation, or the generally benign international climate foster it.

In the contemporary world the debate over the legitimate limits to the scope for markets and the values that inspire them takes the form of a struggle between nativism and globalisers. Christian socialists have long argued that 'The market system has to be guarded by moral values if it is not to play havoc with society';[86] and the sentiment was echoed by various nativising political trends that together allegedly comprise the 'Asian model' of development. At the centre of the debate is the proper role of the state. In some Far Eastern countries not only have the first stages of industrial development been directed by the state, but authoritarian political systems placed limits on the democratic process on the grounds that fragile communities required a paternalistic political shield to restrain the destabilising effects of popular participation. Markets require states, but for Russia the major problem was to decide how big the state should be in conditions of economic and political dependency. Most agreed that the overweening socialist state should be diminished, but to what extent should its powers be redirected to strategic planning, discretionary industrial support, infrastructural development, and so on? Attempts to apply a neo-liberal programme anywhere are fraught with dangers, but in Russia, with its long tradition of patriarchal community reinforced by the egalitarian rhetoric of Soviet communism, this was doubly true. However, the problem was deeper, and just as the institutions and practices of democracy take time to develop, so too the culture of market relations, as Polanyi argued, needs time to mature.

It is useful to compare the democratisation project in Russia with experiences elsewhere. In Africa there has been a long-term failure to institutionalise the democratic process compensated by the over-bureaucratisation of government.[87] At the same time, the states are relatively weak because of their inability to find ways of integrating social structures and interests into the larger state system.[88] Single-party regimes and military intervention were long considered the only antidotes to ethnic conflict and secessionism. African experience clearly demonstrates that ethnocentric or unilinear models of modernisation have to take into account the spontaneous generation of traditional patterns. In Russia the institutionalisation of civic activity appeared to take root very quickly, overcoming political misdevelopment, yet its fragility encouraged the creation of an authoritarian carapace to manage the transition.

The growing class divisions, the emergence of a concentrated monopolistic pseudo-capitalist elite, semi-privatised and state-owned industries allowing as if by sufferance a capitalist sector, and the absence of a strong middle class reminded many of Latin American patterns.[89] There, small elites maintained their rule with the occasional intervention of the military when societal and political contradictions became too great. Russia's destiny appeared not Western Europe but an unstable political order built on a corrupt and unequal social system. This model does have some points in its favour, yet the differences between earlier Latin American patterns and the Russian situation are significant. In Russia, for example, the military did not serve as the midwife of the new polity and therefore lacked the legitimacy to intervene directly in politics. Russia did not have a stable society based on an oligarchic property system developed over the centuries and linked to foreign concerns. The civilian political elite in Russia was able to achieve a relative autonomy from social and military elites, and indeed its isolation was part of the problem and necessitated the generation of alliances and patronage systems with the emerging elite structure. Russia generated its own synthesis of tradition and modernity, of old and new elites, of legal-rationality and charismatic rule.

The enormous destructive creativity and creative destructiveness of Western civilisation embroiled all other cultures and civilisations in its expansive dynamism. Other societies either had to find a way of incorporating Western values within a transformed tradition, or find that tradition ruthlessly subverted and granted only a pastiche of civilisational independence. Russia had been one of the first to confront the problem, and had spent much of its modern history inventing strategies to cope with it. After the fall of communism the problem returned with redoubled force. Old debates between Slavophiles and Westernisers, patriots and liberals, were not simply exhumed but re-energised to confront the problems of post-communist Russia, and indeed to respond to universal problems of modernity and modernisation. The liberals were portrayed as a fifth column hastening the disintegration of Russian civilisation, whereas the patriots portrayed themselves as the zealots defending the last citadel of the nation's spiritual identity. The paradox of Russia's post-communist communists is particularly vivid here: a movement that had begun life as internationalist in the 1990s became patriotic and anti-globalist.

Conclusion

Barrington Moore described three main routes to the 'modern world': the path of 'bourgeois revolution' that combined capitalism and parliamentary democracy; the reactionary capitalist path that culminated in fascism; and the peasant and/or communist road. The failure of the last two in the twentieth century leaves only the first, although in this respect many are called but few are chosen. The 'modern world' for the great majority and a growing proportion of humanity appears elusive, and the most common path in large parts of the world appears to be under-development (both political and economic) and an inability to reach 'modern society' but to live forever in its shadow. This may be the fate of some of the post-Soviet republics, and possibly Russia itself.

The USSR/Russia had little choice but to adapt itself to Western and world patterns of life. In the 1990s, the great utopian social experiment conducted in Russia under the flag of democratisation was in effect an attempt at 're-civilising' the country. Overcoming the legacy of misdevelopment was no less arduous than trying to overcome under-development, and in certain respects it is more difficult because it entails destroying more of the old to allow scope for new forms to take root. Hence the enormous destructiveness, condemned by the national-patriots, of the first post-communist generation as they tried to eradicate the old system, good and bad alike. Universal child care, cheap food and housing, and a whole cultural universe were swept away together with command planning and obsolete enterprises. A society that had barely endured the catastrophic upheaval of modernisation under Stalin and his successors was now subjected to a grandiose programme of re-modernisation. Democracy and destructiveness went hand in hand in popular perceptions. All the landmarks of the old regime, ownership relations, claims to internationalism, promises of social justice and a whole network of cultural values, were swept away in the tide and a new civilisation was born. The nature of this new order is not yet clear.

While the literature on comparative transitions is instructive, it has to be tailored to the specific circumstances of societies emerging not from authoritarian regimes but from totalitarianism, however decayed. The restructuring of political systems is one thing, but the complete reshaping of social and economic structures is another. In terms of urbanisation, educational achievements and occupational structure Russia was already a modernised country. The social, economic and cultural preconditions for democracy are, however, only one aspect of achieving successful change from authoritarianism. There is also the question of political leadership and coalition building, the problem of defining a political strategy and sustaining it by ensuring that sufficient elite groups can identify with that strategy. Successful democratisation, in other words, requires both agency and structure, a reform coalition sustained by social interests and classes. It also requires a certain cultural 'fit' between political institutions and the national and cultural aspirations of society.

19 Pluralism, elites, regime and leadership

> Our object in the construction of the state is the greatest happiness of the whole, and not that of any one class.
>
> (Plato)[1]

We are now in a position to reflect more broadly on the nature of post-communist political development in Russia. We will begin by examining the ambiguities in Russian pluralism, the social nature of the transition, the emergence of a quasi-democratic regime system of rule, and conclude with an examination of the role of Yeltsin and Putin in post-communist Russian politics.

Russian pluralism

The political system was marked by the following features. First, although formally the presidency under Yeltsin gained enormous powers, its authority and powers were fragmented: the presidential system was prey to factionalism and competing policy lobbies. Under Putin the presidency sought to reassert its autonomy while at the same time differentiating the state from the economy and unmediated social pressure. Second, the fragmented nature of political authority allowed the 'power' and political ministries, the only bodies with the bureaucratic muscle to do so, to devise and pursue their own agendas and policies, often in contradiction to officially proclaimed policy. Third, the government was relatively marginalised, concerned mainly with the economy. Fourth, while parliament emerged as an effective legislative agency, its political influence was relatively weak because authority had been transferred to the presidency and the government. In terms of principal–agent theory, the accountability of the agent (the executive authorities) to the principal (the sovereign people's representatives in parliament) was extraordinarily weak. Fifth, the numerous political parties did not yet add up to a viable multi-party system. In short, a modified bureaucratic politics model clearly applies to post-communist Russian politics.

Democratisation is usually defined as the extension of mass democracy through active citizenship. The stunted development of popular representation in Russia and the limited reach of parties means that, although formally a democracy, the quality of democratic life in Russia remains impoverished. Political parties serve more as a means of communicating within the elite and of mobilising ideological and political resources in intra-elite struggle than a way of representing social interests. The communicative functions between state and society are fulfilled more by the mass media and various lobbying groups than by parties. Parties are an expression of the attempt to institutionalise the diverse interests of civil society, but Russia's fragmented pluralism allowed parties only fitfully to achieve this function. No efficient mechanism exists to channel popular feelings into legislative affairs, or then to support parliamentary politics in society. The formation of a structured party system is inhibited by the intrinsic weakness of Russian civil society, by the institutional framework of government, and by the general failure of the legal order to defend the autonomy of social interests. While Putin's reform of the party system sought to overcome the atomisation of the Russian party system, it failed adequately to ensure the autonomy of the representative system. Some of the cruder forms of the antagonism between state and society ended with the fall of the Soviet system, but the gulf between power and the individual remained. A structured party system is an essential element in pluralist democracy, but only the rudiments of such a system have emerged in Russia.

The weakness of parties was compensated by the growth of a dense network of interest and pressure groups. The mere existence of numerous interest and other groups, however, does not automatically betoken a pluralistic system. Despite some 15,000 interest groups in the United States, power is allegedly concentrated in what president Dwight D. Eisenhower in 1959 called 'the military industrial complex' and C. Wright Mills 'the power elite'. In Russia the problem of the genuine pluralisation of politics and the dispersal of influence, if not power, is all the sharper. Pluralist writers like Robert Dahl suggest that power in America is exercised not by any particular elite or social class but by competing groups whose influence depends on their strategic location and resources in regard to any particular issue.[2] In what Dahl calls polyarchy – the rule of the many – he describes a system of competing elites in which the state is limited to providing an environment in which various interests compete over policy. A polyarchical system presupposes a basic consensus over the aims and purpose of policy, something which is lacking in Russia today. The decline of totalitarianism and the end of the elite rule of the Communist Party have been replaced by a society marked by the presence of many interest and pressure groups, but the organised representation of these groups is only in its infancy, and the structural aggregation of interests at the level of the state is embryonic. Dahl's model of a polyarchy of countervailing interests is not yet applicable.

State socialism had undermined the autonomy and scope for reciprocal interaction of groups in society, and instead the limited pluralism that did exist was limited to interest groups like the military, industry and agriculture competing for scarce resources allocated by the central administrative system. Links were primarily vertical, between a group and the government, rather than horizontal, between groups themselves. The old regime had maintained a very high degree of monopoly over the distribution of the social and political goods of society, and pressure groups and lobbies emerged out of the power structures of the regime itself. Government at the centre and the localities was in certain respects not much more than a general committee for co-ordinating the affairs of sectoral interests generated by the system itself. Social groups and interests were patterned into a relationship of dependence on the party-state. This dependence eroded as the system decayed, and the rudiments of a pluralistic society were emerging even within the carapace of the old society, but this was a type of sectoral or departmental pluralism rather than a pluralism originating in society itself.

The new pluralism, therefore, bore the stamp of its provenance under the old regime. Vertical links were replicated as struggling enterprises sought credits, and privatisation was in part an attempt by the state to divest itself of direct budgetary responsibility. Groups that had been strong under the old regime found themselves strategically placed to take advantage of the new conditions. Sectoral groups lost their strategic location at the heart of governmental structures but retained privileged access to decision-making. Groups like the military, the heavy industry or agricultural lobbies were no longer part of the system itself but gained a corporate identity within the new system, something achieved with outstanding success by the Ministry of Oil and Gas (Minneftegazprom), which in 1989 became the state concern 'Gazprom', and some major oil companies. Outsider groups now fought their cause on a more level playing field and gained greater scope for independent lobbying, but the development of a genuinely pluralistic system was distorted by the predominance of corporate interests, once again part of a new power elite. The breakdown of the old system revealed the degree to which Soviet society had become fragmented. Groups, no longer constrained by the Party and the security apparatus, began to carve out fiefdoms for themselves and exerted direct pressure on parliament and regional assemblies. In post-communist conditions the concept of the 'revenge of the *nomenklatura*' means the ability of strategically placed groups to take advantage of the new freedoms to consolidate themselves. A pseudo-pluralistic system emerged.

While the political situation remains fluid the emergence of a distinctive Russian 'power elite', a structured pattern of interest and pressure group politics, can be identified.[3] In Yeltsin's final years the boundary between the political and economic spheres was blurred, but following the August 1998 financial crisis, and even more under Putin, the line was redrawn. At the same time, the tendency for regional leaders to combine public office with private business has declined. This has been accompanied, however, by 'a revitalisation of power exerted by former *nomenklatura* members and an activation of previous social networks'.[4] In addition to and often part of the reconstituted *nomenklatura* elite, the economic reforms saw the emergence of powerful financial-industrial groups (FIGs) who for a time became the main arbiters of power struggles in Moscow. The policy gulf between new entrepreneurs and traditional state managers was gradually eroded as the rudiments of a financial and trade market system emerged. In short, the old Soviet bureaucratic corporatism disintegrated in the late 1980s and in its place a new pattern of oligarchical corporatism emerged.[5]

The multi-party system in Russia developed in the interstices of political life; parties were only one of the forms in which post-communist politics was structured. Parties were rivalled by social associations like trade unions and business organisations, and there were also various organised but not necessarily institutionalised social forces such as the 'mafia' or elements of the old *nomenklatura*. Pressure groups emerged to promote specific causes and interests, and the common complaint against MPs was that they had become lobbyists for particular interests rather than representatives of the general good. Khasbulatov's parliament became a forum for unrestrained lobbying, but in both the old and the new parliament *flaws .*

deputies openly acted on behalf of special interests. The absence of either a law in general concerning lobbying, or detailed parliamentary procedures to regulate it, meant that the scale of the interpenetration between political elites and special-interest groups is hard to quantify.

There was an enormous growth of divergent social and economic interests but their ability to be represented at the political level was unequal. Some groups had privileged access and greater resources to make their voice heard, while others, above all those dependent on the state budget like teachers and health workers, let alone pensioners and unskilled workers, were unrepresented. Putin's rise is in part explained by his appeal to these previously disenfranchised groups, promising the payment of back wages, increases in pensions and the revalidation of their life experiences. He also sought to ensure that corporate interests were removed to arms length from the government. On two occasions in his first year in power as president he met with leading oligarchs and lectured them on the need for a separation of spheres of activity: politicians with politics, and business people with business. No longer would it be true to say that the business of Russian politics is business.

Corporate interests, however, remain the best organised. Notable among them is Arkadii Vol'skii's Russian Union of Industrialists and Entrepreneurs (Employers) (RUIE), acting at first largely as a pressure group for the industrialists who, having lost the privileged access to the ministries that they had enjoyed in the past, turned to parliamentary lobbying. By 2001, the RUIE had changed its structures and represented some 80 per cent of Russian industry.[6] However, the unity of the industrialists should not be exaggerated, with deep regional and sectoral divisions.[7] The new elites are by no means homogeneous, with divisions between industrialists and entrepreneurs, with the former on the whole for state subsidies while the latter favour macro-economic stabilisation, a stable currency and low inflation. Even traditional elites were forced to find new ways of advancing their interests, and their special-interest lobbying became increasingly professional. One of these forms was the formation of so-called 'elite clubs' like the Council for Foreign and Defence Policy (SVOP) or Yurii Petrov's Club of Realists, where their members could meet behind closed doors, share their views and issue influential policy papers. Entrepreneurial groups sought to influence elections but found that support for various apparently sympathetic candidates and groups gave little return on their 'investment' once in parliament. A number of pressure groups, both from business and labour, participated directly in the 1995 elections, but these attempts failed miserably and none of the numerous business groups crossed the 5 per cent threshold, and in later elections they were more wary. The politics of pressure and lobbying was as fragmented as the party system that it shadowed.[8]

Old and new elites

Under late communism nepotism and patron–client relations undermined the political criteria of elite recruitment in the *nomenklatura* system.[9] The political elite began to degenerate into a social class, perhaps one of the most economically useless in history. As Milovan Djilas had long ago noted, the Party fostered a class that grew at its expense and began to transform itself into a traditional oligarchy.[10] Under the cover of the declining communist regime a vigorous network of informal relations emerged directed towards gaining benefits of the system, a phenomenon identified by Zvi Gitelman as constituting a 'second polity', paralleling the 'second economy' of 'really existing socialism'.[11] The 'new class', as Djilas termed it, eventually outgrew the system that had given it birth. August 1991 can thus be seen as the revolt not of society but of a rebellious section of the old elite against the tutelage of its progenitor, the communist system, and in this scheme of things there was no room for popular democratic mobilisation or anything more than superficial de-communisation. One section of the elite was politically expropriated by another representing the emerging economically based class system. The decapitation of the Party in 1991 did not destroy these networks of communication and patronage but forced them to adapt to a more open environment and new rules of operation. From this perspective it was no longer a question of the new society bearing the deformations of its tragic birth pangs, but that the new society *was* the old society in a new guise.

The post-communist regime system emerged out of the old *nomenklatura* system and in its way represented the reconstitution of late Soviet forms of rule – but without the CPSU. Regional Communist Party bosses, as Hough described them in his classic work *The Soviet Prefects*, performed numerous functions, few of them directly connected with politics but mostly associated with lobbying for resources, getting supplies for local enterprises, and in general managing local labour and wage funds.[12] Party, state and economic management overlapped, with all responsible positions being filled exclusively through the *nomenklatura* appointments system. With Gorbachev's attempts to restrict the Party more narrowly to the sphere of politics, and with the prestige of the CPSU falling rapidly from 1990, some of the more far-sighted party officials shifted over to state posts to join the economic managers already heavily represented in the ranks of the local soviets and their executive bodies – and continued to do what they had always done but in new ways.[13]

The *nomenklatura* class did not disappear with the fall of the old regime; it only lost its role in the Party-led system of power but generated its own interests (however fragmented). The KGB and regional Party officialdom in particular survived the dissolution of communist power largely intact. More broadly, the informers and executioners of the secret police, the corrupt judges, the dedicated communists building socialism on the bones of the peasantry, all became 'citizens' of the new Russia. The transition was in many respects an incomplete revolution, with profound continuities in elite structures and political practices. If the collapse of communist power in 1991 was something akin to an 'abdication', in which its leadership relinquished power without much of a struggle, the elite structures at the heart of the old regime did not by any means renounce their advantages. So-called 'outsiders', like dissidents, had little chance of coming to power, and in Russia (like most other post-Soviet states) even nationalists found the path of political insurgency blocked by the consensual (if not negotiated) pattern of political transition that left much of the old system in place, losing *only* the obviously politically dysfunctional political apparatus of Party rule and the intellectually obsolescent claim to be 'building socialism'. Shorn of this political and intellectual incubus, which far-seeing elements even within the system had long realised to be antithetical to the effective development of the polity and society, the old elites forged an alliance with the new authorities and thus secured themselves a place in the new order. Only in Chechnya was the fall of the old regime accompanied by a full-blooded popular revolution that swept away the thin layer of a Sovietised Chechen elite together with the old Party-state apparatus – with consequences that were learnt by other national republics who used Chechnya as a warning against the excesses of popular sovereignty. Too much democracy in the transition, they warned, threatened inter-ethnic peace and could explode, as in Tajikistan between 1992–7, into civil war. In contrast to Germany after the Second World War, where its traditional order had been destroyed by defeat and Allied intervention, it was out of the old Soviet order that the new Russia was born. Full-scale democratisation soon ran into the sands of this stubborn socio-political reality.

The late Soviet years were marked by the bifurcation of elite structures between a Party elite and a nascent middle class, and, more specifically, the final Gorbachev years saw the accelerated divergence between Party and state officialdom, with the latter beginning to distance itself from the communist regime. The anti-communist revolution thus entailed only a partial transformation of the social order: certain groups ascended, others fell, but most adapted to the new regime. The losers were the old Party *apparatchiki*, the military top brass, and the military-industrial complex as a whole. However, many of these, particularly the regional elites, were able to make the transition with relatively few losses, and much of the old *nomenklatura* did very well by converting their privileges into material assets, often in the form of real estate and stakes in enterprises through *nomenklatura* privatisation. More clearly winners were the new class of entrepreneurs and those who had been able to use civic activity as a path of upward social mobility, often as a substitute for economic initiative. The *nomenklatura*, strictly speaking, refers not only to former Party officials (the *apparatchiki*) but to the top managers and administrators, who went on to become elected regional deputies and from whom most governors were drawn.

In the late Soviet era, the term 'mafia' took on a broad meaning, encompassing the fused political and semi-criminal priviligentsia. Telman Gdlyan's book *Mafia of the Lawless Times* exposed the luxurious lifestyles of the Party mafia in the Soviet Far East and Moscow.[14] Even before the *coup*, the *nomenklatura* elite adapted to post-communist forms of social organisation as they valorised or 'capitalised' their assets, converting privileges enjoyed by custom into property defended by right. Top Party officials, for example, crossed over to take positions in the state apparatus, assisted by Gorbachev's aide, Valerii Boldin.[15] The old elite transformed itself into the new by shifting from Party to state posts, creating economic structures subordinate to the party, and by joining emerging independent commercial organisations where they exploited personal contacts and knowledge of the system. State assets, in theory owned by everyone but concretely owned by no one, were privatised to become personal assets. Ownership (or lack of it) had proven to be the Achilles' heel of the old system, and now became the cornerstone of the new.[16] The late Soviet 'mafia' imperceptibly became part of the class of 'new Russians', those able to take advantage of emerging opportunities and the lax legal framework to enrich themselves. It is for this reason that Govorukhin describes post-communist Russia as 'the great criminal revolution'.[17]

Democratic institutions need a stable class structure to sustain them, and in many respects a post-communist psycho-social order was already highly developed within the framework of the communist system. One of the reasons commonly given for the failure of the 1991 *coup* was that sections of the old elite were already becoming incorporated into the new. A post-revolutionary settlement was already in the making in which the second echelon of the office-holding *nomenklatura* were turning themselves into capitalists and officials of the new order. It is hardly surprising that they were unwilling to jeopardise their chances by defending the crumbling old order. In other words, the old political class saw its best hopes of survival by transforming itself into a new social elite.

But what is the *nomenklatura* and is it still valid to use the term?[18] Should we continue to call the demobilised army of officials and administrators by their old name? After all, over a decade has passed since someone was last appointed by recommendation of a department of the Central Committee. The temptation to continue to use the term, however, is great; after all, words give substance to abstractions and make the intangible real, but ultimately the term will become increasingly anachronistic. In the post-communist context the concept of the *nomenklatura* is less of a precise occupational category than a way of identifying a broad social class. The academic Dmitrii Furman, for example, talks of the *nomenklatura* as 'a vast network of personal relationships and clans'.[19] This encompasses the former Party bosses, enterprise managers, officials of the old regime and many more who were formed in the same school and recognise certain common interests, irrespective of whether they called themselves democrats, patriots or whatever. The transformation of the Politburo member into the president, the *oblast* Party secretary into the mayor, the criminal entrepreneur into a businessman, all suggest not so much the formation of a new elite as the *reformation* of the old. It is this, among other things, that gives Russia's current social transformation its hall-of-mirrors quality.

Despite the hopes of the activists of the democratic insurgency in 1989–91, following the *coup* Yeltsin concentrated on economic reform at the expense of democratic renewal, and remarkably little de-communisation took place. This had never been part of Gorbachev's strategy, and even though Yeltsin's programme in the insurgency phase was permeated by an anti-communist rhetoric, this was not translated into purges against the communist elite. There was remarkably little turnover in the regional and local elites, and in 1994 82.3 per cent of senior administrative staff and legislators were still made up of former *nomenklatura* officials.[20] According to Kryshtanovskaya, 75 per cent of the new political elite and 61 per cent of the new business elite comes from the old Soviet *nomenklatura*. The businessmen mostly came from the Komsomol (38 per cent) and from the old economic bureaucracy (38 per cent). She notes the central role played by a small number of banks favoured by the government in unifying the new elite in the wake of the collapse of the old system.[21]

This elite dominates many of Russia's regions and republics, and indeed some of the other successor states. In this context Yeltsin's refusal to sanction purges of the *nomenklatura* through lustration laws and the like, as demanded by the radical democrats, makes more sense. There is a normative element to the 'self-limiting' nature of Russia's democratic transition, the attempt to bring an end to the cycle of violence and retribution characteristic of Russian history, but more prosaic concerns also play their part: the need to draw on the skills of the old elite, to secure their loyalty to the new dispensation, and, above all, to preserve the gains of the reformed old/new class. While the 'democrats' were disappointed by the absence of significant de-communisation, experience suggests that their political activists were often incompetent administrators, and so by necessity the Yeltsin regime was forced to rely on the old guard. This, however, is only a partial explanation: far more importantly, Yeltsin forged a strategic alliance with the old administrative elites by choice to secure a social base to his own rule and at the time to free himself from dependence on any particular constituency, the democrats included. Thus, the refusal to hold elections in the aftermath of the August *coup*, when the democratic wave was at its peak, can be understood as part of Yeltsin's strategy to consolidate his alliance with regional and central administrators. Stability took precedence over deepening the anti-communist revolution.

The option was only possible because of the virtual self-destruction of the commanding heights of the political system during the August putsch: Yeltsin's ban on the CPSU was no more than the *coup de grâce*. Yeltsin decapitated the political leadership of the old regime and placed himself at the head of its elite hierarchy. The Party was destroyed as a functioning political organism and its administrators in the regions, now firmly ensconced in the local soviets, were free to forge new alliances. The confiscation of the CPSU's property allowed local soviets to dispose of these assets as they saw fit, an important factor in buying their allegiance to the new system. This analysis, of course, leaves out the important question of political preferences, and the residual tension between the new regime in Moscow and the provincial elites was an important factor shaping post-communist politics. The main point, however, is that the regime's self-image, as a progressive reforming government in the centre combating the conservative inertia of the regions, greatly simplifies the true state of affairs.

Corporate clans combining new financial entrepreneurs with some of the traditional industrial and administrative elite represented an enormous concentration of resources. Not only did they sponsor parties and politicians who could represent their interests, in a certain sense they became the functional substitute of political parties. The concept of the 'party of bosses' (*partiya nachal'stva*) is used to describe administrative and state economic managers who not only enjoy important positions in the country's management structures but who enter politics in their own right and who, without being affiliated to any particular party, achieve considerable electoral successes.[22] They continue to exercise significant political influence in the centre and in the regions. Chernomyrdin's Russia Our Home party was created to channel this spontaneous development and incorporate it into the existing alignment of political forces, a task that was then continued by Unity. The election of the oligarch Roman Abramovich, first as a deputy and then as governor of Chukotka, is perhaps the most striking example of a business leader entering politics and affiliating with the 'party of power'.

The post-communist class system in Russia is represented schematically in Table 19.1. While the political shift from a communist to a nominally democratic order could be achieved fairly swiftly, there could be no such direct transition in the social sphere. The emergence of the unofficial or shadow system inhibited the transformation of the old officialdom into a democratic class system, acting as a barrier and in many cases a vale of tears for those trying to make that transition. In other words,

Table 19.1 The class structure of post-communist Russia

Official	*Nomenklatura*, operating according to command principles. After August 1991, the old class of communism is reformed to become one element of the new class of democracy
Unofficial or shadow system	Based on patronage and client relations, bribery, the second economy, black market mechanisms, allied often with criminal elements and corrupt sections of the co-operative movement. The official system began to merge with this shadow class to create the politico-economic 'mafia' or the criminal bourgeoisie. To capitalise on their political advantages they asset-strip their old contacts and knowledge; a political class becomes a degenerate economic class
Democratic class system	Based on meritocracy, market and competition; officialdom becomes a civil service

between the old elite and the new class system there lay a whole series of social networks that derived from the past but at the same time looked to the future. In social terms, there could be no simple leap from the past to the future. Between the official mono-class system and the democratic meritocratic class system lay a third system entirely, a feature typical of post-communist societies.

The new capitalists are a thoroughly syncretic and heterogeneous class, including outright criminals, the mafia, shady dealers from the black economy and the co-operative sector, officials from the KGB and the old Party structures, the corrupted new democrats 'grabbing' (from *prikhvatizatisiya*, a pun on *privatizatsiya*) as fast as they can for the limited period they find themselves at the trough and, occasionally, some genuine new entrepreneurs. The priviligentsia only gradually turned into a middle class. The proto-bourgeoisie converted its power and privileges into property and rights, and they were aided in this endeavour by the state. Just as under communism, politics came first in the sense that the new class was consolidated as a result of an exercise of political will rather than emerging as a spontaneous process of class formation. Tensions remained between the political elite and the emerging new bourgeoisie, yet both realised that they were in a fateful dependency on each other.

The old elite metamorphosed into a new one, but at the same a multiplicity of new elite structures emerged. The scale of elite fragmentation is a matter of some controversy; the American diplomat Thomas Graham in late 1995, indeed, suggested that Russian government was an oligarchy in which political and economic power was held by narrow cliques.[25] The structure and context of elite politics changed as recruitment became more open and caste-type and politically driven methods of recruitment (typical of the *nomenklatura* system) were undermined. The new Russian elite, however, is still far from representative of society at large, with the old Party-state and managerial structures greatly over-represented.

While the notion of a *nomenklatura* revolution reflects important elements of Russia's current social and political transformation, it is far from revealing the whole truth. Although there was some popular mobilisation, notably between 1989 and 1991 with marches, meetings, strikes and flag-waving, this was not a genuine popular revolution and not even a negotiated revolution, with the orderly transfer of power from a ruling group to an organised opposition. The transition can be characterised as the consensual and evolutionary political self-transcendence or self-transformation of an unviable order into one more consonant with the modern age. A defunct ruling class shakes off the ideology and structures that stifled its development and, emerging from the chrysalis, takes wing, legitimised by the language of democracy and the market but neither democratic in conviction nor prepared to submit to the free play of market *forces*. The democratic insurgency can thus be seen as an auxiliary in the struggle between elites, to be dispensed with when no longer required. This does not mean that Russia's democracy is no more than a masquerade or that its rudimentary market system is no more than a convenient mechanism for the new class to enrich itself, but it does suggest the flawed hegemony of the new historical order.[24]

Regime politics

The tension between the weakness of the Russian state (characterised by the poor reach of the judicial authorities, fiscal confusion, inept administration and the like) and the hypertrophy of the state apparatus promoted the development of what we call 'regime politics'. The elimination of the political monopoly of the CPSU in Russia was not replaced by multi-party governance as such but by a regime system in which power was concentrated in the instruments of executive authority in an unstable relationship with legislative power, popular movements and powerful social interests. The pluralism of the system (however distorted) is not in doubt; what is questionable is the degree to which open democratic forms of adjudicating these interests has been institutionalised. The factors that inhibit the development of a multi-party system are not necessarily the same as those that hinder the development of a functioning democratic system, but one way or another the fate of democracy depends on the integration of the new political forces into the system of government.

While the main structural features of the old system have disappeared (the one-party state, the command economy, the ubiquitous security system), elements of what Rigby called 'bureaucratic crypto-politics' have continued in a new form,[25] but now joined by a number of public policy spheres – the presidency, parliament, the media, business and the like. A variety of terms have been advanced to describe the syncretic mix of authoritarianism, corporatism, liberalism, managerialism and democracy that emerged, characterised as authoritarian democracy in the first edition of this book. In the general literature, however, one of the best-known terms is 'delegative democracy'. In weakly established democracies a leader can become so strong that he or she can ignore those whom they are meant to represent. O'Donnell characterises these countries as having 'delegative' rather than representative democracy with the electorate allegedly having delegated to the executive the right to do what it sees fit for the country.[26] Thus, a government emerges that is 'inherently hostile to the patterns of representation normal in established democracies' by 'depoliticising the population except for brief moments in which it demands its plebiscitary support'.[27] A large literature deals with questions of the efficacy and justification of delegative democracy in the context of the developing world, focusing on questions like the function of authoritarian institutions in economic policy-making and the related issue of the role of democratic representation and representative institutions. The evidence suggests no clear conclusion that authoritarian forms of modernisation (as in Taiwan or Singapore) are more effective than in democratic societies, and indeed contemporary thinking highlights the increasing costs associated with authoritarian policy-making.[28]

In Russia the concept of delegative democracy has been fruitfully applied to the study of regional and central politics.[29] It does not, however, adequately convey some of the nuances of the post-communist syndrome, where the elite structure is unstable, social interests fluid, and the relative autonomy of the ruling elite all that much stronger than, for example, in Latin America, the region for which the term was first devised. Another term that has been used to describe the emerging Russian reality is Fareed Zakaria's notion of 'illiberal democracy'.[30] According to Zakaria, states like Germany in the nineteenth century were ruled by law but were not democracies, and until its reincorporation into China Hong Kong was also an illiberal democracy. Russia, too, is in principle governed by the norms established by the constitution and the law, but the quality of its democracy remains decidedly thin. However, the tension between economic and political liberalism is blurred by the use of the term, and although it does provide some insights does not capture the distinctive features of post-communist Russian politics.

We will argue that the concept of regime politics best captures the complexity of Russia's semi-consolidated democracy. Regime politics limits the scope of democratic consolidation but cannot be defined as full-blown authoritarianism. The 1993 constitution now lies at the basis of the polity, committing Russia to liberal rights and freedoms, the separation of powers, federalism and the rule of law. Although often honoured more in the breach than in practice, these commitments remain at the centre of Russian political life. However, there is a tension, on the one hand, between the formal arrangements outlined in the constitution and succeeding normative acts, what we may call the political system, and, on the other hand, the regime that until Yeltsin's resignation on 31 December 1999 centred on the president himself, his family and associates, and a group (conventionally called 'the oligarchs') that were able to take personal advantage of the grand redistribution of state property to enrich themselves and to become key players in the new system.[31] Yeltsin himself was re-elected in 1996 with the collective support of the oligarchs, who put aside their own divisions to rally around the defence of Yeltsin's regime, fearing that a victory of the CPRF led by Zyuganov would put an end to their dominance. In the event, Yeltsin's second term was characterised by policy drift, Yeltsin's own physical incapacity, and a growing demand for changes to the polity through constitutional reform.

Under Yeltsin there was no clear distinction between the regime and the state, and both succumbed to clientilistic pressures exerted by powerful interests in society, some of whom (above all the so-called oligarchs) the regime itself had spawned. The oligarchy and its allies represented a fusion of financial and industrial capital with direct access to government. The traditional distinction between the market and the state was eroded, and lobbying interests enjoyed an extraordinarily close relationship with government. Russian politics became characterised by the salience not so much of the formal institutional structures of government and management but by informal relationships. Above all, given the weakness of the state, the emergence of what might be termed quasi-state actors became particularly important. For example, the banks (including the Central Bank), and the large energy companies (above all Gazprom), acted as substitute sinews of the state, providing financial resources not available through taxation, and served as indirect enforcers of federal policy, while at the same time ensuring that federal policy was not hostile to their interests.

The tension between system and regime was also one between formal and informal political relationships, between law and politics, and between the institutionalisation and personalisation of political authority. In this system of 'regime politics' personalised leadership promoted the under-development of institutions. Behind the formal façade of democratic politics conducted at the level of the state, the regime considered itself largely free from genuine democratic accountability and popular oversight. If under the Soviet system a 'party-state' had emerged, where the CPSU exercised leadership and prevented the state from gaining political autonomy, then we can describe the system that emerged under Yeltsin as a 'regime-state', where the regime focused on the presidency exerted extra-constitutional authority over the political system as represented in the institutions of the state. Political practices that were once associated with 'the Party' were now exercised by 'the regime'. The result was the continued debilitation of the state, unable to assert the principles of the constitutional autonomy of the political system *vis-à-vis* the regime.

We apply the concept of 'regime' to describe not the character of the system as a whole but in the word's other meaning, of a relatively small group of political leaders gaining relative independence of systemic constraints and allied with the socio-economic beneficiaries of post-communist economic transformation. Political integration in post-communist Russia took place at the level of the regime rather than at the level of the political system (the state). The political system is regulated by constitutional norms, laws and judicial decisions; the regime, however, operated according to patterns of personalised ties, patron–client relations and attempts to retain its autonomy. The consequences of this pattern of politics can be seen to be threefold:

1   Although political institutions are established, political processes remain under-institutionalised. They are focused on personalised ties rather than administrative procedures.
2   The greater the institutionalisation of the political system, the more ordered is the state. In Russia, however, not only does the regime undermine the routinisation of systemic power, it is also more broadly parasitic on the state itself. Indeed, an ordered state would threaten the very existence of the relatively autonomous regime. Thus, the crisis of the post-communist Russia state, among many other factors, is in part at least due to the emergence of the Yeltsinite regime. The state, to use Michael Mann's terms,[32] was unable to develop its infrastructural resources in any consistent way, and, instead, at moments of crisis, resorted to the use of despotic force (October 1993, Chechnya) in defence of the regime if not of the state itself. The infrastructural power of the regime is corruption, bribes, electoral manipulation and indeed

the systematic subversion of the constitutional principles of the political system itself. In short, power remained power, and was not converted into authority. Any legitimacy that the regime may have had was derived not from what the regime was itself, but from what it represented. Yeltsinism came to symbolise 'reform', but the form in which these reforms were pursued undermined the substantive content.

3   In an effective liberal democratic society there is a strange alchemy whereby power is converted into legitimate authority. This alchemy works in other respects as well, above all in the sphere of political economy. Marx devoted his life to understanding the mysterious way that money is converted into capital. In Russia's mutant capitalism this transformation of money into capital has barely begun.[33] Money resolutely remains money, to be carted around in suitcases (cardboard boxes) or to be spirited out of the country as capital flight. Similarly, economic relationships remain heavily administrative rather than determined by the rationality of the juridico-market framework. In a semi-marketised and heavily bureaucratised economy like Russia's, personalised links act as the substitute for genuine market relations.

In Yeltsin's order political and economic interests were thoroughly entwined. This, however, was not corporatism of the traditional type since each of the three elements traditionally associated with it (the state, employers and labour) were too weak taken individually or together to strike and maintain corporatist deals. Instead, a 'regime system' emerged based on informal but regularised relationships between the major societal interests and the unclear separation between political office and economic concerns. This was accompanied by a hybrid type of 'regime democracy' in which democratic proceduralism was tempered by the manipulation of democratic processes. Russian democracy was not a sham, but neither was it consolidated.

It might be noted that post-war Japan has also been characterised by a form of regime politics, institutionalised until 1992 by the dominance of the Liberal Democratic Party (LDP) in the Diet and by innumerable informal links with business and other constituencies. A comparison with pre-1989 Italy is also useful. Even the much-vaunted French presidential system is riven by problems and gave rise, according to one observer, to 'the death of politics' under president François Mitterrand, marked by the centralisation of government, the fusion of administrative and political elites, the dominance of the head of state and the corresponding marginalisation of the prime minister and the cabinet, and above all by the etiolation of parliament.[34]

These international comparisons put into perspective 'culturalist' interpretations of post-communist Russian political development. While Russian traditions, and in particular the legacy of institutional confusion and arbitrariness, played an important part in forming the mental world of those who shaped the post-Soviet system, these traditions on their own are an inadequate explanation for these developments. Reissinger *et al.* have proposed, in a different but equally fruitful context, what they call a 'political economy' perspective that stresses 'the evolving concrete material interests of different members of society during a time of rapid change'.[35] Factors like intra-elite conflict and the political economy of economic reform as much as inherited cultural norms shape post-communist political development. Inherited elites seek to maximise their economic advantages in a time of dramatic opportunities, but equally they seek to underwrite their gains in the political sphere; legal guarantees on their own at a time of 'revolution' (if that, indeed, is what Russia is engaged in) are barely worth the paper on which they are written. Thus, the regime system has emerged as a function of the inadequate differentiation between politics and economics, and as a response to the political needs of the dominant groups in post-communist Russia.

Regime politics in the post-communist context, however, is not like traditional authoritarianism, and the regime could not insulate itself from aspects of modern liberal democratic politics like media criticism, parliamentary oversight (if not accountability) and, above all, from the electoral cycle. The legitimacy of the new regime-state rested firmly on its commitment to the classical postulates of liberal democracy and to the marketisation of the economy. Thus, regime-type politics looked both ways: backwards to old-style command politics and the bureaucratic regulation of the economy (hence the enormous opportunity for rent-seeking by elites with access to the regime); and forwards to the genuine separation of powers, the differentiation of politics from economics, the subordination of politics to law, and the genuine application of democratic choice in elections. Regime politics thus represented a hybrid system, not foreclosing further development towards democracy but at the same time replicating many of the practices associated with the past, although in radically new forms and based on an entirely different legitimating idiom. This was the very mixed legacy of Yeltsin's rule, and helps explain why very different evaluations of his presidency are possible.

Leadership and regime change

Yeltsin was above all a master politician, pursuing several policies, often mutually exclusive, simultaneously, and playing off groups and institutions against each other. For most of his rule Yeltsin's appointments were tactical combinations to maintain a balance pivoted on himself. Above all, Yeltsinism looked in two directions at once: forwards towards democracy, international integration and a less bureaucratised and genuinely market economy; while at the same time it inherited, and indeed not only perpetuated but also reinforced, many features of the past – the pervasiveness of bureaucratic arbitrariness in politics and the economy, knee-jerk anti-Westernism, pervasive patron–client relations rather than meritocracy, and widespread corruption. This was the legacy facing Putin, and although he retained many features of the regime politics typical of the Yeltsin era, he subjected that regime to significant change.

Yeltsin's farewell

While it is not unusual for there to be a qualitative difference between the first and second terms of a presidency, no one could have predicted quite how different the two Yeltsin terms would be. If in the first term Yeltsin still retained the capacity for policy innovation, in the second he became reactive and lost much of a sense of strategic direction. We now know that Yeltsin's health first started to deteriorate badly in 1995, and soon after his re-election in June–July 1996 he was forced to undergo a multiple heart bypass operation. From at least March 1997 and the establishment of the government of 'young reformers' (represented above all by Boris Nemtsov), it was clear that Yeltsin's main priority was the succession. It is this factor that helps explain the rapid succession of prime ministers from March 1998, when Chernomyrdin was sacked and Sergei Kirienko was appointed in his place.

The MP and political commentator Vyacheslav Nikonov argued that 'we will only be able to talk of Russia as a democratic or civilised state when the country for the first time in its thousand-year history has a constitutional change of power'.[36] In the event, the *dénouement* to Yeltsin's presidency was as dramatic as the way in which it had been conducted. In his resignation speech of 31 December 1999, Yeltsin asked for forgiveness:

> Not all our dreams came to fulfilment...we thought we could jump from the grey, stagnatory totalitarian past to a light, rich and civilised future in one leap. I believed that myself....But it took more than one jump.

He stressed that he was not resigning for health reasons, although it had long been clear that he had been losing his physical powers. Yeltsin's resignation reflected his view that an opportunity had arisen for him to leave the scene without endangering his political achievements. One of Putin's first moves as acting president was to sign a decree granting Yeltsin and future Russian presidents immunity from criminal prosecution, arrest, search or interrogation. The former president was entitled to 75 per cent of his monthly salary, state protection for himself and his family, and access to VIP lounges in Russia's airports, railway stations and ports.[37] While the interests of the country may have been served by Yeltsin's premature exit, democracy was not best served by the timing. As Yeltsin himself admitted in his resignation speech, his premature exit meant that Russia would not see one democratically elected leader transfer power to another in direct accordance with the expectations laid down in the constitution. Instead, there was an attempt to pre-empt the choice of the voters by transferring power to a designated successor for whom the most benign political environment had been established. However, the succession did take place according to the constitutional norms established earlier in the decade, and this was no mean achievement.

For all of its many faults the Yeltsin era, on the political level at least, was one that did not foreclose the option of democratic development. The basic democratic openings of the late 1980s and early 1990s were not entirely lost, although by the end of the decade they were undermined. Parliament had not developed effective monitoring mechanisms over the executive, media freedoms were being eroded, in the regions various political fiefdoms were being established, the legal system lacked funding and autonomy, the security services once again began to emerge as an independent political force, and in general the quality of political relations had been degraded by the tawdry pursuit of narrow institutional and personal self-interest. Yet a basically co-operative relationship had been established with the West, no one had been prosecuted for views expressed in the media, and basic political freedoms and rights could be exercised. As the Yeltsin era entered its closing stages, the basic question remained: Did the system established by Yeltsin have an evolutionary potential, or did Russia once again have to enter a period of revolutionary upheaval?

Putin's 'third way'

The accession of Putin to the presidency suggested that the answer was 'no'. He came to power committed to the maintenance of the existing constitutional system, although as we have seen in his early years he engaged in significant quasi-constitutional change (as in the establishment of the State Council and the seven federal districts). Putin's politics were centrist, but of a distinctive kind. For Victor Sheinis victory in the December 1999 Duma elections went to a 'quasi-centre',[38] whose basic policy orientations were right wing (i.e. liberal) economics and left wing politics: economic liberalism accompanied by statist great-power politics. Privatisation and other economic reforms would continue, but allied to the continued iron grip of the bureaucracy over the 'market'. According to him, the elections revealed 'the minimal movement towards a self-sustaining civil society' and 'the isolation of the political class from the deep layers of society'. This gulf between the power system and society was something noted by many other commentators. This is why Sheinis's notion of a quasi-centre is so suggestive. It does not come from a historical convergence on the centre ground of policy, but from the opportunistic co-optation of policies to ensure regime survival.

A genuine 'third way', according to Giddens, is derived not simply from the repudiation of idealised notions of left and right, reflected in traditional class politics, but from attempts to create a genuinely radical politics of the centre.[39] While the 'third way' in the West is an attempt to come to terms with the apparent exhaustion of traditional social democracy and represents an attempt to renew it, Russia's third way, or genuine politics of the centre, is drawn from an older tradition, liberal conservatism. Writers like Peter Struve and Semyon Frank are drawn on to sustain the emerging consensus over a Russian 'third way' based on support for the reconstitution of state authority while continuing market reforms and international economic integration. Under Putin the outlines of a distinctive Russian 'third way' have emerged, although shot through with contradictions. The politics of Russia's third way emerge out of traditional 'centrist' positions but the degree to which they represent a development of them is unclear.

Putinism reflects the political amorphousness of the quasi-centre but at the same time potentially transcends it. His intensification of the reforms launched in 1992 represented a second wave of liberal transformation of Russia. The framework, however, was more statist than under Yeltsin, leading to suggestions that his policies represented a programme of authoritarian modernisation: attacking economic institutions and social practices inherited from the Soviet period while reasserting elements of Soviet-style centralisation. Putin systematically dismantled the system of checks and balances that had been established during Yeltsin's rule, basing his power on both bureaucratic and charismatic elements. Putin himself remains an enigma. It was clear that support for Putin in the 2000 presidential elections was not based on any real appreciation of his policies, since, other than the vigorous pursuit of the war in Chechnya, it was unclear what these policies were. Instead support went to mythologised conceptions of what he was taken to represent: youth and vigour in contrast to Yeltsin's senescent debility; the impersonal pursuit of Russian national goals as opposed to selfish and irresponsible pursuit of enrichment and aggrandisement of personal power by Yeltsin and his acolytes; the continuation of economic reform accompanied by a crackdown on corruption, lawlessness and banditry; good relations with the West based on genuine partnership rather than Russian kowtowing to Washington. Some of these mythologised representations turned out to be accurate but, perhaps more importantly, the extraordinary speed and scale of his rise reflected Yeltsin's own political trajectory in the late 1980s, suggesting the need for hero figures in Russian politics, unconnected with parties, programmes or specific interests.

Putin's room for manœuvre is limited, with the scope for radical political intervention and change constrained by earlier institutional development and by Russia's socio-economic structure. In his 'manifesto' posted on the Web in the last days of 1999, Putin was evidently trying to move beyond traditional amorphous definitions of centrism towards a more radical future-oriented model.[40] Putin committed himself to the maintenance of the existing constitution unamended. His basic approach was of a more statist and socially oriented model of liberal capitalism. He did not directly challenge the economic and political privileges and semi-feudal power of the neo-*nomenklatura* elite, although he did distance it from direct access to the state and thus undermined one of the central elements of Yeltsin-style regime politics. Putin sought to transform his broad but shallow political support into a genuine political coalition but his tendency to rely on administrative methods to do so undermined the autonomous development of representative parties and interests in society. Putin's rise represented the triumph of a nativist strand of liberal patriotism; but as the development of the national liberals in late nineteenth-century Germany showed, there are many dangers associated with this combination. The social and international context has changed radically, but history continues to provide warnings if not lessons.

Conclusion

A new political order emerged in Russia, based on a distinctive social relationship with the former political elite, regional forces and economic interests, but its democratic features are tempered by the political characteristics of poorly structured pluralism, elite continuity and regime politics. Russia under Yeltsin was constantly in danger of sailing into what former president Lech Walesa in Poland called the 'Bermuda triangle' between a weak presidency, a fragmented parliament and an ineffective government. State-building in Russia was impeded by the struggle between numerous centres of power: the presidency, the two houses of the Federal assembly, the government and regional authorities. The weakness of institutions put the premium on individuals, yet the creation of presidential rule failed to overcome the crisis of executive power. Under Yeltsin the presidency became the focus of regime relations, subverting the laws and institutions that the executive had itself sponsored but achieving a precarious supremacy in the newly pluralistic system.

Powerful elite groupings, however, by the late 1990s threatened to subordinate the regime to their own ends. In the event, a programme of state reconstitution was launched by Putin, focusing above all on separating the economy from politics, the oligarchs from the state, and subordinating regional bosses to the normative framework of the federal system. The state began to be 're-nationalised', with the influence of the oligarchs curbed and state functions restored to the state.

20 Democracy in Russia

It is absolutely ridiculous to attribute to the high capitalism which is today being imported into Russia and already exists in America – this 'inevitable' economic development – any elective affinity with 'democracy' let alone with 'liberty' (in *any* sense of the word). The question should be: how can these things exist at all for any length of time under the domination of capitalism? In fact they are only possible where they are backed up by the determined *will* of a nation not to be ruled like a flock of sheep.

(Max Weber)[1]

The problems facing the Russian transition have now become clear, but their solutions rather less so. It is still too early to know whether the reconstruction of Russia will take longer than the post-war rebuilding of Germany or Japan, but we do know that it will not be any easier. We cannot even be sure what the end point of this new Russian 'time of troubles' will be: liberalism, neo-socialism, or some new type of authoritarianism. In the years covered by this book Russia underwent a revolution, but a revolution of a distinctive type: mostly not accompanied by bodies of armed men on the streets but a profound revolution of adaptation to a set of norms and governing principles devised elsewhere but at the same time also generated by profound domestic aspirations and pressures. The ambiguity in the reception and incorporation of these norms – of liberal democracy, a market economy and private property, an autonomous arena of public association and a public sphere, individualism and human rights, and international integration – was reflected in the contradictions apparent in Putin's presidency. Rhetorically committed to all of the above, in practice political and social pressures intervened to weaken their fulfilment. A revolution represents a change in power, property and of the ruling class. Russia has undergone an incomplete revolution: the structure of power has changed; property relations are being transformed; but the ruling class and some of its traditional principles of governance remain in place. In this chapter we will provide a brief concluding assessment of the achievements to date.

Democracy, liberalism and the Russian state

In the 1990s, Russia became caught up in multiple processes of accelerated transition focusing on changes in politics, economics, national identity and culture. The Russian Federation, while in certain respects the successor to the Russian Empire and the Soviet Union, differed from its predecessors politically (in trying to become a democracy), economically (in trying to place market relations at the centre of economic life), geographically (Russia had never existed in its present borders) and civilisationally (joining the international community as an equal). The attempt to change everything simultaneously led to numerous tensions. Democratisation, for example, entailed the creation of forms of representative government based on popular sovereignty and the rule of law, while the challenge of economic modernisation posed a somewhat different set of challenges – privatisation, stable property rights, the weakening of Soviet welfarism, market prices for public goods – whose resolution at times appeared incompatible with democratisation; while the demands of state-building came into contradiction with the principles of national self-determination. The Bismarckian Second Reich in Germany at the end of the nineteenth century had been a *Rechtsstaat* (law-based state) rather than a democracy, and post-communist Russia assumed aspects of such an 'illiberal' democracy.

Problems of democracy

Moore defined democracy as: 'a long and certainly incomplete struggle to do three closely related things: 1) to check arbitrary rulers, 2) to replace arbitrary rules with just and rational ones, and 3) to obtain a share for the underlying population in the making of rules.'[2] In the 1990s, Russia only imperfectly achieved these objectives for a variety of reasons. Political demobilisation and problems in structuring political associations were one factor, the hesitant development of democratic state institutions another, while leadership factors were perhaps determining. At the same time, Russia appeared to be a pre-state society in which a pre-political society lived according to its own logic and internal structures. Society appeared to impose its rules on the state, rather than the other way round; while the state itself once again, as so often in Russia's past, increasingly divorced itself from civil society.

One of the most acute observers of the development of democratic states, Alexis de Tocqueville, argued that the political institutions of the United States reflected the spirit and ethos of the people.[3] Democracy is both a system of government and a way of life; and it is not clear how democratic institutions could be grafted on to a society whose traditions were apparently antithetical to democratic norms (but see Chapter 14). The mere presence of numerous political parties and a democratic constitution are no guarantee of democratic practices. Democracy can only with difficulty be 'built from the roof down' but requires the elements of a civic culture like toleration and restraint in society to allow the growth of democracy from below. Tocqueville had warned against 'democratic despotism', although he insisted on the need to create a social state in which popular beliefs (*moeurs*) would sustain a 'free social state'. He noted in *Democracy in America* that 'In America, free mores have made the political institutions freely; in France it is up to the free political institutions to create the mores.' In Russia, too, the political institutions of post-communism were faced with the challenge of developing the social basis on which they could rest.

The very concept of democracy became an element in intra-elite power struggles and lost much of its allure to society and to the elites themselves. A survey of deputies in legislative assemblies in a sample of Russia's regions (Khabarovsk, St Petersburg and Volgograd), for example, found that out of eighty-nine asked, forty-three insisted that Russia could not be characterised as a democratic state, thirty-two tended to that view, while only twelve answered in the affirmative.[4] How can we explain the emergence of this high level of disenchantment? Part of the problem is the distinction, drawn by Larry Diamond and others, between electoral and consolidated democracy: consolidated democracy is when the practices of government are in conformity with the substantive stipulations of the legal-normative provisions of the constitution.[5] The attempt to remake Russian democracy was bound by bureaucratic institutions and traditions. The 'new' political order was a peculiar hybrid: on the one hand, adapting old state structures to new conditions; and, on the other, introducing genuinely new ideas and approaches. It is the unstable balance between these two elements that caused so many problems in the first post-communist years and gave rise to 'a contradiction between the content and form of state power'.[6] The democratic state-building slogans of the early years were trampled in the rush for power and privileges of a narrow political and social elite. In short, while the achievements of democratic institutional building in Russia are substantial and real, they are mediated by asymmetries in access to power and weaknesses in the accountability of that power to society's representatives.

Liberalism and post-Soviet conservatism

Liberalism in the West had developed over a long time as private property, individual freedoms and rationalist thinking developed, whereas in Russia all three had been absent or were severely limited. The main problem in Russia was that the subject of liberalism, *homo economicus*, was largely absent, and therefore liberalism found its main support among the urban liberal intelligentsia.[7] In the West liberalism (including private property, individualism and the defence of the individual and property rights in law) had come before democracy, but in Russia it was the democratic revolution itself that had to create the bases of liberalism. This it tried to do by diffusing the economic power that is associated with private property to establish the basis for individual rights; but at the same time asserted the need for

Table 20.1 Five arenas of consolidated democracy

Arena	Conditions
Civil society	Self-organising groups, movements and individuals. Articulates values and advances interests
Political society	Legitimate contestation for public power, above all through political parties in multi-candidate elections
Rule of law	Constitutional governance regulated by courts and an impartial judiciary
State efficacy	A usable bureaucracy and governing elite that defends an impartial view of state interests; effective tax and budget processes
Economic society	Set of norms and laws that regulate relations between the state and the market

Source: Adapted from Juan J. Linz and Alfred Stepan, *Problems of Democratic Transition and Consolidation: Southern Europe, South America, and Post-Communist Europe* (Baltimore, Johns Hopkins University Press, 1996).

the concentration of political power, a post-communist Leviathan, in the form of presidential power. Economic liberalism but not necessarily fully fledged democracy was on the agenda. The deconcentration of economic power, moreover, succeeded in establishing a class of 'new Russians' and oligarchs, but appeared to do little for the mass of the population, a large proportion of whom lost the social guarantees of the Soviet period and gained very little in return. Liberalism remained far from hegemonic, challenged by the counter-ideology of statism, and neither was it universal, limited to certain enclaves of globalism in Russia, Moscow, St Petersburg and some other cities. Nevertheless, despite the loss of territory and the collapse of the comforting certainties of an all-embracing ideology it would be false to argue that liberalism failed to take root in Russia.

At the heart of the liberal democratic revolution is the attempt to establish a market economy and representative government. But how? While the liberal reformers of the 1990s paid lip service to representative government, faced with what to them appeared intractable opposition from the conservatives in parliament many argued in favour of an 'iron hand', the strong presidency acting as a type of enlightened despotism pushing through the reforms. Yeltsin appeared to succeed where Gorbachev failed, in finding a mid-path between representative government and outright coercion, a type of virtual representation of political and social interests described by the various labels of delegative, illiberal or regime democracy. The collapse of communist power and the weak development of a democratic counter-system allowed bureaucratic and elite structures to establish a relatively high degree of autonomy. This was most evident in the government itself, established as a sort of technocratic high command of the economic transition. In the regions, too, the control functions once fulfilled by the Communist Party were only weakly replaced by the system of federal representatives at the regional or federal district level. While social change and economic transformation were perhaps prerequisites for a liberal order, political development and democratisation require more.

In reaction to the attempt to achieve a liberal modernisation without liberals a type of post-communist Russian conservatism emerged. Conservatism in Russia has much deeper roots and philosophical traditions to draw on than liberalism; but at the turn of the century attempts were made to combine the two in a distinctive Russian ideology of liberal conservatism. Religious philosophers like Sergei Bulgakov and Semyon Frank represent one strand of Russian conservatism, the historians Vladimir Solovyev and V.O. Klyuchevskii another, and a modified form of Eurasianism yet a third. Perhaps the most potent source of post-communist conservatism, however, was the patriotic view of the need for a strong state combined with individual rights and a constitutional system. Thus, in Russia a unique synthesis of liberalism and conservatism took shape and assumed political form in Putin's rise to power.

Russian liberal conservatism of the transition period drew on pre-revolutionary traditions, those of the Soviet period, and in the post-Soviet period on world experience of liberal and social conservatism. It sought to combine the liberal emphasis on individual, political and economic freedoms with an organic conception of the larger community, the attempt to preserve Russia's distinctive traditions and to salvage something of the social policies of the Soviet period. While re-modernisation in

Russia entailed the development of the egoism of civil society (*Gesellschaft*), based on contract and the anonymity of social actors, all modern societies suffer from the nostalgia for the community (*Gemeinschaft*) allegedly typical of traditional societies.[8] In Russia the *Gemeinschaft* represented by the Soviet regime was attractive to the neo-communists and some national-patriots, but others espoused a distinctive brand of liberal conservatism that sought the roots of the new community in Russian traditions. Putin's rule represented a powerful combination of these attributes, and, although shot through with contradictions (how could liberal individualism and collectivism be reconciled?), represented the nativisation of reform, the adaptation of abstract values of reform and transition to Russian conditions. 'Path dependency' approaches, which suggest that history precludes certain developments, are useful in the Russian context to the extent that they focus on certain institutional legacies (above all ethno-federalism), but they are inadequate in understanding the precise pattern of innovation and continuity in post-communist Russian politics.

State, nation and democratisation

Russia's struggle for democracy and statehood took place at a time when the traditional notion of the nation-state itself is facing unprecedented challenges. While the nation-state remains the most important unit of analysis in contemporary international and domestic politics, our study demonstrates the limitations of an exclusively state-centred view. At the international level the state is squeezed from above by globalism (UN), globalisation (IMF, World Bank, WTO), universalism (International Criminal Court), intercontinentalism (Nato), continental supra-state regionalism (EU, OSCE, Council of Europe), and from below by various forms of sub-national regionalism, reflected above all in the Council of the Regions established by the EU and the regionalism of the Council of Europe. Regionalism operates both at the inter-state level, creating cross-national regional identities (Benelux, Turkestan, the East Slavic Community), and at the sub-national level in strengthening regional identities within nation-states (Catalonia, Bavaria, Volga–Urals, Siberia). The discipline of state borders has been eroded by the proliferation of international organisations, the communications revolution, and the globalisation of entertainment and leisure, while from within, republics, civil associations and economic agencies increasingly enter into autonomous relations with the international community. Russian Greenpeace and other environmental organisations engaged in various transnational campaigns, such as the attempt to stop the importation of nuclear waste into Russia for reprocessing or to highlight the dangers of the rusting nuclear submarines in the Barents Sea.

The slogan of strong 'statehood' (*gosudarstvennost*) was a response to the profound crisis of the post-communist Russian state. The very territory that was to be recognised as Russia remained contested, with part of the political community refusing to accept the finality of Russia's existing borders and claiming special rights to defend the interests of Russians abroad. Internally, the consolidation of a state both ruling by law and itself subordinate to law faced awesome difficulties. Under Yeltsin the institutional development of the Russian state in the Weberian sense, as an ordered administrative hierarchy able to make decisions backed by force over its entire territory, remained rudimentary, and it was precisely this problem that Putin sought to tackle. In the 1990s, the breakdown of effective vertical structures was accompanied by the growth of a segmented regionalism that threatened the unity of the state; in particular, the legacy of ethno-federalism raised doubts whether the new Russian federalism would be strong enough to contain separatist tendencies. The erosion of executive authority itself allowed bureaucratic agencies and personalistic networks a relatively free hand. The emergence of a rich political society found itself weakly integrated into the political institutions of the new polity, and to a degree isolated from social processes and structures. The scale of the economic collapse accompanying the transition jeopardised all the other processes of social and national renewal. The class structure of the transitional period was made up of fragmented social and political groups that provided a very unsure footing for the growth of democratic political institutions and market structures. And, finally, the ambiguity over Russia's own national identity inhibited the development of a stable pattern of international relations.

The break-up of the Soviet Union fragmented the single large dictatorship into numerous smaller dictatorships, many worse than the decayed communist regime because of the energy with which they imposed themselves on the population, demanding conformity to communities defined by culture and ethnicity. Shards of the old tyranny took root not only in the new states, but also in the institutions and regions of Russia itself. This was no longer the old monolith but the anarchic tyranny of incipient warlordism. Faced by the breakdown in the rule of law and civil peace, the rise of criminality, armed security services, regional separatism and so on, the very existence of the state was threatened. There was privatisation of parts of the apparatus of order and the use of non-state agencies for contract enforcement, the monstrous growth of private security agencies at times indistinguishable from the police to provide both physical security for businesses and protection (the infamous *krysha*) from rapacious criminal and state bodies.[9] All this suggested that the state was dissolving back into society as pre-modern patterns of social segmentation re-emerged.

It is important, however, to keep this in perspective. Russia did not become a 'quasi-state' in anything like the way defined by Robert Jackson, where the internal attributes of statehood are residual but external recognition sustains the myth of sovereignty.[10] Although there were legitimate concerns about the failure of the state to impose its order over domestic processes while retaining its effectiveness at the inter-state level, for many liberals the problem was quite the opposite – the excessive power of the state to regulate and intervene in the affairs of society. The problem was exacerbated by the peculiar rootlessness of those arguing in favour of a liberal adaptation to global processes, talking in terms of 'universal human values' and joining the 'civilised world', leaving the language of patriotism, national interests and state reassertion to nativists of various stripes.

The events of 1991 undermined two central elements in the country's national identity. The first was the specifically Soviet factor, residually acknowledging the force of the Marxist and Leninist critique of capitalism, defending collectivist values and justifying the Soviet state as a bulwark against capitalist militarism. The disintegration of the geopolitical space of the USSR challenged a second element, the notion of a larger community encompassing Russians, Ukrainians and many other peoples. Whether this should be called the 'Russian imperial' national identity or something more benign remains a moot point. This is precisely one of the issues over which the post-communist Russian national identity remains divided. A specifically democratic identity was undermined because of the countervailing sense of loss of national prestige and the lack of dignity of the new social institutions. Russian nationalism itself remained a fragmented political and intellectual force because of the sheer richness of the Russian national tradition and the multiplicity of often contradictory elements that could be drawn on.

The nation-state was traditionally an inadequate political form for the development of the Eurasian land mass: the steppes, tundra and *taiga* of Russia and the plains of Central Asia are very different from the market squares, little shops, factories and fields of Western and Central Europe.[11] While the inadequacy of the nation-state model in Eurasian conditions was marked, the alternative supranational model was not clear: the 'imperialist' form would be difficult (but not impossible) to reconcile with democratic aspirations; while the liberal internationalist type presupposed market-oriented economies and democratic polities. State- and nation-building remain relatively under-developed in post-communist Russia.

In contrast to the more developed East European countries like Poland and the Czech Republic, where the 'national idea' united an already existing civil society, in Russia civil society remained amorphous and thus national sentiments were in danger of becoming nationalist. Russia developed as an empire before it became a nation, and even today it is unclear whether a Russian nation as such has developed. How is it to be defined: by ethnicity, by culture, by territory, or some other principle? All remained contested. The weakness of civil society and the indefinability of Russian nationhood once again stimulated the notion of *derzhavnost*, a typically Russian concept denoting the idea of great-power statehood; in short, the predominance of the state over society.[12] Whether Putin could finesse the contradiction to establish *both* a liberal economy and an effective democratic state remained to be seen.

A struggling democracy?

Yelena Bonner criticised Yeltsin for not taking stronger action following the *coup* in 1991: Yeltsin should have discarded democratic principles for the sake of expediency, dissolved the Russian parliament, and held new elections. This would have made possible economic reform and constitutional government. 'We lost our August victory....The hope that it could be built on and developed by parliamentary means was Yeltsin's main historic error.'[13] Sergei Stankevich, a political adviser to Yeltsin in the immediate post-*coup* period, talked of 'Russia's lost decade of reform'. While Poland had turned the economic corner in 1994 and thereafter registered strong growth and low inflation, Russia remained on an economic and political precipice even after steady economic growth resumed in 2000. Political stabilisation in Poland was based on the rise of a middle class that provided some 60 per cent of the country's GDP, while in Russia whatever advances had been made by the middle class were knocked back by the August 1998 crisis and were only slowly restored thereafter. In Russia the presidency, in Stankevich's words, waged 'a permanent cold war against parliament' and 'regional barons' pursued separatist agendas, facilitated by the lack of a national party system. After a lost decade of reforms Russia, in Stankevich's view, had returned to almost the same situation it had been in at the beginning of the 1990s, with the difference that the idea of reform itself had been discredited.[14]

The tensions between democracy, order and economic liberalisation remain unresolved in post-communist Russia. The apparent democratic consensus among the political elite in the early post-Soviet period soon dissolved and gave way to a complex interaction between democratisation and authoritarianism. Agreement on the basic rules of the political game at the fall of communism was undermined by the struggle between Yeltsin and the old Soviet legislature, and doubts over the legitimacy of the new constitution and disagreement over its provisions mean that the 'polity' question, the shape of the constitutional order, remains open. The factionalisation of politics, the concentration of power in court attendants and bodyguards, the arbitrary rule of bureaucrats, the growth of corruption and the unpredictability of government suggested that Russia's democratic experiment had run into the sands. The fundamental question was whether the constitutional order inaugurated in the early 1990s was robust enough to allow political and constitutional evolution within its framework, or whether some new system should be devised. As so often in the past, the choice lay between evolution and revolution.

De-democratisation?

The internal resources for the stability of most post-Soviet national democracies are probably less than their counterparts in inter-war Europe, but the international environment is not only benign but positively activist in espousing a set of democratic normative principles. The struggle for democracy, however, will be resolved in the individual states and not by the abstraction we call 'the international community'.

Rather than 'the transition' inexorably leading to a liberal democracy of the Western sort, by the end of Yeltsin's presidency there was fear that the democratic aspirations of the *perestroika* years and the achievements of the early post-communist period were being undermined. Without the compensation of economic growth, the abuse of power, the corruption and the shabby stratagems to gain state property stood out all the more starkly: 'Corrupt, demoralised, unstable: such a Russia poses a risk to itself and the world.'[15] The moral outrage that had been the hallmark of popular politics during *perestroika* gave way to political demobilisation. The very concept of democracy in the 1990s appeared de-legitimised, while the word itself was used as a term of opprobrium. The credibility gap between the statements of the leadership and the realities of daily life gave rise to what has been called a 'mistrust culture' and a pervading sense of social nihilism. While socialism in the early Soviet years had been built with enthusiasm, capitalism was now being built with resignation and a sullen sense of betrayal.

The success of the communists in the 1995 elections provoked Gaidar to argue that they had been 'a defeat for Russian democracy'.[16] The first Chechen war had already served to divide the democratic camp and to expose the shortcomings of the new regime. The campaign by Sergei Kovalev to bring to the attention of the

Russian and world public the human consequences did incalculable damage to Yeltsin's reputation. While supported by the liberals in Russia, Kovalev's criticisms brought abuse from the presidential entourage. The defence minister Grachev called him 'an enemy of the people' in a grisly reminder of attitudes still prevalent in sections of the Russian elite, while Korzhakov attacked 'unstable liberals who denigrate the idea of human rights'.[17] The very basis of the Russian state was questioned by the denunciation of the Belovezh Accords by the Duma in March 1996, while the shortcomings of the 1996 presidential campaign have been noted above. The renewed Chechen war from 1999 was accompanied by the brutality characteristic of the first.

If the regime substituted for the state, a complex elite system substituted for the development of civil society. The typical political expressions of civil society, such as parliament and the rule of law, were subverted by intra-elite negotiations based on personal ties and informal bargaining processes. To prevent intra-elite struggles threatening the stability of the system, the presidency emerged as the arbitrator of the whole. While the *legitimation* of the regime remained democratic, to reduce the unpredictability typically associated with elections elites at the federal and regional level employed a range of 'administrative resources'. While elections were accepted by the regime and opposition alike as the way to manage public politics, much remained hidden and unaccountable behind the scenes.

Weimar Russia

The long shadow of 1917 warned of the danger from the left, while the destruction of inter-war German democracy provided an equally strong warning of the threat from the right. A constituency for non-democratic authoritarianism and populism clearly existed in the form of disgruntled communists and chauvinistic nationalists, fuelled by economic crisis, the loss of national identity and by the squabbling of elites. The rejectionists considered the Belovezh Accords an act of treason akin to the alleged betrayal of the military by civilian politicians in Germany in 1918–19, and this was gradually woven into a national-patriotic counter-myth that considered Yeltsin, and increasingly Putin too, as 'traitors' to Russia. Extremist forces lurked to left and right waiting to take advantage of social unrest and economic dislocation, much as Hitler took advantage of the weakness of the Weimar republic. Before his death in 1920, Max Weber had voiced doubts about the viability of democracy in Germany following the collapse of the Second Reich in 1918, and insisted that Germany needed a strong leader of a plebiscitary or Caesarist type like Bismarck.[18] The fate of Weimar Germany and the rise of Hitler seemed to bear out Weber's pessimism.

The applicability of the 'Weimar Russia' scenario, however, should be tempered by the fact that the world of the 1990s and 2000s is a very different one from that of the 1920s or 1930s, or indeed from the world torn by war in 1917. The growth of economic interdependence, a dense network of human rights legislation and international organisations, all raise the threshold of toleration that extremist reaction would have to negotiate. In addition, for all its faults the Soviet regime had appealed to a form of democratic legitimacy and values that was supportive of democracy, whereas the Wilhelmine Reich had espoused militaristic and elitist values. Nor was it clear what the social basis for fascism or a recrudescent communism in Russia would be. The middle class in Weimar Germany never really accepted 'bourgeois democracy' in the inter-war years, whereas in Russia the nascent middle class and the intelligentsia aspire to live like their counterparts in the West. The analogy with inter-war Germany is instructive but not wholly appropriate. A society that has just freed itself from seventy-odd years of dictatorship was hardly likely to embrace another so soon; the idea of dictatorship remains deeply unpopular among Russians. While the values of order and democracy are often contrasted in public opinion polls, it seems clear that a combination of the two was the desired social ideal for the mass of Russians.

The presidency, regime politics and democracy

Yeltsin insisted that strong presidential power compensated for the weakness of democracy 'in a country accustomed to Tsars and leaders, in which defined group interests are not yet clearly established'.[19] Although formally a strong presidency was established in 1993, its powers are constrained by a number of formal institutional limitations and, perhaps more importantly, by informal pressures, above all those emanating from the regions. At the same time, the formal powers granted parliament are limited. The removal of the president through impeachment, for example, is extremely difficult. Large areas of policy-making have become the direct prerogative of the president, above all in foreign policy and national security policy. The president, moreover, has extensive decree powers. Yet all of this does not make the president all-powerful. The need to achieve parliamentary approval for legislation places it at the shared centre of Russian politics. The constitution, moreover, requires parliamentary confidence in the prime minister, and thus by implication in the government.

The adoption of the constitution inaugurated a new period in the development of politics in Russia. Fears that the new legislature would be a 'pocket' parliament proved exaggerated. The legislature was not converted into a branch of the executive; nor can it claim the prerogatives of the executive. The Duma was able to carve out an important role for itself *despite* the formal provisions of the constitution but *within* the constitution's framework. The constitution, moreover, does not regulate in detail the relations between the executive and the legislative branches of government, and it is these very ambiguities that potentially allow the development of a viable political system in Russia.

The institution of the presidency was strengthened to compensate for the absence of more organic forms of social solidarity and social management. The choice appeared to lie between anarchy and authoritarianism, but however much power Yeltsin took the polity was marked by a crisis of governance as decrees were left unimplemented and the state fragmented. Civil society was weak and there were few deep-rooted democratic traditions. The presidency was new and untested, and existed less as an institution and more as an emanation of Yeltsin's own personality. Under Putin the political institutions of the state became more ordered, leadership more resolute and consistent, but even the young leadership was forced to govern through negotiation and concession. Huntington argued that societies in transition to modernity require firm, if not military, leadership to negotiate the enormous strains placed on society by period of rapid change.[20] In Russia the 'praetorian' role was fulfilled by the presidency rather than the army. The presidency began to recreate a centre not only for the nation but also for political society, the centre that had crumbled under Gorbachev. There remained fears, however, that the strong presidency would not act as a bulwark against lawlessness but would itself be the vehicle for a new form of arbitrariness.[21]

Russia today has a hybrid political system, both democratic and authoritarian. The freedoms that had begun during *glasnost* blossomed into genuine freedom of speech and the press, and the variety of publications and the openness of their content are unparalleled in Russia's history. Censorship is explicitly forbidden and only the courts can permanently ban newspapers, and then only on specific grounds and after due warning. However, the assault against the privileges of certain oligarchs under Putin appeared to threaten the independence of radio and television. Corruption marred the development of Russia as a democracy. While the old regime lacked freedom, it did at least ensure a degree of security. The new freedoms after the fall of communism have been accompanied by such a degree of job and physical insecurity that many yearned for the old days. The interpenetration of organised crime and politics led some to argue that Russia's second revolution had been 'stolen' by an unholy alliance of communists-turned-speculators and the criminal underworld.

The hybrid nature of authoritarianism democracy in Russia arose out of the conflict between ends and means and had a dual function: to undermine the old structures of social and political power, while at the same time to provide the framework for the growth of democratic forms that could ultimately stand on their own. The second or maturity phase of the democratic revolution is marked by free and *fair* elections, the establishment of the 'civic culture' of toleration and institutionalised conflict over resources and decisions, and a peaceful and fully constitutional change of government. Regime-based politics probably only represented a phase in Russian politics, and sources of weakness became increasingly apparent. The development of a more robust and autonomous party system, for example, would offer an alternative means of national integration and popular representation. Under Putin, moreover, federal politics became more insulated from the pressures of economic interests, and the presidency operated less as a free-loading operator in the interstices of the state and society, as it had done under Yeltsin, but as part of a state order seeking support in society.

The disintegration of the USSR was one of the greatest events in European and Asian history. The fall of communism was accompanied by the reversal of the centuries-long Russian process of the 'gathering' of the lands. While the transitions in some of the East European countries entailed elements of re-democratisation, the re-privatisation of property and the re-liberalisation of social relations as a whole, there was little 're' about Russia's transition, except the rediscovery and recovery of native memory and indigenous traditions and re-modernisation. The social, economic and political infrastructure of democratic and liberal systems had to be built for the first time with building blocks that had been thoroughly subverted by the Bolshevik attempt to create an alternative modernity. Ken Jowitt notes the multiple fragmentation in what he calls the post-Leninist world, and stresses the ambiguities in the political culture:

To put it bluntly: the Leninist legacy, understood as the impact of Party organisation, practice, and ethos, *and* the initial charismatic ethical opposition to it favour an authoritarian, not a liberal democratic capitalist, way of life; the obstacles to which are not simply how to privatise and marketise the economy, or organise an electoral campaign, but rather how to institutionalise public virtues.[22]

The dramatic changes in the economy and polity would be inadequate if the public side of human identity was not also cherished, and a way found to establish a balance between 'ethics' and 'interests'.

While to all intents and purposes 'the transition' in Russia is largely over, it is still too early to talk of the establishment of a functioning democracy. The multiparty system is embryonic, the legal system mired in the problems of the past, and elections have been less than fair. Solzhenitsyn condemned Russia's new 'false democracy' and described Russia's retreat from communism as 'the clumsiest and most painful possible' imposing yet another 'heartless experiment on unhappy Russia'.[23] The very project of democracy did not command universal legitimacy. For many, like Metropolitan Innokenti of Khabarovsk, democracy in Russia was a transitional phenomenon and would in time disappear altogether to be replaced (perhaps in a generation or two) by something more in the Russian tradition of *sobornost*. For national-patriots, liberal democracy is antithetical to Russian traditions and cannot provide a solution to problems that are distinctively Russian.

So does Russia have no more than a simulacrum of democracy, a parody of the rule of law, trapped in a cycle of 'democratisation' but unable to achieve democracy itself? There are no guarantees that the moment of liberation following the fall of communist power will be anchored in effective democratic institutions and processes. The greatest achievement of the post-Soviet system in Russia is not the establishment of democracy, a task that will take many years and which in any case is ambiguous, but the restoration of the autonomy of politics, the end of dogmatic and reductionist approaches to power based on an understanding that political decision-making is an open-ended and contentious process. The restoration of politics means the end of the totalitarian impulse and is the first but essential step on the road to liberal democracy. The Russian transition was an attempt to provide an institutional framework for pluralism in society, to guarantee property rights and to overcome Russia's isolation from global processes. While democratic institutions have appeared, it will take longer for the democratic culture and economic structures that can sustain them to emerge, for the unwritten rules of convention to impress themselves onto the written word of the constitution. The first post-communist Russian leadership laid the foundations of a new political order in the belief that Russian could only enter world civilisation if it remade its own. By the beginning of the twenty-first century it was clear that both Russia *and* the world faced challenges that could not be resolved in isolation from each other.

Notes

1 Soviet communism and its dissolution

1 Fyodor Dostoyevsky, 'One of Today's Falsehoods', 1875, in *A Writer's Diary, Volume 1, 1873–1876*, trans. and annotated by Kenneth Lantz (London, Quartet Books, 1994), p. 288.
2 David Remnick, *Lenin's Tomb: The Last Days of the Soviet Empire* (London, Viking, 1993), pp. 294–5.
3 Mikhail Gorbachev, *Perestroika: New Thinking for Our Country and the World* (London, Collins, 1987), p. 10.
4 Gorbachev, *Perestroika*, p. 25.
5 This is the theme of E.A. Hewett, *Reforming the Soviet Economy: Equality vs Efficiency* (Washington, DC, Brookings, 1988).
6 László Póti, 'The Soviet Reform: Domestic Aspects and Implications for East-Central Europe', in *European Conference on 'Similarities and Differences in the Adaptation of the Countries of Central Europe to the European Community'* (Budapest 28–30 November 1991, Euration), p. 32.
7 For example, Graeme Gill, 'Liberalization and Democratization in the Soviet Union and Russia', *Democratization*, Vol. 2, No. 3 (autumn 1995), pp. 313–36.
8 Neil Robinson, 'Gorbachev and the Place of the Party in Soviet Reform, 1985–91', *Soviet Studies*, Vol. 44, No. 3, 1992, pp. 423–44.
9 *Izvestiya*, 11 June 1989.
10 'Dekret o vlasti', *Argumenty i fakty*, No. 25 (23–9 June 1990), p. 1.
11 For example, the First Secretary of the Komi Republic (Yu. Spiridonov) and the city Party leader in Kursk (N. Golovin).
12 Póti, 'The Soviet Reform', p. 32.
13 David Remnick, *New York Review of Books*, 17 May 1990, p. 3.
14 Nina Andreeva, 'I Cannot Forgo My Principles', *Sovetskaya Rossiya*, 13 March 1988.
15 For a description of these events, see John Morrison, *Boris Yeltsin* (London, Penguin Books, 1991), and, for Yeltsin's own view, see *Against the Grain: An Autobiography* (London, Pan, 1991).
16 Estimate by V. Vorotnikov in *Pravda*, 26 March 1990, p. 2.
17 Brendan Kiernan, *The End of Soviet Politics* (Boulder, CO, Westview, 1993), p. 181.
18 L. Efimova, A. Sobyanin and D. Yur'ev, *Argumenty i fakty*, No. 29 (1990), p. 2.
19 Milovan Djilas, *The New Class: An Analysis of the Communist System* (New York, Praeger, 1957).
20 Yitzhak M. Brudny, *Reinventing Russia: Russian Nationalism and the Soviet State, 1953–1991* (Cambridge, MA, Harvard University Press, 1999).
21 Edward Allworth, 'Ambiguities in Russian Group Identity and Leadership of the RSFSR', in Allworth (ed.), *Ethnic Russia in the USSR* (New York, 1980), pp. 24–5.
22 Ruslan Khasbulatov, *The Struggle for Russia: Power and Change in the Democratic Revolution*, edited by Richard Sakwa (London and New York, Routledge, 1993), p. 46.
23 *Soviet News*, 2 August 1989, p. 260.
24 *Soviet News*, 30 August 1989, p. 288.

25 *Pravda* and *Sovetskaya Rossiya*, 7 June 1989, p. 2; also in John Dunlop, *The Rise of Russia and the Fall of the Soviet Empire* (Princeton, NJ, Princeton University Press, 1993), pp. 16–17.

26 *Sovetskaya Rossiya*, 31 May 1990.

27 'Deklaratsiya o gosudarstvennom suverenitete RSFSR', *Argumenty i fakty*, No. 24 (16–22 June 1990), p. 1.

28 Alexei Zverev, 'Qualified Sovereigny: The Tatarstan Model for Resolving Conflicting Loyalties', in Michael Waller, Bruno Coppieters and Alexei Malashenko (eds), *Conflicting Loyalties and the State in Post-Soviet Eurasia* (London, Frank Cass, 1998), p. 123.

29 M.S. Gorbachev, *On My Country and the World* (New York, Columbia University Press, 2000), p. 110.

30 Khasbulatov, *The Struggle for Russia*, p. 222.

31 'O mekhanizme narodovlastiya v RSFSR', *Argumenty i fakty*, No. 25 (June 1990), p. 1.

32 Khasbulatov, *The Struggle for Russia*, p. 36.

33 Steven L. Solnick, *Stealing the Soviet State: Control and Collapse in Soviet Institutions* (Cambridge, MA, Harvard University Press, 1998), p. 232 and *passim*.

34 Michael Urban, with Vyacheslav Igrunov and Sergei Mitrokhin, *The Rebirth of Politics in Russia* (Cambridge, Cambridge University Press, 1997).

35 For a study of the dilemmas facing the insurgency at this time and its state-centredness, see M. Stephen Fish, *Democracy from Scratch: Opposition and Regime in the New Russian Revolution* (Princeton, NJ, Princeton University Press, 1995).

36 *Pravda*, 28 May 1989, p. 1.

37 Gorbachev's most developed attempt to reconceptualise the role of the CPSU appeared in his 'Sotsialisticheskaya ideya i revolyutsionnaya perestroika', *Pravda*, 26 November 1989.

38 Michael Waller, *Democratic Centralism: An Historical Commentary* (New York, St Martin's, 1981).

39 The Marxist Platform was published in *Pravda*, 16 April 1990.

40 For an analysis of Gorbachev's attempts to reform the party, see Ronald J. Hill, 'The CPSU: Decline and Collapse', *Irish Slavonic Studies*, No. 12 (1991), pp. 97–119; and also his 'The Communist Party and After', in S. White *et al.* (eds), *Developments in Soviet and Post-Soviet Politics* (London, Macmillan, 1992), pp. 68–87.

41 *Moscow News*, No. 27 (15 July 1990), p. 5.

42 Hill, 'The CPSU', pp. 113–14.

43 *Moscow News*, No. 24 (24 June 1990), pp. 8–9.

44 *Current Politics of the Soviet Union*, Vol. 1, No. 2 (1990), p. 173. At the Twenty-seventh Party Congress in February–March 1986 membership stood at 18.3 million full and 728,253 candidate members, a total of 19 million, *Izvestiya TsK KPSS*, No. 1, 1990.

45 By 259,605 (1.3 per cent); of these, 136,600 left at their own request, a cumbersome procedure whereby communists had to write a formal letter of resignation and then seek permission to leave from a meeting of the local Party group, *Izvestiya TsK KPSS*, No. 2 (1989), p. 138, and No. 4 (1990), p. 113.

46 Report of the Central Auditing Commission to the Twenty-eighth CPSU Congress, *Pravda*, 4 July 1990.

47 Oleg Vite, *Moscow News*, No. 24 (16 June 1991), p. 8.

48 *Izvestiya*, 10 July 1991, pp. 1, 3.

49 For a lachrymose analysis of Gorbachev's reforms by the former prime minister, see Nikolai Ryzhkov, *Perestroika: istoriya predatel'stv* (Moscow, Novosti, 1992).

50 *Guardian*, 28 December 1991.

51 A point made by Anatolii Sobchak, *Khozhdenie vo vlasti* (Moscow, Novosti, 1991), p. 269.

2 The disintegration of the USSR

1 Francis Bacon, 'Of Empire', in *The Essays* (London, Odhams Press, n.d.), p. 74.

2 Cited by Boris Pankin, *The Moscow Times*, 27 June 2001, p. 11.

3 *Izvestiya*, 22 July 1991, p. 1; and for Gorbachev's condemnation, *Pravda*, 26 July 1991.

4 The draft programme was published in *Pravda*, 8 August, *Sovetskaya Rossiya*, 9 August 1991, under the title 'Socialism, Democracy, Progress'.

5 *Sovetskaya Rossiya*, 23 July 1991, p. 1; *Current Digest of the Soviet Press* (henceforth *CDSP*), Vol. XLIII, No. 30 (1991), pp. 8–10.

6 For an analysis of the *coup*, see Richard Sakwa, 'The Revolution of 1991 in Russia: Interpretations of the Moscow Coup', *Coexistence*, Vol. 29, No. 4 (December 1992), pp. 27–67; and for a different version 'A Cleansing Storm: The August Coup and the Triumph of Perestroika', *Journal of Communist Studies*, Vol. 9, No. 1 (spring 1993), pp. 131–49. Some of the more useful collections of materials on the *coup* include *Putch: khronika trevozhnykh dnei* (Moscow, Progress, 1991); *Avgust-91* (Moscow, Izd. politicheskoi literatury, 1991); *Korichnevyi putch krasnykh Avgust '91* (Moscow, Tekst, 1991); *Smert' zagovora: belaya kniga* (Moscow, Novosti, 1992); and an account by the investigators V. Stepankov and E. Lisov, *Kremlevskii zagovor* (Moscow, Ogonek, 1992).

7 Mikhail Gorbachev, *The August Coup: The Truth and the Lessons* (London, Harper Collins, 1991), pp. 20–1.

8 Amy Knight, *Spies without Cloaks: The KGB's Successors* (Princeton, NJ, Princeton University Press, 1996), p. 17. In her chapter 'The Myth of the August Coup', Knight marshals all the evidence about Gorbachev's alleged complicity in the *coup* but the case against him remains circumstantial.

9 See Archie Brown, *The Gorbachev Factor* (Oxford, Oxford University Press, 1996), pp. 295–9.

10 *Izvestiya*, 10 October 1991.

11 Boris Yeltsin, 'To the Citizens of Russia', 19 August 1991, *CDSP*, Vol. XLIII, No. 33 (1991), pp. 6–7.

12 *Rossiiskaya gazeta*, 9 November 1991, p. 2.

13 See Ivan Bunich, *Zoloto partii* (St Petersburg, Shans, 1992); *Soviet Weekly*, 19 September 1991, p. 5; *Panorama*, BBC TV, 13 July 1992.

14 See Dmitrii Volkogonov, *Argumenty i fakty*, No. 6 (February 1992), p. 4. For the links with the Communist Party of Great Britain, see Nina Fishman, 'Britain: the Road to the Democratic Left', in Martin J. Bull and Paul Heywood (eds), *West European Communist Parties after the Revolutions of 1989* (London, Macmillan, 1994), p. 170.

15 S. Akhromeev and G. Kornienko, *Glazami marshala i diplomata* (Moscow, Mezhdunarodnye otnosheniya, 1992).

16 Remnick, *Lenin's Tomb*, p. xi.

17 Gerd Ruge, *Der Putsch* (Frankfurt, Fischer, 1991), pp. 129, 185.

18 *Moscow News*, No. 37 (1991), p. 1.

19 Gorbachev, *The August Coup*, p. 38.

20 *Moscow News*, No. 37 (1991), p. 1.

21 *Izvestiya*, 7 September 1991.

22 Khasbulatov, *Rossiiskaya gazeta*, 29 October 1991, p. 3.

23 Khasbulatov, *The Struggle for Russia*, p. 223.

24 Boris El'tsyn, *Zapiski prezidenta* (Moscow, Ogonek, 1994), pp. 165–6.

25 *Moscow News*, No. 37 (1991), p. 6.

26 M.S. Gorbachev, *On My Country and the World* (New York, Columbia University Press, 2000), p. 144.

27 The five Union Treaties were published in *Izvestiya*: 24 November 1990; 9 March 1991; 27 June 1991; 15 August 1991; and 25 November 1991.

28 Gorbachev, *On My Country and the World*, p. 145.

29 Roman Szporluk *Russia, Ukraine and the Breakup of the Soviet Union* (Stanford, Hoover Institution Press, 2000), p. xxiv.

30 For Gorbachev's view of these events and his comments on Burbulis's long memorandum proposing the break-up of the USSR, see *Neokonchennaya istoriya: Besedy Mikhaila Gorbacheva s politologom Borisom Slavinym* (Moscow, Olma-Press, 2001), pp. 41–7, 54–5.

31 A point made by Yegor Ligachev, *Inside Gorbachev's Kremlin* (Boulder, Westview Press, 1996), p. 372.
32 The idea of something approximating the (British) Commonwealth had first been proposed by Sakharov at the First USSR Congress of People's Deputies in May 1989, and had been promoted by Democratic Russia and Yeltsin.
33 Leonid Kravchuk interviewed in *Kyivska pravda*, 7 July 1995, cited in *Transition*, 11 August 1995, pp. 80–1, where he also notes that the name CIS was suggested by the Ukrainian delegation.
34 *Transition*, 11 August 1995, p. 81.
35 *Rossiiskaya gazeta*, 10 December 1991, p. 1.
36 *Rossiiskaya gazeta*, 24 December 1991, p. 1.
37 A number of books chart the dramatic personal relationship between Gorbachev and Yeltsin, for example *Rossiya segodnya: politicheskii portret v dokumentakh, 1985–1990* (Moscow, Mezhdunarodnye otnosheniya, 1991), pp. 393–511; *Gorbachev–El'tsin: 1500 dnei politicheskogo protivosostoyaniya* (Moscow, Terra, 1992). Gorbachev's own harsh criticisms of Yeltsin's behaviour at this time are in Gorbachev, *On My Country and the World*, Part Two; while Yeltsin's views are presented in his *The View from the Kremlin*, (London, Harper Collins, 1994), Chapter 3.
38 The proportion of those supporting Yeltsin to those not supporting him was 69:5, Shevardnadze 52:11, Khasbulatov 48:10, while Gorbachev's proportion was 19:37, *Rossiiskaya gazeta*, 13 December 1991, p. 2.
39 *Guardian*, 28 December 1991.
40 Speech to the Fifth Russian Congress of People's Deputies, *Rossiiskaya gazeta*, 29 October 1991, p. 1.
41 X (George Kennan), 'The Sources of Soviet Conduct', *Foreign Affairs*, July 1947, pp. 566–82, at p. 580.

3 The new constitutional order

1 Alexander Solzhenitsyn, *Rebuilding Russia* (London, Harvill, 1991), p. 9.
2 For a 'revisionist' account of the legislature and an institutional explanation for its failure, see Joel M. Ostrow, *Comparing Post-Soviet Legislatures: A Theory of Institutional Design and Political Conflict* (Columbus, OH, Ohio State University Press, 2000).
3 Article 104 of the amended 1978 constitution.
4 *Sed'moi s"ezd narodnykh deputatov Rossiiskoi Federatsii: byulleten'*, No. 23 (14 December 1992), pp. 12–13.
5 For Nikolai Travkin's comments, see *Demokraticheskaya gazeta*, No. 8 (July 1991), p. 2.
6 *Rossiiskaya gazeta*, 29 October 1991, p. 1.
7 'Ob izmeneniyakh i dopolneniyakh Konstitutsii (Osnovnogo Zakona) RSFSR', in *Rossiya segodnya: politicheskii portret v dokumentakh, 1991–1992* (Moscow, Mezhdunarodnye otnosheniya, 1993), pp. 24–7.
8 *Izvestiya*, 12 March 1992, p. 1.
9 See Archie Brown, 'The October Crisis of 1993: Context and Implications', *Post-Soviet Affairs*, Vol. 9, No. 3 (1993), pp. 183–95.
10 By mid-1993, the constitution had been amended over 300 times, and the incremental nature of constitutional revision gave rise to numerous contradictions. Chief among them was the vesting of supreme power in both the legislative and the executive.
11 For criticisms of Khasbulatov, see Otto Latsis, *Izvestiya*, 28 August 1992, p. 3; *Nezavisimaya gazeta*, 1 September 1992; Maria Bogatykh, *Rossiya*, No. 36 (94), 2 September 1992, p. 1; Georgi Ivanov-Smolenskii, *Izvestiya*, 3 September 1992, p. 2; interview with Sergei Yushenkov, co-ordinator of the Radical Democrats faction, *Rossiiskie vesti*, 10 September 1992, p. 2.
12 Article 104 of the amended 1978 constitution, *Konstitutsiya (osnovnoi zakon) RSFSR* (Moscow, Sovetskaya Rossiya), 1991, pp. 32–3.
13 The balance of forces was as follows: some 294 deputies were grouped under the umbrella of the Coalition of Reforms; 170 with the Bloc of Constructive Forces; some

269 independents with another 63 independent-minded deputies in the Sovereignty and Equality faction; and 290 in the oppositional bloc 'Russian Unity', A.A. Sobyanin (ed.), *VI s"ezd narodnykh deputatov Rossii: politicheskie itogi i perspektivy* (Moscow, Organisational Department of the Presidium of the Supreme Soviet of the Russian Federation, 1992), p. 11.

14 Viktor Sheinis, *Nezavisimaya gazeta*, 23 May 1992, p. 2.

15 *Izvestiya*, 11 June 1992.

16 *Rossiiskaya gazeta*, 30 July 1992, pp. 1–2.

17 Some 267 deputies were grouped under the umbrella of the Coalition of Reforms; 155 with the Bloc of Constructive Forces; some 208 independents with another 51 independent-minded deputies in the Sovereignty and Equality faction; and 359 in the oppositional bloc 'Russian Unity', *Sed'moi s"ezd narodnykh deputatov Rossiiskoi Federatsii: byulleten'*, No. 24 (14 December 1992), p. 15.

18 *Rossiiskaya gazeta*, 11 December 1992, pp. 1–2.

19 *Pravda*, 4 March 1993.

20 Alexander Rahr, 'Roots of the Power Struggle', *RFE/RL Research Report* (14 May 1993), p. 12.

21 Khasbulatov, *The Struggle for Russia*, pp. 7–8 and *passim*.

22 *Izvestiya*, 13 August 1993, p. 2.

23 *Moscow News*, No. 39 (24 September 1993), pp. 1–2.

24 Julia Wishnevsky, 'Corruption Allegations Undermine Russia's Leaders', *RFE/RL Research Report*, Vol. 2, No. 37 (17 September 1993), pp. 16–22.

25 *Rossiiskie vesti*, 2 September 1993, p. 1.

26 'O poetapnoi konstitutsionnoi reforme v Rossiiskoi Federatsii', *Konstitutsionnoe soveshchanie*, No. 2 (October 1993), pp. 15–19; *Izvestiya*, 22 September 1993, p. 1.

27 *Izvestiya*, 22 September 1993, p. 1.

28 Described, for example, by Leon Aron, *Boris Yeltsin: A Revolutionary Life* (London, HarperCollins, 2000), pp. 540–8.

29 *Izvestiya*, 25 December 1993, p. 1.

30 Ulrich K. Preuss, 'The Political Meaning of Constitutionalism', in Richard K. Bellamy (ed.), *Constitutionalism, Democracy and Sovereignty: American and European Perspectives* (Aldershot, Avebury, 1996), pp. 22–4.

31 Max Weber, 'Bourgeois Democracy in Russia', in *The Russian Revolutions*, trans. and ed. Gordon C. Wells and Peter Baehr (Oxford, Polity Press, 1995).

32 See Geoffrey Hosking, *The Russian Constitutional Experiment: Government and Duma, 1907–1914* (Cambridge, Cambridge University Press, 1973); also Lothar Schultz, 'Constitutional Law in Russia', in G. Katkov *et al.* (eds), *Russia Enters the Twentieth Century* (London, Temple Smith, 1971), pp. 34–59, esp. pp. 44–7.

33 Gorbachev, *On My Country and the World*, p. 21.

34 See Aryeh L. Unger, *Constitutional Developments in the USSR: A Guide to the Soviet Constitutions* (London, Methuen, 1981).

35 Gorbachev introduced these ideas in his speech to the Nineteenth Party Conference on 28 June 1988 (*Izbrannye rechi i stat'i*, Vol. 6 (Moscow, 1989), pp. 373–6), and developed them in his Supreme Soviet speech of 29 November 1988, 'K polnovlastiyu Sovetov i sozdaniyu sotsialisticheskogo pravovogo gosudarstvo', *Izbrannye rechi i stat'i*, Vol. 7 (Moscow, 1990), pp. 150–75.

36 See L.V. Lazarev and A. Ya. Sliva, *Konstitutsionnaya reforma: pervyi etap* (Moscow, Znanie, 1989).

37 See Jon Elster, Claus Offe and Ulrich K. Preuss, *Institutional Design in Post-Communist Societies: Rebuilding the Boat in the Open Sea* (Cambridge, Cambridge University Press, 1997).

38 An extended version of this part of the chapter can be found in Richard Sakwa, 'The Struggle for the Constitution in Russia and the Triumph of Ethical Individualism', *Studies in East European Thought*, Vol. 48, Nos 2–4 (September 1996), pp. 115–57.

39 *Argumenty i fakty*, No. 47 (November 1990), whole issue; in *Konstitutsionnyi vestnik*, No. 4 (1990), pp. 55–120; a popular edition was published as *Konstitutsii Rossiiskoi*

Federatsii: proekt s kommentariyami (Moscow and Krasnoyarsk, newspaper *Svoi golos* and Krasnoyarsk Press and Information Agency, 1991).

40 *Sovetskaya Rossiya*, 19 April 1991; an earlier version appeared in *Sovetskaya Rossiya*, 24 November 1990.

41 *Rossiiskaya gazeta*, 11 October 1991, special section, with an 'explanatory note' on p. 7.

42 Oleg Rumyantsev, 'Zachem nuzhna novaya konstitutsiya', *Konstitutsionnyi vestnik*, No. 8 (1991), pp. 3–7.

43 *Konstitutsionnyi vestnik*, No. 8 (1991), pp. 68–72.

44 *Konstitutsionnyi vestnik*, No. 8 (1991), p. 74; and pp. 84–148 for the revised draft of 24 October.

45 *Rossiiskaya gazeta*, 5 November 1991, p. 1.

46 *Argumenty i fakty*, No. 12 (March 1992), whole issue; republished in *Proekt konstitutsii Rossiiskoi Federatsii: sbornik materialov* (Moscow, Respublika, 1992), pp. 19–81.

47 Vladimir Kuznechevskii, *Rossiiskaya gazeta*, 3 April 1992, pp. 1–2.

48 The Federation Treaty was made up of three separate documents: an agreement (published in *Rossiiskaya gazeta*, 18 March 1992) signed by eighteen out of the twenty republics, excluding the Chechen and Tatarstan republics; a document signed by Russia's *oblasts* and *krais*; and an agreement with the autonomous *okrugs* and the Jewish Autonomous Oblast. The Russian Federation was a separate signatory to the Treaty. *Federativnyi dogovor. Dokumenty. Kommentarii* (Moscow, Izd-vo 'Respublika', 1992).

49 'O proekte konstitutsii Rossiiskoi Federatsii i poryadke dal'neishei raboty nad nim', 18 April 1992, in *Proekt konstitutsii Rossiiskoi Federatsii: sbornik materialov*, pp. 3–4.

50 *Rossiiskaya gazeta*, 16 May 1992, pp. 3–5.

51 By that time, seven laws making 340 amendments had been adopted: in 1990 there were fifty-three amendments and in 1991 twenty-nine, Rumyantsev in *Konstitutsionnyi vestnik*, No. 15 (March 1993), p. 8.

52 *Konstitutsionnyi vestnik*, No. 13 (November 1992), pp. 25–115.

53 *Konstitutsionnyi vestnik*, No. 13, p. 7.

54 *Nezavisimaya gazeta*, 24 November 1993, p. 2.

55 This version was published as 'Konstitutsiya (osnovnoi zakon) Rossiiskoi Federatsii: proekt' in *Izvestiya*, 30 April 1993, pp. 3–5; reprinted in *Konstitutsionnyi vestnik*, No. 16 (May 1993), pp. 65–108.

56 *Izvestiya*, 13 May 1993, p. 1.

57 *Stolitsa*, No. 22 (132) (1993), pp. 6–7.

58 For example, Marina Shakina, 'Istoriya s konstitutsiei', *Novoe vremya*, No. 23, 1993, pp. 3–5.

59 *Konstitutsionnyi vestnik*, No. 16 (May 1993), p. 202.

60 Shakhrai, for example, argued that it would be legal and constitutional for a Constituent Assembly to adopt a new constitution and declare new parliamentary elections, especially since presidential powers had been re-legitimised in the referendum of 25 April 1993, *Izvestiya*, 30 April 1993, p. 2.

61 'Konstitutsiya Rossiiskoi Federatsii: proekt', *Konstitutsionnyi vestnik*, No. 16 (May 1993), pp. 9–64.

62 *Nezavisimaya gazeta*, 26 June 1993, p. 1.

63 'O zavershenii raboty nad proektom Konstitutsii Rossiiskoi Federatsii', Supreme Soviet resolution of 29 April 1993, *Konstitutsionnyi vestnik*, No. 16 (May 1993), pp. 201–2.

64 *Rossiiskaya gazeta*, 3 April 1992, pp. 1–2; *Nezavisimaya gazeta*, 26 January 1993, p. 5.

65 'O sozyve Konstitutsionnogo soveshchanie i zavershenii podgotovki proekta Konstitutsii Rossiiskoi Federatsii', *Konstitutsionnoe soveshchanii*, No. 1 (August 1993), pp. 7–8.

66 *Konstitutsionnoe soveshchanie*, No. 1, pp. 12–20; *Rossiiskie vesti*, 8 June 1993, p. 2.

67 *Moskovskie novosti*, No. 25 (20 June 1993), p. A8.

68 Kronid Lyubarskii, 'Konets sovetskoi vlasti', *Novoe vremya*, No. 24 (1993), pp. 4–5.

69 B.A. Strashun, 'O "smeshannoi" forme pravleniya v proekte Konstitutsii Rossiiskoi Federatsii', *Konstitutsionnoe soveshchanie*, No. 2 (1993), pp. 51–7; and V.E. Chirkin, '"Chistye" i "smeshannye" formy pravleniya: plyusy i minusy razlichnykh sistem', ibid., pp. 57–65.

70 *Konstitutsionnoe soveshchanie: informatsionnyi byulleten'*, No. 1 (August 1993), pp. 109–57; *Rossiiskie vesti*, 15 July 1993.
71 The Assembly envisaged a broad process of consultation, in particular with the subjects of federation, and a referendum before the draft could be adopted, 'Zakon "O poryadke prinyatiya Konstitutsii Rossiiskoi Federatsii" (proekt)', *Konstitutsionnoe soveshchanie*, No. 1 (August 1993), pp. 155–7.
72 *Izvestiya*, 14 August 1993, p. 1.
73 24 September 1993, 'Ob obrazovanii Obshchestvennoi palaty Konstitutsionnogo soveshchaniya', *Konstitutsionnoe soveshchanie*, No. 2 (October 1993), p. 81.
74 *Rossiiskaya gazeta*, 10 November 1993, pp. 3–6.
75 'O provedenii vsenarodnogo golosovaniya po proektu konstitutsii Rossiiskoi Federatsii'; accompanied on the same date by 'Polozhenie o vsenarodnom golosovanii po proektu konstitutsii Rossiiskoi Federatsii 12 dekabrya 1993 goda', in *Rossiiskaya Federatsiya*, 1 (13), 1993, pp. 22–4; *Rossiiskie vesti*, 21 October 1993. The word 'plebiscite' (*golosovanie*) was used rather than referendum.
76 The October 1990 RSFSR Referendum Law stipulated that matters affecting the constitution could be adopted by a simple majority of all registered voters, while non-constitutional matters could be decided by a simple majority of those participating in the referendum. A referendum would only be valid if turnout exceeded 50 per cent of registered voters, *Rossiiskaya gazeta*, 2 December 1990.
77 A trenchant critique of adopting the constitution by referendum was made by Rumyantsev, *Nezavisimaya gazeta*, 24 November 1993, p. 2.
78 These figures have been the subject of considerable controversy, given in *Rossiiskaya gazeta*, 21 December 1993, p. 1 and in full in *Byulleten' Tsentral'noi izbiratel'noi kommissii Rossiiskoi Federatsii* (henceforth *Byulleten' TsIK*), No. 1 (12) (1994), p. 38.
79 Seven republics voted against the constitution: Adygeya, Bashkortostan, Chuvashia, Dagestan, Karachai-Cherkessia, Mordovia and Tuva; and 10 *oblasts*: Belgorod, Bryansk, Kursk, Lipetsk, Orël, Smolensk, Tambov, Penza, Volgograd and Voronezh, mainly in the Russian south-west where support for the Communist Party was strongest (*Byulleten' TsIK*, No. 1 (12), 1994, pp. 34–8). In Tatarstan the referendum was declared invalid since not enough turned up to vote, but of those who did 74 per cent supported the constitution; *Nezavisimaya gazeta*, 18 December 1993, p. 1. No vote took place in the Chechen Republic.
80 *Rossiiskaya gazeta*, 25 December 1993.
81 Sergei S. Alekseev, *Demokraticheskie reformy i konstitutsiya* (Koscow, Pozitsiya, 1992), p. 4.
82 *Nezavisimaya gazeta*, 9 November 1993, p. 1.
83 *Segodnya*, 13 November 1993, p. 2.
84 *Moskovskie novosti*, No. 47 (21 November 1993), p. A13.
85 Cf. *Nezavisimaya gazeta*, 30 December 1993, p. 2.
86 Cf. Irina Koptel'skaya, 'Konstitutsionnue zakony – novoe yavlenie v zakonodatel'stve Rossii', *Konstitutsionnyi vestnik*, No. 1 (17) (1994), pp. 59–63.
87 *Rossiiskaya gazeta*, 17 December 1993, p. 1.
88 *Nezavisimaya gazeta*, 4 December 1993, p. 2.
89 *Stolitsa*, No. 50 (160) (December 1993), p. 4.
90 *Pravda*, 19 January 1994.
91 *Financial Times*, 10 November 1993.
92 For example, Vyacheslav Nikonov, *Nezavisimaya gazeta*, 23 December 1993, pp. 1, 2.
93 'Ob izmeneniyakh i dopolneniyakh Konstitutsii (Osnovnogo Zakona) RSFSR', in *Rossiya segodnya: politicheskii portret v dokumentakh, 1991–1992* (Moscow, Mezhdunar. otnosheniya, 1993), pp. 24–7.
94 Wendy Slater, 'Head of Russian Constitutional Court under Fire', *RFE/RL Research Report*, Vol. 2, No. 26 (25 June 1993), pp. 1–5.
95 *Sovetskaya Rossiya*, 23 September 1993, p. 1. On 30 September the Constitutional Court suspended the membership of three of the judges (one on health grounds), though the other two (Ernst Ametistov and Nikolai Vitruk) had already declared that they would no longer participate in the Court's work.

96 Cf. Robert Sharlet, 'The Russian Constitutional Court: The First Term', *Post-Soviet Affairs*, Vol. 9, No. 1 (1993), pp. 1–39.

97 See Robert Sharlet, 'Russian Constitutional Crisis: Law and Politics under Yel'tsin', *Post-Soviet Affairs*, Vol. 9, No. 4 (1993), pp. 314–36.

98 *Russkaya mysl'*, No. 4064 (9–15 February 1995), p. 20. Of the 'old' judges, nine had condemned the president's action in September 1993 (Nikolai Vedernikov, Valerii Zor'kin, Victor Luchin, Gadis Gadzhiev, Boris Ebzeev, Nikolai Seleznev, Oleg Tyunov, Vladimir Oleinik and Yurii Rudnik), four had supported the president (Ernst Ametistov, Tamara Morshchakova, Nikolai Vitruk and Anatolii Kononov), while the views of the six newcomers (Vladimir Tumanov, Olga Khokhryakova, Yurii Danilov, Vladimir Yaroslavtsev, Vladimir Strekozov and Marat Baglai, the last to be appointed) remained to be determined.

99 *Moskovskie novosti*, No. 17 (12–19 March 1995), p. 11.

100 For a detailed analysis, see Robert Sharlet, 'Russia's Second Constitutional Court: Politics, Law, and Stability', in V.E. Bonnell and G.W. Breslauer (eds), *Russia in the New Century: Stability or Disorder?* (Boulder, Westview, 2001), pp. 59–77.

101 Ralf Dahrendorf, *Reflections on the Revolution in Europe* (London, Chatto & Windus, 1990), pp. 79, 85.

102 The distinction is made by Hellmut Wollmann, 'Change and Continuity of Political and Administrative Elites from Communist to Post-Communist Russia', *Governance: An International Journal of Policy and Administration*, Vol. 6, No. 3 (July 1993), pp. 325–40.

103 Valerii Zor'kin, 'Uroki oktyabrya-93', *Konstitutsionnyi vestnik*, No. 1 (17), 1994, p. 11.

104 For a theoretical discussion of the issues, see Giuseppe Di Palma, *To Craft Democracies: An Essay in Democratic Transition* (Berkeley, University of California Press, 1990).

105 A classic statement of this argument was made by M.J.C. Vile, *Constitutionalism and the Separation of Powers* (Oxford, Clarendon Press, 1967).

106 For an extended discussion of this issue, see Oleg Rumyantsev, *Osnovy konstitutsionnogo stroya Rossii* (Moscow, Yurist, 1994). See also O.G. Rumyantsev, 'Osnovy konstitutsionnogo stroya: ponyatie, soderzhanie, otrazhenie v konstitutsii', *Gosudarstvo i pravo*, No. 10 (1993), pp. 3–15, and see note 54 above.

107 V.V. Leontovich, *Istoriya liberalizma v Rossii, 1762–1914* (Paris, YMCA-Press, 1980), p. 539.

108 Donald D. Barry (ed.), *Toward the 'Rule of Law' in Russia?: Political and Legal Reform in the Transition Period* (Armonk and London, M.E. Sharpe, 1992), p. xvi.

109 Cf. A. Walicki, *Legal Philosophies of Russian Liberalism* (Oxford, Oxford University Press, 1987), pp. 165–212. See also Jonathan Sutton, *The Religious Philosophy of Vladimir Solovyov* (London, Macmillan, 1988).

110 Sutton, *The Religious Philosophy of Vladimir Solovyov*, p. 114.

111 See Barry (ed.), *Toward the 'Rule of Law' in Russia?*, p. 4.

112 *Moscow News*, No. 46 (12 November 1993), p. 2.

4 Law and society

1 Raymond Aron, *Democracy and Totalitarianism* (London, Weidenfeld & Nicolson, 1965), pp. 109–10.

2 Law of 24 October 1990, 'O deistvii aktov organov SSSR na territorii RSFSR', in *Sbornik zakonodatel'nykh aktov RSFSR o gosudarstvennom suverenitete, soyuznom dogovore i referendume* (Moscow, RSFSR Supreme Soviet, 1991), pp. 16–17.

3 *Ugolovnyi kodeks Rossiiskoi Federatsii* (Moscow, 1997).

4 *Law on the Procuracy*, 1995 (*SZ RF*, 1995, No. 47, #4472).

5 *Federal Constitutional Law on the Court System*, 31 December 1996 (*SZ RF*, 1997, No. 1, #1).

6 *Soviet Weekly*, 24 October 1991, p. 2.

7 For example, Genri Reznik, *Novaya ezhednevnaya gazeta*, 24 December 1993, p. 1.

8 *RFE/RL Newsline*, 26 June 2001.

9 *RFE/RL Newsline*, 18 January 2002.

10 *Nezavisimaya gazeta*, 15 December 2000, p. 8.

11 *Nezavisimaya gazeta*, 13 August 1992, p. 1.

12 *Moskovskie novosti*, No. 17 (12–19 March 1995), p. 11.

13 Stephen Handelman, 'The Russian "Mafiya"', *Foreign Affairs*, Vol. 73, No. 2 (March–April 1994), p. 90.

14 Stephen Handelman, *Comrade Criminal: The Theft of the Second Russian Revolution* (London, Michael Joseph, 1994), p. 8.

15 Georgii Podlesskikh and Andrei Tereshok, *Vory v zakone: brosok k vlasti* (Moscow, Khudozhestvennaya literatura, 1994), p. 27.

16 Tanya Frisby, 'The Rise of Organised Crime in Russia: Its Roots and Social Significance', *Europe–Asia Studies*, Vol. 50, No. 1 (1998), p. 40.

17 *RFE/RL Newsline*, 26 March 2001.

18 According to Moscow region police chief Alexander Kulikov, *Interfax*, 13 June 1997.

19 *The Observer*, 11 September 1994, p. 6.

20 *Nezavisimaya gazeta*, 21 April 1993, p. 2.

21 *Nezavisimaya gazeta*, 11 April 1995, p. 1.

22 Some 289 in 1993 and 562 in 1994; *Nezavismaya gazeta*, 11 April 1995, p. 1; *The Observer*, 21 April 1995, p. 23.

23 *Moskovskie novosti*, No. 80 (19–26 November 1995), p. 21.

24 *The Observer*, 26 March 1995, p. 6.

25 *The Observer*, 16 April 1995, p. 21.

26 Phil Williams (ed.), *Russian Organized Crime: The New Threat* (London, Frank Cass, 1997).

27 RIA-Novosti, 2 July 1997.

28 Handelman, *Comrade Criminal*.

29 *Rossiiskie vesti*, 23 July 1997.

30 Georgy Satarov, 'Corruption, Western and Russian', in Yuri Senokosov and Edward Skidelsky (eds), *Corruption in Russia*, Issue 4 of *Russia on Russia* (Moscow and London, Moscow School of Political Studies and Centre for Post-Collectivist Studies, March 2001), pp. 8–9.

31 Yuri Levada, 'Corruption in Public Opinion', in *ibid.*, pp. 49–58, at pp. 51–2.

32 Alena V. Ledeneva, *Russia's Economy of Favours: Blat, Networking and Informal Exchange* (Cambridge, Cambridge University Press, 1998).

33 For a brilliant analysis of this, see Igor' Klyamkin and Lev Timofeev, *Tenevaya Rossiya: Ekonomiko-sotsiologicheskoe issledovanie* (Moscow, RGGU, 2000).

34 For the development of this argument, see my 'Russia: From a Corrupt System to a System with Corruption', in Robert Williams (ed.), *Party Finance and Political Corruption* (Basingstoke and London, Macmillan; New York, St Martin's Press, 2000), pp. 123–61.

35 The classic statement of this is Milovan Djilas, *The New Class* (New York, Praeger, 1957); with the profound political corruption described later by Mikhail Voslenskii, *Nomenklatura: Anatomy of the Soviet Ruling Class* (London, Bodley Head, 1984); and the social corruption by Konstantin Simis, *USSR: Secrets of a Corrupt Society* (London, Dent, 1982).

36 Leslie Holmes, *The End of Communist Power: Anti-Corruption Campaigns and Legitimation Crisis* (Cambridge, Polity Press, 1993).

37 *Anticorruption in Transition: A Contribution to the Policy Debate* (Washington, DC, World Bank, 2000), pp. xv–xviii.

38 *Novaya gazeta*, No. 35 (1–7 September 1997).

39 Rustam Narzikulov, *Nezavisimaya gazeta*, 11 March 1997.

40 Yeltsin declared an expenditure of 14.4 billion roubles (3.1 million dollars). See 'El'tsyn deneg ne zhalel', in *Ot El'tsina k…El'tsinu: prezidentskaya gonka-96* (Moscow, Terra, 1997), pp. 547–9. For the full income reports of Yeltsin and the other sixteen candidates, see *Deklaratsii o dokhodakh kandidatov v prezidenty na vyborakh 16 iyunya 1996*, compiled by G. Belonuchkin (Moscow, Panorama, 1996). Zyuganov officially spent 11.3 billion roubles ($2.1 million).

41 Peter Reddaway, 'The West's Spoilt Russian Son', *New Statesman*, 22 August 1997, p. 26.
42 *Izvestiya*, 1 July 1997.
43 *Izvestiya*, 5 July 1997.
44 See Janine R. Wedel, *Collision and Collusion: The Strange Case of Western Aid to Eastern Europe 1989–1998* (Basingstoke and London, Macmillan, 1998), in particular Chapter 4.
45 In the event, perhaps taking advantage of his enforced leisure, Kokh did actually write a book, called appropriately *The Selling of the Soviet Empire*.
46 *Russia Briefing*, Vol. 5, No. 3 (30 May 1997), p. 2.
47 Yves Mény, 'Fin de Siècle Corruption', *International Social Science Journal*, No. 149 (September 1996), p. 313.
48 John Girling, *Corruption, Capitalism and Democracy* (London, Routledge, 1997), p. vii.
49 For a discussion of the issue, see Natasha Kogan, 'Thinking About Corruption', *Transitions*, March 1998, pp. 46–9.
50 Leslie Holmes, 'Corruption and the Crisis of the Post-Communist State', *Crime, Law & Social Change*, Vol. 27, No. 3/4 (1997), pp. 1–23.
51 *Moscow Times*, 10 January 1998, p. 11.
52 *Transitions*, March 1998, p. 61.
53 Jamestown Foundation, *Monitor*, 28 June 2001.
54 Above all by Susan Rose-Ackerman, *Corruption: A Study in Political Economy* (New York, Academic Press, 1978).
55 In his analysis Federico Varese stresses precisely this, making reference to the 'tragedy of the commons' where the pursuit of individually rational goals leads to a less-than-optimal outcome, 'The Transition to the Market and Corruption in Post-socialist Russia', *Political Studies*, Vol. 45, No. 3 (1997), pp. 579–96.
56 *Novye izvestiya*, 6 November 1997.
57 Svetlana P. Glinkina, 'The Ominous Landscape of Russian Corruption', *Transitions*, March 1998, pp. 16–17.
58 Tsarist experience is discussed by William A. Clark, *Crime and Punishment in Soviet Officialdom: Combatting Corruption in the Political Elite, 1965–1990* (Armonk, New York, M.E. Sharpe, 1993), pp. 30–8.
59 This is a point made by Paul Goble in relation to anti-corruption campaigns in Kazakhstan, 'The Corruption of Power', *RFE/RL Newsline*, 14 July 1998.
60 *Moskovskii komsomolets*, 8 October 1997.
61 *OMRI Daily Digest*, 6 March 1997.
62 *RFE/RL Newsline*, 3 April 1998.
63 *RFE/RL Newsline*, 30 March 1998.
64 In the Czech Republic the ruling Civic Democratic Party (ODS) stood accused of corrupt financial deals whereby secret business donations were rewarded with political influence. It was even suggested that the prime minister himself, Vaclav Klaus, had built himself a villa in Switzerland out of party funds. An ironic twist in the story was that Klaus's arrogance had provoked some ODS leaders to expose the scandal (using *kompromat* that they had long known about) in order to unseat him and to take revenge on his dictatorial style of government that had humiliated them all.
65 For an analysis of Boldyrev's career, see 'Kontroler-ispytatel'', *Figury i litsa: Nezavisimaya gazeta*, No. 11 (12), June 1998, pp. 9, 11.
66 See Brian Whitmore, 'Russia's Top Crime Fighter', *Transitions*, March 1998, pp. 35–9.
67 *Russia Journal*, 29 June–2 July 2001, p. 2.
68 Girling, *Corruption, Capitalism and Democracy*, p. xi.
69 Peter Rutland and Natasha Kogan, 'The Russian Mafia: Between Hype and Reality', *Transitions*, March 1998, p. 32.
70 It remains a moot point whether criminal ties subvert democracy. It has been alleged, for example, that up to a third of sitting MPs in India are criminals.
71 Vladimir Wozniuk, 'In Search of Ideology: The Politics of Religion and Nationalism in the New Russia (1991–1996)', *Nationalities Papers*, Vol. 25, No. 2 (1997), p. 203.
72 *RFE/RL Newsline*, 4 February 1998.
73 *Moscow News*, No. 47 (19 November 1993), p. 2.

74 For example, in the mid-1997 gubernatorial campaign in Nizhnii Novgorod State Duma deputy and Communist-backed candidate Gennadii Khodyrev charged that the Carnegie Endowment's Moscow Centre was financing the campaign of Ivan Sklyarov, then mayor of Nizhnii Novgorod city and ultimate victor in the campaign, *RFE/RL Newsline*, Vol 1, No. 57, Part I (20 June 1997).

75 Anders Aslund, 'Economic Causes of Crime in Russia', in Jeffrey D. Sachs and Katharina Pistor (eds), *The Rule of Law and Economic Reform in Russia* (Boulder, CO, Westview Press, 1997).

76 Yves Mény, 'Politics, Corruption and Democracy: The 1995 Stein Rokkan Lecture', *European Journal of Political Research*, Vol. 30, No. 2 (1996), pp. 111–23. On the covert funding of parties and the like, see his *La corruption de la République* (Paris, Fayard, 1992).

77 Pal Vastagh, the Hungarian justice minister, noted that some corrupt practices that had developed under communist rule continued to flourish in post-communist Hungary. He admitted that 'at the time of the change of regime, it was believed corruption would no longer pose a big problem in an emerging market economy, since the reasons for it would have ceased to exist. This expectation, unfortunately, proved to be wrong'; *RFE/RL Newsline*, Part II (13 June 1997).

78 *Soviet Weekly*, 5 December 1991, p. 2.

79 Vadim Bakatin, appointed head of the KGB after the *coup*, describes the process in *Izbavlenie ot KGB* (Moscow, Novosti, 1992), pp. 197–220.

80 *Soviet Weekly*, 10 October 1991, p. 4.

81 *Rossiiskaya gazeta*, 11 August 1992, p. 4.

82 *Moskovskaya pravda*, 4 September 1992.

83 Victor Yasmann, 'Corruption in Russia: A Threat to Democracy?', *RFE/RL Research Report*, Vol. 2, No. 10 (5 March 1993), pp. 15–18.

84 See Alexander Rahr, 'Reform of Russia's State Security Apparatus', *RFE/RL Research Report*, Vol. 3, No. 8 (25 February 1994), pp. 19–30.

85 *Nezavisimaya gazeta*, 10 January 1995, p. 3.

86 *Rossiiskaya gazeta*, 28 May 1994, pp. 1, 4.

87 The law 'On Federal Security Service Bodies of the Russian Federation' of April 1995 introduced the name Federal Security Service; and a presidential decree of 23 June 1995 gave details on its implementation.

88 Victor Yasmann, 'Where has the KGB Gone?', *RFE/RL Research Report*, Vol. 2, No. 2 (8 January 1993), pp. 17–20, at p.18.

89 *Rossiiskaya gazeta*, 12 August 1992, p. 1.

90 *Rossiiskaya gazeta*, 12 July 2001.

91 J. Michael Waller, *Secret Empire: The KGB in Russia Today* (Oxford, Westview, 1994), p. 285.

92 *Moskovskie novosti*, No. 9 (5–12 February 1995), p. 6.

93 Amy Knight, *The Security Services and the Decline of Democracy in Russia: 1996–1999*, The Henry M. Jackson School of International Studies, The University of Washington, Seattle, The Donald W. Treadgold Papers, No. 23, October 1999, p. 8.

94 *Nezavisimaya gazeta*, 29 May 2001.

95 See Peter Solomon, 'Limits of Legal Order', *Post-Soviet Affairs*, Vol. 11, No. 2 (1995), pp. 89–114.

5 The executive

1 Thomas Paine, *Rights of Man* (London, Penguin, 1984), p. 191.

2 Eugene Huskey, *Presidential Power in Russia* (Armonk, NY, M.E. Sharpe, 1999).

3 See Juan Linz, 'The Perils of Presidentialism', *Journal of Democracy*, Vol. 1, No. 1 (winter 1990), pp. 72–84.

4 Arend Lijphart (ed.), *Parliamentary versus Presidential Government* (Oxford, Oxford University Press, 1992), p. 19.

5 Juan J. Linz, 'Presidential or Parliamentary Democracy: Does it Make a Difference?', in Juan J. Linz and Arturo Valenzuela (eds), *The Failure of Presidential Democracy: Comparative Perspectives* (Baltimore, Johns Hopkins University Press, 1994), p. 7.

6 *Rossiiskaya gazeta*, 8 April 1992, pp. 1–4.

7 Thomas M. Nichols, *The Russian Presidency: Society and Politics in the Second Russian Republic* (Basingstoke, Macmillan, 2000), p.7.

8 See Stephen White, 'The Presidency and Political Leadership', in Peter Lentini (ed.), *Elections and Political Order in Russia* (Budapest, Central European University Press, 1995), pp. 202–25.

9 *Moscow News*, No. 25 (23 June 1991), p. 1.

10 Ann Sheehy, 'The All-Union and RSFSR Referendums', *Radio Liberty Report on the USSR*, Vol. 3, No. 13 (26 March 1991), p. 23.

11 Law on the Presidency, *Vedemosti S"ezda narodnykh deputatov RSFSR i verkhovnogo Soveta RSFSR*, No. 17 (1991), p. 512.

12 For details of the vote, including regional analysis, see D. Yurev, *Prezidentskie vybory* (Moscow, 1991).

13 *Rossiiskaya gazeta*, 31 October and 1 November 1991; *Izvestiya*, 2 and 4 November 1991.

14 *Demokraticheskaya gazeta*, 12 (15) (12–19 September 1991), p. 3.

15 See Eugene Huskey, 'The State-Legal Administration and the Politics of Redundancy', *Post-Soviet Affairs*, Vol. 11, No. 2 (1995), pp. 115–43.

16 EastWest Institute, *Russian Regional Report*, Vol. 5, No. 13 (5 April 2000).

17 *Strana.ru*, 18 January 2001.

18 The core of the State Council consisted of five presidential advisers (also known as state councillors) and the heads of the nine most important ministries.

19 Namely, state secretary of the RSFSR, secretary of the State Council (19 July 1991), state secretary of the RSFSR (7 April 1992), state secretary to the president (8 May 1992), and finally, adviser without title (14 December 1992); Lesage, 'The Crisis of Public Administration in Russia', p. 129.

20 At the Institute of the USSR Ministry of Non-ferrous Metallurgy.

21 *Rossiiskaya gazeta*, 11 June 1992, p. 5.

22 See Lieutenant-General Valeri Manilov's interview in *Moskovskie novosti*, No. 23 (5–12 June 1994), p. 11.

23 *Moskovskie novosti*, No. 63 (11–18 December 1994), p. 4.

24 *Rossiiskaya gazeta*, 16 July 1996, p. 4.

25 *Rossiiskaya gazeta*, 5 November 1991, p. 1.

26 Alexander Rahr, 'Liberal-centrist Coalition Takes over in Russia', *RFE/RL Research Report*, Vol. 1, No. 29 (21 August 1992), pp. 22–5, at p. 23.

27 *Nezavisimaya gazeta*, 26 May 1992.

28 *Rossiiskaya gazeta*, 7 November 1992, pp. 1, 5.

29 Matthew Campbell, 'The Invisible Coup', *Sunday Times*, 20 December 1992, p. 11.

30 OMRI Special Report: Russian Election Survey, No. 13 (12 December 1995).

31 Igor' Klyamkin and Liliya Shevtsova, *Vnesistemnyi rezhim Borisa II: nekotorye osobennosti politicheskogo razvitiya postsovetskoi Rossii* (Moscow, Carnegie Centre, 1999), p. 12.

32 See Michel Lesage, 'The Crisis of Public Administration in Russia', *Public Administration*, Vol. 71 (spring/summer 1993), pp. 121–33.

33 *Literaturnaya gazeta*, 19 February 1992, p. 3.

34 T.H. Rigby, *The Changing Soviet System: Mono-organisational Socialism from its Origins to Gorbachev's Restructuring* (Aldershot, Edward Elgar, 1990).

35 See Aleksandr Obolonskii, 'Rossiiskoe chinovnichestvo i problemy ego reformirovaniya', *Konstitutsionnoe Pravo: Vostochnoevropeiskie Obozrenie*, No. 4 (33), 2000/No. 1 (34) (2001), pp. 2–9.

36 *Trud*, 27 July 1995.

37 *Izvestiya*, 28 June 2001, p. 1.

38 S. Filatov, 'Power and Business', *Rossiiskaya gazeta*, 30 December 1992; *Rossiiskie vesti*, 30 December 1992.

6 The legislature

1 Edmund Burke, 'Causes of Present Discontents', in *Edmund Burke on Revolution*, edited by Robert A. Smith (New York, Harper & Row, 1968), pp. 30–1.
2 *Izvestiya*, 24 December 1993, pp. 1–2.
3 N. Shelyutto, 'Osobennosti novykh vyborov', *Rossiiskaya Federatsiya: Obshchestvenno-politicheskii zhurnal* (formerly *Narodnyi deputat*), No. 1 (13) (1993), p. 27.
4 For his views, see Ivan Rybkin, *Gosudarstvennaya duma: pytaya popytka* (Moscow, 1994); *My obrecheny na soglasie* (Moscow, Mezhdunarodnye otnosheniya, 1994).
5 *Segodnya*, 18 January 1996, p. 1.
6 *Rossiiskaya gazeta*, 23 December 1993, p. 1.
7 Sergei Mdoyants and Aleksei Salmin, 'Pobedit sluchainyi', *Moskovskie novosti*, No. 71 (15–22 October 1995), p. 6.
8 *Nezavisimaya gazeta*, 12 January 1996, p. 2.
9 Ludmila Telen, *Moskovskie novosti*, No. 87 (1995), p. 8.
10 *RFE/RL Newsline*, 18 January 1999; Ol'ga Tropkina, 'Veshnyakov ne verit v massovye fal'sifikatsii na vyborakh', *Nezavisimaya gazeta*, 28 December 1999, p. 3 gave a slightly higher figure: 175.
11 *Vestnik Tsentral'noi izbiratel'noi komissii Rossiiskoi Federatsii*, No. 1 (91) (2000), p. 231.
12 Laura Belin, 'Early Presidential Election Secures Duma Majority for Putin', *RFE/RL Russian Election Report*, No. 8 (7 January 2000).
13 Leonid Radzikhovskii, *Segodnya*, 6 February 2001.
14 Ivan Rodin, *Nezavisimaya gazeta*, 6 February 2001.
15 *Moskovskie novosti*, No. 69 (8–15 October 1995), p. 7.
16 OMRI *Regional Report*, Vol. 1, No. 2 (4 September 1996), Part 1.
17 *Nezavisimaya gazeta*, 6 December 1995, p. 1.
18 *Rossiiskie vesti*, 24 January 1996, p. 1.
19 *Nezavisimaya gazeta*, 19 May 2000.
20 The Jamestown Foundation, *Monitor*, 19 July 2000.
21 Sarah Karush, 'Governors Give up Federation Fight', *The St. Petersburg Times*, 28 July 2000, p. 2.
22 Sarah Karush, 'Governors Give up Federation Fight', p. 2.
23 The Jamestown Foundation, *Monitor*, 23 May 2000, 25 May 2000.
24 The public chamber of the Constitutional Assembly had opposed granting the FC rather than the Duma powers endorsing presidential decrees on a state of emergency, martial law and the deployment of troops abroad, but had been over-ruled; Viktor Sheinis, *Moscow News*, No. 46 (12 November 1993), p. 2.
25 *RRR*, Vol. 5, No. 29 (26 July 2000).
26 The head of the North-west Federal District, Viktor Cherkesov (a close Putin ally), on 21 July 2000 did in fact suggest that in future both houses could be elected, *RRR*, Vol. 5, No. 29 (26 July 2000).
27 Alfred B. Evans, Jnr, 'Problems of Conflict Management in Russian Politics', *The Journal of Communist Studies*, Vol. 9, No. 2 (June 1993), pp. 1–19.

7 Electoral politics

1 Alexander Pope, *Essay on Man*, Epistle 3.
2 For details, see Stephen White, Richard Rose and Ian McAllister, *How Russia Votes* (Chatham, NJ, Chatham House Publishers, 1996).
3 See Jeffrey Hahn, 'An Experiment in Competition: The 1987 Elections to the Local Soviets', *Slavic Review*, Vol. 47, No. 2 (1988), pp. 434–47; and Stephen White, 'Reforming the Electoral System', *The Journal of Communist Studies*, Vol. 4, No. 4 (1988), pp. 1–17.
4 The revised electoral law was published in *Izvestiya*, 28 October 1989.
5 An example of this is given for Yaroslavl region by Gavin Helf and Jeffrey Hahn, 'Old Dogs and New Tricks: Party Elites in the Russian Regional Elections of 1990', *Slavic Review*, Vol. 51, No. 3 (fall 1992), p. 526.

6 Khasbulatov, *The Struggle for Russia*, p. 242.
7 B.N. Yeltsin, in *Chetvertyi s"ezd narodnykh deputatov RSFSR: stenograficheskii otchet*, 21–25 May 1991 (Moscow, Izd. Verkhovnogo Soveta RSFSR, 1991), Vol. 1, p. 3.
8 Vitalii Vorotnikov, the outgoing chairman of the RSFSR Supreme Soviet, was elected from Adygeya; Alexander Vlasov, the former RSFSR prime minister who ran against Yeltsin in May 1990 for the post of chairman of the Russian Supreme Soviet, was nominated from Yakutia; and F. Bobkov, formerly Victor Chebrikov's right hand in the KGB, from North Ossetia, although none of them had previously had anything to do with these republics.
9 Michael E. Urban, 'El'tsin, Democratic Russia and the Campaign for the Russian Presidency', *Soviet Studies*, Vol. 44, No. 2 (1992), pp. 187–207.
10 Philippe C. Schmitter, 'Reflexions on Revolutionary and Evolutionary Transitions: The Russian Case in Comparative Perspective', in A. Dallin (ed.), *Political Parties in Russia* (Berkeley, University of California Press, 1993), p. 31.
11 See Yitzhak M. Brudny, 'The Dynamics of "Democratic Russia", 1990–1993', *Post-Soviet Affairs*, Vol. 9, No. 2 (1993), pp. 141–70.
12 For a fuller analysis than can be given here, see Richard Sakwa, 'The Russian Elections of December 1993', *Europe–Asia Studies*, Vol. 47, No. 2 (1995), pp. 195–227.
13 *Izvestiya*, 24 September 1993, pp. 3–5.
14 Yeltsin's decree of 11 October allowed the election of the upper house ('O vyborakh v Sovet Federatsii Federal'nogo Sobraniya Rossiiskoi Federatsii'); and the decree of 6 November added yet another clause ensuring that a category of votes 'against all' was added to ballot papers; *Rossiiskaya Federatsiya*, 1 (13) (1993), pp. 7–20; *Moscow News*, 43 (22 October 1993), p. 1.
15 Decree of 11 October; *Rossiiskaya Federatsiya*, No. 1 (13), (1993), p. 17.
16 Nikolai Ryabov, *Rossiiskaya gazeta*, 11 December 1993, p. 1.
17 Cited by Victor Sheinis in *ONS: Obshchestvennye nauki i sovremenost'*, No. 1 (1995), p. 9.
18 Michael Urban, 'December 1993 as a Replication of Late-Soviet Electoral Practices', *Post-Soviet Affairs*, Vol. 10, No. 2 (April–June 1994), p. 128.
19 Yeltsin decreed the increase in numbers to the State Duma on 1 October, 'Polozhenie o vyborakh deputatov Gosudarstvennoi Dumy v 1993 godu', *Rossiiskaya Federatsiya*, 1 (13) (1993), pp. 7–20; *The Political Situation in Russia: Political Parties in Russia*, (Moscow, 'EPIcenter', 1993), p. 26.
20 'Polozhenie o vyborakh deputatov Gosudarstvennoi Dumy', *Izvestiya*, 24 September 1993, pp. 3–5.
21 *Moskovskie novosti*, No. 25 (20 June 1993), p. A9.
22 *The Guardian*, 8 October 1993.
23 *Izvestiya*, 4 May 1994, p. 4.
24 *Rossiiskaya gazeta*, 11 December 1993, p. 1.
25 Alexander Rahr, 'The Future of the Russian Democrats', *RFE/RL Research Report*, Vol. 2, No. 39 (1 October 1993), p. 4.
26 *Rossiiskaya gazeta*, 14 October 1993, p. 3.
27 *Izvestiya*, 14 October 1993, p. 4.
28 For example, for the RCDM, *Put'*, 1 (31) (1994), p. 3.
29 *The Guardian*, 11 November 1993.
30 *Rossiiskaya gazeta*, 11 December 1993, p. 1.
31 This was the main argument of the commission into electoral fraud led by Aleksandr Sobyanin, *Izvestiya*, 4 May 1994, p. 4.
32 *Segodnya*, 10 March 1994; *Izvestiya*, 4 May 1994, p. 4; *Nezavisimaya gazeta*, 19 July 1994, p. 2.
33 Cf. Wendy Slater, 'Russia's Plebiscite on a New Constitution', *RFE/RL Research Report*, Vol. 3, No. 3 (21 January 1994), pp. 1–7.
34 For an analysis of the various figures of registered voters and the differing turnout figures, see Alexander Minkin, *Moskovskii komsomolets*, 11 January 1994, p. 1, and *Pravda*, 28 December 1993, p. 1.
35 Kronid Lyubarskii, *Novoe vremya*, No. 9 (March 1994), pp. 10–13.

36 See Mary Cline, 'Nizhnii Novgorod: A Regional View of the Russian Elections', *RFE/RL Research Report*, Vol. 3, No. 4 (28 January 1994), pp. 48–54.
37 Cf. Elizabeth Teague, 'North–South Divide: Yeltsin and Russia's Provincial Leaders', *RFE/RL Research Report*, Vol. 2, No. 47 (26 November 1993).
38 *Novoe vremya*, No. 7 (February 1994), pp. 8–12.
39 See A.A. Sobyanin and V.G. Sukhovolskii, *Demokratiya, ogranichennaya falsifikatsii* [*Democracy, Limited by Falsification*] (Moscow, Planning Group on Human Rights, 1995).
40 *Byulleten' TsIK*, No. 1 (27) (1995), pp. 8–14; *Nezavisimaya gazeta*, 21 December 1994.
41 Yurii Vedeneev and Vladimir Lysenko, 'Konstitutsionnye vybory: inogo ne dano', *Nezavisimaya gazeta*, 19 July 1994, pp. 1, 3; 20 July 1994, pp. 1, 3.
42 *Moskovskie novosti*, No. 15 (26 February–5 March 1995), p. 8.
43 *Kommersant-Daily*, 18 November 1995.
44 *Nezavisimaya gazeta*, 16 November 1995.
45 Vyacheslav Nikonov, *Moskovskie novosti*, No. 73 (22–9 October 1995), p. 5.
46 *Moskovskie novosti*, No. 73 (22–9 October 1995), p. 6.
47 *Moskovskie novosti*, No. 75 (29 October–5 November 1995), p. 7.
48 This is an argument made by Gleb Cherkasov, political correspondent for *Segodnya*, cited in *OMRI Special Report: Russian Election Survey*, No. 8 (21 November 1995).
49 *Moskovskie novosti*, No. 69 (8–15 October 1995), p. 6.
50 *Moskovskii komsomolets*, 19 December 1995.
51 *Moskovskie novosti*, No. 73 (22–9 October 1995), p. 6.
52 *Independent*, 17 October 1995, p. 13.
53 *Moskovskie novosti*, No. 71 (15–22 October 1995), p. 6; *Sovetskaya Rossiya*, 18 November 1995.
54 *The Economist*, 7 October 1995, p. 55.
55 *Moskovskie novosti*, No. 61 (10–17 September 1995), p. 5.
56 *The Observer*, 1 October 1995, p. 23.
57 *Moskovskie novosti*, No. 61 (10–17 September 1995), p. 4.
58 *Moskovskie novosti*, No. 71 (15–22 October 1995), p. 7.
59 For example, *Moskovskie novosti*, No. 77 (5–12 November 1995), p. 7.
60 *Segodnya*, 27 September 1995, p. 2.
61 The term 'soft' backlash is from Urban, 'December 1993', p. 135, fn 19.
62 *Moskovskie novosti*, No. 44 (25 June-2 July 1995), p. 4.
63 *Nezavisimaya gazeta*, 27 April 1996.
64 On this, see Michael McFaul, *Russia's 1996 Presidential Election: The End of Polarised Politics* (Stanford, CA, Hoover Institution Press, 1997).
65 This section draws on my 'Russia's "Permanent" (Uninterrupted) Elections of 1999–2000', *Journal of Communist Studies and Transition Politics*, Vol. 16, No. 3 (September 2000), pp. 85–112.
66 The SPS included Gaidar's Democratic Choice of Russia, Kirienko's 'New Force' (Novaya sila), Nemtsov's 'Young Russia' (Molodaya Rossiya), Khakamada's 'Common Cause' (Obshche delo), Titov's 'Russia's Voice' (Golos Rossii), Konstantin Borovoi's Party of Economic Freedom, Vladimir Lysenko's Republican Party and a number of other small groups.
67 Sarah Karush, 'Kremlin Loses Control of Election Panel', *Moscow Times*, 25 March 1999.
68 Of the 441 deputies elected, 225 came from the party-lists and 216 from single-member districts. A second round of voting was scheduled for the eight SMD seats where the majority of the electorate voted against all of the candidates on the ballot paper. Elections were not held in Chechnya, the ninth vacant seat.
69 EastWest Institute, *Russian Regional Report*, Vol. 4, No. 48 (22 December 1999).
70 *Izvestiya*, 25 February 2000, p. 5.
71 Yevgenia Borisova, 'And the Winner Is?', *Moscow Times*, 9 September 2000.
72 The point is made by Laura Belin, 'Commission Releases Final Results', *RFE/RL, Russian Election Report*, No. 5 (13) (7 April 2000).

73 The terms were used by Ian Traynor, 'Weary Nation Turns to Putin', *Guardian*, 16 March 2000, p.20

74 See, for example, Stephen White, 'Democratizing Eastern Europe: The Elections of 1990', *Electoral Studies*, Vol. 9, No. 4 (1990), pp. 277–87; Vernon Bogdanor, 'Founding Elections and Regime Change', *Electoral Studies*, Vol. 9, No. 4 (1990), pp. 288–94.

75 Cf. Sergei Mdoyants and Aleksei Salmin, 'Dozhivem li do "rutinoi" demokratii', *Moskovskie novosti*, No. 63 (17–24 September 1995), p. 6.

76 For a discussion of the manipulation of electoral systems, see Arend Lijphart, *Electoral Systems and Party Systems: A Study of Twenty-Seven Democracies, 1945–1990* (Oxford, Oxford University Press, 1994).

77 *Moskovskie novosti*, No. 25 (20 June 1993), p. A9.

78 *Byulleten' Tsentral'noi izbiratel'noi kommissii*, 1 (12) (1994), p. 28.

79 Sergei Mdoyants, Aleksei Salmin, 'Vybor nakanune vyborov', *Nezavisimaya gazeta*, 30 March 1995, p. 3.

80 On this, see Richard Rose, Neil Munro and Stephen White, 'Voting in a Floating Party System: The 1999 Duma Election', *Europe–Asia Studies*, Vol. 53, No. 3 (May 2001), pp. 419–43.

81 This argument is made by Salvatore d'Albergo and Pier Paolo Frassinelli, 'Electoral Typologies and Democracy', *Representation*, Vol. 36, No. 1 (1999), pp. 73–7.

82 For a discussion of the issues, see Stephen White and Ian McAllister, 'Reforming the Russian Electoral System', *Journal of Communist and Transition Politics*, Vol. 15, No. 4 (December 1999), pp. 17–40.

83 Anatolii Luk'yanov, 'Kontrol'naya nad demokratiya', *Nezavisimaya gazeta*, 2 March 2000, p. 3.

84 *O vyborakh deputatov Gosudarstvennoi Dumy Federal'nogo Sobraniya Rossiiskoi Federatsii: Federal'nyi zakon* (Moscow, Izdatel'stvo PRIOR, 1999).

85 For a discussion of the issue, see Andreas Auer (ed.), *Direct Democracy: The Eastern and Central European Experience* (Aldershot, Ashgate, 2001). On the broader issues of direct democracy, see also Ian Budge, *The New Challenge of Direct Democracy* (Cambridge, Polity Press, 1996), and John Haskell, *Direct Democracy or Representive Government: Dispelling the Populist Myth* (Boulder, CO, Westview Press, 2000).

86 Art. 37, sect. 2 of the law, *Sobranie Zakonodatel'stva RF 1995*, No. 42, pos. 3921.

87 These are discussed by Geoffrey Evans and Stephen Whitefield, 'Identifying the Bases of Party Competition in Eastern Europe', *British Journal of Political Science*, Vol. 23, No. 4 (1993), pp. 521–48.

88 See the work by Evans and Whitefield on this issue, most recently Stephen Whitefield and Geoffrey Evans, 'Class, Markets and Partisanship in Post-Soviet Russia' *Electoral Studies*, Vol. 18, No. 2, (1999), pp.155–78.

89 For a detailed discussion, see Matthew Wyman, Stephen White and Sarah Oates (eds), *Elections and Voters in Post-communist Russia* (Cheltenham, Edward Elgar, 1998).

8 Party development

1 James Bryce, *Studies of History and Jurisprudence*, Vol. 1 (Oxford, 1901), p. 166.

2 This chapter develops the themes in my 'Parties and Organized Interests' in Stephen White *et al.* (eds), *Developments in Russian Politics 5* (Basingstoke, Palgrave, 2001), Chapter 15.

3 Giovanni Sartori, *Parties and Party Systems: A Framework for Analysis* (Cambridge, Cambridge University Press, 1976) and his *The Theory of Democracy Revisited* (Chatham, Chatham House Publishers, 1987); see also Jean Blondel, *Comparative Government: An Introduction* (Hemel Hempstead, Simon & Schuster, 1990), Part II.

4 See Judith B. Sedaitis and Jim Butterfield (eds), *Perestroika from Below: Social Movements in the Soviet Union* (London, Westview, 1991). See also Gail Lapidus, 'State and Society: Toward the Emergence of Civil Society in the Soviet Union', in Alexander Dallin and Gail Lapidus (eds), *The Soviet System in Crisis* (Boulder, Westview Press,

1991), pp. 130–47; Victoria Bonnell, 'Voluntary Associations in Gorbachev's Reform Program', also in *The Soviet System in Crisis*, pp. 151–60.

5 Cf. Steven Fish, 'The Emergence of Independent Associations and the Transformation of Russian Political Society', *The Journal of Communist Studies*, Vol. 7, No. 3 (September 1991), pp. 299–334.

6 For perhaps the best analysis of these problems, see Michael Urban, with Vyacheslav Igrunov and Sergei Mitrokhin, *The Rebirth of Politics in Russia* (Cambridge, Cambridge University Press, 1997).

7 A.V. Gromov and O.S. Kuzin, *Neformaly: kto est' kto?* (Moscow, mysl', 1990), pp. 11–15.

8 For example, *Neformaly: kto oni? Kuda zovut?*, ed. V.A. Pecheneva (Moscow, Izd. politicheskoi literatury, 1990).

9 Vladimir Pribylovskii, *Dictionary of Political Parties and Organisations* (Moscow, PostFactum; Washington, DC, Center for Strategic and International Studies, 1992), pp. 28–32.

10 *Svobodnoe Slovo*, No. 5 (107) (1992), p. 1.

11 See Geoffrey Evans and Stephen Whitefield, 'Social and Ideological Cleavage Formation in Post-communist Hungary', *Europe–Asia Studies*, Vol. 47, No. 7 (1995), pp. 1,177–1,204.

12 The figure comes from V.N. Berezovskii *et al.*, *Partii, assotsiatsii, soyuzy, kluby: spravochnik* (Moscow, RAU Press, 1991), Vol. 1 (1), p. 3, with a discussion of classification on pp. 5–9.

13 A survey of a hundred political parties and groups is provided by Vladimir Pribylovskii in *Slovar' oppozitsii: novye politicheskie partii i organizatsii Rossii*, *Analiticheskie vestniki informatsionnogo agenstva Postfactum*, No. 4/5 (April 1991).

14 Andranik Migranyan, 'Prospects for the Russian National Movement', *Nezavisimaya gazeta*, 14 November 1991, p. 5.

15 Cf. Michael Waller, 'Political Actors and Political Roles in East-Central Europe', *The Journal of Communist Studies*, Vol. 9, No. 4 (December 1993), pp. 21–36.

16 L. Gordon and E. Klopov (eds), *Novye sotsial'nye dvizheniya v Rossii* (Moscow, Progress-Kompleks, 1993), p. 25.

17 Michael Urban and Vladimir Gel'man, 'The Development of Political Parties in Russia', in Karen Dawisha and Bruce Parrott (eds), *Democratic Change and Authoritarian Reactions in Russia, Ukraine, Belarus and Moldova* (Cambridge, Cambridge University Press, 1997), pp. 175–219.

18 Vyacheslav Nikonov, *Nezavisimaya gazeta*, 7 August 1992, p. 5.

19 Giovanni Sartori, *Parties and Party Systems: A Framework for Analysis* (Cambridge, Cambridge University Press, 1976), p. 63.

20 *Narodnyi deputat*, No. 8 (1992), pp. 96–100, at p. 96.

21 *Izvestiya*, 20 April 1992, p. 2.

22 *Moscow News*, No. 22 (28 May 1993), p. 1.

23 Maurice Duverger, *Political Parties: Their Organization and Activity in the Modern State* (London, Methuen, 1954).

24 See V.G. Golovin, 'Ekonomicheskie vzglyady politicheskikh partii i blokov Rossii', in *Partii i partiinye sistemy sovremennoi evropy* (Moscow, INION, 1994), pp. 142–71.

25 *Izvestiya*, 24 August 1992.

26 See Yitzhak M. Brudny, 'The Dynamics of "Democratic Russia", 1990–1993', *Post-Soviet Affairs*, Vol. 9, No. 2 (1993), pp. 141–70; on the Civic Union, see Michael McFaul, 'Russian Centrism and Revolutionary Transitions', *Post-Soviet Affairs*, Vol. 9, No. 3 (1993), pp. 196–222.

27 *Izvestiya*, 3 August 1992, p. 3.

28 Alexander Vladislavlev of the Renewal League, *Nezavisimaya gazeta*, 11 July 1992, p. 4.

29 Vladimir Shumeiko, a co-founder of Renewal, in *Moscow News*, No. 24 (14 June 1992), p. 6.

30 *Segodnya*, 31 March 1994, p. 2.

31 Konstantin Medvedev, 'V Rossii vozmozhna smena kursa', *Nezavisimaya gazeta*, 7 December 1991, p. 2.

32 This characterised the Slavic Assembly (*Slavyanskii sobor*), an alliance of Soviet and Russian nationalists; the *Nashi* (Ours) movement that brought together Alexander Nevzorov, the presenter of the investigative Leningrad television programme '600 Seconds', Victor Alksnis of the Soyuz group, and Sergei Kurginyan, one of the leading conservative intellectuals and leader of the 'Postperestroika' group; and the Russian Popular Union (*Russkii obshchenarodnii soyuz*, ROS), led by Sergei Baburin and Nikolai Pavlov. A lawyer by training, Baburin insisted that Russia *was* the former USSR and supported a strong state, collective property and mystical notions of Russian community.

33 *Obozrevatel'*, No. 2–3 (1992), prilozhenie, p. 21.

34 Including the writers Valentin Rasputin, V. Belov, A. Prokhanov, Academician I. Shafarevich, the well-known figures from the old Soviet Congress Viktor Alksnis and A. Makashov, as well as Baburin and Mikhail Astaf'ev (leader of the Constitutional Democratic Party). The core of the NSF was the oppositional parliamentary bloc 'Russian Unity'.

35 *Rossiya*, No. 27 (86) (July 1992), p. 3.

36 Vyacheslav Nikonov, *Nezavisimaya gazeta*, 7 August 1992, p. 5.

37 The decree of 23 August 1991 halted the activity of the CPSU; the decree of 25 August confiscated its property; and the decree of 6 November banned the party in Russia. The appeal is in *Konstitutsionnyi vestnik*, No. 13 (November 1992), pp. 221–5.

38 *Konstitutsionnyi vestnik*, No. 13 (November 1992), pp. 226–42.

39 For example, Sergei Shakhrai, *Moscow News*, No. 22 (31 May 1992), p. 2.

40 *Rossiiskaya gazeta*, 16 December 1992, p. 6.

41 *Konstitutsionnoe soveshchanie*, No. 1 (August 1993), p. 33.

42 Vera Tolz, 'The Civic Accord: Contributing to Russia's Stability?', *RFE/RL Research Report*, Vol. 3, No. 19 (13 May 1994), pp. 1–5.

43 *Izvestiya*, 29 April 1994, p. 1.

44 NTV 19 December 1995, in *OMRI Daily Digest*, Part 1 (19 December 1995).

45 *Washington Post*, 8 September 2000.

46 Anatolii Khimenko, 'Partiinoe stroitel'stvo zamorozheno rossiiskimi "verkhami"', *Nezavisimaya gazeta*, 4 March 1993, p. 2.

47 Alexander Solzhenitsyn, *Rebuilding Russia*, pp. 54–90, at p. 70.

48 Herbert Kitschelt, Zdenka Mansfeldova, Radoslav Markowski and Gabor Toka, *Post-communist Party Systems* (Cambridge, Cambridge University Press, 1999), p. 1.

49 Robert Michels, *Political Parties: A Sociological Study of the Oligarchical Tendencies of Modern Democracies* (New York, Free Press, 1962).

50 As reported by the Minister of Justice, Yurii Chaika, *RFE/RL Newsline*, 25 January 2001. This number differs from other reports.

51 *Obshchaya gazeta*, No. 40 (1994), p. 8.

52 Richard Rose, Neil Munro and Stephen White, *The 1999 Duma Vote: A Floating Party System*, Studies in Public Policy Number 331 (Glasgow, University of Strathclyde, 2000), p. 7.

53 Gleb Cherkasov, *Segodnya*, 9 December 1995, p. 2.

54 Robert G. Moser, *Unexpected Outcomes: Electoral Systems, Political Parties, and Representation in Russia* (Pittsburgh, PA, University of Pittsburgh Press, 2001).

55 *Izvestiya*, 18 August 2000.

56 For a discussion of the background to the law and various alternative drafts, see Z. Zotova, *Politicheskie partii Rossii: organizatsiya i deyatel'nost'* (Moscow, Rossiiskii tsentr obucheniya izbiratel'nym tekhnologiyam, 2001).

57 These criticisms were made by the Independent Expert Legal Council, *Novye Izvestiya*, 2 February 2001; *RFE/RL Newsline*, 5 February 2001.

58 S.M. Lipset and S. Rokkan, 'Cleavage Structures, Party Systems and Voter Alignments: An Introduction', in *Party Systems and Voter Alignments: Cross National Perspectives*, ed. S.M. Lipset and S. Rokkan (New York, The Free Press, 1967); see also S. Rokkan, *Citizens, Elections, Parties* (Oslo, Universitetsforlaget, 1970). For an attempt to apply Rokkanian analysis, see Maurizio Cotta, 'Building Party Systems after the Dictatorship: The East European Cases in a Comparative Perspective', in Geoffrey Pridham and Tatu

Vanhanen (eds), *Democratization in Eastern Europe* (London, Routledge, 1994), pp. 99–127.

59 Mikhail Afanas'ev, *Klientelizm i rossiiskaya gosudarstvennost'* (Moscow, Moskovskii Obshchestvennyi Nauchnyi Fond, 1997).

60 Lipset and Rokkan, pp. 50–1.

61 Cf. Geoffrey Evans and Stephen Whitefield, 'Identifying the Bases of Party Competition in Eastern Europe', *British Journal of Political Science*, Vol. 23, No. 4 (1993), pp. 521–48.

62 See, for example, Erwin Oberlander, 'The Role of the Political Parties', in K. Katkov *et al.* (eds), *Russia Enters the Twentieth Century* (London, Temple, Smith, 1971), pp. 60–84.

63 Cf. Terence Emmons, *The Formation of Political Parties and the First National Elections in Russia* (Cambridge, MA, Harvard University Press, 1983).

64 A.I. Zevelev (ed.), *Istoriya politicheskikh partii Rossii* (Moscow, Vysshaya shkola, 1994); N.V. Orlova, *Politicheskie partii Rossii: stranitsy istorii* (Moscow, Yurist, 1994).

65 Igor' Malov, Maksim Khrustalev, 'Mnogopartiinost'' v Rossii, 1917–1990', *Problemy vostochnoi evropy*, No. 31–2 (Washington, 1991), pp. 79–163.

66 For example, Nikolai Biryukov and V.M. Sergeev, *Russia's Road to Democracy: Parliament, Communism and Traditional Culture* (Aldershot, Edward Elgar, 1993).

67 Stephen Welch, *The Concept of Political Culture* (Basingstoke, Macmillan, 1993).

68 This change is analysed by Richard Hofstadter, *The Idea of a Party System: The Rise of Legitimate Opposition in the United States, 1780–1840* (Berkeley, University of California Press, 1970).

69 G.V. Golosov, 'Proiskhozhdenie sovremennykh rossiiskikh politicheskikh partii, 1987–1993', in V. Gel'man, G. Golosov and E. Meleshkina (eds), *Pervyi elektoral'nyi tsikl v Rossii, 1993–1996gg.* (Moscow, Ves' Mir, 2000), pp. 77–105. See also A. Panebianco, *Political Parties: Organisation and Power* (Cambridge, Cambridge University Press, 1998), p. 50.

70 M. Stephen Fish, *Democracy from Scratch: Opposition and Regime in the New Russian Revolution* (Princeton, NJ, Princeton University Press, 1995).

71 *Kommersant*, No. 48 (98) (16 December 1991), p. 23. A few groups favoured by Burbulis did get premises, but Yeltsin's reneging on this promise for the others was yet another reason for the bitter hostility against him of part of the new political elite.

72 *Sovetskaya Rossiya*, 31 May 1990.

73 V. Ya. Gel'man, 'Institutsional'nyi dizain: sozdavaya "pravila igry"', in V. Gel'man, G. Golosov and E. Meleshkina (eds), *Pervyi elektoral'nyi tsikl v Rossii, 1993–1996gg.* (Moscow, Ves' Mir, 2000), pp. 44–76.

74 *Moscow News*, No. 25 (18 June 1993), p. 2.

75 Sergei Mndoyants and Aleksei Salmin, *Moskovskie novosti*, No. 67 (1–8 October 1995), p. 6.

76 *Moskovskie novosti*, No. 75 (29 October–5 November 1995), p. 6.

77 *Prism*, Vol. VI, Issue 9, Part 4 (2000).

78 A. Kulik, 'Posttotalitarnye partii v politicheskom protsesse', *MEMO*, No. 2 (1994), pp. 27–38, at p. 29.

79 Vladimir Gel'man and Grigorii Golosov, 'Regional Party System Formation in Russia: The Deviant Case of Sverdlovsk Oblast'', *Journal of Communist Studies and Transition Politics*, Vol. 14, No. 1/2, 1998, pp. 31–53.

80 Philippe C. Schmitter, 'Interest Systems and the Consolidation of Democracies', in G. Marks and L. Diamond (eds), *Reexamining Democracy* (London, Sage, 1992), pp. 156–81, at p. 160.

81 Fyodor Gavrilov, 'Russia's Right has to Decide What's Right', *St. Petersburg Times*, 23 July 1999.

82 See Evans and Whitefield, 'Identifying the Bases of Party Competition in Eastern Europe', op. cit..

83 Lyudmila Alekseeva, 'Nesvobodnye profsoyuzy', *Moskovskie novosti*, No. 3 (15–22 January 1995), p. 14.

84 This issue is discussed in the Eastern European context by Sten Berglund and Jan Ake Dellenbrant, 'The Evolution of Party Systems in Eastern Europe', *The Journal of Communist Studies*, Vol. 8, No. 1 (March 1992), pp. 148–59, esp. p. 154.

85 R. Inglehart, 'The Changing Structure of Political Cleavages in Western Societies', in R.J. Dalton *et al.* (eds), *Electoral Change in Advanced Industrial Democracies: Realignment or Dealignment?* (Princeton, Princeton University Press, 1984).
86 Richard S. Katz and Peter Mair *How Parties Organise: Change and Adaptation in Party Organizations in Western Democracies* (London, Sage, 1994).
87 Alan Ware, *Political Parties and Party Systems* (Oxford, Oxford University Press, 1996), Chapter 7.
88 Daniel Bell, *The End of Ideology: On the Exhaustion of Political Ideas in the Fifties* (New York, Free Press of Glencoe, 1960).
89 Francis Fukuyama, 'The End of History', *The National Interest*, summer 1989, pp. 3–17; *The End of History and the Last Man* (New York, Free Press, 1992).
90 Cf. Richard Flacks, 'The Party's Over – So What is to Be Done?', *Social Research*, Vol. 60, No. 3 (fall 1993), pp. 445–70.
91 Jacques Derrida, *Spectres of Marx* (London, Routledge, 1994); see also his 'Spectres of Marx', *New Left Review*, No. 205 (May–June 1994), pp. 31–58.

Part III Federalism, regionalism and nationalism

1 S.A. Smith, 'Citizenship and the Russian Nation during World War I: A Comment', *Slavic Review*, Vol. 59, No. 2 (summer 2000), pp. 316–35, at p. 322.
2 Gorbachev, *On My Country and the World*, p. 164.

9 Federalism and the state

1 Niccolo Machiavelli, *Discourses on the First Decade of Titus Livius* (London, 1883), p. 175.
2 Cited in Paul Dukes, *The Last Great Game: USA versus USSR* (London, Pinter, 1989), p. 147.
3 E.H. Carr, *The Bolshevik Revolution, 1917–1921*, Vol. 1 (London, Penguin, 1966), p. 272.
4 On the creation of the USSR, see A.M. Salmin, *SNG: sostoyanie i perspektivy razvitiya* (Moscow, Gorbachev-Fond, 1992); Victor Swoboda, 'Was the Soviet Union Really Necessary?', *Soviet Studies*, Vol. 44, No. 5 (1992), pp. 761–84.
5 The primary units consisted of sixteen Autonomous Soviet Socialist Republics (ASSR), six *krais* (territories), forty-nine *oblasts* (regions) and the cities of Moscow and St Petersburg, which ranked as *oblasts*. The fifteen secondary units consisted of five autonomous *oblasts* within the *krais*, and ten autonomous *okrugs* (districts), two of which were part of *krais* and the rest part of *oblasts* (see Figure 9.1). There were also 1,834 rural *raions* (districts) and 1,067 cities, thirteen with a population of over a million.
6 *USSR: Facts and Figures Annual*, edited by Alan P. Pollard, Vol. 15, 1991 (Gulf Breeze, FL, Academic International Press, 1991), pp. 2, 504.
7 Ann Sheehy, 'Russia Republic's: A Threat to its Territorial Integrity?', *RFE/RL Research Report*, Vol. 2, No. 20 (14 May 1993), p. 36.
8 This certainly was the view of Khasbulatov, and in August 1990 he devised a constitution for a new federation of sovereign states, *The Struggle for Russia*, pp. 128–36.
9 Adygeya had been subordinate to Krasnodar *krai*; Gorno-Altai to Altai *krai*; Khakassia to Krasnoyarsk *krai*; and Karachai-Cherkessia to Stavropol *krai*.
10 The area of the RSFSR occupied by autonomous territories increased from 40.7 per cent in 1922 (27.7 per cent in the 1989 borders) to 53.3 per cent in 1989; *SNG: sostoyanie i perspektivy razvitiya*, pp. 12, 19.
11 Titular nationalities were an absolute majority in Dagestan (80.2 per cent), Chechen-Ingushetia (70.7 per cent, Chechens alone comprised 58 per cent of Chechen-Ingushetia), Chuvashia (67.8 per cent), Tyva (64.3 per cent), Komi-Permyak *okrug* (60.2 per cent), Kabardino-Balkaria (57.7 per cent), Buryats of the Aga-Buryat autonomous *okrug* (54.9 per cent) and North Ossetia (53.0 per cent); *All-Union Census of the Population of 1989* (Moscow, 1991), pp. 28–33.

12 Titular nationalities comprised comparative majorities in Tatarstan (48.5 per cent), Kalmykia (45.4 per cent) and Marii El (43.3 per cent); *All-Union Census of the Population of 1989* (Moscow, 1991), pp. 28–33.

13 Calculations by A.I. Vdovin in A.S. Barsenkov *et al.*, *Towards a Nationalities Policy in the Russian Federation*, Centre for Soviet and East European Studies, University of Aberdeen, 1993, p. 16.

14 *Politicheskii monitoring Rossii*, No. 3 (July–September 1992), pp. 44–5.

15 The LDPR won 35.34 per cent of the party-list vote in Mordovia, 22 per cent in Tatarstan, 27.45 per cent in Khakassia and 22.53 per cent in Chuvashia (*Byulleten' TsIK*, No. 1 (12), 1994, pp. 52–4). Zhirinovskii's support was strongest where identities were the most divided, as in Tatarstan, as well as among Russian soldiers in Tajikistan and the Russian population of Kaliningrad.

16 Ryszard Kapuscinski, *Imperium*, trans. from the Polish by Klara Glowczewska (London, Granta Books, 1994), p. 172.

17 R. Khakim (Khakimov), *Sumerki imperii: k voprosu o natsii i gosudarstve* (Kazan, 1993), p. 16.

18 R. Khakim (Khakimov), *Sumerki imperii*, p. 62. See also Alexei Zverev, 'Qualified Sovereignty: The Tatarstan Model for Resolving Conflicting Loyalties', in Michael Waller, Bruno Coppieters and Alexei Malashenko (eds), *Conflicting Loyalties and the State in Post-Soviet Eurasia* (London, Frank Cass, 1998), pp. 118–44 for a discussion of the features of the 'Tatarstan model'.

19 Ryszard Kapuscinski, *Imperium*, pp. 162, 163.

20 Space does not allow us to discuss Chechnya here. For an extended discussion of normative aspects of the Chechen bid for independence, see my *Chechnya: The Pre-politics of Partition*, Research Group on Ethics and Transnational Politics, London Centre of International Relations, Working Paper No. 4, 2001.

21 EastWest Institute, *Russian Regional Report*, Vol. 5, No. 21 (31 May 2000).

22 On 5 October 1990 Adygeya raised its status to an autonomous republic; on 8 October the Koryak autonomous *okrug* declared itself sovereign; on 10 October Buryatia; on 11 October Bashkiria; on 16 October Yamalo-Nenets autonomous *okrug*; on 18 October Kalmykiya; on 22 October Mari ASSR; on 24 October Chuvashia; on 25 October Gorno-Altai; and so on until Dagestan on 13 May 1991 and, last of all and not to be left out, Birobijan (Jewish autonomous *oblast*) on 5 November 1991 declared itself sovereign.

23 *Literaturnaya gazeta*, 15 August 1990.

24 Excerpts of Yeltsin's speech can be found in *Nezavisimaya gazeta*, 27 March 1992.

25 *Rossiiskaya gazeta*, 29 October 1991, p. 2.

26 Yelena Bonner, *Nezavisimaya gazeta*, 5 January 1992; *Guardian*, 6 January 1992.

27 Shakhrai in *Gubernatorskie novosti*, No. 9 (March 1993), pp. 3–4.

28 Vladimir Lysenko, Deputy Chairman of the State Committee for Nationality Policy of the Russian Federation, *Rossiiskaya gazeta*, 1 December 1992, p. 4.

29 *Rossiiskaya gazeta*, 1 December 1992, p. 4.

30 *Rossiiskaya gazeta*, 5 November 1991, p. 1.

31 The plan is explained at some length by Rumyantsev, *Rossiiskaya gazeta*, 11 October 1991, p. 7.

32 *Rossiiskaya gazeta*, 11 October 1991, p. 7.

33 *Nezavisimaya gazeta*, 27 November 1991.

34 *Federativnyi dogovor: dokumenty, kommentarii* (Moscow, Supreme Soviet of the Russian Federation, 1992).

35 The three Federal Treaties are in *Konstitutsiya (osnovnoi zakon) Rossiiskoi Federatsii-Rossii* (Moscow, Izvestiya, 1992), pp. 81–108.

36 *Nezavisimaya gazeta*, 1 April 1992, p. 1.

37 These points are made by Abdulatipov in his analysis of the treaties; *Federativnyi dogovor*, p. 4.

38 Abdulatipov insisted that the Federal Treaty gave the regions extensive economic and other powers that were not used by them; *Gubernatorskie novosti*, No. 9 (March 1993), p. 1.

39 *Izvestiya*, 14 August 1992; *Nezavisimaya gazeta*, 15 August 1992.
40 See M. Burgess and A.G. Gagnon (eds), *Comparative Federalism and Federation* (Hemel Hempstead, Harvester Wheatsheaf, 1993).
41 *Konstitutsiya respubliki Tatarstan*, adopted on 6 November 1992 (Kazan, Tatarskoe knizhnoe izd., 1993), p. 14.
42 The Seventh Congress failed to adopt a constitutional amendment that would have allowed the Constitutional Court to rescind legislative acts of the republics if it found them unlawful; *Moscow News*, No. 6 (4 February 1993), p. 3.
43 Sergei Khrushchev, 'The Political Economy of Russia's Regional Fragmentation', in Douglas Blum (ed.), *Russia's Future: Consolidation or Disintegration?* (Boulder, CO, Westview Press, 1994), pp. 93–4.
44 For example, Sergei Shakhrai, *Kommersant-Daily*, 31 August 1995, pp. 1, 3.

10 Regional and local politics

1 Bertrand De Jouvenal, *Sovereignty: An Inquiry into the Political Good*, trans. J.F. Huntington (Cambridge, Cambridge University Press, 1957), p. 139.
2 A theme explored by Kathryn Stoner-Weiss, *Local Heroes: The Political Economy of Russian Regional Governance* (Princeton, NJ, Princeton University Press, 1997).
3 In Rostov *oblast*, for example, the governor was a former Party secretary who went on to appoint former *apparatchiki* as heads of administration; see A. Nikolenko, 'Vivat, nomenklatura?', *Narodny deputat*, No. 5 (1992). For accusations of betrayal, see *Zerkalo*, Vestnik Obshchestvennyi Komitet Rossiiskikh Reform, No. 2 (February 1992), p. 6.
4 The elections designated for 8 December 1991 were postponed by the Fifth CPD on 1 November 1991 to December 1992, and the president was granted the right to appoint heads of administration in the interim. Yeltsin conceded that new heads of administration would have to be approved by the corresponding soviet and Russian MPs from that territory; *Rossiiskaya gazeta*, 5 November 1991, p. 1.
5 Robert Orttung, 'Resourceful Governors Able to Counter the Kremlin', EastWest Institute, *Russian Regional Report*, Vol. 5, No. 10 (15 March 2000); which contains an analysis of the advantages of incumbency.
6 'Ob obshchikh printsipakh organizatsii zakonodatel'nykh (predstavitel'nykh) i ispolnitel'nykh organov gosudarstvennoi vlasti sub'ektov Rossiiskoi Federatsii', *Rossiiskaya gazeta*, 19 October 1999, pp. 4–5.
7 The driving force behind the letter was governor Mikhail Prusak of Novgorod, and it was signed by Belgorod governor Evgenii Savchenko and Kurgan governor Oleg Bogomolov, 'I vlast', i ekonomika, i prezident na 7 let', *Nezavisimaya gazeta*, 25 February 2000, pp. 1, 4.
8 For an instructive comparative discussion of particularism, see Stein Rokkan, 'The Survival of Peripheral Identity', in *State Formation. Nation Building, and Mass Politics in Europe: The Theory of Stein Rokkan*, ed. Peter Flora with Stein Kuhle and Derek Urwin (Oxford, Oxford University Press, 1999), pp. 191–208.
9 'Titov protiv naznacheniya gubernatorov', *Nezavisimaya gazeta*, 3 March 2000; see also *Moscow Times*, 3 March 2000; and EastWest Institute, *Russian Regional Report*, Vol. 5, No. 9 (9 March 2000).
10 The decree establishing 'representatives of the presidium of the Supreme Soviet of the RSFSR' had already been drafted in mid-June, but was shelved until a more opportune moment, provided by the *coup*; *Demokraticheskya gazeta*, No. 12 (15) (12 September 1991), p. 3. Following the *coup*, the 'temporary instructions' made them envoys of the president rather than parliament, causing parliament yet more umbrage.
11 Democratic Russia's objections are voiced in 'My podderzhivaem Eltsyna uslovno', *Izvestiya*, 7 October 1991, p. 2.
12 For their responsibilities, see 'Glaza i ushi prezidenta', *Trud*, 30 January 1992, p. 3; *Izvestiya*, 11 January 1992, p. 2.
13 'Rasporyazhenie B. El'tsina o predstavitel'stve', *Izvestiya* and *Rossiiskaya gazeta*, 6 September 1991, p. 2.

14 *Rossiiskaya gazeta*, 6 September 1991, p. 2.

15 *Rossiiskaya gazeta*, 17 July 1997.

16 Ludmila Telen, *Moscow News*, No. 13 (29 March 1992), p. 7.

17 For comment on this, see Michael Urban, 'The Politics of Identity in Russia's Postcommunist Transition: The Nation against Itself', *Slavic Review*, Vol. 53, No. 3 (fall 1994), p. 760.

18 *Vedemosti Mossoveta*, No. 1 (1992), pp. 4–11. It had become increasingly difficult anyway to gain the necessary two-thirds quorum for meetings of the Mossoviet.

19 *Rossiiskaya gazeta*, 12 October 1993.

20 Some of the themes of this section have been examined in my 'Russian Regionalism, Policy-Making and State Development', in Stefanie Harter and Gerald Easter (eds), *Shaping the Economic Space in Russia: Decision Making Processes, Institutions and Adjustment to Change in the El'tsin Era* (Aldershot, Ashgate, 2000), Chapter 1, pp. 11–34.

21 For a useful discussion, see S.D. Valentei, *Federalizm: Rossiiskaya istoriya i Rossiiskaya real'nost'* (Moscow, Institute of the Economy, Centre for the Socio-Economic Problems of Federalism, RAS, 1998).

22 This is argued, for example, by James Hughes, 'Moscow's Bilateral Treaties Add to Confusion', *Transition*, 20 September 1996, pp. 39–43.

23 Richard Sakwa, 'The Republicanisation of Russia: Federalism and Democratization in Transition I', in Chris Pierson and Simon Tormey (eds), *Politics at the Edge*, The PSA Yearbook 1999 (Basingstoke, Macmillan, 1999), Chapter 16, pp. 215–26. See also the chapter by Cameron Ross in the same volume, pp. 227–40.

24 Kathryn Stoner-Weiss, 'Central Weakness and Provincial Autonomy: Observations on the Devolution Process in Russia', *Post-Soviet Affairs*, Vol. 15, No. 1 (1999), pp. 87–106.

25 Mikhail A. Alexseev, 'Introduction: Challenges to the Russian Federation', in Alexseev (ed.), *Center–Periphery Conflict in Post-Soviet Russia: A Federation Imperiled* (Basingstoke, Macmillan, 1999), p. 1.

26 *Izvestiya*, 4 November 1997; EastWest Institute, *Russian Regional Report* 2 (38), 6 November 1997.

27 *RFE/RL Newsline*, 20 January 1998.

28 *Rossiiskaya gazeta*, 30 June 1999.

29 *RFE/RL Russian Federation Report*, 4 July 2001.

30 *Nezavisimaya gazeta*, 30 June 2001, p. 3.

31 James Hughes, 'Moscow's Bilateral Treaties Add to Confusion', *Transition*, 20 September 1996, pp. 39–43, at p. 39.

32 EastWest Institute, *Russian Regional Report*, Vol. 6, No. 26 (July 2001).

33 *Rossiiskaya gazeta*, 5 November 1991, p. 1.

34 *Politicheskii monitoring Rossii*, No. 3 (July–September 1992), p. 43; *Sotsial'no-politicheskii monitoring Rossii*, p. 28.

35 From west to east the economic regions are: Northern, North-Western, the Kaliningrad exclave (in effect part of the North-Western region but separated physically from Russia), Central, Central Black Earth, Volga, North Caucasian, Urals, Western Siberia, Eastern Siberia, and Far Eastern.

36 *Izvestiya*, 30 March 1992, p. 2.

37 Michael J. Bradshaw, 'Siberia Poses a Challenge to Russian Federalism', *RFE/RL Research Report*, Vol. 1, No. 41 (16 October 1992), p. 6.

38 RIA *Novosti* 9 March 2000, in Tacis, The European Union's project for Capacity Development in Election Monitoring, 10 March 2000.

39 The issue is examined in A. Lavrov (ed.), *Federal'nyi byudzhet i regiony: opyt analiza finansovykh potokov* (Moscow, Dialog-MGU, 1999). See also S.D. Valentei (ed.), *Ekonomicheskie problemy stanovleniya Rossiiskogo federalizma* (Moscow, Nauka, 1999).

40 EastWest Institute, *Russian Regional Report*, Vol. 4, No. 20 (27 May 1999).

41 For example in Pskov; see Darrell Slider, 'Pskov Under the LDPR: Elections and Dysfunctional Federalism in One Region', *Europe–Asia Studies*, Vol. 51, No. 5 (1999), p. 764.

42 Daniel Treisman, 'The Politics of Intergovernmental Transfers in Post-Soviet Russia', *British Journal of Political Science*, Vol. 26, No. 3 (July 1996), pp. 299–335. See also his

'Deciphering Russia's Federal Finance: Fiscal Appeasement in 1995 and 1996', *Europe–Asia Studies*, Vol. 50, No. 5 (July 1998), pp. 893–906.

43 Daniel Treisman, *After the Deluge: Regional Crises and Political Consolidation in Russia* (Ann Arbor, MI, The University of Michigan Press, 1999).

44 Alistair McAuley, 'The Determinants of Russian Federal–Regional Fiscal Relations: Equity or Political Influence', *Europe–Asia Studies*, Vol. 49, No. 3 (May 1997), pp. 431–44.

45 A.M. Lavrov and Alexei G. Makushkin, with a foreword by Alexander G. Granberg, *The Fiscal Structure of the Russian Federation: Financial Flows between the Centre and the Regions* (Armonk, New York and London, M.E. Sharpe, 2000).

46 *Nezavisimaya gazeta*, 24 May 2001.

47 Lavrov's study provides detailed analysis of regional differentiation, using comparisons based on the calculation Gross Regional Product (GRP); Lavrov and Makushkin, *The Fiscal Structure of the Russian Federation*.

48 Martin Nicholson, *Towards a Russia of the Regions*, Adelphi Paper 330 (London, International Institute for Strategic Studies, 1999), p. 35.

49 Mikhail S. Alexseev and Tamara Troyakova, 'A Mirage of the "Amur California": Regional Identity and Economic Incentives for Political Separatism and Primorskiy Kray', in Alexseev (ed.), *Center–Periphery Conflict in Post-Soviet Russia*, Chapter 6, pp. 205–46.

50 See Neil Robinson, 'The Global Economy, Reform and Crisis in Russia', *Review of International Political Economy*, Vol. 6, No. 4 (winter 1999), pp. 531–64.

51 Robert McIntyre, 'Regional Stabilisation Policy under Transitional Period Conditions in Russia: Price Controls, Regional Trade Barriers and Other Local-Level Measures', *Europe–Asia Studies*, Vol. 50, No. 5 (July 1998), pp. 859–72.

52 Darrell Slider, 'Pskov Under the LDPR: Elections and Dysfunctional Federalism in One Region', *Europe–Asia Studies*, Vol. 51, No. 5 (1999), p. 761.

53 EastWest Institute, *Russian Regional Report*, Vol. 4, No. 24 (24 June 1999).

54 *Nezavisimaya gazeta*, 26 June 1999; *Izvestiya*, 30 June 1999.

55 Alan James, 'The Practice of Sovereign Statehood in Contemporary International Society', *Political Studies*, Vol. XLVII, special issue (1999), p. 472.

56 *Kommersant-Daily*, 31 October 1997.

57 EWI, *Russian Regional Report*, Vol. 6, No. 4 (31 January 2001).

58 For example, in the case of Gorno-Altai, discussed below, *Rossiiskaya gazeta*, 21 June 2000, pp. 5–6.

59 Some of the arguments of this section were outlined in Richard Sakwa, 'Putin's New Federalism', EastWest Institute, *Russian Regional Report*, Vol. 5, No. 21 (31 May 2000), pp. 12–17.

60 Natalia Dinello, *What's So Great about Novgorod-The-Great: Trisectoral Cooperation and Symbolic Management* (Washington, DC, NCEEER, 2001), p. iii. For a more positive evaluation, see Nicolai Petro, 'The Novgorod Region: A Russian Success Story', *Post-Soviet Affairs*, Vol. 15, No. 3 (1999), pp. 235–61.

61 For a critique of this, see Grigorii Yavlinskii, 'The Last Phase of Agony', *Obshchaya gazeta*, 10–16 June 1999.

62 Vladimir Putin, *First Person: An Astonishingly Frank Self-Portrait by Russia's President Vladimir Putin*, with Nataliya Gevorkyan, Natalya Timakova and Andrei Kolesnikov, trans. Catherine A. Fitzpatrick (London, Hutchinson, 2000), pp. 182–3.

63 *Rossiiskaya gazeta*, 16 May 2000.

64 The seven capitals of the new Federal Districts (FD) are: Moscow for the Central FD, St Petersburg for the North-west FD, Rostov-na-Donu for the Caucasus FD, Nizhnii Novgorod for the Volga FD, Ekaterinburg for the Urals FD, Novosibirsk for the Siberian FD and Khabarovsk for the Far East FD.

65 The full list is as follows: Sergei Kirienko, the former prime minister and one of the leaders of the Union of Rightist Forces (SPS) headed the Volga Federal District (FD); CIS Affairs Minister and former Russian ambassador to Poland, Leonid Drachevskii, headed the Siberian FD; Viktor Cherkesov, the First Deputy Director of the FSB, headed the North-west FD; General Viktor Kazantsev, who had directed the latest

onslaught against Chechnya, the North Caucasus (later renamed the South Russian FD); First Deputy Interior Minister Petr Latyshev, the Urals FD; former presidential representative to Leningrad Oblast (and before that with years of service in the KGB), Georgi Poltavchenko, headed the Central FD; and Lieutenant-General Konstantin Pulikovskii, who had been a commander in the Chechen war of 1994–6, headed the Far East FD.

66 *RRR*, Vol. 5, No. 29 (26 July 2000).

67 Luzhkov continued to remain obdurate, however, insisting on 23 July 2000 that the city had no intention of dropping registration requirements, arguing that they were necessary 'protective measures' for the capital; *Moscow Times*, 25 July 2000. Not only was it unclear how Luzhkov could be forced to comply with the law, Moscow *oblast* also intended to introduce a similar registration system.

68 *RRR*, Vol. 5, No. 29 (26 July 2000); *Nezavisimaya gazeta*, 26 July 2000.

69 http:/www.president.kremlin.ru/events/34.html.

70 Sarah Karush and Catherine Belton, 'Putin to Tighten Grip on Regions', *Moscow Times*, 18 May 2000.

71 *RFE/RL Newsline*, 18 May 2000.

72 Julie A. Corwin, 'The New Centralizer', *RFE/RL Newsline*, 21 June 2000.

73 'On Removing from Office the Regional Leaders of Legislative and Executive Bodies', *Izvestiya*, 20 July 2000; *RFE/RL Newsline*, 19 July 2000.

74 With the launching of radical economic reform the law was modified by the Fifth Congress on 1 November 1991 and later; 'Zakon RF o mestnom samoupravlenii v RF' (Moscow, Izvestiya, 1993).

75 *Rossiiskaya gazeta*, 29 October 1991, p. 1. Discussion of the administrative reorganisation of Moscow continued into 1992; see *Vestnik merii Moskvy*, No. 12 (June 1992), pp. 3–15.

76 Decree of 9 October, 'O reforme predstavitel'nykh organov vlasti i organov mestnogo samoupravleniya v Rossiiskoi Federatsii', *Rossiiskaya Federatsiya*, 1 (13) (1993), p. 25.

77 The framework for local elections was established by presidential decree on 27 October 1993, *Byulleten' Tsentral'noi izbiratel'noi kommissii Rossiiskoi Federatsii*, No. 1 (12) (1994), pp. 6–27.

78 Decree of 22 October 1993, 'Ob osnovnykh nachalakh organizatsii gosudarstvennoi vlasti v sub'ektakh Rossiiskoi Federatsii', *Byulleten' TsIK*, No. 1 (12) (1994), pp. 3–6.

79 *Rossiiskaya gazeta*, 29 December 1993, p. 4.

80 For a discussion of these issues, see Galina Kurlyandskaya, *Budgetary Pluralism of Russian Authorities*, Open Society Institute, Local Government and Public Service Reform Initiative, Discussion Papers, No. 17, Budapest, 2001.

81 For the earlier period, see Stephen Whitefield, *Industrial Power and the Soviet State* (Oxford, Clarendon Press, 1993).

82 John F. Young, 'At the Bottom of the Heap: Local Self-government and Regional Politics in the Russian Federation', in Peter J. Stavrakis, Joan DeBardeleben and Larry Blank (eds), *Beyond the Monolith: The Emergence of Regionalism in Post-Soviet Russia* (Baltimore, Johns Hopkins University Press, 1997), pp. 81–102.

83 Mary McAuley, 'Politics, Economics and Elite Realignment in Russia: A Case Study', Vol. 8, No. 1 (1992), pp. 46–88.

84 Solzhenitsyn gives details of his scheme in *Rebuilding Russia*, pp. 75–8.

85 *Nezavisimaya gazeta*, 19 May 2000.

86 *Vremya*, 16 May 2001, p. 1.

87 'Intervyu s prezidentom Rossii', *Komsomol'skaya pravda*, 22 March 2001, p. 3.

11 National identity and state-building

1 Valery Tishkov, *Ethnicity, Nationalism and Conflict in and after the Soviet Union: The Mind Aflame* (London, Sage, 1996), p. 246.

2 Hans Kohn, 'Western and Eastern Nationalism', in John Hutchinson and Anthony D. Smith (eds), *Nationalism* (Oxford, Oxford University Press, 1994), pp. 162–5.

3 *Vestnik statistiki*, No. 10 (1990), p. 72.

4 Mark R. Beissinger, 'The Persisting Ambiguity of Empire', *Post-Soviet Affairs*, Vol. 11, No. 2 (1995), pp. 149–84, at p. 158.

5 For an exploration of the tension between nation and empire, see Geoffrey Hosking, *People and Empire, 1552–1917* (London, HarperCollins, 1997).

6 Cited by Margot Light, 'Foreign Policy Thinking', in Neil Malcolm *et al.* (eds), *Internal Factors in Russian Foreign Policy* (Oxford, Clarendon Press, 1996), p. 36.

7 The term 'state-nation' is from Juan J. Linz and Alfred Stepan, 'Toward Consolidated Democracies', *Journal of Democracy*, Vol. 7, No. 1 (April 1996), p. 27, where they are defined as 'those multicultural or even multinational states that nonetheless still manage to engender strong identification and loyalty from their diverse citizens', p. 27. The United States, Switzerland and India are cited as examples of state-nations.

8 For good analyses of the rebirth of Russian nationalism, see: Yitzhak M. Brudny, *Reinventing Russia: Russian Nationalism and the Soviet State, 1953–1991* (Cambridge, MA, Harvard University Press, 1999); Stephen K. Carter, *Russian Nationalism* (London, Pinter, 1990); and Peter Duncan, *Russian Messianism: Third Rome, Revolution, Communism and After* (London, Routledge, 2000).

9 Alexander Solzhenitsyn, *Letter to the Soviet Leaders* (New York, Harper & Row, 1974).

10 Igor Shafarevich, 'Separation or Reconciliation? – The Nationalities Question in the USSR' and 'Does Russia Have a Future?', in Alexander Solzhenitsyn (ed.), *From Under the Rubble* (London, Fontana, 1976), pp. 88–104, 279–94; and see also his 'Russofobiya', *Nash sovremennik*, No. 6 (1989); on allied questions see G. Popov and N. Adzhubei, 'Pamyat' i "Pamyat'": o problemakh istoricheskoi pamyati i sovremennykh natsional'nykh otnoshenii', *Znamya*, No. 1 (1988).

11 The character of this apparent *mésalliance* is analysed, for example, by S.V. Cheshko, *Raspad Sovetskogo Soyuza: Etnopoliticheskii Analiz*, 2nd edn, (Moscow, Institut Etnologii RAN, 2000).

12 The roots of this thinking, the relationship between Nikolai Trubetskoi's anti-Western polemic *Europe and Humanity* (1921) and Nikolai Ustryalov's 'changing landmarks' (*smenovekhovtsy*) movement that endorsed the Bolshevik revolution since it appeared to augment Russian national power, are discussed by Jane Burbank, *Intelligentsia and Revolution* (Oxford, Oxford University Press, 1986), pp. 208–37.

13 Igor Klyamkin, *Ogonek*, No. 47 (1995), p. 19.

14 E.A. Pozdnyakov, *Natsiya, natsionalizm, natsional'nye interesy* (Moscow, Progress-kultura, 1994), p. 61.

15 Pozdnyakov, *Natsiya, natsionalizm, natsional'nye interesy*, p. 74.

16 Solzhenitsyn, *Rebuilding Russia*, p. 15.

17 Sergei Kondrashov, *Nationalism and the Drive for Sovereignty in Tatarstan, 1988–92* (New York, St Martin's Press, 2000).

18 Vladimir Ilyushenko, *Literaturnaya gazeta*, 19 February 1992, p. 11.

19 *Moscow News*, No. 37 (1991), p. 5.

20 Len Karpinskii, cited by Tony Barber 'Democracy Tears Russia to Shreds', *Independent on Sunday*, 22 March 1992.

21 For example, Mykhailo Hrushevs'kyi in S. Frederick Starr (ed.), *The Legacy of History on the Foreign Policies of the New States of the Former Soviet Union* (New York, M.E. Sharpe, 1994).

22 Alexander Zinoviev, *Katastroika* (London, Claridge Press, 1990).

23 This was the view of the 'patriots' associated with the newspaper *Den'* (*Day*) edited by Prokhanov, sponsored by the Union of Russian Writers.

24 Rogers Brubaker, *Nationalism Reframed: Nationhood and the National Question in the New Europe* (Cambridge, Cambridge University Press, 1996).

25 P. Kolsto, *Russians in the Former Soviet Republics* (Bloomington, Indiana University Press, 1995), p. 50.

26 Cited by Roman Szporluk, 'The Imperial Legacy and the Soviet Nationalities Problem' in L. Hajda and M. Beissinger (eds), *The Nationalities Factor in Soviet Politics and Society* (Cambridge, Cambridge University Press, 1990), p. 13.

27 In Hajda and Beissinger (eds), *The Nationalities Factor in Soviet Politics and Society*, pp. 17–18.

28 See Vera Tolz, 'Forging the Nation: National Identity and Nation Building in Post-Communist Russia', *Europe-Asia Studies*, Vol. 50, No. 6 (1998), pp. 993–1,022.
29 For example, Henry A. Kissinger, 'The New Russian Question', *Newsweek*, 10 February 1991, pp. 12–13, at p. 13.
30 Likhachev described his experiences in the 1988 film about the prison, *Solovetskii Power*.
31 Dmitrii S. Likhachev, *Reflections on Russia* (Boulder, Westview Press, 1991), quotation from p. 80; his popular works in Russian include *Proshloe-budushchemu: stat'i i ocherki* (Leningrad, Nauka, 1985) and *Ya vospominayu* (Moscow, Progress, 1991).
32 Cf. Ronald Grigor Suny, 'States, Empires and Nations', *Post-Soviet Affairs*, Vol. 11, No. 2 (1995), pp. 185–96, at p. 190.
33 Vittorio Strada, 'Old and New Borders: Soviet and Russian Borders as a Phenomenon', *Nezavisimaya gazeta*, 6 November 1991.
34 Ken Jowitt, *New World Disorder: The Leninist Extinction* (Berkeley, University of California Press, 1992), pp. 319–26, analyses the 'civic/ethnic' identity issue.
35 *Politicheskii monitoring Rossiii*, No. 3 (July–September 1992), p. 7.
36 *OMRI Daily Digest*, No. 11, Part I, 16 January 1996.
37 *Pravda*, 30 January 1992.
38 *Moscow News*, No. 37 (1991), p. 6.
39 *Soviet Weekly*, 10 October 1991, p. 5.
40 For details, see *Documents on British Foreign Policy, 1919–1939*, First Series, Vol. XI, *Upper Silesia, Poland, and the Baltic States, January 1920–March 1921* (London, HMSO, 1961), pp. 1–197.
41 Alexander Golts, *Krasnaya zvezda*, 18 July 1992, p. 2.
42 Andrei Kozyrev, 'Vneshnyaya politika preobrazhayushcheisya Rossii', *Voprosy istorii*, No. 1 (1994), p. 8.
43 Solzhenitsyn, *Rebuilding Russia*, p. 14.
44 Loc. cit.
45 Ibid., p. 24.
46 *Nezavisimaya gazeta*, 3 July 1992, p. 3; *CDSP*, Vol. XLIV, No. 27 (1992), pp. 11–12.
47 *Rossiiskaya gazeta*, 6 February 1992.
48 *Rossiiskaya gazeta*, 14 July 1993.
49 *Nezavismaya gazeta*, 16 December 2000, p. 3.
50 Lowell Barrington, 'The Domestic and International Consequences of Citizenship in the Soviet Successor States', *Europe-Asia Studies*, Vol. 47, No. 5 (July 1995), pp. 731–63.
51 See Paul Goble, RFE/RL, *Russian Federation Report*, 7 March 2001.
52 *RFE/RL Newsline*, 3 January 2001.
53 Ryszard Kapuscinski, *Imperium*, p. 179.

12 Marketising the economy

1 Boris El'tsin, *Zapiski prezidenta* (Moscow, Ogonek, 1994), p. 300.
2 Mancur Olson, *Power and Prosperity: Outgrowing Communist and Capitalist Dictatorships* (New York, Basic Books, 1999).
3 *Transition Report: Economic Transition in Eastern Europe and the Former Soviet Union* (London, EBRD, October 1994), p. 45.
4 Armenia, Belarus, Kazakhstan, Kyrgyzstan, Russia, Tajikistan, Turkmenistan and Uzbekistan.
5 *Soviet Weekly*, 31 October 1991, pp. 6–7.
6 See Bert van Selm, *The Economics of Soviet Breakup* (London, Routledge, 1997).
7 Alistair McAuley, 'The Economic Consequences of Soviet Disintegration', *Soviet Economy*, Vol. 7, No. 3 (1991), pp. 189–214, suggests a high degree of interdependence.
8 V. Samonis, 'Who Subsidized Whom? The Distorted World of Baltic–Soviet Economic Relations', *Current Politics and Economics of Russia*, Vol. 2, No. 3 (1991), pp. 241–3.
9 *OECD Economic Surveys: The Russian Federation, 1995* (Paris, OECD, 1995), pp. 12–13.
10 *Soviet Weekly*, 5 December 1991, p. 10; John Tedstrom, 'Economic Crisis Deepens', *RFE/RL Research Report*, Vol. 1, No. 1 (3 January 1992), pp. 22–6; Keith Bush, 'The

Disastrous Last Year of the USSR', *RFE/RL Research Report*, Vol. 1, No. 12 (20 March 1992), pp. 39–41.

11 Keith Bush, 'An Overview of the Russian Economy', *RFE/RL Research Report*, Vol. 1, No. 25 (19 June 1992), p. 50.

12 *Soviet Weekly*, 10 October 1991, p. 11.

13 Anatolii B. Chubais and Sergei V. Vasil'ev, 'Privatisation as a Necessary Condition for Structural Change in the USSR', *Communist Economies and Economic Transformation*, Vol. 3, No. 1 (1991), pp. 57–62, at p. 57.

14 See, for example, Michael Ellman and Vladimir Kontorovich (eds), *The Destruction of the Soviet Economic System: An Insiders' History* (New York, M.E. Sharpe, 1998).

15 *Rossiiskaya gazeta*, 29 October 1991.

16 *Rossiiskaya gazeta*, 2 November 1991, p. 1.

17 Janos Kornai, *The Road to a Free Economy: Shifting from a Socialist System: The Example of Hungary* (New York, Norton, 1990).

18 John Kenneth Galbraith, 'Revolt in Our Time: The Triumph of Simplistic Ideology', in Gwyn Prins (ed.), *Spring in Winter: The 1989 Revolutions* (Manchester, Manchester University Press, 1990), pp. 1–12.

19 *Moskovskie novosti*, No. 78 (12–19 November 1995), p. 5.

20 For their views, see Alec Nove, 'New Thinking on the Soviet Economy', in Archie Brown (ed.), *New Thinking in Soviet Politics* (London, Macmillan, 1992), pp. 29–38.

21 *Russian Economic Trends*, Vol. 1, No. 1 (1992), p. 5.

22 *Ekonomika i zhizn'*, No. 51 (1991), p. 1.

23 Chubais and Vasil'ev, 'Privatisation', p. 59.

24 *OECD Economic Surveys*, p. 8.

25 Anders Aslund, 'Reform Vs. "Rent-Seeking" in Russia's Economic Transformation', *Transition*, 26 January 1996, p. 13.

26 Joel S. Hellman, 'Winners Take All: The Politics of Partial Reform in Postcommunist Transitions', *World Politics*, Vol. 50 (1998), pp. 203–34.

27 Dmitrii S. L'vov, 'The Social and Economic Problems of Perestroika', *Communist Economies and Economic Transformation*, Vol. 4, No. 1 (1992), pp. 75–83, at pp. 78–9.

28 Vladimir Capelik, 'The Development of Antimonopoly Policy in Russia', *RFE/RL Research Report*, Vol. 1, No. 34 (28 August 1992), pp. 66–70.

29 *OECD Economic Reviews*, p. 88. In Russia small firms (1–249 employees) made up 53 per cent of the total; in the United States 98 per cent.

30 *Rossiiskaya gazeta*, 10 January 1992, pp. 3–4, with an appendix on 15 January, p. 2.

31 See Alexander Bim *et al.*, 'Privatization in the Former Soviet Union and the New Russia', in Saul Estrin (ed.), *Privatization in Central and Eastern Europe* (London, Longman, 1994), pp. 252–78.

32 *OECD Economic Surveys*, p. 72; Bim *et al.*, 'Privatization in the Former Soviet Union and the New Russia', pp. 262–7.

33 'Interview with Richard Layard', in Keith Bush, *From the Command Economy to the Market: A Collection of Interviews* (Aldershot, Dartmouth Publishing, 1991), pp. 142–7, at p. 143.

34 'Interview with Anders Aslund', in Bush, *From the Command Economy to the Market*, pp. 7–12, at p. 8.

35 'Interview with Milton Friedman', in Bush, *From the Command Economy to the Market*, pp. 49–57, at p. 51.

36 For a discussion of these issues, see Elizabeth Teague (ed.), 'Is Equity Compatible with Efficiency?', *RFE/RL Research Report*, Vol. 1, No. 17 (1992), pp. 9–14.

37 Ivan Ustinov, *Nezavisimaya gazeta – politekonomiya*, 17 April 2001, cited in *RFE/RL Newsline*, 18 April 2001.

38 Boris Slavin and Valentin Davydov, 'Stanovlenie mnogopartiinosti', *Partiinaya zhizn'*, No. 18 (September 1991), pp. 6–16, at p. 15.

39 EastWest Institute, *Russian Regional Report*, 16 July 2001.

40 *RFE/RL Newsline*, 14 February 2001.

41 These were figures given by Sergei Dubinin, then head of the Central Bank, in July 1997.

For details, see 'Krupneiskie banki Rossii', *Finansovye izvestiya*, No. 58 (508), 11 August 1998.
42 *RFE/RL Newsline*, 4 January 2001.
43 *Moscow News*, No. 37 (1991), p. 2.
44 *RFE/RL Newsline*, 3 January 2001.
45 Vladimir Gimpelson, 'Russia's New Independent Entrepreneurs', *RFE/RL Research Report*, Vol. 2, No. 36 (10 September 1993), pp. 44–8.
46 John Tedstrom, 'Russia: Progress Report on Industrial Privatization', *RFE/RL Research Report*, Vol. 1, No. 17 (April 1991), p. 49.
47 *Soviet Weekly*, 10 October 1991, p. 11.
48 'Sotsial'no-ekonomicheskoe polozhenie Rossiiskoi Federatsii v 1991 godu', *Ekonomika i zhizn'*, No. 4 (1992), pp. 4–5.
49 *Moscow News*, No. 37 (1991), pp. 8–9.
50 The Jamestown Foundation, *Monitor*, 5 July 2001.
51 Tedstrom, 'Russia: Progress Report on Industrial Privatization', p. 49.
52 The phrase comes from Roy D. Laird and Edward Crowley (eds), *Soviet Agriculture: The Permanent Crisis* (New York, Praeger, 1965). See also Stefan Hedlund, *Crisis in Soviet Agriculture* (New York, St Martin's Press, 1985). For a discussion of the historical context and Gorbachev's approach to agriculture, see the special issue of *Studies in Comparative Communism*, Vol. 23, No. 2 (summer 1990).
53 The words are those of a speaker at the founding congress of the USSR Peasants' Union in June 1990, *Pravitel'stvennyi vestnik*, No. 25 (51) (June 1990), p. 5.
54 Stephen K. Wegren, 'Private Farming and Agrarian Reform in Russia', *Problems of Communism*, Vol. XLI, No. 3 (May–June 1992), pp. 107–21.
55 *Pravda*, 7 March 1990.
56 *Sovetskaya Rossiya*, 17 March 2001, p. 2.
57 *Monitor*, 5 January 2001.
58 Dariusz Rosati *et al.*, *Transition Countries in the First Quarter 1998: Widening Gap Between Fast and Slow Reformers*, Vienna Institute for Comparative Economic Studies, Research Report No. 248, Vienna, June 1998, p. 25.
59 Ruslan Grinberg, 'Desyat' let sistemnoi transformatsii', *Nezavismaya gazeta*, 22 December 1999, p. 4.
60 *OECD Economic Surveys*, p. iii.
61 Yeltin press conference, 21 August 1992.
62 Marshall I. Goldman, *Lost Opportunity: Why Economic Reforms in Russia Have not Worked* (London, Norton, 1995).
63 See Douglass North, *Institutions, Institutional Change, and Economic Performance* (Cambridge, Cambridge University Press, 1990), p. 1 and *passim*.
64 Peter Evans, *Embedded Autonomy: States and Industrial Transformation* (Princeton, Princeton University Press, 1995).
65 Jude Wanniski, 'The Future of Russian Capitalism', *Foreign Affairs*, Vol. 71, No. 2 (spring 1992), pp. 17–25, at p. 17.
66 *The Moscow Times*, 28 April 2001, p. 9.
67 *The Economist*, 13 May 2000, p. 146.

13 Society and social movements

1 Adam Smith, *The Wealth of Nations* (London, Penguin, 1970), p. 8.
2 Solzhenitsyn, *Rebuilding Russia*, p. 33.
3 *Soviet Weekly*, 24 October 1991, p. 5.
4 Solzhenitsyn, *Rebuilding Russia*, p. 33.
5 Barrington Moore, Jnr, *Social Origins of Dictatorship and Democracy: Lord and Peasant in the Making of the Modern World* (Harmondsworth, Peregrine, 1967), p. 418.
6 The Russian fertility rate is comparable to that in Estonia (1.44), Germany (1.39), Greece (1.35) and Italy (1.25), while in the former GDR it fell to 0.98 in 1991, Penny Morvant, 'Alarm over Falling Life Expectancy', *Transition*, 20 October 1995, p. 41.

7 In 1960, there were 23.2 births per thousand and 7.4 deaths per thousand, giving a natural growth of 15.8 per thousand, and the figure declined therafter; B.P. Pockney, *Soviet Statistics since 1950* (Aldershot, Dartmouth, 1991), p. 74.

8 *Nezavisimaya gazeta*, 26 January 1993, p. 1.

9 *Demograficheskii ezhegodnik RF, 1993* (Moscow, Goskomstat, 1994), p. 83; *Pravda*, 28 November 1995.

10 Report to State Duma on 17 November 2000 by Aleksandr Pochinok, Minister of Labour and Social Development, in Paul Goble, 'Compounding a Demographic Disaster', *Monitor*, 20 November 2000.

11 *Independent*, 9 November 1992. In 1991, the birth rate fell from 12.1 to 11.1 per thousand population, while the death rate increased from 11.4 to 11.9 per thousand; *Nezavisimaya gazeta*, 26 January 1992, p. 1.

12 *Rossiya v tsifrakh*, 2000, p. 70. Part of the reason for the peak is that in 1993 Russia adopted international standards of measurement.

13 *RFE/RL Newsline*, 8 January 2001.

14 For example, Vadim Pervyshin, 'Genotsid kak sistema', *Den'*, No. 36 (51) (6 September 1992), p. 3; see also Boris Khodov in *Pravda*, 30 March 1995. The theme is reflected in Stanislav Govorukhin's film of 1994, *The Russia that We Have Lost*.

15 *RFE/RL Newsline*, 22 June 2001; *Rossiya v tsifrakh*, 2000, p. 70.

16 Victoria Clark, *The Observer*, 26 November 1995, p. 26.

17 *Rossiya v tsifrakh*, 2000, p. 71.

18 *Monitor*, 5 January 2001.

19 *Komsomolskaya pravda*, 25 July 1995. Hungary still has the highest suicide rate out of eighty-four developed countries, but Russia now comes in third.

20 Figures from Dr Alexander Nemtsov, in *The Observer*, 26 November 1995, p. 26.

21 On the anti-alcohol campaign, see Stephen White, *Russia Goes Dry: Alcohol, State and Society* (Cambridge, Cambridge University Press, 1995).

22 Stephen White, 'Hangover Cure for the Bear with a Sore Head', *Times Higher Educational Supplement*, 28 July 1995, pp. 17, 19.

23 Stephen Castles and Mark J. Miller, *The Age of Migration: International Population Movements in the Modern World* (London, Macmillan, 1993).

24 For detailed studies, see Hilary Pilkington, *Migration, Displacement and Identity in Post-Soviet Russia* (London and New York, Routledge, 1998); V.A. Tishkov (ed.), *Vynuzhdennye migranty: integratsiya i vozvrashchenie* (Moscow, Institute of Ethnology and Anthropology, RAS, 1997).

25 See Benedict Anderson, *Imagined Communities: Reflections on the Origin and Spread of Nationalism* (London, Verso, 1983).

26 Konstantin Zatulin, 'We May not Ignore These Problems', *Delovoi mir*, 2 December 1995, p. 6.

27 *The Independent*, 19 April 1995, p. 8.

28 *OECD Economic Surveys*, p. 130.

29 *Rossiiskie vesti*, 5 May 1994, p. 4.

30 *Monitor*, 5 January 2001.

31 *Rossiya*, No. 19 (18–24 May 1994), p. 4.

32 *Izvestiya*, 9 July 1992, p. 3.

33 The Jamestown Foundation, *Prism*, June 2001.

34 Gaidar's report to parliament, 22 September 1992.

35 *Rossiiskaya gazeta*, 5 May 1994, p. 4.

36 *Independent*, 8 May 1992.

37 *Rezultaty sotsiologicheskogo issledovaniya 'Sotsial' no-aktivnye sily Rossii: usloviya i puti ikh konsolidatsii* (Moscow, Institut sotsial'nykh i politicheskikh tekhnologii, 1991), pp. 10–11.

38 This issue is discussed by several contributors in Murray Yanovitch (ed.), *New Directions in Soviet Social Thought* (New York, M.E. Sharpe, 1989).

39 A. Putko, *Soviet Weekly*, 5 December 1991, p. 4.

40 B.P. Pockney, *Soviet Statistics since 1950*, pp. 63, 67.

41 A study by the Economic Analysis Bureau, reported in *Finansovaya Rossii*, No. 4 (2001), cited in *RFE/RF Newsline*, 13 February 2001.

42 For a detailed sociological study of the differentiated outcomes, see L. Gordon and E. Klopov, *Poteri I obreteniya v Rossii 90-kh: istoriko-sotsiologicheskie ocherki ekonomicheskogo polozheniya narodnogo bol'shinstva*, Vol. 1, *Menyayushchayasya strana v menyayushchemsya mire: predposylki peremen v usloviyakh truda i urovnya zhizni* (Moscow, Editorial URSS, 2000).

43 *Rossiiskaya gazeta*, 12 July 2001.

44 Cf. Christopher M. Davies, 'Eastern Europe and the Former USSR: An Overview', *RFE/RL Research Report*, Vol. 2, No. 40 (8 October 1993), pp. 31–43.

45 Jamestown Foundation, *Russia's Week*, 11 July 2001.

46 S.A. Sidorenko, 'Moskovskie bezdomnye – pervye shagi v izuchenii problemy', *Ekonomicheskie i sotsial'nye peremeny: monitoring obshchestvennogo mneniya*, No. 4 (July–August 1995), p. 46.

47 Sheila Marnie, 'Economic Reform and the Social Safety Net', *RFE/RL Research Report*, Vol. 2, No. 17 (23 April 1993), p. 2.

48 Sheila Marnie, 'Economic Reform and the Social Safety Net', pp. 17–23.

49 Khasbulatov, *The Struggle for Russia*, p. 96.

50 *Soviet Weekly*, 3 October 1991, p. 7.

51 *Obshchaya gazeta*, 15 February 2001.

52 *Izvestiya*, 23 January 1996.

53 See Richard Rose, 'The Value of Fringe Benefits in Russia', *RFE/RL Research Report*, Vol. 3, No. 15 (15 April 1994), pp. 16–21.

54 Details of presidential decrees, governmental acts and laws on social policy are in *Sotsial'naya politika v Rossii: sbornik dokumentov* (Moscow, Respublika, 1992).

55 *RFE/RL Newsline*, 27 June 2001.

56 *Trud*, 5 January 2001; *RFE/RL Newsline*, 8 January 2001.

57 *Ekonomika i zhizn'*, No. 22, 1991.

58 *OMRI Daily Digest*, No. 19, Part I (26 January 1996).

59 *RFE/RL Newsline*, 25 June 2001.

60 *The Economist*, 20 November 1993, pp. 47–8.

61 *Rossiiskie vesti*, 5 May 1994, p. 4.

62 Alexander Shokhin, 'Labour Market Regulation in the USSR', *Communist Economies*, Vol. 3, No. 4 (1991), pp. 499–509, at p. 505.

63 *Vremya*, 19 March 2001, p. 1.

64 For details, see Sheila Marnie, 'How Prepared is Russia for Mass Unemployment?', *RFE/RL Research Report*, Vol. 1, No. 48 (4 December 1992), pp. 44–50; see also her 'Who and Where Are the Russian Unemployed?', ibid., Vol. 2, No. 33 (20 August 1993), pp. 36–42.

65 Linda J. Cook, *The Soviet Social Contract and Why it Failed: Welfare Policy and Workers' Politics from Brezhnev to Yeltsin* (Cambridge, MA, Harvard University Press, 1993).

66 See, for example, Russell Bova, 'Worker Activism: The Role of the State', Judith B. Sedaitis and Jim Butterfield (eds), *Perestroika from Below: Social Movements in the Soviet Union* (Boulder, Westview Press, 1991), pp. 29–42.

67 For details on each union, see *Kto est' chto: politicheskaya Moskva 1993* (Moscow, Catallaxy, 1993), pp. 501–624; *Kyo est' chto*, Vol. 2, *Profsoyuznye ob"edineniya i tsentry* (Moscow, 1994).

68 *Soviet Weekly*, 17 October 1991, p. 4.

69 Linda Cook, *Labor and Liberalization: Trade Unions in the New Russia* (New York, Twentieth Century Press, 1997).

70 Stephen Crowley, 'Barriers to Collective Action: Steelworkers and Mutual Dependence in the Former Soviet Union', *World Politics*, Vol. 46, No. 4 (July 1994), pp. 589–615.

71 For details, see Linda J. Cook, 'Russia's Labor Relations', in D.W. Blum (ed.), *Russia's Future* (Boulder, Westview, 1994), pp. 69–89.

72 See John Thirkell, Richard Scase and Sarah Vickerstaff (eds), *Labour Relations and Political Change in Eastern Europe: a Comparative Perspective* (London, UCL Press, 1995).

73 *Goskomstat*, 1999, p. 93.

74 Penny Morvant, 'The Beleaguered Coal-Mining Industry Strikes Back', *Transition*, 30 June 1995, pp. 56–61, 70.

75 See Bela Greskovits, *The Political Economy of Protest and Patience: East European and Latin American Transformations Compared* (Budapest, Central European University Press, 1998).

76 See Boris Kagarlitskii, 'Profsoyuzy stoyat pered vyborom', *Nezavisimaya gazeta*, 25 August 1994, p. 4.

77 The most influential were the Independent Miners' Union, Sotsprof, the Kuzbass Confederation of Labour, and the trade unions for dockers, sailors, pilots, air traffic controllers, and locomotive railway workers; Lyudmila Alekseeva, 'Nesvobodnye profsoyuzy', *Moskovskie novosti*, No. 3 (22 January 1995), p. 14.

78 See Matthew Wyman, *Public Opinion in Postcommunist Russia* (London, Macmillan, 1996), pp. 116–19.

79 For an analysis of the question, see E.B. Gruzdeva and E.S. Chertikhina, 'Polozhenie zhenshchiny v obshchestve: konflikt rolei', in *Obshchestvo v raznykh izmereniyakh: sotsiologi otvechayut na voprosy*, compiled by V.E. Gimpel'son and A.K. Nazimova (Moscow, Moskovskii rabochii, 1990), pp. 147–67.

80 Pockney, *Soviet Statistics since 1950*, pp. 48–9.

81 Pockney, *Soviet Statistics since 1950*, p. 47.

82 Grigorii Gendler and Marina Gildingersh, 'A Socioeconomic Portrait of the Unemployed in Russia', *RFE/RL Research Report*, Vol. 3, No. 3 (21 January 1994), p. 35.

83 *Rossiiskaya gazeta*, 18 February 1994.

84 Mikhail Gorbachev, *Perestroika: New Thinking for Our Country and the World* (London, Collins, 1987), p. 117.

85 See Penny Morvant, 'Bearing the "Double Burden" in Russia', *Transition*, 8 September 1995, pp. 4–9.

86 *RFE/RL Newsline*, 25 October 2000.

87 In 1970 the figure was thirty out of a hundred, and in 1980 forty; *Naselenie Rossii* (Moscow, Goskomstat, 1993).

88 Viktor Perevedentsev, *Moskovskie novosti*, No. 49 (5 December 1993), p. 6.

89 Valentina Bodrova, 'The Russian Family in Flux', *Transition*, 8 September 1995, pp. 10–11.

90 *Izvestiya*, 2 December 1993, p. 4.

91 Peter Lentini, 'Women and the 1989 Elections to the USSR Congress of People's Deputies', *Coexistence*, Vol. 31 (1994), pp. 1–28.

92 *Rossiiskaya gazeta*, 3 December 1992, p. 1; women comprised 8.9 per cent of the Supreme Soviet.

93 Wendy Slater, 'Female Representation in Russian Politics', *RFE/RL Research Report*, Vol. 3, No. 22 (3 June 1994), pp. 27–33.

94 S.V. Polenina, 'Zhenshchiny, vlast', demokratiya', *Byulleten' TsIK*, No. 1 (27) (1995), p. 15.

95 See Svetlana Aivazova, 'Zhenskoe dvizhenie v Rossii: traditsii i sovremennost'', *ONS*, No. 2 (1995), pp. 121–30.

96 *Nezavisimaya gazeta*, 12 January 1996, p. 2.

97 *Vek*, No. 15, 2000.

98 For an analysis of this, see Valerie Sperling, *Organizing Women in Contemporary Russia: Engendering Transition* (Cambridge, Cambridge University Press, 1999).

99 Cited in *Itogovyi otchet o rabote I nezavisimogo zhenskogo foruma* (Moscow, 1991), p. 7.

100 Elzbieta Matynia, 'Women After Communism: A Bitter Freedom', *Social Research*, Vol. 62, No. 2 (summer 1994), pp. 351–77.

101 Cf. Mira Marody, 'Why I am not a Feminist', *Social Research*, Vol. 60, No. 4 (winter 1993), pp. 853–64.

102 David Holloway, 'The Politics of Catastrophe', *The New York Review of Books*, 10 June 1993, p. 36.

103 Mark Popovskii, *Delo akademika Vavilova* (Moscow, Kniga, 1991).

104 Douglas Weiner, *Models of Nature: Ecology, Conservation, and Cultural Revolution in Soviet Russia* (Bloomington, Indiana University Press, 1988).

105 See Charles E. Ziegler, 'Environmental Politics and Policy under Perestroika', pp. 113–32.

106 *Soviet Weekly*, 31 October 1991, p. 4.

107 For more details see Georgii S. Golitsyn, 'Ecological Problems in the CIS During the Transitional Period', *RFE/RL Research Report*, Vol. 2, No. 2 (8 January 1993), pp. 33–46; on the Caspian Sea, *Izvestiya*, 11 December 1993, p. 15; on sunken nuclear reactors, *Independent*, 10 November 1993; and on whaling, *The Guardian*, 12 February 1994, p. 12.

108 *Soviet Weekly*, 31 October 1991, p. 4.

109 William Millinship, *Observer*, 31 May 1992, p. 49. For details of the crisis, see Murray Feshbach and Alfred Friendly, *Ecocide in the USSR: Health and Nature under Siege* (New York, Basic Books, 1992).

110 Divish Petrof, 'Siberian Forests under Threat', *The Ecologist*, Vol. 22, No. 6 (1992), pp. 267–70.

111 *Moscow News*, No. 6 (4 February 1993), p. 3.

112 See Zhores Medvedev, *The Legacy of Chernobyl* (Oxford, Blackwell, 1991); see also Piers Paul Reed, *Ablaze: The Story of the Heroes and Victims of Chernobyl* (New York, Random House, 1992).

113 See David R. Marples, 'Nuclear Power in the CIS: A Reappraisal', *RFE/RL Research Report*, Vol. 3, No. 22 (3 June 1994), pp. 21–6.

114 *Independent*, 25 January 1992.

115 Cf. Jeremy Russell, *Energy and Environmental Conflicts in East/Central Europe: The Case of Power Generation* (London, RIIA/World Conservation Union, 1991).

116 *The Observer*, 26 March 1995, p. 1.

117 Cf. Duncan Fisher, *Paradise Deferred: Environmental Policymaking in Central and Eastern Europe* (London, RIIA/Ecological Studies Institute, 1992).

118 *Vedemosti S"ezda narodnykh deputatov Rossiiskoi Federatsii i Verkhovhogo Soveta Rossiiskoi federatsii*, No. 10 (5 March 1992), pp. 592–630.

119 D.J. Peterson, 'The Environment in the Post-Soviet Era', *RFE/RL Research Report*, Vol. 2, No. 2 (8 January 1993), pp. 43–6.

120 *Russian Conservation News*, No. 3 (May 1995), p. 4. As of 30 March 1995, Russia had eighty-nine *Zapovedniki* covering a total area of 29.1 million hectares (1.42 per cent of Russia's territory), and twenty-nine National Parks, covering 6.6 million hectares, or 0.38 per cent of the Federation, with the final total expected to settle at about a hundred; ibid., p. 11.

121 Cf. M. Waller and F. Millard, 'Environmental Politics in Eastern Europe', *Environmental Politics*, Vol. 2 (1992), p. 171.

14 Cultural transformation

1 Alexei Podberezkin, leader of the 'Spiritual Heritage' movement, quoted by Eric Black, 'Russia's Heritage Sets it Apart', *Star Tribune*, 29 October 1999, in Johnson's Russia List, No. 3595/6.

2 For a discussion of the re-evaluation of history, see R.W. Davies, *Soviet History in the Gorbachev Revolution* (Basingstoke, Macmillan, 1989); the story is taken further in his *Soviet History in the Yeltsin Era* (Basingstoke, Macmillan, 1997).

3 *Soviet Weekly*, 10 October 1991, p. 3.

4 *Rossiiskaya gazeta*, 8 February 1992, pp. 3–4.

5 *RFE/RL Newsline*, 15 June 2001.

6 *Partiinaya zhizn'*, No. 18 (September 1991), p. 3.

7 Stjepan G. Mestrovic, 'Series Editor's Statement', in Joseph Gibbs, *Gorbachev's Glasnost: The Soviet Media in the First Phase of Perestroika* (College Station, Texas A & M University Press, 1999), p. x.

8 *RFE/RL Newsline*, 26 January 2001.

9 *http://www.scrf.gov.ru/*

10 Rosalind Marsh, 'The Death of Soviet Literature: Can Russian Literature Survive?', *Europe-Asia Studies*, Vol. 45, No. 1 (1993), pp. 115–39.

11 *Rossiiskaya gazeta*, 29 October 1991, p. 2.

12 For a discussion of plans, see *Nezavisimaya gazeta*, 28 June 2001, p. 8.

13 *Literaturnaya gazeta*, 22 July 1992, p. 5.

14 On the role of the intelligentsia from a different perspective, see K.G. Barbakova and V.A. Mansurov, *Intelligentsiya i vlast'* (Moscow, Institute of Sociology, 1991).

15 *Guardian*, 3 December 1992.

16 This was the view of Kozyrev, *Izvestiya*, 30 June 1992.

17 *Rossiya*, No. 1 (9), (4–10 January 1991), p. 1.

18 *Religion in Communist Dominated Areas*, 30, 1 (1991), p. 9.

19 John B. Dunlop, 'KGB Subversion of Russian Orthodox Church', *RFE/RL Research Report*, Vol. 1, No. 12 (20 March 1992), pp. 51–3; Oxana Antic, 'Orthodox Church Reacts to Criticism of KGB Links', *RFE/RL Research Report*, Vol. 1, No. 23 (5 June 1992), pp. 61–3.

20 See Edwin Bacon, 'Religion and Politics in Russia', in Mike Bowker and Cameron Ross (eds), *Russia After the Cold War* (Harlow, Longman, 2000), pp. 185–98, at p. 188.

21 Deacon Andrei Kurayev, *Moscow News*, No. 7 (11 February 1993), p. 11.

22 *RFE/RL Newsline*, 30 May 2001.

23 According to Mikhail Tul'skii (*Nezavisimaya gazeta – religii*, April 2001), there were 10,913 Orthodox congregations, 3,048 Muslim groups, 197 Jewish communities and 193 Buddhist temples. The growth of Protestant groups was marked, with 2,910 Evangelical churches, 330 Jehovah's Witness groups, 213 Presbyterian congregations and 476 other communities. In addition, there were 106 registered Hare Krishna groups, twenty Bahai communities and seventeen Unification Church branches.

24 Max Weber, *The Protestant Ethic and the Spirit of Capitalism* (London, Allen & Unwin, 1976); R.H. Tawney, *Religion and the Rise of Capitalism* (London, Pelican, 1938).

25 See Harry Eckstein, Frederic J. Fleron Jnr, Erik P. Hoffmann and William M. Reissinger, *Can Democracy Take Root in Post-Soviet Russia? Explorations in State–Society Relations* (Lanham, MD, Rowman & Littlefield Publishers, Inc., 1998).

26 G.A. Almond and S. Verba, *The Civic Culture: Political Attitudes and Democracy in Five Nations* (Princeton, NJ, Princeton University Press, 1963); G.A. Almond and S. Verba (eds), *The Civic Culture Revisited* (Boston, Little, Brown, 1980); L.W. Pye and S. Verba (eds), *Political Culture and Political Development* (Princeton, NJ, Princeton University Press, 1965).

27 Nikolai Biryukov and V.M. Sergeev, *Russia's Road to Democracy: Parliament, Communism and Traditional Culture* (Aldershot, Edward Elgar, 1993); see also their *Russian Politics in Transition: Institutional Conflict in a Nascent Democracy* (Aldershot, Ashgate Publishing, 1997).

28 Alexander Lukin, *Political Culture of Russian Democrats* (Oxford, Oxford University Press, 1999), p. 298.

29 The classic example of this approach was the comparative analysis of the past and present of several communist countries in Archie Brown and Jack Gray (eds), *Political Culture and Change in Communist Systems* (London, Macmillan, 1977). See also Archie Brown (ed.), *Political Culture and Communist Studies* (London, Macmillan, 1984), and Stephen White, *Political Culture and Soviet Politics* (London, Macmillan, 1979).

30 Robert D. Putnam, *Making Democracy Work: Civic Traditions in Modern Italy* (Princeton, NJ, Princeton University Press, 1993).

31 See, for example, Sergei Pushkarev, *Self-Government and Freedom in Russia* (Boulder, CO, Westview Press, 1988); Nicolai N. Petro (ed.), *Christianity and Russian Culture in Soviet Society* (Boulder, CO, Westview Press, 1990).

32 Letter to the author, 18 November 1992. This is the core of his argument in Nicolai N. Petro, *The Rebirth of Russian Democracy: An Interpretation of Russian Political Culture* (Cambridge, MA, Harvard University Press, 1995).

33 J.R. Millar (ed.), *Politics, Work and Daily Life in the USSR* (Cambridge, Cambridge University Press, 1987).

34 Some 18,000 people were questioned in twenty-five regions of Russia, including a representative sample from Moscow, *Rezultaty sotsiologicheskogo issledovaniya 'Sotsial'no-aktivnye sily Rossii: usloviya i puti ikh konsolidatsii'* (Moscow, Institut sotsial'nykh i politicheskikh tekhnologii, 1991), p. 7.

35 *Rezultaty sotsiologicheskogo issledovaniya*, p. 12.

36 Study conducted by the Russian Independent Institute for Social and Nationality Problems, *Nezavisimaya gazeta*, 8 August 1992, p.2.

37 Weekly poll conducted by the independent Institute of the Sociology of Parliamentarianism, *Izvestiya*, 17 August 1992, p. 2.

38 This trend is reflected in numerous polls and traced in those conducted by the Media and Opinion Research (MOR) Department of the RFE/RL Research Institute: *RFE/RL Research Report*, Vol. 1, No. 19 (8 May 1992), pp. 57–8; No. 25 (19 June 1992), pp. 72–3; No. 41 (16 October 1992), pp. 64–5; Vol. 2, No. 3 (15 January 1993), pp. 42–4.

39 Jeffrey W. Hahn, 'Continuity and Change in Russian Political Culture', *British Journal of Political Science*, Vol. 21, pp. 393–412.

40 Some 70 per cent were in favour of strong government in November 1991, *Nezavisimaya gazeta*, 7 November 1991.

41 In February 1992, 33 per cent out of 1985 agreed that the market was 'our only salvation', whereas 20 per cent saw it as 'the cause of our destruction', and in the same poll 43 per cent saw more negative than positive in the transition, and only 22 per cent saw more positive, *Mir mnenii i mneniya o mire*, No. 8 (August 1992), pp. 4–5.

42 *Soviet Weekly*, 10 October 1991, p. 6.

43 Leonid Gordon and Natal'ya Pliskevich, 'Lyudi ustali ot nasiliya', *Nezavisimaya gazeta*, 7 December 1991, p. 2.

44 *Rezultaty sotsiologicheskogo issledovaniya*, op. cit., pp. 21–2.

45 For earlier discussions of social justice, see David S. Mason and Svetlana Sidorenko, 'Perestroika, Social Justice and Soviet Public Opinion', *Problems of Communism*, Vol. 34, No. 6 (November–December 1990), pp. 34–43.

46 *RFE/RL Research Report*, Vol. 1, No. 47 (27 October 1992), pp. 60–2.

47 Leonid Gordon and Natal'ya Pliskevich, 'Lyudi ustali ot nasiliya', *Nezavisimaya gazeta*, 7 December 1991, p. 2.

48 James Gibson, 'A Mile Wide but an Inch Deep? The Structure of Democratic Commitments in the Former USSR', *American Journal of Political Science*, Vol. 40, No. 2 (May 1996), pp. 396–420.

49 Leonid Sedov, *Nezavisimaya gazeta – Stsenarii*, No. 5, 2000.

50 For a report on a detailed survey of the question, see *Izvestiya*, 30 June 2001, p. 4.

51 William L. Miller, Stephen White and Paul Heywood, *Values and Political Change in Postcommunist Europe* (Basingstoke, Macmillan, 1998), p. 28.

52 Timothy J. Colton and Michael McFaul, *Are Russians Undemocratic?* (Carnegie Endowment for International Peace, Russian Domestics Politics Project, Russian and Eurasian Program, Working Paper No. 20, June 2001), p. 8.

53 Ibid., p. 11.

54 Ibid., pp. 15–16.

55 Ibid., p. 22.

56 Alexander Zinoviev, *The Yawning Heights* (Harmondsworth, Penguin, 1981), p. 621.

57 *Soviet Weekly*, 19 September 1991, p. 4.

58 This is one of the questions posed by Karl Marx, and paradoxically the fall of communism might well have made his analysis, if not his solutions, more relevant to Russian society than before.

Part V Foreign policies

1 *Trud*, 11 January 2001.
2 *Medium-Term Strategy for the Development of Relations between the RF and the EU (2000–2010)*, mimeo 1999, point 1.1.

15 Foreign policy

1 G.P. Fedotov, *Russia, Europe and Us: Collected Essays*, Vol. 2 (Paris, YMCA Press, 1973), p. 232.
2 A.V. Kozyrev, 'Vneshnyaya politika preobrazhayushcheisya Rossii', *Voprosy istorii*, No. 1 (1994), p. 4.
3 Boris Pankin, *The Last Hundred Days of the Soviet Union* (London, I.B. Tauris, 1996), p. 104.
4 Suzanne Crow, 'Personnel Changes in the Russian Foreign Ministry', *RFE/RL Research Report*, Vol. 1, No. 16 (17 April 1992), pp. 18–22, at p. 18.
5 Cited in Kozyrev, 'Vneshnyaya politika', p. 6.
6 Andrei Kozyrev, 'Russia: A Chance of Survival', *Foreign Affairs* (spring 1992), pp. 1–16, at p. 4.
7 For example, *Izvestiya*, 30 June 1992.
8 Pavel Baev, *The Russian Army in a Time of Trouble* (London, Sage, 1996).
9 *Nezavisimaya gazeta*, 28 March 1992. Andranik Migranyan later claimed to have redis-covered the notion of the Monroe Doctrine for Russia, 'Russia and the Near Abroad', *Nezavisimaya gazeta*, 12 January 1994.
10 'A Strategy for Russia', *Nezavisimaya gazeta*, 19 August 1992, p. 4.
11 Suzanne Crow, 'Russia Seeks Leadership in Regional Peacekeeping', *RFE/RL Research Report*, Vol. 2, No. 15 (9 April 1993).
12 Kozyrev, 'Vneshnyaya politika', p. 3.
13 *Izvestiya*, 8 October 1993.
14 See Andrei Kozyrev, 'Partnership or Cold Peace?', *Foreign Policy*, No. 99 (summer 1995), pp. 3–14.
15 For example, Andranik Migranyan, *Nezavisimaya gazeta*, 10 December 1994.
16 *Moskovskie novosti*, No. 63 (11–18 December 1994), pp. 4, 6.
17 *Izvestiya*, 10 February 1996, p. 3.
18 *Independent*, 13 January 1996, p. 9.
19 *RFE/RL Newsline*, 27 March 2000.
20 http://www.mid.ru/mid/eng/econcept.htm, in English.
21 http://www.president.kremlin.ru/events/145.html
22 *Soviet Weekly*, 26 September 1991, p. 6.
23 *Diplomaticheskii vestnik*, No. 16 (31 March 1992).
24 *Rossiiskaya gazeta*, 31 March 1995, p. 5.
25 Konstantin Eggert, *Izvestiya*, 16 December 1995, p. 3.
26 *Izvestiya*, 30 June 1992.
27 *Nezavisimaya gazeta*, 27 May 1994, p. 5.
28 Cited in Suzanne Crow, 'Russia Prepares to Take a Hard Line on "Near Abroad"', *RFE/RL Research Report*, Vol. 1, No. 32 (1992), pp. 21–4.
29 *Nezavisimaya gazeta*, 19 August 1992, p. 4.
30 *Nezavisimaya gazeta*, 27 May 1994, pp. 4–5.
31 *Nezavisimaya gazeta*, 27 May 1994, p. 4.
32 Cf. the testimony of the former deputy foreign minister from October 1991 to October 1992, Fedor Shelov-Kovedyaev, *Segodnya*, 31 August 1993.
33 *Moscow News*, No. 37 (10 September 1993), p. 7.
34 Konstantin Eggert, *Izvestiya*, 16 December 1995, p. 3.
35 Vladimir Zubok, 'Tyranny of the Weak: Russia's New Foreign Policy', *World Policy Journal*, Vol. IX, No. 2 (spring 1992), pp. 191–218.
36 *Moscow News*, No. 52 (31 December 1993), p. 1.
37 *Pravda*, 29 June–2 July 2001, p. 3.

38 Cf. V.P. Lukin, 'Rossiya i ee interesy', *Diplomaticheskii vestnik*, No. 21–2 (15–30 November 1992), pp. 48–53.
39 Sergei Stankevich, *Nezavisimaya gazeta*, 28 March 1992, p. 4.
40 Cf. Elgiz Pozdnyakov, 'National, State, and Class Interests in International Relations', in *MEMO: New Soviet Voices on Foreign and Economic Policy*, edited by Steve Hirsch (Washington, DC, Bureau of National Affairs, 1989), pp. 471–90; originally in *MEMO*, No. 5 (May 1988).
41 For example, Sergei Goncharov, head of the Sino-Russian relations department at the Institute of the Far East, RAN, *Izvestiya*, 25 February 1992, p. 6.
42 Pozdnyakov, *Natsiya, natsionalizm, natsional'nye interesy*, p. 78.
43 Sergei Stankevich, 'A Power in Search of Itself', *Nezavisimaya gazeta*, 28 March 1992, p. 4. See also Alexander Rahr, 'Atlanticists versus Eurasians in Russian Foreign Policy', *RFE/RL Research Report*, Vol. 1, No. 22 (1992), pp. 17–22.
44 Tibor Szamuely, *The Russian Tradition* (London, Fontana, 1988), p. 10.
45 Szamuely, *The Russian Tradition*, p. 10.
46 Dmitrii Likhachev, *Reflections on Russia* (Boulder, Westview Press, 1991), p. 80.
47 See Elgiz Pozdnyakov, 'The Problem of Returning the Soviet Union to European Civilisation', *Paradigms: The Kent Journal of International Relations*, Vol. 5, Nos. 1/2 (1991), pp. 45–57. See also Milan Hauner, *What is Asia for Us? Russia's Asian Heartland Yesterday and Today* (London, Unwin Hyman, 1990); and Mark Bassin, 'Russia Between Europe and Asia: The Ideological Construction of Geographical Space', *Slavic Review*, Vol. 50, No. 1 (spring 1991), pp. 1–17.
48 Assen Ignatow, *Der "Eurasismus" und die Suche nach einer neuen russischen Kulturidentität. Die Neubelebung des "Jewrasijstwo"-Mythos* (Cologne, Berichte des BIOst 15, 1992).
49 Halford J. Mackinder, 'The Geographical Pivot of History', in his *Democratic Ideals and Reality* (New York, W.W. Norton & Co., 1962).
50 Cited in John M. Letiche and Basil Dmytryshyn, *Russian Statecraft: The Politika of Iurii Krizhanich* (Oxford, Basil Blackwell, 1985), p. 128.
51 Sergei N. Goncharov, 'Russia's Special Interests: What are They?', *Izvestiya*, 25 February 1992, p. 6.
52 P. Ya. Chaadaev, *Polnoe sobranie sochinenii i izbrannye pis'ma* (Moscow, Nauka, 1991), pp. 320–39.
53 Elgiz Pozdnyakov, 'Russia is a Great Power', *International Affairs* (Moscow), No. 1 (1993), pp. 3, 5.
54 Andrei Zagorsky, 'Russia and Europe', *International Affairs* (Moscow), No. 1 (1993), pp. 43–51.
55 *The Observer*, 10 September 1995, p. 23.
56 A point made already under Gorbachev by, for example, Jack Snyder, 'International Leverage on Soviet Domestic Change', *World Politics*, Vol. 42, No. 1 (1990), pp. 1–30.
57 For a general discussion of the 'democratic peace' hypothesis, see, *inter alia*, Michael Brown, Sean Lynn-Jones and Steven Miller (eds), *Debating the Democratic Peace* (Cambridge, MA, MIT Press, 1996); John Oneal and Bruce Russett, 'The Classical Liberals were Right: Democracy, Interdependence and Conflict, 1950–1985', *International Studies Quarterly*, Vol. 41, No. 2 (1997), pp. 267–94; Randall Schweller, 'Domestic Structure and Preventive War: Are Democracies More Pacific?', *World Politics*, Vol. 44, No. 2, pp. 235–69.
58 The link between democratisation and war was suggested by E. Mansfield and J. Snyder, 'Democratization and the Danger of War', *International Security*, Vol. 20, No. 1 (1995), pp. 26–31. It was challenged by Neil Malcolm and Alex Pravda, 'Democratization and Russian Foreign Policy', *International Affairs*, Vol. 72, No. 3 (1996), pp. 537–52. See also B.F. Braumoeller, 'Deadly Doves: Liberal Nationalism and the Democratic Peace in the Soviet Successor States', *International Studies Quarterly*, Vol. 41 (1997), pp. 375–402; Michael McFaul, 'A Precarious Peace: Domestic Politics in the Making of Russian Foreign Policy', *International Security*, Vol. 22, No. 3 (1998), pp. 5–35. Snyder develops his argument in his *From Voting to Violence: Democratization and Nationalist Conflict* (New York, W.W. Norton, 2000).

59 *Literaturnaya gazeta*, 13 September 1995, cited in *Transition*, 3 November 1995, p. 68.
60 The question is discussed by Aleksei Podberezkin, 'Problemy global'nogo mira: vzglyad sleva', *NG-Stsenarii*, No. 5 (61), 16 May 2001, pp. 9, 13.
61 *Independent*, 18 June 1992.
62 For example, Stephen F. Cohen, *Failed Crusade: America and the Tragedy of Post-Communist Russia* (New York, W.W. Norton, 2000).
63 *Frankfurter Allgemeine Zeitung*, 31 July 1998, cited in *The Guardian*, 15 April 1999, p. 19.
64 *Russkaya mysl'*, 19 April 1991.
65 *The Independent*, 18 March 1995.
66 *The Independent*, 16 February 1995.
67 *RFE/RL Newsline*, 3 July 2001.
68 *The Common Strategy of the EU on Russia*, 4 June 1999, at http://europa.eu.int/council/off/conclu/June 1999/annexe_en.htm#a2. The Madrid European Council of December 1995 had commissioned the *European Action Plan for Russia* of May 1996 (*Bulletin of the European Union*, No. 5 (1996)) that had already outlined five priorities for Russia–EU relations: the promotion of Russia's democratic reforms, economic co-operation, co-operation in the areas of justice and home affairs, security in Europe, and foreign policy.
69 These four points are discussed in Hannes Adomeit *et al.*, *Russia's Futures: Assessment of the CPN Russia Team as of February 2000* (Brussels, Conflict Prevention Network (CPN), 2000), pp. 14–15.
70 For further details, see Jackie Gower, 'Russia and the European Union', in Mark Webber (ed.), *Russia and Europe: Conflict and Cooperation* (Basingstoke, Macmillan, 2000), pp. 66–98.
71 *Nezavisimaya gazeta*, 20 August 1992, p. 4.
72 Watanabe Koji, 'Introduction', in W. Koji (ed.), *Engaging Russia in Asia Pacific (Tokyo, Japan Center for International Exchange*, 1999), p. 13.
73 Zbigniew Brzezinski, *The Grand Chessboard: American Primacy and Its Geostrategic Imperatives* (New York, Basic Books, 1997).
74 Akino Yutaka, 'Welcome for a New Russia', in Koji (ed.), *Engaging Russia*, p. 162.
75 V.I. Lenin, *Polnoe sobranie sochinenii*, 5th edn (Moscow, 1958–70), Vol. 30, p. 236.
76 See Millan Hauner, *What is Asia for Us? Russia's Asian Heartland Yesterday and Today* (London, Unwin Hyman, 1990).
77 *Russkaya mysl'*, 19 April 1991.
78 See E. Valkenier, *The Soviet Union and the Third World: The Economic Bind* (New York, Praeger, 1983); J.F. Hough, *The Struggle for the Third World: Soviet Debates and American Options* (Washington, DC, Brookings, 1986).
79 Solzhenitsyn, *Rebuilding Russia*, p. 27.
80 *Nezavisimaya gazeta*, 1 April 1992, p. 3.

16 Commonwealth, community and fragmentation

1 Elie Kedourie, *Nationalism*, 4th edn (Oxford, Blackwell, 1993), p. xvii.
2 For an overview, see Richard Sakwa and Mark Webber, 'The Commonwealth of Independent States, 1991–1998: Stagnation and Survival', *Europe-Asia Studies*, Vol. 51, No. 3 (May 1999), pp. 379–415.
3 *Pravda*, 27 November 1991.
4 The Alma Ata agreements of 21 December are in *Rossiiskaya gazeta*, 24 December 1991, p. 1.
5 Mikhail Gorbachev, 'Mir na perelome', *Svobodnaya mysl'*, No. 16 (1992), pp. 3–18, at p. 9.
6 M.A. Khrustalev, 'Evolyutsiya SNG i vneshnepoliticheskaya strategiya Rossii', *Diplomaticheskii vestnik*, No. 21–2 (15–30 November 1992), pp. 31–3.
7 Andrei Zagorskii *et al.*, *The Commonwealth of Independent States: Developments and Prospects* (Moscow, Centre for International Studies, MGIMO, 1992), p. 6.
8 See Andrei Zagorskii, *SNG: ot dezintegratsii k reintegratsii?* (Moscow, MGIMO, 1994).

9 *Literaturnaya gazeta*, 19 August 1992, p. 11.

10 *Nezavisimaya gazeta*, 18 August 1992, p. 2. Gorbachev remained consistent in this view, developed at length in his *Dekabr'-91: moya pozitsiya* (Moscow, Novosti, 1992).

11 Alexei Malashenko, 'Rossiya i islam', *Nezavisimaya gazeta*, 22 February 1992, p. 3.

12 *Nezavisimaya gazeta*, 9 October 1992, p. 3.

13 Andrei Zagorskii, 'Reintegration in the Former USSR?', *Aussenpolitik*, No. 3 (1994), pp. 263–72.

14 *Nezavisimaya gazeta*, 17 May 2001, p. 5.

15 Robert Cottrell, 'In Search of a Policy', *Financial Times*, 21 February 2001.

16 *Nezavisimaya gazeta*, 1 September 1992.

17 Suzanne Crow, 'Russia's Relations with Members of the Commonwealth', *RFE/RL Research Report*, Vol. 1, No. 19 (8 May 1992), pp. 8–12, at p. 11.

18 *Rossiiskaya gazeta*, 23 September 1995, p. 4.

19 Survey conducted by the 'Obshchestvennoe mnenie' agency, reported in *Sovetskaya Rossiya*, 17 March 2001, p. 1.

20 *Nezavisimaya gazeta*, 19 August 1992; Suzanne Crow, 'Competing Blueprints for Russian Foreign Policy', *RFE/RL Research Report*, Vol. 1, No. 50 (18 December 1992), pp. 48–9.

21 Andrei Zagorskii *et al.*, *After the Disintegration of the Soviet Union: Russia in a New World* (Moscow, MGIMO, February 1992).

22 C. Macartney, *National States and National Minorities* (London, Oxford University Press, 1934), p. 275 and *passim*. See also Hugh Miall (ed.), *Minority Rights in Europe* (London, Pinter, 1994).

23 *Nezavisimaya gazeta*, 28 June 2001, pp. 1, 5.

24 Andrei Kozyrev, 'Peace with a Sword', *Moscow News*, No. 36 (9–15 September 1994).

25 Suzanne Crow, 'The Theory and Practice of Peacekeeping in the Former USSR', *RFE/RL Research Report*, Vol. 1, No. 37 (18 September 1992).

26 The text is in Stephen Foye, 'The Soviet Legacy', *RFE/RL Research Report*, Vol. 2, No. 25 (18 June 1993), pp. 4–5.

27 Pavel Baev, 'Russia's Experiments and Experience in Conflict Management and Peacemaking', *International Peacekeeping*, Vol. 1, No. 3 (Autumn 1994).

28 *Segodnya*, 25 December 1993, p. 1.

29 A development examined by Dmitrii Trenin, 'Collective Security and Collective Defence', *Nezavisimaya gazeta*, 4 November 1994.

30 See, for example, General V.M. Barynkin, 'Local Wars at the Present Stage', *Voennaya mysl'*, No. 6 (June 1994), pp. 7–11.

31 Yurii Afanas'ev and Len Karpinskii, *Moskovskie novosti*, No. 32 (7–14 May 1995).

32 For Gorbachev's views, see his *Soyuz mozhno bylo sokhranit'* (Moscow, izd. 'aprel'-85', 1995).

33 Neil Melvin, *Forging the New Russian Nation* (London, RIIA Discussion Paper 50, 1994), p. 3.

34 *Constitution of Ukraine*, adopted at the Fifth Session of the Verkhovna Rada of Ukraine on 28 June 1996, in *The Ukrainian Review*, Vol. 43, No. 4 (winter 1996), p. 4.

35 Ann Sheehy, 'The CIS: A Shaky Edifice', *RFE/RL Research Report*, Vol. 2, No. 1 (1 January 1993), p. 39.

36 See Chauncy D. Harris, 'The New Russian Minorities: A Statistical Overview', *Post-Soviet Geography*, Vol. 34, No. 1 (1993), pp. 1–27.

37 Melvin, *Forging the New Russian Nation*, p. 3.

38 *Rossiiskaya gazeta*, 29 October 1991, p. 2.

39 For a good analysis of the 'Russians abroad' issue, see the Gorbachev Foundation's report, *Nezavisimaya gazeta*, 7 September 1993.

40 Emil Pain, 'Russia and the Post-Soviet Space', *Moscow News*, No. 8 (25 February–3 March 1994).

41 Speech of 29 April 1995, *OMRI Daily Digest*, No. 85, Part I, 2 May 1995.

42 *The Independent*, 19 April 1995, p. 8.

17 Defence and security policy

1 Osip Mandelstam, cited by Vasily Grossman, *Life and Fate* (London, The Harvill Press, 1995), p. 267.

2 Paul Hirst, 'The State, Civil Society and the Collapse of Soviet Communism', *Economy and Society*, Vol. 20, No. 2, pp. 217–42. For a discussion of the size of the defence sector, see *Kommunist*, No. 1 (1991), pp. 54–64.

3 William E. Odom, *The Collapse of the Soviet Military* (New Haven, CT, Yale University Press, 1998), Chapter 16.

4 For a discussion of the army's ambiguous legal status at this time, see *Nezavisimaya gazeta*, 2 February 1992, p. 1.

5 *Soviet Weekly*, 19 September 1991, p. 2.

6 Shaposhnikov observed 'I am a citizen of Russia…whom do I serve if not Russia? But it is Russia whose vital interests are conjugated with the interests of the other CIS nations'; *Moscow News*, No. 6 (4 February 1993), p. 4.

7 *Izvestiya*, 3 July 1992, pp. 1–2.

8 *RFE/RL Research Report*, Vol. 1, No. 42 (23 October 1992), p. 41.

9 The defence minister, Konstantin Morozov, argued that the decision was prompted by Moscow's refusal to release around 20,000 officers of Ukrainian origin serving outside the republic who had asked to return to serve in Ukraine's armed forces; *Independent*, 8 June 1992.

10 *The Military Balance 1994–1995* (London, Brasseys for The International Institute for Strategic Studies, 1994), p. 104.

11 Cf. Adrian Karatnycky, 'The Ukrainian Factor', *Foreign Affairs*, Vol. 71, No. 3 (summer 1992), p. 94.

12 For details, see Douglas L. Clarke, 'Implementing the CFE Treaty', *RFE/RL Research Report*, Vol. 1, No. 23 (5 June 1992), pp. 50–5.

13 *The Military Balance 1994–1995*, p. 108.

14 Cf. Douglas L. Clarke, 'The Russian Military and the CFE Treaty', *RFE/RL Research Report*, Vol. 2, No. 42 (22 October 1993), pp. 38–43.

15 *Krasnaya zvezda*, 9 May 1992.

16 *Moscow News*, No. 7 (11 February 1993), p. 3.

17 *Krasnaya zvezda*, 17 February 1993, p. 1.

18 Dzintra Bungs, 'Soviet Troops in Latvia' *RFE/RL Research Report*, Vol. 1, No. 34 (28 August 1992), pp. 18–28.

19 Stephen Foye, 'Russia's Defense Establishment in Disarray', *RFE/RL Research Report*, Vol. 2, No. 36 (10 September 1993), pp. 49–54.

20 *RFE/RL Research Report*, Vol. 1, No. 31 (31 July 1992), p. 61.

21 *The Military Balance 1994–1995*, p. 109.

22 *Nezavisimaya gazeta*, 21 February 2001.

23 *Pravda*, 8 December 1988.

24 Estimates range as high as 15 million; Keith Bush, 'Conversion and Employment in Russia', *RFE/RL Research Report*, Vol. 2, No. 2 (8 January 1993), p. 30; Brenda Hoorigan, 'How Many People Worked in the Soviet Defence Industry?', *RFE/RL Research Report*, Vol. 1, No. 33 (21 August 1992), pp. 33–9.

25 *Rossiiskie vesti*, 22 May 1992.

26 Julian Cooper, *The Soviet Defence Industry: Conversion and Reform* (London, RIIA/Pinter, 1991), pp. 10–11, 14.

27 Keith Bush, 'Russia's Latest Program for Military Conversion', *RFE/RL Research Report*, Vol. 1, No. 35 (4 September 1992), pp. 32–5, at p. 33.

28 See V.N. Tsygichko, 'Geopolitical Aspects of Shaping Russia's Nuclear Policy', *Military Thought/Voennaya Mysl'*, No. 3 (March 1994), pp. 2–9.

29 According to one report the Soviet nuclear arsenal included 45,000 warheads at its peak in 1986, 12,000 more than had been thought; *The Independent*, 27 September 1993.

30 Stephen Van Evera, 'Managing the Eastern Crisis: Preventing War in the Former Soviet Empire', *Security Studies*, Vol. 1, No. 3 (spring 1992).

31 Bohdan Nahaylo, 'The Shaping of Ukrainian Attitudes towards Nuclear Arms', *RFE/RL Research Report*, Vol. 2, No. 8 (19 February 1993), pp. 21–33.
32 *Nezavisimaya gazeta*, 7 December 1991, p. 1.
33 See John W.R. Lepingwell, 'Ukraine, Russia, and the Control of Nuclear Weapons', *RFE/RL Research Report*, Vol. 2, No. 8 (19 February 1993), pp. 4–20.
34 In his book, *Poslednii brosok na yug* (Moscow, Svetoton, 1994), Zhirinovskii argued that Russia's arrival on the shores of the Indian Ocean and the Mediterranean would signal the salvation of the Russian nation, removing the threat to Russia from the South forever.
35 *Segodnya*, 18 July 1995, p. 3.
36 *Nezavisimaya gazeta*, 20 February 2001.
37 *Moscow News*, No. 30 (1990), p. 11.
38 *Independent*, 12 May 1992.
39 Anne White, *Democratization in Russia under Gorbachev 1985–91: The Birth of a Voluntary Sector* (Basingstoke, Macmillan, 1999), p. 123.
40 For a debate over the issue, see *Trud*, 27 March 1991.
41 *The Military Balance 1994–1995*, p. 109.
42 *Vek*, 23 February 2001.
43 *Izvestiya*, 25 June 2001.
44 For example, V.K. Demedyuk and Yu. S. Kortunenko, 'On Organizational Structure of the Armed Forces', *Military Thought/Voennaya mysl'*, No. 5 (May 1994), pp. 2–6, who had defended a separate ADF.
45 Douglas L. Clarke, 'Rusting Fleet Renews Debate on Navy's Mission', *RFE/RL Research Report*, Vol. 2, No. 25 (18 June 1993), p. 30.
46 Sergei Parkhomenko, *Segodnya*, 19 November 1994.
47 Chris Donnelly, 'Civil–Military Relations in the New Democracies', in David Betz and John Löwenhardt (eds), 'Army and State in Postcommunist Europe', special issue of *The Journal of Communist Studies and Transition Politics*, Vol. 17, No. 1, March 2001, p. 9.
48 'Evolutionary Problems in the Former Soviet Armed Forces', *Survival*, Autumn 1992, p. 37.
49 *Moscow News*, No. 5 (28 January 1993), p. 4.
50 For Yeltsin's vivid depiction of these events, see his *Zapiski prezidenta*, pp. 382–7.
51 *Independent*, 28 October 1995, p. 11.
52 *Independent*, 28 October 1995, p. 11.
53 Andrei Nikolaev, *Rossiya na perelome* (Moscow, Sovremennyi pisatel', 1999).
54 Stephen Foye, 'The Defense Ministry and the New Military "Opposition"', *RFE/RL Research Report*, Vol. 2, No. 20 (14 May 1993), pp. 68–73.
55 *Moscow News*, No. 7 (11 February 1992), p. 1.
56 *RFE/RL Research Report*, Vol. 1, No. 36 (11 September 1992), p. 72. According to unofficial figures, some 25,000 officers had been dismissed by the end of 1992 for disagreeing with the government; *Guardian*, 13 January 1993.
57 For a detailed analysis, see Sven Gunnar Simonsen, 'Marching to a Different Drum? Political Orientations and Nationalism in Russia's Armed Forces', in Betz and Löwenhardt (eds), op. cit., pp. 43–64.
58 *Moskovskie novosti*, No. 59 (3–10 September 1995), p. 7.
59 Pavel K. Baev, 'The Russian Armed Forces: Failed reform Attempts and Creeping Regionalization', in Betz and Löwenhardt (eds), op. cit., p. 23.
60 *Segodnya*, 5 August 1994; *Rossiiskaya gazeta*, 6 August 1994.
61 *Moscow News*, No. 5 (28 January 1993), p. 4.
62 Scott McMichael, 'Russia's New Military Doctrine', *RFE/RL Research Report*, Vol. 1, No. 40 (9 October 1992), p. 45. For a fascinating discussion of Soviet military doctrine, see A.A. Kokoshin, *Armiya I politika: Sovetskaya voenno-politicheskaya i voenno-strategichsekaya mysl', 1918–1991* (Moscow, Mezhdunarodnye otnosheniya, 1995).
63 The draft was published in a special issue of *Voennaya mysl'*, May 1992.
64 The document was discussed by the Security Council on 3 March and 6 October 1993, and accepted at its session of 2 November, on which date the president decreed its

adoption, 'Osnovnye polozheniya voennoi doktriny Rossiiskoi Federatsii', special issue of *Voennaya mysl'*, November 1993, also in *Izvestiya*, 18 November 1993.
65 Ibid., p. 4.
66 Both are available at the Security Council's website: www.scrf.gov.ru/documents.
67 Andrei Zagorskii, 'Khel'sinki: budushchee v tumane', *Moskovskie novosti*, No. 13 (29 March 1991), p. 5.
68 See Donald D. Asmus *et al.*, 'NATO Expansion: The Next Steps', *Survival*, Vol. 37, No. 1 (spring 1995).
69 For a concise overview, see Caroline Kennedy-Pipe, 'Russia and the North Atlantic Treaty Organization', in Mark Webber (ed.), *Russia and Europe: Conflict or Cooperation?* (Basingstoke, Macmillan, 2000), pp. 46–65.
70 For a discussion of the issues, see *Transition*, 15 December 1995, pp. 5–43.
71 Kozyrev, 'Partnership or Cold Peace?, p. 13.
72 *Soviet Weekly*, 31 October 1991, p. 4.
73 *Izvestiya*, 6 September 1994.
74 *RFE/RL Newsline*, 3 July 2001.
75 For details, see J.L. Black, *NATO Expansion: Bearing Gifts or Bearing Arms?* (Lanham, Rowman & Littlefield, 2000).
76 The Basic Document of the EAPC, adopted at Sintra, Portugal, on 30 May 1997, is in *Nato Review*, No. 4 (July–August 1997), special insert.
77 *NATO Review*, No. 3 (May 1995), p. 5.
78 'Founding Act on Mutual Relations, Cooperation and Security between NATO and the Russian Federation', *NATO Review*, Vol. 45, No. 4 (1997), special insert, pp. 7–10.
79 Andrei Zagorski, 'Great Expectations', *NATO Review*, Vol. 49 (spring 2001), pp. 24–7, at p. 25.
80 The impact of enlargement on Russian domestic opinion is discussed extensively by Black, *NATO Expansion*.
81 *Nezavisimaya gazeta*, 3 February 1995; see also the CFDP's theses on how Russia should respond to Nato expansion, *Nezavisimaya gazeta*, 21 June 1995, reproduced in *Transition*, 15 December 1995, pp. 27–32.
82 *Russkaya mysl'*, No. 4,062 (26 January–1 February 1995), p. 20.
83 Benjamin S. Lambeth, 'Russia's Wounded Military', *Foreign Affairs*, Vol. 74, No. 2 (March/April 1995), pp. 86–7.
84 Pavel Baev, letter to the author, 23 March 1993.
85 *Nezavisimaya gazeta*, 19 August 1992.

18 Problems of transition

1 Vladimir Putin meeting with representatives of non-governmental organisations on 12 June 2001, at which he noted that many had 'a more effective influence on society than do political parties'; *RFE/RL Newsline*, 13 June 2001.
2 'The Case of the Russian Archives: An Interview with Iurii N. Afanas'ev', *Slavic Review*, Vol. 52, No. 2 (summer 1993), p. 315.
3 For an evaluation of Western 'Sovietology' see Michael Cox (ed.), *Rethinking Soviet Collapse: Sovietology, the Death of Communism and the New Russia* (London and New York, Pinter, 1998).
4 Paul Kennedy, *The Rise and Fall of the Great Powers: Economic Change and Military Conflict from 1500 to 2000* (London, Unwin Hyman, 1988).
5 Philip G. Roeder, *Red Sunset: The Failure of Soviet Politics* (Princeton, NJ, Princeton University Press, 1993).
6 For a defence of the concept of totalitarianism, see William E. Odom, 'Soviet Politics and After: Old and New Concepts', *World Politics*, Vol. 45, No. 1 (1992), pp. 66–98; and for the view that the so-called 'totalitarianism' versus 'pluralism' debate obscured as much as it revealed, George Breslauer, 'In Defense of Sovietology', *Post-Soviet Affairs*, Vol. 8, No. 3 (1992), pp. 197–238, esp. pp. 216–22.

7 Robert O. Crummey, 'Introduction', in Crummey (ed.), *Reform in Russia and the USSR: Past and Prospects* (Urbana, University of Illinois Press, 1989), p. 9.

8 Loc. cit.

9 See, for example, Ian Kershaw and Moshe Lewin (eds), *Stalinism and Nazism: Dictatorships in Comparison* (Cambridge, Cambridge University Press, 1997).

10 See, for example, Tim Mason, *Social Policy in the Third Reich: The Working Class and the National Community* (Providence, RI, Berg, 1993); and his *Nazism, Fascism and the Working Class* (Cambridge, Cambridge University Press, 1994). During the transition to NEP, as we have seen, Lenin, fearing for the stability of the regime, intensified the political dictatorship.

11 Ralf Dahrendorf, *Society and Democracy in Germany* (London, Weidenfeld & Nicolson, 1968), p. 342.

12 The problem of Russia's 'asocial subjectivity' and allied issues are discussed in my 'Subjectivity, Politics and Order in Russian Political Evolution', *Slavic Review*, Vol. 54, No. 4 (winter 1995), pp. 943–64.

13 For a discussion of history and time, see Robert C. Tucker, 'Kakoe vremya pokazyvayut seichas chasy Rossiiskoi istorii' ('What Time is it in Russia's History'), *Problemy vostochnoi evropy*, Nos. 31–2 (1991), pp. 58–78.

14 John Miller, *Mikhail Gorbachev and the End of Soviet Power* (London, Macmillan, 1993), p. 8.

15 *Political Archives of the Soviet Union*, Vol. 2, No 2 (1991), p. 119.

16 Petro, *The Rebirth of Russian Democracy*, Chapter 2.

17 N. Berdyaev *et al.*, *Vekhi: sbornik statei o Russkoi intelligentsii* (Moscow, 1909; reprinted Frankfurt, Posev, 1967).

18 Geoffrey Hosking, *The Russian Constitutional Experiment: Government and Duma, 1907–1914* (Cambridge, Cambridge University Press, 1973).

19 Richard Pipes, *Russian under the Old Regime* (London, Weidenfeld & Nicolson, 1974).

20 *Izvestiya*, 16 November 1993.

21 Peter Reddaway and Dmitri Glinski, *The Tragedy of Russia's Reforms: Market Bolshevism against Democracy* (Washington, DC, The United States Institute of Peace Press, 2001).

22 See, for example, Sergei Pushkarev, *Self-Government and Freedom in Russia* (Boulder, CO, Westview Press, 1988); Nicolai N. Petro (ed.), *Christianity and Russian Culture in Soviet Society* (Boulder, CO, Westview Press, 1990).

23 A.V. Obolenskii, 'Mekhanizm tormozheniya: chelovecheskoe izmerenie', *Sovetskoe gosudarstvo i pravo*, No. 1 (1990), pp. 80–7; see also his 'Russian Politics in the Time of Troubles', in Amin Saikal and William Maley (eds), *Russia in Search of its Future* (Cambridge, Cambridge University Press, 1995), pp. 12–27.

24 Petro, *The Rebirth of Russian Democracy*, pp. 2–3 and *passim*.

25 For example at the State Conference on 12–15 August 1917 in speeches by Georgi Plekhanov ('There can be no bourgeois revolution in which the bourgeoisie do not take part. There can be no capitalism in which there are no capitalists'), and Alexander Guchkov, a leader of the Octobrist Party, who urged the establishment of a strong government; *Moscow News*, No. 24 (16 June 1991), p. 9.

26 *Izvestiya*, 16 November 1993.

27 Alexander Yakovlev, 'Wake up Brother Russia', *Guardian*, 6 May 1992.

28 For recent assessments of 1917 in Russia, see Edward Acton, *Rethinking the Russian Revolution* (London, Edward Arnold, 1990); Edith Rogovin Frankel, Jonathen Frankel and Baruch Knei-Paz (eds), *Revolution in Russia: Reassessments of 1917* (Cambridge, Cambridge University Press, 1992). The best of recent analyses of the intelligentsia in revolution includes Jane Burbank, *Intelligentsia and Revolution: Russian Views of Bolshevism, 1917–1922* (Oxford, Oxford University Press, 1986); Christopher Read, *Culture and Power in Revolutionary Russia: The Intelligentsia and the Transition from Tsarism to Communism* (London, Macmillan, 1990).

29 For a discussion of the issue, see Luc Huyse, 'Justice After Transition: On the Choices Successor Elites Make in Dealing with the Past', *Law and Social Enquiry*, Vol. 20, No. 1 (winter 1995), pp. 51–78.

30 Solzhenitsyn, *Rebuilding Russia*, p. 29.
31 Gerd Ruge, *Der Putsch* (Frankfurt, Fischer, 1991), p. 153.
32 Gorbachev, *The August Coup*, p. 48.
33 *Zerkalo*, Vestnik Obshchestvennyi Komitet Rossiiskikh Reform, No. 2 (February 1992), pp. 1–2.
34 *Moscow News*, No. 5 (28 January 1993), p. 13.
35 See Tina Rosenberg, 'Overcoming the Legacies of Dictatorship', *Foreign Affairs*, Vol. 74, No. 3, May–June 1995, pp. 134–52.
36 Cf. Geoffrey Best, *War and Law Since 1945* (Oxford, Clarendon, 1994).
37 C. Charles Bertschi, 'Lustration and the Transition to Democracy: The Cases of Poland and Bulgaria', *East European Quarterly*, Vol. 28, No. 4 (January 1995), pp. 435–51.
38 Knight, *Spies Without Cloaks*, p. 204.
39 For the reasons why West Germany pursued the issue so aggressively in the East, see A. James McAdams, 'Reappraising the Conditions of Transitional Justice in Unified Germany' *East European Constitutional Review*, winter 2001, pp. 53–9.
40 Amos Elon, 'East Germany: Crime and Punishment', *The New York Review of Books*, 14 May 1992, pp. 6–11.
41 Peggy Morvant, 'Yakovlev on Communist Repression of Religion', *OMRI Daily Digest*, No. 230, Part I (28 November 1995).
42 See Vladimir Wozniuk, 'In Search of Ideology: The Politics of Religion and Nationalism in the New Russia (1991–1996)', *Nationalities Papers*, Vol. 25, No. 2 (1997), p. 201.
43 *Moscow News*, No. 5 (28 January 1993), p. 13.
44 Zdenek Mlynar, *Can Gorbachev Change the Soviet Union? The International Dimension of Political Reform* (Boulder, CO, Westview Press, 1990).
45 Francis Fukuyama, 'The End of History', *The National Interest* (summer 1989), pp. 3–17; *The End of History and the Last Man* (New York, Free Press, 1992).
46 For a discussion of mismodernisation, see Richard Sakwa, *Postcommunism* (Milton Keynes, Open University Press, 1999), pp. 24–5.
47 *Rossiiskaya gazeta*, 29 October 1991, p. 1.
48 Michel Foucault, 'The Politics of Health in the Eighteenth Century', in *Power/Knowledge: Selected Interviews and Other Writings, 1972–1977* (London, Harvester Wheatsheaf, 1980), edited by Colin Gordon, p. 171.
49 Seymour Martin Lipset, 'Some Social Requisites of Democracy', *American Political Science Review*, Vol. 53, No. 1 (March 1959), pp. 69–105; 'Economic Development and Democracy', in S.M. Lipset, *Political Man* (London, Mercury Books, 1963), pp. 45–76; 'The Social Requisites of Democracy Revisited', *American Sociological Review*, Vol. 59, No. 1 (February 1994), pp. 1–22; 'On the General Conditions for Democracy', in Lisa Anderson (ed.), *Transitions to Democracy* (New York, Columbia University Press, 1999).
50 Lucian W. Pye, 'Political Science and the Crisis of Authoritarianism', *American Political Science Review*, Vol. 84, No. 1 (March 1990), pp. 3–19.
51 For a sophisticated attempt to analyse the relationship between modernisation and political development, see Andrew C. Janos, 'Social Science, Communism, and the Dynamics of Political Change', *World Politics*, Vol. 44, No. 1 (October 1991), pp. 81–112.
52 See Boris Kapustin, *Sovremmenost' kak predmet politicheskoi teorii* (Moscow, Rosspen, 1998).
53 Dankwart Rustow, 'Democracy: A Global Revolution', *Foreign Affairs*, Vol. 69, No. 4 (fall 1990), p. 75.
54 Clifford G. Gaddy and Barry W. Ickes, 'Russia's Virtual Economy', *Foreign Affairs*, September–October 1998, pp. 53–67.
55 Karl Polanyi, *The Great Transformation: The Political and Economic Origins of our Times* (New York, Rinehart, 1944).
56 For a stimulating comparison of the governmental technologies of the Bolsheviks and the early modern police, see Agnes Horvath and Arpad Szakolczai, *The Dissolution of Communist Power: The Case of Hungary* (London, Routledge, 1992), especially Chapter 8.

57 Guillermo O'Donnell and Philippe Schmitter, *Transitions from Authoritarian Rule: Tentative Conclusions about Uncertain Democracies* (Baltimore, Johns Hopkins University Press, 1986).

58 For a classic example of the maturation argument, see Moshe Lewin, *The Gorbachev Phenomenon: A Historical Interpretation* (London, Hutchinson Radius, 1988).

59 Chris Brown, '"Really Existing Liberalism" and International Order', *Millenium*, Vol. 21, No. 3 (1992), pp. 313–28; see also his *International Relations Theory: New Normative Approaches* (Hemel Hempstead, Harvester Wheatsheaf, 1992).

60 Moore, *Social Origins of Dictatorship and Democracy*, p. 418.

61 For example, Charles Lindblom, *Politics and Markets* (New York, Basic Books, 1977); John Freeman, *Democracy and Markets* (Ithaca, NY, Cornell University Press, 1989).

62 For a stimulating discussion of the weakness of post-communist liberalism and its 'economistic' turn, see Jerzy Szacki, *Liberalism after Communism* (Budapest, Central European University Press, 1995).

63 For a challenging analysis of 'populist' and 'pluralist' definitions of democracy and the emergence of parliamentarianism in Russia, see Biryukov and Sergeev, *Russia's Road to Democracy*.

64 Samuel P. Huntington, *The Third Wave: Democratization in the Late Twentieth Century* (Norman, University of Oklahoma Press, 1991); see also his 'How Countries Democratize', *Political Science Quarterly*, Vol. 106, No. 4 (1991–2), pp. 579–616.

65 Samuel P. Huntington, 'After Twenty Years: The Future of the Third Wave', *Journal of Democracy*, Vol. 8, No. 1 (January 1997), pp. 111–26.

66 For a sustained analysis of methodological problems from a Russian perspective, see Andrei Yu. Melvil', *Demokraticheskie tranzity (teoretiko-metodologicheskie in prikladnye aspekty)* (Moscow, 1999); and one of the most sustained attempts to apply political science approaches to the Russian transition, Vladimir Gel'man, *Transformatsiya v Rossii: politicheskii rezhim i demokraticheskaya oppozitsiya* (Moscow, 1999).

67 O'Donnell and Schmitter, *Tentative Conclusions*, pp. 15–36.

68 Alfred Stepan, 'Paths toward Redemocratisation: Theoretical and Comparative Considerations', in Guillermo O'Donnell, Philippe Schmitter and Laurence Whitehead (eds), *Transitions from Authoritarian Rule: Comparative Perspectives* (Baltimore, Johns Hopkins University Press, 1986), pp. 64–84.

69 The classic statement is Samuel Huntington, *Political Order in Changing Societies* (New Haven, Yale University Press, 1968).

70 Dankwart Rustow, 'Transitions to Democracy: Toward a Dynamic Model', *Comparative Politics*, Vol. 2, No. 3 (1970), pp. 337–63, at pp. 352–61.

71 Claus Offe, 'Capitalism by Democratic Design? Democratic Theory facing the Triple Transition in East Central Europe', *Social Research*, Vol. 58, No. 4 (1991), pp. 876–92. Also in Claus Offe, *Varieties of Transition: The East European and East German Experience* (Cambridge, Polity Press, 1996), Chapter 3, pp. 29–49.

72 For an extended discussion of the various spheres, see Juan J. Linz and Alfred Stepan, *Problems of Democratic Transition and Consolidation: Southern Europe, South America, and Post-Communist Europe* (Baltimore, Hopkins University Press, 1996), especially Chapter 1.

73 Valerie Bunce, 'Should Transitologists be Grounded?, *Slavic Review*, Vol. 54, No. 1 (spring 1995), pp. 111–27. See also Valerie Bunce, 'Comparing East and South', *Journal of Democracy*, Vol. 6, No. 3 (1995), pp. 87–100.

74 On the idea of a fourth wave, see Klaus von Beyme, *Transition to Democracy in Eastern Europe* (London, Macmillan, 1996), p. 3; cf. M. Stephen Fish, 'Russia's Fourth Transition', in Larry Diamond and Marc F. Plattner (eds), *The Global Resurgence of Democracy* (Baltimore, Johns Hopkins University Press, 1996).

75 The issue was debated by Sarah Meiklejohn Terry, 'Thinking about Post-Communist Transitions: How Different Are They?, *Slavic Review*, Vol. 52, No. 2 (summer 1993), pp. 333–7; Philippe C. Schmitter with Terry Lynn Karl, 'The Conceptual Travails of Transitologists and Consolidologists: How Far East Should They Attempt to Go?', *Slavic Review*, Vol. 53, No. 1 (spring 1994), pp. 173–85; Terry Lynn Karl and Philippe C.

Schmitter, 'From an Iron Curtain to a Paper Curtain: Grounding Transitologists or Students of Postcommunism?, *Slavic Review*, Vol. 54, No. 4 (winter 1995), pp. 965–87.
76 Rustow, 'Transitions to Democracy', p. 337.
77 Rustow, 'Transitions to Democracy', p. 352; Adam Przeworski, 'Some Problems in the Study of the Transition to Democracy', Guillermo O'Donnell *et al*. (eds), *Comparative Perspectives*, pp. 47–63, at p. 58; and Giuseppe Di Palma, *To Craft Democracies: An Essay in Democratic Transitions* (Berkeley, University of California Press, 1990), pp. 54 ff.
78 Cf. Joseph Schumpeter, *Capitalism, Socialism and Democracy* (London, 1942/76); for a discussion of Schumpeter's relevance to the post-communist transitions, see Richard Bellamy, 'Schumpeter and the Transformation of Capitalism, Liberalism and Democracy', *Government and Opposition*, Vol. 26, No. 4 (1991), pp. 500–19.
79 Rustow, 'Democracy: A Global Revolution', p. 79.
80 For a perceptive attempt to 'deconstruct' the discursive framework of the globalisation paradigm, see Colin Hay and David Marsh (eds), *Demystifying Globalization* (Basingstoke, Macmillan, 2000).
81 *Financial Times*, 14 May 2001, p. 21.
82 Jadwiga Staniszkis, *The Dynamics of Breakthrough in Eastern Europe* (Berkely, CA, California University Press, 1991).
83 Samuel P. Huntington, 'The Clash of Civilizations?', *Foreign Affairs*, Vol. 72, No. 3 (summer 1993), pp. 22–49; Zyuganov's views are in 'Rossiya i mir', in *Sovremennaya Russkaya ideya i gosudarstvo* (Moscow, Obozrevatel', 1995), pp. 10–26; see also his *Za gorizontom* (Moscow, 1995), p.8 and *passim*; and his collected essays *Postizhenie Rossii* (Moscow, Mysl', 2000), Part III.
84 Jadwiga Staniszkis, 'The Worrying Power Shift in the Kremlin', *European Brief*, Vol. 2, No. 4 (1993), pp. 73–4.
85 Laurence Whitehead, 'International Aspects of Democratisation', in Guillermo O'Donnell, Philippe Schmitter and Laurence Whitehead (eds), *Transitions from Authoritarian Rule: Comparative Perspectives* (Baltimore, Johns Hopkins University Press, 1986), pp. 3–46.
86 Frank Field review of Ronald H. Preston, *Religion and the Ambiguities of Capitalism* (London, SCM, 1992), *Independent*, 4 June 1992.
87 See, for example, Michael Bratton and Nicolas van de Walle, *Democratic Experiments in Africa: Regime Transitions in Comparative Perspective* (Cambridge, Cambridge University Press, 1997); Richard Joseph (ed.), *State, Conflict, and Democracy in Africa* (Boulder and London, Lynne Rienner Publishers, 1999). For a general discussion, see Robin Luckham and Gordon White (eds), *Democratization in the South: The Jagged Wave* (Manchester, Manchester University Press, 1996).
88 Joel Migdal, *Strong Societies and Weak States: State–Society Relations and State Capacities in the Third World* (Princeton, Princeton University Press, 1988).
89 Melvin Croan *et al.*, 'Is Latin America the Future of Eastern Europe?', *Problems of Communism*, Vol. XLI, No. 3 (May–June 1992), pp. 44–57.

19 Pluralism, elites, regime and leadership

1 Plato, 'The Philosopher Ruler', *The Republic*, Part 7, Book 7 (London, Penguin, 1955), pp. 284–5 (modified translation).
2 See Robert A. Dahl, *A Preface to Democratic Theory* (Chicago, University of Chicago Press, 1956); *Who Governs? Democracy and Power in an American City* (New Haven, CT, Yale University Press, 1961); *Dilemmas of Pluralist Democracy* (New Haven, CT, Yale University Press, 1982); *A Preface to Economic Democracy* (Cambridge, Polity Press, 1985).
3 David Lane and Cameron Ross, *The Transition from Communism to Capitalism: Ruling Elites from Gorbachev to Yeltsin* (New York, St Martin's Press, 1999).
4 Peter Kirkow, 'Regional Warlordism in Russia: The Case of Primorskii *Krai*', *Europe–Asia Studies*, Vol. 47, No. 6 (September 1995), p. 923.

5 This is the argument of Sergei Peregudov, Natalya Lapina and Irina Semenenko, *Gruppy interesov i Rossiiskoe gosudarstvo* (Moscow, Editorial URSS, 1999).

6 Sergei Bekov, *Vek*, No. 11 (427), 2001, p. 8.

7 See David Lane (ed.), *Russia in Flux* (Aldershot, Edward Elgar, 1992), in particular his 'Soviet Elites, Monolithic or Polyarchic?', pp. 3–23.

8 See Evgenii Krasnikov, 'Kluby vmesto partii?', *Nezavisimaya gazeta*, 20 July 1994, p. 2.

9 John P. Willerton, *Patronage and Politics in the USSR* (Cambridge, Cambridge University Press, 1992).

10 Milovan Djilas, *The New Class* (New York, Praeger, 1957).

11 Zvi Gitelman, 'Working the Soviet System: Citizens and Urban Bureaucracies', in Henry W. Morton and Robert C. Stuart (eds), *The Contemporary Soviet City* (New York, M.E. Sharpe, 1984), p. 241.

12 J.F. Hough, *The Soviet Prefects: The Local Party Organs in Industrial Decision-making* (Cambridge, MA, Harvard University Press, 1969).

13 See Mary McAuley, 'Politics, Economics and Elite Realignment in Russia: A Regional Perspective', *Soviet Economy*, Vol. 8, pp. 46–88.

14 T. Gdlyan and E. Dodolev, *Mafiya vremen bezzakoniya* (Erevan, Izdatel'stvo AN Armenii, 1991).

15 *Moscow News*, No. 37 (1991), p. 6.

16 We have already (Chapter 1) referred to Solnick's discussion of the issue, *Stealing the State*, which focuses on the way that Komsomol officials took advantage of the relaxation of authority to grab as much former state property as they could.

17 Stanislav Govorukhin, *Velikaya kriminal'naya revolyutsiya* (Moscow, 'Andreevskii flag', 1993).

18 Cf. Michael Voslensky, *Nomenklatura: Anatomy of the Soviet Ruling Class* (London, Bodley Head, 1980).

19 *Moscow News*, No. 37 (10 September 1993), p. 7.

20 Olga Kryshtanovskaya, 'Transformatsiya staroi nomenklatury v novuyu Rossiiskuyu elitu', *Obshchestvennye nauki i sovremennost'*, No. 1 (1995), p. 64.

21 Olga Kryshtanovskaya, *Izvestiya*, 10 January 1996; see also her 'The Transformation of the Old *Nomenklatura* into a New Russian Elite', *Izvestiya*, 18 May 1994, p. 2, and 'Transformatsiya staroi nomenklatury v novuyu rossiiskuyu elitu', *ONS: Obshchestvennye nauki i sovremennost'*, No. 1 (1995), pp. 51–65.

22 The idea of a 'party of bosses' comes from Grigorii V. Golosov, 'Russian Political Parties and the "Bosses": Evidence from the 1994 Provincial Elections in Western Siberia', *Party Politics*, Vol. 3, No. 1, 1997, pp. 5–21.

23 Thomas Graham, 'The New Russian Regime', *Nezavisimaya gazeta*, 23 November 1995.

24 On this, see Jeremy Lester, *Modern Tsars and Princes: The Struggle for Hegemony in Russia* (London and New York, Verso, 1995).

25 For a collection of Rigby's articles on the Soviet system see T.H. Rigby, *The Changing Soviet System: Mono-Organisational Socialism from its Origins to Gorbachev's Restructuring* (Aldershot, Edward Elgar, 1990).

26 Guillermo O'Donnell, 'Delegative Democracy', *Journal of Democracy*, Vol. 5, No. 1 (January 1994), pp. 55–69.

27 Guillermo O'Donnell, 'On the State, Democratization and Some Conceptual Problems (A Latin American View with Glances at Some Postcommunist Countries)', *World Development*, Vol. 21, No. 8 (1993), pp. 1,355–69, at p. 1,367.

28 See Adam Przeworski, *Democracy and the Market: Political and Economic Reforms in Eastern Europe and Latin America* (Cambridge, Cambridge University Press, 1991); John F. Helliwell, 'Empirical Linkages Between Democracy and Economic Growth', *British Journal of Political Science*, Vol. 24, No. 2 (1994), pp. 225–48.

29 For example, V. Gel'man, S. Ryzhenkov and M. Bri (eds), *Rossiya regionov: transformatsiya politicheskikh rezhimov* (Moscow, Ves' Mir, 2000).

30 Fareed Zakaria, 'The Rise of Illiberal Democracy', *Foreign Affairs*, Vol. 76, No. 6 (November/December 1997), pp. 22–43.

31 A similar distinction is made by Igor' Klyamkin and Liliya Shevtsova, *Vnesistemnyi rezhim Boris II: nekotorye osobennosti politicheskogo razvitiya postsovetskoi Rossii*

(Moscow, Carnegie Centre, 1999), although operationalised in a different way. For an earlier approach to the question, see my 'The Regime System in Russia', *Contemporary Politics*, Vol. 3, No. 1 (1997), pp. 7–25.

32 Michael Mann, 'The Autonomous Power of the State: Its Origins, Mechanisms and Results', in John A. Hall (ed.), *States in History* (Oxford, Basil Blackwell, 1986).

33 Cf. David Woodruff, *Money Unmade: Barter and the Fate of Russian Capitalism* (Ithaca and London, Cornell University Press, 1999).

34 John Laughland, *The Death of Politics under Mitterrand* (London, Michael Joseph, 1994).

35 W.M. Reissinger, A.H. Miller and V.L. Hesli, 'Political Norms in Rural Russia', *Europe–Asia Studies*, Vol. 47, No. 6 (September 1995), p. 1,030.

36 *Nezavisimaya gazeta*, 23 June 1994, p. 2.

37 *RFE/RL Newsline*, 3 January 2000.

38 Viktor Sheinis, 'Posle bitvy: itogi parlamentskikh vyborov i novaya Gosudarstvennaya Duma', *Nezavisimaya gazeta*, 29 December 1999, p. 8.

39 Anthony Giddens, *The Third Way: The Renewal of Social Democracy* (Cambridge, Polity Press, 1998).

40 Vladimir Putin, 'Rossiya na rubezhe tysyacheletii', *Nezavisimaya gazeta*, 30 December 1999, p. 4; www.pravitelstvo.gov.ru. See also his book of interviews, Vladimir Putin, *First Person: An Astonishingly Frank Self-Portrait by Russia's President Vladimir Putin*, with Nataliya Gevorkyan, Natalya Timakova and Andrei Kolesnikov, trans. Catherine A. Fitzpatrick (London, Hutchinson, 2000).

20 Democracy in Russia

1 Max Weber, 'Bourgeois Democracy in Russia', in *The Russian Revolutions*, ed. and trans. Gordon C. Wells and Peter Baehr (Cambridge, Polity Press, 1995), p. 109.

2 Moore, *Social Origins of Dictatorship and Democracy*, p. 414.

3 Alexis de Tocqueville, *Democracy in America* (New York, Random House, 1981).

4 Bo Petersson, *National Self-Images and Regional Identities in Russia* (Aldershot, Ashgate, 2001), p. 146.

5 Larry Diamond, *Developing Democracy: Towards Consolidation* (Baltimore and London, Johns Hopkins University Press, 1999).

6 See V.B. Pastukhov, 'Stanovlenie Rossiiskoi gosudarstvennosti i konstitutsionnyi protsess: politologicheskii aspekt', *Gosudarstvo i pravo*, No. 2 (1993), pp. 89–96, at p. 89.

7 Andrei Ryabov, 'Integrativnaya ideologiya i modernizatsiya sovremennoi Rossii', *Svobodnaya mysl'*, No. 15 (1992), pp. 58–69.

8 On these questions, see Charles Taylor, *Sources of the Self: The Making of Modern Identity* (Cambridge, Cambridge University Press, 1989).

9 See, for example, Vadim Volkov, 'Violent Entrepreneurship in Post-Communist Russia', *Europe–Asia Studies*, Vol. 51, No. 5, July 1999, pp. 741–54.

10 Robert Jackson, *Quasi States: Sovereignty, International Relations, and the Third World* (Cambridge, Cambridge University Press, 1990).

11 In his *August 1914* Solzhenitsyn vividly portrays the shock experienced by General Samsonov's troops as they entered East Prussia (now Kaliningrad) at the beginning of the Great War, only to be defeated by the Germans.

12 These ideas are discussed by Thomas Graham, *Moskovskie novosti*, No. 78 (12–19 November 1995), p. 23.

13 'Yeltsin and Russia: Two Views', *The New York Review of Books*, 22 April 1993, p. 17.

14 Sergei Stankevich, 'Russia's Lost Decade of Reforms', *Transitions*, March 1999, pp. 61–2.

15 Jeffrey Sachs, *Moscow News*, No. 51 (28 December 1995), p. 3.

16 *Izvestiya*, 26 December 1995, p. 5.

17 *The Observer*, 19 February 1995, p. 21.

18 Gordon A. Craig, 'Demonic Democracy', *New York Review of Books*, 13 February 1992,

pp. 39–43, at p. 43; see also Wolfgang J. Mommsen, *Max Weber and German Politics, 1890–1920*, trans. Michael S. Steinberg (Chicago, University of Chicago Press, 1984).

19 *Izvestiya*, 16 November 1993.
20 Huntington, *Political Order in Changing Societies*.
21 As Schmitter demonstrated, presidential systems in Latin America were conducive to dictatorships, G. O'Donnell, P. Schmitter and L. Whitehead (eds), *Transitions from Authoritarian Rule* (Baltimore, MD, Johns Hopkins University Press, 1986): Vol. 2, *Latin America*, p. 9.
22 Ken Jowitt, *New World Disorder: The Leninist Extinction* (Berkeley, University of California Press, 1992), p. 293.
23 *Izvestiya*, 4 May 1994, p. 5; *The Observer*, 29 May 1994.

Select bibliography

Adelman, Jonathan A., *Torrents of Spring: Soviet and Post-Soviet Politics* (New York, McGraw-Hill, 1995).

Aron, Leon, *Boris Yeltsin: A Revolutionary Life* (London, HarperCollins, 2000).

Barner-Barry, Carol and Cynthia Hody, *The Politics of Change: The Transformation of the Former Soviet Union* (London, Macmillan, 1995).

Beyme, Klaus Von, *Transition to Democracy in Eastern Europe* (London, Macmillan, 1996).

Billington, James H., *Russia Transformed: Breakthrough to Hope* (New York, Free Press, 1993).

Blum, Douglas W., *Russia's Future: Consolidation or Disintegration?* (Oxford, Boulder Press, 1994).

Bonnell, Victoria E. and George W. Breslauer (eds), *Russia in the New Century: Stability or Disorder?* (Boulder, CO, Westview Press, 2000).

Bowker, Mike and Cameron Ross (eds), *Russia after the Cold War* (Harlow, Longman, 2000).

Brown, Archie (ed.), *Contemporary Russian Politics: A Reader* (Oxford, Oxford University Press, 2001).

Buckley, Mary, *Redefining Russian Society and Polity* (Oxford, Westview Press, 1993).

Clark, Bruce, *An Empire's New Clothes: The End of Russia's Liberal Dream* (London, Vintage, 1997).

Cohen, Ariel, *Russian Imperialism: Development and Crisis* (New York, Praeger, 1996).

Cohen, Stephen F., *Failed Crusade: America and the Tragedy of Post-communist Russia* (New York, W.W. Norton, 2000).

Danks, Catherine, *Russian Politics and Society* (Harlow, Longman, 2001).

Davies, R.W., *Soviet History in the Yeltsin Era* (London, Macmillan, 1996).

DeBardeleben, Joan, *Russian Politics in Transition*, second edn (Abingdon, Houghton Mifflin, 1997).

Devlin, Judith, *The Rise of the Russian Democrats: The Causes and Consequences of the Elite Revolution* (Aldershot, Edward Elgar, 1995).

Dunlop, John B., *The Rise of Russia and the Fall of the Soviet Empire* (Princeton, NJ, Princeton University Press, 1993).

Eckstein, Harry, Frederic J. Fleron Jnr, Erik P. Hoffmann and William M. Reissinger, *Can Democracy Take Root in Post-Soviet Russia? Explorations in State–Society Relations* (Lanham, MD, Rowman & Littlefield Publishers, Inc., 1998).

Freeland, Chrystia, *Sale of the Century: Russia's Wild Ride from Communism to Capitalism* (New York, Crown Business, 2000).

Gill, Graeme and Roger D. Markwick, *Russia's Stillborn Democracy? From Gorbachev to Yeltsin* (Oxford, Oxford University Press, 2000).

Gustafson, Thane, *Capitalism Russian-Style* (Cambridge, Cambridge University Press, 1999).

Harter, Stefanie and Gerald Easter (eds), *Shaping the Economic Space in Russia: Decision Making Processes, Institutions and Adjustment to Change in the El'tsin Era* (Aldershot, Ashgate, 2000).

Isham, Heyward (ed.), *Remaking Russia: Voices from Within* (New York, M.E. Sharpe, 1995).

Isham, Heyward, with Natan M. Shklyar (eds), *Russia's Fate through Russian Eyes: Voices of a New Generation* (Boulder, CO, Westview Press, 2000).

Jones, Mark, *Russia in the Emergent World System* (London, Pluto Press, 1999).

Kampfner, John, *Inside Yeltsin's Russia* (London, Cassell, 1994).

Kagarlitsky, Boris, *Russia under Yeltsin and Putin: Neo-liberal Autocracy*, trans. Renfrey Clarke (London, Verso, 2001).

——, *Mirage of Modernisation* trans. Renfrey Clarke (London, Verso, 1995).

——, *Restoration in Russia: Why Capitalism Failed*, trans. Renfrey Clarke (London, Verso, 1995).

Klein, Lawrence and Marshall Pomer (eds), *The New Russia: Transition Gone Awry* (Cambridge, Cambridge University Press, 2001).

Kolste, Pal, *Political Construction Sites: Nation Building in Russia and the Post-Soviet States* (Boulder, CO, Westview Press, 2000).

Ledeneva, Alena V., *Russia's Economy of Favours: Blat, Networking and Informal Exchange* (Cambridge, Cambridge University Press, 1998).

Lane, David (ed.), *Russia in Transition: Politics, Privatisation and Inequality* (Harlow, Longman, 1995).

Lapidus, Gail W. (ed.), *The New Russia: Troubled Transformation* (Boulder, CO, Westview Press, 1994).

Lloyd, John, *Rebirth of a Nation: An Anatomy of Russia* (London, Michael Joseph, 1998).

Löwenhardt, John, *The Reincarnation of Russia: Struggling with the Legacy of Communism, 1990–94* (Harlow, Longman, 1995).

Lupher, Mark, *Power Restructuring in China and Russia* (Boulder, Westview, 1996).

McFaul, Michael, *Post-Communist Politics: Democratic Prospects in Russia and East Europe* (Washington, DC, Centre for Strategic and International Studies, 1993).

——, *The Troubled Birth of Russian Democracy* (Stanford, Hoover Press, 1993).

Medvedev, Roy, *A Journey through the Yeltsin Era* (New York, Columbia University Press, 2000).

Morrison, John, *Boris Yeltsin: From Bolshevik to Democrat* (London, Penguin Books, 1991).

Murray, Donald, *A Democracy of Despots* (Boulder, CO, Westview Press, 1996).

Murrell, G.D.G., *Russia's Transition to Democracy: An Internal Political History, 1989–1996* (Brighton, Sussex Academic Press, 1997).

Nelson, Lynn D. and Irina Kuzes, *Radical Reform in Yeltsin's Russia: What Went Wrong?* (Armonk, NY, M.E. Sharpe, 1995).

Nogee, Joseph L. and R. Judson Mitchell, *Russian Politics: The Struggle for Order* (Hemel Hempstead, Allyn & Bacon, 1997).

Orlovsky, Daniel (ed.), *Beyond Soviet Studies* (Washington, The Woodrow Wilson Center Press, 1995).

Petro, Nicolai N., *The Rebirth of Russian Democracy: An Interpretation of Political Culture* (Cambridge, MA, Harvard University Press, 1995).

Ragsdale, Hugh, *The Russian Tragedy: The Burden of History* (New York, M.E. Sharpe, 1996).

Reddaway, Peter and Dmitri Glinski, *The Tragedy of Russia's Reforms: Market Bolshevism against Democracy* (Washington, DC, The United States Institute of Peace Press, 2001).

Remington, Thomas, *Politics in Russia*, 2nd edn (Harlow, Longman, 2001).

Remnick, David, *Resurrection: The Struggle for a New Russia* (New York, Random House, 1997).

Robinson, Neil (ed.), *Institutions and Political Change in Russia* (Basingstoke, Macmillan, 2000).

Rutland, Peter (ed.), *Business and the State in Contemporary Russia* (Boulder, CO, Westview Press, 2000).

Saivetz, Carol R. and Anthony Jones (eds), *In Search of Pluralism: Soviet and Post-Soviet Politics* (Boulder, CO, Westview, 1994).

Saikal, Amin and William Maley (eds), *Russian in Search of its Future* (Cambridge, Cambridge University Press, 1994).

Shaw, D.J.B., *The Post-Soviet Republics: A Systematic Geography* (London, Longman, 1995).

Simes, Dmitri K., *After the Collapse: Russia Seeks its Place as a Great Power* (New York, Simon & Schuster, 1999).

Smith, Gordon B., *State-Building in Russia: The Yeltsin Legacy and the Challenge of the Future* (Armonk, NY, M.E. Sharpe, 1998).

Smith, Graham, *The Post-Soviet States: Mapping the Politics of Transition* (London, Arnold, 1999).

Solzhenitsyn, Alexander, *The Russian Question at the End of the Twentieth Century* (London, Harvill Press, 1995).

——, *Rebuilding Russia: Reflections and Tentative Proposals* (London, Harvill Press, 1991).

Sperling, Valerie (ed.), *Building the Russian State: Institutional Crisis and the Quest for Democratic Governance* (Boulder, CO, Westview Press, 2000).

Starr, S. Frederick (ed.), *The Legacy of History in Russia and the New States of Eurasia* (New York, M.E. Sharpe, 1994).

Steele, Jonathan, *Eternal Russia* (London, Faber, 1994).

Surovell, Jeffrey, *Capitalist Russia and the West* (Aldershot, Ashgate, 2000).

Thatcher, Ian (ed.), *Regime and Society in Twentieth Century Russia* (London, Macmillan, 1997).

Tikhomirov, Vladimir (ed.), *Russia After Yeltsin* (Aldershot, Ashgate, 2001).

Tismaneanu, Vladimir (ed.), *Political Culture in Russia and the New States of Eurasia* (New York, M.E. Sharpe, 1995).

Truscott, Peter, *Russia First: Breaking with the West* (London, I.B. Tauris, 1997).

Weigle, Marcia A., *Russia's Liberal Project: State–Society Relations in the Transition from Communism* (University Park, PA, Penn State University Press, 2000).

White, Stephen, *Russia's New Politics: The Management of a Postcommunist Society* (Cambridge, Cambridge University Press, 2000).

White, Stephen, Grame Gill and Darrell Slider *The Politics of Transition: Shaping a Post-Soviet Future* (Cambridge, Cambridge University Press, 1993).

White, Stephen, Alex Pravda and Zvi Gitelman (eds), 5th edn, *Developments in Russian Politics* (London, Palgrave, 2001).

Wyman, Matthew and Edwin Bacon, *Contemporary Russia* (Basingstoke, Palgrave, 2001).

Yergin, Daniel and Thane Gustafson, *Russia 2010 and What it Means for the World* (New York, Random House, 1993).

Zwass, Adam, *From Failed Communism to Underdeveloped Capitalism: Transformation of Eastern Europe, the Post-Soviet Union, and China* (New York, M.E. Sharpe, 1995).

Index

Note: Page numbers followed by '*t*' indicate tables and those followed by '*f*' indicate figures.